DUMBARTON OAKS
MEDIEVAL LIBRARY

Jan M. Ziolkowski, General Editor

THE VULGATE BIBLE

VOLUME I

DOML I

The Vulgate
Bible

VOLUME I

THE PENTATEUCH

DOUAY-RHEIMS TRANSLATION

Edited by

SWIFT EDGAR

DUMBARTON OAKS
MEDIEVAL LIBRARY

HARVARD UNIVERSITY PRESS
CAMBRIDGE, MASSACHUSETTS
LONDON, ENGLAND
2010

Library of Congress Cataloging-in-Publication Data
Bible. English. Douai. 2010
　The Vulgate Bible : Douay-Rheims translation / edited by Swift Edgar.
　　v. cm. — (Dumbarton Oaks medieval library ; DOML 1)
　English and Latin text on facing pages.
　Includes bibliographical references.
　Contents: v. 1. The Pentateuch
　ISBN 978-0-674-05534-6 (alk. paper)
　I. Edgar, Swift, 1985– II. Dumbarton Oaks. III. Title.
　BS180 2010
　222′.1047—dc22　　　2010015238

Contents

Introduction

The Vulgate Bible is a collection of Latin texts compiled and translated in large part by Saint Jerome (ca. 345–420) in the late fourth and early fifth centuries CE. Roughly speaking, Jerome translated the Old Testament—except for the books of Wisdom, Ecclesiasticus, Baruch and 1 and 2 Maccabees— and he revised existing Latin versions of the Psalms and the Gospels. Jerome's Bible was used widely in the Western European Christian (and later, specifically Catholic) tradition from the early Middle Ages through the twentieth century.

The adjective "Vulgate" (from the Latin verb *vulgare,* meaning "to disseminate") lacks the connotation of coarseness often inherent in its relative "vulgar," but both words imply commonness. Indeed, the Vulgate Bible was so widespread that its significance can hardly be overstated. It made critical contributions to literature, visual art, music and education during the Middle Ages and the Renaissance, and it informed much of the Western theological, intellectual, artistic and even political history of that period. Students of almost any aspect of European civilization from the seventh century (when the Latin Bible existed more or less in the form we know today) through the sixteenth century (when translations of scripture into various European vernaculars

became widely available to the public and acceptable to religious authorities) must refer frequently to the Vulgate Bible and have a thorough knowledge of it.

In this edition, the Latin is presented opposite the first English version of the Bible sanctioned by the Roman Catholic Church. This English Bible is typically referred to as the Douay-Rheims Version, after the present-day names of its places of publication. The New Testament was published in 1582 by the English College at Rheims, and the Old Testament (to call it the Hebrew Bible would be inaccurate, since it includes nine books that have never belonged to the Hebrew canon) was published in 1609 and 1610, in two volumes, by the English College at Douay. The entire Douay-Rheims Bible was revised several times, notably by Bishop Dr. Richard Challoner (1691–1781) in 1749 and 1750.

In this introduction, I use the terms "Catholic" and "Protestant" in their current senses. Adherents of the Church of England in the sixteenth century at times referred to themselves as Catholics and to those who followed the religious authorities in Rome as Popish or Papists. The members of the Roman Church called their Anglican rivals various names, such as heretics, Protestants, Lutherans and Calvinists, but they would not have called them Catholics.

Douay and Rheims were major centers of learning for English-speaking Catholics, who faced hostility in Protestant England. The English College, a prominent Catholic institution, was exiled from Douay to Rheims in 1578, near the beginning of the Eighty Years' War between the Netherlands (to which Douay at the time belonged) and Philip II of Spain, who had founded the college.[1] The exile lasted until 1593. The college undertook these translations of the Bi-

ble primarily in response to the English versions produced under the Church of England that did not treat Jerome's text as the ultimate authority. Protestant English translators did use the Vulgate, but they also consulted the German rendering by Martin Luther (1482–1546), the Greek Septuagint and New Testament, testimonia in Hebrew and other sources. In contrast, the Douay-Rheims Version was directly translated from the Latin Bible as it was known to the professors at the English College in 1582.

While the English College was working on its translations at Douay and Rheims, Pope Sixtus V (r. 1585–1590) called for the preparation of an authoritative Latin text. This Latin Bible was published in 1590, just prior to his death, but it contained errors and was soon suppressed for fear that Protestants would use them to attack the Catholic Church.[2] Three corrected printings followed, in 1592, 1593 and 1598, during the papacy of Clement VIII (r. 1592–1605). These four editions, substantially the same, are referred to collectively as the Sixto-Clementine Version. While it strongly resembles the Latin Bible that evidently served as the basis for the Douay-Rheims translation, the two are not identical. The Dumbarton Oaks Medieval Library (DOML) here presents a reconstructed Latin text of the lost Bible used by the professors at Douay and Rheims, and Challoner's revision of the English translation faces the Latin. Challoner's text, discussed in detail below ("The English Text of This Edition"), sometimes reflects the Sixto-Clementine Bible more closely than did the English College translations of 1582, 1609 and 1610, but many of the revision's features are not at all related to the Sixto-Clementine Bible, and some lead the translation even further from the Latin.

Although the Douay Old Testament was not published until 1609–1610, most of the work on the translation seems to have been completed much earlier, before any Sixto-Clementine edition. Despite its publication date, therefore, this section of the English translation still provides a valuable witness to a Latin text that predated the Sixto-Clementine Version. Most scholars accept the conclusion by Charles Dodd that "the work may be entirely ascribed to Mr. [Gregory] Martin [who died a decade before publication of the Sixto-Clementine edition] . . . He translated the whole Bible; tho' it was not publish'd all at one time."[3] There is good reason to believe that Dodd was right: an entry in the "Douay Diaries,"[4] records of the activities at the young English College, attests that Martin began translating the Bible in October 1578 and that he translated two chapters a day, which were revised by two other professors. Since there are 1,353 chapters in the Bible—including the Books of Tobit, Judith, Wisdom, Ecclesiasticus, Baruch, 1 and 2 Maccabees and 3 and 4 Ezra, and counting the Prayer of Manasseh as one chapter—the task would have taken Martin and his team slightly more than 676 days, far less time than the thirty years that elapsed between the project's commencement and the complete publication of the Bible. Indeed, this calculation is confirmed in the address "To the right vvelbeloved English reader" in the first volume of the Old Testament (1609), which states that the Bible was translated "about thirtie yeares since" (fifth page of the section). The translation thus almost certainly preceded the Sixto-Clementine text, which immediately became the standard edition upon its printing in 1592. The lag between translation and publication is explained on the first page of the

same section: "As for the impediments, which hitherto haue hindered this worke, they al proceded (as manie do know) of one general cause, our poore estate in banishment"—that is, the exile of the English College to Rheims.

The Douay-Rheims translation used here mostly follows the version printed in 1899, a slight revision of Challoner's editions, incorporating elements from the 1749, 1750 and 1752 printings. Challoner's principal contribution was to make the original Douay-Rheims easier to read by updating obscure phraseology and obsolete words. This volume modifies the 1899 version to bring the punctuation and the transliteration of proper nouns and adjectives into line with modern practice (see Alternate Spellings in the endmatter for this edition's policies regarding transliterations) and to restore some readings from Challoner's 1750 and 1752 editions that had been changed (mostly due to printers' errors) in the 1899 version. In addition, the whole text has been prepared according to the guidelines of the fifteenth edition of the *Chicago Manual of Style*. This policy has resulted in significant alterations to Challoner's edition, which superabounds in colons and commas, lacks quotation marks and begins each verse on a new line, sometimes making the text difficult to understand. In contrast to most English Bibles, this volume renders all of the text as prose, even the parts that were originally in verse, since neither the Latin nor the English is poetic. The Latin text has been punctuated according to the English translation to allow easy movement between the two languages. In the rare instances when they diverge, the text in each language has been punctuated according to its most natural meaning (see, for example, Gen 31:1–4).

Readers of the Dumbarton Oaks Medieval Library who wish to compare either the English or the Latin version presented here with another Bible should bear in mind that the versification in the Vulgate and the numbering of psalms differ from those in Bibles translated from languages other than Latin. Furthermore, the books in this volume have been selected and ordered according to Challoner's revisions, which follow the Sixto-Clementine Bible. This policy has resulted in the inclusion of some chapters and books commonly considered "apocryphal" or "deuterocanonical" (Tobit, Judith, Wisdom, Ecclesiasticus, Baruch, 1 and 2 Maccabees, Daniel 3:24–90, Daniel 13 and 14) and the omission of others that were relegated to appendices even in early printed versions of the Bible (3 and 4 Ezra and the Prayer of Mannaseh). The names of some books differ from the ones that may be familiar to many readers: for instance, 1 and 2 Kings in this volume are commonly called 1 and 2 Samuel; 3 and 4 Kings are usually 1 and 2 Kings; 1 and 2 Paralipomenon equate to 1 and 2 Chronicles; 1 Ezra is usually simply Ezra, while 2 Ezra is typically Nehemiah; the Canticle of Canticles is also known as the Song of Songs; Ecclesiasticus is Sirach and in some Latin Bibles is known as Iesu Filii Sirach; and, last, the Apocalypse of St. John the Apostle may be known to most readers as the Book of Revelation.

The Latin Text of This Edition

The Latin in this edition presents as closely as possible the text from which the Douay-Rheims translators worked. It would have been a version of the Bible known to many Europeans from the eighth through the sixteenth century. Be-

fore Jerome, translations of parts of the Bible into Latin existed; we call these disparate texts the Old Latin Bible. After Jerome finished his work, versions of his Vulgate proliferated. According to one count, a third of the biblical manuscripts we have today dating to about one hundred years after Jerome's death are from the Vulgate, and a century later "manuscripts of the Vulgate start to outnumber those of the Old Latin by about two to one. In the seventh century, the ratio has risen to about six to one."[5] The early ninth century brought the stabilization of a recension that was overseen by Alcuin, the schoolmaster from York who played a major role in the cultural revival promoted by Charlemagne. The so-called Alcuin Bibles, of which some thirty survive, became the standard text outside Italy during the Carolingian period. They were the products of monastic copy centers known as scriptoria. In the thirteenth century, the Alcuin Bibles gave way to the so-called Paris Bibles, which were written by professional scribes. The text of the Paris Bibles, a direct descendent of the Alcuin Bibles, was in turn closely related to the Sixto-Clementine Bibles of the late sixteenth century. In large part, the DOML text corresponds to Robert Weber's edition (2007). Most adjustments to bring the Latin closer to the English coincide with an edition of the Sixto-Clementine Bible (1959) that preserves the majority of the readings from the second Clementine edition (1593) and occasionally replaces that text with readings from the other two Clementine editions, which were very similar to each other. For consistency's sake, the spellings and inflections of adjustments based on the Sixto-Clementine Bible have been brought into line with Weber's text.

When neither the Weber nor the Sixto-Clementine text

provides the reading that the Douay-Rheims translators appear to have seen, the critical apparatuses in Weber and in Quentin's edition (1926–[1995]) have been consulted. Often the readings attested in early printed editions of the Bible, such as the famous "42-line Bible" printed by Johannes Gutenberg in 1454, come closest to the translation. In rare instances it has been necessary to print reconstructions of the text theoretically used by the translators, since neither the Sixto-Clementine, Weber and Quentin editions nor the citations in their apparatus provide a suitable reading. These reconstructions, often closer to the Greek Septuagint than to any Vulgate edition, follow the Old Latin Bible.

In trying to identify the Latin source or sources of the Douay-Rheims translation, some scholars have pointed to the Louvain Bible,[6] an early printed edition that strongly resembles the Sixto-Clementine Version. However, the readings in the Douay-Rheims Version do not support the conclusion that Martin based his translation on either the Louvain Bible of 1547 or the correction of that edition published at Rome in 1574. Furthermore, the preface of the Douay-Rheims Version addressed "To the right vvelbeloved English reader" states (and Greenslade accepts) that the editors of the Old Testament "conformed it to the most perfect Latin Edition"—presumably, given the publication date, the Sixto-Clementine Version.[7] To take just one illustration of the danger of assuming that the translators used a single identifiable source, consider Ex 16:29, which in the Douay translation reads in part, "and let none goe forth": of the many sources considered by Quentin (including the Louvain Bible), only two—both early printed editions and neither of them the Sixto-Clementine or the Louvain edition—begin

the relevant Latin clause with a conjunction. Moreover, while the translators claimed their work was "diligently conferred with the Hebrew, Greeke, and other Editions in diuers languages,"[8] the relative paucity of readings different from well-established Latin sources and the inconsistency in the nature of the divergences suggest that they were working with a now lost Latin text of idiosyncratic nature rather than a still extant one that they chose to ignore from time to time. Since several people collaborated on that translation, the translators may also have followed different editions of the Bible and therefore produced a translation for which there is no single surviving Latin source.

Unlike the Latin as edited by Weber, the Sixto-Clementine edition (to whose family the Douay-Rheims translation belongs) often regularizes the language found in earlier manuscripts. In general, the Sixto-Clementine rarely accepts the *lectio difficilior,* while most editors since the eighteenth century, including Weber, tend to choose the "more difficult reading" from among multiple possibilities. For example, at Gen 32:5, the Weber edition reads, "habeo boves et asinos oves et servos atque ancillas," while the Sixto-Clementine editors preferred to avoid the variations of asyndeton after *asinos* and of *atque,* so their text reads, "Habeo boves et asinos et oves et servos et ancillas." In this instance, the Douay-Rheims translators evidently saw a conjunction between *asinos* and *oves* and also between *servos* and *ancillas.* In this edition, an *et* has been inserted in the former case, but the *atque* has remained in the latter, because we cannot know which of the many options for the English "and" the translators encountered in their Latin.

At times, the translation reflects a base text closer to We-

ber's than to the Sixto-Clementine edition. For example, at Gen 1:14, Weber reads "fiant luminaria in firmamento caeli ut dividant diem ac noctem," while for *ut,* the Sixto-Clementine edition reads *et.* However, the Douay-Rheims translation (as revised by Challoner, but here retaining the grammatical construction of the original) reads, "Let there be lights made in the firmament of heaven to divide the day and the night," clearly translating *ut.* The Sixto-Clementine choice was probably made by analogy to verses like Gen 1:6, which reads in both editions "Fiat firmamentum in medio aquarum, et dividat."

The English Text of This Edition

The "Douay-Rheims Version" is an imperfect name for the translation of the Vulgate Bible used in this volume. Indeed, one anonymous scholar in 1836 went so far as to write that calling a translation similar to the one printed here "the Douay or Rhemish version is an abuse of terms."[9] The English here follows a text that was published in 1899. Although this text has been understood routinely as being the Douay-Rheims Version without any qualification, it in fact offers an English translation that derives not directly from the work of the English College of Douay and Rheims, but rather from a nineteenth-century form of a revision by Challoner. Challoner published at least five revisions of the New Testament and two of the Old (the New Testaments appeared in 1749, 1750, 1752, 1764 and 1772, the Old Testaments in 1750 and 1763–1764); after his death, others produced many more. Since the editions of 1582, 1609 and 1610, many subsequent revisions have purported to be simple reprints.

Indeed, the frontispiece to the 1899 edition has a message of approbation by James Cardinal Gibbons, then archbishop of Baltimore, who writes that the text "is an accurate reprint of the Rheims and Douay edition with Dr. Challoner's notes." But if we are to understand the "Rheims and Douay edition" to mean the translations originally printed in those cities in the late sixteenth and early seventeenth centuries, the text we have is by no means an accurate reprint of that.

Because the versions issued between 1610 and 1899 can be difficult to come by, and because the only work approaching a systematic collation of various "Douay-Rheims" Bibles is a bitterly anti-Catholic work from 1855,[10] many scholars regard the Douay-Rheims translation as a text that has barely changed (if at all) since its first printing. Some are aware of Challoner's extensive revisions in the mid-eighteenth century, which updated the language of the Douay-Rheims Version and toned down the polemical annotations, but few know the extent of his alterations, or that they make it more distant from the Latin Vulgate, or that they took place over several editions or that the editions published after his death often contain the work of other scholars.

Many factors complicate analysis of the modifications that the Douay-Rheims Version has undergone over the past four centuries. The most significant is the doctrinal conservatism of the Catholic Church. Owing to both the primacy of Jerome's Vulgate (another inadequate label, since Jerome hardly produced the Latin text by himself), recognized at the Council of Trent (1545–1563), and the desire of the Church to exert some control over access to scripture, the translation of the Bible into vernacular tongues was dis-

couraged. Yet after Protestant churches made the text of the Bible available to speakers of English and German, it became easier for reformist thinkers to disseminate their teachings. Some English-speaking Catholics then sought to produce their own translation, but since the point of this work was to regulate the message read by the flock, the translation required authorization to insure that it was appropriate. A letter of 1580 from William Allen, the president of the English College at Douay, to a colleague, Professor Jean de Vendeville, expresses the need for papal sanctioning of the translation: "We on our part will undertake, if His Holiness shall think proper, to produce a faithful, pure, and genuine version of the Bible in accordance with the version approved by the Church."[11] The printed edition was approved not by the pope but by three professors at Allen's own college (Douay-Rheims 1609, *Approbatio*).

Conservatism demanded the Church's approbation and made revision difficult. How could a reviser supplant something that had already been declared acceptable to the Church? Revisions required approval of their own, yet they could not directly contradict previously approved editions. For this reason, the only reference to a difference between Challoner's 1750 edition and the printings of 1582, 1609 and 1610 comes on the title page, which describes the work as "Newly revised and corrected, according to the Clementine Edition of the Scriptures." As the phrasing shows, Challoner was careful to note that his version derived from the Latin Bible first authorized by Pope Clement VIII in 1592, ten years after the Rheims New Testament, but he obscured the extent of his revisions. Despite the popularity of Challoner's revision and of the Bibles still in print that descend from it,

the English translations and revisions of scripture were not created under a directive from the Vatican. There is no single, indisputably "official" translation of the Latin Bible into English. All the translations lay claim to official status without criticizing other Catholic versions, and none of them has clear primacy.

This confusing (and confused) climate has misled modern readers into believing precisely what the editors and translators of English Catholic Bibles from the sixteenth through the nineteenth century wanted them to think: a single standard English translation of the Bible existed, and the reader in question was holding a copy of it. One well-respected medievalist cautioned against using the King James Version for medieval studies (because it lacks a close relationship to the Vulgate text), implying that the Douay-Rheims Version is preferable. While correct about the King James Version, he shows himself to be unaware of the Douay-Rheims's own modern tradition, writing, "The English translation of [the Vulgate] is the one known as the 'Douai-Rheims' translation . . . also available in many modern editions," and later quoting the translation of Ct 2:4 in the Douay-Rheims as "he set in order charity in me."[12] This quotation comes from Challoner's revision of the translation from 1750; the 1610 translation reads, "he hath ordered in me charitie."

The particular case of Ct 2:4 does not perfectly illustrate the danger of using Challoner's revision of the Douay-Rheims translation, because his rendering still matches the Vulgate text ("ordinavit in me caritatem"). But in many places (italicized in this edition) Challoner strayed from the Latin, usually to revise some particularly awkward phrasing

in the older Douay-Rheims edition. For example, at Gen 6:13, he changed "the earth is replenished with iniquitie from the face of them" to "the earth is filled with iniquity through them." Four points are important about this revision. The first is that Challoner updated the spelling of "iniquitie." Second, here, as elsewhere, he translated very logically an ordinary Latin word *(repleta)* with an equally common English one ("filled"), rather than with a cognate ("replenished"). Thus, he followed a policy that contrasts with the Latinate qualities that pervade the earlier translation. Third, "through" is not found in any Latin edition; while the meaning of "from the face of them" is obscure in English, it is a literal rendition of all the transmitted Vulgate texts of this verse. The fourth point is the trickiest one to address: the preposition "through" instead of "from the face of" is in fact found in the King James Version, which was in Challoner's day the more or less official Anglican (and of course Protestant) Bible.

Gen 6:13 illustrates how Challoner revised the Douay-Rheims Bible on literary grounds. One peculiarity of Bible studies is that many areas of interest are plagued with partisanship, and it can be difficult to make any argument without seeming to side with one religious (or secular) establishment against another. In trying to articulate the relationship between the King James and Douay-Rheims Versions, many otherwise useful sources emphasize the effects of one on the other according to the publisher's disposition: that is to say, Catholic sources underscore the similarities between the 1582 New Testament and the 1611 King James text, while Protestant reference works point to Challoner's alleged in-

debtedness to the King James Version. A notable exception is the anonymous article quoted above, which in its passionate call for a responsible, authorized translation of the Sixto-Clementine Vulgate rightly commented on a difference between the 1582 New Testament and Challoner's revision: "This correction is taken verbatim from the Protestant version."[13] Without delving into the differences in the theological programs of the editors of the Douay-Rheims and King James Versions or calling one preferable to the other, one could argue convincingly (as many have done) that the King James Bible has far greater—or at the very least, more enduring—literary merit than the original Douay-Rheims Version.

To understand the relative qualities of these English Bibles, compare, for example, the translations of Dt 30:19. The Douay-Rheims reads: "I cal for witnesses this day heauen and earth, that I haue proposed to you life and death, blessing and cursing. Choose therefore life, that both thou mayest liue, and thy seede." The King James Version has "I call heauen and earth to record this day against you, that I haue set before you life and death, blessing and cursing: therefore choose life, that both thou and thy seed may liue." Significantly, the King James Version is more natural and memorable; we should also note that the most awkward phrasing in the Douay-Rheims translation ("proposed to") has, in Challoner, been replaced by "set before," the King James reading.

The literary superiority of the King James Version is worth bearing in mind, because Challoner (whose schoolboy nickname, we are told, was Book)[14] revised the Douay-

Rheims text primarily on the basis of literary sensibilities. His version significantly departs from the Douay-Rheims when that text is most stilted, and not infrequently in such instances, Challoner's revision closely matches the sense or wording (or both) of the King James Bible.

A word of caution should be issued to those who would accept the implication of the subtitle of Challoner's Bible: "Newly revised and corrected, according to the Clementine Edition of the Scriptures." This description suggests that Challoner updated the Douay-Rheims translation in light of the standard text of the Bible that had not been available to the translators at the English College. Through oversight, however, his revision skipped a few phrases that the Douay-Rheims translators had missed as well (mostly when similar Latin words appeared on different parts of the page, causing leaps of the eye).[15] These omissions suggest strongly that Challoner's primary task was to make the English of the Douay-Rheims version more readable; it was not a revision on textual grounds. Otherwise, a careful collation of the Douay-Rheims Version with the Sixto-Clementine Bible would have been essential. More often than not, Challoner appears simply to have read the Douay-Rheims and fixed the poor or awkward style, occasionally turning to the King James, Latin, Greek or possibly Hebrew texts for help. He does not seem to have compared the Douay-Rheims systematically with the Latin (or any other version).

If we are not prepared to credit the magnum opus of the Anglican Church as a major source for Challoner, we can say that many of his revisions came from Hebrew and Greek sources (the same texts that the King James editors read,

possibly accounting for the similarities). Why Challoner often turned to sources other than the Latin Vulgate, which had existed in stable and authorized form since 1592, is unclear, especially in view of his title-page statement that he had updated the Douay-Rheims according to the Sixto-Clementine Bible. The period in which Challoner published his first edition of the New Testament (1749) was one of lively productivity for biblical scholars. The monumental edition of the pre-Vulgate Latin Bible credited to Pierre Sabatier, a Benedictine monk, was in production (Rheims 1739, 1749; Paris 1751). This text was meant to reconstruct the Bible as it was known to the Church fathers writing in Latin before the general acceptance of Jerome's text, and it received the approbation of two vicars general and Sabatier's own abbot. It relies frequently on Greek and Hebrew sources, indicating that the study of those texts was not as distasteful to the Church elite in the eighteenth century as it had been in 1609, when the Douay-Rheims translators prefaced their edition with the following words:

> But here an other question may be proposed: VVhy we translate the Latin text, rather than the Hebrew, or Greke, which Protestantes preferre, as the fountaine tongues, wherin holie Scriptures were first written? To this we answer, that if in dede those first pure Editions were now extant, or if such as be extant, were more pure than the Latin, we would also preferre such fountaines before the riuers, in whatsoeuer they should be found to disagree. But the ancient best lerned Fathers, & Doctors of the Church, do much complaine, and

testifie to vs, that both the Hebrew and Greke Editions are fouly corrupted by Iewes, and Heretikes, since the Latin was truly translated out of them, whiles they were more pure.[16]

Indeed, by 1750 the Counter-Reformational motives of the Douay-Rheims Version of 1582, 1609 and 1610 had become largely irrelevant, and the polemical annotations of the first translation were either omitted or stripped of their vehemence. Even the notes in the Old Testament of 1609–1610 contain less vitriol than those in the 1582 New Testament. Strict adherence to the Vulgate Bible mattered less to Challoner than to the original translators, although he still evidently favored literalism in his renderings. Consequently, he may have preferred to replace poorly worded translations with a new literal translation of a different source, rather than to print loose constructions of the Latin text. Nonetheless, the translation on the whole adheres faithfully to the Vulgate, the official Bible of the Catholic Church; after all, Challoner wrote a pamphlet entitled "The Touchstone of the New Religion: or, Sixty Assertions of Protestants, try'd by their own Rule of Scripture alone, and condemned by clear and express Texts of their own Bible" (London 1735). Interestingly, this tract reveals Challoner's familiarity with, or at least access to, the King James Version of the Bible. As one scholar put it, "He sought to establish the Roman Church's credentials out of the mouths of her enemies."[17]

It may be fitting that the DOML Bible is an artificial one. After all, in whatever language or languages the texts collectively called the Bible are read, they are heterogeneous, cobbled together over centuries, having been composed (or re-

vealed) and varied by oral tradition throughout the preceding millennia. With only minor revisions, we use Challoner's edition of the Douay-Rheims Bible because his text preserves the character of the English translation that brings us closest to the end of the medieval period while still being fairly elegant and readable. This edition differs from the 1899 printing in restoring readings from the 1750 and 1752 editions which had been spuriously altered in the 1899 version and in updating the biblical names and the punctuation of the earlier edition. Challoner's notes have been excised, though his chapter summaries remain.

With its rich and somewhat thorny history, Challoner's English is important to scholars of many disciplines, and its proximity to the literal translation of the most important book of the medieval period—namely, the Latin Bible—makes it invaluable to English-speakers studying the Middle Ages.

A NOTE ON THE TRANSLATION

Every discussion of the Douay-Rheims translation—whether praising or condemning it, whether acknowledging or ignoring Challoner's contribution to the text—affirms its proximity to the Latin. The translation in this volume has, however, a few characteristics that are either difficult for contemporary English-speakers to understand or that make the English less literal than it could be.

Challoner's word choice may sometimes puzzle readers. In the service of literalism, the Douay-Rheims translators and Challoner usually rendered *postquam* by the now obsolete phrase "after that," regardless of whether the Latin

word was a conjunction or an adverb. For example, at Gen 24:22, the translation reads, "And after that the camels had drunk, the man took out golden earrings weighing two sicles and as many bracelets of ten sicles weight," whereas a natural, more modern rendering would eliminate the word "that." Possibly by analogy to the case of *postquam,* or possibly because in the seventeenth century there was little distinction between the meanings of "after" and "after that," the translators occasionally rendered other words as "after that" where the phrase makes little sense in modern usage; see, for example, the temporal *cum* at Gen 8:6. On the whole, though, Challoner avoided trying to fit the square peg of English translation into the round hole of the Latin text. He shied away from the Douay-Rheims tendency to translate Latin words with awkward cognates, such as "invocate" for forms of *invoco* (for example, Gen 4:26); he frequently rendered relative pronouns with a conjunction followed by a demonstrative (Gen 3:1 and elsewhere); and he and his antecedents were free with temporal constructions, rendering, to take one example, *de nocte* as "very early" at Ex 34:4. Furthermore, Challoner translated many conjunctions as "now" that literally mean "and," "but," "moreover" or "therefore" (for example, Gen 16:1 and 3 Rg 1:1); the King James translators were also liberal in their use of "now."

Challoner's breaches of the rule of strict (some have said excessive) literalism also occur in areas other than word choice. The most frequent deviations appear in the translation of participles, the passive voice and especially passive participles. The translation of Nm 20:6 illustrates this program: the verse in Latin begins, "Ingressusque Moses et Aaron dimissa multitudine Tabernaculum Foederis corru-

erunt"; the 1609 translation reads, "And Moyses and Aaron, the multitude being dismissed, entering into the tabernacle of couenant, fel"; whereas Challoner, preferring not to employ the passive voice or more than one construction with a participle, rendered the verse (with my punctuation), "And Moses and Aaron leaving the multitude went into the Tabernacle of the Covenant and fell." The many ablatives absolute and other participial constructions that have been modified by Challoner to fit more neatly into his preferred English style have not been signaled by italics in this volume because they do not illuminate anything about the Latin text and because the renderings are not so loose as to make their relationship to the Latin difficult to perceive.

Another systematic abandonment of literal translations appears in Challoner's rendering of oath formulas and other invocations of God, especially those that begin in Latin *vivo* or *vivit Dominus* or that employ constructions similar to "haec faciat mihi Deus et haec addat." Usually the first two formulas are rendered by adding "as" in English before the subject of the verb, and if the next clause begins with a conjunction, it is excised in translation. See, for example, 1 Rg 14:39, which begins in Latin, "Vivit Dominus, salvator Israhel, quia si" and was translated in the 1609 edition as "Our Lord the sauiour of Israel liueth, that if," which was modified by Challoner to read, "As the Lord liveth who is the saviour of Israel, if." The constructions that substantially resemble "haec faciat mihi Deus et haec addat" as at 1 Rg 14:44 were translated predictably in 1609 as "These thinges doe God to me, and these thinges adde he." Challoner rendered the prayer as "May God do so and so to me and add still more." Both of these divergences from the

Latin are anticipated in the English of the King James Version, and because such renderings are pervasive, they have been noted only here and are not mentioned in the Notes to the Text.

Challoner's antecedents at Douay and Rheims were also at times a bit lax in their translation. The degrees of adjectives and adverbs are not differentiated: *durius* (Gen 31:29) can be rendered as "roughly," *pessima* (Gen 37:20) as "naughtie." *Haec* (Gen 9:8), especially before verbs of saying, is often translated as "thus." Similar lapses in literalism occur with the verbs *volo* and *debeo,* the future tense, the future perfect tense and the subjunctive mood, which are all often rendered as simple futures in English; yet in most cases when the Douay-Rheims translators stuck to a literal translation and Challoner changed it, his variation and its source have been noted. When the Douay-Rheims translators use a turn of phrase that does not square with the Latin, the divergence has been commented upon only if the translation seems to be a useful key to the Latin they worked from; if they seem simply to have rendered the text loosely, no note appears. The most striking translation choices that the professors from Douay and Rheims made were to translate *utinam* (e.g., Ex 16:3) as "would to God," *absit* (e.g., Gen 44:17) as "God forbid," *salve* (e.g., 2 Rg 18:28) as "God save thee" and *vivat Rex* (e.g., 1 Rg 10:24) as "God save the King," even though there is no reference to the Divine. One other consistent policy of the Douay-Rheims translation was to translate *Dominus* as "our Lord." This practice stemmed from theological rather than philological reasons, and Challoner (like the King James translators) rendered this word as "the Lord." In these cases, there can be no other Latin reading,

and since the English is not helpful in illuminating a hitherto unknown Latin text, no note has been made.

Last, the translation and Challoner's revision tried to avoid enjambment as much as possible. For example, Nm 7:18–19 reads in Latin, "Secundo die, obtulit Nathanahel, filius Suar, dux de tribu Isachar: / acetabulum argenteum," whereas at verses 24–25 of the same chapter we find "Tertio die, princeps filiorum Zabulon, Heliab, filius Helon, / obtulit acetabulum argenteum." Syntactically, the verses are identical (the colon is placed in the Latin only on the basis of the translation), but because in the first example *obtulit* appears in a separate verse from its direct object, the translation reads, "The second day, Nethanel, the son of Zuar, prince of the tribe of Issachar, made his offering: / a silver dish," while at verses 24–25 we have "The third day, the prince of the sons of Zebulun, Eliab, the son of Helon, / offered a silver dish."

Apart from these few deviations and the occasional italicized words and phrases, the Challoner revision is an exceptionally literal and readable translation of the Vulgate Bible, and it has proved helpful over the past quarter millennium to those who find the meaning of the Latin obscure.

I am grateful to the many people who have helped me with this project, including readers George Carlisle, Bob Edgar, Sally Edgar, Jim Halporn, Scott Johnson and Christopher Osborne; Alexandra Helprin, for her support and encouragement; Terra Dunham, Ian Stevenson and Sharmila Sen at Harvard University Press; Philip Kim and Julian Yolles for their excellent proofreading; Maria Ascher, for her thought-

ful editing of the Introduction; Andy Kelly, whose generosity was particularly helpful in the introductory paragraphs on Richard Challoner; Michael Herren and Danuta Shanzer for their careful reading and helpful suggestions; and especially Jan Ziolkowski, who conceived of the series, trusted me to see this project through, and supervised my work.

NOTES

1 See Carleton, *The Part of Rheims in the Making of the English Bible,* p. 13.

2 Quentin, *Mémoire sur l'établissement du texte de la Vulgate,* pp. 190–92.

3 Dodd, *The Church History of England,* vol. 2, p. 121, quoted in Pope and Bullough, *English Versions of the Bible,* p. 252.

4 Knox, *The First and Second Diaries of the English College,* p. 145, cited in Carleton, *The Part of Rheims in the Making of the English Bible,* p. 16.

5 de Hamel, *The Book: A History of the Bible,* p. 28.

6 Pope and Bullough, *English Versions of the Bible,* p. 295; Greenslade, *The Cambridge History of the Bible,* p. 163.

7 Greenslade, *The Cambridge History of the Bible,* p. 163.

8 Frontispiece, Douay-Rheims Bible, 1609.

9 A Catholic, "A new Version of the Four Gospels," p. 476, quoted in Cartmell, "English Spiritual Writers," p. 583. Cartmell erroneously cites the passage as appearing on page 276 but attributes it correctly to Nicholas Wiseman, though the review was published anonymously.

10 Cotton, *Rhemes and Doway.*

11 Translated from the Latin by Knox; see Carleton, *The Part of Rheims in the Making of the English Bible,* p. 15.

12 Kaske, *Medieval Christian Literary Imagery,* p. 6.

13 A Catholic, "A new Version of the Four Gospels," p. 476.

14 Duffy, *Challoner and His Church,* p. 6.

15 See Pope and Bullough, *English Versions of the Bible,* pp. 359–71.

16 "To the right vvelbeloved English reader," Douay-Rheims Bible, 1609.

17 Gilley, "Challoner as Controvertionalist," p. 93.

Abbreviations

Gen	Genesis
Ex	Exodus
Lv	Leviticus
Dt	Deuteronomy
Nm	Numbers
Jos	Joshua
Jdg	Judges
Rt	Ruth
1 Kings	1 Kings
2 Kings	2 Kings
3 Kings	3 Kings
4 Kings	4 Kings
1 Par	1 Paralipomenon
2 Par	2 Paralipomenon
1 Ezr	1 Ezra
2 Ezr	2 Ezra
Tb	Tobit
Jdt	Judith
Est	Esther
Job	Job
Ps	Psalms
Prov	Proverbs

Ecl	Ecclesiastes
Ct	Canticle of Canticles
Wis	Wisdom
Sir	Ecclesiasticus
Is	Isaiah
Jer	Jeremiah
Lam	Lamentations
Bar	Baruch
Ez	Ezekiel
Dn	Daniel
Hos	Hosea
Joel	Joel
Am	Amos
Ob	Obadiah
Jon	Jonah
Mi	Micah
Na	Nahum
Hab	Habakkuk
Zeph	Zephaniah
Hag	Haggai
Zech	Zechariah
Mal	Malachi
1 Mcc	1 Maccabees
2 Mcc	2 Maccabees
Mt	Matthew
Mk	Mark
Lk	Luke
John	John
Act	Acts of the Apostles

Rom	Romans
1 Cor	1 Corinthians
2 Cor	2 Corinthians
Gal	Galatians
Eph	Ephesians
Phlp	Philippians
Col	Colossians
1 Th	1 Thessalonians
2 Th	2 Thessalonians
1 Tim	1 Timothy
2 Tim	2 Timothy
Tit	Titus
Phlm	Philemon
Hbr	Hebrews
Ja	James
1 Pt	1 Peter
2 Pt	2 Peter
1 John	1 John
2 John	2 John
3 John	3 John
Jud	Jude
Apc	Apocalypse of St. John the Apostle

LATIN NAMES FOR BOOKS IN THE BIBLE

Gen	Genesis
Ex	Exodi
Lv	Levitici
Nm	Numerorum
Dt	Deuteronomii

Ios	Iosue
Idc	Iudicum
Rt	Ruth
1 Rg	1 Regum
2 Rg	2 Regum
3 Rg	3 Regum
4 Rg	4 Regum
1 Par	1 Paralipomenon
2 Par	2 Paralipomenon
1 Esr	1 Ezrae
2 Esr	2 Ezrae
Tb	Tobiae
Idt	Iudith
Est	Hester
Iob	Iob
Ps	Psalmi
Prv	Proverbiorum
Ecl	Ecclesiastes
Ct	Canticum Canticorum
Sap	Sapientiae
Sir	Sirach (Ecclesiasticus *or* Iesu Filii Sirach)
Is	Isaias
Ier	Hieremias
Lam	Lamentationes
Bar	Baruch
Ez	Hiezechiel
Dn	Danihel
Os	Osee
Ioel	Iohel

Am	Amos
Abd	Abdias
Ion	Iona
Mi	Micha
Na	Naum
Hab	Abacuc
So	Sofonias
Agg	Aggeus
Za	Zaccharias
Mal	Malachi
1 Mcc	1 Macchabeorum
2 Mcc	2 Macchabeorum
Mt	Secundum Mattheum
Mc	Secundum Marcum
Lc	Secundum Lucam
Io	Secundum Iohannem
Act	Actus Apostolorum
Rm	Ad Romanos
1 Cor	Ad Corinthios 1
2 Cor	Ad Corinthios 2
Gal	Ad Galatas
Eph	Ad Ephesios
Phil	Ad Philippenses
Col	Ad Colossenes
1 Th	Ad Thessalonicenses 1
2 Th	Ad Thessalonicenses 2
1 Tim	Ad Timotheum
Tit	Ad Titum
Phlm	Ad Philemonem

Hbr	Ad Hebraeos
Iac	Epistula Iacobi
1 Pt	Epistula Petri 1
2 Pt	Epistula Petri 2
1 Io	Epistula Iohannis 1
2 Io	Epistula Iohannis 2
3 Io	Epistula Iohannis 3
Iud	Epistula Iudae
Apc	Apocalypsis Iohannis

GENESIS

Caput 1

In principio, creavit Deus caelum et terram. 2 Terra autem erat inanis et vacua, et tenebrae super faciem abyssi, et spiritus Dei ferebatur super aquas. 3 Dixitque Deus, "Fiat lux." Et facta est lux. 4 Et vidit Deus lucem quod esset bona, et divisit lucem a tenebris. 5 Appellavitque lucem diem et tenebras noctem; factumque est vespere et mane: dies unus.

6 Dixit quoque Deus, "Fiat firmamentum in medio aquarum, et dividat aquas ab aquis." 7 Et fecit Deus firmamentum divisitque aquas quae erant sub firmamento ab his quae erant super firmamentum, et factum est ita. 8 Vocavitque Deus firmamentum caelum, et factum est vespere et mane dies secundus.

9 Dixit vero Deus, "Congregentur aquae quae sub caelo sunt in locum unum, et appareat arida." Factumque est ita. 10 Et vocavit Deus aridam terram, congregationesque aquarum appellavit maria. Et vidit Deus quod esset bonum.

Chapter 1

God createth heaven and earth and all things therein in six days.

In the beginning, God created heaven and earth. 2 And the earth was void and empty, and darkness was upon the face of the deep, and the spirit of God moved over the waters. 3 And God said, "Be light made." And light was made. 4 And God saw the light that it was good, and he divided the light from the darkness. 5 And he called the light day and the darkness night; and there was evening and morning: one day.

6 And God said, "Let there be a firmament made amidst the waters, and let it divide the waters from the waters." 7 And God made a firmament and divided the waters that were under the firmament from those that were above the firmament, and it was so. 8 And God called the firmament heaven, and the evening and morning were the second day.

9 God also said, "Let the waters that are under the heaven be gathered together into one place, and let the dry land appear." And it was so done. 10 And God called the dry land earth, and the gathering together of the waters he called seas. And God saw that it was good.

11 Et ait, "Germinet terra herbam virentem et facientem semen et lignum pomiferum faciens fructum iuxta genus suum, cuius semen in semet ipso sit super terram." Et factum est ita. 12 Et protulit terra herbam virentem et adferentem semen iuxta genus suum lignumque faciens fructum et habens unumquodque sementem secundum speciem suam. Et vidit Deus quod esset bonum. 13 Factumque est vespere et mane dies tertius.

14 Dixit autem Deus, "Fiant luminaria in firmamento caeli ut dividant diem ac noctem, et sint in signa et tempora et dies et annos 15 ut luceant in firmamento caeli et inluminent terram." Et factum est ita. 16 Fecitque Deus duo magna luminaria—luminare maius ut praeesset diei et luminare minus ut praeesset nocti—et stellas, 17 et posuit eas in firmamento caeli ut lucerent super terram 18 et praeessent diei ac nocti et dividerent lucem ac tenebras. Et vidit Deus quod esset bonum. 19 Et factum est vespere et mane dies quartus.

20 Dixit etiam Deus, "Producant aquae reptile animae viventis et volatile super terram sub firmamento caeli." 21 Creavitque Deus cete grandia et omnem animam viventem atque motabilem quam produxerant aquae in species suas et omne volatile secundum genus suum. Et vidit Deus quod esset bonum. 22 Benedixitque eis, dicens, "Crescite, et multiplicamini, et replete aquas maris, avesque multiplicentur super terram." 23 Et factum est vespere et mane dies quintus.

11 And he said, "Let the earth bring forth the green herb and such as may seed and the fruit tree yielding fruit after its kind, which may have seed in itself upon the earth." And it was so done. 12 And the earth brought forth the green herb and such as yieldeth seed according to its kind and the tree that beareth fruit having seed, each one according to its kind. And God saw that it was good. 13 And the evening and the morning were the third day.

14 And God said, "Let there be lights made in the firmament of heaven to divide the day and the night, and let them be for signs and for seasons and for days and years 15 to shine in the firmament of heaven and to give light upon the earth." And it was so done. 16 And God made two great lights—a greater light to rule the day and a lesser light to rule the night—and the stars, 17 and he set them in the firmament of heaven to shine upon the earth 18 and to rule the day and the night and to divide the light and the darkness. And God saw that it was good. 19 And the evening and morning were the fourth day.

20 God also said, "Let the waters bring forth the creeping creature having life and the fowl that may fly over the earth under the firmament of heaven." 21 And God created the great whales and every living and moving creature which the waters brought forth according to their kinds and every *winged* fowl according to its kind. And God saw that it was good. 22 And he blessed them, saying, "Increase, and multiply, and fill the waters of the sea, and let the birds be multiplied upon the earth." 23 And the evening and morning were the fifth day.

24 Dixit quoque Deus, "Producat terra animam viventem in genere suo, iumenta et reptilia et bestias terrae secundum species suas." Factumque est ita. 25 Et fecit Deus bestias terrae iuxta species suas et iumenta et omne reptile terrae in genere suo. Et vidit Deus quod esset bonum.

26 Et ait, "Faciamus hominem ad imaginem et similitudinem nostram, et praesit piscibus maris et volatilibus caeli et bestiis universaeque terrae omnique reptili quod movetur in terra." 27 Et creavit Deus hominem ad imaginem suam; ad imaginem Dei creavit illum; masculum et feminam creavit eos. 28 Benedixitque illis Deus, et ait, "Crescite, et multiplicamini, et replete terram, et subicite eam, et dominamini piscibus maris et volatilibus caeli et universis animantibus quae moventur super terram."

29 Dixitque Deus, "Ecce! Dedi vobis omnem herbam adferentem semen super terram et universa ligna quae habent in semet ipsis sementem generis sui ut sint vobis in escam 30 et cunctis animantibus terrae omnique volucri caeli et universis quae moventur in terra et in quibus est anima vivens ut habeant ad vescendum." Et factum est ita. 31 Viditque Deus cuncta quae fecerat, et erant valde bona. Et factum est vespere et mane dies sextus.

24 And God said, "Let the earth bring forth the living creature in its kind, cattle and creeping things and beasts of the earth according to their kinds." And it was so done. 25 And God made the beasts of the earth according to their kinds and cattle and every thing that creepeth on the earth after its kind. And God saw that it was good.

26 And he said, "Let us make man to our image and likeness, and let him have dominion over the fishes of the sea and the fowls of the air and the beasts and the whole earth and every creeping creature that moveth upon the earth." 27 And God created man to his own image; to the image of God he created him; male and female he created them. 28 And God blessed them, *saying*, "Increase, and multiply, and fill the earth, and subdue it, and rule over the fishes of the sea and the fowls of the air and all living creatures that move upon the earth."

29 And God said, "Behold! I have given you every herb bearing seed upon the earth and all trees that have in themselves seed of their own kind to be your meat 30 and to all beasts of the earth and to every fowl of the air and to all that move upon the earth and wherein there is life that they may have to feed upon." And it was so done. 31 And God saw all the things that he had made, and they were very good. And the evening and morning were the sixth day.

Caput 2

Igitur perfecti sunt caeli et terra et omnis ornatus eorum. 2 Conplevitque Deus die septimo opus suum quod fecerat, et requievit die septimo ab universo opere quod patrarat. 3 Et benedixit diei septimo et sanctificavit illum quia in ipso cessaverat ab omni opere suo quod creavit Deus ut faceret. 4 Istae generationes caeli et terrae quando creatae sunt in die quo fecit Dominus Deus caelum et terram 5 et omne virgultum agri antequam oreretur in terra omnemque herbam regionis priusquam germinaret, non enim pluerat Dominus Deus super terram, et homo non erat qui operaretur terram.

6 Sed fons ascendebat e terra, inrigans universam superficiem terrae. 7 Formavit igitur Dominus Deus hominem de limo terrae et inspiravit in faciem eius spiraculum vitae, et factus est homo in animam viventem. 8 Plantaverat autem Dominus Deus paradisum voluptatis a principio, in quo posuit hominem quem formaverat. 9 Produxitque Dominus Deus de humo omne lignum, pulchrum visu et ad vescen-

Chapter 2

God resteth on the seventh day and blesseth it. The earthly paradise in which God placeth man. He commandeth him not to eat of the tree of knowledge and formeth a woman of his rib.

So the heavens and the earth were finished and all the furniture of them. 2 And on the seventh day, God ended his work which he had made, and he rested on the seventh day from all his work which he had done. 3 And he blessed the seventh day and sanctified it because in it he had rested from all his work which God created *and made*. 4 These are the generations of the heaven and the earth when they were created in the day that the Lord God made the heaven and the earth 5 and every plant of the field before it sprung up in the earth and every herb of the ground before it grew, for the Lord God had not rained upon the earth, and there was not a man to till the earth.

6 But a spring rose out of the earth, watering all the surface of the earth. 7 And the Lord God formed man of the slime of the earth and breathed into his face the breath of life, and man became a living soul. 8 And the Lord God had planted a paradise of pleasure from the beginning, wherein he placed man whom he had formed. 9 And the Lord God brought forth of the ground all manner of trees, fair to be-

dum suave, lignum etiam vitae in medio paradisi lignumque scientiae boni et mali.

10 Et fluvius egrediebatur de loco voluptatis ad inrigandum paradisum, qui inde dividitur in quattuor capita. 11 Nomen uni Phison: ipse est qui circuit omnem terram Evilat, ubi nascitur aurum. 12 Et aurum terrae illius optimum est. Ibi invenitur bdellium et lapis onychinus. 13 Et nomen fluvio secundo Geon: ipse est qui circuit omnem terram Aethiopiae. 14 Nomen vero fluminis tertii Tigris: ipse vadit contra Assyrios. Fluvius autem quartus ipse est Eufrates.

15 Tulit ergo Dominus Deus hominem, et posuit eum in paradiso voluptatis ut operaretur et custodiret illum. 16 Praecepitque ei, dicens, "Ex omni ligno paradisi comede, 17 de ligno autem scientiae boni et mali ne comedas. In quocumque enim die comederis ex eo, morte morieris."

18 Dixit quoque Dominus Deus, "Non est bonum esse hominem solum; faciamus ei adiutorium similem sui." 19 Formatis igitur Dominus Deus de humo cunctis animantibus terrae et universis volatilibus caeli, adduxit ea ad Adam ut videret quid vocaret ea, omne enim quod vocavit Adam animae viventis, ipsum est nomen eius. 20 Appellavitque Adam nominibus suis cuncta animantia et universa volatilia caeli et omnes bestias terrae, Adam vero non inveniebatur adiutor similis eius.

21 Inmisit ergo Dominus Deus soporem in Adam, cumque obdormisset, tulit unam de costis eius et replevit carnem pro ea. 22 Et aedificavit Dominus Deus costam quam tulerat de Adam in mulierem et adduxit eam ad Adam. 23 Dixitque Adam, "Hoc nunc os ex ossibus meis et caro de

hold and pleasant to eat of, the tree of life also in the midst of paradise and the tree of knowledge of good and evil.

10 And a river went out of the place of pleasure to water paradise, which from thence is divided into four heads. 11 The name of the one is Pishon: that is it which compasseth all the land of Havilah, where gold groweth. 12 And the gold of that land is very good. There is found bdellium and the onyx stone. 13 And the name of the second river is Gihon: the same is it that compasseth all the land of Ethiopia. 14 And the name of the third river is Tigris: the same passeth along by the Assyrians. And the fourth river is Euphrates.

15 And the Lord God took man, and put him into the paradise of pleasure to dress it and to keep it. 16 And he commanded him, saying, "Of every tree of paradise thou shalt eat, 17 but of the tree of knowledge of good and evil thou shalt not eat. For in what day soever thou shalt eat of it, thou shalt die the death."

18 And the Lord God said, "It is not good for man to be alone; let us make him a help like unto himself." 19 And the Lord God having formed out of the ground all the beasts of the earth and all the fowls of the air, brought them to Adam to see what he would call them, for whatsoever Adam called any living creature, the same is its name. 20 And Adam called all the beasts by their names and all the fowls of the air and all the cattle of the field, but for Adam there was not found a helper like himself.

21 Then the Lord God cast a deep sleep upon Adam, and when he was fast asleep, he took one of his ribs and filled up flesh for it. 22 And the Lord God built the rib which he took from Adam into a woman and brought her to Adam. 23 And

carne mea; haec vocabitur virago, quoniam de viro sumpta est. 24 Quam ob rem relinquet homo patrem suum et matrem et adherebit uxori suae; et erunt duo in carne una." 25 Erant autem uterque nudi, Adam, scilicet, et uxor eius, et non erubescebant.

Caput 3

Sed et serpens erat callidior cunctis animantibus terrae quae fecerat Dominus Deus. Qui dixit ad mulierem, "Cur praecepit vobis Deus ut non comederetis de omni ligno paradisi?"

2 Cui respondit mulier, "De fructu lignorum quae sunt in paradiso vescimur, 3 de fructu vero ligni quod est in medio paradisi, praecepit nobis Deus ne comederemus et ne tangeremus illud, ne forte moriamur."

4 Dixit autem serpens ad mulierem, "Nequaquam morte moriemini, 5 scit enim Deus quod in quocumque die comederitis ex eo, aperientur oculi vestri, et eritis sicut dii, scientes bonum et malum."

Adam said, "This now is bone of my bones and flesh of my flesh; she shall be called woman, because she was taken out of man. 24 Wherefore a man shall leave father and mother and shall cleave to his wife; and they shall be two in one flesh." 25 And they were both naked, to wit, Adam and his wife, and were not ashamed.

Chapter 3

The serpent's craft. The fall of our first parents. Their punishment. The promise of a redeemer.

Now the serpent was more subtle than any of the beasts of the earth which the Lord God had made. And he said to the woman, "Why hath God commanded you that you should not eat of every tree of paradise?"

2 And the woman answered him, *saying,* "Of the fruit of the trees that are in paradise we do eat, 3 but of the fruit of the tree which is in the midst of paradise, God hath commanded us that we should not eat and that we should not touch it, lest perhaps we die."

4 And the serpent said to the woman, "No, you shall not die the death, 5 for God doth know that in what day soever you shall eat thereof, your eyes shall be opened, and you shall be as gods, knowing good and evil."

6 Vidit igitur mulier quod bonum esset lignum ad vescendum et pulchrum oculis aspectuque delectabile, et tulit de fructu illius et comedit deditque viro suo, qui comedit. 7 Et aperti sunt oculi amborum, cumque cognovissent esse se nudos, consuerunt folia ficus et fecerunt sibi perizomata.

8 Et cum audissent vocem Domini Dei deambulantis in paradiso ad auram post meridiem, abscondit se Adam et uxor eius a facie Domini Dei in medio ligni paradisi. 9 Vocavitque Dominus Deus Adam et dixit ei, "Ubi es?"

10 Qui ait, "Vocem tuam audivi in paradiso, et timui eo quod nudus essem, et abscondi me."

11 Cui dixit, "Quis enim indicavit tibi quod nudus esses, nisi quod ex ligno de quo tibi praeceperam ne comederes comedisti?"

12 Dixitque Adam, "Mulier quam dedisti sociam mihi dedit mihi de ligno, et comedi."

13 Et dixit Dominus Deus ad mulierem, "Quare hoc fecisti?"

Quae respondit, "Serpens decepit me, et comedi."

14 Et ait Dominus Deus ad serpentem, "Quia fecisti hoc, maledictus es inter omnia animantia et bestias terrae: super pectus tuum gradieris, et terram comedes cunctis diebus vitae tuae. 15 Inimicitias ponam inter te et mulierem et semen tuum et semen illius. Ipsa conteret caput tuum, et tu insidiaberis calcaneo eius."

16 Mulieri quoque dixit, "Multiplicabo aerumnas tuas et

6 And the woman saw that the tree was good to eat and fair to the eyes and delightful to behold, and she took of the fruit thereof and did eat and gave to her husband, who did eat. 7 And the eyes of them both were opened, and when they perceived themselves to be naked, they sewed together fig leaves and made themselves aprons.

8 And when they heard the voice of the Lord God walking in paradise at the afternoon air, Adam and his wife hid themselves from the face of the Lord God amidst the trees of paradise. 9 And the Lord God called Adam and said to him, "Where art thou?"

10 And he said, "I heard thy voice in paradise, and I was afraid because I was naked, and I hid myself."

11 And he said to him, "And who hath told thee that thou wast naked, but that thou hast eaten of the tree whereof I commanded thee that thou shouldst not eat?"

12 And Adam said, "The woman whom thou gavest me to be my companion gave me of the tree, and I did eat."

13 And the Lord God said to the woman, "Why hast thou done this?"

And she answered, "The serpent deceived me, and I did eat."

14 And the Lord God said to the serpent, "Because thou hast done this thing, thou art cursed among all cattle and beasts of the earth: upon thy breast shalt thou go, and earth shalt thou eat all the days of thy life. 15 I will put enmities between thee and the woman and thy seed and her seed. She shall crush thy head, and thou shalt lie in wait for her heel."

16 To the woman also he said, "I will multiply thy sorrows

conceptus tuos. In dolore paries filios, et sub viri potestate eris, et ipse dominabitur tui."

17 Ad Adam vero dixit, "Quia audisti vocem uxoris tuae et comedisti de ligno ex quo praeceperam tibi ne comederes, maledicta terra in opere tuo; in laboribus comedes ex ea cunctis diebus vitae tuae. 18 Spinas et tribulos germinabit tibi, et comedes herbas terrae. 19 In sudore vultus tui vesceris pane donec revertaris in terram de qua sumptus es, quia pulvis es et in pulverem reverteris."

20 Et vocavit Adam nomen uxoris suae Hava, eo quod mater esset cunctorum viventium.

21 Fecit quoque Dominus Deus Adam et uxori eius tunicas pellicias et induit eos. 22 Et ait, "Ecce! Adam factus est quasi unus ex nobis, sciens bonum et malum. Nunc, ergo, ne forte mittat manum suam et sumat etiam de ligno vitae et comedat et vivat in aeternum!" 23 Et emisit eum Dominus Deus de paradiso voluptatis ut operaretur terram de qua sumptus est. 24 Eiecitque Adam et conlocavit ante paradisum voluptatis cherubin et flammeum gladium atque versatilem ad custodiendam viam ligni vitae.

and thy conceptions. In sorrow shalt thou bring forth children, and thou shalt be under thy husband's power, and he shall have dominion over thee."

17 And to Adam he said, "Because thou hast hearkened to the voice of thy wife and hast eaten of the tree whereof I commanded thee that thou shouldst not eat, cursed is the earth in thy work; with *labour and toil* shalt thou eat thereof all the days of thy life. 18 Thorns and thistles shall it bring forth to thee, and thou shalt eat the herbs of the earth. 19 In the sweat of thy face shalt thou eat bread till thou return to the earth out of which thou wast taken, for dust thou art and into dust thou shalt return."

20 And Adam called the name of his wife Eve, because she was the mother of all the living.

21 And the Lord God made for Adam and his wife garments of skins and clothed them. 22 And he said, "Behold! Adam is become as one of us, knowing good and evil. Now, therefore, lest perhaps he put forth his hand and take also of the tree of life and eat and live for ever!" 23 And the Lord God sent him out of the paradise of pleasure to till the earth from which he was taken. 24 And he cast out Adam and placed before the paradise of pleasure cherubim and a flaming sword, turning every way to keep the way of the tree of life.

Caput 4

Adam vero cognovit Havam, uxorem suam, quae concepit et peperit Cain, dicens, "Possedi hominem per Deum." 2 Rursusque peperit fratrem eius, Abel. Fuit autem Abel pastor ovium, et Cain agricola.

3 Factum est autem post multos dies ut offerret Cain de fructibus terrae munera Domino. 4 Abel quoque obtulit de primogenitis gregis sui et de adipibus eorum, et respexit Dominus ad Abel et ad munera eius. 5 Ad Cain vero et ad munera illius non respexit, iratusque est Cain vehementer, et concidit vultus eius.

6 Dixitque Dominus ad eum, "Quare iratus es? Et cur concidit facies tua? 7 Nonne si bene egeris, recipies? Sin autem male, statim in foribus peccatum aderit? Sed sub te erit appetitus eius, et tu dominaberis illius."

8 Dixitque Cain ad Abel, fratrem suum, "Egrediamur foras." Cumque essent in agro, consurrexit Cain adversus Abel, fratrem suum, et interfecit eum.

9 Et ait Dominus ad Cain, "Ubi est Abel, frater tuus?"

Qui respondit, "Nescio: num custos fratris mei sum?"

10 Dixitque ad eum, "Quid fecisti? Vox sanguinis fratris

Chapter 4

The history of Cain and Abel.

And Adam knew Eve, his wife, who conceived and brought forth Cain, saying, "I have gotten a man through God." 2 And again she brought forth his brother, Abel. And Abel was a shepherd, and Cain a husbandman.

3 And it came to pass after many days that Cain offered of the fruits of the earth gifts to the Lord. 4 Abel also offered of the firstlings of his flock and of their fat, and the Lord had respect to Abel and to his offerings. 5 But to Cain and his offerings he had no respect, and Cain was exceedingly angry, and his countenance fell.

6 And the Lord said to him, "Why art thou angry? And why is thy countenance fallen? 7 If thou do well, shalt thou not receive? But if ill, shall not sin forthwith be present at the door? But the lust thereof shall be under thee, and thou shalt have dominion over it."

8 And Cain said to Abel, his brother, "Let us go forth abroad." And when they were in the field, Cain rose up against his brother, Abel, and slew him.

9 And the Lord said to Cain, "Where is thy brother, Abel?"

And he answered, "I know not: am I my brother's keeper?"

10 And he said to him, "What hast thou done? The voice

tui clamat ad me de terra. 11 Nunc, igitur, maledictus eris super terram, quae aperuit os suum et suscepit sanguinem fratris tui de manu tua. 12 Cum operatus fueris eam, non dabit tibi fructus suos. Vagus et profugus eris super terram."

13 Dixitque Cain ad Dominum, "Maior est iniquitas mea quam ut veniam merear. 14 Ecce! Eicis me hodie a facie terrae, et a facie tua abscondar, et ero vagus et profugus in terra. Omnis, igitur, qui invenerit me occidet me."

15 Dixitque ei Dominus, "Nequaquam ita fiet, sed omnis qui occiderit Cain septuplum punietur." Posuitque Dominus Cain signum ut non eum interficeret omnis qui invenisset eum.

16 Egressusque Cain a facie Domini habitavit in terra profugus ad orientalem plagam Eden. 17 Cognovit autem Cain uxorem suam, quae concepit et peperit Enoch. Et aedificavit civitatem vocavitque nomen eius ex nomine filii sui Enoch. 18 Porro Enoch genuit Irad, et Irad genuit Maviahel, et Maviahel genuit Matusahel, et Matusahel genuit Lamech, 19 qui accepit uxores duas: nomen uni Ada, et nomen alteri Sella. 20 Genuitque Ada Iabel, qui fuit pater habitantium in tentoriis atque pastorum. 21 Et nomen fratris eius Iubal; ipse fuit pater canentium cithara et organo. 22 Sella quoque genuit Thubalcain, qui fuit malleator et faber in cuncta opera aeris et ferri. Soror vero Thubalcain Noemma.

23 Dixitque Lamech uxoribus suis, Adae et Sellae, "Audite vocem meam, uxores Lamech; auscultate sermonem meum,

of thy brother's blood crieth to me from the earth. 11 Now, therefore, cursed shalt thou be upon the earth, which hath opened her mouth and received the blood of thy brother at thy hand. 12 When thou shalt till it, it shall not yield to thee its fruit. A fugitive and a vagabond shalt thou be upon the earth."

13 And Cain said to the Lord, "My iniquity is greater than that I may deserve pardon. 14 Behold! Thou dost cast me out this day from the face of the earth, and I shall be hidden from thy face, and I shall be a vagabond and a fugitive on the earth. Every one, therefore, that findeth me shall kill me."

15 And the Lord said to him, "No, it shall not be so, but whosoever shall kill Cain shall be punished sevenfold." And the Lord set a mark upon Cain that whosoever found him should not kill him.

16 And Cain went out from the face of the Lord and dwelt as a fugitive on the earth at the east side of Eden. 17 And Cain knew his wife, and she conceived and brought forth Enoch. And he built a city and called the name thereof by the name of his son Enoch. 18 And Enoch begot Irad, and Irad begot Mehujael, and Mehujael begot Methushael, and Methushael begot Lamech, 19 who took two wives: the name of the one was Adah, and the name of the other Zillah. 20 And Adah brought forth Jabal, who was the father of such as dwell in tents and of herdsmen. 21 And his brother's name was Jubal; he was the father of them that play upon the harp and the organs. 22 Zillah also brought forth Tubalcain, who was a hammerer and artificer in every work of brass and iron. And the sister of Tubalcain was Naamah.

23 And Lamech said to his wives, Adah and Zillah, "Hear my voice, ye wives of Lamech; hearken to my speech, for I

quoniam occidi virum in vulnus meum et adulescentulum in livorem meum. 24 Septuplum ultio dabitur de Cain, de Lamech vero septuagies septies."

25 Cognovit quoque adhuc Adam uxorem suam, et peperit filium vocavitque nomen eius Seth, dicens, "Posuit mihi Deus semen aliud, pro Abel quem occidit Cain."

26 Sed et Seth natus est filius, quem vocavit Enos; iste coepit invocare nomen Domini.

Caput 5

Hic est liber generationis Adam. In die qua creavit Deus hominem, ad similitudinem Dei fecit illum. 2 Masculum et feminam creavit eos et benedixit illis et vocavit nomen eorum Adam, in die qua creati sunt.

3 Vixit autem Adam centum triginta annis et genuit ad similitudinem et imaginem suam vocavitque nomen eius Seth. 4 Et facti sunt dies Adam postquam genuit Seth octingenti anni, genuitque filios et filias. 5 Et factum est omne tempus quod vixit Adam anni nongenti triginta, et mortuus est.

6 Vixit quoque Seth centum quinque annos et genuit Enos. 7 Vixitque Seth postquam genuit Enos octingentis

have slain a man to the wounding of myself and a stripling to my own bruising. 24 Sevenfold vengeance shall be taken for Cain, but for Lamech seventy times sevenfold."

25 Adam also knew his wife again, and she brought forth a son and called his name Seth, saying, "God hath given me another seed, for Abel whom Cain slew."

26 But to Seth also was born a son, whom he called Enosh; this man began to call upon the name of the Lord.

Chapter 5

The genealogy, age and death of the patriarchs from Adam to Noah. The translation of Enoch.

This is the book of the generation of Adam. In the day that God created man, he made him to the likeness of God. 2 He created them male and female and blessed them and called their name Adam in the day when they were created.

3 And Adam lived a hundred and thirty years and begot a son to his own image and likeness and called his name Seth. 4 And the days of Adam after he begot Seth were eight hundred years, and he begot sons and daughters. 5 And all the time that Adam lived came to nine hundred and thirty years, and he died.

6 Seth also lived a hundred and five years and begot Enosh. 7 And Seth lived after he begot Enosh eight hundred and

septem annis genuitque filios et filias. 8 Et facti sunt omnes dies Seth nongentorum duodecim annorum, et mortuus est.

9 Vixit vero Enos nonaginta annis et genuit Cainan, 10 post cuius ortum vixit octingentis quindecim annis et genuit filios et filias. 11 Factique sunt omnes dies Enos nongentorum quinque annorum, et mortuus est.

12 Vixit quoque Cainan septuaginta annis et genuit Malalehel. 13 Et vixit Cainan postquam genuit Malalehel octingentos quadraginta annos genuitque filios et filias. 14 Et facti sunt omnes dies Cainan nongenti decem anni, et mortuus est.

15 Vixit autem Malalehel sexaginta quinque annos et genuit Iared. 16 Et vixit Malalehel postquam genuit Iared octingentis triginta annis et genuit filios et filias. 17 Et facti sunt omnes dies Malalehel octingenti nonaginta quinque anni, et mortuus est.

18 Vixitque Iared centum sexaginta duobus annis et genuit Enoch. 19 Et vixit Iared postquam genuit Enoch octingentos annos et genuit filios et filias. 20 Et facti sunt omnes dies Iared nongenti sexaginta duo anni, et mortuus est.

21 Porro Enoch vixit sexaginta quinque annis et genuit Mathusalam. 22 Et ambulavit Enoch cum Deo et vixit postquam genuit Mathusalam trecentis annis et genuit filios et filias. 23 Et facti sunt omnes dies Enoch trecenti sexaginta quinque anni. 24 Ambulavitque cum Deo et non apparuit quia tulit eum Deus.

25 Vixit quoque Mathusalam centum octoginta septem annos et genuit Lamech. 26 Et vixit Mathusalam postquam genuit Lamech septingentos octoginta duos annos et genuit

seven years and begot sons and daughters. 8 And all the days of Seth were nine hundred and twelve years, and he died.

9 And Enosh lived ninety years and begot Kenan, 10 after whose birth he lived eight hundred and fifteen years and begot sons and daughters. 11 And all the days of Enosh were nine hundred and five years, and he died.

12 And Kenan lived seventy years and begot Mahalalel. 13 And Kenan lived after he begot Mahalalel eight hundred and forty years and begot sons and daughters. 14 And all the days of Kenan were nine hundred and ten years, and he died.

15 And Mahalalel lived sixty-five years and begot Jared. 16 And Mahalalel lived after he begot Jared eight hundred and thirty years and begot sons and daughters. 17 And all the days of Mahalalel were eight hundred and ninety-five years, and he died.

18 And Jared lived a hundred and sixty-two years and begot Enoch. 19 And Jared lived after he begot Enoch eight hundred years and begot sons and daughters. 20 And all the days of Jared were nine hundred and sixty-two years, and he died.

21 And Enoch lived sixty-five years and begot Methuselah. 22 And Enoch walked with God and lived after he begot Methuselah three hundred years and begot sons and daughters. 23 And all the days of Enoch were three hundred and sixty-five years. 24 And he walked with God and was seen no more because God took him.

25 And Methuselah lived a hundred and eighty-seven years and begot Lamech. 26 And Methuselah lived after he begot Lamech seven hundred and eighty-two years and be-

filios et filias. 27 Et facti sunt omnes dies Mathusalae nongenti sexaginta novem anni, et mortuus est.

28 Vixit autem Lamech centum octoginta duobus annis et
genuit filium. 29 Vocavitque nomen eius Noe, dicens, "Iste
consolabitur nos ab operibus et laboribus manuum nostra-
rum in terra cui maledixit Dominus." 30 Vixitque Lamech
postquam genuit Noe quingentos nonaginta quinque annos
et genuit filios et filias. 31 Et facti sunt omnes dies Lamech
septingenti septuaginta septem anni, et mortuus est.

Noe vero cum quingentorum esset annorum genuit Sem,
Ham et Iafeth.

Caput 6

Cumque coepissent homines multiplicari super terram
et filias procreassent, 2 videntes filii Dei filias hominum
quod essent pulchrae, acceperunt uxores sibi ex omnibus
quas elegerant. 3 Dixitque Deus, "Non permanebit spiritus
meus in homine in aeternum, quia caro est, eruntque dies illius centum viginti annorum."

4 Gigantes autem erant super terram in diebus illis, postquam enim ingressi sunt filii Dei ad filias hominum illaeque

got sons and daughters. 27 And all the days of Methuselah were nine hundred and sixty-nine years, and he died.

28 And Lamech lived a hundred and eighty-two years and begot a son. 29 And he called his name Noah, saying, "This same shall comfort us from the works and labours of our hands on the earth which the Lord hath cursed." 30 And Lamech lived after he begot Noah five hundred and ninety-five years and begot sons and daughters. 31 And all the days of Lamech came to seven hundred and seventy-seven years, and he died.

And Noah when he was five hundred years old begot Shem, Ham and Japheth.

Chapter 6

Man's sin is the cause of the deluge. Noah is commanded to build the ark.

And after that men began to be multiplied upon the earth and daughters were born to them, 2 the sons of God, seeing the daughters of men that they were fair, took to themselves wives of all which they chose. 3 And God said, "My spirit shall not remain in man for ever, because he is flesh, and his days shall be a hundred and twenty years."

4 Now giants were upon the earth in those days, for after the sons of God went in to the daughters of men and they

genuerunt; isti sunt potentes a saeculo, viri famosi. 5 Videns autem Deus quod multa malitia hominum esset in terra et cuncta cogitatio cordis intenta esset ad malum omni tempore, 6 paenituit eum quod hominem fecisset in terra. Et tactus dolore cordis intrinsecus, 7 "Delebo," inquit, "hominem quem creavi a facie terrae, ab homine usque ad animantia, a reptili usque ad volucres caeli, paenitet enim me fecisse eos."

8 Noe vero invenit gratiam coram Domino. 9 Hae generationes Noe: Noe vir iustus atque perfectus fuit in generationibus suis; cum Deo ambulavit, 10 et genuit tres filios: Sem, Ham et Iafeth.

11 Corrupta est autem terra coram Deo et repleta est iniquitate. 12 Cumque vidisset Deus terram esse corruptam (omnis quippe caro corruperat viam suam super terram), 13 dixit ad Noe, "Finis universae carnis venit coram me; repleta est terra iniquitate a facie eorum, et ego disperdam eos cum terra. 14 Fac tibi arcam de lignis levigatis. Mansiunculas in arca facies, et bitumine linies intrinsecus et extrinsecus. 15 Et sic facies eam: trecentorum cubitorum erit longitudo arcae, quinquaginta cubitorum latitudo, et triginta cubitorum altitudo illius.

16 "Fenestram in arca facies, et in cubito consummabis summitatem eius, ostium autem arcae pones ex latere; deorsum, cenacula et tristega facies in ea.

17 "Ecce! Ego adducam diluvii aquas super terram ut interficiam omnem carnem in qua spiritus vitae est subter

brought forth children, these are the mighty men of old, men of renown. 5 And God, seeing that the wickedness of men was great on the earth and that all the thought of their heart was bent upon evil at all times, 6 it repented him that he had made man on the earth. And being touched inwardly with sorrow of heart, 7 he said, "I will destroy man whom I have created from the face of the earth, from man even to beasts, from the creeping thing even to the fowls of the air, for it repenteth me that I have made them."

8 But Noah found grace before the Lord. 9 These are the generations of Noah: Noah was a just and perfect man in his generations; he walked with God, 10 and he begot three sons: Shem, Ham and Japheth.

11 And the earth was corrupted before God and was filled with iniquity. 12 And when God had seen that the earth was corrupted (for all flesh had corrupted its way upon the earth), 13 he said to Noah, "The end of all flesh is come before me; the earth is filled with iniquity *through* them, and I will destroy them with the earth. 14 Make thee an ark of timber planks. Thou shalt make little rooms in the ark, and thou shalt pitch it within and without. 15 And thus shalt thou make it: the length of the ark shall be three hundred cubits, the breadth of it fifty cubits, and the height of it thirty cubits.

16 "Thou shalt make a window in the ark, and in a cubit shalt thou finish the top of it, and the door of the ark thou shalt set in the side; with lower middle chambers and third stories shalt thou make it.

17 "Behold! I will bring the waters of a *great* flood upon the earth to destroy all flesh wherein is the breath of life under heaven. All things that are in the earth shall be con-

caelum. Universa quae in terra sunt consumentur. 18 Ponamque foedus meum tecum, et ingredieris arcam, tu et filii tui, uxor tua et uxores filiorum tuorum tecum.

19 "Et ex cunctis animantibus universae carnis bina induces in arcam ut vivant tecum, masculini sexus et feminini. 20 De volucribus iuxta genus suum et de iumentis in genere suo et ex omni reptili terrae secundum genus suum; bina de omnibus ingredientur tecum ut possint vivere.

21 "Tolles igitur tecum ex omnibus escis quae mandi possunt, et conportabis apud te, et erunt tam tibi quam illis in cibum." 22 Fecit ergo Noe omnia quae praeceperat illi Deus.

Caput 7

Dixitque Dominus ad eum, "Ingredere, tu et omnis domus tua, in arcam, te enim vidi iustum coram me in generatione hac. 2 Ex omnibus animantibus mundis, tolle septena et septena masculum et feminam, de animantibus vero non mundis duo et duo masculum et feminam. 3 Sed et de volatilibus caeli, septena et septena, masculum et feminam, ut salvetur semen super faciem universae terrae. 4 Adhuc enim et

sumed. 18 And I will establish my covenant with thee, and thou shalt enter into the ark, thou and thy sons and thy wife and the wives of thy sons with thee.

19 "And of every living creature of all flesh thou shalt bring two of a sort into the ark that they may live with thee, of the male sex and the female. 20 Of fowls according to their kind and of beasts in their kind and of every thing that creepeth on the earth according to its kind; two of every sort shall go in with thee that they may live.

21 "Thou shalt take unto thee of all food that may be eaten, and thou shalt lay it up with thee, and it shall be food for thee and them." 22 And Noah did all things which God commanded him.

Chapter 7

Noah with his family go into the ark. The deluge overflows
the earth.

And the Lord said to him, "Go in, thou and all thy house, into the ark, for thee I have seen just before me in this generation. 2 Of all clean beasts, take seven and seven, the male and the female, but of the beasts that are unclean, two and two, the male and the female. 3 Of the fowls also of the air, seven and seven, the male and the female, that seed may be saved upon the face of the whole earth. 4 For yet a while and

post dies septem ego pluam super terram quadraginta diebus et quadraginta noctibus, et delebo omnem substantiam
quam feci de superficie terrae." 5 Fecit ergo Noe omnia quae
mandaverat ei Dominus.

6 Eratque sescentorum annorum quando diluvii aquae
inundaverunt super terram. 7 Et ingressus est Noe et filii
eius, uxor eius et uxores filiorum eius cum eo in arcam propter aquas diluvii. 8 De animantibus quoque mundis et in-
mundis et de volucribus et ex omni quod movetur super terram, 9 duo et duo ingressa sunt ad Noe in arcam, masculus et
femina, sicut praeceperat Dominus Noe. 10 Cumque transissent septem dies, aquae diluvii inundaverunt super terram.

11 Anno sescentesimo vitae Noe, mense secundo, septi-
modecimo die mensis, rupti sunt omnes fontes abyssi magnae, et cataractae caeli apertae sunt, 12 et facta est pluvia
super terram quadraginta diebus et quadraginta noctibus.
13 In articulo diei illius, ingressus est Noe et Sem et Ham et
Iafeth, filii eius, uxor illius et tres uxores filiorum eius cum
eis in arcam; 14 ipsi et omne animal secundum genus suum
universaque iumenta in genus suum et omne quod movetur
super terram in genere suo cunctumque volatile secundum
genus suum, universae aves omnesque volucres, 15 ingressae
sunt ad Noe in arcam, bina et bina ex omni carne in qua erat
spiritus vitae. 16 Et quae ingressa sunt, masculus et femina
ex omni carne introierunt, sicut praeceperat ei Deus, et in-
clusit eum Dominus de foris.

17 Factumque est diluvium quadraginta diebus super terram, et multiplicatae sunt aquae et elevaverunt arcam in su-
blime a terra, 18 vehementer enim inundaverunt et omnia

after seven days I will rain upon the earth forty days and forty nights, and I will destroy every substance that I have made from the face of the earth." 5 And Noah did all things which the Lord had commanded him.

6 And he was six hundred years old when the waters of the flood overflowed the earth. 7 And Noah went in and his sons, his wife and the wives of his sons with him into the ark because of the waters of the flood. 8 And of beasts clean and unclean and of fowls and of every thing that moveth upon the earth, 9 two and two went in to Noah into the ark, male and female, as the Lord had commanded Noah. 10 And after the seven days were passed, the waters of the flood overflowed the earth.

11 In the six hundredth year of the life of Noah, in the second month, in the seventeenth day of the month, all the fountains of the great deep were broken up, and the floodgates of heaven were opened, 12 and the rain fell upon the earth forty days and forty nights. 13 In the *selfsame* day, Noah and Shem and Ham and Japheth, his sons, his wife and the three wives of his sons with them went into the ark; 14 they and every beast according to its kind and all the cattle in their kind and every thing that moveth upon the earth according to its kind and every fowl according to its kind, all birds and all that fly, 15 went in to Noah into the ark, two and two of all flesh wherein was the breath of life. 16 And they that went in, went in male and female of all flesh, as God had commanded him, and the Lord shut him in on the outside.

17 And the flood was forty days upon the earth, and the waters increased and lifted up the ark on high from the earth, 18 for they overflowed exceedingly and filled all on the

repleverunt in superficie terrae, porro arca ferebatur super aquas. 19 Et aquae praevaluerunt nimis super terram, opertique sunt omnes montes excelsi sub universo caelo. 20 Quindecim cubitis altior fuit aqua super montes quos operuerat.

21 Consumptaque est omnis caro quae movebatur super terram, volucrum, animantium, bestiarum omniumque reptilium quae reptant super terram. Universi homines 22 et cuncta in quibus spiraculum vitae est in terra mortua sunt. 23 Et delevit omnem substantiam quae erat super terram, ab homine usque ad pecus tam reptile quam volucres caeli, et deleta sunt de terra. Remansit autem solus Noe et qui cum eo erant in arca. 24 Obtinueruntque aquae terram centum quinquaginta diebus.

Caput 8

Recordatus autem Deus Noe cunctarumque animantium et omnium iumentorum quae erant cum eo in arca adduxit spiritum super terram, et inminutae sunt aquae. 2 Et clausi sunt fontes abyssi et cataractae caeli et prohibitae sunt pluviae de caelo.

3 Reversaeque aquae de terra, euntes et redeuntes, et coe-

face of the earth, and the ark was carried upon the waters. 19 And the waters prevailed beyond measure upon the earth, and all the high mountains under the whole heaven were covered. 20 The water was fifteen cubits higher than the mountains which it covered.

21 And all flesh was destroyed that moved upon the earth, *both* of fowl and of cattle and of beasts and of all creeping things that creep upon the earth *and all men.* 22 *And* all things wherein there is the breath of life on the earth died. 23 And he destroyed all the substance that was upon the earth, from man even to beast and the creeping things and fowls of the air, and they were destroyed from the earth. And Noah only remained and they that were with him in the ark. 24 And the waters prevailed upon the earth a hundred and fifty days.

Chapter 8

The deluge ceaseth. Noah goeth out of the ark and offereth a sacrifice. God's covenant to him.

And God remembered Noah and all the living creatures and all the cattle which were with him in the ark and brought a wind upon the earth, and the waters were abated. 2 The fountains also of the deep and the floodgates of heaven were shut up, and the rain from heaven was restrained.

3 And the waters returned from off the earth, going and

perunt minui post centum quinquaginta dies. 4 Requievit-
que arca mense septimo, vicesima septima die mensis, super
montes Armeniae. 5 At vero aquae ibant et decrescebant usque ad decimum mensem, decimo enim mense, prima die
mensis, apparuerunt cacumina montium.

6 Cumque transissent quadraginta dies, aperiens Noe fenestram arcae quam fecerat, dimisit corvum, 7 qui egrediebatur et non revertebatur donec siccarentur aquae super
terram. 8 Emisit quoque columbam post eum ut videret si
iam cessassent aquae super faciem terrae, 9 quae cum non
invenisset ubi requiesceret pes eius, reversa est ad eum in arcam, aquae enim erant super universam terram. Extenditque manum et adprehensam intulit in arcam.

10 Expectatis autem ultra septem diebus aliis, rursum dimisit columbam ex arca. 11 At illa venit ad eum ad vesperam,
portans ramum olivae virentibus foliis in ore suo. Intellexit
ergo Noe quod cessassent aquae super terram. 12 Expecta-
vitque nihilominus septem alios dies, et emisit columbam,
quae non est reversa ultra ad eum.

13 Igitur, sescentesimo primo anno, primo mense, prima
die mensis, inminutae sunt aquae super terram, et aperiens
Noe tectum arcae, aspexit viditque quod exsiccata esset su-
perficies terrae. 14 Mense secundo, septima et vicesima die
mensis, arefacta est terra.

15 Locutus est autem Deus ad Noe, dicens, 16 "Egredere
de arca, tu et uxor tua, filii tui et uxores filiorum tuorum
tecum. 17 Cuncta animantia quae sunt apud te ex omni

coming, and they began to be abated after a hundred and fifty days. 4 And the ark rested in the seventh month, the seven and twentieth day of the month, upon the mountains of Armenia. 5 And the waters were going and decreasing until the tenth month, for in the tenth month, the first day of the month, the tops of the mountains appeared.

6 And after that forty days were passed, Noah, opening the window of the ark which he had made, sent forth a raven, 7 which went forth and did not return till the waters were dried up upon the earth. 8 He sent forth also a dove after him to see if the waters had now ceased upon the face of the earth, 9 but she, not finding where her foot might rest, returned to him into the ark, for the waters were upon the whole earth. And he put forth his hand and caught her and brought her into the ark.

10 And having waited yet seven other days, he again sent forth the dove out of the ark. 11 And she came to him in the evening, carrying a bough of an olive tree with green leaves in her mouth. Noah therefore understood that the waters were ceased upon the earth. 12 And he stayed yet other seven days, and he sent forth the dove, which returned not any more unto him.

13 Therefore, in the six hundredth and first year, the first month, the first day of the month, the waters were lessened upon the earth, and Noah, opening the covering of the ark, looked and saw that the face of the earth was dried. 14 In the second month, the seven and twentieth day of the month, the earth was dried.

15 And God spoke to Noah, saying, 16 "Go out of the ark, thou and thy wife, thy sons and the wives of thy sons with thee. 17 All living things that are with thee of all flesh, as well

carne, tam in volatilibus quam in bestiis et universis reptili-
bus quae reptant super terram, educ tecum, et ingredimini
super terram. Crescite, et multiplicamini super eam."

18 Egressus est ergo Noe et filii eius, uxor illius et uxores
filiorum eius cum eo. 19 Sed et omnia animantia, iumenta et
reptilia quae repunt super terram, secundum genus suum,
arcam egressa sunt. 20 Aedificavit autem Noe altare Domino,
et, tollens de cunctis pecoribus et volucribus mundis, obtulit holocausta super altare.

21 Odoratusque est Dominus odorem suavitatis et ait,
"Nequaquam ultra maledicam terrae propter homines, sen-
sus enim et cogitatio humani cordis in malum prona sunt ab
adulescentia sua. Non igitur ultra percutiam omnem animam viventem sicut feci. 22 Cunctis diebus terrae, sementis
et messis, frigus et aestus, aestas et hiemps, nox et dies, non
requiescent."

Caput 9

Benedixitque Deus Noe et filiis eius. Et dixit ad eos,
"Crescite, et multiplicamini, et implete terram. 2 Et terror
vester ac tremor sit super cuncta animalia terrae et super

in fowls as in beasts and all creeping things that creep upon the earth, bring out with thee, and go ye upon the earth. Increase, and multiply upon it."

18 So Noah went out, he and his sons, his wife and the wives of his sons with him. 19 And all living things *and* cattle and creeping things that creep upon the earth, according to their kinds, went out of the ark. 20 And Noah built an altar unto the Lord, and, taking of all cattle and fowls that were clean, offered holocausts upon the altar.

21 And the Lord smelled a sweet savour and said, "I will no more curse the earth for the sake of man, for the imagination and thought of man's heart are prone to evil from his youth. Therefore, I will no more destroy every living soul as I have done. 22 All the days of the earth, seedtime and harvest, cold and heat, summer and winter, night and day, shall not cease."

Chapter 9

God blesseth Noah, forbiddeth blood and promiseth never more to destroy the world by water. The blessing of Shem and Japheth.

And God blessed Noah and his sons. And he said to them, "Increase, and multiply, and fill the earth. 2 And let the fear and dread of you be upon all the beasts of the earth

omnes volucres caeli cum universis quae moventur in terra. Omnes pisces maris manui vestrae traditi sunt. 3 Et omne quod movetur et vivit erit vobis in cibum. Quasi holera virentia tradidi vobis omnia, 4 excepto quod carnem cum sanguine non comedetis, 5 sanguinem enim animarum vestrarum requiram de manu cunctarum bestiarum, et de manu hominis, de manu viri et fratris eius requiram animam hominis. 6 Quicumque effuderit humanum sanguinem, fundetur sanguis illius, ad imaginem quippe Dei factus est homo. 7 Vos autem crescite, et multiplicamini, et ingredimini super terram, et implete eam."

8 Haec quoque dixit Deus ad Noe et ad filios eius cum eo: 9 "Ecce! Ego statuam pactum meum vobiscum et cum semine vestro post vos 10 et ad omnem animam viventem quae est vobiscum, tam in volucribus quam in iumentis et pecudibus terrae cunctis quae egressa sunt de arca, et universis bestiis terrae. 11 Statuam pactum meum vobiscum, et nequaquam ultra interficietur omnis caro aquis diluvii, neque erit deinceps diluvium dissipans terram."

12 Dixitque Deus, "Hoc signum foederis quod do inter me et vos et ad omnem animam viventem quae est vobiscum in generationes sempiternas. 13 Arcum meum ponam in nubibus, et erit signum foederis inter me et inter terram. 14 Cumque obduxero nubibus caelum, apparebit arcus meus in nubibus, 15 et recordabor foederis mei vobiscum et cum omni anima vivente quae carnem vegetat, et non erunt ultra aquae diluvii ad delendam universam carnem. 16 Eritque arcus in nubibus, et videbo illum et recordabor foederis semp-

and upon all the fowls of the air and all that move upon the earth. All the fishes of the sea are delivered into your hand. 3 And every thing that moveth and liveth shall be meat for you. Even as the green herbs have I delivered them all to you, 4 saving that flesh with blood you shall not eat, 5 for I will require the blood of your lives at the hand of every beast, and at the hand of man, at the hand of every man and of his brother will I require the life of man. 6 Whosoever shall shed man's blood, his blood shall be shed, for man was made to the image of God. 7 But increase you, and multiply, and go upon the earth, and fill it."

8 Thus also said God to Noah and to his sons with him: 9 "Behold! I will establish my covenant with you and with your seed after you 10 and with every living soul that is with you, as well in all birds as in cattle and beasts of the earth that are come forth out of the ark, and in all the beasts of the earth. 11 I will establish my covenant with you, and all flesh shall be no more destroyed with the waters of a flood, neither shall there be from henceforth a flood to waste the earth."

12 And God said, "This is the sign of the covenant which I give between me and you and to every living soul that is with you for perpetual generations. 13 I will set my bow in the clouds, and it shall be the sign of a covenant between me and between the earth. 14 And when I shall cover the sky with clouds, my bow shall appear in the clouds, 15 and I will remember my covenant with you and with every living soul that beareth flesh, and there shall no more be waters of a flood to destroy all flesh. 16 And the bow shall be in the clouds, and I shall see it and shall remember the everlasting

iterni quod pactum est inter Deum et omnem animam viventem universae carnis quae est super terram."

17 Dixitque Deus Noe, "Hoc erit signum foederis quod constitui inter me et omnem carnem super terram."

18 Erant igitur filii Noe qui egressi sunt de arca Sem, Ham et Iafeth, porro Ham ipse est pater Chanaan. 19 Tres isti sunt filii Noe, et ab his disseminatum est omne hominum genus super universam terram.

20 Coepitque Noe, vir agricola, exercere terram et plantavit vineam 21 bibensque vinum inebriatus est et nudatus in tabernaculo suo. 22 Quod cum vidisset Ham, pater Chanaan, verenda, scilicet, patris sui esse nuda, nuntiavit duobus fratribus suis foras. 23 At vero Sem et Iafeth pallium inposuerunt umeris suis et, incedentes retrorsum, operuerunt verecunda patris sui, faciesque eorum aversae erant, et patris virilia non viderunt.

24 Evigilans autem Noe ex vino, cum didicisset quae fecerat ei filius suus minor, 25 ait, "Maledictus Chanaan; servus servorum erit fratribus suis."

26 Dixitque, "Benedictus Dominus Deus Sem; sit Chanaan servus eius. 27 Dilatet Deus Iafeth, et habitet in tabernaculis Sem, sitque Chanaan servus eius."

28 Vixit autem Noe post diluvium trecentis quinquaginta annis, 29 et impleti sunt omnes dies eius nongentorum quinquaginta annorum, et mortuus est.

covenant that was made between God and every living soul of all flesh which is upon the earth."

17 And God said to Noah, "This shall be the sign of the covenant which I have established between me and all flesh upon the earth."

18 And the sons of Noah who came out of the ark were Shem, Ham and Japheth, and Ham is the father of Canaan. 19 These three are the sons of Noah, and from these was all mankind spread over the whole earth.

20 And Noah, a husbandman, began to till the ground and planted a vineyard 21 and drinking of the wine was made drunk and was uncovered in his tent. 22 Which when Ham, the father of Canaan, had seen, to wit, that his father's nakedness was uncovered, he told it to his two brethren without. 23 But Shem and Japheth put a cloak upon their shoulders and, going backward, covered the nakedness of their father, and their faces were turned away, and they saw not their father's nakedness.

24 And Noah, awaking from the wine, when he had learned what his younger son had done to him, 25 he said, "Cursed be Canaan; a servant of servants shall he be unto his brethren."

26 And he said, "Blessed be the Lord God of Shem; be Canaan his servant. 27 May God enlarge Japheth, and may he dwell in the tents of Shem, and Canaan be his servant."

28 And Noah lived after the flood three hundred and fifty years, 29 and all his days were in the whole nine hundred and fifty years, and he died.

Caput 10

Hae generationes filiorum Noe: Sem, Ham et Iafeth. Natique sunt eis filii post diluvium. 2 Filii Iafeth: Gomer et Magog et Madai et Iavan et Thubal et Mosoch et Thiras. 3 Porro filii Gomer: Aschenez et Rifath et Thogorma. 4 Filii autem Iavan: Elisa et Tharsis, Cetthim et Dodanim. 5 Ab his divisae sunt insulae Gentium in regionibus suis, unusquisque secundum linguam suam et familias suas in nationibus suis.

6 Filii autem Ham: Chus et Mesraim et Fut et Chanaan. 7 Filii Chus: Saba et Hevila et Sabatha et Regma et Sabathaca. Filii Regma: Saba et Dadan. 8 Porro Chus genuit Nemrod; ipse coepit esse potens in terra. 9 Et erat robustus venator coram Domino. Ab hoc exivit proverbium: "Quasi Nemrod, robustus venator coram Domino." 10 Fuit autem principium regni eius Babylon et Arach et Archad et Chalanne in terra Sennaar. 11 De terra illa egressus est Assur et aedificavit Nineven et plateas civitatis et Chale, 12 Resen quoque, inter Nineven et Chale; haec est civitas magna. 13 At vero Mesraim genuit Ludim et Anamim et Laabim, Nepthuim 14 et Phetrusim et Cesluim, de quibus egressi sunt

Chapter 10

The genealogy of the children of Noah, by whom the world was peopled after the flood.

These are the generations of the sons of Noah: Shem, Ham and Japheth. And unto them sons were born after the flood. 2 The sons of Japheth: Gomer and Magog and Madai and Javan and Tubal and Meshech and Tiras. 3 And the sons of Gomer: Ashkenaz and Riphath and Togorma. 4 And the sons of Javan: Elishah and Tarshish, Cetthim and Rodanim. 5 By these were divided the islands of the Gentiles in their lands, every one according to his tongue and their families in their nations.

6 And the sons of Ham: Cush and Mesram and Put and Canaan. 7 And the sons of Cush: Seba and Havilah and Sabtah and Raamah and Sabteca. The sons of Raamah: Seba and Dedan. 8 Now Cush begot Nimrod; he began to be mighty on the earth. 9 And he was a stout hunter before the Lord. Hence came a proverb: "Even as Nimrod, the stout hunter before the Lord." 10 And the beginning of his kingdom was Babylon and Erech and Accad and Chalanne in the land of Shinar. 11 Out of that land came forth Asshur and built Nineveh and the streets of the city and Calah, 12 Resen also, between Nineveh and Calah; this is the great city. 13 And Mesraim begot Ludim and Anamim and Lehabim, Naphtuhim 14 and Pathrusim and Casluhim, of whom came forth

Philisthim et Capthurim. 15 Chanaan autem genuit Sidonem, primogenitum suum, Ettheum 16 et Iebuseum et Amorreum, Gergeseum, 17 Eveum et Araceum, Sineum 18 et Aradium, Samariten et Amatheum. Et post haec disseminati sunt populi Chananeorum. 19 Factique sunt termini Chanaan venientibus a Sidone Geraram usque Gazam donec ingrediaris Sodomam et Gomorram, et Adama et Seboim usque Lesa. 20 Hii filii Ham in cognationibus et linguis et generationibus terrisque et gentibus suis.

21 De Sem quoque nati sunt patre omnium filiorum Eber, fratre Iafeth maiore. 22 Filii Sem: Aelam et Assur et Arfaxad et Lud et Aram. 23 Filii Aram: Us et Hul et Gether et Mes. 24 At vero Arfaxad genuit Sala de quo ortus est Eber. 25 Natique sunt Eber filii duo: nomen uni Faleg, eo quod in diebus eius divisa sit terra, et nomen fratris eius: Iectan. 26 Qui Iectan genuit Helmodad et Saleph et Asarmoth, Iare 27 et Aduram et Uzal et Decla 28 et Ebal et Abimahel, Saba 29 et Ophir et Evila et Iobab. Omnes isti filii Iectan. 30 Et facta est habitatio eorum de Messa pergentibus usque Sephar, montem orientalem. 31 Isti filii Sem secundum cognationes et linguas et regiones in gentibus suis.

32 Hae familiae Noe iuxta populos et nationes suas. Ab his divisae sunt gentes in terra post diluvium.

the Philistines and the Caphtorim. 15 And Canaan begot Sidon, his firstborn, the Hittite 16 and the Jebusite and the Amorite and the Girgashite, 17 the Hivite and the Arkite, the Sinite 18 and the Aradian, the Zemarite and the Hamathite. And afterwards the *families* of the Canaanites were spread abroad. 19 And the limits of Canaan were from Sidon as one comes to Gerar even to Gaza until thou enter Sodom and Gomorrah, and Admah and Zeboiim even to Lasha. 20 These are the children of Ham in their kindreds and tongues and generations and lands and nations.

21 Of Shem also, the father of all the children of Eber, the elder brother of Japheth, sons were born. 22 The sons of Shem: Elam and Asshur and Arpachshad and Lud and Aram. 23 The sons of Aram: Uz and Hul and Gether and Mash. 24 But Arpachshad begot Shelah of whom was born Eber. 25 And to Eber were born two sons: the name of the one was Peleg, because in his days the earth was divided, and his brother's name: Joktan. 26 Which Joktan begot Almodad and Sheleph and Hazarmaveth, Jerah 27 and Hadoram and Uzal and Diklah 28 and Obal and Abimael, Sheba 29 and Ophir and Havilah and Jobab. All these were the sons of Joktan. 30 And their dwelling was from Mesha as we go on as far as Sephar, a mountain in the east. 31 These are the children of Shem according to their kindreds and tongues and countries in their nations.

32 These are the families of Noah according to their peoples and nations. By these were the nations divided on the earth after the flood.

Caput 11

Erat autem terra labii unius et sermonum eorundem. 2 Cumque proficiscerentur de oriente, invenerunt campum in terra Sennaar et habitaverunt in eo. 3 Dixitque alter ad proximum suum, "Venite; faciamus lateres et coquamus eos igni." Habueruntque lateres pro saxis et bitumen pro cemento. 4 Et dixerunt, "Venite; faciamus nobis civitatem et turrem, cuius culmen pertingat ad caelum, et celebremus nomen nostrum antequam dividamur in universas terras."

5 Descendit autem Dominus ut videret civitatem et turrem quam aedificabant filii Adam. 6 Et dixit, "Ecce! Unus est populus, et unum labium omnibus, coeperuntque hoc facere, nec desistent a cogitationibus suis donec eas opere conpleant. 7 Venite, igitur, descendamus et confundamus ibi linguam eorum ut non audiat unusquisque vocem proximi sui."

8 Atque ita divisit eos Dominus ex illo loco in universas terras, et cessaverunt aedificare civitatem. 9 Et idcirco vocatum est nomen eius Babel quia ibi confusum est labium universae terrae, et inde dispersit eos Dominus super faciem cunctarum regionum.

10 Hae generationes Sem: Sem centum erat annorum

Chapter 11

The tower of Babel. The confusion of tongues. The genealogy of Shem down to Abram.

And the earth was of one tongue and of the same speech. 2 And when they removed from the east, they found a plain in the land of Shinar and dwelt in it. 3 And each one said to his neighbour, "Come; let us make brick and bake them with fire." And they had brick instead of stones and slime instead of mortar. 4 And they said, "Come; let us *make* a city and a tower, the top whereof may reach to heaven, and let us make our name famous before we be scattered abroad into all lands."

5 And the Lord came down to see the city and the tower which the children of Adam were building. 6 And he said, "Behold! It is one people, and all have one tongue, and they have begun to do this, neither will they leave off from their designs till they accomplish them in deed. 7 Come ye, therefore, let us go down and there confound their tongue that *they may not understand one another's speech.*"

8 And so the Lord scattered them from that place into all lands, and they ceased to build the city. 9 And therefore the name thereof was called Babel because there the language of the whole earth was confounded, and from thence the Lord scattered them abroad upon the face of all countries.

10 These are the generations of Shem: Shem was a hun-

quando genuit Arfaxad biennio post diluvium. 11 Vixitque Sem postquam genuit Arfaxad quingentos annos et genuit filios et filias.

12 Porro Arfaxad vixit triginta quinque annos et genuit Sale. 13 Vixitque Arfaxad postquam genuit Sale trecentis tribus annis et genuit filios et filias.

14 Sale quoque vixit triginta annis et genuit Eber. 15 Vixitque Sale postquam genuit Eber quadringentis tribus annis et genuit filios et filias.

16 Vixit autem Eber triginta quattuor annis et genuit Faleg. 17 Et vixit Eber postquam genuit Faleg quadringentis triginta annis et genuit filios et filias.

18 Vixit quoque Faleg triginta annis et genuit Reu. 19 Vixitque Faleg postquam genuit Reu ducentis novem annis et genuit filios et filias.

20 Vixit autem Reu triginta duobus annis et genuit Sarug. 21 Vixitque Reu postquam genuit Sarug ducentis septem annis et genuit filios et filias.

22 Vixit vero Sarug triginta annis et genuit Nahor. 23 Vixitque Sarug postquam genuit Nahor ducentos annos et genuit filios et filias.

24 Vixit autem Nahor viginti novem annis et genuit Thare. 25 Vixitque Nahor postquam genuit Thare centum decem et novem annos et genuit filios et filias.

26 Vixitque Thare septuaginta annis et genuit Abram et Nahor et Aran. 27 Hae sunt autem generationes Thare: Thare genuit Abram, Nahor et Aran. Porro Aran genuit Loth. 28 Mortuusque est Aran ante Thare, patrem suum, in terra nativitatis suae in Ur Chaldeorum.

29 Duxerunt autem Abram et Nahor uxores: nomen uxoris Abram Sarai, et nomen uxoris Nahor, Melcha, filia Aran,

dred years old when he begot Arpachshad two years after the flood. 11 And Shem lived after he begot Arpachshad five hundred years and begot sons and daughters.

12 And Arpachshad lived thirty-five years and begot Shelah. 13 And Arpachshad lived after he begot Shelah three hundred and three years and begot sons and daughters.

14 Shelah also lived thirty years and begot Eber. 15 And Shelah lived after he begot Eber four hundred and three years and begot sons and daughters.

16 And Eber lived thirty-four years and begot Peleg. 17 And Eber lived after he begot Peleg four hundred and thirty years and begot sons and daughters.

18 Peleg also lived thirty years and begot Reu. 19 And Peleg lived after he begot Reu two hundred and nine years and begot sons and daughters.

20 And Reu lived thirty-two years and begot Serug. 21 And Reu lived after he begot Serug two hundred and seven years and begot sons and daughters.

22 And Serug lived thirty years and begot Nahor. 23 And Serug lived after he begot Nahor two hundred years and begot sons and daughters.

24 And Nahor lived nine and twenty years and begot Terah. 25 And Nahor lived after he begot Terah a hundred and nineteen years and begot sons and daughters.

26 And Terah lived seventy years and begot Abram and Nahor and Haran. 27 And these are the generations of Terah: Terah begot Abram, Nahor and Haran. And Haran begot Lot. 28 And Haran died before Terah, his father, in the land of his nativity in Ur of the Chaldeans.

29 And Abram and Nahor married wives: the name of Abram's wife was Sarai, and the name of Nahor's wife, Mil-

patris Melchae et patris Ieschae. 30 Erat autem Sarai sterilis nec habebat liberos.

31 Tulit itaque Thare Abram, filium suum, et Loth, filium Aran, filium filii sui, et Sarai, nurum suam, uxorem Abram, filii sui, et eduxit eos de Ur Chaldeorum ut irent in terram Chanaan. Veneruntque usque Haran et habitaverunt ibi. 32 Et facti sunt dies Thare ducentorum quinque annorum, et mortuus est in Haran.

Caput 12

Dixit autem Dominus ad Abram, "Egredere de terra tua et de cognatione tua et de domo patris tui, et veni in terram quam monstrabo tibi. 2 Faciamque te in gentem magnam, et benedicam tibi et magnificabo nomen tuum, erisque benedictus. 3 Benedicam benedicentibus tibi et maledicam maledicentibus tibi, atque in te benedicentur universae cognationes terrae."

4 Egressus est itaque Abram sicut praeceperat ei Dominus, et ivit cum eo Loth. Septuaginta quinque annorum erat Abram cum egrederetur de Haran. 5 Tulitque Sarai, uxorem suam, et Loth, filium fratris sui, universamque substantiam

cha, the daughter of Haran, father of Milcha and father of Iscah. 30 And Sarai was barren and had no children.

31 And Terah took Abram, his son, and Lot, the son of Haran, his son's son, and Sarai, his daughter-in-law, the wife of Abram, his son, and brought them out of Ur of the Chaldeans to go into the land of Canaan. And they came as far as Haran and dwelt there. 32 And the days of Terah were two hundred and five years, and he died in Haran.

Chapter 12

The call of Abram and the promise made to him. He sojourneth in Canaan and then, by occasion of a famine, goeth down to Egypt.

And the Lord said to Abram, "Go forth out of thy country and from thy kindred and out of thy father's house, and come into the land which I shall shew thee. 2 And I will make of thee a great nation, and I will bless thee and magnify thy name, and thou shalt be blessed. 3 I will bless them that bless thee and curse them that curse thee, and in thee shall all the kindred of the earth be blessed."

4 So Abram went out as the Lord had commanded him, and Lot went with him. Abram was seventy-five years old when he went forth from Haran. 5 And he took Sarai, his wife, and Lot, his brother's son, and all the substance which

quam possederant et animas quas fecerant in Haran, et egressi sunt ut irent in terram Chanaan. Cumque venissent in eam, 6 pertransivit Abram terram usque ad locum Sychem usque ad convallem inlustrem.

Chananeus autem tunc erat in terra. 7 Apparuitque Dominus Abram, et dixit ei, "Semini tuo dabo terram hanc." Qui aedificavit ibi altare Domino qui apparuerat ei. 8 Et inde transgrediens ad montem qui erat contra orientem Bethel, tetendit ibi tabernaculum suum, ab occidente habens Bethel et ab oriente Ai; aedificavit quoque ibi altare Domino et invocavit nomen eius.

9 Perrexitque Abram, vadens et ultra progrediens ad meridiem. 10 Facta est autem fames in terra, descenditque Abram in Aegyptum ut peregrinaretur ibi, praevaluerat enim fames in terra.

11 Cumque prope esset ut ingrederetur Aegyptum, dixit Sarai, uxori suae, "Novi quod pulchra sis mulier 12 et quod cum viderint te Aegyptii, dicturi sunt, 'Uxor ipsius est,' et interficient me et te reservabunt. 13 Dic ergo, obsecro te, quod soror mea sis ut bene sit mihi propter te et vivat anima mea ob gratiam tui."

14 Cum itaque ingressus esset Abram Aegyptum, viderunt Aegyptii mulierem quod esset pulchra nimis. 15 Et nuntiaverunt principes Pharaoni et laudaverunt eam apud illum, et sublata est mulier in domum Pharaonis. 16 Abram vero bene usi sunt propter illam. Fueruntque ei oves et boves et asini et servi et famulae et asinae et cameli.

17 Flagellavit autem Dominus Pharaonem plagis maximis et domum eius propter Sarai, uxorem Abram. 18 Vocavitque

they had gathered and the souls which they had gotten in Haran, and they went out to go into the land of Canaan. And when they were come into it, 6 Abram passed through the country into the place of Shechem, as far as the noble vale.

Now the Canaanite was at that time in the land. 7 And the Lord appeared to Abram, and said to him, "To thy seed will I give this land." And he built there an altar to the Lord who had appeared to him. 8 And passing on from thence to a mountain that was on the east side of Bethel, he there pitched his tent, having Bethel on the west and Ai on the east; he built there also an altar to the Lord and called upon his name.

9 And Abram went forward, going and proceeding on to the south. 10 And there came a famine in the country, and Abram went down into Egypt to sojourn there, for the famine was very grievous in the land.

11 And when he was near to enter into Egypt, he said to Sarai, his wife, "I know that thou art a beautiful woman 12 and that when the Egyptians shall see thee, they will say, 'She is his wife,' and they will kill me and keep thee. 13 Say therefore, I pray thee, that thou art my sister that I may be well used for thee and that my soul may live for thy sake."

14 And when Abram was come into Egypt, the Egyptians saw the woman that she was very beautiful. 15 And the princes told Pharaoh and praised her before him, and the woman was taken into the house of Pharaoh. 16 And they used Abram well for her sake. And he had sheep and oxen and he-asses and menservants and maidservants and she-asses and camels.

17 But the Lord scourged Pharaoh and his house with most grievous stripes for Sarai, Abram's wife. 18 And Pha-

Pharao Abram, et dixit ei, "Quidnam est hoc quod fecisti mihi? Quare non indicasti quod uxor tua esset? 19 Quam ob causam dixisti esse sororem tuam, ut tollerem eam mihi in uxorem? Nunc igitur, ecce coniux tua; accipe eam, et vade." 20 Praecepitque Pharao super Abram viris, et deduxerunt eum et uxorem illius et omnia quae habebat.

Caput 13

Ascendit ergo Abram de Aegypto, ipse et uxor eius et omnia quae habebat et Loth cum eo, ad australem plagam. 2 Erat autem dives valde in possessione argenti et auri. 3 Reversusque est per iter quo venerat, a meridie in Bethel, usque ad locum ubi prius fixerat tabernaculum inter Bethel et Ai, 4 in loco altaris quod fecerat prius, et invocavit ibi nomen Domini.

5 Sed et Loth, qui erat cum Abram, fuerunt greges ovium et armenta et tabernacula, 6 nec poterat eos capere terra ut habitarent simul, erat quippe substantia eorum multa, et non quibant habitare communiter. 7 Unde et facta est rixa inter pastores gregum Abram et Loth. Eo autem tempore

raoh called Abram, and said to him, "What is this that thou hast done to me? Why didst thou not tell me that she was thy wife? 19 For what cause didst thou say she was thy sister, that I might take her to my wife? Now therefore, there is thy wife; take her, and go thy way." 20 And Pharaoh gave his men orders concerning Abram, and they led him away and his wife and all that he had.

Chapter 13

Abram and Lot part from each other. God's promise to Abram.

And Abram went up out of Egypt, he and his wife and all that he had and Lot with him, into the south. 2 And he was very rich in possession of gold and silver. 3 And he returned by the way that he came, from the south to Bethel, to the place where before he had pitched his tent between Bethel and Ai, 4 in the place of the altar which he had made before, and there he called upon the name of the Lord.

5 But Lot also, who was with Abram, had flocks of sheep and herds of beasts and tents, 6 neither was the land able to bear them that they might dwell together, for their substance was great, and they could not dwell together. 7 Whereupon also there arose a strife between the herdsmen of Abram and of Lot. And at that time the Canaanite

Chananeus et Ferezeus habitabant in illa terra. 8 Dixit ergo Abram ad Loth, "Ne, quaeso, sit iurgium inter me et te et inter pastores meos et pastores tuos, fratres enim sumus. 9 Ecce: universa terra coram te est. Recede a me, obsecro. Si ad sinistram ieris, ego dexteram tenebo; si tu dexteram elegeris, ego ad sinistram pergam."

10 Elevatis itaque Loth oculis vidit omnem circa regionem Iordanis, quae universa inrigabatur antequam subverteret Dominus Sodomam et Gomorram, sicut paradisus Domini et sicut Aegyptus venientibus in Segor. 11 Elegitque sibi Loth regionem circa Iordanem, et recessit ab oriente, divisique sunt alterutrum a fratre suo.

12 Abram habitavit in terra Chanaan, Loth vero moratus est in oppidis quae erant circa Iordanem et habitavit in Sodomis. 13 Homines autem Sodomitae pessimi erant et peccatores coram Domino nimis. 14 Dixitque Dominus ad Abram, postquam divisus est Loth ab eo, "Leva oculos tuos, et vide a loco in quo nunc es, ad aquilonem et ad meridiem, ad orientem et ad occidentem. 15 Omnem terram quam conspicis tibi dabo et semini tuo usque in sempiternum. 16 Faciamque semen tuum sicut pulverem terrae: si quis potest hominum numerare pulverem terrae, semen quoque tuum numerare poterit. 17 Surge, et perambula terram in longitudine et in latitudine sua, quia tibi daturus sum eam."

18 Movens, igitur, Abram tabernaculum suum venit et habitavit iuxta convallem Mambre, quod est in Hebron, aedificavitque ibi altare Domino.

and the Perizzite dwelled in that country. 8 Abram therefore said to Lot, "Let there be no quarrel, I beseech thee, between me and thee and between my herdsmen and thy herdsmen, for we are brethren. 9 Behold: the whole land is before thee. Depart from me, I pray thee. If thou wilt go to the left hand, I will take the right; if thou choose the right hand, I will pass to the left."

10 And Lot, lifting up his eyes, saw all the country about the Jordan, which was watered throughout before the Lord destroyed Sodom and Gomorrah, as the paradise of the Lord and like Egypt as one comes to Zoar. 11 And Lot chose to himself the country about the Jordan, and he departed from the east, and they were separated one brother from the other.

12 Abram dwelt in the land of Canaan, and Lot abode in the towns that were about the Jordan and dwelt in Sodom. 13 And the men of Sodom were very wicked and sinners before the face of the Lord beyond measure. 14 And the Lord said to Abram, after Lot was separated from him, "Lift up thy eyes, and look from the place wherein thou now art, to the north and *to* the south, to the east and *to* the west. 15 All the land which thou seest I will give to thee and to thy seed for ever. 16 And I will make thy seed as the dust of the earth: if any man be able to number the dust of the earth, he shall be able to number thy seed also. 17 Arise, and walk through the land in the length and in the breadth thereof, for I will give it to thee."

18 So Abram, removing his tent, came and dwelt by the vale of Mamre, which is in Hebron, and he built there an altar to the Lord.

Caput 14

Factum est autem in illo tempore ut Amrafel, rex Sennaar, et Arioch, rex Ponti, et Chodorlahomor, rex Aelamitarum, et Thadal, rex gentium, 2 inirent bellum contra Bara, regem Sodomorum, et contra Bersa, regem Gomorrae, et contra Sennaab, regem Adamae, et contra Semeber, regem Seboim, contraque regem Balae, ipsa est Segor. 3 Omnes hii convenerunt in vallem silvestrem, quae nunc est Mare Salis, 4 duodecim enim annis servierant Chodorlahomor, et tertiodecimo anno recesserunt ab eo. 5 Igitur anno quartodecimo venit Chodorlahomor et reges qui erant cum eo, percusseruntque Rafaim in Astharothcarnaim et Zuzim cum eis et Emim in Savecariathaim 6 et Chorreos in montibus Seir usque ad campestria Pharan, quae est in solitudine.

7 Reversique sunt et venerunt ad fontem Mesfat—ipsa est Cades—et percusserunt omnem regionem Amalechitarum et Amorreum qui habitabat in Asasonthamar. 8 Et egressi sunt rex Sodomorum et rex Gomorrae rexque Adamae et rex Seboim necnon et rex Balae, quae est Segor, et

Chapter 14

The expedition of the four kings. The victory of Abram. He is blessed by Melchizedek.

And it came to pass at that time that Amraphel, king of Shinar, and Arioch, king of Pontus, and Chedorlaomer, king of the Elamites, and Tidal, king of nations, 2 made war against Bera, king of Sodom, and against Birsha, king of Gomorrah, and against Shinab, king of Admah, and against Shemeber, king of Zeboiim, and against the king of Bela, which is Zoar. 3 All these came together into the woodland vale, which now is the Salt Sea, 4 for they had served Chedorlaomer twelve years, and in the thirteenth year they revolted from him. 5 And in the fourteenth year came Chedorlaomer and the kings that were with him, and they smote the Rephaim in Ashteroth-karnaim and the Zuzim with them and the Emim in Shaveh-kiriathaim 6 and the Horites in the mountains of Seir even to the plains of El-paran, which is in the wilderness.

7 And they returned and came to the fountain of En-mishpat—the same is Kadesh—and they smote all the country of the Amalekites and the Amorean that dwelt in Hazazon-tamar. 8 And the king of Sodom and the king of Gomorrah and the king of Admah and the king of Zeboiim and the king of Bela, which is Zoar, went out, and they set themselves against them in battle array in the woodland

direxerunt contra eos aciem in valle silvestri, 9 scilicet, adversum Chodorlahomor, regem Aelamitarum, et Thadal, regem gentium, et Amrafel, regem Sennaar, et Arioch, regem Ponti: quattuor reges adversus quinque.

10 Vallis autem silvestris habebat puteos multos bituminis. Itaque rex Sodomorum et Gomorrae terga verterunt cecideruntque ibi, et qui remanserant fugerunt ad montem. 11 Tulerunt autem omnem substantiam Sodomorum et Gomorrae et universa quae ad cibum pertinent et abierunt, 12 necnon et Loth et substantiam eius, filium fratris Abram, qui habitabat in Sodomis.

13 Et ecce: unus qui evaserat nuntiavit Abram, Hebraeo, qui habitabat in convalle Mambre, Amorrei, fratris Eschol et fratris Aner, hii enim pepigerant foedus cum Abram. 14 Quod cum audisset Abram captum, videlicet, Loth, fratrem suum, numeravit expeditos vernaculos suos trecentos decem et octo et persecutus est eos usque Dan. 15 Et divisis sociis, inruit super eos nocte percussitque eos et persecutus est usque Hoba, quae est ad levam Damasci. 16 Reduxitque omnem substantiam et Loth, fratrem suum, cum substantia illius, mulieres quoque et populum.

17 Egressus est autem rex Sodomorum in occursum eius postquam reversus est a caede Chodorlahomor et regum qui cum eo erant in valle Save, quae est vallis regis. 18 At vero Melchisedech, rex Salem, proferens panem et vinum, erat enim sacerdos Dei altissimi, 19 benedixit ei et ait, "Benedictus Abram Deo excelso, qui creavit caelum et terram. 20 Et benedictus Deus excelsus, quo protegente hostes in manibus tuis sunt." Et dedit ei decimas ex omnibus.

vale, 9 to wit, against Chedorlaomer, king of the Elamites, and Tidal, king of nations, and Amraphel, king of Shinar, and Arioch, king of Pontus: four kings against five.

10 Now the woodland vale had many pits of slime. And the king of Sodom and the king of Gomorrah turned their backs and were overthrown there, and they that remained fled to the mountain. 11 And they took all the substance of the Sodomites and Gomorrites and all *their victuals* and went their way, 12 and Lot also, the son of Abram's brother, who dwelt in Sodom, and his substance.

13 And behold: one that had escaped told Abram, the Hebrew, who dwelt in the vale of Mamre, the Amorite, the brother of Eshcol and the brother of Aner, for these had made league with Abram. 14 Which when Abram had heard, to wit, that his brother Lot was taken, he numbered of the servants born in his house three hundred and eighteen well appointed and pursued them to Dan. 15 And dividing his company, he rushed upon them in the night and defeated them and pursued them as far as Hobah, which is on the left hand of Damascus. 16 And he brought back all the substance and Lot, his brother, with his substance, the women also and the people.

17 And the king of Sodom went out to meet him after he returned from the slaughter of Chedorlaomer and of the kings that were with him in the vale of Shaveh, which is the king's vale. 18 But Melchizedek, the king of Salem, bringing forth bread and wine, for he was the priest of the most high God, 19 blessed him and said, "Blessed be Abram by the most high God, who created heaven and earth. 20 And blessed be the most high God, by whose protection the enemies are in thy hands." And he gave him the tithes of all.

21 Dixit autem rex Sodomorum ad Abram, "Da mihi animas, cetera tolle tibi."

22 Qui respondit ei, "Levo manum meam ad Dominum Deum, excelsum, possessorem caeli et terrae, 23 quod a filo subteminis usque ad corrigiam caligae, non accipiam ex omnibus quae tua sunt, ne dicas, 'Ego ditavi Abram,' 24 exceptis his quae comederunt iuvenes et partibus virorum qui venerunt mecum: Aner, Eschol et Mambre. Isti accipient partes suas."

Caput 15

His itaque transactis, factus est sermo Domini ad Abram per visionem, dicens, "Noli timere, Abram; ego protector tuus sum et merces tua magna nimis."

2 Dixitque Abram, "Domine Deus, quid dabis mihi? Ego vadam absque liberis, et filius procuratoris domus meae iste Damascus Eliezer." 3 Addiditque Abram, "Mihi autem non dedisti semen, et ecce: vernaculus meus heres meus erit."

4 Statimque, sermo Domini factus est ad eum, dicens, "Non erit hic heres tuus, sed qui egredietur de utero tuo, ipsum habebis heredem." 5 Eduxitque eum foras et ait illi,

21 And the king of Sodom said to Abram, "Give me the persons, and the rest take to thyself."

22 And he answered him, "I lift up my hand to the Lord God, the most high, the possessor of heaven and earth, 23 that from the very woof thread unto the shoe latchet, I will not take of any things that are thine, lest thou say, 'I have enriched Abram,' 24 except such things as the young men have eaten and the shares of the men that came with me: Aner, Eshcol and Mamre. These shall take their shares."

Chapter 15

God promiseth seed to Abram. His faith, sacrifice and vision.

Now when these things were done, the word of the Lord came to Abram by a vision, saying, "Fear not, Abram; I am thy protector and thy reward exceeding great."

2 And Abram said, "Lord God, what wilt thou give me? I shall go without children, and the son of the steward of my house is this Damascus Eliezer." 3 And Abram added, "But to me thou hast not given seed, and lo: my servant born in my house shall be my heir."

4 And immediately, the word of the Lord came to him, saying, "He shall not be thy heir, but he that shall come out of thy bowels, him shalt thou have for thy heir." 5 And he

"Suspice caelum, et numera stellas, si potes." Et dixit ei, "Sic erit semen tuum."

6 Credidit Abram Deo, et reputatum est ei ad iustitiam. 7 Dixitque ad eum, "Ego Dominus qui eduxi te de Ur Chaldeorum ut darem tibi terram istam et possideres eam."

8 At ille ait, "Domine Deus, unde scire possum quod possessurus sim eam?"

9 Et respondens Dominus, "Sume," inquit, "mihi vaccam triennem et capram trimam et arietem annorum trium, turturem quoque et columbam." 10 Qui tollens universa haec divisit per medium et utrasque partes contra se altrinsecus posuit, aves autem non divisit. 11 Descenderuntque volucres super cadavera, et abigebat eas Abram.

12 Cumque sol occumberet, sopor inruit super Abram, et horror magnus et tenebrosus invasit eum. 13 Dictumque est ad eum, "Scito praenoscens quod peregrinum futurum sit semen tuum in terra non sua, et subicient eos servituti et adfligent quadringentis annis. 14 Verumtamen gentem cui servituri sunt ego iudicabo, et post haec egredientur cum magna substantia. 15 Tu autem ibis ad patres tuos in pace, sepultus in senectute bona. 16 Generatione autem quarta, revertentur huc, necdum enim conpletae sunt iniquitates Amorreorum usque ad praesens tempus." 17 Cum ergo occubuisset sol, facta est caligo tenebrosa, et apparuit clibanus fumans et lampas ignis transiens inter divisiones illas.

18 In die illo, pepigit Dominus cum Abram foedus, dicens,

brought him forth abroad and said to him, "Look up to heaven, and number the stars, if thou canst." And he said to him, "So shall thy seed be."

6 Abram believed God, and it was reputed to him unto justice. 7 And he said to him, "I am the Lord who brought thee out from Ur of the Chaldeans to give thee this land and that thou mightest possess it."

8 But he said, "Lord God, whereby may I know that I shall possess it?"

9 And the Lord answered, and said, "Take me a cow of three years old and a she-goat of three years and a ram of three years, a turtle also and a pigeon." 10 And he took all these and divided them in the midst and laid the two pieces of each one against the other, but the birds he divided not. 11 And the fowls came down upon the carcasses, and Abram drove them away.

12 And when the sun was setting, a deep sleep fell upon Abram, and a great and darksome horror seized upon him. 13 And it was said unto him, "Know thou beforehand that thy seed shall be a stranger in a land not their own, and they shall bring them under bondage and afflict them four hundred years. 14 But I will judge the nation which they shall serve, and after this they shall come out with great substance. 15 And thou shalt go to thy fathers in peace and be buried in a good old age. 16 But in the fourth generation, they shall return hither, for as yet the iniquities of the Amorites are not at the full until this present time." 17 And when the sun was set, there arose a dark mist, and there appeared a smoking furnace and a lamp of fire passing between those divisions.

18 That day, God made a covenant with Abram, saying,

"Semini tuo dabo terram hanc, a fluvio Aegypti usque ad fluvium magnum Eufraten. 19 Cineos et Cenezeos, Cedmoneos 20 et Hettheos et Ferezeos, Rafaim quoque 21 et Amorreos et Chananeos et Gergeseos et Iebuseos."

Caput 16

Igitur Sarai, uxor Abram, non genuerat liberos, sed habens ancillam, Aegyptiam nomine Agar, 2 dixit marito suo, "Ecce! Conclusit me Dominus ne parerem. Ingredere ad ancillam meam, si forte saltem ex illa suscipiam filios." Cumque ille adquiesceret deprecanti, 3 tulit Agar Aegyptiam, ancillam suam, post annos decem quam habitare coeperant in terra Chanaan, et dedit eam viro suo uxorem. 4 Qui ingressus est ad eam.

At illa, concepisse se videns, despexit dominam suam. 5 Dixitque Sarai ad Abram, "Inique agis contra me. Ego dedi ancillam meam in sinum tuum, quae, videns quod conceperit, despectui me habet. Iudicet Dominus inter me et te."

6 Cui respondens, Abram, "Ecce," ait, "ancilla tua in manu

"To thy seed will I give this land, from the river of Egypt even to the great river Euphrates. 19 The Cineans and Kenizzites, the Cedmonites 20 and the Hittites and the Perizzites, the Rephaim also 21 and the Amorites and the Canaanites and the Girgashites and the Jebusites."

Chapter 16

Abram marrieth Hagar, who bringeth forth Ishmael.

Now Sarai, the wife of Abram, had brought forth no children, but having a handmaid, an Egyptian named Hagar, 2 she said to her husband, "Behold! The Lord hath restrained me from bearing. Go in unto my handmaid; it may be I may have children of her at least." And when he agreed to her request, 3 she took Hagar the Egyptian, her handmaid, ten years after they first dwelt in the land of Canaan, and gave her to her husband to wife. 4 And he went in to her.

But she, perceiving that she was with child, despised her mistress. 5 And Sarai said to Abram, "Thou dost unjustly with me. I gave my handmaid into thy bosom, and she, perceiving herself to be with child, despiseth me. The Lord judge between me and thee."

6 And Abram made answer, and said to her, "Behold: thy

tua est; utere ea ut libet." Adfligente igitur eam Sarai, fugam iniit.

7 Cumque invenisset illam angelus Domini iuxta fontem aquae in solitudine qui est in via Sur in deserto, 8 dixit ad eam, "Agar, ancilla Sarai, unde venis? Et quo vadis?"

Quae respondit, "A facie Sarai, dominae meae, ego fugio."

9 Dixitque ei angelus Domini, "Revertere ad dominam tuam, et humiliare sub manu ipsius." 10 Et rursum, "Multiplicans," inquit, "multiplicabo semen tuum, et non numerabitur prae multitudine." 11 Ac deinceps, "Ecce," ait, "concepisti, et paries filium, vocabisque nomen eius Ismahel eo quod audierit Dominus adflictionem tuam. 12 Hic erit ferus homo: manus eius contra omnes, et manus omnium contra eum, et e regione universorum fratrum suorum figet tabernacula."

13 Vocavit autem nomen Domini qui loquebatur ad eam Tu Deus qui vidisti me. Dixit enim, "Profecto hic vidi posteriora videntis me." 14 Propterea appellavit puteum illum Puteum Viventis et Videntis me. Ipse est inter Cades et Barad. 15 Peperitque Abrae filium qui vocavit nomen eius Ismahel. 16 Octoginta et sex annorum erat Abram quando peperit ei Agar Ismahelem.

handmaid is in thy own hand; use her as it pleaseth thee." And when Sarai afflicted her, she ran away.

7 And the angel of the Lord having found her by a fountain of water in the wilderness which is in the way to Shur in the desert, 8 he said to her, "Hagar, handmaid of Sarai, whence comest thou? And whither goest thou?"

And she answered, "I flee from the face of Sarai, my mistress."

9 And the angel of the Lord said to her, "Return to thy mistress, and humble thyself under her hand." 10 And again he said, *"I will multiply thy seed exceedingly,* and it shall not be numbered for multitude." 11 And again, "Behold," said he, "thou art with child, and thou shalt bring forth a son, and thou shalt call his name Ishmael because the Lord hath heard thy affliction. 12 He shall be a wild man: his hand will be against all men, and all men's hands against him, and he shall pitch his tents over against all his brethren."

13 And she called the name of the Lord that spoke unto her Thou the God who hast seen me. For she said, "Verily here have I seen the hinder parts of him that seeth me." 14 Therefore she called that well the Well of him that Liveth and Seeth me. The same is between Kadesh and Bered. 15 And Hagar brought forth a son to Abram who called his name Ishmael. 16 Abram was four score and six years old when Hagar brought him forth Ishmael.

Caput 17

Postquam vero nonaginta et novem annorum esse coeperat, apparuit ei Dominus dixitque ad eum, "Ego Deus Omnipotens. Ambula coram me, et esto perfectus. 2 Ponamque foedus meum inter me et te, et multiplicabo te vehementer nimis." 3 Cecidit Abram pronus in faciem. 4 Dixitque ei Deus, "Ego sum, et pactum meum tecum, erisque pater multarum gentium. 5 Nec ultra vocabitur nomen tuum Abram, sed appellaberis Abraham, quia patrem multarum gentium constitui te.

6 "Faciamque te crescere vehementissime, et ponam te in gentibus, regesque ex te egredientur. 7 Et statuam pactum meum inter me et te et inter semen tuum post te in generationibus suis foedere sempiterno ut sim Deus tuus et seminis tui post te. 8 Daboque tibi et semini tuo terram peregrinationis tuae, omnem terram Chanaan, in possessionem aeternam, eroque Deus eorum."

9 Dixit iterum Deus ad Abraham, "Et tu ergo custodies pactum meum, et semen tuum post te in generationibus suis. 10 Hoc est pactum meum quod observabitis, inter me et vos et semen tuum post te: circumcidetur ex vobis omne masculinum.

11 "Et circumcidetis carnem praeputii vestri ut sit in sig-

Chapter 17

The covenant of circumcision.

And after he began to be ninety and nine years old, the Lord appeared to him and said unto him, "I am the Almighty God. Walk before me, and be perfect. 2 And I will make my covenant between me and thee, and I will multiply thee exceedingly." 3 Abram fell flat on his face. 4 And God said to him, "I am, and my covenant is with thee, and thou shalt be a father of many nations. 5 Neither shall thy name be called any more Abram, but thou shalt be called Abraham, because I have made thee a father of many nations.

6 "And I will make thee increase exceedingly, and I will make nations of thee, and kings shall come out of thee. 7 And I will establish my covenant between me and thee and between thy seed after thee in their generations by a perpetual covenant to be a God to thee and to thy seed after thee. 8 And I will give to thee and to thy seed the land of thy sojournment, all the land of Canaan, for a perpetual possession, and I will be their God."

9 Again God said to Abraham, "And thou therefore shalt keep my covenant, and thy seed after thee in their generations. 10 This is my covenant which you shall observe, between me and you and thy seed after thee: all the male kind of you shall be circumcised.

11 "And you shall circumcise the flesh of your foreskin

num foederis inter me et vos. 12 Infans octo dierum circumcidetur in vobis, omne masculinum in generationibus vestris. Tam vernaculus quam empticius circumcidetur et
quicumque non fuerit de stirpe vestra. 13 Eritque pactum
meum in carne vestra in foedus aeternum. 14 Masculus cuius
praeputii caro circumcisa non fuerit, delebitur anima illa de
populo suo quia pactum meum irritum fecit."

15 Dixit quoque Deus ad Abraham, "Sarai, uxorem tuam,
non vocabis Sarai, sed Sarram. 16 Et benedicam ei, et ex illa
dabo tibi filium cui benedicturus sum, eritque in nationes,
et reges populorum orientur ex eo."

17 Cecidit Abraham in faciem et risit, dicens in corde
suo, "Putasne centenario nascetur filius? Et Sarra nonagena-
ria pariet?" 18 Dixitque ad Deum, "Utinam Ismahel vivat coram te!"

19 Et ait Deus ad Abraham, "Sarra, uxor tua, pariet tibi filium, vocabisque nomen eius Isaac, et constituam pactum
meum illi in foedus sempiternum et semini eius post eum.
20 Super Ismahel quoque exaudivi te. Ecce! Benedicam ei et
augebo et multiplicabo eum valde: duodecim duces gene-
rabit, et faciam illum in gentem magnam. 21 Pactum vero
meum statuam ad Isaac quem pariet tibi Sarra tempore isto
in anno altero."

22 Cumque finitus esset sermo loquentis cum eo, ascendit
Deus ab Abraham. 23 Tulit autem Abraham Ismahelem, filium suum, et omnes vernaculos domus suae universosque
quos emerat, cunctos mares ex omnibus viris domus suae, et

that it may be for a sign of the covenant between me and you. 12 An infant of eight days old shall be circumcised among you, every man-child in your generations. He that is born in the house as well as the bought servant shall be circumcised and whosoever is not of your stock. 13 And my covenant shall be in your flesh for a perpetual covenant. 14 The male whose flesh of his foreskin shall not be circumcised, that soul shall be destroyed out of his people because he hath broken my covenant."

15 God said also to Abraham, "Sarai, thy wife, thou shalt not call Sarai, but Sarah. 16 And I will bless her, and of her I will give thee a son whom I will bless, and he shall become nations, and kings of people shall spring from him."

17 Abraham fell upon his face and laughed, saying in his heart, "Shall a son, thinkest thou, be born to him that is a hundred years old? And shall Sarah that is ninety years old bring forth?" 18 And he said to God, "O that Ishmael may live before thee!"

19 And God said to Abraham, "Sarah, thy wife, shall bear thee a son, and thou shalt call his name Isaac, and I will establish my covenant with him for a perpetual covenant and with his seed after him. 20 And as for Ishmael I have also heard thee. Behold! I will bless him and increase and multiply him exceedingly: he shall beget twelve chiefs, and I will make him a great nation. 21 But my covenant I will establish with Isaac whom Sarah shall bring forth to thee at this time in the next year."

22 And when he had left off speaking with him, God went up from Abraham. 23 And Abraham took Ishmael, his son, and all that were born in his house and all whom he had bought, every male among the men of his house, and he cir-

circumcidit carnem praeputii eorum statim in ipsa die sicut praeceperat ei Deus. 24 Abraham nonaginta et novem erat annorum quando circumcidit carnem praeputii sui, 25 et Ismahel, filius eius, tredecim annos impleverat tempore circumcisionis suae. 26 Eadem die circumcisus est Abraham et Ismahel, filius eius. 27 Et omnes viri domus illius, tam vernaculi quam empticii et alienigenae, pariter circumcisi sunt.

Caput 18

Apparuit autem ei Dominus in convalle Mambre sedenti in ostio tabernaculi sui in ipso fervore diei. 2 Cumque elevasset oculos, apparuerunt ei tres viri stantes propter eum, quos cum vidisset, cucurrit in occursum eorum de ostio tabernaculi et adoravit in terra. 3 Et dixit, "Domine, si inveni gratiam in oculis tuis, ne transeas servum tuum, 4 sed adferam pauxillum aquae, et lavate pedes vestros, et requiescite sub arbore. 5 Ponamque buccellam panis, et confortate cor vestrum; postea transibitis, idcirco enim declinastis ad servum vestrum."

Qui dixerunt, "Fac ut locutus es."

cumcised the flesh of their foreskin forthwith the very same day as God had commanded him. 24 Abraham was ninety and nine years old when he circumcised the flesh of his foreskin, 25 and Ishmael, his son, was full thirteen years old at the time of his circumcision. 26 The selfsame day was Abraham circumcised and Ishmael, his son. 27 And all the men of his house, as well they that were born in his house as the bought servants and strangers, were circumcised with him.

Chapter 18

Angels are entertained by Abraham. They foretell the birth of Isaac. Abraham's prayer for the men of Sodom.

And the Lord appeared to him in the vale of Mamre as he was sitting at the door of his tent in the very heat of the day. 2 And when he had lifted up his eyes, there appeared to him three men standing near him, and as soon as he saw them, he ran to meet them from the door of his tent and adored down to the ground. 3 And he said, "Lord, if I have found favour in thy sight, pass not away from thy servant, 4 but I will fetch a little water, and wash ye your feet, and rest ye under the tree. 5 And I will set a morsel of bread, and strengthen ye your heart; afterwards you shall pass on, for therefore are you come aside to your servant."

And they said, "Do as thou hast spoken."

6 Festinavit Abraham in tabernaculum ad Sarram dixitque ei, "Adcelera! Tria sata similae commisce, et fac subcinericios panes." 7 Ipse vero ad armentum cucurrit et tulit inde vitulum tenerrimum et optimum deditque puero qui festinavit et coxit illum. 8 Tulit quoque butyrum et lac et vitulum quem coxerat et posuit coram eis, ipse vero stabat iuxta eos sub arbore.

9 Cumque comedissent, dixerunt ad eum, "Ubi est Sarra, uxor tua?"

Ille respondit, "Ecce: in tabernaculo est."

10 Cui dixit, "Revertens veniam ad te tempore isto vita comite, et habebit filium Sarra, uxor tua." Quo audito, Sarra risit post ostium tabernaculi.

11 Erant autem ambo senes provectaeque aetatis, et desierant Sarrae fieri muliebria. 12 Quae risit occulte, dicens, "Postquam consenui et dominus meus vetulus est, voluptati operam dabo?"

13 Dixit autem Dominus ad Abraham, "Quare risit Sarra, dicens, 'Num vere paritura sum anus?' 14 Numquid Deo est quicquam difficile? Iuxta condictum, revertar ad te hoc eodem tempore vita comite, et habebit Sarra filium."

15 Negavit Sarra, dicens, "Non risi," timore perterrita.

Dominus autem, "Non est," inquit, "ita, sed risisti."

16 Cum ergo surrexissent inde viri, direxerunt oculos suos contra Sodomam, et Abraham simul gradiebatur, deducens eos. 17 Dixitque Dominus, "Num celare potero Abraham quae gesturus sum, 18 cum futurus sit in gentem magnam ac

6 Abraham made haste into the tent to Sarah and said to her, "Make haste! Temper together three measures of flour, and make cakes upon the hearth." 7 And he himself ran to the herd and took from thence a calf very tender and very good and gave it to a young man who made haste and boiled it. 8 He took also butter and milk and the calf which he had boiled and set before them, but he stood by them under the tree.

9 And when they had eaten, they said to him, "Where is Sarah, thy wife?"

He answered, "Lo: she is in the tent."

10 And he said to him, "I will return and come to thee at this time life accompanying, and Sarah, thy wife, shall have a son." Which when Sarah heard, she laughed behind the door of the tent.

11 Now they were both old and far advanced in years, and *it had ceased to be with Sarah after the manner of women.* 12 And she laughed secretly, saying, "After I am grown old and my lord is an old man, shall I give myself to pleasure?"

13 And the Lord said to Abraham, "Why did Sarah laugh, saying, 'Shall I who am an old woman bear a child indeed?' 14 Is there any thing hard to God? According to appointment, I will return to thee at this same time life accompanying, and Sarah shall have a son."

15 Sarah denied, saying, "I did not laugh," for she was afraid.

But the Lord said, "*Nay,* but thou didst laugh."

16 And when the men rose up from thence, they turned their eyes towards Sodom, and Abraham walked with them, bringing them on the way. 17 And the Lord said, "Can I hide from Abraham what I am about to do, 18 seeing he shall be-

robustissimam et benedicendae sint in illo omnes nationes terrae? 19 Scio enim quod praecepturus sit filiis suis et domui suae post se ut custodiant viam Domini et faciant iustitiam et iudicium ut adducat Dominus propter Abraham omnia quae locutus est ad eum."

20 Dixit itaque Dominus, "Clamor Sodomorum et Gomorrae multiplicatus est, et peccatum earum adgravatum est nimis. 21 Descendam et videbo utrum clamorem qui venit ad me opere conpleverint an non est ita, ut sciam." 22 Converteruntque se inde et abierunt Sodomam, Abraham vero adhuc stabat coram Domino.

23 Et, adpropinquans, ait, "Numquid perdes iustum cum impio? 24 Si fuerint quinquaginta iusti in civitate, peribunt simul? Et non parces loco illi propter quinquaginta iustos, si fuerint in eo? 25 Absit a te ut rem hanc facias et occidas iustum cum impio fiatque iustus sicut impius; non est hoc tuum; qui iudicas omnem terram nequaquam facies iudicium."

26 Dixitque Dominus ad eum, "Si invenero Sodomis quinquaginta iustos in medio civitatis, dimittam omni loco propter eos."

27 Respondensque, Abraham ait, "Quia semel coepi, loquar ad Dominum meum, cum sim pulvis et cinis. 28 Quid si minus quinquaginta iustis quinque fuerint? Delebis propter quadraginta quinque universam urbem?"

Et ait, "Non delebo si invenero ibi quadraginta quinque."

29 Rursumque locutus est ad eum, "Sin autem quadraginta ibi inventi fuerint, quid facies?"

Ait, "Non percutiam propter quadraginta."

come a great and *mighty* nation and in him all the nations of the earth shall be blessed? 19 For I know that he will command his children and his household after him to keep the way of the Lord and do judgment and justice that for Abraham's sake the Lord may bring to effect all the things he hath spoken unto him."

20 And the Lord said, "The cry of Sodom and Gomorrah is multiplied, and their sin is become exceedingly grievous. 21 I will go down and see whether they have done according to the cry that is come to me or whether it be not so, that I may know." 22 And they turned themselves from thence and went their way to Sodom, but Abraham as yet stood before the Lord.

23 And, drawing nigh, he said, "Wilt thou destroy the just with the wicked? 24 If there be fifty just men in the city, shall they perish withal? And wilt thou not spare that place for the sake of the fifty just, if they be therein? 25 Far be it from thee to do this thing and to slay the just with the wicked and for the just to be in like case as the wicked; this is not beseeming thee; thou who judgest all the earth wilt not make this judgment."

26 And the Lord said to him, "If I find in Sodom fifty just within the city, I will spare the whole place for their sake."

27 And Abraham answered, and said, "Seeing I have once begun, I will speak to my Lord, whereas I am dust and ashes. 28 What if there be five less than fifty just persons? Wilt thou for five and forty destroy the whole city?"

And he said, "I will not destroy it if I *find* five and forty."

29 And again he said to him, "But if forty be found there, what wilt thou do?"

He said, "I will not destroy it for the sake of forty."

30 "Ne, quaeso," inquit, "indigneris, Domine, si loquar. Quid si inventi fuerint ibi triginta?

Respondit, "Non faciam si invenero ibi triginta."

31 "Quia semel," ait, "coepi, loquar ad Dominum meum. Quid si inventi fuerint ibi viginti?"

Dixit, "Non interficiam propter viginti."

32 "Obsecro," inquit, "ne irascaris, Domine, si loquar adhuc semel. Quid si inventi fuerint ibi decem?"

Et dixit, "Non delebo propter decem." 33 Abiitque Dominus postquam cessavit loqui ad Abraham, et ille reversus est in locum suum.

Caput 19

Veneruntque duo angeli Sodomam vespere, et sedente Loth in foribus civitatis. Qui cum vidisset eos, surrexit et ivit obviam eis adoravitque pronus in terra 2 et dixit, "Obsecro, domini, declinate in domum pueri vestri, et manete ibi. Lavate pedes vestros, et mane proficiscemini in viam vestram."

Qui dixerunt, "Minime, sed in platea manebimus." 3 Conpulit illos oppido ut deverterent ad eum, ingressisque

30 "Lord," saith he, "be not angry, I beseech thee, if I speak. What if thirty shall be found there?"

He answered, "I will not do it if I find thirty there."

31 "Seeing," saith he, "I have once begun, I will speak to my Lord. What if twenty be found there?"

He said, "I will not destroy it for the sake of twenty."

32 "I beseech thee," saith he, "be not angry, Lord, if I speak yet once more. What if ten should be found there?"

And he said, "I will not destroy it for the sake of ten."

33 And the Lord departed after he had *left speaking* to Abraham, and Abraham returned to his place.

Chapter 19

Lot, entertaining angels in his house, is delivered from
Sodom, which is destroyed. His wife for looking back is
turned into a statue of salt.

And the two angels came to Sodom in the evening, and Lot was sitting in the gate of the city. And seeing them, he rose up and went to meet them and worshipped prostrate to the ground 2 and said, "I beseech you, my lords, turn in to the house of your servant, and lodge there. Wash your feet, and in the morning you shall go on your way."

And they said, "No, but we will abide in the street." 3 He pressed them very much to turn in unto him, and when they

domum illius, fecit convivium et coxit azyma, et comederunt.

4 Prius autem quam irent cubitum, viri civitatis vallave-
runt domum, a puero usque ad senem, omnis populus simul.
5 Vocaveruntque Loth et dixerunt ei, "Ubi sunt viri qui introierunt ad te nocte? Educ illos huc ut cognoscamus eos."

6 Egressus ad eos Loth post tergum adcludens ostium ait,
7 "Nolite, quaeso, fratres mei, nolite malum hoc facere. 8 Habeo duas filias quae necdum cognoverunt virum. Educam
eas ad vos, et abutimini eis sicut placuerit vobis dummodo
viris istis nihil faciatis mali, quia ingressi sunt sub umbraculum tegminis mei."

9 At illi dixerunt, "Recede illuc." Et rursus, "Ingressus es,"
inquiunt, "ut advena; numquid ut iudices? Te ergo ipsum
magis quam hos adfligemus." Vimque faciebant Loth vehementissime, iamque prope erat ut refringerent fores. 10 Et
ecce: miserunt manum viri et introduxerunt ad se Loth clu-
seruntque ostium. 11 Et eos qui erant foris percusserunt caecitate a minimo usque ad maximum ita ut ostium invenire
non possent.

12 Dixerunt autem ad Loth, "Habes hic tuorum quempiam, generum aut filios aut filias? Omnes qui tui sunt, educ
de urbe hac, 13 delebimus enim locum istum eo quod incre-
verit clamor eorum coram Domino, qui misit nos ut perda-
mus illos."

14 Egressus itaque Loth locutus est ad generos suos qui
accepturi erant filias eius et dixit, "Surgite! Egredimini de

were come into his house, he made them a feast and baked unleavened bread, and they ate.

4 But before they went to bed, the men of the city beset the house, *both* young *and* old, all the people together. 5 And they called Lot and said to him, "Where are the men that came in to thee at night? Bring them out hither that we may know them."

6 Lot went out to them and shut the door after him and said, 7 "Do not so; I beseech you, my brethren, do not commit this evil. 8 I have two daughters who as yet have not known man. I will bring them out to you, and abuse you them as it shall please you so that you do no evil to these men, because they are come in under the shadow of my roof."

9 But they said, "Get thee back thither." And again, "Thou camest in," said they, "as a stranger; was it to be a judge? Therefore we will afflict thee more than them." And they pressed very violently upon Lot, and they were even at the point of breaking open the doors. 10 And behold: the men put out their hand and drew in Lot unto them and shut the door. 11 And them that were without they struck with blindness from the least to the greatest so that they could not find the door.

12 And they said to Lot, "Hast thou here any of thine, son-in-law or sons or daughters? All that are thine, bring them out of this city, 13 for we will destroy this place because their cry is grown loud before the Lord, who hath sent us to destroy them."

14 So Lot went out and spoke to his sons-in-law that were to have his daughters and said, "Arise! Get you out of this

loco isto quia delebit Dominus civitatem hanc." Et visus est eis quasi ludens loqui.

15 Cumque esset mane, cogebant eum angeli, dicentes, "Surge! Tolle uxorem tuam et duas filias quas habes, ne et tu pariter pereas in scelere civitatis."

16 Dissimulante illo, adprehenderunt manum eius et manum uxoris ac duarum filiarum eius eo quod parceret Dominus illi. 17 Et eduxerunt eum posueruntque extra civitatem, ibique locuti sunt ad eum, dicentes, "Salva animam tuam. Noli respicere post tergum, nec stes in omni circa regione, sed in monte salvum te fac ne et tu simul pereas."

18 Dixitque Loth ad eos, "Quaeso, Domine mi, 19 quia invenit servus tuus gratiam coram te et magnificasti misericordiam tuam quam fecisti mecum ut salvares animam meam nec possum in monte salvari ne forte adprehendat me malum et moriar: 20 est civitas haec iuxta ad quam possum fugere, parva, et salvabor in ea. Numquid non modica est, et vivet anima mea?"

21 Dixitque ad eum, "Ecce: etiam in hoc suscepi preces tuas ut non subvertam urbem pro qua locutus es. 22 Festina, et salvare ibi, quia non potero facere quicquam donec ingrediaris illuc." Idcirco vocatum est nomen urbis illius Segor. 23 Sol egressus est super terram, et Loth ingressus est in Segor. 24 Igitur Dominus pluit super Sodomam et Gomorram sulphur et ignem a Domino de caelo. 25 Et subvertit civitates has et omnem circa regionem, universos habitatores urbium et cuncta terrae virentia.

26 Respiciensque uxor eius post se versa est in statuam salis. 27 Abraham autem consurgens mane, ubi steterat prius

place because the Lord will destroy this city." And he seemed to them to speak as it were in jest.

15 And when it was morning, the angels pressed him, saying, "Arise! Take thy wife and the two daughters which thou hast, lest thou also perish in the wickedness of the city."

16 And as he lingered, they took his hand and the hand of his wife and of his two daughters because the Lord spared him. 17 And they brought him forth and set him without the city, and there they spoke to him, saying, "Save thy life. Look not back, neither stay thou in all the country about, but save thyself in the mountain lest thou be also consumed."

18 And Lot said to them, "I beseech thee, my Lord, 19 because thy servant hath found grace before thee and thou hast magnified thy mercy which thou hast *shewn to me in saving my life* and I cannot escape to the mountain lest some evil seize me and I die: 20 there is this city here at hand to which I may flee; *it is* a little one, and I shall be saved in it. Is it not a little one, and my soul shall live?"

21 And he said to him, "Behold: also in this I have heard thy prayers not to destroy the city for which thou hast spoken. 22 Make haste, and be saved there, because I cannot do any thing till thou go in thither." Therefore the name of that city was called Zoar. 23 The sun was risen upon the earth, and Lot entered into Zoar. 24 And the Lord rained upon Sodom and Gomorrah brimstone and fire from the Lord out of heaven. 25 And he destroyed these cities and all the country about, all the inhabitants of the cities and all things that spring from the earth.

26 And his wife looking behind her was turned into a statue of salt. 27 And Abraham got up early in the morning, and in the place where he had stood before with the Lord

cum Domino 28 intuitus est Sodomam et Gomorram et universam terram regionis illius, viditque ascendentem favillam de terra quasi fornacis fumum. 29 Cum enim subverteret Deus civitates regionis illius, recordatus Abrahae liberavit Loth de subversione urbium in quibus habitaverat. 30 Ascenditque Loth de Segor et mansit in monte duae quoque filiae eius cum eo (timuerat enim manere in Segor), et mansit in spelunca, ipse et duae filiae eius cum eo.

31 Dixitque maior ad minorem, "Pater noster senex est, et nullus virorum remansit in terra qui possit ingredi ad nos iuxta morem universae terrae. 32 Veni, inebriemus eum vino, dormiamusque cum eo ut servare possimus ex patre nostro semen." 33 Dederunt itaque patri suo bibere vinum nocte illa, et ingressa est maior dormivitque cum patre, at ille non sensit, nec quando accubuit filia nec quando surrexit.

34 Altera quoque die dixit maior ad minorem, "Ecce: dormivi heri cum patre meo; demus ei bibere vinum etiam hac nocte, et dormies cum eo ut salvemus semen de patre nostro." 35 Dederunt et illa nocte patri bibere vinum, ingressaque minor filia dormivit cum eo, et nec tunc quidem sensit quando concubuerit vel quando illa surrexerit.

36 Conceperunt ergo duae filiae Loth de patre suo. 37 Peperitque maior filium, et vocavit nomen eius Moab. Ipse est pater Moabitarum usque in praesentem diem. 38 Minor quoque peperit filium, et vocavit nomen eius Ammon, id est, filius populi mei. Ipse est pater Ammanitarum usque hodie.

28 he looked towards Sodom and Gomorrah and the whole land of that country, and he saw the ashes rise up from the earth as the smoke of a furnace. 29 Now when God destroyed the cities of that country, remembering Abraham he delivered Lot out of the destruction of the cities wherein he had dwelt. 30 And Lot went up out of Zoar and abode in the mountain and his two daughters with him (for he was afraid to stay in Zoar), and he dwelt in a cave, he and his two daughters with him.

31 And the elder said to the younger, "Our father is old, and there is no man left on the earth to come in unto us after the manner of the whole earth. 32 Come, let us make him drunk with wine, and let us lie with him that we may preserve seed of our father." 33 And they made their father drink wine that night, and the elder went in and lay with her father, but he perceived not, neither when his daughter lay down nor when she rose up.

34 And the next day the elder said to the younger, "Behold: I lay last night with my father; let us make him drink wine also tonight, and thou shalt lie with him that we may save seed of our father." 35 They made their father drink wine that night also, and the younger daughter went in and lay with him, and neither then did he perceive when she lay down nor when she rose up.

36 So the two daughters of Lot were with child by their father. 37 And the elder bore a son, and she called his name Moab. He is the father of the Moabites unto this day. 38 The younger also bore a son, and she called his name Ammon, that is, the son of my people. He is the father of the Ammonites unto this day.

Caput 20

Profectus inde Abraham in terram australem habitavit inter Cades et Sur et peregrinatus est in Geraris. 2 Dixitque de Sarra, uxore sua, "Soror mea est." Misit ergo Abimelech, rex Gerarae, et tulit eam.

3 Venit autem Deus ad Abimelech per somnium nocte, et ait ei, "En! Morieris propter mulierem quam tulisti, habet enim virum."

4 Abimelech vero non tetigerat eam, et ait, "Domine, num gentem ignorantem et iustam interficies? 5 Nonne ipse dixit mihi, 'Soror mea est,' et ipsa ait, 'Frater meus est'? In simplicitate cordis mei et munditia manuum mearum feci hoc."

6 Dixitque ad eum Deus, "Et ego scio quod simplici corde feceris, et ideo custodivi te ne peccares in me, et non dimisi ut tangeres eam. 7 Nunc, igitur, redde uxorem viro suo, quia propheta est, et orabit pro te, et vives. Si autem nolueris reddere, scito quod morte morieris, tu et omnia quae tua sunt."

8 Statimque de nocte consurgens, Abimelech vocavit omnes servos suos et locutus est universa verba haec in auribus

Chapter 20

Abraham sojourneth in Gerar. Sarah is taken into King Abimelech's house but by God's commandment is restored untouched.

Abraham removed from thence to the south country and dwelt between Kadesh and Shur and sojourned in Gerar. 2 And he said of Sarah, his wife, "She is my sister." So Abimelech, the king of Gerar, sent and took her.

3 And God came to Abimelech in a dream by night, and he said to him, "Lo! Thou shalt die for the woman thou hast taken, for she hath a husband."

4 Now Abimelech had not touched her, and he said, "Lord, wilt thou slay a nation that is ignorant and just? 5 Did not he say to me, 'She is my sister,' and she say, 'He is my brother'? In the simplicity of my heart and cleanness of my hands have I done this."

6 And God said to him, "And I know that thou didst it with a sincere heart, and therefore I withheld thee from sinning against me, and I *suffered thee not to* touch her. 7 Now therefore restore the man his wife, for he is a prophet, and he shall pray for thee, and thou shalt live. But if thou wilt not restore her, know that thou shalt surely die, thou and all that are thine."

8 And Abimelech, forthwith rising up in the night, called all his servants and spoke all these words in their hearing,

eorum, timueruntque omnes viri valde. 9 Vocavit autem Abimelech etiam Abraham et dixit ei, "Quid fecisti nobis? Quid peccavimus in te quia induxisti super me et super regnum meum peccatum grande? Quae non debuisti facere fecisti nobis." 10 Rursusque expostulans ait, "Quid vidisti ut hoc faceres?"

11 Respondit Abraham, "Cogitavi mecum, dicens, 'Forsitan non est timor Dei in loco isto, et interficient me propter uxorem meam.' 12 Alias autem, et vere soror mea est, filia patris mei et non filia matris meae, et duxi eam uxorem. 13 Postquam autem eduxit me Deus de domo patris mei dixi ad eam, 'Hanc misericordiam facies mecum: in omni loco ad quem ingrediemur, dices quod frater tuus sim.'"

14 Tulit igitur Abimelech oves et boves et servos et ancillas et dedit Abraham reddiditque illi Sarram, uxorem suam, 15 et ait, "Terra coram vobis est; ubicumque tibi placuerit habita."

16 Sarrae autem dixit, "Ecce: mille argenteos dedi fratri tuo. Hoc erit tibi in velamen oculorum ad omnes qui tecum sunt et quocumque perrexeris. Mementoque te deprehensam." 17 Orante autem Abraham, sanavit Deus Abimelech et uxorem ancillasque eius, et pepererunt, 18 concluserat enim Dominus omnem vulvam domus Abimelech propter Sarram, uxorem Abraham.

and all the men were exceedingly afraid. 9 And Abimelech called also for Abraham and said to him, "What hast thou done to us? What have we offended thee in that thou hast brought upon me and upon my kingdom a great sin? Thou hast done to us what thou oughtest not to do." 10 And again he expostulated *with him* and said, "What sawest thou that thou hast done this?"

11 Abraham answered, "I thought with myself, saying, 'Perhaps there is not the fear of God in this place, and they will kill me for the sake of my wife.' 12 Howbeit otherwise, also she is truly my sister, the daughter of my father and not the daughter of my mother, and I took her to wife. 13 And after God brought me out of my father's house I said to her, 'Thou shalt do me this kindness: in every place to which we shall come, thou shalt say that I am thy brother.'"

14 And Abimelech took sheep and oxen and servants and handmaids and gave to Abraham and restored to him Sarah, his wife, 15 and said, "The land is before you; dwell wheresoever it shall please thee."

16 And to Sarah he said, "Behold: I have given thy brother a thousand pieces of silver. This shall serve thee for a covering of thy eyes to all that are with thee and whithersoever thou shalt go. And remember thou wast taken." 17 And when Abraham prayed, God healed Abimelech and his wife and his handmaids, and they bore children, 18 for the Lord had closed up every womb of the house of Abimelech on account of Sarah, Abraham's wife.

Caput 21

Visitavit autem Dominus Sarram sicut promiserat et implevit quae locutus est. 2 Concepitque et peperit filium in senectute sua tempore quo praedixerat ei Deus. 3 Vocavitque Abraham nomen filii sui quem genuit ei Sarra Isaac. 4 Et circumcidit eum octavo die, sicut praeceperat ei Deus, 5 cum centum esset annorum, hac quippe aetate patris natus est Isaac.

6 Dixitque Sarra, "Risum fecit mihi Deus. Quicumque audierit conridebit mihi." 7 Rursumque ait, "Quis auditurum crederet Abraham quod Sarra lactaret filium quem peperit ei iam seni?" 8 Crevit igitur puer et ablactatus est, fecitque Abraham grande convivium in die ablactationis eius. 9 Cumque vidisset Sarra filium Agar, Aegyptiae, ludentem cum Isaac, filio suo, dixit ad Abraham, 10 "Eice ancillam hanc et filium eius, non enim erit heres filius ancillae cum filio meo Isaac."

11 Dure accepit hoc Abraham pro filio suo. 12 Cui dixit Deus, "Non tibi videatur asperum super puero et super ancilla tua. Omnia quae dixerit tibi Sarra audi vocem eius quia in Isaac vocabitur tibi semen. 13 Sed et filium ancillae faciam in gentem magnam quia semen tuum est." 14 Surrexit itaque

Chapter 21

Isaac is born. Hagar and Ishmael are cast forth.

Ａnd the Lord visited Sarah as he had promised and fulfilled what he had spoken. 2 And she conceived and bore a son in her old age at the time that God had foretold her. 3 And Abraham called the name of his son whom Sarah bore him Isaac. 4 And he circumcised him the eighth day, as God had commanded him, 5 when he was a hundred years old, for at this age of his father was Isaac born.

6 And Sarah said, "God hath made a laughter for me. Whosoever shall hear of it will laugh with me." 7 And again she said, "Who would believe that Abraham should hear that Sarah gave suck to a son whom she bore to him in his old age?" 8 And the child grew and was weaned, and Abraham made a great feast on the day of his weaning. 9 And when Sarah had seen the son of Hagar, the Egyptian, playing with Isaac, her son, she said to Abraham, 10 "Cast out this bondwoman and her son, for the son of the bondwoman shall not be heir with my son Isaac."

11 Abraham took this grievously for his son. 12 And God said to him, "Let it not seem grievous to thee for the boy and for thy bondwoman. In all that Sarah hath said to thee hearken to her voice, for in Isaac shall thy seed be called. 13 But I will make the son also of the bondwoman a great nation because he is thy seed." 14 So Abraham rose up in the

Abraham mane et, tollens panem et utrem aquae, inposuit scapulae eius tradiditque puerum et dimisit eam. Quae cum abisset errabat in solitudine Bersabee.

15 Cumque consumpta esset aqua in utre, abiecit puerum subter unam arborum quae ibi erant. 16 Et abiit seditque e regione procul quantum potest arcus iacere, dixit enim, "Non videbo morientem puerum," et sedens contra, levavit vocem suam et flevit.

17 Exaudivit autem Deus vocem pueri, vocavitque angelus Dei Agar de caelo, dicens, "Quid agis, Agar? Noli timere, exaudivit enim Deus vocem pueri de loco in quo est. 18 Surge; tolle puerum, et tene manum illius, quia in gentem magnam faciam eum." 19 Aperuitque oculos eius Deus, quae videns puteum aquae abiit et implevit utrem deditque puero bibere.

20 Et fuit cum eo, qui crevit et moratus est in solitudine et factus est iuvenis, sagittarius. 21 Habitavitque in deserto Pharan, et accepit illi mater sua uxorem de terra Aegypti.

22 Eodem tempore, dixit Abimelech et Fichol, princeps exercitus eius, ad Abraham, "Deus tecum est in universis quae agis. 23 Iura ergo per Deum ne noceas mihi et posteris meis stirpique meae, sed iuxta misericordiam quam feci tibi, facies mihi et terrae in qua versatus es advena."

24 Dixitque Abraham, "Ego iurabo." 25 Et increpavit Abimelech propter puteum aquae quem vi abstulerant servi illius.

26 Responditque Abimelech, "Nescivi quis fecerit hanc rem, sed et tu non indicasti mihi, et ego non audivi praeter hodie." 27 Tulit itaque Abraham oves et boves et dedit Abi-

morning and, taking bread and a bottle of water, put it upon her shoulder and delivered the boy and sent her away. And she departed and wandered in the wilderness of Beer-sheba.

15 And when the water in the bottle was spent, she cast the boy under one of the trees that were there. 16 And she went her way and sat over against him a great way off as far as a bow can carry, for she said, "I will not see the boy die," and sitting over against, she lifted up her voice and wept.

17 And God heard the voice of the boy, and an angel of God called to Hagar from heaven, saying, "What art thou doing, Hagar? Fear not, for God hath heard the voice of the boy from the place wherein he is. 18 Arise; take up the boy, and hold him by the hand, for I will make him a great nation." 19 And God opened her eyes, and she saw a well of water and went and filled the bottle and gave the boy to drink.

20 And God was with him, and he grew and dwelt in the wilderness and became a young man, an archer. 21 And he dwelt in the wilderness of El-paran, and his mother took a wife for him out of the land of Egypt.

22 At the same time, Abimelech and Phicol, the general of his army, said to Abraham, "God is with thee in all that thou dost. 23 Swear therefore by God that thou wilt not hurt me nor my posterity nor my stock, but according to the kindness that I have done to thee, thou shalt do to me and to the land wherein thou hast lived a stranger."

24 And Abraham said, "I will swear." 25 And he reproved Abimelech for a well of water which his servants had taken away by force.

26 And Abimelech answered, "I knew not who did this thing, and thou didst not tell me, and I heard not of it till today." 27 And Abraham took sheep and oxen and gave them

melech, percusseruntque ambo foedus. 28 Et statuit Abraham septem agnas gregis seorsum. 29 Cui dixit Abimelech, "Quid sibi volunt septem agnae istae quas stare fecisti seorsum?"

30 At ille, "Septem," inquit, "agnas accipies de manu mea ut sint in testimonium mihi quoniam ego fodi puteum istum."

31 Idcirco vocatus est locus ille Bersabee, quia ibi uterque iuraverunt. 32 Et inierunt foedus pro Puteo Iuramenti. 33 Surrexit autem Abimelech et Fichol, princeps militiae eius, reversique sunt in terram Palestinorum. Abraham vero plantavit nemus in Bersabee et invocavit ibi nomen Domini Dei aeterni. 34 Et fuit colonus terrae Philisthinorum diebus multis.

Caput 22

Quae postquam gesta sunt, temptavit Deus Abraham et dixit ad eum, "Abraham, Abraham."

At ille respondit, "Adsum."

2 Ait ei, "Tolle filium tuum unigenitum, quem diligis,

to Abimelech, and both of them made a league. 28 And Abraham set apart seven ewe lambs of the flock. 29 And Abimelech said to him, "What mean these seven ewe lambs which thou hast set apart?"

30 But he said, "Thou shalt take seven ewe lambs at my hand that they may be a testimony for me that I dug this well."

31 Therefore that place was called Beer-sheba, because there both of them did swear. 32 And they made a league for the Well of Oath. 33 And Abimelech and Phicol, the general of his army, arose and returned to the land of the Philistines. But Abraham planted a grove in Beer-sheba and there called upon the name of the Lord God eternal. 34 And he was a sojourner in the land of the Philistines many days.

Chapter 22

The faith and obedience of Abraham is proved in his readiness to sacrifice his son Isaac. He is stayed from the act by an angel. Former promises are renewed to him. His brother Nahor's issue.

*A*fter these things, God tempted Abraham and said to him, "Abraham, Abraham."

And he answered, "Here I am."

2 He said to him, "Take thy only begotten son, Isaac,

Isaac, et vade in terram visionis, atque offeres eum ibi holocaustum super unum montium quem monstravero tibi."
3 Igitur Abraham, de nocte consurgens, stravit asinum suum
ducens secum duos iuvenes et Isaac, filium suum. Cumque
concidisset ligna in holocaustum, abiit ad locum quem praeceperat ei Deus.

4 Die autem tertio, elevatis oculis, vidit locum procul.
5 Dixitque ad pueros suos, "Expectate hic cum asino. Ego et
puer illuc usque properantes, postquam adoraverimus revertemur ad vos."

6 Tulit quoque ligna holocausti et inposuit super Isaac, filium suum, ipse vero portabat in manibus ignem et gladium.
Cumque duo pergerent simul, 7 Dixit Isaac patri suo, "Pater
mi?"

At ille respondit, "Quid vis, fili?"

"Ecce," inquit, "ignis et ligna; ubi est victima holocausti?"

8 Dixit autem Abraham, "Deus providebit sibi victimam
holocausti, fili mi." Pergebant ergo pariter. 9 Veneruntque ad
locum quem ostenderat ei Deus, in quo aedificavit altare et
desuper ligna conposuit. Cumque conligasset Isaac, filium
suum, posuit eum in altari super struem lignorum. 10 Extenditque manum et arripuit gladium ut immolaret filium.

11 Et ecce: angelus Domini de caelo clamavit, dicens,
"Abraham, Abraham!"

Qui respondit, "Adsum."

12 Dixitque ei, "Non extendas manum tuam super pue-

whom thou lovest, and go into the land of vision, and there thou shalt offer him for a holocaust upon one of the mountains which I will show thee." 3 So Abraham, rising up in the night, saddled his ass and took with him two young men and Isaac, his son. And when he had cut wood for the holocaust, he went his way to the place which God had commanded him.

4 And on the third day, lifting up his eyes, he saw the place afar off. 5 And he said to his young men, "Stay you here with the ass. I and the boy will go with speed as far as yonder, and after we have worshipped will return to you."

6 And he took the wood for the holocaust and laid it upon Isaac, his son, and he himself carried in his hands fire and a sword. And as they two went on together, 7 Isaac said to his father, "My father?"

And he answered, "What wilt thou, son?"

"Behold," saith he, "fire and wood; where is the victim for the holocaust?"

8 And Abraham said, "God will provide himself a victim for a holocaust, my son." So they went on together. 9 And they came to the place which God had shown him, where he built an altar and laid the wood in order upon it. And when he had bound Isaac, his son, he laid him on the altar upon the pile of wood. 10 And he put forth his hand and took the sword to sacrifice his son.

11 And behold: an angel of the Lord from heaven called to him, saying, "Abraham, Abraham!"

And he answered, "Here I am."

12 And he said to him, "Lay not thy hand upon the boy, neither do thou any thing to him. Now I know that thou

rum, neque facias illi quicquam. Nunc cognovi quod timeas Deum et non peperceris filio tuo unigenito propter me."

13 Levavit Abraham oculos, viditque post tergum arietem inter vepres herentem cornibus, quem adsumens obtulit holocaustum pro filio. 14 Appellavitque nomen loci illius Dominus Videt. Unde usque hodie dicitur, "In monte Dominus videbit."

15 Vocavit autem angelus Domini Abraham secundo de caelo, dicens, 16 "'Per memet ipsum iuravi,' dicit Dominus. Quia fecisti rem hanc et non pepercisti filio tuo unigenito propter me, 17 benedicam tibi, et multiplicabo semen tuum sicut stellas caeli et velut harenam quae est in litore maris. Possidebit semen tuum portas inimicorum suorum, 18 et benedicentur in semine tuo omnes gentes terrae, quia oboedisti voci meae." 19 Reversus est Abraham ad pueros suos, abieruntque Bersabee simul, et habitavit ibi.

20 His ita gestis, nuntiatum est Abraham quod Melcha quoque genuisset filios Nahor, fratri suo. 21 Hus, primogenitum, et Buz, fratrem eius, et Camuhel, patrem Syrorum, 22 et Chased et Azau, Pheldas quoque et Iedlaph 23 ac Bathuel, de quo nata est Rebecca: octo istos genuit Melcha Nahor, fratri Abraham. 24 Concubina vero illius, nomine Roma, peperit Tabee et Gaom et Thaas et Maacha.

fearest God and hast not spared thy only begotten son for my sake."

13 Abraham lifted up his eyes, and saw behind his back a ram amongst the briers sticking fast by the horns, which he took and offered for a holocaust instead of his son. 14 And he called the name of that place the Lord Seeth. Whereupon even to this day it is said, "In the mountain the Lord will see."

15 And the angel of the Lord called to Abraham a second time from heaven, saying, 16 "'By my own self have I sworn,' saith the Lord. Because thou hast done this thing and hast not spared thy only begotten son for my sake, 17 I will bless thee, and I will multiply thy seed as the stars of heaven and as the sand that is by the sea-shore. Thy seed shall possess the gates of their enemies, 18 and in thy seed shall all the nations of the earth be blessed, because thou hast obeyed my voice." 19 Abraham returned to his young men, and they went to Beer-sheba together, and he dwelt there.

20 *After these things,* it was told Abraham that Milcha also had borne children to Nahor, his brother. 21 Uz, the firstborn, and Buz, his brother, and Kemuel, the father of the Syrians, 22 and Chesed and Hazo and Pildash and Jidlaph 23 and Bethuel, of whom was born Rebekah: these eight did Milcha bear to Nahor, Abraham's brother. 24 And his concubine, named Reumah, bore Tebah and Gaham and Tahash and Maacah.

Caput 23

Vixit autem Sarra centum viginti septem annis, 2 et mortua est in civitate Arbee, quae est Hebron, in terra Chanaan, venitque Abraham ut plangeret et fleret eam. 3 Cumque surrexisset ab officio funeris, locutus est ad filios Heth, dicens, 4 "Advena sum et peregrinus apud vos. Date mihi ius sepulchri vobiscum ut sepeliam mortuum meum."

5 Responderunt filii Heth, dicentes, 6 "Audi nos, domine. Princeps Dei es apud nos. In electis sepulchris nostris sepeli mortuum tuum, nullusque prohibere te poterit quin in monumento eius sepelias mortuum tuum."

7 Surrexit Abraham et adoravit populum terrae, filios, videlicet, Heth, 8 dixitque ad eos, "Si placet animae vestrae ut sepeliam mortuum meum, audite me, et intercedite pro me apud Ephron, filium Soor, 9 ut det mihi speluncam duplicem quam habet in extrema parte agri sui; pecunia digna tradat mihi eam coram vobis in possessionem sepulchri."

10 Habitabat autem Ephron in medio filiorum Heth. Responditque Ephron ad Abraham cunctis audientibus qui ingrediebantur portam civitatis illius, dicens, 11 "Nequaquam ita fiat, domine mi, sed tu magis ausculta quod loquor.

Chapter 23

Sarah's death and burial in the field bought of Ephron.

And Sarah lived a hundred and twenty-seven years, 2 and she died in the city of Arbee, which is Hebron, in the land of Canaan, and Abraham came to mourn and weep for her. 3 And after he rose up from the funeral obsequies, he spoke to the children of Heth, saying, 4 "I am a stranger and sojourner among you. Give me the right of a burying place with you that I may bury my dead."

5 The children of Heth answered, saying, 6 "My lord, hear us. Thou art a prince of God among us. Bury thy dead in our principal sepulchres, and no man shall have power to hinder thee from burying thy dead in his *sepulchre.*"

7 Abraham rose up and bowed down to the people of the land, to wit, the children of Heth, 8 and said to them, "If it please your soul that I should bury my dead, hear me, and intercede for me to Ephron, the son of Zohar, 9 that he may give me the double cave which he hath in the end of his field; for as much money as it is worth he shall give it me before you for a possession of a burying place."

10 Now Ephron dwelt in the midst of the children of Heth. And Ephron made answer to Abraham in the hearing of all that went in at the gate of the city, saying, 11 "Let it not be so, my lord, but do thou rather hearken to what I say. The

Agrum trado tibi et speluncam quae in eo est praesentibus filiis populi mei; sepeli mortuum tuum."

12 Adoravit Abraham coram populo terrae, 13 et locutus est ad Ephron circumstante plebe, "Quaeso ut audias me. Dabo pecuniam pro agro. Suscipe eam, et sic sepeliam mortuum meum in eo."

14 Responditque Ephron, 15 "Domine mi, audi me. Terram quam postulas quadringentis argenti siclis valet. Istud est pretium inter me et te. Sed quantum est hoc? Sepeli mortuum tuum."

16 Quod cum audisset Abraham, adpendit pecuniam quam Ephron postulaverat audientibus filiis Heth, quadringentos siclos argenti probatae monetae publicae. 17 Confirmatusque est ager quondam Ephronis in quo erat spelunca duplex, respiciens Mambre, tam ipse quam spelunca et omnes arbores eius in cunctis terminis eius per circuitum, 18 Abrahae in possessionem videntibus filiis Heth et cunctis qui intrabant portam civitatis illius. 19 Atque ita sepelivit Abraham Sarram, uxorem suam, in spelunca agri duplici qui respiciebat Mambre; haec est Hebron in terra Chanaan. 20 Et confirmatus est ager et antrum quod erat in eo Abrahae in possessionem monumenti a filiis Heth.

field I deliver to thee and the cave that is therein in the presence of the children of my people; bury thy dead."

12 Abraham bowed down before the people of the land, 13 and he spoke to Ephron in the presence of the people, "I beseech thee to hear me. I will give money for the field. Take it, and so I will bury my dead in it."

14 And Ephron answered, 15 "My lord, hear me. The ground which thou desirest is worth four hundred sicles of silver. This is the price between me and thee. But what is this? Bury thy dead."

16 And when Abraham had heard this, he weighed out the money that Ephron had asked in the hearing of the children of Heth, four hundred sicles of silver of common current money. 17 And the field that before was Ephron's wherein was the double cave, looking towards Mamre, both it and the cave and all the trees thereof in all its limits round about, 18 was made sure to Abraham for a possession in the sight of the children of Heth and of all that went in at the gate of his city. 19 And so Abraham buried Sarah, his wife, in a double cave of the field that looked towards Mamre; this is Hebron in the land of Canaan. 20 And the field was made sure to Abraham and the cave that was in it for a possession to bury in by the children of Heth.

Caput 24

Erat autem Abraham senex dierumque multorum, et Dominus in cunctis benedixerat ei. 2 Dixitque ad servum seniorem domus suae, qui praeerat omnibus quae habebat, "Pone manum tuam subter femur meum 3 ut adiurem te per Dominum, Deum caeli et terrae, ut non accipias uxorem filio meo de filiabus Chananeorum inter quos habito 4 sed ad terram et cognationem meam proficiscaris et inde accipias uxorem filio meo Isaac."

5 Respondit servus, "Si noluerit mulier venire mecum in terram hanc, num reducere debeo filium tuum ad locum de quo egressus es?"

6 Dixitque Abraham, "Cave nequando reducas illuc filium meum. 7 Dominus Deus caeli, qui tulit me de domo patris mei et de terra nativitatis meae, qui locutus est mihi et iuravit mihi, dicens, 'Semini tuo dabo terram hanc,' ipse mittet angelum suum coram te, et accipies inde uxorem filio meo. 8 Sin autem noluerit mulier sequi te, non teneberis iuramento; filium tantum meum ne reducas illuc."

9 Posuit ergo servus manum sub femore Abraham, domini sui, et iuravit illi super sermone hoc. 10 Tulitque decem camelos de grege domini sui et abiit, ex omnibus bonis eius

Chapter 24

Abraham's servant, sent by him into Mesopotamia, bringeth from thence Rebekah, who is married to Isaac.

Now Abraham was old and *advanced in age,* and the Lord had blessed him in all things. 2 And he said to the elder servant of his house, who was ruler over all he had, "Put thy hand under my thigh 3 that I may make thee swear by the Lord, the God of heaven and earth, that thou take not a wife for my son of the daughters of the Canaanites among whom I dwell 4 but that thou go to my own country and kindred and take a wife from thence for my son Isaac."

5 The servant answered, "If the woman will not come with me into this land, must I bring thy son back again to the place from whence thou camest out?"

6 And Abraham said, "Beware thou never bring my son back again thither. 7 The Lord God of heaven who took me out of my father's house and out of my native country, who spoke to me and swore to me, saying, 'To thy seed will I give this land,' he will send his angel before thee, and thou shalt take from thence a wife for my son. 8 But if the woman will not follow thee, thou shalt not be bound by the oath; only bring not my son *back thither again."*

9 The servant therefore put his hand under the thigh of Abraham, his lord, and swore to him upon this word. 10 And he took ten camels of his master's herd and departed, carry-

portans secum, profectusque perrexit Mesopotamiam ad urbem Nahor.

11 Cumque camelos fecisset accumbere extra oppidum iuxta puteum aquae vespere eo tempore quo solent mulieres egredi ad hauriendam aquam, dixit, 12 "Domine, Deus domini mei, Abraham, occurre, obsecro, hodie mihi et fac misericordiam cum domino meo, Abraham. 13 Ecce: ego sto propter fontem aquae, et filiae habitatorum huius civitatis egredientur ad hauriendam aquam. 14 Igitur, puella cui ego dixero, 'Inclina hydriam tuam ut bibam,' et illa responderit, 'Bibe, quin et camelis tuis dabo potum,' ipsa est quam praeparasti servo tuo Isaac, et per hoc intellegam quod feceris misericordiam cum domino meo."

15 Necdum intra se verba conpleverat, et ecce: Rebecca egrediebatur, filia Bathuel, filii Melchae, uxoris Nahor, fratris Abraham, habens hydriam in scapula—16 puella decora nimis virgoque pulcherrima et incognita viro—descenderat autem ad fontem et impleverat hydriam ac revertebatur. 17 Occurritque ei servus et ait, "Pauxillum mihi ad sorbendum praebe aquae de hydria tua."

18 Quae respondit, "Bibe, domine mi." Celeriterque deposuit hydriam super ulnam suam et dedit ei potum. 19 Cumque ille bibisset, adiecit, "Quin et camelis tuis hauriam aquam donec cuncti bibant." 20 Effundensque hydriam in canalibus, recurrit ad puteum ut hauriret aquam. Et haustam omnibus camelis dedit.

21 Ille autem contemplabatur eam tacitus, scire volens utrum prosperum fecisset iter suum Dominus an non.

ing something of all his goods with him, and he set forward and went on to Mesopotamia to the city of Nahor.

11 And when he had made the camels lie down without the town near a well of water in the evening at the time when women are wont to come out to draw water, he said, 12 "O Lord, the God of my master, Abraham, meet me today, I beseech thee, and show kindness to my master, Abraham. 13 Behold: I stand nigh the spring of water, and the daughters of the inhabitants of this city will come out to draw water. 14 Now, therefore, the maid to whom I shall say, 'Let down thy pitcher that I may drink,' and she shall answer, 'Drink, and I will give thy camels drink also,' *let it be the same* whom thou hast provided for thy servant Isaac, and by this I shall understand that thou hast shown kindness to my master."

15 He had not yet ended these words within himself, and behold: Rebekah came out, the daughter of Bethuel, son of Milcha, wife to Nahor, the brother of Abraham, having a pitcher on her shoulder— 16 an exceeding comely maid and a most beautiful virgin and not known to man—and she went down to the spring and filled her pitcher and was coming back. 17 And the servant ran to meet her and said, "Give me a little water to drink of thy pitcher."

18 And she answered, "Drink, my lord." And quickly she let down the pitcher upon her arm and gave him drink. 19 And when he had drunk, she said, "I will draw water for thy camels also till they all drink." 20 And, pouring out the pitcher into the troughs, she ran back to the well to draw water. And, *having drawn, she gave* to all the camels.

21 But he, *musing,* beheld her with silence, desirous to know whether the Lord had made his journey prosperous or

22 Postquam autem biberunt cameli, protulit vir inaures aureas adpendentes siclos duos et armillas totidem pondo siclorum decem. 23 Dixitque ad eam, "Cuius es filia? Indica mihi: est in domo patris tui locus ad manendum?"

24 Quae respondit, "Filia Bathuelis sum, filii Melchae, quem peperit Nahor." 25 Et addidit, dicens, "Palearum quoque et faeni plurimum est apud nos et locus spatiosus ad manendum."

26 Inclinavit se homo et adoravit Dominum, 27 dicens, "Benedictus Dominus, Deus domini mei, Abraham, qui non abstulit misericordiam et veritatem suam a domino meo et recto me itinere perduxit in domum fratris domini mei." 28 Cucurrit itaque puella et nuntiavit in domum matris suae omnia quae audierat.

29 Habebat autem Rebecca fratrem nomine Laban qui festinus egressus est ad hominem ubi erat fons. 30 Cumque vidisset inaures et armillas in manibus sororis suae et audisset cuncta verba referentis, "Haec locutus est mihi homo," venit ad virum qui stabat iuxta camelos et propter fontem aquae 31 dixitque ad eum, "Ingredere, benedicte Domini; cur foris stas? Praeparavi domum et locum camelis." 32 Et introduxit eum in hospitium, ac destravit camelos deditque paleas et faenum et aquam ad lavandos pedes eius et virorum qui venerant cum eo. 33 Et adpositus est in conspectu eius panis.

Qui ait, "Non comedam donec loquar sermones meos."

Respondit ei, "Loquere."

34 At ille, "Servus," inquit, "Abraham sum, 35 et Dominus benedixit domino meo valde, magnificatusque est, et dedit

not. 22 And after that the camels had drunk, the man took out golden earrings weighing two sicles and as many bracelets of ten sicles' weight. 23 And he said to her, "Whose daughter art thou? Tell me: is there any place in thy father's house to lodge?"

24 And she answered, "I am the daughter of Bethuel, the son of Milcha, whom she bore to Nahor." 25 And she *said moreover to him,* "We have good store of both straw and hay and a large place to lodge in."

26 The man bowed himself down and adored the Lord, 27 saying, "Blessed be the Lord, God of my master, Abraham, who hath not taken away his mercy and truth from my master and hath brought me the straight way into the house of my master's brother." 28 Then the maid ran and told in her mother's house all that she had heard.

29 And Rebekah had a brother named Laban who went out in haste to the man, *to the well.* 30 And when he had seen the earrings and bracelets in his sister's hands and had heard all *that she related,* saying, *"Thus and thus* the man spoke to me," he came to the man who stood by the camels and near to the spring of water 31 and said to him, "Come in, thou blessed of the Lord; why standest thou without? I have prepared the house and a place for the camels." 32 And he brought him in into his lodging, and he unharnessed the camels and gave straw and hay and water to wash his feet and the feet of the men that were come with him. 33 And bread was set before him.

But he said, "I will not eat till I tell my message."

He answered him, "Speak."

34 And he said, "I am the servant of Abraham, 35 and the Lord hath blessed my master wonderfully, and he is become

ei oves et boves, argentum et aurum, servos et ancillas, camelos et asinos.

36 "Et peperit Sarra, uxor domini mei, filium domino meo in senectute sua, deditque illi omnia quae habuerat. 37 Et adiuravit me dominus meus, dicens, 'Non accipies uxorem filio meo de filiabus Chananeorum in quorum terra habito, 38 sed ad domum patris mei perges et de cognatione mea accipies uxorem filio meo,' 39 ego vero respondi domino meo, 'Quid si noluerit venire mecum mulier?' 40 'Dominus,' ait, 'in cuius conspectu ambulo, mittet angelum suum tecum et diriget viam tuam, accipiesque uxorem filio meo de cognatione mea et de domo patris mei; 41 innocens eris a maledictione mea cum veneris ad propinquos meos et non dederint tibi.'

42 "Veni ergo hodie ad fontem aquae et dixi, 'Domine, Deus domini mei, Abraham, si direxisti viam meam in qua nunc ambulo, 43 ecce: sto iuxta fontem aquae, et virgo quae egredietur ad hauriendam aquam audierit a me, "Da mihi pauxillum aquae ad bibendum ex hydria tua," 44 et dixerit mihi, "Et tu bibe, et camelis tuis hauriam," ipsa est mulier quam praeparavit Dominus filio domini mei.' 45 Dumque haec mecum tacitus volverem, apparuit Rebecca veniens cum hydria, quam portabat in scapula, descenditque ad fontem et hausit aquam. Et aio ad eam, 'Da mihi paululum bibere.'

46 "Quae festina deposuit hydriam de umero et dixit mihi, 'Et tu bibe, et camelis tuis potum tribuam.' Bibi, et adaquavit camelos. 47 Interrogavique eam et dixi, 'Cuius es filia?' Quae respondit, 'Filia Bathuelis sum, filii Nahor, quem pe-

great, and he hath given him sheep and oxen, silver and gold, men-servants and women-servants, camels and asses.

36 "And Sarah, my master's wife, hath borne my master a son in her old age, and he hath given him all that he had. 37 And my master made me swear, saying, 'Thou shalt not take a wife for my son of the *Canaanites* in whose land I dwell, 38 but thou shalt go to my father's house and shalt take a wife of my own kindred for my son,' 39 but I answered my master, 'What if the woman will not come with me?' 40 'The Lord,' said he, 'in whose sight I walk, will send his angel with thee and will direct thy way, and thou shalt take a wife for my son of my own kindred and of my father's house, 41 but thou shalt be clear from my curse when thou shalt come to my kindred *if* they will not give thee *one.*'

42 "And I came today to the well of water and said, 'O Lord, God of my master, Abraham, if thou hast prospered my way wherein I now walk, 43 behold: I stand by the well of water, and the virgin that shall come out to draw water *who shall hear me say,* "Give me a little water to drink of thy pitcher," 44 and shall say to me, "Both drink thou, and I will also draw for thy camels," *let the same be* the woman whom the Lord hath prepared for my master's son.' 45 And whilst I pondered these things secretly with myself, Rebekah appeared coming with a pitcher, which she carried on her shoulder, and she went down to the well and drew water. And I said to her, 'Give me a little to drink.'

46 "And she speedily let down the pitcher from her shoulder and said to me, 'Both drink thou, and to thy camels I will give drink.' I drank, and she watered the camels. 47 And I asked her and said, 'Whose daughter art thou?' And she answered, 'I am the daughter of Bethuel, the son of Nahor,

perit illi Melcha.' Suspendi itaque inaures ad ornandam faciem eius, et armillas posui in manibus. 48 Pronusque adoravi Dominum, benedicens Domino, Deo domini mei, Abraham, qui perduxit me recto itinere ut sumerem filiam fratris domini mei filio eius. 49 Quam ob rem, si facitis misericordiam et veritatem cum domino meo, indicate mihi—sin autem aliud placet, et hoc dicite mihi—ut vadam ad dextram sive ad sinistram."

50 Responderuntque Laban et Bathuel, "A Domino egressus est sermo; non possumus extra placitum eius quicquam aliud tecum loqui.

51 "En: Rebecca coram te est; tolle eam, et proficiscere, et sit uxor filii domini tui, sicut locutus est Dominus." 52 Quod cum audisset puer Abraham, procidens adoravit in terra Dominum. 53 Prolatisque vasis argenteis et aureis ac vestibus, dedit ea Rebeccae pro munere. Fratribus quoque eius et matri dona obtulit. 54 Initoque convivio, vescentes pariter et bibentes manserunt ibi.

Surgens autem mane, locutus est puer, "Dimittite me ut vadam ad dominum meum."

55 Responderuntque frater eius et mater, "Maneat puella saltem decem dies apud nos, et postea proficiscetur."

56 "Nolite," ait, "me retinere, quia Dominus direxit viam meam. Dimittite me ut pergam ad dominum meum."

whom Milcha bore to him.' So I put earrings on her to adorn her face, and I put bracelets on her hands. 48 And, falling down, I adored the Lord, blessing the Lord, God of my master, Abraham, who hath brought me the straight way to take the daughter of my master's brother for his son. 49 Wherefore, if you do according to mercy and truth with my master, tell me—but if it please you otherwise, tell me that also—that I may go to the right hand or to the left."

50 And Laban and Bethuel answered, "The word hath proceeded from the Lord; we cannot speak any other thing to thee but his pleasure.

51 "Behold: Rebekah is before thee; take her, and go thy way, and let her be the wife of thy master's son, as the Lord hath spoken." 52 Which when Abraham's servant heard, falling down to the ground he adored the Lord. 53 And bringing forth vessels of silver and gold and garments, he gave them to Rebekah for a present. He offered gifts also to her brothers and to her mother. 54 *And* a banquet was made, and they ate and drank together and lodged there.

And in the morning, the servant arose and said, "Let me depart that I may go to my master."

55 And her brother and mother answered, "Let the maid stay at least ten days with us, and afterwards she shall depart."

56 "Stay me not," said he, "because the Lord hath *prospered* my way. Send me away that I may go to my master."

57 Et dixerunt, "Vocemus puellam et quaeramus ipsius voluntatem." 58 Cumque vocata, venisset, sciscitati sunt, "Vis ire cum homine isto?"

Quae ait, "Vadam."

59 Dimiserunt ergo eam et nutricem illius servumque Abraham et comites eius, 60 inprecantes prospera sorori suae atque dicentes, "Soror nostra es; crescas in mille milia, et possideat semen tuum portas inimicorum suorum."

61 Igitur Rebecca et puellae illius ascensis camelis secutae sunt virum qui festinus revertebatur ad dominum suum. 62 Eo tempore, Isaac deambulabat per viam quae ducit ad puteum cuius nomen est Viventis et Videntis, habitabat enim in terra australi. 63 Et egressus fuerat ad meditandum in agro, inclinata iam die, cumque levasset oculos, vidit camelos venientes procul. 64 Rebecca quoque, conspecto Isaac, descendit de camelo 65 et ait ad puerum, "Quis est ille homo qui venit per agrum in occursum nobis?"

Dixitque ei, "Ipse est dominus meus." At illa tollens cito pallium operuit se. 66 Servus autem cuncta quae gesserat narravit Isaac, 67 qui introduxit eam in tabernaculum Sarrae, matris suae, et accepit uxorem, et in tantum dilexit ut dolorem qui ex morte matris acciderat temperaret.

57 And they said, "Let us call the maid and ask her will." 58 And they called her, and when she was come, they asked, "Wilt thou go with this man?"

She said, "I will go."

59 So they sent her away and her nurse and Abraham's servant and his company, 60 wishing prosperity to their sister and saying, "Thou art our sister; mayst thou increase to thousands of thousands, and may thy seed possess the gates of their enemies."

61 So Rebekah and her maids being set upon camels followed the man who with speed returned to his master. 62 At the *same* time, Isaac was walking along the way to the well which is called Of the Living and the Seeing, for he dwelt in the south country. 63 And he was gone forth to meditate in the field, the day being now well spent, and when he had lifted up his eyes, he saw camels coming afar off. 64 Rebekah also, when she saw Isaac, lighted off the camel 65 and said to the servant, "Who is that man who cometh towards us along the field?"

And he said to her, "That man is my master." But she quickly took her cloak and covered herself. 66 And the servant told Isaac all that he had done, 67 who brought her into the tent of Sarah, his mother, and took her to wife, and he loved her so much that it moderated the sorrow which was occasioned by his mother's death.

Caput 25

Abraham vero aliam duxit uxorem, nomine Cetthuram, 2 quae peperit ei Zamram et Iexan et Madan et Madian et Iesboch et Sue. 3 Iexan quoque genuit Saba et Dadan. Filii Dadan fuerunt Assurim et Lathusim et Loommim, 4 at vero ex Madian ortus est Epha et Opher et Enoch et Abida et Eldaa. Omnes hii filii Cetthurae. 5 Deditque Abraham cuncta quae possederat Isaac. 6 Filiis autem concubinarum largitus est munera et separavit eos ab Isaac, filio suo, dum adhuc ipse viveret ad plagam orientalem.

7 Fuerunt autem dies vitae Abraham centum septuaginta quinque anni. 8 Et, deficiens, mortuus est in senectute bona provectaeque aetatis et plenus dierum congregatusque est ad populum suum. 9 Et sepelierunt eum Isaac et Ismahel, filii sui, in spelunca duplici quae sita est in agro Ephron, filii Soor, Hetthei, e regione Mambre, 10 quem emerat a filiis Heth. Ibi sepultus est ipse et Sarra, uxor eius.

11 Et post obitum illius, benedixit Deus Isaac, filio eius, qui habitabat iuxta puteum nomine Viventis et Videntis. 12 Hae sunt generationes Ismahel, filii Abraham, quem pe-

Chapter 25

Abraham's children by Keturah. His death and that of Ishmael. Isaac hath Esau and Jacob, twins. Esau selleth his first
birthright to Jacob.

And Abraham married another wife, named Keturah,
2 who bore him Zimran and Jokshan and Medan and Midian
and Ishbak and Shuah. 3 Jokshan also begot Sheba and Dedan. The children of Dedan were Asshurim and Letushim
and Leummim, 4 but of Midian was born Ephah and Epher
and Hanoch and Abida and Eldaah. All these were the children of Keturah. 5 And Abraham gave all his possessions to
Isaac. 6 And to the children of the concubines he gave gifts
and separated them from Isaac, his son, while he yet lived to
the east country.

7 And the days of Abraham's life were a hundred and
seventy-five years. 8 And, decaying, he died in a good old age
and having lived a long time and being full of days and was
gathered to his people. 9 And Isaac and Ishmael, his sons,
buried him in the double cave which was situated in the
field of Ephron, the son of Zohar, the Hittite, over against
Mamre, 10 which he had bought of the children of Heth.
There was he buried and Sarah, his wife.

11 And after his death, God blessed Isaac, his son, who
dwelt by the well named Of the Living and Seeing. 12 These
are the generations of Ishmael, the son of Abraham, whom

perit ei Agar, Aegyptia famula Sarrae, 13 et haec nomina filiorum eius in vocabulis et generationibus suis: primogenitus Ismahelis Nabaioth, dein Cedar et Abdeel et Mabsam, 14 Masma quoque et Duma et Massa, 15 Adad et Thema et Itur et Naphis et Cedma. 16 Isti sunt filii Ismahel, et haec nomina per castella et oppida eorum, duodecim principes tribuum suarum. 17 Et facti sunt anni vitae Ismahel centum triginta septem; deficiensque mortuus est et adpositus ad populum suum. 18 Habitavit autem ab Evila usque Sur, quae respicit Aegyptum, introeuntibus Assyrios. Coram cunctis fratribus suis obiit.

19 Hae quoque sunt generationes Isaac, filii Abraham: Abraham genuit Isaac, 20 qui cum quadraginta esset annorum duxit uxorem Rebeccam, filiam Bathuel, Syri de Mesopotamiam, sororem Laban.

21 Deprecatusque est Isaac Dominum pro uxore sua eo quod esset sterilis, qui exaudivit eum et dedit conceptum Rebeccae. 22 Sed conlidebantur in utero eius parvuli, quae ait, "Si sic mihi futurum erat, quid necesse fuit concipere?" Perrexitque ut consuleret Dominum.

23 Qui respondens ait, "Duae gentes in utero tuo sunt, et duo populi ex ventre tuo dividentur, populusque populum superabit, et maior minori serviet." 24 Iam tempus pariendi venerat, et ecce: gemini in utero repperti sunt. 25 Qui primus egressus est rufus erat et totus in morem pellis hispidus, vocatumque est nomen eius Esau. Protinus alter, egrediens, plantam fratris tenebat manu, et idcirco appellavit eum Iacob.

26 Sexagenarius erat Isaac quando nati sunt ei parvuli.

Hagar, the Egyptian, Sarah's servant, bore unto him, 13 and these are the names of his children according to their calling and generations: the firstborn of Ishmael was Nebaioth, then Kedar and Adbeel and Mibsam 14 and Mishma and Dumah and Massa, 15 Hada and Tema and Jetur and Naphish and Kedemah. 16 These are the sons of Ishmael, and these are their names by their castles and towns, twelve princes of their tribes. 17 And the years of Ishmael's life were a hundred and thirty-seven, and decaying, he died and was gathered unto his people. 18 And he dwelt from Havilah as far as Shur, which looketh towards Egypt, to them that go towards the Assyrians. He died in the presence of all his brethren.

19 These also are the generations of Isaac, the son of Abraham: Abraham begot Isaac, 20 who when he was forty years old took to wife Rebekah, the daughter of Bethuel, the Syrian of Mesopotamia, sister to Laban.

21 And Isaac besought the Lord for his wife because she was barren, and he heard him and made Rebekah to conceive. 22 But the children struggled in her womb, and she said, "If it were to be so with me, what need was there to conceive?" And she went to consult the Lord.

23 And he answering said, "Two nations are in thy womb, and two peoples shall be divided out of thy womb, and one people shall overcome the other, and the elder shall serve the younger." 24 And when her time was come to be delivered, behold: twins were found in her womb. 25 He that came forth first was red and *hairy* like a skin, and his name was called Esau. Immediately the other, coming forth, held his brother's foot in his hand, and therefore *he was called* Jacob.

26 Isaac was threescore years old when the children were

27 Quibus adultis, factus est Esau vir gnarus venandi et homo agricola, Iacob autem, vir simplex, habitabat in tabernaculis. 28 Isaac amabat Esau eo quod de venationibus illius vesceretur, et Rebecca diligebat Iacob. 29 Coxit autem Iacob pulmentum ad quem cum venisset Esau, de agro lassus, 30 ait, "Da mihi de coctione hac rufa, quia oppido lassus sum," quam ob causam vocatum est nomen eius Edom.

31 Cui dixit Iacob, "Vende mihi primogenita tua."

32 Ille respondit, "En! Morior; quid mihi proderunt primogenita?"

33 Ait Iacob, "Iura ergo mihi." Iuravit ei Esau et vendidit primogenita. 34 Et sic, accepto pane et lentis edulio, comedit et bibit et abiit, parvipendens quod primogenita vendidisset.

Caput 26

Orta autem fame super terram post eam sterilitatem quae acciderat in diebus Abraham, abiit Isaac ad Abimelech, regem Palestinorum, in Gerara. 2 Apparuitque ei Dominus et ait, "Ne descendas in Aegyptum, sed quiesce in terra quam dixero tibi 3 et peregrinare in ea, eroque tecum et benedi-

born unto him. 27 And when they were grown up, Esau became a *skillful hunter* and a husbandman, but Jacob, a plain man, dwelt in tents. 28 Isaac loved Esau because he ate of his hunting, and Rebekah loved Jacob. 29 And Jacob boiled pottage to whom Esau, coming faint out of the field, 30 said, "Give me of this red pottage, for I am exceeding faint," for which reason his name was called Edom.

31 And Jacob said to him, "Sell me thy first birthright."

32 He answered, "Lo! I die; what will the first birthright avail me?"

33 Jacob said, "Swear therefore to me." Esau swore to him and sold his first birthright. 34 And so, taking bread and the pottage of lentils, he ate and drank and went his way, making little account of having sold his first birthright.

Chapter 26

Isaac sojourneth in Gerar, where God reneweth to him the promise made to Abraham. King Abimelech maketh league with him.

And when a famine came in the land after that barrenness which had happened in the days of Abraham, Isaac went to Abimelech, king of the Philistines, to Gerar. 2 And the Lord appeared to him and said, "Go not down into Egypt, but stay in the land that I shall tell thee 3 and sojourn

cam tibi, tibi enim et semini tuo dabo universas regiones has conplens iuramentum quod spopondi Abraham, patri tuo. 4 Et multiplicabo semen tuum sicut stellas caeli, daboque posteris tuis universas regiones has, et benedicentur in semine tuo omnes gentes terrae 5 eo quod oboedierit Abraham voci meae et custodierit praecepta et mandata mea et caerimonias legesque servaverit."

6 Mansit itaque Isaac in Geraris. 7 Qui cum interrogaretur a viris loci illius super uxore sua, respondit, "Soror mea est," timuerat enim confiteri quod sibi esset sociata coniugio, reputans ne forte interficerent eum propter illius pulchritudinem.

8 Cumque pertransissent dies plurimi et ibi demoraretur, prospiciens Abimelech, Palestinorum rex, per fenestram, vidit eum iocantem cum Rebecca, uxore sua. 9 Et accersito ait, "Perspicuum est quod uxor tua sit. Cur mentitus es sororem tuam esse?"

Respondit, "Timui ne morerer propter eam."

10 Dixitque Abimelech, "Quare inposuisti nobis? Potuit coire quispiam de populo cum uxore tua, et induxeras super nos grande peccatum." Praecepitque omni populo, dicens, 11 "Qui tetigerit hominis huius uxorem morte morietur."

12 Seruit autem Isaac in terra illa, et invenit in ipso anno centuplum, benedixitque ei Dominus. 13 Et locupletatus est homo, et ibat proficiens atque succrescens donec magnus vehementer effectus est. 14 Habuit quoque possessiones ovium et armentorum et familiae plurimum. Ob haec, invidentes ei, Palestini, 15 omnes puteos quos foderant servi patris illius, Abraham, illo tempore obstruxerunt implentes

in it, and I will be with thee and will bless thee, for to thee and to thy seed I will give all these countries *to fulfill* the oath which I swore to Abraham, thy father. 4 And I will multiply thy seed like the stars of heaven, and I will give to thy posterity all these countries, and in thy seed shall all the nations of the earth be blessed 5 because Abraham obeyed my voice and kept my precepts and commandments and observed my ceremonies and laws."

6 So Isaac abode in Gerar. 7 And when he was asked by the men of that place concerning his wife, he answered, "She is my sister," for he was afraid to confess that she was his wife, thinking lest perhaps they would kill him because of her beauty.

8 And when very many days were passed and he abode there, Abimelech, king of the Philistines, looking out through a window, saw him playing with Rebekah, his wife. 9 And calling for him, he said, "It is evident she is thy wife. Why didst thou feign her to be thy sister?"

He answered, "I feared lest I should die for her sake."

10 And Abimelech said, "Why hast thou deceived us? Some man of the people might have lain with thy wife, and thou hadst brought upon us a great sin." And he commanded all the people, saying, 11 "He that shall touch this man's wife shall *surely* be put to death."

12 And Isaac sowed in that land, and he found that same year a hundredfold, and the Lord blessed him. 13 And the man was enriched, and he went on prospering and increasing till he became exceeding great. 14 And he had possessions of sheep and of herds and a very great family. Wherefore the Philistines, envying him, 15 stopped up at that time all the wells that the servants of his father, Abraham, had

humo, 16 in tantum ut ipse Abimelech diceret ad Isaac, "Recede a nobis, quoniam potentior nostri factus es valde."

17 Et ille, discedens ut veniret ad torrentem Gerarae habitaretque ibi, 18 rursum fodit alios puteos quos foderant servi patris sui, Abraham, et quos, illo mortuo, olim obstruxerant Philisthim, appellavitque eos hisdem nominibus quibus ante pater vocaverat. 19 Foderuntque in torrente et reppererunt aquam vivam. 20 Sed et ibi iurgium fuit pastorum Gerarae adversum pastores Isaac, dicentium, "Nostra est aqua." Quam ob rem nomen putei, ex eo quod acciderat, vocavit Calumniam.

21 Foderunt autem et alium, et pro illo quoque rixati sunt, appellavitque eum Inimicitias. 22 Profectus inde, fodit alium puteum pro quo non contenderunt. Itaque vocavit nomen illius Latitudo, dicens, "Nunc dilatavit nos Dominus et fecit crescere super terram." 23 Ascendit autem ex illo loco in Bersabee, 24 ubi apparuit ei Dominus in ipsa nocte, dicens, "Ego sum Deus Abraham, patris tui; noli metuere, quia tecum sum. Benedicam tibi et multiplicabo semen tuum propter servum meum Abraham. 25 Itaque aedificavit ibi altare et invocato nomine Domini extendit tabernaculum praecepitque servis suis ut foderent puteum. 26 Ad quem locum cum venissent de Geraris Abimelech et Ochozath, amicus illius, et Fichol, dux militum, 27 locutus est eis Isaac, "Quid venistis ad me, hominem quem odistis et expulistis a vobis?"

28 Qui responderunt, "Vidimus tecum esse Dominum, et idcirco nos diximus, 'Sit iuramentum inter nos, et ineamus

digged, filling them up with earth, 16 insomuch that Abimelech himself said to Isaac, "Depart from us, for thou art become much mightier than we."

17 *So he departed and came to the torrent of Gerar to dwell there.* 18 *And* he digged again other wells which the servants of his father, Abraham, had digged and which, after his death, the Philistines had of old stopped up, and he called them by the same names by which his father before had called them. 19 And they digged in the torrent and found living water. 20 But there also the herdsmen of Gerar strove against the herdsmen of Isaac, saying, "It is our water." Wherefore he called the name of the well, on occasion of that which had happened, Calumny.

21 And they digged also another, and for that they quarrelled likewise, and he called the name of it Enmity. 22 Going forward from thence, he digged another well for which they contended not. Therefore he called the name thereof Latitude, saying, "Now hath the Lord given us room and made us to increase upon the earth." 23 And he went up from that place to Beer-sheba, 24 where the Lord appeared to him that same night, saying, "I am the God of Abraham, thy father; do not fear, for I am with thee. I will bless thee and multiply thy seed for my servant Abraham's sake." 25 And he built there an altar and called upon the name of the Lord and pitched his tent and commanded his servants to dig a well. 26 To which place when Abimelech and Ahuzzath, his friend, and Phicol, chief captain of his soldiers, came from Gerar, 27 Isaac said to them, "Why are ye come to me, a man whom you hate and have thrust out from you?"

28 And they answered, "We saw that the Lord is with thee, and therefore we said, 'Let there be an oath between us, and

foedus 29 ut non facias nobis quicquam mali sicut et nos nihil tuorum adtigimus nec fecimus quod te laederet sed cum pace dimisimus auctum benedictione Domini.'"

30 Fecit ergo eis convivium, et, post cibum et potum, 31 surgentes mane iuraverunt sibi mutuo, dimisitque eos Isaac pacifice in locum suum. 32 Ecce autem: venerunt in ipso die servi Isaac adnuntiantes ei de puteo quem foderant atque dicentes, "Invenimus aquam." 33 Unde appellavit eum Abundantiam. Et nomen urbis inpositum est Bersabee usque in praesentem diem.

34 Esau vero quadragenarius duxit uxores: Iudith, filiam Beeri, Hetthei, et Basemath, filiam Helon eiusdem loci. 35 Quae ambae offenderant animum Isaac et Rebeccae.

Caput 27

Senuit autem Isaac, et caligaverunt oculi eius, et videre non poterat. Vocavitque Esau, filium suum maiorem, et dixit ei, "Fili mi?"

Qui respondit, "Adsum."

let us make a covenant 29 that thou do us no harm as we on our part have touched nothing of thine nor have done any thing to hurt thee, but with peace have sent thee away increased with the blessing of the Lord.'"

30 And he made them a feast, and, after they had eaten and drunk, 31 arising in the morning they swore one to another, and Isaac sent them away peaceably to their own home. 32 And behold: the same day, the servants of Isaac came, telling him of a well which they had digged and saying, "We have found water." 33 Whereupon he called it Abundance. And the name of the city was *called* Beer-sheba even to this day.

34 And Esau being forty years old married wives: Judith, the daughter of Beeri, the Hittite, and Basemath, the daughter of Elon of the same place. 35 And they both offended the mind of Isaac and Rebekah.

Chapter 27

Jacob, by his mother's counsel, obtaineth his father's blessing instead of Esau and by her is advised to fly to his uncle, Laban.

Now Isaac was old, and his eyes were dim, and he could not see. And he called Esau, his elder son, and said to him, "My son?"

And he answered, "Here I am."

2 Cui pater, "Vides," inquit, "quod senuerim et ignorem diem mortis meae. 3 Sume arma tua, faretram et arcum, et egredere foras. Cumque venatu aliquid adprehenderis, 4 fac mihi inde pulmentum sicut velle me nosti, et adfer ut comedam et benedicat tibi anima mea antequam moriar."

5 Quod cum audisset Rebecca et ille abisset in agrum ut iussionem patris expleret, 6 dixit filio suo Iacob, "Audivi patrem tuum loquentem cum Esau, fratre tuo, et dicentem ei, 7 'Adfer mihi de venatione tua et fac cibos ut comedam et benedicam tibi coram Domino antequam moriar.' 8 Nunc ergo, fili mi, adquiesce consiliis meis, 9 et pergens ad gregem adfer mihi duos hedos optimos ut faciam ex eis escas patri tuo quibus libenter vescitur, 10 quas cum intuleris et comederit, benedicat tibi priusquam moriatur."

11 Cui ille respondit, "Nosti quod Esau, frater meus, homo pilosus sit et ego lenis. 12 Si adtractaverit me pater meus et senserit, timeo ne putet sibi voluisse inludere et inducam super me maledictionem pro benedictione."

13 Ad quem mater, "In me sit," ait, "ista maledictio, fili mi. Tantum audi vocem meam, et perge; adfer quae dixi."

14 Abiit et adtulit deditque matri. Paravit illa cibos sicut noverat velle patrem illius, 15 et vestibus Esau valde bonis quas apud se habebat domi induit eum, 16 pelliculasque hedorum circumdedit manibus et colli nuda protexit. 17 Dedit-

2 And his father said to him, "Thou seest that I am old and know not the day of my death. 3 Take thy arms, thy quiver and bow, and go abroad. And when thou hast taken some thing by hunting, 4 make me savoury meat thereof as thou knowest I like, and bring it that I may eat and my soul may bless thee before I die."

5 And when Rebekah had heard this and he was gone into the field to fulfill his father's commandment, 6 she said to her son Jacob, "I heard thy father talking with Esau, thy brother, and saying to him, 7 'Bring me of thy hunting and make me meats that I may eat and bless thee in the sight of the Lord before I die.' 8 Now therefore, my son, follow my counsel, 9 and go thy way to the flock; bring me two kids of the best that I may make of them meat for thy father such as he gladly eateth, 10 which when thou hast brought in and he hath eaten, he may bless thee before he die."

11 And he answered her, "Thou knowest that Esau, my brother, is a hairy man and I am smooth. 12 If my father shall feel me and perceive it, I fear lest he will think I would have mocked him, and I shall bring upon me a curse instead of a blessing."

13 And his mother said to him, "Upon me be this curse, my son. Only hear thou my voice, and go; fetch me the things which I have said."

14 He went and brought and gave them to his mother. She dressed meats such as she knew his father liked, 15 and she put on him very good garments of Esau which she had at home with her, 16 and the little skins of the kids she put about his hands and covered the bare of his neck. 17 And she gave him the savoury meat and delivered him bread that she

que pulmentum et panes quos coxerat tradidit. 18 Quibus inlatis dixit, "Pater mi?"

At ille respondit, "Audio. Quis tu es, fili mi?"

19 Dixitque Iacob, "Ego sum Esau, primogenitus tuus. Feci sicut praecepisti mihi. Surge; sede, et comede de venatione mea ut benedicat mihi anima tua."

20 Rursumque Isaac ad filium suum, "Quomodo," inquit, "tam cito invenire potuisti, fili mi?"

Qui respondit, "Voluntas Dei fuit ut cito mihi occurreret quod volebam."

21 Dixitque Isaac, "Accede huc ut tangam te, fili mi, et probem utrum tu sis filius meus Esau an non." 22 Accessit ille ad patrem, et palpato eo dixit Isaac, "Vox quidem vox Iacob est, sed manus manus sunt Esau." 23 Et non cognovit eum, quia pilosae manus similitudinem maioris expresserant. Benedicens ergo illi, 24 ait, "Tu es filius meus Esau?"

Respondit, "Ego sum."

25 At ille, "Offer," inquit, "mihi cibos de venatione tua, fili mi, ut benedicat tibi anima mea." Quos cum oblatos comedisset, obtulit ei etiam vinum, quo hausto 26 dixit ad eum, "Accede ad me, et da mihi osculum, fili mi." 27 Accessit et osculatus est eum. Statimque ut sensit vestimentorum illius fragrantiam, benedicens illi, ait, "Ecce! Odor filii mei sicut odor agri pleni cui benedixit Dominus. 28 Det tibi Deus de rore caeli et de pinguedine terrae abundantiam frumenti et vini. 29 Et serviant tibi populi et adorent te tribus. Esto dominus fratrum tuorum, et incurventur ante te filii matris

had baked. 18 Which when he had carried in, he said, "My father?"

But he answered, "I hear. Who art thou, my son?"

19 And Jacob said, "I am Esau, thy firstborn. I have done as thou didst command me. Arise; sit, and eat of my venison that thy soul may bless me."

20 And Isaac said to his son, "How couldst thou find it so quickly, my son?"

He answered, "It was the will of God that what I sought came quickly in my way."

21 And Isaac said, "Come hither that I may feel thee, my son, and may prove whether thou be my son Esau or not." 22 He came near to his father, and when he had felt him Isaac said, "The voice indeed is the voice of Jacob, but the hands are the hands of Esau." 23 And he knew him not, because his hairy hands made him like to the elder. Then blessing him, 24 he said, "Art thou my son Esau?"

He answered, "I am."

25 Then he said, "Bring me the meats of thy hunting, my son, that my soul may bless thee." And when they were brought and he had eaten, he offered him wine also, which after he had drunk 26 he said to him, "Come near me, and give me a kiss, my son." 27 He came near and kissed him. And immediately as he smelled the fragrant smell of his garments, blessing him, he said, "Behold! The smell of my son is as the smell of a plentiful field which the Lord hath blessed. 28 God give thee of the dew of heaven and of the fatness of the earth abundance of corn and wine. 29 And let peoples serve thee and tribes worship thee. Be thou lord of thy brethren, and let thy mother's children bow down before

tuae. Qui maledixerit tibi sit maledictus et qui benedixerit benedictionibus repleatur."

30 Vix Isaac sermonem impleverat et, egresso Iacob foras, venit Esau, 31 coctosque de venatione cibos intulit patri, dicens, "Surge, pater mi, et comede de venatione filii tui ut benedicat mihi anima tua."

32 Dixitque illi Isaac, "Quis enim es tu?"

Qui respondit, "Ego sum primogenitus filius tuus, Esau."

33 Expavit Isaac, stupore vehementi, et ultra quam credi potest admirans ait, "Quis igitur ille est qui dudum captam venationem adtulit mihi et comedi ex omnibus priusquam tu venires? Benedixique ei et erit benedictus."

34 Auditis Esau sermonibus patris inrugiit clamore magno et consternatus ait, "Benedic etiam mihi, pater mi."

35 Qui ait, "Venit germanus tuus fraudulenter et accepit benedictionem tuam."

36 At ille subiunxit, "Iuste vocatum est nomen eius Iacob, subplantavit enim me, en, altera vice. Primogenita mea ante tulit, et nunc secundo subripuit benedictionem meam." Rursumque ad patrem, "Numquid non reservasti," ait, "et mihi benedictionem?"

37 Respondit Isaac, "Dominum tuum illum constitui et omnes fratres eius servituti illius subiugavi. Frumento et vino stabilivi eum, et tibi post haec, fili mi, ultra quid faciam?"

thee. Cursed be he that curseth thee, and let him that blesseth thee be filled with blessings."

30 Isaac had scarce ended his words when, Jacob being now gone out abroad, Esau came, 31 and brought in to his father meats made of *what he had taken in hunting,* saying, "Arise, my father, and eat of thy son's venison that thy soul may bless me."

32 And Isaac said to him, "Why! who art thou?"

He answered, "I am thy firstborn son, Esau."

33 Isaac was struck with fear and astonished exceedingly and wondering beyond what can be believed said, "Who is he then that even now brought me venison that he had taken and I ate of all before thou camest? And I have blessed him, and he shall be blessed."

34 Esau having heard his father's words roared out with a great cry and being in a *great* consternation said, "Bless me also, my father."

35 And he said, "Thy brother came deceitfully and got thy blessing."

36 But he said again, "Rightly is his name called Jacob, for he hath supplanted me, lo, this second time. My first birth-right he took away before, and now this second time he hath stolen away my blessing." And again he said to his father, "Hast thou not reserved me also a blessing?"

37 Isaac answered, "I have appointed him thy lord and have made all his brethren his servants. I have established him with corn and wine, and after this what shall I do more for thee, my son?"

38 Cui Esau, "Num unam," inquit, "tantum benedictionem habes, pater? Mihi quoque, obsecro ut benedicas."

Cumque heiulatu magno fleret, 39 motus Isaac dixit ad eum, "In pinguedine terrae et in rore caeli desuper 40 erit benedictio tua. Vives gladio et fratri tuo servies, tempusque veniet cum excutias et solvas iugum eius de cervicibus tuis."

41 Oderat ergo semper Esau Iacob pro benedictione qua benedixerat ei pater, dixitque in corde suo, "Venient dies luctus patris mei, et occidam Iacob, fratrem meum."

42 Nuntiata sunt haec Rebeccae, quae mittens et vocans Iacob, filium suum, dixit ad eum, "Ecce: Esau, frater tuus, minatur ut occidat te. 43 Nunc ergo, fili mi, audi vocem meam, et consurgens fuge ad Laban, fratrem meum, in Haran. 44 Habitabisque cum eo dies paucos donec requiescat furor fratris tui 45 et cesset indignatio eius obliviscaturque eorum quae fecisti in eum. Postea mittam et adducam te inde huc. Cur utroque orbabor filio in una die?"

46 Dixit quoque Rebecca ad Isaac, "Taedet me vitae meae propter filias Heth. Si acceperit Iacob uxorem de stirpe huius terrae, nolo vivere."

38 And Esau said to him, "Hast thou only one blessing, father? I beseech thee, bless me also."

And when he wept with a loud cry, 39 Isaac being moved said to him, "In the fat of the earth and in the dew of heaven from above 40 shall thy blessing be. Thou shalt live by the sword and shalt serve thy brother, and the time shall come when thou shalt shake off and loose his yoke from thy neck."

41 Esau therefore always hated Jacob for the blessing wherewith his father had blessed him, and he said in his heart, "The days will come of the mourning of my father, and I will kill my brother, Jacob."

42 These things were told to Rebekah, and she sent and called Jacob, her son, and said to him, "Behold: Esau, thy brother, threateneth to kill thee. 43 Now therefore, my son, hear my voice: arise and flee to Laban, my brother, to Haran. 44 And thou shalt dwell with him a few days till the wrath of thy brother be assuaged 45 and his indignation cease and he forget the things thou hast done to him. Afterwards I will send and bring thee from thence hither. Why shall I be deprived of both my sons in one day?"

46 And Rebekah said to Isaac, "I am weary of my life because of the daughters of Heth. If Jacob take a wife of the stock of this land, I *choose* not to live."

Caput 28

Vocavit itaque Isaac Iacob et benedixit eum praecepitque ei, dicens, "Noli accipere coniugem de genere Chanaan,
2 sed vade, et proficiscere in Mesopotamiam Syriae, ad domum Bathuel, patrem matris tuae, et accipe tibi inde uxorem de filiabus Laban, avunculi tui. 3 Deus autem omnipotens benedicat tibi et crescere te faciat atque multiplicet ut
sis in turbas populorum 4 et det tibi benedictiones Abraham
et semini tuo post te ut possideas terram peregrinationis
tuae, quam pollicitus est avo tuo." 5 Cumque dimisisset eum
Isaac, profectus venit in Mesopotamiam Syriae, ad Laban,
filium Bathuel Syri, fratrem Rebeccae, matris suae.

6 Videns autem Esau quod benedixisset pater suus Iacob
et misisset eum in Mesopotamiam Syriae ut inde uxorem
duceret et quod post benedictionem praecepisset ei, dicens,
"Non accipies coniugem de filiabus Chanaan," 7 quodque
oboediens Iacob parentibus isset in Syriam, 8 probans quoque quod non libenter aspiceret filias Chanaan pater suus,
9 ivit ad Ismahelem et duxit uxorem, absque his quas prius
habebat, Maeleth, filiam Ismahel, filii Abraham, sororem
Nabaioth.

10 Igitur egressus Iacob de Bersabee pergebat Haran.

Chapter 28

And Isaac called Jacob and blessed him and charged him, saying, "Take not a wife of the stock of Canaan, 2 but go, and take a journey to Mesopotamia of Syria, to the house of Bethuel, thy mother's father, and take thee a wife thence of the daughters of Laban, thy uncle. 3 And God almighty bless thee and make thee to increase and multiply thee that thou mayst be a multitude of people 4 and give the blessings of Abraham to thee and to thy seed after thee that thou mayst possess the land of thy sojournment, which he promised to thy grandfather." 5 And when Isaac had sent him away, he took his journey and went to Mesopotamia of Syria, to Laban, the son of Bethuel, the Syrian, brother to Rebekah, his mother.

6 And Esau, seeing that his father had blessed Jacob and had sent him into Mesopotamia of Syria to marry a wife thence and that after the blessing he had charged him, saying, "Thou shalt not take a wife of the daughters of Canaan," 7 and that Jacob obeying his parents was gone into Syria, 8 experiencing also that his father *was not well pleased with* the daughters of Canaan, 9 he went to Ishmael and took to wife, besides them he had before, Mahalath, the daughter of Ishmael, Abraham's son, the sister of Nebaioth.

10 But Jacob being departed from Beer-sheba went on to

11 Cumque venisset ad quendam locum et vellet in eo requiescere post solis occubitum, tulit de lapidibus qui iacebant et subponens capiti suo dormivit in eodem loco. 12 Viditque in somnis scalam stantem super terram et cacumen illius tangens caelum, angelos quoque Dei ascendentes et descendentes per eam 13 et Dominum innixum scalae, dicentem sibi, "Ego sum Dominus, Deus Abraham, patris tui, et Deus Isaac. Terram in qua dormis tibi dabo et semini tuo. 14 Eritque semen tuum quasi pulvis terrae. Dilataberis ad occidentem et orientem et septentrionem et meridiem, et benedicentur in te et in semine tuo cunctae tribus terrae. 15 Et ero custos tuus quocumque perrexeris et reducam te in terram hanc, nec dimittam nisi conplevero universa quae dixi."

16 Cumque evigilasset Iacob de somno, ait, "Vere Dominus est in loco isto, et ego nesciebam." 17 Pavensque, "Quam terribilis," inquit, "est locus iste! Non est hic aliud nisi domus Dei et porta caeli." 18 Surgens ergo Iacob mane tulit lapidem quem subposuerat capiti suo et erexit in titulum, fundens oleum desuper. 19 Appellavitque nomen urbis Bethel, quae prius Luza vocabatur. 20 Vovit etiam votum, dicens, "Si fuerit Deus mecum et custodierit me in via per quam ambulo et dederit mihi panem ad vescendum et vestem ad induendum 21 reversusque fuero prospere ad domum patris mei, erit mihi Dominus in Deum. 22 Et lapis iste quem erexi in titulum vocabitur domus Dei, cunctorumque quae dederis mihi decimas offeram tibi."

Haran. 11 And when he was come to a certain place and would rest in it after sunset, he took of the stones that lay there and putting under his head slept in the same place. 12 And he saw in his sleep a ladder standing upon the earth and the top thereof touching heaven, the angels also of God ascending and descending by it 13 and the Lord leaning upon the ladder, saying to him, "I am the Lord God of Abraham, thy father, and the God of Isaac. The land wherein thou sleepest I will give to thee and to thy seed. 14 And thy seed shall be as the dust of the earth. Thou shalt spread abroad to the west and to the east and to the north and to the south, and in thee and thy seed all the tribes of the earth shall be blessed. 15 And I will be thy keeper whithersoever thou goest and will bring thee back into this land, neither will I leave thee till I shall have accomplished all that I have said."

16 And when Jacob awaked out of sleep, he said, "Indeed the Lord is in this place, and I knew it not." 17 And trembling he said, "How terrible is this place! This is no other but the house of God and the gate of heaven." 18 And Jacob arising in the morning took the stone which he had laid under his head and set it up for a title, pouring oil upon the top of it. 19 And he called the name of the city Bethel, which before was called Luz. 20 And he made a vow, saying, "If God shall be with me and shall keep me in the way by which I walk and shall give me bread to eat and raiment to put on 21 and I shall return prosperously to my father's house, the Lord shall be my God. 22 And this stone which I have set up for a title shall be called the house of God, and of all things that thou shalt give to me I will offer tithes to thee."

Caput 29

Profectus ergo Iacob venit ad terram orientalem. 2 Et vidit puteum in agro tresque greges ovium accubantes iuxta eum, nam ex illo adaquabantur pecora, et os eius grandi lapide claudebatur. 3 Morisque erat ut cunctis ovibus congregatis devolverent lapidem et refectis gregibus rursum super os putei ponerent. 4 Dixitque ad pastores, "Fratres, unde estis?"

Qui responderunt, "De Haran."

5 Quos interrogans, "Numquid," ait, "nostis Laban, filium Nahor?"

Dixerunt, "Novimus."

6 "Sanusne est?" inquit.

"Valet," inquiunt, "et ecce: Rahel, filia eius, venit cum grege suo."

7 Dixitque Iacob, "Adhuc multum diei superest, nec est tempus ut reducantur ad caulas greges. Date ante potum ovibus et sic ad pastum eas reducite."

8 Qui responderunt, "Non possumus donec omnia pecora congregentur et amoveamus lapidem de ore putei ut adaquemus greges." 9 Adhuc loquebantur, et ecce: Rahel

Chapter 29

Jacob serveth Laban seven years for Rachel but is deceived with Leah. He afterwards marrieth Rachel. Leah bears him four sons.

Then Jacob went on in his journey and came into the east country. 2 And he saw a well in the field and three flocks of sheep lying by it, for the beasts were watered out of it, and the mouth thereof was closed with a great stone. 3 And the custom was when all the sheep were gathered together to roll away the stone and after the sheep were watered to put it on the mouth of the well again. 4 And he said to the shepherds, "Brethren, whence are you?"

They answered, "Of Haran."

5 And he asked them, saying, "Know you Laban, the son of Nahor?"

They said: "We know him."

6 He said, "Is he in health?"

"He is in health," say they, "and behold: Rachel, his daughter, cometh with his flock."

7 And Jacob said, "There is yet much day remaining, neither is it time to bring the flocks into the folds again. First give the sheep drink and so lead them back to feed."

8 They answered, "We cannot till all the cattle be gathered together and we remove the stone from the well's mouth that we may water the flocks." 9 They were yet speak-

veniebat cum ovibus patris sui, nam gregem ipsa pascebat. 10 Quam cum vidisset Iacob et sciret consobrinam suam ovesque Laban, avunculi sui, amovit lapidem quo puteus claudebatur. 11 Et adaquato grege, osculatus est eam elevataque voce flevit. 12 Et indicavit ei quod frater esset patris eius et filius Rebeccae, at illa festinans nuntiavit patri suo, 13 qui, cum audisset venisse Iacob, filium sororis suae, cucurrit obviam conplexusque eum et in oscula ruens duxit in domum suam.

Auditis autem causis itineris, 14 respondit, "Os meum es et caro mea." Et postquam expleti sunt dies mensis unius, 15 dixit ei, "Num quia frater meus es, gratis servies mihi? Dic quid mercedis accipias."

16 Habebat vero filias duas: nomen maioris Lia; minor vero appellabatur Rahel. 17 Sed Lia lippis erat oculis; Rahel decora facie et venusto aspectu. 18 Quam diligens Iacob ait, "Serviam tibi pro Rahel, filia tua minore, septem annis."

19 Respondit Laban, "Melius est ut tibi eam dem quam viro alteri; mane apud me." 20 Servivit igitur Iacob pro Rahel septem annis, et videbantur illi pauci dies prae amoris magnitudine.

21 Dixitque ad Laban, "Da mihi uxorem meam, quia iam tempus expletum est, ut ingrediar ad eam." 22 Qui vocatis multis amicorum turbis ad convivium fecit nuptias. 23 Et vespere filiam suam Liam introduxit ad eum 24 dans ancillam filiae Zelpham nomine.

ing, and behold: Rachel came with her father's sheep, for she fed the flock. 10 And when Jacob saw her and knew her to be his cousin-german and that they were the sheep of Laban, his uncle, he removed the stone wherewith the well was closed. 11 And having watered the flock, he kissed her and lifting up his voice wept. 12 And he told her that he was her father's brother and the son of Rebekah, but she went in haste and told her father, 13 who, when he heard that Jacob, his sister's son, was come, ran forth to meet him and embracing him and heartily kissing him brought him into his house.

And when he had heard the causes of his journey, 14 he answered, "Thou art my bone and my flesh." And after the days of one month were expired, 15 he said to him, "Because thou art my brother, shalt thou serve me without wages? Tell me what wages thou wilt have."

16 Now he had two daughters: the name of the elder was Leah and the younger was called Rachel. 17 But Leah was blear eyed; Rachel was well favoured and of a beautiful countenance. 18 And Jacob being in love with her said, "I will serve thee seven years for Rachel, thy younger daughter."

19 Laban answered, "It is better that I give her to thee than to another man; stay with me." 20 So Jacob served seven years for Rachel, and they seemed but a few days because of the greatness of his love.

21 And he said to Laban, "Give me my wife, for now the time is fulfilled, that I may go in unto her." 22 And he having invited a great number of his friends to the feast made the marriage. 23 And at night he brought in Leah his daughter to him 24 giving his daughter a handmaid named Zilpah.

Ad quam cum ex more Iacob fuisset ingressus, facto mane, vidit Liam, 25 et dixit ad socerum, "Quid est quod facere voluisti? Nonne pro Rahel servivi tibi? Quare inposuisti mihi?"

26 Respondit Laban, "Non est in loco nostro consuetudinis ut minores ante tradamus ad nuptias. 27 Imple ebdomadem dierum huius copulae, et hanc quoque dabo tibi pro opere quo serviturus es mihi septem annis aliis." 28 Adquievit placito et ebdomade transacta Rahel duxit uxorem 29 cui pater servam Balam dederat. 30 Tandemque potitus optatis nuptiis, amorem sequentis priori praetulit serviens apud eum septem annis aliis.

31 Videns autem Dominus quod despiceret Liam aperuit vulvam eius, sorore sterili permanente. 32 Quae conceptum genuit filium vocavitque nomen eius Ruben, dicens, "Vidit Dominus humilitatem meam; nunc amabit me vir meus." 33 Rursumque concepit et peperit filium et ait, "Quoniam audivit Dominus haberi me contemptui, dedit etiam istum mihi," vocavitque nomen illius Symeon. 34 Concepitque tertio et genuit alium filium dixitque, "Nunc quoque copulabitur mihi maritus meus eo quod pepererim illi tres filios," et idcirco appellavit nomen eius Levi. 35 Quarto concepit et peperit filium et ait, "Modo confitebor Domino," et ob hoc vocavit eum Iudam. Cessavitque parere.

Now when Jacob had gone in to her according to custom, when morning was come, he saw it was Leah, 25 and he said to his father-in-law, "What is it that thou didst mean to do? Did not I serve thee for Rachel? Why hast thou deceived me?"

26 Laban answered, "It is not the custom in *this* place to give the younger in marriage first. 27 Make up the week of days of this match, and I will give thee her also for the service that thou shalt render me other seven years." 28 He yielded to his pleasure, and after the week was past he married Rachel 29 to whom her father gave Bilhah for her servant. 30 And having at length obtained the marriage he wished for, he preferred the love of the latter before the former and served with him other seven years.

31 And the Lord seeing that he despised Leah opened her womb, but her sister remained barren. 32 And she conceived and bore a son and called his name Reuben, saying, "The Lord saw my affliction; now my husband will love me." 33 And again she conceived and bore a son and said, "Because the Lord heard that I was despised, he hath given this also to me," and she called his name Simeon. 34 And she conceived the third time and bore another son and said, "Now also my husband will be joined to me because I have borne him three sons," and therefore she called his name Levi. 35 The fourth time she conceived and bore a son and said, "Now will I praise the Lord," and for this she called him Judah. And she left bearing.

Caput 30

Cernens autem Rahel quod infecunda esset, invidit sorori et ait marito suo, "Da mihi liberos; alioquin moriar."

2 Cui iratus respondit Iacob, "Num pro Deo ego sum, qui privavit te fructu ventris tui?"

3 At illa, "Habeo," inquit, "famulam, Balam. Ingredere ad eam ut pariat super genua mea et habeam ex ea filios." 4 Deditque illi Balam in coniugium quae, 5 ingresso ad se viro, concepit et peperit filium.

6 Dixitque Rahel, "Iudicavit mihi Dominus et exaudivit vocem meam, dans mihi filium," et idcirco appellavit nomen illius Dan. 7 Rursumque Bala concipiens peperit alterum, 8 pro quo ait Rahel, "Conparavit me Deus cum sorore mea, et invalui," vocavitque eum Nepthalim.

9 Sentiens Lia quod parere desisset, Zelpham, ancillam suam, marito tradidit. 10 Qua post conceptum edente filium,

Chapter 30

Rachel being barren delivereth her handmaid to Jacob. She beareth two sons. Leah ceasing to bear giveth also her handmaid, and she beareth two more. Then Leah beareth other two sons and one daughter. Rachel beareth Joseph. Jacob, desirous to return home, is hired to stay for a certain part of the flock's increase, whereby he becometh exceeding rich.

And Rachel, seeing *herself without children,* envied her sister and said to her husband, "Give me children; otherwise I shall die."

2 And Jacob being angry with her answered, "Am I as God, who hath deprived thee of the fruit of thy womb?"

3 But she said, "I have here my servant, Bilhah. Go in unto her that she may bear upon my knees and I may have children by her." 4 And she gave him Bilhah in marriage who, 5 when her husband had gone in unto her, conceived and bore a son.

6 And Rachel said, "The Lord hath judged for me and hath heard my voice, giving me a son," and therefore she called his name Dan. 7 And again Bilhah conceived and bore another, 8 for whom Rachel said, "God hath compared me with my sister, and I have prevailed," and she called him Naphtali.

9 Leah, perceiving that she had left off bearing, gave Zilpah, her handmaid, to her husband. 10 And when she had

11 dixit, "Feliciter," et idcirco vocavit nomen eius Gad. 12 Peperit quoque Zelpha alterum, 13 dixitque Lia, "Hoc pro beatitudine mea, beatam quippe me dicent mulieres." Propterea appellavit eum Aser.

14 Egressus autem Ruben tempore messis triticeae in agro, repperit mandragoras quos matri, Liae, detulit. Dixitque Rahel, "Da mihi partem de mandragoris filii tui."

15 Illa respondit, "Parumne tibi videtur quod praeripueris maritum mihi nisi etiam mandragoras filii mei tuleris?"

Ait Rahel, "Dormiat tecum hac nocte pro mandragoris filii tui."

16 Redeuntique ad vesperam de agro Iacob, egressa est in occursum Lia et, "Ad me," inquit, "intrabis quia mercede conduxi te pro mandragoris filii mei." Dormivitque cum ea nocte illa. 17 Et exaudivit Deus preces eius, concepitque et peperit filium quintum, 18 et ait, "Dedit Deus mercedem mihi quia dedi ancillam meam viro meo." Appellavitque nomen illius Isachar. 19 Rursum Lia concipiens peperit sextum filium 20 et ait, "Dotavit me Deus dote bona; etiam hac vice mecum erit maritus meus eo quod genuerim ei sex filios," et idcirco appellavit nomen eius Zabulon, 21 post quem peperit filiam nomine Dinam.

22 Recordatus quoque Dominus Rahelis exaudivit eam et aperuit vulvam illius. 23 Quae concepit et peperit filium, dicens, "Abstulit Deus obprobrium meum." 24 Et vocavit nomen illius Ioseph, dicens, "Addat mihi Dominus filium alterum."

25 Nato autem Ioseph, dixit Iacob socero suo, "Dimitte

conceived and brought forth a son, 11 she said, "Happily," and therefore called his name Gad. 12 Zilpah also bore another, 13 and Leah said, "This is for my happiness, for women will call me blessed." Therefore she called him Asher.

14 And Reuben, going out in the time of the wheat harvest into the field, found mandrakes which he brought to his mother, Leah. And Rachel said, "Give me part of thy son's mandrakes."

15 She answered, "Dost thou think it a small matter that thou hast taken my husband from me unless thou take also my son's mandrakes?"

Rachel said, "He shall sleep with thee this night for thy son's mandrakes."

16 And when Jacob returned at even from the field, Leah went out to meet him and said, "Thou shalt come in unto me because I have hired thee for my son's mandrakes." And he slept with her that night. 17 And God heard her prayers, and she conceived and bore the fifth son, 18 and said, "God hath given me a reward because I gave my handmaid to my husband." And she called his name Issachar. 19 And Leah conceived again and bore the sixth son 20 and said, "God hath endowed me with a good dowry; this turn also my husband will be with me because I have borne him six sons," and therefore she called his name Zebulun, 21 after whom she bore a daughter named Dinah.

22 The Lord also remembering Rachel heard her and opened her womb. 23 And she conceived and bore a son, saying, "God hath taken away my reproach." 24 And she called his name Joseph, saying, "The Lord give me also another son."

25 And when Joseph was born, Jacob said to his father-in-law, "Send me away that I may return into my country and to

me ut revertar in patriam et ad terram meam. 26 Da mihi uxores et liberos meos pro quibus servivi tibi ut abeam. Tu nosti servitutem qua servivi tibi."

27 Ait ei Laban, "Inveniam gratiam in conspectu tuo. Experimento didici quod benedixerit mihi Deus propter te. 28 Constitue mercedem tuam quam dem tibi."

29 At ille respondit, "Tu nosti quomodo servierim tibi et quanta in manibus meis fuerit possessio tua. 30 Modicum habuisti antequam venirem ad te, et nunc dives effectus es, benedixitque tibi Dominus ad introitum meum. Iustum est igitur ut aliquando provideam etiam domui meae."

31 Dixitque Laban, "Quid dabo tibi?"

At ille ait, "Nihil volo, sed si feceris quod postulo, iterum pascam et custodiam pecora tua. 32 Gyra omnes greges tuos, et separa cunctas oves varias et sparso vellere, et quodcumque furvum et maculosum variumque fuerit tam in ovibus quam in capris erit merces mea. 33 Respondebitque mihi cras iustitia mea quando placiti tempus advenerit coram te. Et omnia quae non fuerint varia et maculosa et furva tam in ovibus quam in capris furti me arguent."

34 Dixitque Laban, "Gratum habeo quod petis." 35 Et separavit in die illo capras et oves et hircos et arietes varios atque maculosos, cunctum autem gregem unicolorem, id est, albi et nigri velleris, tradidit in manu filiorum suorum.

36 Et posuit spatium itineris inter se et generum dierum trium, qui pascebat reliquos greges eius. 37 Tollens ergo Iacob virgas populeas virides et amigdalinas et ex platanis

my land. 26 Give me my wives and my children for whom I have served thee that I may depart. Thou knowest the service that I have rendered thee."

27 Laban said to him, "Let me find favour in thy sight. I have learned by experience that God hath blessed me for thy sake. 28 Appoint thy wages which I shall give thee."

29 But he answered, "Thou knowest how I have served thee and how great thy possession hath been in my hands. 30 Thou hadst but little before I came to thee, and now thou art become rich, and the Lord hath blessed thee at my coming. It is reasonable therefore that I should now provide also for my own house."

31 And Laban said, "What shall I give thee?"

But he said, "I require nothing, but if thou wilt do what I demand, I will feed and keep thy sheep again. 32 Go round through all thy flocks, and separate all the sheep of divers colours and *speckled,* and all that is brown and spotted and of divers colours as well among the sheep as among the goats shall be my wages. 33 And my justice shall answer for me tomorrow before thee when the time of the bargain shall come. And all that is not of divers colours and spotted and brown as well among the sheep as among the goats shall accuse me of theft."

34 And Laban said, "I like well what thou demandest." 35 And he separated the same day the she-goats and the sheep and the he-goats and the rams of divers colours and spotted, and all the flock of one colour, that is, of white and black fleece, he delivered into the hands of his sons.

36 And he set the space of three days' journey betwixt himself and his son-in-law, who fed the rest of his flock. 37 And Jacob took green rods of poplar and of almond and of

ex parte decorticavit eas detractisque corticibus in his quae spoliata fuerant, candor apparuit, illa vero quae integra erant viridia permanserunt, atque in hunc modum color effectus est varius. 38 Posuitque eas in canalibus ubi effundebatur aqua ut cum venissent greges ad bibendum ante oculos haberent virgas et in aspectu earum conciperent. 39 Factumque est ut in ipso calore coitus, oves intuerentur virgas et parerent maculosa et varia et diverso colore respersa. 40 Divisitque gregem Iacob et posuit virgas in canalibus ante oculos arietum, erant autem alba quaeque et nigra Laban, cetera vero Iacob separatis inter se gregibus.

41 Igitur quando primo tempore ascendebantur oves, ponebat Iacob virgas in canalibus aquarum ante oculos arietum et ovium ut in earum contemplatione conciperent, 42 quando vero serotina admissura erat et conceptus extremus, non ponebat eas. Factaque sunt ea quae erant serotina Laban, et quae primi temporis, Iacob. 43 Ditatusque est homo ultra modum, et habuit greges multos, ancillas et servos, camelos et asinos.

plane trees and pilled them in part *so* when the bark was taken off in the parts that were pilled, there appeared whiteness, but the parts that were whole remained green, and by this means the colour was divers. 38 And he put them in the troughs where the water was poured out that when the flocks should come to drink they might have the rods before their eyes and in the sight of them might conceive. 39 And it came to pass that in the very heat of coition, the sheep beheld the rods and brought forth spotted and of divers colours and *speckled*. 40 And Jacob separated the flock and put the rods in the troughs before the eyes of the rams, and all the white and the black were Laban's, and the rest were Jacob's when the flocks were separated one from the other.

41 So when the ewes went first to ram, Jacob put the rods in the troughs of water before the eyes of the rams and of the ewes that they might conceive while they were looking upon them, 42 but when the latter coming was and the last conceiving, he did not put them. And those that were lateward became Laban's, and they of the first time, Jacob's. 43 And the man was enriched exceedingly, and he had many flocks, maid-servants and men-servants, camels and asses.

Caput 31

Postquam autem audivit verba filiorum Laban dicentium, "Tulit Iacob omnia quae fuerunt patris nostri et de illius facultate ditatus factus est inclitus," 2 animadvertit quoque faciem Laban quod non esset erga se sicut heri et nudius tertius, 3 maxime dicente sibi Domino, "Revertere in terram patrum tuorum et ad generationem tuam, eroque tecum," 4 misit et vocavit Rahel et Liam in agrum ubi pascebat greges 5 dixitque eis, "Video faciem patris vestri quod non sit erga me sicut heri et nudius tertius, Deus autem patris mei fuit mecum. 6 Et ipsae nostis quod totis viribus meis servierim patri vestro. 7 Sed et pater vester circumvenit me et mutavit mercedem meam decem vicibus, et tamen non dimisit eum Deus ut noceret mihi. 8 Si quando dixit, 'Variae erunt mercedes tuae,' pariebant omnes oves varios fetus, quando vero e contrario ait, 'Alba quaeque accipies pro mercede,' omnes greges alba pepererunt. 9 Tulitque Deus substantiam patris vestri et dedit mihi, 10 postquam enim conceptus ovium tempus advenerat, levavi oculos meos et vidi in somnis ascendentes mares super feminas varios et maculosos et diversorum colorum.

Chapter 31

Jacob's departure. He is pursued and overtaken by Laban. They make a covenant.

But after that he heard the words of the sons of Laban saying, "Jacob hath taken away all that was our father's and being enriched by his substance is become great," 2 and perceiving also that Laban's countenance was not towards him as yesterday and the other day, 3 especially the Lord saying to him, "Return into the land of thy fathers and to thy kindred, and I will be with thee," 4 he sent and called Rachel and Leah into the field where he fed the flocks 5 and said to them, "I see your father's countenance is not towards me as yesterday and the other day, but the God of my father hath been with me. 6 And you know that I have served your father to the uttermost of my power. 7 Yea, your father also hath overreached me and hath changed my wages ten times, and yet God hath not suffered him to hurt me. 8 If at any time he said, 'The speckled shall be thy wages,' all the sheep brought forth speckled, but when he said on the contrary, 'Thou shalt take all the white ones for thy wages,' all the flocks brought forth white ones. 9 And God hath taken your father's substance and given it to me, 10 for after that time came of the ewes conceiving, I lifted up my eyes and saw in my sleep that the males which leaped upon the females were of divers colours and spotted and speckled.

11 "Dixitque angelus Dei ad me in somnis, 'Iacob?' Et ego respondi, 'Adsum.' 12 Qui ait, 'Leva oculos tuos, et vide universos masculos ascendentes super feminas varios respersos atque maculosos, vidi enim omnia quae fecit tibi Laban. 13 Ego sum Deus Bethel ubi unxisti lapidem et votum vovisti mihi. Nunc ergo surge, et egredere de terra hac, revertens in terram nativitatis tuae.'"

14 Responderuntque Rahel et Lia, "Numquid habemus residui quicquam in facultatibus et hereditate domus patris nostri? 15 Nonne quasi alienas reputavit nos et vendidit comeditque pretium nostrum? 16 Sed Deus tulit opes patris nostri et nobis eas tradidit ac filiis nostris; unde omnia quae praecepit tibi Deus fac." 17 Surrexit itaque Iacob et inpositis liberis et coniugibus suis super camelos abiit. 18 Tulitque omnem substantiam et greges et quicquid in Mesopotamiam quaesierat pergens ad Isaac, patrem suum, in terram Chanaan.

19 Eo tempore Laban ierat ad tondendas oves, et Rahel furata est idola patris sui. 20 Noluitque Iacob confiteri socero quod fugeret.

21 Cumque abisset, tam ipse quam omnia quae iuris eius erant, et amne transmisso pergeret contra Montem Galaad, 22 nuntiatum est Laban die tertio quod fugeret Iacob, 23 qui adsumptis fratribus suis persecutus est eum diebus septem et conprehendit eum in Monte Galaad. 24 Viditque in somnis dicentem sibi Deum, "Cave ne quicquam aspere loquaris contra Iacob." 25 Iamque Iacob extenderat in monte tabernaculum, cumque ille consecutus fuisset eum cum fratribus suis, in eodem Monte Galaad fixit tentorium.

11 "And the angel of God said to me in my sleep, 'Jacob?' And I answered, 'Here I am.' 12 And he said, 'Lift up thy eyes, and see that all the males leaping upon the females are of divers colours spotted and speckled, for I have seen all that Laban hath done to thee. 13 I am the God of Bethel where thou didst anoint the stone and make a vow to me. Now therefore arise, and go out of this land, and return into thy native country.'"

14 And Rachel and Leah answered, "Have we any thing left among the goods and inheritance of our father's house? 15 Hath he not counted us as strangers and sold us and eaten up the price of us? 16 But God hath taken our father's riches and delivered them to us and to our children; wherefore do all that God hath commanded thee." 17 Then Jacob rose up and having set his children and wives upon camels went his way. 18 And he took all his substance and flocks and whatsoever he had gotten in Mesopotamia and went forward to Isaac, his father, to the land of Canaan.

19 At that time Laban was gone to shear his sheep, and Rachel stole away her father's idols. 20 And Jacob would not confess to his father-in-law that he was flying away.

21 And when he was gone, together with all that belonged to him, and having passed the river was going on towards Mount Gilead, 22 it was told Laban on the third day that Jacob fled, 23 and he took his brethren with him and pursued after him seven days and overtook him in the Mount of Gilead. 24 And he saw in a dream God saying to him, "Take heed thou speak not any thing harshly against Jacob." 25 Now Jacob had pitched his tent in the mountain, and when he with his brethren had overtaken him, he pitched his tent in the same Mount of Gilead.

26 Et dixit ad Iacob, "Quare ita egisti, ut clam me abigeres filias meas quasi captivas gladio? 27 Cur ignorante me fugere voluisti nec indicare mihi ut prosequerer te cum gaudio et canticis et tympanis et citharis? 28 Non es passus ut oscularer filios meos ac filias; stulte operatus es, et nunc 29 valet quidem manus mea reddere tibi malum. Sed Deus patris vestri heri dixit mihi, 'Cave ne loquaris contra Iacob quicquam durius.' 30 Esto ad tuos ire cupiebas et desiderio tibi erat domus patris tui: cur furatus es deos meos?"

31 Respondit Iacob, "Quod inscio te profectus sum, timui ne violenter auferres filias tuas. 32 Quod autem furti arguis: apud quemcumque inveneris deos tuos necetur coram fratribus nostris. Scrutare; quicquid tuorum apud me inveneris, et aufer."

Haec dicens ignorabat quod Rahel furata esset idola. 33 Ingressus itaque Laban tabernaculum Iacob et Liae et utriusque famulae non invenit. Cumque intrasset tentorium Rahelis, 34 illa festinans abscondit idola subter stramen cameli et sedit desuper, scrutantique omne tentorium et nihil invenienti 35 ait, "Ne irascatur dominus meus quod coram te adsurgere nequeo, quia iuxta consuetudinem feminarum nunc accidit mihi." Sic delusa sollicitudo quaerentis est.

36 Tumensque Iacob cum iurgio ait, "Quam ob culpam meam et ob quod peccatum meum sic exarsisti post me 37 et scrutatus es omnem supellectilem meam? Quid invenisti

26 And he said to Jacob, "Why hast thou done thus, to carry away without my knowledge my daughters as captives taken with the sword? 27 Why wouldst thou run away *privately* and not acquaint me that I might have brought thee on the way with joy and with songs and with timbrels and with harps? 28 Thou hast not suffered me to kiss my sons and daughters; thou hast done foolishly, and now indeed 29 it is in my power to return thee evil. But the God of your father said to me yesterday, 'Take heed thou speak not any thing harshly against Jacob.' 30 Suppose thou didst desire to go to thy friends and hadst a longing after thy father's house: why hast thou stolen away my gods?"

31 Jacob answered, "That I departed unknown to thee, it was for fear lest thou wouldst take away thy daughters by force. 32 But whereas thou chargest me with theft: with whomsoever thou shalt find thy gods let him be slain before our brethren. Search, *and if* thou find any of thy things with me, *take them* away."

Now when he said this he knew not that Rachel had stolen the idols. 33 So Laban went into the tent of Jacob and of Leah and of both the handmaids and found them not. And when he was entered into Rachel's tent, 34 she in haste hid the idols under the camel's furniture and sat upon them, and when he had searched all the tent and found nothing 35 she said, "Let not my lord be angry that I cannot rise up before thee, because it has now happened to me according to the custom of women." So *his careful search was in vain.*

36 And Jacob being angry said in a chiding manner, "For what fault of mine and for what offence on my part hast thou so hotly pursued me 37 and searched all my household stuff? What hast thou found of all the substance of thy

de cuncta substantia domus tuae? Pone hic coram fratribus meis et fratribus tuis, et iudicent inter me et te. 38 Idcirco viginti annis fui tecum? Oves tuae et caprae steriles non fuerunt; arietes gregis tui non comedi, 39 nec captum a bestia ostendi tibi; ego damnum omne reddebam. Quicquid furto perierat a me exigebas. 40 Die noctuque aestu urebar et gelu, fugiebatque somnus ab oculis meis. 41 Sicque per viginti annos in domo tua servivi tibi: quattuordecim pro filiabus et sex pro gregibus tuis. Inmutasti quoque mercedem meam decem vicibus. 42 Nisi Deus patris mei Abraham et timor Isaac adfuisset mihi, forsitan modo nudum me dimisisses. Adflictionem meam et laborem manuum mearum respexit Deus et arguit te heri."

43 Respondit ei Laban, "Filiae meae et filii et greges tui et omnia quae cernis mea sunt. Quid possum facere filiis et nepotibus meis? 44 Veni ergo; ineamus foedus ut sit in testimonium inter me et te."

45 Tulit itaque Iacob lapidem et erexit illum in titulum. 46 Dixitque fratribus suis, "Adferte lapides." Qui congregantes fecerunt tumulum, comederuntque super eum. 47 Quem vocavit Laban Tumulus Testis, et Iacob, Acervum Testimonii, uterque iuxta proprietatem linguae suae.

48 Dixitque Laban, "Tumulus iste testis erit inter me et te hodie." Et idcirco appellatum est nomen eius Galaad, id est, Tumulus Testis.

49 "Intueatur Dominus et iudicet inter nos quando recesserimus a nobis. 50 Si adflixeris filias meas, et si introduxeris

house? Lay it here before my brethren and thy brethren, and let them judge between me and thee. 38 Have I therefore been with thee twenty years? Thy ewes and goats were not barren; the rams of thy flocks I did not eat, 39 neither did I show thee that which the beast had torn; I made good all the damage. Whatsoever was lost by theft thou didst exact it of me. 40 Day and night was I parched with heat and with frost, and sleep departed from my eyes. 41 And in this manner have I served thee in thy house twenty years: fourteen for thy daughters and six for thy flocks. Thou hast changed also my wages ten times. 42 Unless the God of my father Abraham and the fear of Isaac had stood by me, peradventure now thou hadst sent me away naked. God beheld my affliction and the labour of my hands and rebuked thee yesterday."

43 Laban answered him, "The daughters are mine, and the children and thy flocks and all things that thou seest are mine. What can I do to my children and grandchildren? 44 Come therefore; let us enter into a league that it may be for a testimony between me and thee."

45 And Jacob took a stone and set it up for a title. 46 And he said to his brethren, "Bring hither stones." And they gathering stones together made a heap, and they ate upon it. 47 And Laban called it the Witness Heap, and Jacob, the Hillock of Testimony, each of them according to the propriety of his language.

48 And Laban said, "This heap shall be a witness between me and thee this day." And therefore the name thereof was called Galeed, that is, the Witness Heap.

49 "The Lord behold and judge between us when we shall be gone one from the other. 50 If thou afflict my daughters,

uxores alias super eas, nullus sermonis nostri testis est absque Deo, qui praesens respicit." 51 Dixitque rursus ad Iacob, "En: tumulus hic et lapis quem erexi inter me et te 52 testis erit. Tumulus, inquam, iste et lapis, sint in testimonio: si aut ego transiero illum pergens ad te aut tu praeterieris malum mihi cogitans, 53 Deus Abraham et Deus Nahor iudicet inter nos, Deus patris eorum." Iuravit Iacob per timorem patris sui, Isaac. 54 Immolatisque victimis in monte, vocavit fratres suos ut ederent panem. Qui cum comedissent, manserunt ibi. 55 Laban vero de nocte consurgens osculatus est filios et filias suas et benedixit illis reversusque in locum suum.

Caput 32

Iacob quoque abiit itinere quo coeperat, fueruntque ei obviam angeli Dei. 2 Quos cum vidisset ait, "Castra Dei sunt haec," et appellavit nomen loci illius Manaim, id est, Castra. 3 Misit autem et nuntios ante se ad Esau, fratrem suum, in terram Seir, in regionem Edom, 4 praecepitque eis, dicens,

and if thou bring in other wives over them, none is witness of our speech but God, who is present and beholdeth." 51 And he said again to Jacob, "Behold: this heap and the stone which I have set up between me and thee 52 shall be a witness. This heap, I say, and the stone, be they for a testimony: if either I shall pass beyond it going towards thee or thou shalt pass beyond it thinking harm to me, 53 the God of Abraham and the God of Nahor, the God of their father, judge between us." And Jacob swore by the fear of his father, Isaac. 54 And after he had offered sacrifices in the mountain, he called his brethren to eat bread. And when they had eaten, they lodged there. 55 But Laban arose in the night and kissed his sons and daughters and blessed them and returned to his place.

Chapter 32

Jacob's vision of angels. His message and presents to Esau. His wrestling with an angel.

Jacob also went on the journey he had begun, and the angels of God met him. 2 And when he saw them he said, "These are the camps of God," and he called the name of that place Mahanaim, that is, Camps. 3 And he sent messengers before him to Esau, his brother, to the land of Seir, to the country of Edom, 4 and he commanded them, say-

"Sic loquimini domino meo Esau: 'Haec dicit frater tuus, Iacob: "Apud Laban peregrinatus sum et fui usque in praesentem diem. 5 Habeo boves et asinos et oves et servos atque ancillas, mittoque nunc legationem ad dominum meum ut inveniam gratiam in conspectu tuo."'"

6 Reversique sunt nuntii ad Iacob, dicentes, "Venimus ad Esau, fratrem tuum, et ecce: properat in occursum tibi cum quadringentis viris."

7 Timuit Iacob valde et perterritus divisit populum qui secum erat greges quoque et oves et boves et camelos in duas turmas, 8 dicens, "Si venerit Esau ad unam turmam et percusserit eam, alia turma quae reliqua est salvabitur." 9 Dixitque Iacob, "Deus patris mei Abraham et Deus patris mei Isaac, Domine, qui dixisti mihi, 'Revertere in terram tuam et in locum nativitatis tuae, et benefaciam tibi,' 10 minor sum cunctis miserationibus tuis et veritate tua quam explesti servo tuo. In baculo meo transivi Iordanem istum, et nunc cum duabus turmis regredior. 11 Erue me de manu fratris mei Esau, quia valde eum timeo ne forte veniens percutiat matrem cum filiis. 12 Tu locutus es quod bene mihi faceres et dilatares semen meum sicut harenam maris quae prae multitudine numerari non potest."

13 Cumque dormisset ibi nocte illa, separavit de his quae habebat munera Esau fratri suo: 14 capras ducentas, hircos viginti, oves ducentas et arietes viginti, 15 camelos fetas cum pullis suis triginta, vaccas quadraginta et tauros viginti, asinas viginti et pullos earum decem.

ing, "Thus shall ye speak to my lord Esau: 'Thus saith thy brother, Jacob: "I have sojourned with Laban and have been with him until this day. 5 I have oxen and asses and sheep and men-servants and women-servants, and now I send a message to my lord that I may find favour in thy sight."'"

6 And the messengers returned to Jacob, saying, "We came to Esau, thy brother, and behold: he cometh with speed to meet thee with four hundred men."

7 Then Jacob was greatly afraid and in his fear divided the people that was with him and the flocks and the sheep and the oxen and the camels into two companies, 8 saying, "If Esau come to one company and destroy it, the other company that is left shall escape." 9 And Jacob said, "O God of my father Abraham and God of my father Isaac, O Lord, who saidst to me, 'Return to thy land and to the place of thy birth, and I will do well for thee,' 10 *I am not worthy of the least of* all thy mercies and of thy truth which thou hast fulfilled to thy servant. With my staff I passed over this Jordan, and now I return with two companies. 11 Deliver me from the hand of my brother Esau, for I am greatly afraid of him lest perhaps he come and kill the mother with the children. 12 Thou didst say that thou wouldst do well by me and multiply my seed like the sand of the sea which cannot be numbered for multitude."

13 And when he had slept there that night, he set apart of the things which he had presents for his brother Esau: 14 two hundred she-goats, twenty he-goats, two hundred ewes and twenty rams, 15 thirty milch camels with their colts, forty kine and twenty bulls, twenty she-asses and ten of their foals.

16 Et misit per manus servorum suorum, singulos seorsum greges, dixitque pueris suis, "Antecedite me, et sit spatium inter gregem et gregem." 17 Et praecepit priori, dicens, "Si obvium habueris Esau, fratrem meum, et interrogaverit te, 'Cuius es?' aut, 'Quo vadis?' aut, 'Cuius sunt ista quae sequeris?' 18 respondebis, 'Servi tui Iacob: munera misit domino meo Esau, ipse quoque post nos venit.'" 19 Similiter mandata dedit secundo ac tertio et cunctis qui sequebantur greges, dicens, "Hisdem verbis loquimini ad Esau cum inveneritis eum. 20 Et addetis, 'Ipse quoque servus tuus Iacob iter nostrum insequitur, dixit enim, "Placabo illum muneribus quae praecedunt, et postea videbo; forsitan propitiabitur mihi."'"

21 Praecesserunt itaque munera ante eum, ipse vero mansit nocte illa in castris. 22 Cumque mature surrexisset tulit duas uxores suas et totidem famulas cum undecim filiis et transivit vadum Iaboc. 23 Transductisque omnibus quae ad se pertinebant, 24 remansit solus, et ecce: vir luctabatur cum eo usque mane. 25 Qui cum videret quod eum superare non posset, tetigit nervum femoris eius, et statim emarcuit.

26 Dixitque ad eum, "Dimitte me, iam enim ascendit aurora."

Respondit, "Non dimittam te nisi benedixeris mihi."

27 Ait ergo, "Quod nomen est tibi?"

Respondit, "Iacob."

16 And he sent them by the hands of his servants, every drove by itself, and he said to his servants, "Go before me, and let there be a space between drove and drove." 17 And he commanded the first, saying, "If thou meet my brother, Esau, and he ask thee, 'Whose art thou?' or, 'Whither goest thou?' or, 'Whose are these *before thee?*' 18 thou shalt answer, 'Thy servant Jacob's: he hath sent them as a present to my lord Esau, and he cometh after us.'" 19 In like manner he commanded the second and the third and all that followed the droves, saying, "Speak ye the same words to Esau when ye find him. 20 And ye shall add, 'Thy servant Jacob himself also followeth after us, for he said, "I will appease him with the presents that go before, and afterwards I will see him; perhaps he will be gracious to me."'"

21 So the presents went before him, but himself lodged that night in the camp. 22 And rising early he took his two wives and his *two* handmaids with his eleven sons and passed over the ford of Jabbok. 23 And when all things were brought over that belonged to him, 24 he remained alone, and behold: a man wrestled with him till morning. 25 And when he *[the man]* saw that he could not overcome him *[Jacob],* he *[the man]* touched the sinew of his *[Jacob's]* thigh, and forthwith it shrank.

26 And he *[the man]* said to him, "Let me go, for it is break of day."

He answered, "I will not let thee go except thou bless me."

27 And he said, "What is thy name?"

He answered, "Jacob."

28 At ille, "Nequaquam," inquit, "Iacob appellabitur nomen tuum, sed Israhel, quoniam si contra Deum fortis fuisti, quanto magis contra homines praevalebis?"

29 Interrogavit eum Iacob, "Dic mihi: quo appellaris nomine?"

Respondit, "Cur quaeris nomen meum?" Et benedixit ei in eodem loco. 30 Vocavitque Iacob nomen loci illius Phanuhel, dicens, "Vidi Deum facie ad faciem, et salva facta est anima mea."

31 Ortusque est ei statim sol postquam transgressus est Phanuhel, ipse vero claudicabat pede. 32 Quam ob causam non comedunt filii Israhel nervum qui emarcuit in femore Iacob usque in praesentem diem, eo quod tetigerit nervum femoris eius et obstipuerit.

Caput 33

Levans autem Iacob oculos suos vidit venientem Esau et cum eo quadringentos viros, divisitque filios Liae et Rahel ambarumque famularum. 2 Et posuit utramque ancillam et liberos earum in principio Liam vero et filios eius in secundo loco Rahel autem et Ioseph novissimos. 3 Et ipse praegrediens adoravit pronus in terram septies donec adpropinqua-

28 But he said, "Thy name shall not be called Jacob, but Israel, for if thou hast been strong against God, how much more shalt thou prevail against men?"

29 Jacob asked him, "Tell me: by what name art thou called?"

He answered, "Why dost thou ask my name?" And he blessed him in the same place. 30 And Jacob called the name of the place Peniel, saying, "I have seen God face to face, and my soul has been saved."

31 And immediately the sun rose upon him after he was past Penuel, but he halted on his foot. 32 Therefore the children of Israel unto this day eat not the sinew that shrank in Jacob's thigh, because he touched the sinew of his thigh and it shrank.

Chapter 33

Jacob and Esau meet. Jacob goeth to Salem, where he raiseth an altar.

And Jacob lifting up his eyes saw Esau coming and with him four hundred men, and he divided the children of Leah and of Rachel and of the two handmaids. 2 And he put both the handmaids and their children foremost and Leah and her children in the second place and Rachel and Joseph last. 3 And he went forward and bowed down with his face to the

ret frater eius. 4 Currens itaque Esau obviam fratri suo amplexatus est eum, stringensque collum et osculans, flevit. 5 Levatisque oculis vidit mulieres et parvulos earum et ait, "Quid sibi volunt isti? Et si ad te pertinent?"

Respondit, "Parvuli sunt quos donavit mihi Deus, servo tuo."

6 Et adpropinquantes ancillae et filii earum incurvati sunt. 7 Accessitque Lia cum liberis suis, et cum similiter adorassent, extremi Ioseph et Rahel adoraverunt. 8 Dixitque Esau, "Quaenam sunt istae turmae quas obvias habui?"

Respondit, "Ut invenirem gratiam coram domino meo."

9 At ille, "Habeo," ait, "plurima, frater mi; sint tua tibi."

10 Dixitque Iacob, "Noli ita, obsecro, sed si inveni gratiam in oculis tuis, accipe munusculum de manibus meis, sic enim vidi faciem tuam quasi viderim vultum Dei. Esto mihi propitius, 11 et suscipe benedictionem quam adtuli tibi et quam donavit mihi Deus, tribuens omnia."

Vix fratre conpellente suscipiens 12 ait, "Gradiamur simul, eroque socius itineris tui."

13 Dixitque Iacob, "Nosti, domine mi, quod parvulos habeam teneros et oves ac boves fetas mecum, quas si plus in ambulando fecero laborare, morientur una die cuncti greges. 14 Praecedat dominus meus ante servum suum, et ego sequar paulatim vestigia eius sicut videro posse parvulos meos donec veniam ad dominum meum in Seir."

ground seven times until his brother came near. 4 Then Esau ran to meet his brother and embraced him and, clasping him fast about the neck and kissing him, wept. 5 And lifting up his eyes he saw the women and their children and said, "What mean these? And do they belong to thee?"

He answered, "They are the children which God hath given to me, thy servant."

6 Then the handmaids and their children came near and bowed themselves. 7 Leah also with her children came near and bowed down in like manner, and last of all Joseph and Rachel bowed down. 8 And Esau said, "What are the droves that I met?"

He answered, "That I might find favour before my lord."

9 But he said, "I have plenty, my brother; keep what is thine for thyself."

10 And Jacob said, "Do not so, I beseech thee, but if I have found favour in thy eyes, receive a little present at my hand, for I have seen thy face as if I should have seen the countenance of God. Be gracious to me, 11 and take the blessing which I have brought thee and which God hath given me, who giveth all things."

He took it with much ado at his brother's earnest pressing him 12 and said, "Let us go on together, and I will accompany thee in thy journey."

13 And Jacob said, "My lord, thou knowest that I have with me tender children and sheep and kine with young, which if I should cause *to be overdriven,* in one day all the flocks will die. 14 May it please my lord to go before his servant, and I will follow softly after him as I shall see my children to be able until I come to my lord in Seir."

15 Respondit Esau, "Oro te ut de populo qui mecum est, saltem, socii remaneant viae tuae."

"Non est," inquit, "necesse. Hoc uno indigeo: ut inveniam gratiam in conspectu tuo, domine mi."

16 Reversus est itaque illo die Esau itinere quo venerat in Seir. 17 Et Iacob venit in Soccoth ubi, aedificata domo et fixis tentoriis, appellavit nomen loci illius Soccoth, id est, Tabernacula. 18 Transivitque in Salem, urbem Sycimorum, quae est in terra Chanaan, postquam regressus est de Mesopotamiam Syriae, et habitavit iuxta oppidum, 19 emitque partem agri in qua fixerat tabernacula a filiis Emor, patris Sychem, centum agnis. 20 Et erecto ibi altari, invocavit super illud fortissimum Deum Israhel.

Caput 34

Egressa est autem Dina, filia Liae, ut videret mulieres regionis illius. 2 Quam cum vidisset Sychem, filius Emor, Evei, princeps terrae illius, adamavit et rapuit et dormivit cum illa, vi opprimens virginem. 3 Et conglutinata est anima eius cum ea, tristemque blanditiis delinivit. 4 Et pergens ad

15 Esau answered, "I beseech thee that some of the people, at least, who are with me may stay to accompany thee in the way."

And he said, "There is no necessity. I want *nothing else but* only to find favour, my lord, in thy sight."

16 So Esau returned that day the way that he came to Seir. 17 And Jacob came to Succoth where, having built a house and pitched tents, he called the name of the place Succoth, that is, Tents. 18 And he passed over to Salem, a city of the Shechemites, which is in the land of Canaan, after he returned from Mesopotamia of Syria, and he dwelt by the town, 19 and he bought that part of the field in which he pitched his tents of the children of Hamor, the father of Shechem, for a hundred lambs. 20 And raising an altar there, he invoked upon it the most mighty God of Israel.

Chapter 34

Dinah is ravished, for which the Shechemites are destroyed.

And Dinah, the daughter of Leah, went out to see the women of that country. 2 And when Shechem, the son of Hamor, the Hivite, the prince of that land, saw her, he was in love with her and took her away and lay with her, ravishing the virgin. 3 And his soul was fast knit unto her, and *whereas she was* sad, he comforted her with sweet words. 4 And going

Emor, patrem suum, "Accipe mihi," inquit, "puellam hanc coniugem." 5 Quod cum audisset Iacob, absentibus filiis et in pastu occupatis pecorum, siluit donec redirent.

6 Egresso autem Emor, patre Sychem, ut loqueretur ad Iacob, 7 ecce: filii eius veniebant de agro, auditoque quod acciderat irati sunt valde eo quod foedam rem esset operatus in Israhel et violata filia Iacob rem inlicitam perpetrasset. 8 Locutus est itaque Emor ad eos, "Sychem filii mei adhesit anima filiae vestrae; date eam illi uxorem, 9 et iungamus vicissim conubia. Filias vestras tradite nobis, et filias nostras accipite, 10 et habitate nobiscum. Terra in potestate vestra est: exercete, negotiamini, et possidete eam."

11 Sed et Sychem ad patrem et ad fratres eius ait, "Inveniam gratiam coram vobis, et quaecumque statueritis dabo. 12 Augete dotem, et munera postulate, et libenter tribuam quod petieritis. Tantum date mihi puellam hanc uxorem."

13 Responderunt filii Iacob Sychem et patri eius in dolo, saevientes ob stuprum sororis, 14 "Non possumus facere quod petitis nec dare sororem nostram homini incircumciso, quod inlicitum et nefarium est apud nos. 15 Sed in hoc valebimus foederari, si esse volueritis nostri similes et circumcidatur in vobis omne masculini sexus. 16 Tunc dabimus et accipiemus mutuo filias nostras ac vestras, et habitabimus vobiscum erimusque unus populus. 17 Sin autem circumcidi nolueritis, tollemus filiam nostram et recedemus."

18 Placuit oblatio eorum Emor et Sychem, filio eius, 19 nec distulit adulescens, quin statim quod petebatur expleret,

to Hamor, his father, he said, "Get me this damsel to wife."
5 But when Jacob had heard this, his sons being absent and
employed in feeding the cattle, he held his peace till they
came back.

6 And when Hamor, the father of Shechem, was come out
to speak to Jacob, 7 behold: his sons came from the field, and
hearing what had passed they were exceeding angry because
he had done a foul thing in Israel and committed an unlawful act in ravishing Jacob's daughter. 8 And Hamor spoke to
them, "The soul of my son Shechem has a longing for your
daughter; give her him to wife, 9 and let us contract marriages one with another. Give us your daughters, and take
you our daughters, 10 and dwell with us. The land is at your
command: till, trade, and possess it."

11 Shechem also said to her father and to her brethren,
"Let me find favour in your sight, and whatsoever you shall
appoint I will give. 12 Raise the dowry, and ask gifts, and I
will gladly give what you shall demand. Only give me this
damsel to wife."

13 The sons of Jacob answered Shechem and his father
deceitfully, being enraged at the deflowering of their sister,
14 "We cannot do what you demand nor give our sister to
one that is uncircumcised, which with us is unlawful and
abominable. 15 But in this we may be allied with you, if you
will be like us and all the male sex among you be circumcised. 16 Then will we mutually give and take your daughters
and ours, and we will dwell with you and will be one people.
17 But if you will not be circumcised, we will take our daughter and depart."

18 Their offer pleased Hamor and Shechem, his son,
19 and the young man made no delay, but forthwith fulfilled

amabat enim puellam valde et ipse erat inclitus in omni domo patris sui.

20 Ingressique portam urbis locuti sunt populo, 21 "Viri isti pacifici sunt et volunt habitare nobiscum. Negotientur in terra et exerceant eam, quae spatiosa et lata cultoribus indiget. Filias eorum accipiemus uxores, et nostras illis dabimus. 22 Unum est quo differtur tantum bonum: si circumcidamus masculos nostros, ritum gentis imitantes, 23 et substantia eorum et pecora et cuncta quae possident nostra erunt. Tantum in hoc adquiescamus, et habitantes simul unum efficiemus populum." 24 Adsensique sunt omnes circumcisis cunctis maribus.

25 Et ecce: die tertio quando gravissimus vulnerum dolor est, arreptis duo Iacob filii, Symeon et Levi, fratres Dinae, gladiis ingressi sunt urbem confidenter interfectisque omnibus masculis. 26 Emor et Sychem pariter necaverunt tollentes Dinam de domo Sychem sororem suam. 27 Quibus egressis, inruerunt super occisos ceteri filii Iacob et depopulati sunt urbem in ultionem stupri. 28 Oves eorum et armenta et asinos, cunctaque vastantes quae in domibus et in agris erant, 29 parvulos quoque et uxores eorum duxere captivas. 30 Quibus patratis audacter, Iacob dixit ad Symeon et Levi, "Turbastis me et odiosum fecistis me Chananeis et Ferezeis, habitatoribus terrae huius. Nos pauci sumus. Illi congregati percutient me, et delebor ego et domus mea."

31 Responderunt, "Numquid ut scorto abuti debuere sorore nostra?"

what was required, for he loved the damsel exceedingly and he was the greatest man in all his father's house.

20 And going into the gate of the city they spoke to the people, 21 "These men are peaceable and willing to dwell with us. Let them trade in the land and till it, which being large and wide wanteth men to till it. We shall take their daughters for wives, and we will give them ours. 22 One thing there is for which so great a good is deferred: we must circumcise every male among us, following the manner of the nation, 23 and their substance and cattle and all that they possess shall be ours. Only in this let us condescend, and by dwelling together we shall make one people." 24 And they all agreed and circumcised all the males.

25 And behold: the third day, when the pain of the wound was greatest, two of the sons of Jacob, Simeon and Levi, the brothers of Dinah, taking their swords entered boldly into the city and slew all the men. 26 And they killed also Hamor and Shechem and took away their sister Dinah out of Shechem's house. 27 And when they were gone out, the other sons of Jacob came upon the slain and plundered the city in revenge of the rape. 28 And *they took* their sheep and their herds and their asses, wasting all they had in their houses and in the fields, 29 and their children and wives they took captive. 30 And when they had boldly perpetrated these things, Jacob said to Simeon and Levi, "You have troubled me and made me hateful to the Canaanites and Perizzites, the inhabitants of this land. We are few. They will gather themselves together and kill me, and both I and my house shall be destroyed."

31 They answered, "Should they abuse our sister as a strumpet?"

Caput 35

Interea, locutus est Deus ad Iacob, "Surge, et ascende Bethel, et habita ibi, facque altare Deo qui apparuit tibi quando fugiebas Esau, fratrem tuum."

2 Iacob vero convocata omni domo sua ait, "Abicite deos alienos qui in medio vestri sunt, et mundamini, ac mutate vestimenta vestra. 3 Surgite, et ascendamus in Bethel ut faciamus ibi altare Deo qui exaudivit me in die tribulationis meae et fuit socius itineris mei." 4 Dederunt ergo ei omnes deos alienos quos habebant et inaures quae erant in auribus eorum, at ille infodit ea subter terebinthum quae est post urbem Sychem. 5 Cumque profecti essent, terror Dei invasit omnes per circuitum civitates, et non sunt ausi persequi recedentes.

6 Venit igitur Iacob Luzam, quae est in terra Chanaan, cognomento Bethel, ipse et omnis populus cum eo. 7 Aedificavitque ibi altare et appellavit nomen loci illius Domus Dei, ibi enim apparuit ei Deus cum fugeret fratrem suum. 8 Eodem tempore mortua est Debbora, nutrix Rebeccae, et

Chapter 35

Jacob purgeth his family from idols, goeth by God's commandment to Bethel and there buildeth an altar. God appearing again to Jacob blesseth him and changeth his name into Israel. Rachel dieth in childbirth. Isaac also dieth.

In the meantime, God said to Jacob, "Arise, and go up to Bethel, and dwell there, and make *there* an altar to God who appeared to thee when thou didst flee from Esau, thy brother."

2 And Jacob having called together all his household said, "Cast away the strange gods that are among you, and be cleansed, and change your garments. 3 Arise, and let us go up to Bethel that we may make there an altar to God who heard me in the day of my affliction and accompanied me in my journey." 4 So they gave him all the strange gods they had and the earrings which were in their ears, and he buried them under the turpentine tree that is behind the city of Shechem. 5 And when they were departed, the terror of God fell upon all the cities round about, and they durst not pursue after them as they went away.

6 And Jacob came to Luz, which is in the land of Canaan, surnamed Bethel, he and all the people that were with him. 7 And he built there an altar and called the name of that place the House of God, for there God appeared to him when he fled from his brother. 8 At the same time Deborah,

sepulta ad radices Bethel subter quercum. Vocatumque est nomen loci illius Quercus Fletus. 9 Apparuit autem iterum Deus Iacob postquam reversus est de Mesopotamiam Syriae, benedixitque ei, 10 dicens, "Non vocaberis ultra Iacob, sed Israhel erit nomen tuum." Et appellavit eum Israhel 11 dixitque ei, "Ego Deus omnipotens; cresce, et multiplicare. Gentes et populi nationum erunt ex te, reges de lumbis tuis egredientur. 12 Terramque quam dedi Abraham et Isaac dabo tibi et semini tuo post te." 13 Et recessit ab eo. 14 Ille vero erexit titulum lapideum in loco quo locutus ei fuerat Deus, libans super eum libamina et effundens super eum oleum 15 vocansque nomen loci illius Bethel.

16 Egressus autem inde, venit verno tempore ad terram quae ducit Efratham in qua cum parturiret Rahel. 17 Ob difficultatem partus periclitari coepit, dixitque ei obsetrix, "Noli timere, quia et hunc habebis filium." 18 Egrediente autem anima prae dolore et inminente iam morte, vocavit nomen filii sui Benoni, id est, filius doloris mei, pater vero appellavit eum Beniamin, id est, filius dexterae. 19 Mortua est ergo Rahel et sepulta in via quae ducit Efratham; haec est Bethleem. 20 Erexitque Iacob titulum super sepulchrum eius. Hic est titulus monumenti Rahel usque in praesentem diem.

21 Egressus inde fixit tabernaculum trans Turrem Gregis. 22 Cumque habitaret in illa regione, abiit Ruben et dormivit cum Bala, concubina patris sui, quod illum minime latuit. Erant autem filii Iacob duodecim. 23 Filii Liae: primogenitus, Ruben, et Symeon et Levi et Iudas et Isachar et Zabu-

the nurse of Rebekah, died and was buried at the foot of Bethel under an oak. And the name of that place was called the Oak of Weeping. 9 And God appeared again to Jacob after he returned from Mesopotamia of Syria, and he blessed him, 10 saying, "Thou shalt not be called any more Jacob, but Israel shall be thy name." And he called him Israel 11 and said to him, "I am God almighty; increase thou, and be multiplied. Nations and peoples of nations shall be from thee, and kings shall come out of thy loins. 12 And the land which I gave to Abraham and Isaac I will give to thee and to thy seed after thee." 13 And he departed from him. 14 But he set up a monument of stone in the place where God had spoken to him, pouring drink offerings upon it and pouring oil thereon 15 and calling the name of that place Bethel.

16 And going forth from thence, he came in the springtime to the land which leadeth to Ephrath wherein when Rachel was in travail. 17 By reason of her hard labour she began to be in danger, and the midwife said to her, "Fear not, for thou shalt have this son also." 18 And when her soul was departing for pain and death was now at hand, she called the name of her son Ben-oni, that is, the son of my pain, but his father called him Benjamin, that is, the son of the right hand. 19 So Rachel died and was buried in the highway that leadeth to Ephrath; this is Bethlehem. 20 And Jacob erected a pillar over her sepulchre. This is the pillar of Rachel's monument to this day.

21 Departing thence he pitched his tent beyond the Flock Tower. 22 And when he dwelt in that country, Reuben went and slept with Bilhah, the concubine of his father, which he was not ignorant of. Now the sons of Jacob were twelve. 23 The sons of Leah: Reuben, the first born, and Simeon and

lon. 24 Filii Rahel: Ioseph et Beniamin. 25 Filii Balae, ancillae
Rahelis: Dan et Nepthalim. 26 Filii Zelphae, ancillae Liae:
Gad et Aser. Hii filii Iacob qui nati sunt ei in Mesopotamiam
Syriae.

27 Venit etiam ad Isaac, patrem suum, in Mambre, civitatem Arbee; haec est Hebron in qua peregrinatus est Abraham et Isaac. 28 Et conpleti sunt dies Isaac centum octoginta
annorum. 29 Consumptusque aetate mortuus est et adpositus populo suo senex et plenus dierum, et sepelierunt eum
Esau et Iacob, filii sui.

Caput 36

Hae sunt autem generationes Esau; ipse est Edom. 2 Esau
accepit uxores de filiabus Chanaan: Ada, filiam Elom, Hetthei, et Oolibama, filiam Anae, filiae Sebeon, Evei, 3 Basemath quoque, filiam Ismahel, sororem Nabaioth. 4 Peperit
autem Ada Eliphaz; Basemath genuit Rauhel; 5 Oolibama
edidit Hieus et Hielom et Core. Hii filii Esau qui nati sunt ei
in terra Chanaan.

Levi and Judah and Issachar and Zebulun. 24 The sons of Rachel: Joseph and Benjamin. 25 The sons of Bilhah, Rachel's handmaid: Dan and Naphtali. 26 The sons of Zilpah, Leah's handmaid: Gad and Asher. These are the sons of Jacob that were born to him in Mesopotamia of Syria.

27 And he came to Isaac, his father, in Mamre, the city of Arbee; this is Hebron wherein Abraham and Isaac sojourned. 28 And the days of Isaac were a hundred and eighty years. 29 And being spent with age he died and was gathered to his people being old and full of days, and his sons, Esau and Jacob, buried him.

Chapter 36

Esau with his wives and children parteth from Jacob. An
account of his descendants and of the first kings of Edom.

And these are the generations of Esau; the same is Edom. 2 Esau took wives of the daughters of Canaan: Adah, the daughter of Elon, the Hittite, and Oholibamah, the daughter of Anah, the daughter of Zibeon, the Hivite, 3 and Basemath, the daughter of Ishmael, sister of Nebaioth. 4 And Adah bore Eliphaz; Basemath bore Reuel; 5 Oholibamah bore Jeush and Jalam and Korah. These are the sons of Esau that were born to him in the land of Canaan.

6 Tulit autem Esau uxores suas et filios et filias et omnem animam domus suae et substantiam et pecora et cuncta quae habere poterat in terra Chanaan et abiit in alteram regionem recessitque a fratre suo Iacob, 7 divites enim erant valde et simul habitare non poterant, nec sustinebat eos terra peregrinationis eorum prae multitudine gregum. 8 Habitavitque Esau in Monte Seir; ipse est Edom.

9 Hae autem sunt generationes Esau, patris Edom, in Monte Seir, 10 et haec nomina filiorum eius: Eliphaz, filius Ada, uxoris Esau, Rauhel quoque, filius Basemath, uxoris eius. 11 Fueruntque filii Eliphaz: Theman, Omar, Sephu et Gatham et Cenez. 12 Erat autem Thamna concubina Eliphaz, filii Esau, quae peperit ei Amalech. Hii sunt filii Adae, uxoris Esau. 13 Filii autem Rauhel Naath et Zara, Semma et Meza. Hii filii Basemath, uxoris Esau.

14 Isti quoque erant filii Oolibama, filiae Ana, filiae Sebeon, uxoris Esau, quos genuit ei: Hieus et Hielom et Core.

15 Hii duces filiorum Esau. Filii Eliphaz, primogeniti Esau: Dux Theman, Dux Omar, Dux Sephu, Dux Cenez, 16 Dux Core, Dux Gatham, Dux Amalech. Hii filii Eliphaz in terra Edom et hii filii Adae.

17 Hii quoque filii Rauhel, filii Esau: Dux Naath, Dux Zara, Dux Semma, Dux Meza. Hii autem duces Rauhel in terra Edom, isti filii Basemath, uxoris Esau.

6 And Esau took his wives and his sons and daughters and every soul of his house and his substance and cattle and all that he was able to acquire in the land of Canaan and went into another country and departed from his brother Jacob, 7 for they were exceeding rich and could not dwell together, neither was the land in which they sojourned able to bear them for the multitude of their flocks. 8 And Esau dwelt in Mount Seir; he is Edom.

9 And these are the generations of Esau, the father of Edom, in Mount Seir, 10 and these the names of his sons: Eliphaz, the son of Adah, the wife of Esau, and Reuel, the son of Basemath, his wife. 11 And Eliphaz had sons: Teman, Omar, Zepho and Gatam and Kenaz. 12 And Timna was the concubine of Eliphaz, the son of Esau, and she bore him Amalek. These are the sons of Adah, the wife of Esau. 13 And the sons of Reuel were Nahath and Zerah, Shammah and Mizzah. These were the sons of Basemath, the wife of Esau.

14 And these were the sons of Oholibamah, the daughter of Anah, the daughter of Zibeon, the wife of Esau, whom she bore to him: Jeush and Jalam and Korah.

15 These were dukes of the sons of Esau, the sons of Eliphaz, the firstborn of Esau: Duke Teman, Duke Omar, Duke Zepho, Duke Kenaz, 16 Duke Korah, Duke Gatam, Duke Amalek. These are the sons of Eliphaz in the land of Edom and these the sons of Adah.

17 And these were the sons of Reuel, the son of Esau: Duke Nahath, Duke Zerah, Duke Shammah, Duke Mizzah. And these are the dukes of Reuel in the land of Edom, these the sons of Basemath, the wife of Esau.

18 Hii autem filii Oolibama, uxoris Esau: Dux Hieus, Dux Hielom, Dux Core. Hii duces Oolibama, filiae Ana, uxoris Esau. 19 Isti filii Esau, et hii duces eorum; ipse est Edom.

20 Isti filii Seir, Horrei, habitatores terrae: Lotham et Sobal et Sebeon et Anan 21 et Dison et Eser et Disan. Hii duces Horrei, filii Seir in terra Edom.

22 Facti sunt autem filii Lotham: Horrei et Heman. Erat autem soror Lotham Thamna.

23 Et isti filii Sobal: Alvam et Maneeth et Hebal et Sephi et Onam.

24 Et hii filii Sebeon: Ahaia et Anam. Iste est Ana qui invenit aquas calidas in solitudine cum pasceret asinos Sebeon, patris sui, 25 habuitque filium, Disan, et filiam, Oolibama.

26 Et isti filii Disan: Amdan et Esban et Iethran et Charan. 27 Hii quoque filii Eser: Balaan et Zevan et Acham. 28 Habuit autem filios Disan: Hus et Aran. 29 Isti duces Horreorum: Dux Lothan, Dux Sobal, Dux Sebeon, Dux Ana, 30 Dux Dison, Dux Eser, Dux Disan; isti duces Horreorum qui imperaverunt in terra Seir.

31 Reges autem qui regnaverunt in terra Edom antequam haberent regem filii Israhel fuerunt hii: 32 Bale, filius Beor, nomenque urbis eius, Denaba. 33 Mortuus est autem Bale, et regnavit pro eo Iobab, filius Zare de Bosra. 34 Cumque mortuus esset Iobab, regnavit pro eo Husan de terra Themanorum. 35 Hoc quoque mortuo, regnavit pro eo Adad, filius Ba-

18 And these the sons of Oholibamah, the wife of Esau: Duke Jeush, Duke Jalam, Duke Korah. These are the dukes of Oholibamah, the daughter of Anah and wife of Esau. 19 These are the sons of Esau, and these the dukes of them; the same is Edom.

20 These are the sons of Seir, the Horite, the inhabitants of the land: Lotan and Shobal and Zibeon and Anah 21 and Dishon and Ezer and Dishan. These are dukes of the Horites, the sons of Seir in the land of Edom.

22 And Lotan had sons: Hori and Heman. And the sister of Lotan was Timna.

23 And these the sons of Shobal: Alvan and Manahat and Ebal and Shepho and Onam.

24 And these the sons of Zibeon: Aiah and Anah. This is Anah that found the hot waters in the wilderness when he fed the asses of Zibeon, his father, 25 and he had a son, Dishon, and a daughter, Oholibamah.

26 And these were the sons of Dishon: Hemdan and Eshban and Ithran and Cheran. 27 These also were the sons of Ezer: Bilhan and Zaavan and Akan. 28 And Dishan had sons: Uz and Aran. 29 These were dukes of the Horites: Duke Lotan, Duke Shobal, Duke Zibeon, Duke Anah, 30 Duke Dishon, Duke Ezer, Duke Dishan; these were dukes of the Horites that ruled in the land of Seir.

31 And the kings that ruled in the land of Edom before the children of Israel had a king were these: 32 Bela, the son of Beor, and the name of his city, Dinhabah. 33 And Bela died, and Jobab, the son of Zerah of Bozrah, reigned in his stead. 34 And when Jobab was dead, Husham of the land of the Temanites reigned in his stead. 35 And after his death, Hadad, the son of Bedad, reigned in his stead, who defeated

dadi, qui percussit Madian in regione Moab, et nomen urbis eius, Ahuith.

36 Cumque mortuus esset Adad, regnavit pro eo Semla de Maserecha. 37 Hoc quoque mortuo, regnavit pro eo Saul de fluvio Rooboth. 38 Cumque et hic obisset, successit in regnum Baalanam, filius Achobor. 39 Isto quoque mortuo, regnavit pro eo Adad, nomenque urbis eius Phau, et appellabatur uxor illius Meezabel, filia Matred, filiae Mizaab.

40 Haec ergo nomina ducum Esau in cognationibus et locis et vocabulis suis: Dux Thamna, Dux Alva, Dux Ietheth, 41 Dux Oolibama, Dux Ela, Dux Phinon, 42 Dux Cenez, Dux Theman, Dux Mabsar, 43 Dux Mabdiel, Dux Iram. Hii duces Edom habitantes in terra imperii sui; ipse est Esau, pater Idumeorum.

Caput 37

Habitavit autem Iacob in terra Chanaan in qua peregrinatus est pater suus, 2 et hae sunt generationes eius.

Ioseph cum sedecim esset annorum pascebat gregem

the Midianites in the country of Moab, and the name of his city was Avith.

36 And when Hadad was dead, there reigned in his stead Samlah of Masrekah. 37 And he being dead, Shaul of the river Rehoboth reigned in his stead. 38 And when he also was dead, Baal-hanan, the son of Achbor, succeeded to the kingdom. 39 This man also being dead, Hadad reigned in his place, and the name of his city was Pau, and his wife was called Mehetabel, the daughter of Matred, daughter of Mezahab.

40 And these are the names of the dukes of Esau in their kindreds and places and callings: Duke Timna, Duke Alvan, Duke Jetheth, 41 Duke Oholibamah, Duke Elah, Duke Pinon, 42 Duke Kenaz, Duke Teman, Duke Mibzar, 43 Duke Magdiel, Duke Iram. These are the dukes of Edom dwelling in the land of their government; the same is Esau, the father of the Edomites.

Chapter 37

Joseph's dreams. He is sold by his brethren and carried into Egypt.

And Jacob dwelt in the land of Canaan wherein his father sojourned, 2 and these are his generations.

Joseph when he was sixteen years old was feeding the flock with his brethren, being but a boy, and he was with the

cum fratribus suis, adhuc puer, et erat cum filiis Balae et Zelphae, uxorum patris sui, accusavitque fratres suos apud patrem crimine pessimo. 3 Israhel autem diligebat Ioseph super omnes filios suos eo quod in senectute genuisset eum, fecitque ei tunicam polymitam. 4 Videntes autem fratres eius quod a patre plus cunctis filiis amaretur, oderant eum nec poterant ei quicquam pacifice loqui. 5 Accidit quoque ut visum somnium referret fratribus quae causa maioris odii seminarium fuit.

6 Dixitque ad eos, "Audite somnium meum quod vidi: 7 putabam ligare nos manipulos in agro, et quasi consurgere manipulum meum, et stare, vestrosque manipulos circumstantes adorare manipulum meum."

8 Responderunt fratres eius, "Numquid rex noster eris? Aut subiciemur dicioni tuae?" Haec ergo causa somniorum atque sermonum invidiae et odii fomitem ministravit.

9 Aliud quoque vidit somnium quod narrans fratribus ait, "Vidi per somnium quasi solem et lunam et stellas undecim adorare me."

10 Quod cum patri suo et fratribus rettulisset, increpavit eum pater et dixit, "Quid sibi vult hoc somnium quod vidisti? Num ego et mater tua et fratres adorabimus te super terram?"

11 Invidebant igitur ei fratres sui, pater vero rem tacitus considerabat. 12 Cumque fratres illius in pascendis gregibus patris morarentur in Sychem, 13 dixit ad eum Israhel, "Fratres tui pascunt oves in Sycimis. Veni; mittam te ad eos." Quo respondente, 14 "Praesto sum," ait ei, "Vade, et vide si

sons of Bilhah and of Zilpah, his father's wives, and he accused his brethren to his father of a most wicked crime. 3 Now Israel loved Joseph above all his sons because he had him in his old age, and he made him a coat of divers colours. 4 And his brethren, seeing that he was loved by his father more than all his sons, hated him and could not speak *peaceably* to him. 5 Now it fell out also that he told his brethren a dream that he had dreamed which occasioned them to hate him the more.

6 And he said to them, "Hear my dream which I dreamed: 7 I thought we were binding sheaves in the field, and my sheaf arose, as it were, and stood, and your sheaves standing about bowed down before my sheaf."

8 His brethren answered, "Shalt thou be our king? Or shall we be subject to thy dominion?" Therefore this matter of his dreams and words ministered nourishment to their envy and hatred.

9 He dreamed also another dream, which he told his brethren, saying, "I saw in a dream as it were the sun and the moon and eleven stars worshipping me."

10 And when he had told this to his father and brethren, his father rebuked him and said, "What meaneth this dream that thou hast dreamed? Shall I and thy mother and thy brethren worship thee upon the earth?"

11 His brethren therefore envied him, but his father considered the thing with himself. 12 And when his brethren abode in Shechem feeding their father's flocks, 13 Israel said to him, "Thy brethren feed the sheep in Shechem. Come; I will send thee to them." And when he answered, 14 "I am ready," he said to him, "Go, and see if all things be well with

cuncta prospera sint erga fratres tuos et pecora, et renuntia mihi quid agatur."

Missus de valle Hebron, venit in Sychem, 15 invenitque eum vir errantem in agro et interrogavit quid quaereret. 16 At ille respondit, "Fratres meos quaero; indica mihi ubi pascant greges."

17 Dixitque ei vir, "Recesserunt de loco isto, audivi autem eos dicentes, 'Eamus in Dothain.'"

Perrexit ergo Ioseph post fratres suos et invenit eos in Dothain. 18 Qui cum vidissent eum procul antequam accederet ad eos, cogitaverunt illum occidere. 19 Et mutuo loquebantur, "Ecce! Somniator venit. 20 Venite; occidamus eum et mittamus in cisternam veterem, dicemusque, 'Fera pessima devoravit eum,' et tunc apparebit quid illi prosint somnia sua."

21 Audiens autem hoc Ruben nitebatur liberare eum de manibus eorum et dicebat, 22 "Non interficiatis animam eius, nec effundatis sanguinem, sed proicite eum in cisternam hanc quae est in solitudine, manusque vestras servate innoxias." Hoc autem dicebat volens eripere eum de manibus eorum et reddere patri suo. 23 Confestim igitur ut pervenit ad fratres, nudaverunt eum tunica talari et polymita 24 miseruntque in cisternam veterem quae non habebat aquam. 25 Et sedentes ut comederent panem, viderunt viatores Ismahelitas venire de Galaad et camelos eorum portare aromata et resinam et stacten in Aegyptum.

26 Dixit ergo Iudas fratribus suis, "Quid nobis prodest si occiderimus fratrem nostrum et celaverimus sanguinem ipsius? 27 Melius est ut vendatur Ismahelitis et manus nostrae

thy brethren and the cattle, and bring me word again what is doing."

So being sent from the vale of Hebron, he came to Shechem, 15 and a man found him there wandering in the field and asked what he sought. 16 But he answered, "I seek my brethren; tell me where they feed the flocks."

17 And the man said to him, "They are departed from this place, for I heard them say, 'Let us go to Dothan.'"

And Joseph went forward after his brethren and found them in Dothan. 18 And when they saw him afar off before he came nigh them, they thought to kill him. 19 And said one to another, "Behold! The dreamer cometh. 20 Come; let us kill him and cast him into some old pit, and we will say, 'Some evil beast hath devoured him,' and then it shall appear what his dreams avail him."

21 And Reuben, hearing this, endeavoured to deliver him out of their hands and said, 22 "Do not take away his life, nor shed his blood, but cast him into this pit that is in the wilderness, and keep your hands harmless." Now he said this being desirous to deliver him out of their hands and to restore him to his father. 23 And as soon as he came to his brethren, they forthwith stript him of his outside coat that was of divers colours 24 and cast him into an old pit where there was no water. 25 And sitting down to eat bread, they saw some Ishmaelites on their way coming from Gilead with their camels carrying spices and balm and myrrh to Egypt.

26 And Judah said to his brethren, "What will it profit us to kill our brother and conceal his blood? 27 It is better

non polluantur, frater enim et caro nostra est." Adquieverunt fratres sermonibus eius. 28 Et praetereuntibus Madianitis negotiatoribus, extrahentes eum de cisterna vendiderunt Ismahelitis viginti argenteis, qui duxerunt eum in Aegyptum.

29 Reversusque Ruben ad cisternam non invenit puerum, 30 et scissis vestibus pergens ad fratres ait, "Puer non conparet, et ego quo ibo?"

31 Tulerunt autem tunicam eius et in sanguinem hedi quem occiderant tinxerunt, 32 mittentes qui ferrent ad patrem et dicerent, "Hanc invenimus: vide utrum tunica filii tui sit an non."

33 Quam cum agnovisset pater, ait, "Tunica filii mei est; fera pessima comedit eum; bestia devoravit Ioseph." 34 Scissisque vestibus indutus est cilicio, lugens filium multo tempore. 35 Congregatis autem cunctis liberis eius ut lenirent dolorem patris, noluit consolationem recipere sed ait, "Descendam ad filium meum lugens in infernum." Et illo perseverante in fletu, 36 Madianei vendiderunt Ioseph in Aegypto Putiphar, eunucho Pharaonis, magistro militiae.

that he be sold to the Ishmaelites and that our hands be not defiled, for he is our brother and our flesh." His brethren agreed to his words. 28 And when the Midianite merchants passed by, they drew him out of the pit and sold him to the Ishmaelites for twenty pieces of silver, and they led him into Egypt.

29 And Reuben, returning to the pit, found not the boy, 30 and rending his garments he went to his brethren and said, "The boy doth not appear, and whither shall I go?"

31 And they took his coat and dipped it in the blood of a kid which they had killed, 32 sending some to carry it to their father and to say, "This we have found: see whether it be thy son's coat or not."

33 And the father, acknowledging it, said, "It is my son's coat; an evil wild beast hath eaten him; a beast hath devoured Joseph." 34 And tearing his garments he put on sackcloth, mourning for his son a long time. 35 And, all his children being gathered together to comfort their *father in his sorrow,* he would not receive comfort but said, "I will go down to my son into hell, mourning." And whilst he continued weeping, 36 the Midianites sold Joseph in Egypt to Potiphar, an eunuch of Pharaoh, captain of the soldiers.

Caput 38

Eodem tempore, descendens Iudas a fratribus suis divertit ad virum Odollamitem nomine Hiram. 2 Viditque ibi filiam hominis Chananei vocabulo Suae. Et, uxore accepta, ingressus est ad eam. 3 Quae concepit et peperit filium vocavitque nomen eius Her. 4 Rursumque concepto fetu, natum filium nominavit Onam. 5 Tertium quoque peperit quem appellavit Sela, quo nato parere ultra cessavit.

6 Dedit autem Iudas uxorem primogenito suo, Her, nomine Thamar. 7 Fuitque Her, primogenitus Iudae, nequam in conspectu Domini et ab eo occisus est. 8 Dixit ergo Iudas ad Onam, filium suum, "Ingredere ad uxorem fratris tui, et sociare illi ut suscites semen fratri tuo." 9 Ille, sciens non sibi nasci filios, introiens ad uxorem fratris sui semen fundebat in terram ne liberi fratris nomine nascerentur. 10 Et idcirco percussit eum Dominus, quod rem detestabilem faceret.

11 Quam ob rem dixit Iudas Thamar, nurui suae, "Esto vidua in domo patris tui donec crescat Sela, filius meus," timebat enim ne et ipse moreretur sicut fratres eius. Quae abiit et habitavit in domo patris sui.

12 Evolutis autem multis diebus, mortua est filia Suae,

Chapter 38

The sons of Judah. The death of Er and Onan. The birth of Perez and Zerah.

*A*t *that* time, Judah went down from his brethren and turned in to a *certain* Adullamite named Hirah. 2 And he saw there the daughter of a man of Canaan called Shua. And, taking her to wife, he went in unto her. 3 And she conceived and bore a son and called his name Er. 4 And conceiving again, she bore a son and called him Onan. 5 She bore also a third whom she called Shelah, after whose birth she ceased to bear any more.

6 And Judah took a wife for Er, his firstborn, whose name was Tamar. 7 And Er, the firstborn of Judah, was wicked in the sight of the Lord and was slain by him. 8 Judah therefore said to Onan, his son, "Go in to thy brother's wife, and marry her that thou mayst raise seed to thy brother." 9 He, knowing that the children should not *be his,* when he went in to his brother's wife spilled his seed upon the ground lest children should be born in his brother's name. 10 And therefore the Lord slew him, because he did a detestable thing.

11 Wherefore Judah said to Tamar, his daughter-in-law, "Remain a widow in thy father's house till Shelah, my son, grow up," for he was afraid lest he also might die as his brethren did. She went her way and dwelt in her father's house.

12 And after many days were past, the daughter of Shua,

uxor Iudae, qui post luctum consolatione suscepta, ascendebat ad tonsores ovium suarum, ipse et Hiras, opilio gregis,
Odollamita, in Thamnas. 13 Nuntiatumque est Thamar quod
socer illius ascenderet in Thamnas ad tondendas oves.
14 Quae depositis viduitatis vestibus, adsumpsit theristrum
et, mutato habitu, sedit in bivio itineris quod ducit Tham-
nam eo quod crevisset Sela et non eum accepisset maritum.
15 Quam cum vidisset Iudas, suspicatus est esse meretricem,
operuerat enim vultum suum ne cognosceretur.

16 Ingrediensque ad eam ait, "Dimitte me ut coeam
tecum," nesciebat enim quod nurus sua esset.

Qua respondente, "Quid mihi dabis ut fruaris concubitu
meo?" 17 dixit, "Mittam tibi hedum de gregibus."

Rursumque illa dicente, "Patiar quod vis si dederis mihi
arrabonem donec mittas quod polliceris," 18 ait Iudas, "Quid
vis tibi pro arrabone dari?"

Respondit, "Anulum tuum et armillam et baculum quem
manu tenes."

Ad unum igitur coitum concepit mulier. 19 Et surgens
abiit depositoque habitu quem adsumpserat, induta est viduitatis vestibus. 20 Misit autem Iudas hedum per pastorem
suum, Odollamitem, ut reciperet pignus quod dederat mulieri. Qui cum non invenisset eam, 21 interrogavit homines
loci illius, "Ubi est mulier quae sedebat in bivio?" Respon-
dentibus cunctis, "Non fuit in loco isto meretrix," 22 reversus est ad Iudam et dixit ei, "Non inveni eam; sed et homines
loci illius dixerunt mihi numquam ibi sedisse scortum."

the wife of Judah, died, and when he had taken comfort after his mourning, he went up to Timnah, to the shearers of his sheep, he and Hirah, the Adullamite, the shepherd of his flock. 13 And it was told Tamar that her father-in-law was come up to Timnah to shear his sheep. 14 And she put off the garments of her widowhood and took a veil and, changing her dress, sat in the crossway that leadeth to Timnah because Shelah was grown up and she had not been married to him. 15 When Judah saw her, he thought she was a harlot, for she had covered her face lest she should be known.

16 And going to her he said, "Suffer me to lie with thee," for he knew her not to be his daughter-in-law.

And she answered, "What wilt thou give me to enjoy my company?"

17 He said, "I will send thee a kid out of the flock."

And when she said again, "I will suffer what thou wilt if thou give a pledge till thou send what thou promisest," 18 Judah said, "What wilt thou have for a pledge?"

She answered, "Thy ring and bracelet and the staff which thou holdest in thy hand."

The woman therefore at one copulation conceived. 19 And she arose and went her way and, putting off the apparel which she had taken, put on the garments of her widowhood. 20 And Judah sent a kid by his shepherd, the Adullamite, that he might receive the pledge again which he had given to the woman. But he, not finding her, 21 asked the men of that place, "Where is the woman that sat in the crossway?" And when they all made answer, "There was no harlot in this place," 22 he returned to Judah and said to him, "I have not found her; moreover, the men of that place said to me that there never sat a harlot there."

23 Ait Iudas, "Habeat sibi. Certe mendacii nos arguere non poterit: ego misi hedum quem promiseram, et tu non invenisti eam."

24 Ecce autem: post tres menses nuntiaverunt Iudae dicentes, "Fornicata est Thamar, nurus tua, et videtur uterus illius intumescere."

Dixitque Iudas, "Producite eam ut conburatur."

25 Quae cum duceretur ad poenam, misit ad socerum suum, dicens, "De viro cuius haec sunt concepi. Cognosce cuius sit anulus et armilla et baculus."

26 Qui agnitis muneribus ait, "Iustior me est quia non tradidi eam Sela, filio meo." Attamen, ultra non cognovit illam. 27 Instante autem partu, apparuerunt gemini in utero, atque in ipsa effusione infantum unus protulit manum in qua obsetrix ligavit coccinum, dicens, 28 "Iste egredietur prior." 29 Illo vero retrahente manum, egressus est alter, dixitque mulier, "Quare divisa est propter te maceria?" et ob hanc causam vocavit nomen eius Phares. 30 Postea, egressus est frater in cuius manu erat coccinum, quem appellavit Zara.

23 Judah said, "Let her take it to herself. Surely she cannot charge us with a lie: I sent the kid which I promised, and thou didst not find her."

24 And behold: after three months they told Judah, saying, "Tamar, thy daughter-in-law, hath played the harlot, and *she appeareth to have a big belly.*"

And Judah said, "Bring her out that she may be burnt."

25 But when she was led to execution, she sent to her father-in-law, saying, "By the man to whom these things belong I am with child. See whose ring and bracelet and staff this is."

26 But he acknowledging the gifts said, "She is juster than I because I did not give her to Shelah, my son." However, he knew her no more. 27 And when she was ready to be brought to bed, there appeared twins in her womb, and in the very delivery of the infants one put forth a hand whereon the midwife tied a scarlet thread, saying, 28 "This shall come forth the first." 29 But he drawing back his hand, the other came forth, and the woman said, "Why is the partition divided for thee?" and therefore called his name Perez. 30 Afterwards, his brother came out on whose hand was the scarlet thread, and she called him Zerah.

Caput 39

Igitur Ioseph ductus est in Aegyptum, emitque eum Putiphar, eunuchus Pharaonis, princeps exercitus, vir Aegyptius, de manu Ismahelitarum a quibus perductus erat. 2 Fuitque Dominus cum eo, et erat vir in cunctis prospere agens, habitabatque in domo domini sui, 3 qui optime noverat esse Dominum cum eo et omnia quae gereret ab eo dirigi in manu illius. 4 Invenitque Ioseph gratiam coram domino suo et ministrabat ei, a quo praepositus omnibus, gubernabat creditam sibi domum et universa quae tradita fuerant. 5 Benedixitque Dominus domui Aegyptii propter Ioseph et multiplicavit tam in aedibus quam in agris cunctam eius substantiam, 6 nec quicquam aliud noverat nisi panem quo vescebatur. Erat autem Ioseph pulchra facie et decorus aspectu. 7 Post multos itaque dies, iecit domina oculos suos in Ioseph et ait, "Dormi mecum."

8 Qui nequaquam adquiescens operi nefario dixit ad eam, "Ecce: dominus meus omnibus mihi traditis ignorat quid habeat in domo sua, 9 nec quicquam est quod non in mea sit potestate vel non tradiderit mihi praeter te quae uxor eius es. Quomodo ergo possum malum hoc facere et peccare in

Chapter 39

Joseph hath charge of his master's house, rejecteth his mistress's solicitations, is falsely accused by her and cast into prison, where he hath the charge of all the prisoners.

And Joseph was brought into Egypt, and Potiphar, an eunuch of Pharaoh, chief captain of the army, an Egyptian, bought him of the Ishmaelites by whom he was brought. 2 And the Lord was with him, and he was a prosperous man in all things, and he dwelt in his master's house, 3 who knew very well that the Lord was with him and made all that he did to prosper in his hand. 4 And Joseph found favour in the sight of his master and ministered to him, and, being set over all by him, he governed the house committed to him and all things that were delivered to him. 5 And the Lord blessed the house of the Egyptian for Joseph's sake and multiplied all his substance both at home and in the fields, 6 neither knew he any other thing but the bread which he ate. And Joseph was of a beautiful countenance and comely to behold. 7 And after many days, his mistress cast her eyes on Joseph and said, "Lie with me."

8 But he in no wise consenting to that wicked act said to her, "Behold: my master hath delivered all things to me and knoweth not what he hath in his own house, 9 neither is there any thing which is not in my power or that he hath not delivered to me but thee who art his wife. How then can I

Deum meum?" 10 Huiuscemodi verbis per singulos dies et mulier molesta erat adulescenti, et ille recusabat stuprum.

11 Accidit autem quadam die ut intraret Ioseph domum et operis quippiam absque arbitris faceret, 12 et illa, adprehensa lacinia vestimenti eius, diceret, "Dormi mecum." Qui, relicto in manu illius pallio, fugit et egressus est foras. 13 Cumque vidisset mulier vestem in manibus suis et se esse contemptam, 14 vocavit ad se homines domus suae et ait ad eos, "En: introduxit virum Hebraeum ut inluderet nobis. Ingressus est ad me ut coiret mecum, cumque ego succlamassem 15 et audisset vocem meam, reliquit pallium quod tenebam et fugit foras."

16 In argumentum ergo fidei retentum pallium ostendit marito revertenti domum 17 et ait, "Ingressus est ad me servus Hebraeus quem adduxisti ut inluderet mihi, 18 cumque audisset me clamare, reliquit pallium quod tenebam et fugit foras." 19 His auditis dominus et nimium credulus verbis coniugis iratus est valde 20 tradiditque Ioseph in carcerem ubi vincti regis custodiebantur, et erat ibi clausus.

21 Fuit autem Dominus cum Ioseph et, misertus illius, dedit ei gratiam in conspectu principis carceris 22 qui tradidit in manu ipsius universos vinctos qui in custodia tenebantur et quicquid fiebat sub ipso erat. 23 Nec noverat aliquid, cunctis ei creditis, Dominus enim erat cum illo et omnia eius opera dirigebat.

do this wicked thing and sin against my God?" 10 With such words as these day by day both the woman was importunate with the young man, and he refused the adultery.

11 Now it happened on a certain day that Joseph went into the house and was doing some business without *any man with him,* 12 and she, catching the skirt of his garment, said, "Lie with me." But he, leaving the garment in her hand, fled and went out. 13 And when the woman saw the garment in her hands and herself disregarded, 14 she called to her the men of her house and said to them, "See: he hath brought in a Hebrew to abuse us. He came in to me to lie with me, and when I cried out 15 and he heard my voice, he left the garment that I held and got him out."

16 For a proof therefore of her fidelity she kept the garment and shewed it to her husband when he returned home 17 and said, "The Hebrew servant whom thou hast brought came to me to abuse me, 18 and when he heard me cry, he left the garment which I held and fled out." 19 His master hearing these things and giving too much credit to his wife's words was very angry 20 and cast Joseph into the prison where the king's prisoners were kept, and he was there shut up.

21 But the Lord was with Joseph and, having mercy upon him, gave him favour in the sight of the chief keeper of the prison 22 who delivered into his hand all the prisoners that were kept in custody and whatsoever was done was under him. 23 Neither did he himself know any thing, having committed all things to him, for the Lord was with him and made all that he did to prosper.

Caput 40

His ita gestis, accidit ut peccarent duo eunuchi, pincerna regis Aegypti et pistor, domino suo. 2 Iratusque Pharao contra eos (nam alter pincernis praeerat, alter pistoribus), 3 misit eos in carcerem principis militum in quo erat vinctus et Ioseph. 4 At custos carceris tradidit eos Ioseph, qui et ministrabat eis. Aliquantulum temporis fluxerat, et illi in custodia tenebantur. 5 Videruntque ambo somnium nocte una, iuxta interpretationem congruam sibi.

6 Ad quos cum introisset Ioseph mane et vidisset eos tristes, 7 sciscitatus est, dicens, "Cur tristior est hodie solito facies vestra?"

8 Qui responderunt, "Somnium vidimus, et non est qui interpretetur nobis."

Dixitque ad eos Ioseph, "Numquid non Dei est interpretatio? Referte mihi quid videritis."

9 Narravit prior praepositus pincernarum somnium: "Videbam coram me vitem 10 in qua erant tres propagines crescere paulatim gemmas, et post, flores uvas maturescere. 11 Calicemque Pharaonis in manu mea, tuli ergo uvas et ex-

Chapter 40

Joseph interpreteth the dreams of two of Pharaoh's servants in prison. The event declareth the interpretations to be true, but Joseph is forgotten.

After this, it came to pass that two eunuchs, the butler and the baker of the king of Egypt, offended their lord. 2 And Pharaoh being angry with them (now the one was chief butler, the other, chief baker), 3 he sent them to the prison of the commander of the soldiers in which Joseph also was prisoner. 4 But the keeper of the prison delivered them to Joseph, and he served them. Some little time passed, and they were kept in custody. 5 And they both dreamed a dream the same night, according to the interpretation agreeing to themselves.

6 And when Joseph was come in to them in the morning and saw them sad, 7 he asked them, saying, "Why is your countenance sadder today than usual?"

8 They answered, "We have dreamed a dream, and there is nobody to interpret it to us."

And Joseph said to them, "Doth not interpretation belong to God? Tell me what you have dreamed."

9 The chief butler first told his dream: "I saw before me a vine 10 on which were three branches, which by little and little sent out buds, and after, the blossoms brought forth ripe grapes. 11 And the cup of Pharaoh was in my hand, and I

pressi in calicem quem tenebam, et tradidi poculum Pharaoni."

12 Respondit Ioseph, "Haec est interpretatio somnii: tres propagines tres adhuc dies sunt, 13 post quos recordabitur Pharao ministerii tui et restituet te in gradum pristinum, dabisque ei calicem iuxta officium tuum sicut facere ante consueveras. 14 Tantum memento mei cum tibi bene fuerit, et facias mecum misericordiam: ut suggeras Pharaoni ut educat me de isto carcere, 15 quia furto sublatus sum de terra Hebraeorum et hic innocens in lacum missus sum."

16 Videns pistorum magister quod prudenter somnium dissolvisset ait, "Et ego vidi somnium quod haberem tria canistra farinae super caput meum, 17 et in uno canistro quod erat excelsius portare me omnes cibos qui fiunt arte pistoria avesque comedere ex eo."

18 Respondit Ioseph, "Haec est interpretatio somnii: tria canistra tres adhuc dies sunt, 19 post quos auferet Pharao caput tuum ac suspendet te in cruce, et lacerabunt volucres carnes tuas."

20 Exin dies tertius natalicius Pharaonis erat, qui faciens grande convivium pueris suis recordatus est inter epulas magistri pincernarum et pistorum principis. 21 Restituitque alterum in locum suum ut porrigeret ei poculum; 22 alterum suspendit in patibulo ut coniectoris veritas probaretur. 23 Et tamen succedentibus prosperis praepositus pincernarum oblitus est interpretis sui.

took the grapes and pressed them into the cup which I held, and I gave the cup to Pharaoh."

12 Joseph answered, "This is the interpretation of the dream: the three branches are yet three days, 13 after which Pharaoh will remember thy service and will restore thee to thy former place, and thou shalt present him the cup according to thy office as before thou wast wont to do. 14 Only remember me when it shall be well with thee, and do me this kindness: to put Pharaoh in mind to take me out of this prison, 15 for I was stolen away out of the land of the Hebrews and here without any fault was cast into the dungeon."

16 The chief baker seeing that he had wisely interpreted the dream said, "I also dreamed a dream that I had three baskets of meal upon my head, 17 and that in one basket which was uppermost I carried all meats that are made by the art of baking and that the birds ate out of it."

18 Joseph answered, "This is the interpretation of the dream: the three baskets are yet three days, 19 after which Pharaoh will take thy head from thee and hang thee on a cross, and the birds shall tear thy flesh."

20 The third day after this was the birthday of Pharaoh, and he made a great feast for his servants and at the banquet remembered the chief butler and the chief baker. 21 And he restored the one to his place to present him the cup; 22 the other he hanged on a gibbet that the truth of the interpreter might be shewn. 23 But the chief butler when things prospered with him forgot his interpreter.

Caput 41

Post duos annos, vidit Pharao somnium. Putabat se stare super fluvium 2 de quo ascendebant septem boves, pulchrae et crassae nimis, et pascebantur in locis palustribus. 3 Aliae quoque septem emergebant de flumine, foedae confectae-que macie, et pascebantur in ipsa amnis ripa in locis virenti-bus. 4 Devoraveruntque eas quarum mira species et habi-tudo corporum erat.

Expergefactus Pharao, 5 rursum dormivit, et vidit alte-rum somnium. Septem spicae pullulabant in culmo uno, ple-nae atque formonsae. 6 Aliae quoque totidem spicae, tenues et percussae uredine, oriebantur, 7 devorantes omnem prio-rum pulchritudinem.

Evigilans Pharao post quietem, 8 et facto mane, pavore perterritus, misit ad omnes coniectores Aegypti cunctos-que sapientes. Et accersitis, narravit somnium, nec erat qui interpretaretur. 9 Tunc demum, reminiscens pincernarum magister ait, "Confiteor peccatum meum: 10 iratus rex ser-vis suis me et magistrum pistorum retrudi iussit in carce-rem principis militum, 11 ubi una nocte uterque vidimus somnium praesagum futurorum. 12 Erat ibi puer, He-braeus, eiusdem ducis militum famulus, cui narrantes som-

Chapter 41

Joseph interpreteth the two dreams of Pharaoh. He is made
ruler over all Egypt.

After two years, Pharaoh had a dream. He thought he
stood by the river 2 out of which came up seven kine, very
beautiful and fat, and they fed in marshy places. 3 Other
seven also came up out of the river, ill favoured and *lean-
fleshed,* and they fed on the very bank of the river in green
places. 4 And they devoured them whose *bodies were very
beautiful and well conditioned, so Pharaoh awoke.*

5 *He slept again,* and dreamed another dream. Seven ears
of corn came up upon one stalk, full and fair. 6 Then seven
other ears sprung up, thin and *blasted,* 7 and devoured all the
beauty of the former.

Pharaoh awaked after his rest, 8 and when morning was
come, being struck with fear, he sent to all the interpreters
of Egypt and to all the wise men. And, they being called for,
he told them his dream, and there was not any one that
could interpret it. 9 Then at length, the chief butler remembering said, "I confess my sin: 10 the king being angry with
his servants commanded me and the chief baker to be cast
into the prison of the captain of the soldiers, 11 where in one
night both of us dreamed a dream foreboding things to
come. 12 There was there a young man, a Hebrew, servant to
the same captain of the soldiers, to whom we told our

nia, 13 audivimus quicquid postea rei probavit eventus, ego enim redditus sum officio meo et ille suspensus est in cruce."

14 Protinus ad regis imperium eductum de carcere Ioseph totonderunt ac veste mutata obtulerunt ei. 15 Cui ille ait, "Vidi somnia, nec est qui edisserat. Quae audivi te prudentissime conicere."

16 Respondit Ioseph, "Absque me, Deus respondebit prospera Pharaoni."

17 Narravit ergo Pharao quod viderat: "Putabam me stare super ripam fluminis, 18 et septem boves de amne conscendere, pulchras nimis et obesis carnibus, quae in pastu paludis virecta carpebant. 19 Et ecce: has sequebantur aliae septem boves, in tantum deformes et macilentae ut numquam tales in terra Aegypti viderim, 20 quae devoratis et consumptis prioribus 21 nullum saturitatis dedere vestigium sed simili macie et squalore torpebant. Evigilans rursum sopore depressus 22 vidi somnium: septem spicae pullulabant in culmo uno, plenae atque pulcherrimae. 23 Aliae quoque septem, tenues et percussae uredine, oriebantur stipula, 24 quae priorum pulchritudinem devorarunt. Narravi coniectoribus somnium, et nemo est qui edisserat."

25 Respondit Ioseph, "Somnium regis unum est; quae facturus est Deus ostendit Pharaoni.

26 "Septem boves pulchrae et septem spicae plenae septem ubertatis anni sunt, eandemque vim somnii conprehendunt. 27 Septem quoque boves tenues atque macilentae quae ascenderunt post eas et septem spicae tenues et vento

dreams, 13 and we heard what afterwards the event of the thing proved to be so, for I was restored to my office and he was hanged upon a gibbet."

14 Forthwith at the king's command Joseph was brought out of the prison, and they shaved him, and changing his apparel brought him in to him. 15 And he said to him, "I have dreamed dreams, and there is no one that can expound them. Now I have heard that thou art very wise at interpreting them."

16 Joseph answered, "Without me, God shall give Pharaoh a prosperous answer."

17 So Pharaoh told what he had dreamed: "Methought I stood upon the bank of the river, 18 and seven kine came up out of the river, exceeding beautiful and full of flesh, and they grazed on green places in a marshy pasture. 19 And behold: there followed these other seven kine, so very ill favoured and lean that I never saw the like in the land of Egypt, 20 and they devoured and consumed the former 21 and yet gave no mark of their being full but *were as lean and ill favoured as before.* I awoke and then fell asleep again 22 and dreamed a dream: seven ears of corn grew upon one stalk, full and very fair. 23 Other seven also, thin and blasted, sprung of the stock, 24 and they devoured the beauty of the former. I told this dream to the conjecturers, and there is no man that can expound it."

25 Joseph answered, "The king's dream is one; God hath shewn to Pharaoh what he is about to do.

26 "The seven beautiful kine and the seven full ears are seven years of plenty, and both contain the same meaning of the dream. 27 And the seven lean and thin kine that came up after them and the seven thin ears that were blasted

urente percussae septem anni sunt venturae famis, 28 qui hoc ordine conplebuntur— 29 ecce: septem anni venient fertilitatis magnae in universa terra Aegypti, 30 quos sequentur septem anni alii tantae sterilitatis ut oblivioni tradatur cuncta retro abundantia, consumptura est enim fames omnem terram, 31 et ubertatis magnitudinem perditura inopiae magnitudo. 32 Quod autem vidisti secundo ad eandem rem pertinens somnium, firmitatis indicium est eo quod fiat sermo Dei et velocius impleatur. 33 Nunc ergo provideat rex virum sapientem et industrium et praeficiat eum terrae Aegypti 34 qui constituat praepositos per singulas regiones et quintam partem fructuum per septem annos fertilitatis 35 qui iam nunc futuri sunt congreget in horrea, et omne frumentum sub Pharaonis potestate condatur serveturque in urbibus. 36 Et paretur futurae septem annorum fami quae pressura est Aegyptum, et non consumetur terra inopia."

37 Placuit Pharaoni consilium et cunctis ministris eius. 38 Locutusque est ad eos, "Num invenire poterimus talem virum qui spiritu Dei plenus sit?" 39 Dixit ergo ad Ioseph, "Quia ostendit Deus tibi omnia quae locutus es, numquid sapientiorem et similem tui invenire potero? 40 Tu eris super domum meam, et ad tui oris imperium cunctus populus oboediet. Uno tantum regni solio te praecedam."

41 Dixitque rursum Pharao ad Ioseph, "Ecce: constitui te super universam terram Aegypti." 42 Tulitque anulum de manu sua et dedit in manu eius vestivitque eum stola byssina

with the burning wind are seven years of famine to come, 28 which shall be fulfilled in this order— 29 behold: there shall come seven years of great plenty in the whole land of Egypt, 30 after which shall follow other seven years of so great scarcity that all the abundance before shall be forgotten, for the famine shall consume all the land, 31 and the greatness of the scarcity shall destroy the greatness of the plenty. 32 And for that thou didst see the second time a dream pertaining to the same thing, it is a token of the certainty and that the word of God cometh to pass and is fulfilled speedily. 33 Now therefore let the king provide a wise and industrious man and make him ruler over the land of Egypt 34 that he may appoint overseers over all the countries and gather into barns the fifth part of the fruits during the seven fruitful years 35 that shall now presently ensue, and let all the corn be laid up under Pharaoh's hands and be reserved in the cities. 36 And let it be in readiness against the famine of seven years to come which shall oppress Egypt, and the land shall not be consumed with scarcity."

37 The counsel pleased Pharaoh and all his servants. 38 And he said to them, "Can we find such another man that is full of the spirit of God?" 39 He said therefore to Joseph, "Seeing God hath shewn thee all that thou hast said, can I find one wiser and one like unto thee? 40 Thou shalt be over my house, and at the commandment of thy mouth all the people shall obey. Only in the kingly throne will I be above thee."

41 And again Pharaoh said to Joseph, "Behold: I have appointed thee over the whole land of Egypt." 42 And he took his ring from his own hand and gave it into his hand, and he put upon him a robe of silk and put a chain of gold about his

et collo torquem auream circumposuit. 43 Fecitque ascendere super currum suum secundum, clamante praecone ut omnes coram eo genuflecterent et praepositum esse scirent universae terrae Aegypti. 44 Dixit quoque rex ad Ioseph, "Ego sum Pharao; absque tuo imperio non movebit quisquam manum aut pedem in omni terra Aegypti." 45 Vertitque nomen illius et vocavit eum lingua Aegyptiaca Salvatorem Mundi. Dedit quoque illi uxorem Aseneth, filiam Putiphare, sacerdotis Heliopoleos.

Egressus itaque Ioseph ad terram Aegypti 46 (triginta autem erat annorum quando stetit in conspectu Regis Pharaonis), et circuivit omnes regiones Aegypti. 47 Venitque fertilitas septem annorum, et in manipulos redactae segetes congregatae sunt in horrea Aegypti. 48 Omnis etiam frugum abundantia in singulis urbibus condita est. 49 Tantaque fuit abundantia tritici ut harenae maris coaequaretur, et copia mensuram excederet. 50 Nati sunt autem Ioseph filii duo antequam veniret fames, quos ei peperit Aseneth, filia Putiphare, sacerdotis Heliopoleos. 51 Vocavitque nomen primogeniti Manasse, dicens, "Oblivisci me fecit Deus omnium laborum meorum et domum patris mei." 52 Nomen quoque secundi appellavit Ephraim, dicens, "Crescere me fecit Deus in terra paupertatis meae."

53 Igitur transactis septem annis ubertatis qui fuerant in Aegypto, 54 coeperunt venire septem anni inopiae, quos praedixerat Ioseph, et in universo orbe fames praevaluit, in cuncta autem terra Aegypti erat panis. 55 Qua esuriente, clamavit populus ad Pharaonem alimenta petens, quibus ille respondit, "Ite ad Ioseph, et quicquid vobis dixerit facite."

neck. 43 And he made him go up into his second chariot, the crier proclaiming that all should bow their knee before him and that they should know he was made governor over the whole land of Egypt. 44 And the king said to Joseph, "I am Pharaoh; without thy commandment no man shall move hand or foot in all the land of Egypt." 45 And he turned his name and called him in the Egyptian tongue the Saviour of the World. And he gave him to wife Asenath, the daughter of Potiphera, priest of Heliopolis.

Then Joseph went out to the land of Egypt 46 (now he was thirty years old when he stood before King Pharaoh), and he went round all the countries of Egypt. 47 And the fruitfulness of the seven years came, and the corn being bound up into sheaves was gathered together into the barns of Egypt. 48 And all the abundance of grain was laid up in every city. 49 And there was so great abundance of wheat that it was equal to the sand of the sea, and the plenty exceeded measure. 50 And before the famine came, Joseph had two sons born, whom Asenath, the daughter of Potiphera, priest of Heliopolis, bore unto him. 51 And he called the name of the firstborn Manasseh, saying, "God hath made me to forget all my labours and my father's house." 52 And he named the second Ephraim, saying, "God hath made me to grow in the land of my poverty."

53 Now when the seven years of the plenty that had been in Egypt were past, 54 the seven years of scarcity, which Joseph had foretold, began to come, and the famine prevailed in the whole world, but there was bread in all the land of Egypt. 55 And when there also they began to be famished, the people cried to Pharaoh for food, and he said to them, "Go to Joseph, and do all that he shall say to you."

56 Crescebat autem cotidie fames in omni terra, aperuit-que Ioseph universa horrea et vendebat Aegyptiis, nam et illos oppresserat fames. 57 Omnesque provinciae veniebant in Aegyptum ut emerent escas et malum inopiae tempera-rent.

Caput 42

Audiens autem Iacob quod alimenta venderentur in Ae-gypto dixit filiis suis, "Quare neglegitis? 2 Audivi quod triti-cum venundetur in Aegypto. Descendite, et emite nobis ne-cessaria ut possimus vivere et non consumamur inopia." 3 Descendentes igitur fratres Ioseph decem ut emerent fru-menta in Aegypto, 4 Beniamin domi retento ab Iacob, qui dixerat fratribus eius, "Ne forte in itinere quicquam patiatur mali." 5 Ingressi sunt terram Aegypti cum aliis qui pergebant ad emendum, erat autem fames in terra Chanaan.

6 Et Ioseph princeps in terra Aegypti, atque ad illius nu-tum frumenta populis vendebantur. Cumque adorassent eum fratres sui 7 et agnovisset eos, quasi ad alienos durius loquebatur, interrogans eos, "Unde venistis?"

56 And the famine increased daily in all the land, and Joseph opened all the barns and sold to the Egyptians, for the famine had oppressed them also. 57 And all provinces came into Egypt to buy food and to *seek some relief of their want*.

Chapter 42

Jacob sendeth his ten sons to buy corn in Egypt. Their treatment by Joseph.

And Jacob hearing that food was sold in Egypt said to his sons, "Why are ye careless? 2 I have heard that wheat is sold in Egypt. Go ye down, and buy us necessaries that we may live and not be consumed with want." 3 So the ten brethren of Joseph went down to buy corn in Egypt, 4 whilst Benjamin was kept at home by Jacob, who said to his brethren, "Lest perhaps he take any harm in the journey." 5 And they entered into the land of Egypt with others that went to buy, for the famine was in the land of Canaan.

6 And Joseph was governor in the land of Egypt, and corn was sold by his direction to the people. And when his brethren had bowed down to him 7 and he knew them, he spoke as it were to strangers somewhat roughly, asking them, "Whence came you?"

Qui responderunt, "De terra Chanaan ut emamus victui necessaria."

8 Et tamen fratres ipse cognoscens, non est agnitus ab eis. 9 Recordatusque somniorum quae aliquando viderat, ait ad eos, "Exploratores estis. Ut videatis infirmiora terrae venistis."

10 Qui dixerunt, "Non est ita, domine, sed servi tui venerunt ut emerent cibos. 11 Omnes filii unius viri sumus; pacifici venimus, nec quicquam famuli tui machinantur mali."

12 Quibus ille respondit, "Aliter est. Inmunita terrae huius considerare venistis."

13 At illi, "Duodecim," inquiunt, "servi tui, fratres sumus, filii viri unius in terra Chanaan. Minimus cum patre nostro est; alius non est super."

14 "Hoc est," ait, "quod locutus sum: exploratores estis. 15 Iam nunc experimentum vestri capiam. Per salutem Pharaonis, non egrediemini hinc donec veniat frater vester minimus. 16 Mittite e vobis unum ut adducat eum, vos autem eritis in vinculis donec probentur quae dixistis, utrum falsa an vera sint, alioquin, per salutem Pharaonis, exploratores estis."

17 Tradidit ergo eos custodiae tribus diebus. 18 Die autem tertio, eductis de carcere, ait, "Facite quod dixi, et vivetis, Deum enim timeo. 19 Si pacifici estis, frater vester unus ligetur in carcere, vos autem abite, et ferte frumenta quae emistis in domos vestras. 20 Et fratrem vestrum minimum ad me adducite ut possim vestros probare sermones et non moriamini."

Fecerunt ut dixerat, 21 et locuti sunt invicem: "Merito haec patimur quia peccavimus in fratrem nostrum, videntes

They answered, "From the land of Canaan to buy necessaries of life."

8 And though he knew his brethren, he was not known by them. 9 And remembering the dreams which formerly he had dreamed, he said to them, "You are spies. You are come to view the weaker parts of the land."

10 But they said, "It is not so, my lord, but thy servants are come to buy food. 11 We are all the sons of one man; we are come as peaceable men, neither do thy servants go about any evil."

12 And he answered them, "It is otherwise. You are come to consider the unfenced parts of this land."

13 But they said, "We, thy servants, are twelve brethren, the sons of one man in the land of Canaan. The youngest is with our father; the other is not living."

14 He saith, "This is it that I said: you are spies. 15 I shall now presently *try what you are.* By the health of Pharaoh, you shall not depart hence until your youngest brother come. 16 Send one of you to fetch him, and you shall be in prison till what you have said be proved, whether it be true or false, or else, by the health of Pharaoh, you are spies."

17 So he put them in prison three days. 18 And the third day, he brought them out of prison and said, "Do as I have said, and you shall live, for I fear God. 19 If you be peaceable men, let one of your brethren be bound in prison, and go ye your ways, and carry the corn that you have bought unto your houses. 20 And bring your youngest brother to me that I may find your words to be true and you may not die."

They did as he had said, 21 and they talked one to another: "We deserve to suffer these things because we have sinned

angustiam animae illius cum deprecaretur nos et non audivimus. Idcirco venit super nos ista tribulatio."

22 E quibus unus, Ruben, ait, "Numquid non dixi vobis, 'Nolite peccare in puerum,' et non audistis me? En: sanguis eius exquiritur." 23 Nesciebant autem quod intellegeret Ioseph, eo quod per interpretem loquebatur ad eos. 24 Avertitque se parumper et flevit, et reversus locutus est ad eos. 25 Tollensque Symeon et ligans illis praesentibus, iussit ministris ut implerent saccos eorum tritico et reponerent pecunias singulorum in sacculis suis datis supra cibariis in via, qui fecerunt ita.

26 At illi portantes frumenta in asinis profecti sunt. 27 Apertoque unus sacco ut daret iumento pabulum in diversorio, contemplatus pecuniam in ore sacculi, 28 dixit fratribus suis, "Reddita est mihi pecunia; en: habetur in sacco."

Et obstupefacti turbatique dixerunt mutuo, "Quidnam est hoc quod fecit nobis Deus?" 29 Veneruntque ad Iacob, patrem suum, in terra Chanaan, et narraverunt ei omnia quae accidissent sibi, dicentes, 30 "Locutus est nobis dominus terrae dure et putavit nos exploratores provinciae, 31 cui respondimus, 'Pacifici sumus, nec ullas molimur insidias. 32 Duodecim fratres uno patre geniti sumus; unus non est super; minimus cum patre est in terra Chanaan.' 33 Qui ait nobis, 'Sic probabo quod pacifici sitis: fratrem vestrum unum dimittite apud me, et cibaria domibus vestris necessaria sumite, et abite, 34 fratremque vestrum minimum adducite ad me ut sciam quod non sitis exploratores, et istum qui

against our brother, seeing the anguish of his soul when he besought us and we would not hear. Therefore is this affliction come upon us."

22 And Reuben, one of them, said, "Did not I say to you, 'Do not sin against the boy,' and you would not hear me? Behold: his blood is required." 23 And they knew not that Joseph understood, because he spoke to them by an interpreter. 24 And he turned himself away a little while and wept, and returning he spoke to them. 25 And taking Simeon and binding him in their presence, he commanded his servants to fill their sacks with wheat and to put every man's money again in their sacks and to give them besides provisions for the way, and they did so.

26 But they having loaded their asses with the corn went their way. 27 And one of them, opening his sack to give his beast provender in the inn, saw the money in the sack's mouth 28 and said to his brethren, "My money is given me again; behold: it is in the sack."

And they were astonished and troubled and said to one another, "What is this that God hath done unto us?" 29 And they came to Jacob, their father, in the land of Canaan, and they told him all things that had befallen them, saying, 30 "The lord of the land spoke roughly to us and took us to be spies of the country, 31 and we answered him, 'We are peaceable men, and we mean no plot. 32 We are twelve brethren born of one father; one is not living; the youngest is with our father in the land of Canaan.' 33 And he said to us, 'Hereby shall I know that you are peaceable men: leave one of your brethren with me, and take ye necessary provision for your houses, and go your ways, 34 and bring your youngest brother to me that I may know you are not spies, and

tenetur in vinculis recipere possitis ac deinceps emendi quae vultis habeatis licentiam.'"

35 His dictis, cum frumenta effunderent, singuli reppererunt in ore saccorum ligatas pecunias, exterritisque simul omnibus, 36 dixit pater Iacob, "Absque liberis me esse fecistis: Ioseph non est super, Symeon tenetur in vinculis, et Beniamin auferetis. In me haec mala omnia reciderunt."

37 Cui respondit Ruben, "Duos filios meos interfice si non reduxero illum tibi. Trade in manu mea, et ego eum tibi restituam."

38 At ille, "Non descendet," inquit, "filius meus vobiscum. Frater eius mortuus est, et ipse solus remansit. Si quid ei adversi acciderit in terra ad quam pergitis, deducetis canos meos cum dolore ad inferos."

Caput 43

Interim, fames omnem terram vehementer premebat. 2 Consumptisque cibis quos ex Aegypto detulerant, dixit Iacob ad filios suos, "Revertimini, et emite nobis pauxillum escarum."

3 Respondit Iudas, "Denuntiavit nobis vir ille sub attesta-

you may receive this man again that is kept in prison and afterwards may have leave to buy what you will.'"

35 When they had told this, they poured out their corn, and every man found his money tied in the mouth of his sack, and all being astonished together, 36 their father Jacob said, "You have made me to be without children: Joseph is not living, Simeon is kept in bonds, and Benjamin you will take away. All these evils are fallen upon me."

37 And Reuben answered him, "Kill my two sons if I bring him not again to thee. Deliver him into my hand, and I will restore him to thee."

38 But he said, "My son shall not go down with you. His brother is dead, and he is left alone. If any mischief befall him in the land to which you go, you will bring down my gray hairs with sorrow to hell."

Chapter 43

The sons of Jacob go again into Egypt with Benjamin. They are entertained by Joseph.

In the meantime, the famine *was heavy* upon all the land. 2 And when they had eaten up all the corn which they had brought out of Egypt, Jacob said to his sons, "Go again, and buy us a little food."

3 Judah answered, "The man declared unto us with the at-

tione iurandi, dicens, 'Non videbitis faciem meam nisi fratrem vestrum minimum adduxeritis vobiscum.' 4 Si, ergo, vis mittere eum nobiscum, pergemus pariter et ememus tibi necessaria. 5 Si autem non vis, non ibimus, vir enim, ut saepe diximus, denuntiavit nobis, dicens, 'Non videbitis faciem meam absque fratre vestro minimo.'"

6 Dixit eis Israhel, "In meam hoc fecistis miseriam ut indicaretis ei et alium habere vos fratrem."

7 At illi responderunt, "Interrogavit nos homo per ordinem nostram progeniem: si pater viveret; si haberemus fratrem; et nos respondimus ei consequenter, iuxta id quod fuerat sciscitatus. Numquid scire poteramus quod dicturus esset, 'Adducite vobiscum fratrem vestrum'?"

8 Iudas quoque dixit patri suo, "Mitte puerum mecum ut proficiscamur et possimus vivere ne moriamur nos et parvuli nostri. 9 Ego suscipio puerum; de manu mea require illum. Nisi reduxero et tradidero eum tibi, ero peccati in te reus omni tempore. 10 Si non intercessisset dilatio, iam vice altera venissemus."

11 Igitur Israhel, pater eorum, dixit ad eos, "Si sic necesse est, facite quod vultis. Sumite de optimis terrae fructibus in vasis vestris, et deferte viro munera: modicum resinae et mellis et styracis, stactes, terebinthi et amigdalarum. 12 Pecuniamque duplicem ferte vobiscum, et illam quam invenistis in sacculis reportate, ne forte errore factum sit. 13 Sed et fratrem vestrum tollite, et ite ad virum. 14 Deus autem meus omnipotens faciat vobis eum placabilem et remittat vobiscum fratrem vestrum quem tenet et hunc Beniamin. Ego autem, quasi orbatus absque liberis ero." 15 Tulerunt ergo

testation of an oath, saying, 'You shall not see my face unless you bring your youngest brother with you.' 4 If, therefore, thou wilt send him with us, we will set out together and will buy necessaries for thee. 5 But if thou wilt not, we will not go, for the man, as we have often said, declared unto us, saying, 'You shall not see my face without your youngest brother.'"

6 Israel said to them, "You have done this for my misery in that you told him you had also another brother."

7 But they answered, "The man asked us in order concerning our kindred: if our father lived; if we had a brother; and we answered him regularly, according to what he demanded. Could we know that he would say, 'Bring hither your brother with you'?"

8 And Judah said to his father, "Send the boy with me that we may set forward and may live lest both we and our children perish. 9 I take the boy upon me; require him at my hand. Unless I bring him again and restore him to thee, I will be guilty of sin against thee forever. 10 If delay had not been made, we had been here again the second time."

11 Then *Israel* said to them, "If it must needs be so, do what you will. Take of the best fruits of the land in your vessels, and carry down presents to the man: a little balm and honey and storax, myrrh, turpentine and almonds. 12 And take with you double money, and carry back what you found in your sacks, lest perhaps it was done by mistake. 13 And take also your brother, and go to the man. 14 And may my almighty God make him favourable to you and send back with you your brother whom he keepeth and this Benjamin. And as for me, I shall be desolate without children." 15 So the

viri munera et pecuniam duplicem et Beniamin descenderuntque in Aegyptum et steterunt coram Ioseph.

16 Quos cum ille vidisset et Beniamin simul, praecepit
dispensatori domus suae, dicens, "Introduc viros domum, et
occide victimas, et instrue convivium, quoniam mecum sunt
comesuri meridie." 17 Fecit ille sicut fuerat imperatum et introduxit viros domum.

18 Ibique exterriti dixerunt mutuo, "Propter pecuniam
quam rettulimus prius in saccis nostris introducti sumus ut
devolvat in nos calumniam et violenter subiciat servituti et
nos et asinos nostros."

19 Quam ob rem, in ipsis foribus accedentes ad dispensatorem domus, 20 locuti sunt, "Oramus, domine, ut audias
nos. Iam ante descendimus ut emeremus escas, 21 quibus
emptis cum venissemus ad diversorium aperuimus sacculos
nostros et invenimus pecuniam in ore saccorum, quam nunc
eodem pondere reportamus. 22 Sed et aliud adtulimus argentum ut emamus quae nobis necessaria sunt. Non est in nostra conscientia quis eam posuerit in marsuppiis nostris."

23 At ille respondit, "Pax vobiscum; nolite timere. Deus
vester et Deus patris vestri dedit vobis thesauros in sacculis
vestris, nam pecuniam quam dedistis mihi probatam ego
habeo." Eduxitque ad eos Symeon. 24 Et introductis domum,
adtulit aquam, et laverunt pedes suos, deditque pabula asinis eorum. 25 Illi vero parabant munera donec ingrederetur
Ioseph meridie, audierant enim quod ibi comesuri essent
panem.

men took the presents and double money and Benjamin and went down into Egypt and stood before Joseph.

16 And when he had seen them and Benjamin with them, he commanded the steward of his house, saying, "Bring in the men into the house, and kill victims, and prepare a feast, because they shall eat with me at noon." 17 He did as he was commanded and brought the men into the house.

18 And they being much afraid said there, one to another, "Because of the money which we carried back the first time in our sacks we are brought in that he may bring upon us a false accusation and by violence make slaves of us and our asses."

19 Wherefore, going up to the steward of the house at the door, 20 they said, "Sir, we desire thee to hear us. We came down once before to buy food, 21 and when we had bought and come to the inn we opened our sacks and found our money in the mouths of the sacks, which we have now brought again in the same weight. 22 And we have brought other money besides to buy what we want. *We cannot tell* who put it in our bags."

23 But he answered, "Peace be with you; fear not. Your God and the God of your father hath given you treasure in your sacks, for the money which you gave me I have for good." And he brought Simeon out to them. 24 And having brought them into the house, he fetched water, and they washed their feet, and he gave provender to their asses. 25 But they made ready the presents against Joseph came at noon, for they had heard that they should eat bread there.

26 Igitur ingressus est Ioseph domum suam, obtuleruntque ei munera, tenentes in manibus, et adoraverunt proni in
terram. 27 At ille clementer resalutatis eis, interrogavit, dicens, "Salvusne est pater vester, senex de quo dixeratis mihi?
Adhuc vivit?"

28 Qui responderunt, "Sospes est servus tuus pater noster;
adhuc vivit." Et incurvati adoraverunt eum. 29 Adtollens
autem oculos Ioseph vidit Beniamin, fratrem suum uteri-
num, et ait, "Iste est frater vester parvulus de quo dixeratis
mihi?" Et rursum, "Deus," inquit, "misereatur tui, fili mi."
30 Festinavitque quia commota fuerant viscera eius super
fratre suo, et erumpebant lacrimae, et introiens cubiculum
flevit.

31 Rursusque lota facie egressus, continuit se et ait, "Ponite panes." 32 Quibus adpositis seorsum Ioseph et seorsum
fratribus, Aegyptiis quoque qui vescebantur simul seorsum
(inlicitum est enim Aegyptiis comedere cum Hebraeis et
profanum putant huiuscemodi convivium), 33 sederunt coram eo: primogenitus iuxta primogenita sua et minimus
iuxta aetatem suam. Et mirabantur nimis, 34 sumptis partibus quas ab eo acceperant. Maiorque pars venit Beniamin
ita ut quinque partibus excederet. Biberuntque et inebriati
sunt cum eo.

26 Then Joseph came into his house, and they offered him the presents, holding them in their hands, and they bowed down with their face to the ground. 27 But he, courteously saluting them again, asked them, saying, "Is the old man, your father, in health of whom you told me? Is he yet living?"

28 And they answered, "Thy servant our father is in health; he is yet living." And bowing themselves they made obeisance to him. 29 And Joseph lifting up his eyes saw Benjamin, his brother by the same mother, and said, "Is this your young brother of whom you told me?" And he said, "God be gracious to thee, my son." 30 And he made haste because his heart was moved upon his brother, and tears gushed out, and going into his chamber he wept.

31 And when he had washed his face, coming out again, he refrained himself and said, "Set bread on the table." 32 And when it was set on for Joseph apart and for his brethren apart, for the Egyptians also that ate with him apart (for it is unlawful for the Egyptians to eat with the Hebrews and they think such a feast profane), 33 they sat before him: the firstborn according to his birthright and the youngest according to his age. And they wondered very much, 34 taking the messes which they received of him. And the greater mess came to Benjamin so that it exceeded by five parts. And they drank and were *merry* with him.

Caput 44

Praecepit autem Ioseph dispensatori domus suae, dicens, "Imple saccos eorum frumento, quantum possunt capere, et pone pecuniam singulorum in summitate sacci. 2 Scyphum autem meum argenteum et pretium quod dedit tritici pone in ore sacci iunioris." Factumque est ita. 3 Et orto mane, dimissi sunt cum asinis suis. 4 Iamque urbem exierant et processerant paululum, tum Ioseph, arcessito dispensatore domus, "Surge," inquit, "et persequere viros, et adprehensis dicito, 'Quare reddidistis malum pro bono? 5 Scyphum quem furati estis ipse est in quo bibit dominus meus et in quo augurari solet. Pessimam rem fecistis.'"

6 Fecit ille ut iusserat. Et adprehensis per ordinem locutus est. 7 Qui responderunt, "Quare sic loquitur dominus noster, ut servi tui tantum flagitii commiserint? 8 Pecuniam quam invenimus in summitate saccorum reportavimus ad te de terra Chanaan. Et quomodo consequens est ut furati simus de domo domini tui aurum vel argentum? 9 Apud quemcumque fuerit inventum servorum tuorum quod quaeris, moriatur, et nos servi erimus domini nostri."

Chapter 44

Joseph's contrivance to stop his brethren. The humble supplication of Judah.

And Joseph commanded the steward of his house, saying, "Fill their sacks with corn, as much as they can hold, and put the money of every one in the top of his sack. 2 And in the mouth of the younger's sack put my silver cup and the price which he gave for the wheat." And it was so done. 3 And when the morning arose, they were sent away with their asses. 4 And when they were now departed out of the city and had gone forward a little way, Joseph sending for the steward of his house said, "Arise, and pursue after the men, and when thou hast overtaken them, say to them, 'Why have you returned evil for good? 5 The cup which you have stolen is that in which my lord drinketh and in which he is wont to divine. You have done a very evil thing.'"

6 He did as he had commanded him. And having overtaken them, he spoke to them *the same words.* 7 And they answered, "Why doth our lord speak so, as though thy servants had committed so heinous a fact? 8 The money that we found in the top of our sacks we brought back to thee from the land of Canaan. How then *should it be* that we should steal out of thy lord's house gold or silver? 9 With whomsoever of thy servants shall be found that which thou seekest, let him die, and we will be the bondmen of *my* lord."

10 Qui dixit eis, "Fiat iuxta vestram sententiam: apud quemcumque fuerit inventum ipse sit servus meus, vos autem eritis innoxii."

11 Itaque festinato deponentes in terram saccos, aperuerunt singuli. 12 Quos scrutatus, incipiens a maiore usque ad minimum, invenit scyphum in sacco Beniamin. 13 At illi scissis vestibus oneratisque rursum asinis reversi sunt in oppidum. 14 Primusque Iudas cum fratribus ingressus est ad Ioseph (necdum enim de loco abierat), omnesque ante eum in terra pariter corruerunt. 15 Quibus ille ait, "Cur sic agere voluistis? An ignoratis quod non sit similis mei in augurandi scientia?"

16 Cui Iudas, "Quid respondebimus," inquit, "domino meo? Vel quid loquemur aut iuste poterimus obtendere? Deus invenit iniquitatem servorum tuorum. En: omnes servi sumus domini mei, et nos et apud quem inventus est scyphus."

17 Respondit Ioseph, "Absit a me ut sic agam. Qui furatus est scyphum, ipse sit servus meus, vos autem abite liberi ad patrem vestrum."

18 Accedens autem propius Iudas confidenter ait, "Oro, domine mi, loquatur servus tuus verbum in auribus tuis, et ne irascaris famulo tuo, tu es enim post Pharaonem 19 dominus meus. Interrogasti prius servos tuos, 'Habetis patrem aut fratrem?' 20 Et nos respondimus tibi, domino meo, 'Est nobis pater, senex, et puer parvulus qui in senecta illius natus est cuius uterinus frater est mortuus, et ipsum solum habet mater sua, pater vero tenere diligit eum.' 21 Dixistique servis tuis, 'Adducite eum ad me, et ponam oculos meos super illum.' 22 Suggessimus domino meo, 'Non potest puer

10 And he said to them, "Let it be according to your sentence: with whomsoever it shall be found let him be my servant, and you shall be blameless."

11 Then they speedily took down their sacks to the ground, and every man opened his sack. 12 Which when he had searched, beginning at the eldest and ending at the youngest, he found the cup in Benjamin's sack. 13 Then they rent their garments and loading their asses again returned into the town. 14 And Judah at the head of his brethren went in to Joseph (for he was not yet gone out of the place), and they all together fell down before him on the ground. 15 And he said to them, "Why would you do so? Know you not that there is no one like me in the science of divining?"

16 And Judah said to him, "What shall we answer my lord? Or what shall we say or be able justly to allege? God hath found out the iniquity of thy servants. Behold: we are all bondmen to my lord, both we and he with whom the cup was found."

17 Joseph answered, "God forbid that I should do so. He that stole the cup, he shall be my bondman, and go you away free to your father."

18 Then Judah, coming nearer, said boldly, "I beseech thee, my lord, let thy servant speak a word in thy ears, and be not angry with thy servant, for after Pharaoh thou art 19 my lord. Thou didst ask thy servants the first time, 'Have you a father or a brother?' 20 And we answered thee, my lord, 'We have a father, an old man, and a young boy that was born in his old age whose brother by the mother is dead, and *he alone is left of his mother,* and his father loveth him tenderly.' 21 And thou saidst to thy servants, 'Bring him hither to me, and I will set my eyes on him.' 22 We suggested to my lord,

relinquere patrem suum, si enim illum dimiserit, morietur.' 23 Et dixisti servis tuis, 'Nisi venerit frater vester minimus vobiscum, non videbitis amplius faciem meam.' 24 Cum ergo ascendissemus ad famulum tuum patrem nostrum, narravimus ei omnia quae locutus est dominus meus. 25 Et dixit pater noster, 'Revertimini, et emite nobis parum tritici.' 26 Cui diximus, 'Ire non possumus. Si frater noster minimus descendet nobiscum, proficiscemur simul. Alioquin, illo absente non audemus videre faciem viri.' 27 Ad quae ille respondit, 'Vos scitis quod duos genuerit mihi uxor mea. 28 Egressus est unus, et dixistis, "Bestia devoravit eum, et hucusque non conparet." 29 Si tuleritis et istum et aliquid ei in via contigerit, deducetis canos meos cum maerore ad inferos.' 30 Igitur si intravero ad servum tuum patrem nostrum, et puer defuerit (cum anima illius ex huius anima pendeat), 31 videritque eum non esse nobiscum, morietur, et deducent famuli tui canos eius cum dolore ad inferos. 32 Ego proprie servus tuus sim qui in meam hunc recepi fidem et spopondi, dicens, 'Nisi reduxero eum, peccati reus ero in patrem meum omni tempore.' 33 Manebo itaque, servus tuus, pro puero in ministerium domini mei, et puer ascendat cum fratribus suis, 34 non enim possum redire ad patrem absente puero, ne calamitatis quae oppressura est patrem meum testis adsistam."

'The boy cannot leave his father, for if he leave him, he will die.' 23 And thou saidst to thy servants, 'Except your youngest brother come with you, you shall see my face no more.' 24 Therefore when we were gone up to thy servant our father, we told him all that my lord had said. 25 And our father said, 'Go again, and buy us a little wheat.' 26 And we said to him, 'We cannot go. If our youngest brother go down with us, we will set out together. Otherwise, without him we dare not see the man's face.' 27 Whereunto he answered, 'You know that my wife bore me two. 28 One went out, and you said, "A beast devoured him, and hitherto he appeareth not." 29 If you take this also and any thing befall him in the way, you will bring down my gray hairs with sorrow unto hell.' 30 Therefore if I shall go to thy servant our father, and the boy be wanting (whereas his life dependeth upon the life of him), 31 and he shall see that he is not with us, he will die, and thy servants shall bring down his gray hairs with sorrow unto hell. 32 Let me be thy proper servant who took him into my trust and promised, saying, 'If I bring him not again, I will be guilty of sin against my father forever.' 33 Therefore I, thy servant, will stay instead of the boy in the service of my lord, and let the boy go up with his brethren, 34 for I cannot return to my father without the boy, lest I *be* a witness of the calamity that will oppress my father."

Caput 45

Non se poterat ultra cohibere Ioseph multis coram adstantibus, unde praecepit ut egrederentur cuncti foras, et nullus interesset alienus agnitioni mutuae. 2 Elevavitque vocem cum fletu, quam audierunt Aegyptii omnisque domus Pharaonis. 3 Et dixit fratribus suis, "Ego sum Ioseph. Adhuc pater meus vivit?" Non poterant respondere fratres, nimio timore perterriti. 4 Ad quos ille clementer, "Accedite," inquit, "ad me." Et cum accessissent prope, "Ego sum," ait, "Ioseph, frater vester, quem vendidistis in Aegypto. 5 Nolite pavere, nec vobis durum esse videatur quod vendidistis me in his regionibus, pro salute enim vestra misit me Deus ante vos in Aegyptum, 6 biennium est enim quod fames esse coepit in terra et adhuc quinque anni restant quibus nec arari poterit nec meti. 7 Praemisitque me Deus ut reservemini super terram et escas ad vivendum habere possitis. 8 Non vestro consilio sed Dei huc voluntate missus sum qui fecit me quasi patrem Pharaonis et dominum universae domus eius ac principem in omni terra Aegypti.

9 "Festinate, et ascendite ad patrem meum, et dicetis ei, 'Haec mandat filius tuus Ioseph: "Deus me fecit dominum

Chapter 45

Joseph maketh himself known to his brethren and sendeth for his father.

J oseph could no longer refrain himself before many that stood by, whereupon he commanded that all should go out, and no stranger be present at their knowing one another. 2 And he lifted up his voice with weeping, which the Egyptians and all the house of Pharaoh heard. 3 And he said to his brethren, "I am Joseph. Is my father yet living?" His brethren could not answer him, being struck with exceeding great fear. 4 And he said mildly to them, "Come nearer to me." And when they were come near him, he said, "I am Joseph, your brother, whom you sold into Egypt. 5 Be not afraid, and let it not seem to you a hard case that you sold me into these countries, for God sent me before you into Egypt for your preservation, 6 for it is two years since the famine began to be upon the land and five years more remain wherein there can be neither ploughing nor reaping. 7 And God sent me before that you may be preserved upon the earth and may have food to live. 8 Not by your counsel was I sent hither but by the will of God who hath made me as it were a father to Pharaoh and lord of his whole house and governor in all the land of Egypt.

9 "Make haste, and go ye up to my father, and say to him, 'Thus saith thy son Joseph: "God hath made me lord of the

universae terrae Aegypti. Descende ad me; ne moreris, 10 et habitabis in terra Gessen, erisque iuxta me, tu et filii tui et filii filiorum tuorum, oves tuae et armenta tua et universa quae possides. 11 Ibique te pascam (adhuc enim quinque anni residui sunt famis) ne et tu pereas et domus tua et omnia quae possides.'"

12 "En: oculi vestri et oculi fratris mei Beniamin vident quod os meum loquatur ad vos. 13 Nuntiate patri meo universam gloriam meam et cuncta quae vidistis in Aegypto. Festinate, et adducite eum ad me."

14 Cumque amplexatus recidisset in collum Beniamin fratris sui flevit, illo quoque flente similiter super collum eius. 15 Osculatusque est Ioseph omnes fratres suos et ploravit super singulos, post quae ausi sunt loqui ad eum.

16 Auditumque est, et celebri sermone vulgatum in aula regis: "Venerunt fratres Ioseph," et gavisus est Pharao atque omnis familia eius. 17 Dixitque ad Ioseph ut imperaret fratribus suis, dicens, "Onerantes iumenta ite in terram Chanaan, 18 et tollite inde patrem vestrum et cognationem, et venite ad me, et ego dabo vobis omnia bona Aegypti ut comedatis medullam terrae. 19 Praecipe etiam ut tollant plaustra de terra Aegypti ad subvectionem parvulorum suorum et coniugum, ac dicito, 'Tollite patrem vestrum, et properate quantocius venientes, 20 nec dimittatis quicquam de supellectili vestra, quia omnes opes Aegypti vestrae erunt.'"

21 Feceruntque filii Israhel ut eis mandatum fuerat. Quibus dedit Ioseph plaustra secundum Pharaonis imperium et cibaria in itinere. 22 Singulisque proferri iussit binas stolas,

whole land of Egypt. Come down to me; linger not, 10 and thou shalt dwell in the land of Goshen, and thou shalt be near me, thou and thy sons and thy sons' sons, thy sheep and thy herds and all things that thou hast. 11 And there I will feed thee (for there are yet five years of famine remaining) lest both thou perish and thy house and all things that thou hast.'"

12 "Behold: your eyes and the eyes of my brother Benjamin see that it is my mouth that speaketh to you. 13 *You shall tell* my father of all my glory and all things that you have seen in Egypt. Make haste, and bring him to me."

14 And falling upon the neck of his brother Benjamin he embraced him and wept, and Benjamin in like manner wept also on his neck. 15 And Joseph kissed all his brethren and wept upon every one of them, after which they were emboldened to speak to him.

16 And it was heard, and the fame was abroad in the king's court: "The brethren of Joseph are come," and Pharaoh with all his family was glad. 17 And he spoke to Joseph that he should give orders to his brethren, saying, "Load your beasts, and go into the land of Canaan, 18 and bring away from thence your father and kindred, and come to me, and I will give you all the good things of Egypt that you may eat the marrow of the land. 19 Give orders also that they take wagons out of the land of Egypt for the carriage of their children and their wives, and say, 'Take up your father, and make haste to come with all speed, 20 and leave nothing of your household stuff, for all the riches of Egypt shall be yours.'"

21 And the sons of Israel did as they were bid. And Joseph gave them wagons according to Pharaoh's commandment and provisions for the way. 22 He ordered also to be brought

Beniamin vero dedit trecentos argenteos cum quinque stolis optimis, 23 tantundem pecuniae et vestium mittens patri suo, addens et asinos decem qui subveherent ex omnibus divitiis Aegypti et totidem asinas triticum in itinere panesque portantes. 24 Dimisit ergo fratres suos et proficiscentibus ait, "Ne irascamini in via."

25 Qui ascendentes ex Aegypto venerunt in terram Chanaan ad patrem suum, Iacob. 26 Et nuntiaverunt ei, dicentes, "Ioseph, filius tuus, vivit et ipse dominatur in omni terra Aegypti." Quo audito Iacob quasi de gravi somno evigilans tamen non credebat eis. 27 Illi, contra, referebant omnem ordinem rei.

Cumque vidisset plaustra et universa quae miserat, revixit spiritus eius, 28 et ait, "Sufficit mihi si adhuc Ioseph filius meus vivit; vadam et videbo illum antequam moriar."

Caput 46

Profectusque Israhel cum omnibus quae habebat, venit ad Puteum Iuramenti, et, mactatis ibi victimis Deo patris sui Isaac, 2 audivit eum per visionem nocte vocantem se et dicentem sibi, "Iacob, Iacob."

out for every one of them two robes, but to Benjamin he gave three hundred pieces of silver with five robes of the best, 23 sending to his father as much money and raiment, adding besides ten he-asses to carry of all the riches of Egypt and as many she-asses carrying wheat and bread for the journey. 24 So he sent away his brethren and at their departing said to them, "Be not angry in the way."

25 And they went up out of Egypt and came into the land of Canaan to their father, Jacob. 26 And they told him, saying, "Joseph, thy son, is living, and he is ruler in all the land of Egypt." Which when Jacob heard, he awaked as it were out of a deep sleep yet did not believe them. 27 They, on the other side, told the whole order of the thing.

And when he saw the wagons and all that he had sent, his spirit revived, 28 and he said, "It is enough for me if Joseph my son be yet living; I will go and see him before I die."

Chapter 46

Israel, warranted by a vision from God, goeth down into Egypt with all his family.

And Israel, taking his journey with all that he had, came to the Well of the Oath, and, killing victims there to the God of his father Isaac, 2 he heard him by a vision in the night calling him and saying to him, "Jacob, Jacob."

Cui respondit, "Ecce, adsum."

3 Ait illi Deus, "Ego sum fortissimus Deus patris tui. Noli timere; descende in Aegyptum, quia in gentem magnam faciam te ibi. 4 Ego descendam tecum illuc et ego inde adducam te revertentem. Ioseph quoque ponet manus suas super oculos tuos."

5 Surrexit autem Iacob a Puteo Iuramenti, tuleruntque eum filii cum parvulis et uxoribus suis in plaustris quae miserat Pharao ad portandum senem 6 et omnia quae possederat in terra Chanaan, venitque in Aegyptum cum omni semine suo, 7 filii eius et nepotes, filiae et cuncta simul progenies. 8 Haec sunt autem nomina filiorum Israhel qui ingressi sunt in Aegyptum, ipse cum liberis suis: primogenitus, Ruben; 9 filii Ruben: Enoch et Phallu et Esrom et Charmi; 10 filii Symeon: Iemuhel et Iamin et Ahod et Iachin et Saher et Saul, filius Chananitidis; 11 filii Levi: Gerson et Caath et Merari; 12 filii Iuda: Her et Onan et Sela et Phares et Zara—mortui sunt autem Her et Onan in terra Chanaan. Natique sunt filii Phares: Esrom et Amul. 13 Filii Isachar: Thola et Phua et Iob et Semron; 14 filii Zabulon: Sared et Helon et Iahelel. 15 Hii filii Liae quos genuit in Mesopotamiam Syriae cum Dina, filia sua. Omnes animae filiorum eius et filiarum: triginta tres.

16 Filii Gad: Sephion et Haggi et Suni et Esebon et Heri et Arodi et Areli. 17 Filii Aser: Iamne et Iesua et Iesui et Beria, Sara quoque, soror eorum. Filii Beria: Heber et Melchihel. 18 Hii filii Zelphae quam dedit Laban Liae, filiae suae. Et hos genuit Iacob: sedecim animas.

And he answered him, "Lo, here I am."

3 God said to him, "I am the most mighty God of thy father. Fear not; go down into Egypt, for I will make a great nation of thee there. 4 I will go down with thee thither and will bring thee back again from thence. Joseph also shall put his hands upon thy eyes."

5 And Jacob rose up from the Well of the Oath, and his sons took him up with their children and wives in the wagons which Pharaoh had sent to carry the old man 6 and all that he had in the land of Canaan, and he came into Egypt with all his seed, 7 his sons and grandsons, daughters and all his offspring together. 8 And these are the names of the children of Israel that entered into Egypt, he and his children: his firstborn, Reuben; 9 the sons of Reuben: Hanoch and Phallu and Hezron and Carmi; 10 the sons of Simeon: Jemuel and Jamin and Ohad and Jachin and Zohar and Shaul, the son of a woman of Canaan; 11 the sons of Levi: Gershon and Kohath and Merari; 12 the sons of Judah: Er and Onan and Shelah and Perez and Zerah—and Er and Onan died in the land of Canaan. And sons were born to Perez: Hezron and Hamul. 13 The sons of Issachar: Tola and Puvah and Jashub and Shimron; 14 the sons of Zebulun: Sered and Elon and Jahleel. 15 These are the sons of Leah whom she bore in Mesopotamia of Syria with Dinah, his daughter. All the souls of her sons and daughters: thirty-three.

16 The sons of Gad: Ziphion and Haggi and Shuni and Ezbon and Eri and Arodi and Areli. 17 The sons of Asher: Imnah and Ishvah and Ishvi and Beriah, and Serah, their sister. The sons of Beriah: Heber and Malchiel. 18 These are the sons of Zilpah whom Laban gave to Leah, his daughter. And these she bore to Jacob: sixteen souls.

19 Filii Rahel, uxoris Iacob: Ioseph et Beniamin. 20 Natique sunt Ioseph filii in terra Aegypti quos genuit ei Aseneth, filia Putiphare, sacerdotis Heliopoleos: Manasses et Ephraim. 21 Filii Beniamin: Bela et Bechor et Asbel et Gera et Naaman et Ehi et Ros et Mophim et Opphim et Ared. 22 Hii filii Rahel quos genuit Iacob; omnes animae: quattuordecim.

23 Filii Dan: Usim. 24 Filii Nepthalim: Iasihel et Guni et Hieser et Sallem. 25 Hii filii Balae quam dedit Laban Raheli, filiae suae, et hos genuit Iacob; omnes animae: septem.

26 Cunctae animae quae ingressae sunt cum Iacob in Aegyptum et egressae de femore illius, absque uxoribus filiorum: sexaginta sex. 27 Filii autem Ioseph qui nati sunt ei in terra Aegypti: animae duae. Omnes animae domus Iacob quae ingressa est Aegyptum fuere septuaginta.

28 Misit autem Iudam ante se ad Ioseph ut nuntiaret ei et ille occurreret in Gessen. 29 Quo cum pervenisset, iuncto Ioseph curru suo ascendit obviam patri ad eundem locum, vidensque eum inruit super collum eius et inter amplexus flevit. 30 Dixitque pater ad Ioseph, "Iam laetus moriar quia vidi faciem tuam et superstitem te relinquo."

31 Et ille locutus est ad fratres et ad omnem domum patris sui, "Ascendam et nuntiabo Pharaoni dicamque ei, 'Fratres mei et domus patris mei qui erant in terra Chanaan venerunt ad me, 32 et sunt viri pastores ovium, curamque habent alendorum gregum; pecora sua et armenta et omnia quae habere potuerunt adduxerunt secum.' 33 Cumque vocaverit vos et dixerit, 'Quod est opus vestrum?' 34 responde-

19 The sons of Rachel, Jacob's wife: Joseph and Benjamin. 20 And sons were born to Joseph in the land of Egypt whom Asenath, the daughter of Potiphera, priest of Heliopolis, bore him: Manasseh and Ephraim. 21 The sons of Benjamin: Bela and Becher and Ashbel and Gera and Naaman and Ehi and Rosh and Muppim and Huppim and Ard. 22 These are the sons of Rachel whom she bore to Jacob; all the souls: fourteen.

23 The sons of Dan: Husham. 24 The sons of Naphtali: Jahzeel and Guni and Jezer and Shillem. 25 These are the sons of Bilhah whom Laban gave to Rachel, his daughter, and these she bore to Jacob; all the souls: seven.

26 All the souls that went with Jacob into Egypt and that came out of his thigh, besides his sons' wives: sixty-six. 27 And the sons of Joseph that were born to him in the land of Egypt: two souls. All the souls of the house of Jacob that entered into Egypt were seventy.

28 And he sent Judah before him to Joseph to tell him and that he should meet him in Goshen. 29 And when he was come thither, Joseph made ready his chariot and went up to meet his father in the same place, and seeing him he fell upon his neck and embracing him wept. 30 And the father said to Joseph, "Now shall I die with joy because I have seen thy face and leave thee alive."

31 And Joseph said to his brethren and to all his father's house, "I will go up and will tell Pharaoh and will say to him, 'My brethren and my father's house that were in the land of Canaan are come to me, 32 and the men are shepherds, and their occupation is to feed cattle; their flocks and herds and all they *have* they have brought with them.' 33 And when he shall call you and shall say, 'What is your occupation?' 34 you

bitis, 'Viri pastores sumus servi tui ab infantia nostra usque in praesens, et nos et patres nostri.' Haec autem dicetis ut habitare possitis in terra Gessen quia detestantur Aegyptii omnes pastores ovium."

Caput 47

Ingressus ergo Ioseph nuntiavit Pharaoni, dicens, "Pater meus et fratres, oves eorum et armenta et cuncta quae possident venerunt de terra Chanaan. Et ecce: consistunt in terra Gessen."

2 Extremos quoque fratrum suorum, quinque viros, constituit coram rege, 3 quos ille interrogavit, "Quid habetis operis?"

Responderunt, "Pastores ovium sumus servi tui, et nos et patres nostri. 4 Ad peregrinandum in terra tua venimus quoniam non est herba gregibus servorum tuorum, ingravescente fame in regione Chanaan, petimusque ut esse nos iubeas, servos tuos, in terra Gessen."

5 Dixit itaque rex ad Ioseph, "Pater tuus et fratres tui venerunt ad te. 6 Terra Aegypti in conspectu tuo est: in optimo

shall answer, 'We, thy servants, are shepherds from our infancy until now, both we and our fathers.' And this you shall say that you may dwell in the land of Goshen because the Egyptians have all shepherds in abomination."

Chapter 47

Jacob and his sons are presented before Pharaoh. He giveth
them the land of Goshen. The famine forceth the Egyptians
to sell all their possessions to the king.

Then Joseph went in and told Pharaoh, saying, "My father and brethren, their sheep and their herds and all that they possess are come out of the land of Canaan. And behold: they stay in the land of Goshen."

2 Five men also, the last of his brethren, he presented before the king, 3 and he asked them, "What is your occupation?"

They answered, "We, thy servants, are shepherds, both we and our fathers. 4 We are come to sojourn in thy land because there is no grass for the flocks of thy servants, the famine being very grievous in the land of Canaan, and we pray thee to give orders that we, thy servants, may be in the land of Goshen."

5 The king therefore said to Joseph, "Thy father and thy brethren are come to thee. 6 The land of Egypt is before

loco fac habitare eos et trade eis terram Gessen. Quod si nosti esse in eis viros industrios, constitue illos magistros pecorum meorum."

7 Post haec, introduxit Ioseph patrem suum ad regem et statuit eum coram eo, qui benedicens illi, 8 et interrogatus ab eo, "Quot sunt dies annorum vitae tuae?" 9 respondit, "Dies peregrinationis vitae meae centum triginta annorum sunt, parvi et mali, et non pervenerunt usque ad dies patrum meorum quibus peregrinati sunt." 10 Et, benedicto rege, egressus est foras.

11 Ioseph vero patri et fratribus suis dedit possessionem in Aegypto in optimo loco terrae, Ramesses, ut praeceperat Pharao. 12 Et alebat eos omnemque domum patris sui, praebens cibaria singulis, 13 in toto enim orbe panis deerat, et oppresserat fames terram, maxime Aegypti et Chanaan, 14 e quibus omnem pecuniam congregavit pro venditione frumenti et intulit eam in aerarium regis. 15 Cumque defecisset emptoribus pretium, venit cuncta Aegyptus ad Ioseph, dicens, "Da nobis panes: quare morimur coram te, deficiente pecunia?"

16 Quibus ille respondit, "Adducite pecora vestra, et dabo vobis pro eis cibos, si pretium non habetis." 17 Quae cum adduxissent, dedit eis alimenta pro equis et ovibus et bubus et asinis, sustentavitque eos illo anno pro commutatione pecorum.

18 Veneruntque anno secundo, et dixerunt ei, "Non celabimus dominum nostrum quod deficiente pecunia pecora simul defecerint, nec clam te est quod absque corporibus et terra nihil habeamus. 19 Cur ergo moriemur te vidente? Et

thee: make them dwell in the best place and give them the land of Goshen. And if thou knowest that there are industrious men among them, make them rulers over my cattle."

7 After this, Joseph brought in his father to the king and presented him before him, and he blessed him, 8 and being asked by him, "How many are the days of the years of thy life?" 9 he answered, "The days of my *pilgrimage* are a hundred and thirty years, few and evil, and they are not come up to the days of the *pilgrimage of my fathers.*" 10 And, blessing the king, he went out.

11 But Joseph gave a possession to his father and his brethren in Egypt in the best place of the land, in Rameses, as Pharaoh had commanded. 12 And he nourished them and all his father's house, allowing food to every one, 13 for in the whole world there was want of bread, and a famine had oppressed the land, *more* especially of Egypt and Canaan, 14 out of which he gathered up all the money for the *corn which they bought* and brought it into the king's treasure. 15 And when the buyers wanted money, all Egypt came to Joseph, saying, "Give us bread: why should we die in thy presence, having now no money?"

16 And he answered them, "Bring me your cattle, and for them I will give you food, if you have no money." 17 And when they had brought them, he gave them food in exchange for their horses and sheep and oxen and asses, and he maintained them that year for the exchange of their cattle.

18 And they came the second year, and said to him, "We will not hide from our lord how that our money is spent and our cattle also are gone, neither art thou ignorant that we have nothing now left but our bodies and our lands. 19 Why

nos et terra nostra tui erimus. Eme nos in servitutem regiam, et praebe semina ne pereunte cultore redigatur terra in solitudinem."

20 Emit igitur Ioseph omnem terram Aegypti, vendentibus singulis possessiones suas, prae magnitudine famis. Subiecitque eam Pharaoni 21 et cunctos populos eius a novissimis terminis Aegypti usque ad extremos fines eius, 22 praeter terram sacerdotum, quae a rege tradita fuerat eis, quibus et statuta cibaria ex horreis publicis praebebantur et idcirco non sunt conpulsi vendere possessiones suas.

23 Dixit ergo Ioseph ad populos, "En: ut cernitis, et vos et terram vestram Pharao possidet. Accipite semina, et serite agros, 24 ut fruges habere possitis. Quintam partem regi dabitis; quattuor reliquas permitto vobis in sementem et in cibos famulis et liberis vestris."

25 Qui responderunt, "Salus nostra in manu tua est. Respiciat nos tantum dominus noster, et laeti serviemus regi."

26 Ex eo tempore usque in praesentem diem, in universa terra Aegypti, regibus quinta pars solvitur, et factum est quasi in legem, absque terra sacerdotali, quae libera ab hac condicione fuit. 27 Habitavit ergo Israhel in Aegypto, id est, in terra Gessen, et possedit eam auctusque est et multiplicatus nimis.

28 Et vixit in ea decem et septem annis, factique sunt omnes dies vitae illius centum quadraginta septem annorum. 29 Cumque adpropinquare cerneret mortis diem, vocavit filium suum Ioseph et dixit ad eum, "Si inveni gratiam in conspectu tuo, pone manum sub femore meo, et facies mihi

therefore shall we die before thy eyes? We will be thine, both we and our lands. Buy us to be the king's servants, and give us seed lest for want of tillers the land be turned into a wilderness."

20 So Joseph bought all the land of Egypt, every man selling his possessions, because of the greatness of the famine. And he brought it into Pharaoh's hands 21 and all its people from one end of the borders of Egypt even to the other end thereof, 22 except the land of the priests, which had been given them by the king, to whom also a certain allowance of food was given out of the public stores and therefore they were not forced to sell their possessions.

23 Then Joseph said to the people, "Behold: as you see, both you and your lands belong to Pharaoh. Take seed, and sow the fields, 24 that you may have corn. The fifth part you shall give to the king; the other four *you shall have* for seed and for food for your families and children."

25 And they answered, "Our life is in thy hand. Only let my lord look favourably upon us, and we will gladly serve the king."

26 From that time unto this day, in the whole land of Egypt, the fifth part is paid to the king, and it is become as a law, except the land of the priests, which was free from this covenant. 27 So Israel dwelt in Egypt, that is, in the land of Goshen, and possessed it and grew and was multiplied exceedingly.

28 And he lived in it seventeen years, and all the days of his life came to a hundred and forty-seven years. 29 And when he saw that the day of his death drew nigh, he called his son Joseph and said to him, "If I have found favour in thy sight, put thy hand under my thigh, and thou shalt shew me

misericordiam et veritatem: ut non sepelias me in Aegypto. 30 Sed dormiam cum patribus meis, et auferas me de hac terra condasque in sepulchro maiorum."

Cui respondit Ioseph, "Ego faciam quod iussisti."

31 Et ille, "Iura ergo," inquit, "mihi." Quo iurante, adoravit Israhel Deum, conversus ad lectuli caput.

Caput 48

His ita transactis, nuntiatum est Ioseph quod aegrotaret pater eius, qui adsumptis duobus filiis, Manasse et Ephraim, perrexit. 2 Dictumque est seni, "Ecce: filius tuus Ioseph venit ad te." Qui confortatus sedit in lectulo.

3 Et ingresso ad se ait, "Deus Omnipotens apparuit mihi in Luza, quae est in terra Chanaan, benedixitque mihi, 4 et ait, 'Ego te augebo et multiplicabo, et faciam in turbas populorum, daboque tibi terram hanc et semini tuo post te in possessionem sempiternam.' 5 Duo igitur filii tui qui nati

this kindness and truth: not to bury me in Egypt. 30 But I will sleep with my fathers, and thou shalt take me away out of this land and bury me in the burying place of my ancestors."

And Joseph answered him, "I will do what thou hast commanded."

31 And he said, "Swear then to me." And as he was swearing, Israel adored God, turning to the bed's head.

Chapter 48

Joseph visiteth his father in his sickness, who adopteth his two sons, Manasseh and Ephraim, and blesseth them, preferring the younger before the elder.

After these things, it was told Joseph that his father was sick, and he *set out to go to him,* taking his two sons, Manasseh and Ephraim. 2 And it was told the old man, "Behold: thy son Joseph cometh to thee." And being strengthened he sat on his bed.

3 And when Joseph was come in to him, he said, "God Almighty appeared to me at Luz, which is in the land of Canaan, and he blessed me, 4 and he said, 'I will cause thee to increase and multiply, and I will make *of thee a multitude* of people, and I will give this land to thee and to thy seed after thee for an everlasting possession.' 5 So thy two sons who

sunt tibi in terra Aegypti antequam huc venirem ad te mei erunt. Ephraim et Manasses sicut Ruben et Symeon reputabuntur mihi. 6 Reliquos autem quos genueris post eos tui erunt et nomine fratrum suorum vocabuntur in possessionibus suis, 7 mihi enim quando veniebam de Mesopotamiam, mortua est Rahel in terra Chanaan in ipso itinere, eratque vernum tempus, et ingrediebar Ephratam, et sepelivi eam iuxta viam Ephratae, quae alio nomine appellatur Bethleem."

8 Videns autem filios eius, dixit ad eum, "Qui sunt isti?"

9 Respondit, "Filii mei sunt quos dedit mihi Deus in hoc loco."

"Adduc," inquit, "eos ad me ut benedicam illis," 10 oculi enim Israhel caligabant prae nimia senectute, et clare videre non poterat. Adplicitosque ad se, deosculatus et circumplexus 11 dixit ad filium, "Non sum fraudatus aspectu tuo; insuper, ostendit mihi Deus semen tuum." 12 Cumque tulisset eos Ioseph de gremio patris, adoravit pronus in terram. 13 Et posuit Ephraim ad dexteram suam, id est, ad sinistram Israhel, Manassen vero in sinistra sua, ad dexteram, scilicet, patris, adplicuitque ambos ad eum.

14 Qui extendens manum dextram posuit super caput Ephraim, iunioris fratris, sinistram autem super caput Manasse, qui maior natu erat, commutans manus. 15 Benedixitque Iacob filiis Ioseph et ait, "Deus, in cuius conspectu ambulaverunt patres mei Abraham et Isaac, Deus qui pascit me ab adulescentia mea usque in praesentem diem, 16 angelus qui eruit me de cunctis malis, benedicat pueris istis, et invo-

were born to thee in the land of Egypt before I came hither to thee shall be mine. Ephraim and Manasseh shall be reputed to me as Reuben and Simeon. 6 But the rest whom thou shalt have after them shall be thine and shall be called by the name of their brethren in their possessions, 7 for when I came out of Mesopotamia, Rachel died from me in the land of Canaan in the very journey, and it was springtime, and I was going to Ephrath, and I buried her near the way of Ephrath, which by another name is called Bethlehem."

8 Then seeing his sons, he said to him, "Who are these?"

9 He answered, "They are my sons whom God hath given me in this place."

And he said, "Bring them to me that I may bless them," 10 for Israel's eyes were dim by reason of his great age, and he could not see clearly. And when they were brought to him, he kissed and embraced them 11 and said to his son, "I am not deprived of seeing thee; moreover, God hath shewed me thy seed." 12 And when Joseph had taken them from his father's lap, he bowed down with his face to the ground. 13 And he set Ephraim on his right hand, that is, towards the left hand of Israel, but Manasseh on his left hand, to wit, towards his father's right hand, and brought them near to him.

14 But he stretching forth his right hand put it upon the head of Ephraim, the younger brother, and the left upon the head of Manasseh, who was the elder, changing his hands. 15 And Jacob blessed the sons of Joseph and said, "God, in whose sight my fathers Abraham and Isaac walked, God that feedeth me from my youth until this day, 16 the angel that delivereth me from all evils, bless these boys, and let my

cetur super eos nomen meum, nomina quoque patrum meorum Abraham et Isaac, et crescant in multitudinem super
terram."

17 Videns autem Ioseph quod posuisset pater suus dexteram manum super caput Ephraim, graviter accepit, et adprehensam patris manum levare conatus est de capite
Ephraim et transferre super caput Manasse. 18 Dixitque ad
patrem, "Non ita convenit, pater, quia hic est primogenitus.
Pone dexteram tuam super caput eius."

19 Qui rennuens ait, "Scio, fili mi; scio. Et iste quidem erit
in populos et multiplicabitur, sed frater eius iunior maior
illo erit, et semen illius crescet in gentes."

20 Benedixitque eis in ipso tempore, dicens, "In te benedi-
cetur Israhel, atque dicetur, 'Faciat tibi Deus sicut Ephraim
et sicut Manasse.'" Constituitque Ephraim ante Manassen.

21 Et ait ad Ioseph, filium suum, "En: ego morior, et erit
Deus vobiscum reducetque vos ad terram patrum vestrorum. 22 Do tibi partem unam extra fratres tuos quam tuli de
manu Amorrei in gladio et arcu meo."

name be called upon them and the names of my fathers Abraham and Isaac, and may they grow into a multitude upon the earth."

17 And Joseph, seeing that his father had put his right hand upon the head of Ephraim, *was much displeased,* and taking his father's hand he tried to lift it from Ephraim's head and to remove it to the head of Manasseh. 18 And he said to his father, "It *should not be so, my father,* for this is the firstborn. Put thy right hand upon his head."

19 But he refusing, said, "I know, my son; I know. And this also shall become peoples and shall be multiplied, but this younger brother shall be greater than he, and his seed shall grow into nations." 20 And he blessed them at that time, saying, "In thee shall Israel be blessed, and it shall be said, 'God do to thee as to Ephraim and as to Manasseh.'" And he set Ephraim before Manasseh.

21 And he said to Joseph, his son, "Behold: I die, and God will be with you and will bring you back into the land of your fathers. 22 I give thee a portion above thy brethren which I took out of the hand of the Amorite with my sword and bow."

Caput 49

Vocavit autem Iacob filios suos et ait eis, "Congregamini ut adnuntiem quae ventura sunt vobis diebus novissimis. 2 Congregamini, et audite, filii Iacob; audite Israhel, patrem vestrum.

3 "Ruben, primogenitus meus, tu fortitudo mea et principium doloris mei, prior in donis, maior imperio. 4 Effusus es sicut aqua. Non crescas, quia ascendisti cubile patris tui et maculasti stratum eius.

5 "Symeon et Levi, fratres, vasa iniquitatis, bellantia, 6 in consilio eorum ne veniat anima mea et in coetu illorum non sit gloria mea, quia in furore suo occiderunt virum, et in voluntate sua suffoderunt murum. 7 Maledictus furor eorum quia pertinax et indignatio illorum quia dura. Dividam eos in Iacob et dispergam illos in Israhel.

8 "Iuda, te laudabunt fratres tui. Manus tua in cervicibus inimicorum tuorum; adorabunt te filii patris tui. 9 Catulus leonis Iuda. Ad praedam, fili mi, ascendisti. Requiescens, accubuisti ut leo et quasi leaena; quis suscitabit eum? 10 Non auferetur sceptrum de Iuda et dux de femore eius donec ve-

Chapter 49

Jacob's prophetical blessings of his twelve sons. His death.

And Jacob called his sons and said to them, "Gather yourselves together that I may tell you the things that shall befall you in the last days. 2 Gather yourselves together, and hear, O ye sons of Jacob; hearken to Israel, your father.

3 "Reuben, my firstborn, thou art my strength and the beginning of my sorrow, excelling in gifts, greater in command. 4 Thou art poured out as water. Grow thou not, because thou wentest up to thy father's bed and didst defile his couch.

5 "Simeon and Levi, brethren, vessels of iniquity, waging war, 6 let not my soul go into their counsel nor my glory be in their assembly, because in their fury they slew a man, and in their selfwill they undermined a wall. 7 Cursed be their fury because it was stubborn and their wrath because it was cruel. I will divide them in Jacob and will scatter them in Israel.

8 "Judah, thee shall thy brethren praise. Thy hands shall be on the necks of thy enemies; the sons of thy father shall bow down to thee. 9 Judah is a lion's whelp. To the prey, my son, thou art gone up. Resting, thou hast couched as a lion and as a lioness; who shall rouse him? 10 The sceptre shall not be taken away from Judah nor a ruler from his thigh till he come that is to be sent, and he shall be the expectation of

niat qui mittendus est, et ipse erit expectatio gentium, 11 ligans ad vineam pullum suum et ad vitem, O fili mi, asinam suam; lavabit vino stolam suam et sanguine uvae pallium suum. 12 Pulchriores oculi eius vino, et dentes lacte candidiores.

13 "Zabulon in litore maris habitabit et in statione navium, pertingens usque ad Sidonem.

14 "Isachar asinus fortis accubans inter terminos. 15 Vidit requiem quod esset bona et terram quod optima, et subposuit umerum suum ad portandum factusque est tributis serviens.

16 "Dan iudicabit populum suum sicut et alia tribus Israhel. 17 Fiat Dan coluber in via, cerastes in semita, mordens ungulas equi ut cadat ascensor eius retro.

18 "Salutare tuum expectabo, Domine.

19 "Gad, accinctus, proeliabitur ante eum, et ipse accingetur retrorsum.

20 "Aser, pinguis panis eius, et praebebit delicias regibus.

21 "Nepthalim, cervus emissus et dans eloquia pulchritudinis.

22 "Filius adcrescens Ioseph, filius adcrescens et decorus aspectu. Filiae discurrerunt super murum. 23 Sed exasperaverunt eum et iurgati sunt invideruntque illi habentes iacula. 24 Sedit in forti arcus eius, et dissoluta sunt vincula brachiorum et manuum illius per manus potentis Iacob. Inde pastor egressus est, lapis Israhel. 25 Deus patris tui erit adiutor tuus, et Omnipotens benedicet tibi benedictionibus caeli desuper, benedictionibus abyssi iacentis deorsum, benedictionibus uberum et vulvae. 26 Benedictiones patris tui confortatae sunt benedictionibus patrum eius. Donec veniret

nations, 11 tying his foal to the vineyard and his ass, O my son, to the vine; he shall wash his robe in wine and his garment in the blood of the grape. 12 His eyes are more beautiful than wine, and his teeth whiter than milk.

13 "Zebulun shall dwell on the sea-shore and in the road of ships, reaching as far as Sidon.

14 "Issachar shall be a strong ass lying down between the borders. 15 He saw rest that it was good and the land that it was excellent, and he bowed his shoulder to carry and became a servant under tribute.

16 "Dan shall judge his people like another tribe in Israel. 17 Let Dan be a snake in the way, a serpent in the path, that biteth the horse's heels that his rider may fall backward.

18 "I will look for thy salvation, O Lord.

19 "Gad, being girded, shall fight before him, and he himself shall be girded backward.

20 "Asher, his bread shall be fat, and he shall yield dainties to kings.

21 "Naphtali, a hart let loose and giving words of beauty.

22 "Joseph is a growing son, a growing son and comely to behold. The daughters run to and fro upon the wall. 23 But they that held darts provoked him and quarrelled with him and envied him. 24 His bow rested upon the strong, and the bands of his arms and his hands were loosed by the hands of the mighty one of Jacob. Thence he came forth a pastor, the stone of Israel. 25 The God of thy father shall be thy helper, and the Almighty shall bless thee with the blessings of heaven above, with the blessings of the deep that lieth beneath, with the blessings of the breasts and of the womb. 26 The blessings of thy father are strengthened with the blessings of his fathers. Until the desire of the everlasting

desiderium collium aeternorum, fiant in capite Ioseph et in vertice Nazarei inter fratres suos.

27 "Beniamin, lupus rapax, mane comedet praedam et vespere dividet spolia."

28 Omnes hii in tribubus Israhel duodecim. Haec locutus est eis pater suus, benedixitque singulis benedictionibus propriis. 29 Et praecepit eis, dicens, "Ego congregor ad populum meum. Sepelite me cum patribus meis in spelunca duplici quae est in agro Ephron, Hetthei, 30 contra Mambre in terra Chanaan, quam emit Abraham cum agro ab Ephron, Hettheo, in possessionem sepulchri. 31 Ibi sepelierunt eum et Sarram, uxorem eius. Ibi sepultus est Isaac cum Rebecca, coniuge. Ibi et Lia condita iacet."

32 Finitisque mandatis quibus filios instruebat, collegit pedes suos super lectulum et obiit, adpositusque est ad populum suum.

Caput 50

Quod cernens Ioseph, ruit super faciem patris, flens et deosculans eum. 2 Praecepitque servis suis, medicis, ut aromatibus condirent patrem. 3 Quibus iussa explentibus, trans-

hills should come, may they be upon the head of Joseph and upon the crown of the Nazirite among his brethren.

27 "Benjamin, a ravenous wolf, in the morning shall eat the prey and in the evening shall divide the spoil."

28 All these are the twelve tribes of Israel. These things their father spoke to them, and he blessed every one with their proper blessings. 29 And he charged them, saying, "I am now going to be gathered to my people. Bury me with my fathers in the double cave which is in the field of Ephron, the Hittite, 30 over against Mamre in the land of Canaan, which Abraham bought together with the field of Ephron, the Hittite, for a possession to bury in. 31 There they buried him and Sarah, his wife. There was Isaac buried with Rebekah, his wife. There also Leah doth lie buried."

32 And when he had ended the commandments wherewith he instructed his sons, he drew up his feet upon the bed and died, and he was gathered to his people.

Chapter 50

The mourning for Jacob, and his interment. Joseph's kindness towards his brethren. His death.

And when Joseph saw this, he fell upon his father's face, weeping and kissing him. 2 And he commanded his servants, the physicians, to *embalm* his father. 3 And while they were

ierunt quadraginta dies, iste quippe mos erat cadaverum conditorum, flevitque eum Aegyptus septuaginta diebus. 4 Et expleto planctus tempore, locutus est Ioseph ad familiam Pharaonis, "Si inveni gratiam in conspectu vestro, loquimini in auribus Pharaonis, 5 eo quod pater meus adiuraverit me, dicens, 'En: morior. In sepulchro meo quod fodi mihi in terra Chanaan sepelies me.' Ascendam igitur et sepeliam patrem meum ac revertar."

6 Dixitque ei Pharao, "Ascende, et sepeli patrem tuum sicut adiuratus es." 7 Quo ascendente, ierunt cum eo omnes senes domus Pharaonis cunctique maiores natu terrae Aegypti, 8 domus Ioseph cum fratribus suis, absque parvulis et gregibus atque armentis, quae dereliquerant in terra Gessen. 9 Habuit quoque in comitatu currus et equites, et facta est turba non modica. 10 Veneruntque ad aream Atad, quae sita est trans Iordanem, ubi celebrantes exequias planctu magno atque vehementi, impleverunt septem dies.

11 Quod cum vidissent habitatores terrae Chanaan, dixerunt, "Planctus magnus est iste Aegyptiis." Et idcirco, vocatum est nomen loci illius Planctus Aegypti. 12 Fecerunt ergo filii Iacob sicut praeceperat eis. 13 Et portantes eum in terram Chanaan, sepelierunt in spelunca duplici quam emerat Abraham cum agro in possessionem sepulchri, ab Ephron, Hettheo, contra faciem Mambre. 14 Reversusque est Ioseph in Aegyptum cum fratribus suis et omni comitatu sepulto patre.

15 Quo mortuo, timentes fratres eius et mutuo conlo-

fulfilling his commands, there passed forty days, for this was the manner with bodies that were embalmed, and Egypt mourned for him seventy days. 4 And the time of the mourning being expired, Joseph spoke to the family of Pharaoh, "If I have found favour in your sight, speak in the ears of Pharaoh, 5 for my father made me swear to him, saying, 'Behold: I die. Thou shalt bury me in my sepulchre which I have digged for myself in the land of Canaan.' So I will go up and bury my father and return."

6 And Pharaoh said to him, "Go up, and bury thy father according as he made thee swear." 7 So he went up, and there went with him all the ancients of Pharaoh's house and all the elders of the land of Egypt 8 and the house of Joseph with his brethren, except their children and their flocks and herds, which they left in the land of Goshen. 9 He had also in his train chariots and horsemen, and *it was a great company.* 10 And they came to the threshingfloor of Atad, which is situated beyond the Jordan, where celebrating the exequies with a great and vehement lamentation, they spent full seven days.

11 And when the inhabitants of Canaan saw this, they said, "This is a great mourning to the Egyptians." And therefore, the name of that place was called the Mourning of Egypt. 12 So the sons of Jacob did as he had commanded them. 13 And carrying him into the land of Canaan, they buried him in the double cave which Abraham had bought together with the field for a possession of a burying place, of Ephron, the Hittite, over against Mamre. 14 And Joseph returned into Egypt with his brethren and all that were in his company after he had buried his father.

15 Now he being dead, his brethren were afraid and talked

quentes, "Ne forte memor sit iniuriae quam passus est et reddat nobis malum omne quod fecimus," 16 mandaverunt ei, dicentes, "Pater tuus praecepit nobis antequam moreretur 17 ut haec tibi verbis illius diceremus: 'Obsecro ut obliviscaris sceleris fratrum tuorum et peccati atque malitiae quam exercuerunt in te.' Nos quoque oramus ut servis Dei patris tui dimittas iniquitatem hanc." Quibus auditis, flevit Ioseph. 18 Veneruntque ad eum fratres sui, et proni adorantes in terram dixerunt, "Servi tui sumus."

19 Quibus ille respondit, "Nolite timere. Num Dei possumus resistere voluntati? 20 Vos cogitastis de me malum, sed Deus vertit illud in bonum ut exaltaret me sicut inpraesentiarum cernitis et salvos faceret multos populos. 21 Nolite metuere. Ego pascam vos et parvulos vestros." Consolatusque est eos et blande ac leniter est locutus.

22 Et habitavit in Aegypto cum omni domo patris sui vixitque centum decem annis. Et vidit Ephraim filios usque ad tertiam generationem. Filii quoque Machir, filii Manasse, nati sunt in genibus Ioseph, 23 quibus transactis locutus est fratribus suis, "Post mortem meam Deus visitabit vos et ascendere faciet de terra ista ad terram quam iuravit Abraham, Isaac et Iacob." 24 Cumque adiurasset eos atque dixisset, "Deus visitabit vos. Asportate vobiscum ossa mea de loco isto," 25 mortuus est expletis centum decem vitae suae annis. Et conditus aromatibus, repositus est in loculo in Aegypto.

one with another, "Lest perhaps he should remember the wrong he suffered and requite us all the evil that we did to him," 16 and they sent a message to him, saying, "Thy father commanded us before he died 17 that we should say thus much to thee *from him:* 'I beseech thee to forget the wickedness of thy brethren and the sin and malice they practiced against thee.' We also pray thee to forgive the servants of the God of thy father this wickedness." And when Joseph heard this, he wept. 18 And his brethren came to him, and worshipping prostrate on the ground they said, "We are thy servants."

19 And he answered them, "Fear not. Can we resist the will of God? 20 You thought evil against me, but God turned it into good that he might exalt me as at present you see and might save many people. 21 Fear not. I will feed you and your children." And he comforted them and spoke gently and mildly.

22 And he dwelt in Egypt with all his father's house and lived a hundred and ten years. And he saw the children of Ephraim to the third generation. The children also of Machir, the son of Manasseh, were born on Joseph's knees, 23 after which he told his brethren, "God will visit you after my death and will make you go up out of this land to the land which he swore to Abraham, Isaac and Jacob." 24 And he made them swear to him, saying, "God will visit you. Carry my bones with you out of this place." 25 And he died being a hundred and ten years old. And being *embalmed,* he was laid in a coffin in Egypt.

EXODUS

Caput 1

Haec sunt nomina filiorum Israhel qui ingressi sunt Aegyptum cum Iacob—singuli cum domibus suis introierunt—2 Ruben, Symeon, Levi, Iuda, 3 Isachar, Zabulon et Beniamin, 4 Dan et Nepthalim, Gad et Aser. 5 Erant igitur omnes animae qui egressi sunt de femore Iacob septuaginta, Ioseph autem in Aegypto erat.

6 Quo mortuo et universis fratribus eius omnique cognatione illa, 7 filii Israhel creverunt et quasi germinantes multiplicati sunt, ac roborati nimis impleverunt terram. 8 Surrexit interea rex novus super Aegyptum qui ignorabat Ioseph, 9 et ait ad populum suum, "Ecce: populus filiorum Israhel multus et fortior nobis. 10 Venite; sapienter opprimamus eum ne forte multiplicetur, et si ingruerit contra nos bellum, addatur inimicis nostris expugnatisque nobis egrediatur e terra."

11 Praeposuit itaque eis magistros operum ut adfligerent eos oneribus, aedificaveruntque urbes tabernaculorum Pharaoni: Phiton et Ramesses. 12 Quantoque opprimebant eos,

Chapter 1

The Israelites are multiplied in Egypt. They are oppressed by a new king who commandeth all their male children to be killed.

These are the names of the children of Israel that went into Egypt with Jacob—they went in, every man with his household—2 Reuben, Simeon, Levi, Judah, 3 Issachar, Zebulun and Benjamin, 4 Dan and Naphtali, Gad and Asher. 5 And all the souls that came out of Jacob's thigh were seventy, but Joseph was in Egypt.

6 After he was dead and all his brethren and all that generation, 7 the children of Israel increased and *sprung up into multitudes,* and growing exceedingly strong they filled the land. 8 In the mean time there arose a new king over Egypt that knew not Joseph, 9 and he said to his people, "Behold: the people of the children of Israel are numerous and stronger than we. 10 Come; let us wisely oppress them lest they multiply and, if any war shall rise against us, join with our enemies and having overcome us depart out of the land."

11 Therefore he set over them masters of the works to afflict them with burdens, and they built for Pharaoh cities of tabernacles: Pithom and Rameses. 12 But the more they oppressed them, the more they were multiplied and in-

tanto magis multiplicabantur et crescebant, 13 oderantque filios Israhel Aegyptii et adfligebant inludentes eis. 14 Atque ad amaritudinem perducebant vitam eorum operibus duris luti et lateris omnique famulatu quo in terrae operibus premebantur. 15 Dixit autem rex Aegypti obsetricibus Hebraeorum, quarum una vocabatur Sephra, altera, Phua, 16 praecipiens eis, "Quando obsetricabitis Hebraeas et partus tempus advenerit, si masculus fuerit, interficite illum, si femina, reservate."

17 Timuerunt autem obsetrices Deum et non fecerunt iuxta praeceptum regis Aegypti sed conservabant mares. 18 Quibus ad se accersitis rex ait, "Quidnam est hoc quod facere voluistis ut pueros servaretis?"

19 Quae responderunt, "Non sunt Hebraeae sicut Aegyptiae mulieres, ipsae enim obsetricandi habent scientiam, et priusquam veniamus ad eas pariunt." 20 Bene ergo fecit Deus obsetricibus, et crevit populus confortatusque est nimis. 21 Et quia timuerunt obsetrices Deum, aedificavit illis domos.

22 Praecepit ergo Pharao omni populo suo, dicens, "Quicquid masculini sexus natum fuerit, in flumen proicite; quicquid feminei, reservate."

creased, 13 and the Egyptians hated the children of Israel and afflicted them and mocked them. 14 And they made their life bitter with hard works in clay and brick and with all manner of service wherewith they were overcharged in the works of the earth. 15 And the king of Egypt spoke to the midwives of the Hebrews, of whom one was called Shiphrah, the other, Puah, 16 commanding them, "When you shall do the office of midwives to the Hebrew women and the time of delivery is come, if it be a man-child, kill it, if a woman, keep it alive."

17 But the midwives feared God and did not do as the king of Egypt had commanded but saved the men-children. 18 And the king called for them and said, "What is that you meant to do that you would save the men-children?"

19 They answered, "The Hebrew women are not as the Egyptian women, for they themselves are skillful in the office of a midwife, and they are delivered before we come to them." 20 Therefore God dealt well with the midwives, and the people multiplied and grew exceedingly strong. 21 And because the midwives feared God, he built them houses.

22 Pharaoh therefore charged all his people, saying, "Whatsoever shall be born of the male sex, *ye shall cast* into the river; whatsoever of the female, *ye shall save alive.*"

Caput 2

Egressus est post haec vir de domo Levi et accepit uxorem stirpis suae. 2 Quae concepit et peperit filium et, videns eum elegantem, abscondit tribus mensibus. 3 Cumque iam celare non posset, sumpsit fiscellam scirpeam et linivit eam bitumine ac pice posuitque intus infantulum et exposuit eum in carecto ripae fluminis, 4 stante procul sorore eius et considerante eventum rei. 5 Ecce autem: descendebat filia Pharaonis ut lavaretur in flumine, et puellae eius gradiebantur per crepidinem alvei. Quae cum vidisset fiscellam in papyrione, misit unam e famulis suis, et adlatam, 6 aperiens cernensque in ea parvulum vagientem, miserta eius ait, "De infantibus Hebraeorum est hic."

7 Cui soror pueri, "Vis," inquit, "ut vadam et vocem tibi Hebraeam mulierem quae nutrire possit infantulum?"

8 Respondit, "Vade."

Perrexit puella et vocavit matrem eius, 9 ad quam locuta filia Pharaonis, "Accipe," ait, "puerum istum, et nutri mihi; ego tibi dabo mercedem tuam." Suscepit mulier et nutrivit

Chapter 2

Moses is born and exposed on the bank of the river, where he is taken up by the daughter of Pharaoh and adopted for her son. He killeth an Egyptian and fleeth into Midian, where he marrieth a wife.

After this, there went a man of the house of Levi and took a wife of his own kindred. 2 And she conceived and bore a son and, seeing him a goodly child, hid him three months. 3 And when she could hide him no longer, she took a basket made of bulrushes and daubed it with slime and pitch and put the little babe therein and laid him in the sedges by the river's brink, 4 his sister standing afar off and taking notice *what would be done.* 5 And behold: the daughter of Pharaoh came down to wash herself in the river, and her maids walked by the river's brink. And when she saw the basket in the sedges, she sent one of her maids *for it,* and when it was brought, 6 she opened it, and, seeing within it an infant crying, having compassion on it, she said, "This is one of the babes of the Hebrews."

7 And the child's sister said to her, "Shall I go and call to thee a Hebrew woman to nurse the babe?"

8 She answered, "Go."

The maid went and called her mother, 9 and Pharaoh's daughter said to her, "Take this child, and nurse him for me; I will give thee thy wages." The woman took and nursed the

puerum, adultumque tradidit filiae Pharaonis. 10 Quem illa adoptavit in locum filii vocavitque nomen eius Mosi, dicens, "Quia de aqua tuli eum."

11 In diebus illis postquam creverat Moses, egressus est ad fratres suos viditque adflictionem eorum et virum Aegyptium percutientem quendam de Hebraeis, fratribus suis. 12 Cumque circumspexisset huc atque illuc et nullum adesse vidisset, percussum Aegyptium abscondit sabulo. 13 Et egressus die altero, conspexit duos Hebraeos rixantes, dixitque ei qui faciebat iniuriam, "Quare percutis proximum tuum?"

14 Qui respondit, "Quis constituit te principem et iudicem super nos? Num occidere me tu vis sicut heri occidisti Aegyptium?"

Timuit Moses et ait, "Quomodo palam factum est verbum istud?" 15 Audivitque Pharao sermonem hunc et quaerebat occidere Mosen, qui fugiens de conspectu eius moratus est in terra Madian, et sedit iuxta puteum.

16 Erant autem sacerdoti Madian septem filiae quae venerunt ad hauriendam aquam et, impletis canalibus, adaquare cupiebant greges patris sui. 17 Supervenere pastores et eiecerunt eas, surrexitque Moses et, defensis puellis, adaquavit oves earum. 18 Quae cum revertissent ad Raguhel, patrem suum, dixit ad eas, "Cur velocius venistis solito?"

19 Responderunt, "Vir Aegyptius liberavit nos de manu pastorum, insuper et hausit aquam nobiscum potumque dedit ovibus."

20 At ille, "Ubi est?" inquit, "Quare dimisistis hominem? Vocate eum ut comedat panem."

child, and when he was grown up, she delivered him to Pharaoh's daughter. 10 And she adopted him for a son and called *him* Moses, saying, "Because I took him out of the water."

11 In those days after Moses was grown up, he went out to his brethren and saw their affliction and an Egyptian striking one of the Hebrews, his brethren. 12 And when he had looked about this way and that way and saw no one there, he slew the Egyptian and hid him in the sand. 13 And going out the next day, he saw two Hebrews quarrelling, and he said to him that did the wrong, "Why strikest thou thy neighbour?"

14 But he answered, "Who hath appointed thee prince and judge over us? Wilt thou kill me as thou didst yesterday kill the Egyptian?"

Moses feared and said, "How is this come *to be known?*" 15 And Pharaoh heard of this word and sought to kill Moses, but he fled from his sight and abode in the land of Midian, and he sat down by a well.

16 And the priest of Midian had seven daughters who came to draw water and, when the troughs were filled, desired to water their father's flocks. 17 And the shepherds came and drove them away, and Moses arose and, defending the maids, watered their sheep. 18 And when they returned to Reuel, their father, he said to them, "Why are ye come sooner than usual?"

19 They answered, "A man of Egypt delivered us from the hands of the shepherds, and he drew water also with us and gave the sheep to drink."

20 But he said, "Where is he? Why have you let the man go? Call him that he may eat bread."

21 Iuravit ergo Moses quod habitaret cum eo. Accepitque Seffram, filiam eius, uxorem, 22 quae peperit ei filium, quem vocavit Gersam, dicens, "Advena fui in terra aliena." Alterum vero peperit, quem vocavit Eliezer, dicens, "Deus enim patris mei, adiutor meus, eripuit me de manu Pharaonis."

23 Post multum vero temporis, mortuus est rex Aegypti, et ingemescentes filii Israhel propter opera vociferati sunt, ascenditque clamor eorum ad Deum ab operibus. 24 Et audivit gemitum eorum ac recordatus foederis quod pepigit cum Abraham, Isaac et Iacob. 25 Et respexit Dominus filios Israhel, et cognovit eos.

Caput 3

Moses autem pascebat oves Iethro, soceri sui, sacerdotis Madian, cumque minasset gregem ad interiora deserti, venit ad montem Dei, Horeb. 2 Apparuitque ei Dominus in flamma ignis de medio rubi, et videbat quod rubus arderet et non conbureretur. 3 Dixit ergo Moses, "Vadam et videbo visionem hanc magnam, quare non conburatur rubus."

21 And Moses swore that he would dwell with him. And he took Zipporah, his daughter, to wife, 22 and she bore him a son, whom he called Gershom, saying, "I have been a stranger in a foreign country." And she bore another, whom he called Eliezer, saying, "For the God of my father, my helper, hath delivered me out of the hand of Pharaoh."

23 Now after a long time, the king of Egypt died, and the children of Israel, groaning, cried out because of the works, and their cry went up unto God from the works. 24 And he heard their groaning and remembered the covenant which he made with Abraham, Isaac and Jacob. 25 And the Lord looked upon the children of Israel, and he knew them.

Chapter 3

God appeareth to Moses in a bush and sendeth him to deliver Israel.

Now Moses fed the sheep of Jethro, his father-in-law, the priest of Midian, and he drove the flock to the inner parts of the desert and came to the mountain of God, Horeb. 2 And the Lord appeared to him in a flame of fire out of the midst of a bush, and he saw that the bush was on fire and was not burnt. 3 And Moses said, "I will go and see this great sight, why the bush is not burnt."

4 Cernens autem Dominus quod pergeret ad videndum, vocavit eum de medio rubi et ait, "Moses, Moses."

Qui respondit, "Adsum."

5 At ille, "Ne adpropies," inquit, "huc. Solve calciamentum de pedibus tuis, locus enim in quo stas terra sancta est." 6 Et ait, "Ego sum Deus patris tui, Deus Abraham, Deus Isaac et Deus Iacob." Abscondit Moses faciem suam, non enim audebat aspicere contra Deum. 7 Cui ait Dominus, "Vidi adflictionem populi mei in Aegypto, et clamorem eius audivi propter duritiam eorum qui praesunt operibus. 8 Et, sciens dolorem eius, descendi ut liberem eum de manibus Aegyptiorum et educam de terra illa in terram bonam et spatiosam, in terram quae fluit lacte et melle, ad loca Chananei et Hetthei et Amorrei et Ferezei et Evei et Iebusei. 9 Clamor ergo filiorum Israhel venit ad me, vidique adflictionem eorum qua ab Aegyptiis opprimuntur. 10 Sed veni, et mittam te ad Pharaonem, ut educas populum meum, filios Israhel, de Aegypto."

11 Dixitque Moses ad Deum, "Quis ego sum ut vadam ad Pharaonem et educam filios Israhel de Aegypto?"

12 Qui dixit ei, "Ero tecum, et hoc habebis signum quod miserim te: cum eduxeris populum meum de Aegypto, immolabis Deo super montem istum."

13 Ait Moses ad Deum, "Ecce: ego vadam ad filios Israhel et dicam eis, 'Deus patrum vestrorum misit me ad vos.' Si dixerint mihi, 'Quod est nomen eius?' quid dicam eis?"

4 And when the Lord saw that he went forward to see, he called to him out of the midst of the bush and said, "Moses, Moses."

And he answered, "Here I am."

5 And he said, "Come not nigh hither. Put off the shoes from thy feet, for the place whereon thou standest is holy ground." 6 And he said, "I am the God of thy father, the God of Abraham, the God of Isaac and the God of Jacob." Moses hid his face, for he durst not look at God. 7 And the Lord said to him, "I have seen the affliction of my people in Egypt, and I have heard their cry because of the rigour of them that are over the works. 8 And, knowing their sorrow, I am come down to deliver them out of the hands of the Egyptians and to bring them out of that land into a good and spacious land, into a land that floweth with milk and honey, to the places of the Canaanite and Hittite and Amorite and Perizzite and Hivite and Jebusite, 9 *for* the cry of the children of Israel is come unto me, and I have seen their affliction wherewith they are oppressed by the Egyptians. 10 But come, and I will send thee to Pharaoh, that thou mayst bring forth my people, the children of Israel, out of Egypt."

11 And Moses said to God, "Who am I that I should go to Pharaoh and should bring forth the children of Israel out of Egypt?"

12 And he said to him, "I will be with thee, and this thou shalt have for a sign that I have sent thee: when thou shalt have brought my people out of Egypt, thou shalt offer sacrifice to God upon this mountain."

13 Moses said to God, "Lo: I shall go to the children of Israel and say to them, 'The God of your fathers hath sent me to you.' If they should say to me, 'What is his name?' what shall I say to them?"

14 Dixit Deus ad Mosen, "Ego sum qui sum." Ait, "Sic dices filiis Israhel: 'Qui est misit me ad vos.'" 15 Dixitque iterum Deus ad Mosen, "Haec dices filiis Israhel: 'Dominus, Deus patrum vestrorum, Deus Abraham, Deus Isaac et Deus Iacob, misit me ad vos.' Hoc nomen mihi est in aeternum, et hoc memoriale meum in generationem et generatione.

16 "Vade, et congrega seniores Israhel, et dices ad eos, 'Dominus, Deus patrum vestrorum apparuit mihi, Deus Abraham, Deus Isaac et Deus Iacob, dicens, "Visitans visitavi vos, et vidi omnia quae acciderunt vobis in Aegypto, 17 et dixi ut educam vos de adflictione Aegypti, in terram Chananei et Hetthei et Amorrei et Ferezei et Evei et Iebusei, ad terram fluentem lacte et melle."' 18 Et audient vocem tuam, ingredierisque, tu et seniores Israhel, ad regem Aegypti, et dices ad eum, 'Dominus, Deus Hebraeorum, vocavit nos; ibimus viam trium dierum in solitudinem ut immolemus Domino, Deo nostro.' 19 Sed ego scio quod non dimittet vos rex Aegypti ut eatis nisi per manum validam, 20 extendam enim manum meam et percutiam Aegyptum in cunctis mirabilibus meis quae facturus sum in medio eorum. Post haec dimittet vos. 21 Daboque gratiam populo huic coram Aegyptiis.

"Et cum egrediemini, non exibitis vacui, 22 sed postulabit mulier a vicina sua et ab hospita sua vasa argentea et aurea ac vestes, ponetisque eas super filios et filias vestras et spoliabitis Aegyptum."

14 God said to Moses, "I am who I am." He said, "Thus shalt thou say to the children of Israel: 'He who is hath sent me to you.'" 15 And God said again to Moses, "Thus shalt thou say to the children of Israel: 'The Lord, God of your fathers, the God of Abraham, the God of Isaac and the God of Jacob, hath sent me to you.' This is my name for ever, and this is my memorial *unto all generations.*

16 "Go, and gather together the ancients of Israel, and thou shalt say to them, 'The Lord, God of your fathers, the God of Abraham, the God of Isaac and the God of Jacob, hath appeared to me, saying, "Visiting I have visited you, and I have seen all that hath befallen you in Egypt. 17 And I have said the word to bring you forth out of the affliction of Egypt, into the land of the Canaanite and Hittite and Amorite and Perizzite and Hivite and Jebusite, to a land that floweth with milk and honey."' 18 And they shall hear thy voice, and thou shalt go in, thou and the ancients of Israel, to the king of Egypt, and thou shalt say to him, 'The Lord, God of the Hebrews, hath called us; we will go three days' journey into the wilderness to sacrifice unto the Lord, our God.' 19 But I know that the king of Egypt will not *let you go* but by a mighty hand, 20 for I will stretch forth my hand and will strike Egypt with all my wonders which I will do in the midst of them. After these he will let you go. 21 And I will give favour to this people in the sight of the Egyptians.

"And when you go forth, you shall not depart empty, 22 but every woman shall ask of her neighbour and of her that is in her house vessels of silver and of gold and raiment, and you shall put them on your sons and daughters and shall spoil Egypt."

Caput 4

Respondens Moses ait, "Non credent mihi neque audient vocem meam, sed dicent, 'Non apparuit tibi Dominus.'"

2 Dixit ergo ad eum, "Quid est quod tenes in manu tua?" Respondit, "Virga."

3 Dixitque Dominus, "Proice eam in terram." Proiecit, et versa est in colubrum ita ut fugeret Moses. 4 Dixitque Dominus, "Extende manum tuam, et adprehende caudam eius." Extendit et tenuit, versaque est in virgam. 5 "Ut credant," inquit, "quod apparuerit tibi Dominus, Deus patrum suorum, Deus Abraham, Deus Isaac et Deus Iacob."

6 Dixitque Dominus rursum, "Mitte manum in sinum tuum." Quam cum misisset in sinum, protulit leprosam instar nivis. 7 "Retrahe," ait, "manum in sinum tuum." Retraxit et protulit iterum, et erat similis carni reliquae. 8 "Si non crediderint," inquit, "tibi neque audierint sermonem signi prioris, credent verbo signi sequentis. 9 Quod si nec duobus quidem his signis crediderint neque audierint vocem tuam,

Chapter 4

Moses is empowered to confirm his mission with miracles.
His brother Aaron is appointed to assist him.

M oses answered and said, "They will not believe me nor
hear my voice, but they will say, 'The Lord hath not appeared
to thee.'"

2 Then he said to him, "What is that thou holdest in thy
hand?"

He answered, "A rod."

3 And the Lord said, "Cast it down upon the ground." He
cast it down, and it was turned into a serpent so that Moses
fled from it. 4 And the Lord said, "Put out thy hand, and take
it *by the tail.*" He put forth his hand and took hold of it, and
it was turned into a rod. 5 "That they may believe," saith he,
"that the Lord, God of their fathers, the God of Abraham,
the God of Isaac and the God of Jacob, hath appeared to
thee."

6 And the Lord said again, "Put thy hand into thy bosom."
And when he had put it into his bosom, he brought it forth
leprous as snow. 7 And he said, "Put back thy hand into thy
bosom." He put it back and brought it out again, and it was
like the other flesh. 8 "If they will not believe thee," saith he,
"nor hear the voice of the former sign, they will believe the
word of the latter sign. 9 But if they will not even believe
these two signs nor hear thy voice, take of the river water,

sume aquam fluminis, et effunde eam super aridam, et quicquid hauseris de fluvio vertetur in sanguinem."

10 Ait Moses, "Obsecro, Domine. Non sum eloquens ab
heri et nudius tertius, et ex quo locutus es ad servum tuum,
inpeditioris et tardioris linguae sum."

11 Dixit Dominus ad eum, "Quis fecit os hominis? Aut
quis fabricatus est mutum et surdum, videntem et caecum?
Nonne ego? 12 Perge, igitur, et ego ero in ore tuo, doceboque
te quid loquaris."

13 At ille, "Obsecro," inquit, "Domine, mitte quem missurus es."

14 Iratus Dominus in Mosen ait, "Aaron, frater tuus, Levites; scio quod eloquens sit. Ecce: ipse egreditur in occursum
tuum vidensque te laetabitur corde. 15 Loquere ad eum, et
pone verba mea in ore eius, et ego ero in ore tuo et in ore illius et ostendam vobis quid agere debeatis. 16 Ipse loquetur
pro te ad populum et erit os tuum, tu autem eris ei in his
quae ad Deum pertinent. 17 Virgam quoque hanc sume in
manu tua in qua facturus es signa."

18 Abiit Moses et reversus est ad Iethro, socerum suum,
dixitque ei, "Vadam et revertar ad fratres meos in Aegyptum
ut videam si adhuc vivant."

Cui ait Iethro, "Vade in pace."

19 Dixit ergo Dominus ad Mosen in Madian, "Vade, et
revertere in Aegyptum, mortui sunt enim omnes qui quae-
rebant animam tuam." 20 Tulit ergo Moses uxorem et filios
suos et inposuit eos super asinum reversusque est in Aegyptum, portans virgam Dei in manu sua.

and pour it out upon the dry land, and whatsoever thou drawest out of the river shall be turned into blood."

10 Moses said, "I beseech thee, Lord. I am not eloquent from yesterday and the day before, and since thou hast spoken to thy servant, I have more impediment and slowness of tongue."

11 The Lord said to him, "Who made man's mouth? Or who made the dumb and the deaf, the seeing and the blind? Did not I? 12 Go, therefore, and I will be in thy mouth, and I will teach thee what thou shalt speak."

13 But he said, "I beseech thee, Lord, send whom thou wilt send."

14 The Lord being angry at Moses said, "Aaron, the Levite, is thy brother; I know that he is eloquent. Behold: he cometh forth to meet thee and seeing thee shall be glad at heart. 15 Speak to him, and put my words in his mouth, and I will be in thy mouth and in his mouth and will shew you what you must do. 16 He shall speak in thy stead to the people and shall be thy mouth, but thou shalt be to him in those things that pertain to God. 17 And take this rod in thy hand wherewith thou shalt do the signs."

18 Moses went his way and returned to Jethro, his father-in-law, and said to him, "I will go and return to my brethren into Egypt that I may see if they be yet alive."

And Jethro said to him, "Go in peace."

19 And the Lord said to Moses in Midian, "Go, and return into Egypt, for they are all dead that sought thy life." 20 Moses therefore took his wife and his sons and set them upon an ass and returned into Egypt, carrying the rod of God in his hand.

21 Dixitque ei Dominus revertenti in Aegyptum, "Vide ut omnia ostenta quae posui in manu tua facias coram Pharaone. Ego indurabo cor eius, et non dimittet populum. 22 Dicesque ad eum, 'Haec dicit Dominus: "Filius meus primogenitus Israhel. 23 Dixi tibi, 'Dimitte filium meum ut serviat mihi,' et noluisti dimittere eum. Ecce! Ego interficiam filium tuum primogenitum.""""

24 Cumque esset in itinere, in diversorio, occurrit ei Dominus et volebat occidere eum. 25 Tulit ilico Seffora acutissimam petram et circumcidit praeputium filii sui tetigitque pedes eius et ait, "Sponsus sanguinum tu mihi es."

26 Et dimisit eum postquam dixerat, "Sponsus sanguinum tu mihi es," ob circumcisionem. 27 Dixit autem Dominus ad Aaron, "Vade in occursum Mosi in desertum." Qui perrexit ei obviam in montem Dei et osculatus est eum. 28 Narravitque Moses Aaron omnia verba Domini quibus miserat eum et signa quae mandaverat. 29 Veneruntque simul, et congregaverunt cunctos seniores filiorum Israhel. 30 Locutusque est Aaron omnia verba quae dixerat Dominus ad Mosen, et fecit signa coram populo, 31 et credidit populus. Audieruntque quod visitasset Dominus filios Israhel et quod respexisset adflictionem eorum. Et proni adoraverunt.

21 And the Lord said to him as he was returning into Egypt, "See that thou do all the wonders before Pharaoh which I have put in thy hand. I shall harden his heart, and he will not let the people go. 22 And thou shalt say to him, 'Thus saith the Lord: "Israel is my son, *my firstborn.* 23 I have said to thee, 'Let my son go that he may serve me,' and thou wouldst not let him go. Behold! I will kill thy son, *thy first-born.*"'"

24 And when he was in his journey, in the inn, the Lord met him and would have killed him. 25 Immediately, Zipporah took a very sharp stone and circumcised the foreskin of her son and touched his feet and said, "A bloody spouse art thou to me."

26 And he let him go after she had said, "A bloody spouse art thou to me," because of the circumcision. 27 And the Lord said to Aaron, "Go into the desert to meet Moses." And he went forth to meet him in the mountain of God and kissed him. 28 And Moses told Aaron all the words of the Lord by which he had sent him and the signs that he had commanded. 29 And they came together, and they assembled all the ancients of the children of Israel. 30 And Aaron spoke all the words which the Lord had said to Moses, and he wrought the signs before the people, 31 and the people believed. And they heard that the Lord had visited the children of Israel and that he had looked upon their affliction. And *falling down,* they adored.

Caput 5

Post haec, ingressi sunt Moses et Aaron et dixerunt Pharaoni, "Haec dicit Dominus, Deus Israhel: 'Dimitte populum meum ut sacrificet mihi in deserto.'"

2 At ille respondit, "Quis est Dominus ut audiam vocem eius et dimittam Israhel? Nescio Dominum, et Israhel non dimittam."

3 Dixeruntque, "Deus Hebraeorum vocavit nos ut eamus viam trium dierum in solitudinem et sacrificemus Domino, Deo nostro, ne forte accidat nobis pestis aut gladius."

4 Ait ad eos rex Aegypti, "Quare, Moses et Aaron, sollicitatis populum ab operibus suis? Ite ad onera vestra." 5 Dixitque Pharao, "Multus est populus terrae; videtis quod turba succreverit; quanto magis si dederitis eis requiem ab operibus?"

6 Praecepit ergo in die illo praefectis operum et exactoribus populi, dicens, 7 "Nequaquam ultra dabitis paleas populo ad conficiendos lateres sicut prius, sed ipsi vadant et colligant stipulam. 8 Et mensuram laterum quam prius faciebant inponetis super eos, nec minuetis quicquam, va-

Chapter 5

Pharaoh refuseth to let the people go. They are more oppressed.

Afer these things, Moses and Aaron went in and said to Pharaoh, "Thus saith the Lord, God of Israel: 'Let my people go that they may sacrifice to me in the desert.'"

2 But he answered, "Who is the Lord that I should hear his voice and let Israel go? I know not the Lord, neither will I let Israel go."

3 And they said, "The God of the Hebrews hath called us to go three days' journey into the wilderness and to sacrifice to the Lord, our God, lest a pestilence or the sword fall upon us."

4 The king of Egypt said to them, "Why do you, Moses and Aaron, draw off the people from their works? Get you gone to your burdens." 5 And Pharaoh said, "The people of the land is numerous; you see that the multitude is increased; how much more if you give them rest from their works?"

6 Therefore he commanded the same day the overseers of the works and the taskmasters of the people, saying, 7 "You shall give straw no more to the people to make brick as before, but let them go and gather straw. 8 And you shall lay upon them the task of bricks which they did before, neither shall you diminish any thing thereof, for they are idle,

cant enim, et idcirco vociferantur, dicentes, 'Eamus et sacrificemus Deo nostro.' 9 Opprimantur operibus, et expleant ea ut non adquiescant verbis mendacibus."

10 Igitur egressi praefecti operum et exactores ad populum dixerunt, "Sic dicit Pharao: 'Non do vobis paleas. 11 Ite, et colligite sicubi invenire poteritis. Nec minuetur quicquam de opere vestro.'" 12 Dispersusque est populus per omnem terram Aegypti ad colligendas paleas.

13 Praefecti quoque operum instabant, dicentes, "Conplete opus vestrum cotidie ut prius facere solebatis quando dabantur vobis paleae." 14 Flagellatique sunt qui praeerant operibus filiorum Israhel ab exactoribus Pharaonis, dicentibus, "Quare non impletis mensuram laterum sicut prius nec heri nec hodie?"

15 Veneruntque praepositi filiorum Israhel et vociferati sunt ad Pharaonem, dicentes, "Cur ita agis contra servos tuos? 16 Paleae non dantur nobis, et lateres similiter imperantur. En! Famuli tui flagellis caedimur, et iniuste agitur contra populum tuum."

17 Qui ait, "Vacatis otio, et idcirco dicitis, 'Eamus et sacrificemus Domino.' 18 Ite, ergo, et operamini. Paleae non dabuntur vobis, et reddetis consuetum numerum laterum."

19 Videbantque se praepositi filiorum Israhel in malo, eo quod diceretur eis, "Non minuetur quicquam de lateribus per singulos dies." 20 Occurreruntque Mosi et Aaron, qui stabant ex adverso, egredientes a Pharaone.

and therefore they cry, saying, 'Let us go and sacrifice to our God.' 9 Let them be oppressed with works, and let them fulfill them that they may not regard lying words."

10 And the overseers of the works and the taskmasters went out and said to the people, "Thus saith Pharaoh: 'I allow you no straw. 11 Go, and gather it where you can find it. Neither shall any thing of your work be diminished.'" 12 And the people was scattered through all the land of Egypt to gather straw.

13 And the overseers of the works pressed them, saying, "Fulfill your work every day as before you were wont to do when straw was given you." 14 And they that were over the works of the children of Israel were scourged by Pharaoh's taskmasters, saying, "Why have you not made up the task of bricks both yesterday and today as before?"

15 And the officers of the children of Israel came and cried out to Pharaoh, saying, "Why dealest thou so with thy servants? 16 Straw is not given us, and bricks are required of us as before. Behold! We, thy servants, are beaten with whips, and thy people is unjustly dealt withal."

17 And he said, "You are idle, and therefore you say, 'Let us go and sacrifice to the Lord.' 18 Go, therefore, and work. Straw shall not be given you, and you shall deliver the accustomed number of bricks."

19 And the officers of the children of Israel saw that they were in evil case, because it was said to them, "There shall not a whit be diminished of the bricks for every day." 20 And they met Moses and Aaron, who stood over against them as they came out from Pharaoh.

21 Et dixerunt ad eos, "Videat Dominus et iudicet quoniam fetere fecistis odorem nostrum coram Pharao et servis eius, et praebuistis ei gladium ut occideret nos."

22 Reversusque est Moses ad Dominum et ait, "Domine, cur adflixisti populum istum? Quare misisti me? 23 Ex eo enim quo ingressus sum ad Pharaonem ut loquerer in nomine tuo adflixit populum tuum, et non liberasti eos."

Caput 6

Dixitque Dominus ad Mosen, "Nunc videbis quae facturus sum Pharaoni, per manum enim fortem dimittet eos, et in manu robusta eiciet illos de terra sua." 2 Locutusque est Dominus ad Mosen, dicens, "Ego Dominus 3 qui apparui Abraham, Isaac et Iacob in Deo Omnipotente; et nomen meum, Adonai, non indicavi eis. 4 Pepigique cum eis foedus ut darem illis terram Chanaan, terram peregrinationis eorum in qua fuerunt advenae. 5 Ego audivi gemitum filiorum Israhel quo Aegyptii oppresserunt eos, et recordatus sum pacti mei. 6 Ideo dic filiis Israhel, 'Ego Dominus qui educam

21 And they said to them, "The Lord see and judge because you have made our savour to stink before Pharaoh and his servants, and you have given him a sword to kill us."

22 And Moses returned to the Lord and said, "Lord, why hast thou afflicted this people? Wherefore hast thou sent me? 23 For since the time that I went in to Pharaoh to speak in thy name he hath afflicted thy people, and thou hast not delivered them."

Chapter 6

God reneweth his promise. The genealogies of Reuben, Simeon and Levi down to Moses and Aaron.

And the Lord said to Moses, "Now thou shalt see what I will do to Pharaoh, for by a mighty hand shall he let them go, and with a strong hand shall he cast them out of his land." 2 And the Lord spoke to Moses, saying, "I am the Lord 3 that appeared to Abraham, to Isaac and to Jacob by the name of God Almighty; and my name, Adonai, I did not shew them. 4 And I made a covenant with them to give them the land of Canaan, the land of their pilgrimage wherein they were strangers. 5 I have heard the groaning of the children of Israel wherewith the Egyptians have oppressed them, and I have remembered my covenant. 6 Therefore say to the children of Israel, 'I am the Lord who will bring

vos de ergastulo Aegyptiorum et eruam de servitute ac redimam in brachio excelso et iudiciis magnis. 7 Et adsumam vos mihi in populum; et ero vester Deus, scietisque quod ego sim Dominus, Deus vester, qui eduxerim vos de ergastulo Aegyptiorum 8 et induxerim in terram super quam levavi manum meam ut darem eam Abraham, Isaac et Iacob, daboque illam vobis possidendam; ego Dominus.'" 9 Narravit ergo Moses omnia filiis Israhel, qui non adquieverunt ei propter angustiam spiritus et opus durissimum.

10 Locutusque est Dominus ad Mosen, dicens, 11 "Ingredere, et loquere ad Pharao, regem Aegypti, ut dimittat filios Israhel de terra sua."

12 Respondit Moses coram Domino, "Ecce: filii Israhel non me audiunt, et quomodo audiet me Pharao, praesertim cum sim incircumcisus labiis?"

13 Locutusque est Dominus ad Mosen et Aaron, et dedit mandatum ad filios Israhel et ad Pharao, regem Aegypti, ut educerent filios Israhel de terra Aegypti.

14 Isti sunt principes domorum per familias suas.

Filii Ruben, primogeniti Israhelis: Enoch et Phallu, Aesrom et Charmi. 15 Hae cognationes Ruben.

Filii Symeon: Iamuhel et Iamin et Aod et Iachin et Soer et Saul, filius Chananitidis. Hae progenies Symeon.

16 Et haec nomina filiorum Levi per cognationes suas: Gerson et Caath et Merari. Anni autem vitae Levi fuerunt centum triginta septem. 17 Filii Gerson: Lobeni et Semei, per cognationes suas. 18 Filii Caath: Amram et Isuar et He-

you out from the work-prison of the Egyptians and will deliver you from bondage and redeem you with a high arm and great judgments. 7 And I will take you to myself for my people; *I* will be your God, and you shall know that I am the Lord, your God, who brought you out from the work-prison of the Egyptians 8 and brought you into the land concerning which I lifted up my hand to give it to Abraham, Isaac and Jacob, and I will give it you to possess; I am the Lord.'" 9 And Moses told all this to the children of Israel, but they did not hearken to him for anguish of spirit and most painful work.

10 And the Lord spoke to Moses, saying, 11 "Go in, and speak to Pharaoh, king of Egypt, that he let the children of Israel go out of his land."

12 Moses answered before the Lord, "Behold: the children of Israel do not hearken to me, and how will Pharaoh hear *me,* especially as I am of uncircumcised lips?"

13 And the Lord spoke to Moses and Aaron, and he gave them a charge unto the children of Israel and unto Pharaoh, the king of Egypt, that they should bring forth the children of Israel out of the land of Egypt.

14 These are the heads of their house by their families.

The sons of Reuben, the firstborn of Israel: Hanoch and Pallu, Hezron and Caarmi. 15 These are the kindreds of Reuben.

The sons of Simeon: Jemuel and Jamin and Ohad and Jachin and Zohar and Shaul, the son of a Canaanitess. These are the families of Simeon.

16 And these are the names of the sons of Levi by their kindreds: Gershon and Kohath and Merari. And the years of the life of Levi were a hundred and thirty seven. 17 The sons of Gershon: Libni and Shimei, by their kindreds. 18 The sons

bron et Ozihel. Annique vitae Caath centum triginta tres. 19 Filii Merari: Mooli et Musi. Hae cognationes Levi per familias suas.

20 Accepit autem Amram uxorem Iocabed, patruelem suam, quae peperit ei Aaron et Mosen. Fueruntque anni vitae Amram centum triginta septem. 21 Filii quoque Isuar: Core et Napheg et Zechri. 22 Filii quoque Ozihel: Misahel et Elsaphan et Sethri. 23 Accepit autem Aaron uxorem Elisabe, filiam Aminadab, sororem Naasson, quae peperit ei Nadab et Abiu et Eleazar et Ithamar. 24 Filii quoque Core: Asir et Helcana et Abiasab. Hae sunt cognationes Coritarum. 25 At vero Eleazar, filius Aaron, accepit uxorem de filiabus Phutihel, quae peperit ei Finees. Hii sunt principes familiarum Leviticarum per cognationes suas.

26 Iste est Aaron et Moses, quibus praecepit Dominus ut educerent filios Israhel de terra Aegypti per turmas suas. 27 Hii sunt qui loquuntur ad Pharao, regem Aegypti, ut educant filios Israhel de Aegypto. Iste Moses et Aaron 28 in die qua locutus est Dominus ad Mosen in terra Aegypti.

29 Et locutus est Dominus ad Mosen, dicens, "Ego Dominus. Loquere ad Pharao, regem Aegypti, omnia quae ego loquor tibi."

30 Et ait Moses coram Domino, "En: incircumcisus labiis sum; quomodo audiet me Pharao?"

of Kohath: Amram and Izhar and Hebron and Uzziel. And the years of Kohath's life were a hundred and thirty-three. 19 The sons of Merari: Mahli and Mushi. These are the kindreds of Levi by their families.

20 And Amram took to wife Jochebed, his aunt by the father's side, and she bore him Aaron and Moses. And the years of Amram's life were a hundred and thirty-seven. 21 The sons also of Izhar: Korah and Nepheg and Zichri. 22 The sons also of Uzziel: Mishael and Elzaphan and Sithri. 23 And Aaron took to wife Elisheba, the daughter of Amminadab, sister of Nahshon, who bore him Nadab and Abihu and Eleazar and Ithamar. 24 The sons also of Korah: Assir and Elkanah and Abiasaph. These are the kindreds of the Korahites. 25 But Eleazar, the son of Aaron, took a wife of the daughters of Putiel, and she bore him Phinehas. These are the heads of the Levitical families by their kindreds.

26 These are Aaron and Moses, whom the Lord commanded to bring forth the children of Israel out of the land of Egypt by their companies. 27 These are they that speak to Pharaoh, king of Egypt, in order to bring out the children of Israel from Egypt. These are that Moses and Aaron 28 in the day when the Lord spoke to Moses in the land of Egypt.

29 And the Lord spoke to Moses, saying, "I am the Lord. Speak thou to Pharaoh, king of Egypt, all that I say to thee."

30 And Moses said before the Lord, "Lo: I am of uncircumcised lips; how will Pharaoh hear me?"

Caput 7

Dixitque Dominus ad Mosen, "Ecce: constitui te deum Pharaonis, et Aaron, frater tuus, erit propheta tuus. 2 Tu loqueris ei omnia quae mando tibi, et ille loquetur ad Pharaonem ut dimittat filios Israhel de terra sua. 3 Sed ego indurabo cor eius et multiplicabo signa et ostenta mea in terra Aegypti, 4 et non audiet vos. Inmittamque manum meam super Aegyptum et educam exercitum et populum meum, filios Israhel, de terra Aegypti per iudicia maxima. 5 Et scient Aegyptii quod ego sim Dominus, qui extenderim manum meam super Aegyptum et eduxerim filios Israhel de medio eorum.

6 Fecit itaque Moses et Aaron sicut praeceperat Dominus; ita egerunt. 7 Erat autem Moses octoginta annorum et Aaron octoginta trium quando locuti sunt ad Pharaonem. 8 Dixitque Dominus ad Mosen et Aaron, 9 "Cum dixerit vobis Pharao, 'Ostendite signa,' dices ad Aaron, 'Tolle virgam tuam, et proice eam coram Pharao, ac vertetur in colubrum.'" 10 Ingressi itaque Moses et Aaron ad Pharaonem fe-

Chapter 7

Moses and Aaron go into Pharaoh. They turn the rod into a serpent and the waters of Egypt into blood, which was the first plague. The magicians do the like, and Pharaoh's heart is hardened.

And the Lord said to Moses, "Behold: I have appointed thee the god of Pharaoh, and Aaron, thy brother, shall be thy prophet. 2 Thou shalt speak to him all that I command thee, and he shall speak to Pharaoh that he let the children of Israel go out of his land. 3 But I shall harden his heart and shall multiply my signs and wonders in the land of Egypt, 4 and he will not hear you. And I will lay my hand upon Egypt and will bring forth my army and my people, the children of Israel, out of the land of Egypt by very great judgments. 5 And the Egyptians shall know that I am the Lord, who have stretched forth my hand upon Egypt and have brought forth the children of Israel out of the midst of them."

6 And Moses and Aaron did as the Lord had commanded; so did they. 7 And Moses was eighty years old and Aaron eighty-three when they spoke to Pharaoh. 8 And the Lord said to Moses and Aaron, 9 "When Pharaoh shall say to you, 'Shew signs,' thou shalt say to Aaron, 'Take thy rod, and cast it down before Pharaoh, and it shall be turned into a serpent.'" 10 So Moses and Aaron went in unto Pharaoh and did

cerunt sicut praeceperat Dominus. Tulitque Aaron virgam coram Pharao et servis eius, quae versa est in colubrum.

11 Vocavit autem Pharao sapientes et maleficos, et fecerunt etiam ipsi per incantationes Aegyptias et arcana quaedam similiter. 12 Proieceruntque singuli virgas suas, quae versae sunt in dracones, sed devoravit virga Aaron virgas eorum. 13 Induratumque est cor Pharaonis, et non audivit eos sicut praeceperat Dominus.

14 Dixit autem Dominus ad Mosen, "Ingravatum est cor Pharaonis; non vult dimittere populum. 15 Vade ad eum mane. Ecce: egredietur ad aquas, et stabis in occursum eius super ripam fluminis, et virgam quae conversa est in draconem tolles in manu tua, 16 dicesque ad eum, 'Dominus, Deus Hebraeorum, misit me ad te, dicens, "Dimitte populum meum ut mihi sacrificet in deserto," et usque ad praesens audire noluisti. 17 Haec igitur dicit Dominus: "In hoc scies quod Dominus sim. Ecce! Percutiam virga quae in manu mea est aquam fluminis, et vertetur in sanguinem. 18 Pisces quoque qui sunt in fluvio morientur, et conputrescent aquae, et adfligentur Aegyptii bibentes aquam fluminis."'" 19 Dixit quoque Dominus ad Mosen, "Dic ad Aaron, 'Tolle virgam tuam, et extende manum tuam super aquas Aegypti et super fluvios eorum et rivos ac paludes et omnes lacus aquarum ut vertantur in sanguinem.' Et sit cruor in omni terra Aegypti, tam in ligneis vasis quam in saxeis."

20 Feceruntque Moses et Aaron sicut praeceperat Dominus, et elevans virgam percussit aquam fluminis coram

as the Lord had commanded. And Aaron took the rod before Pharaoh and his servants, and it was turned into a serpent.

11 And Pharaoh called the wise men and the magicians, and they also by Egyptian enchantments and certain secrets did in like manner. 12 And they every one cast down their rods, and they were turned into serpents, but Aaron's rod devoured their rods. 13 And Pharaoh's heart was hardened, and he did not hearken to them as the Lord had commanded.

14 And the Lord said to Moses, "Pharaoh's heart is hardened; he will not let the people go. 15 Go to him in the morning. Behold: he will go out to the waters, and thou shalt stand to meet him on the bank of the river, and thou shalt take in thy hand the rod that was turned into a serpent, 16 and thou shalt say to him, 'The Lord, God of the Hebrews, sent me to thee, saying, "Let my people go to sacrifice to me in the desert," and hitherto thou wouldst not hear. 17 Thus therefore saith the Lord: "In this thou shalt know that I am the Lord. Behold! I will strike with the rod that is in my hand the water of the river, and it shall be turned into blood. 18 And the fishes that are in the river shall die, and the waters shall be corrupted, and the Egyptians shall be afflicted when they drink the water of the river."'" 19 The Lord also said to Moses, "Say to Aaron, 'Take thy rod, and stretch forth thy hand upon the waters of Egypt and upon their rivers and streams and pools and all the ponds of waters that they may be turned into blood.' And let blood be in all the land of Egypt, both in vessels of wood and of stone."

20 And Moses and Aaron did as the Lord had commanded, and lifting up the rod he struck the water of the river be-

Pharao et servis eius, quae versa est in sanguinem. 21 Et pisces qui erant in flumine mortui sunt, conputruitque fluvius, et non poterant Aegyptii bibere aquam fluminis, et fuit sanguis in tota terra Aegypti.

22 Feceruntque similiter malefici Aegyptiorum incantationibus suis, et induratum est cor Pharaonis, nec audivit eos, sicut praeceperat Dominus. 23 Avertitque se et ingressus est domum suam, nec adposuit cor etiam hac vice. 24 Foderunt autem omnes Aegyptii per circuitum fluminis aquam ut biberent, non enim poterant bibere de aqua fluminis. 25 Impletique sunt septem dies postquam percussit Dominus fluvium.

Caput 8

Dixitque Dominus ad Mosen, "Ingredere ad Pharao, et dices ad eum, 'Haec dicit Dominus: "Dimitte populum meum ut sacrificet mihi. 2 Sin autem nolueris dimittere, ecce: ego percutiam omnes terminos tuos ranis. 3 Et ebulliet fluvius ranas quae ascendent et ingredientur domum tuam et cubiculum lectuli tui et super stratum tuum et in domos

fore Pharaoh and his servants, and it was turned into blood. 21 And the fishes that were in the river died, and the river corrupted, and the Egyptians could not drink the water of the river, and there was blood in all the land of Egypt.

22 And the magicians of the Egyptians with their enchantments did in like manner, and Pharaoh's heart was hardened, neither did he hear them, as the Lord had commanded. 23 And he turned himself away and went into his house, neither did he set his heart to it this time also. 24 And all the Egyptians dug round about the river for water to drink, for they could not drink of the water of the river. 25 And seven days were fully ended after that the Lord struck the river.

Chapter 8

The second plague is of frogs. Pharaoh promiseth to let the Israelites go but breaketh his promise. The third plague is of sciniphs. The fourth is of flies. Pharaoh again promiseth to dismiss the people but doth it not.

And the Lord said to Moses, "Go in to Pharaoh, and thou shalt say to him, 'Thus saith the Lord: "Let my people go to sacrifice to me. 2 But if thou wilt not let them go, behold: I will strike all thy coasts with frogs. 3 And the river shall *bring forth an abundance of* frogs which shall come up and enter into thy house and thy bedchamber and upon thy bed and in

servorum tuorum et in populum tuum et in furnos tuos et in reliquias ciborum tuorum. 4 Et ad te et ad populum tuum et ad omnes servos tuos intrabunt ranae.""" 5 Dixitque Dominus ad Mosen, "Dic Aaron, 'Extende manum tuam super fluvios et super rivos ac paludes, et educ ranas super terram Aegypti.'"

6 Et extendit Aaron manum super aquas Aegypti, et ascenderunt ranae operueruntque terram Aegypti. 7 Fecerunt autem et malefici per incantationes suas similiter, eduxeruntque ranas super terram Aegypti. 8 Vocavit autem Pharao Mosen et Aaron et dixit eis, "Orate Dominum ut auferat ranas a me et a populo meo, et dimittam populum ut sacrificet Domino."

9 Dixitque Moses Pharaoni, "Constitue mihi quando deprecer pro te et pro servis tuis et pro populo tuo ut abigantur ranae a te et a domo tua et a servis tuis et a populo tuo et tantum in flumine remaneant."

10 Qui respondit, "Cras."

At ille, "Iuxta verbum," inquit, "tuum faciam ut scias quoniam non est sicut Dominus, Deus noster. 11 Et recedent ranae a te et a domo tua et a servis tuis et a populo tuo et tantum in flumine remanebunt."

12 Egressique sunt Moses et Aaron a Pharaone, et clamavit Moses ad Dominum pro sponsione ranarum quam condixerat Pharaoni. 13 Fecitque Dominus iuxta verbum Mosi, et mortuae sunt ranae de domibus et de villis et de agris. 14 Congregaveruntque eas in inmensos aggeres, et conpu-

the houses of thy servants and to thy people and into thy ovens and into the remains of thy meats. 4 And the frogs shall come in to thee and to thy people and to all thy servants.'"" 5 And the Lord said to Moses, "Say to Aaron, 'Stretch forth thy hand upon the streams and upon the rivers and the pools, and bring forth frogs upon the land of Egypt.'"

6 And Aaron stretched forth his hand upon the waters of Egypt, and the frogs came up and covered the land of Egypt. 7 And the magicians also by their enchantments did in like manner, and they brought forth frogs upon all the land of Egypt. 8 But Pharaoh called Moses and Aaron and said to them, "Pray ye to the Lord to take away the frogs from me and from my people, and I will let the people go to sacrifice to the Lord."

9 And Moses said to Pharaoh, "Set me *a time* when I shall pray for thee and for thy servants and for thy people that the frogs may be driven away from thee and from thy house and from thy servants and from thy people and may remain only in the river."

10 And he answered, "Tomorrow."

But he said, "I will do according to thy word that thou mayst know that there is none like to the Lord, our God. 11 And the frogs shall depart from thee and from thy house and from thy servants and from thy people and shall remain only in the river."

12 And Moses and Aaron went forth from Pharaoh, and Moses cried to the Lord for the promise which he had made to Pharaoh concerning the frogs. 13 And the Lord did according to the word of Moses, and the frogs died out of the houses and out of the villages and out of the fields. 14 And they gathered them together into immense heaps, and the

truit terra. 15 Videns autem Pharao quod data esset requies ingravavit cor suum et non audivit eos, sicut praeceperat Dominus.

16 Dixitque Dominus ad Mosen, "Loquere ad Aaron, 'Extende virgam tuam, et percute pulverem terrae, et sint scinifes in universa terra Aegypti.'" 17 Feceruntque ita. Et extendit Aaron manum, virgam tenens, percussitque pulverem terrae, et facti sunt scinifes in hominibus et in iumentis. Omnis pulvis terrae versus est in scinifes per totam terram Aegypti. 18 Feceruntque similiter malefici incantationibus suis ut educerent scinifes, et non potuerunt, erantque scinifes tam in hominibus quam in iumentis.

19 Et dixerunt malefici ad Pharao, "Digitus Dei est hic." Induratumque est cor Pharaonis, et non audivit eos, sicut praeceperat Dominus.

20 Dixit quoque Dominus ad Mosen, "Consurge diluculo, et sta coram Pharaone, egredietur enim ad aquas, et dices ad eum, 'Haec dicit Dominus: "Dimitte populum meum ut sacrificet mihi. 21 Quod si non dimiseris eum, ecce: ego inmittam in te et in servos tuos et in populum tuum et in domos tuas omne genus muscarum, et implebuntur domus Aegyptiorum muscis diversi generis et universa terra in qua fuerint. 22 Faciamque mirabilem in die illa terram Gessen, in qua populus meus est, ut non sint ibi muscae, et scias quoniam ego Dominus in medio terrae. 23 Ponamque divisionem inter populum meum et populum tuum. Cras erit signum istud."'" 24 Fecitque Dominus ita.

land was corrupted. 15 And Pharaoh seeing that rest was given hardened his own heart and did not hear them, as the Lord had commanded.

16 And the Lord said to Moses, "Say to Aaron, 'Stretch forth thy rod, and strike the dust of the earth, and may there be sciniphs in all the land of Egypt.'" 17 And they did so. And Aaron stretched forth his hand, holding the rod, and he struck the dust of the earth, and there came sciniphs on men and on beasts. All the dust of the earth was turned into sciniphs through all the land of Egypt. 18 And the magicians with their enchantments practiced in like manner to bring forth sciniphs, and they could not, and there were sciniphs as well on men as on beasts.

19 And the magicians said to Pharaoh, "This is the finger of God." And Pharaoh's heart was hardened, and he hearkened not unto them, as the Lord had commanded.

20 The Lord also said to Moses, "Arise early, and stand before Pharaoh, for he will go forth to the waters, and thou shalt say to him, 'Thus saith the Lord: "Let my people go to sacrifice to me. 21 But if thou wilt not let them go, behold: I will send in upon thee and upon thy servants and upon thy houses all kind of flies, and the houses of the Egyptians shall be filled with flies of divers kinds and the whole land wherein they shall be. 22 And I will make the land of Goshen, wherein my people is, wonderful in that day, so that flies shall not be there, and thou shalt know that I am the Lord in the midst of the earth. 23 And I will put a division between my people and thy people. Tomorrow shall this sign be."'" 24 And the Lord did so.

Et venit musca gravissima in domos Pharaonis et servorum eius et in omnem terram Aegypti, corruptaque est terra ab huiuscemodi muscis. 25 Vocavitque Pharao Mosen et Aaron et ait eis, "Ite, et sacrificate Deo vestro in terra hac."

26 Et ait Moses, "Non potest ita fieri, abominationes enim Aegyptiorum immolabimus Domino, Deo nostro. Quod si mactaverimus ea quae colunt Aegyptii, coram eis, lapidibus nos obruent. 27 Via trium dierum pergemus in solitudinem, et sacrificabimus Domino, Deo nostro, sicut praeceperit nobis."

28 Dixitque Pharao, "Ego dimittam vos ut sacrificetis Domino, Deo vestro, in deserto, verumtamen longius ne abeatis. Rogate pro me."

29 Et ait Moses, "Egressus a te orabo Dominum, et recedet musca a Pharaone et a servis suis et a populo eius cras, verumtamen noli ultra fallere ut non dimittas populum sacrificare Domino." 30 Egressusque Moses a Pharao oravit Dominum.

31 Qui fecit iuxta verbum illius, et abstulit muscas a Pharao et a servis suis et a populo eius; non superfuit ne una quidem. 32 Et ingravatum est cor Pharaonis ita ut ne hac quidem vice dimitteret populum.

And there came a very grievous swarm of flies into the houses of Pharaoh and of his servants and into all the land of Egypt, and the land was corrupted by this kind of flies. 25 And Pharaoh called Moses and Aaron, and said to them, "Go, and sacrifice to your God in this land."

26 And Moses said, "It cannot be so, for we shall sacrifice the abominations of the Egyptians to the Lord, our God. Now if we kill those things which the Egyptians worship, in their presence, they will stone us. 27 We will go three days' journey into the wilderness, and we will sacrifice to the Lord, our God, as he hath commanded us."

28 And Pharaoh said, "I will let you go to sacrifice to the Lord, your God, in the wilderness, but go no farther. Pray for me."

29 And Moses said, "I will go out from thee and will pray to the Lord, and the flies shall depart from Pharaoh and from his servants and from his people tomorrow, but do not deceive any more *in not letting the people go* to sacrifice to the Lord." 30 So Moses went out from Pharaoh and prayed to the Lord.

31 And he did according to his word, and he took away the flies from Pharaoh and from his servants and from his people; there was not left so much as one. 32 And Pharaoh's heart was hardened so that neither this time would he let the people go.

Caput 9

Dixit autem Dominus ad Mosen, "Ingredere ad Pharaonem, et loquere ad eum, 'Haec dicit Dominus, Deus Hebraeorum: "Dimitte populum meum ut sacrificet mihi. 2 Quod si adhuc rennuis et retines eos, 3 ecce: manus mea erit super agros tuos et super equos et asinos et camelos et boves et oves pestis valde gravis. 4 Et faciet Dominus mirabile inter possessiones Israhel et possessiones Aegyptiorum ut nihil omnino intereat ex his quae pertinent ad filios Israhel."'" 5 Constituitque Dominus tempus, dicens, "Cras faciet Dominus verbum istud in terra."

6 Fecit ergo Dominus verbum hoc altero die, mortuaque sunt omnia animantia Aegyptiorum, de animalibus vero filiorum Israhel nihil omnino periit. 7 Et misit Pharao ad videndum, nec erat quicquam mortuum de his quae possidebat Israhel. Ingravatumque est cor Pharaonis, et non dimisit populum. 8 Et dixit Dominus ad Mosen et Aaron, "Tollite plenas manus cineris de camino, et spargat illud Moses in caelum coram Pharao. 9 Sitque pulvis super omnem terram Aegypti, erunt enim in hominibus et iumentis ulcera et ve-

Chapter 9

The fifth plague is a murrain among the cattle, the sixth, of boils in men and beasts, the seventh, of hail. Pharaoh promiseth again to let the people go and breaketh his word.

And the Lord said to Moses, "Go in to Pharaoh, and speak to him, 'Thus saith the Lord, God of the Hebrews: "Let my people go to sacrifice to me. 2 But if thou refuse and withhold them still, 3 behold: my hand shall be upon thy fields and a very grievous murrain upon thy horses and asses and camels and oxen and sheep. 4 And the Lord will make a *wonderful difference* between the possessions of Israel and the possessions of the Egyptians that nothing at all shall die of those things that belong to the children of Israel."'" 5 And the Lord appointed a time, saying, "Tomorrow will the Lord do this thing in the land."

6 The Lord therefore did this thing the next day, and all the beasts of the Egyptians died, but of the beasts of the children of Israel there died not one. 7 And Pharaoh sent to see, and there was not any thing dead of that which Israel possessed. And Pharaoh's heart was hardened, and he did not let the people go. 8 And the Lord said to Moses and Aaron, "Take to you handfuls of ashes out of the chimney, and let Moses sprinkle it in the air in the presence of Pharaoh. 9 And be there dust upon all the land of Egypt, for there shall be boils and swelling blains *both* in men and

sicae turgentes in universa terra Aegypti." 10 Tuleruntque cinerem de camino et steterunt coram Pharao, et sparsit illud Moses in caelum, factaque sunt ulcera vesicarum turgentium in hominibus et iumentis.

11 Nec poterant malefici stare coram Mosen propter ulcera quae in illis erant et in omni terra Aegypti. 12 Induravitque Dominus cor Pharaonis, et non audivit eos, sicut locutus est Dominus ad Mosen. 13 Dixit quoque Dominus ad Mosen, "Mane consurge, et sta coram Pharao, et dices ad eum, 'Haec dicit Dominus, Deus Hebraeorum: "Dimitte populum meum ut sacrificet mihi. 14 Quia in hac vice mittam omnes plagas meas super cor tuum et super servos tuos et super populum tuum ut scias quod non sit similis mei in omni terra. 15 Nunc enim extendens manum percutiam te et populum tuum peste, peribisque de terra. 16 Idcirco autem posui te ut ostendam in te fortitudinem meam, et narretur nomen meum in omni terra. 17 Adhuc retines populum meum, et non vis eum dimittere? 18 En! Pluam hac ipsa hora cras grandinem multam nimis qualis non fuit in Aegypto a die qua fundata est usque in praesens tempus. 19 Mitte ergo iam nunc, et congrega iumenta tua et omnia quae habes in agro, homines enim et iumenta et universa quae inventa fuerint foris nec congregata de agris cecideritque super ea grando morientur."'"

20 Qui timuit verbum Domini de servis Pharao fecit confugere servos suos et iumenta in domos, 21 qui autem neglexit sermonem Domini dimisit servos suos et iumenta in agris. 22 Et dixit Dominus ad Mosen, "Extende manum tuam

beasts in the whole land of Egypt." 10 And they took ashes out of the chimney and stood before Pharaoh, and Moses sprinkled it in the air, and there came boils *with* swelling blains in men and beasts.

11 Neither could the magicians stand before Moses for the boils that were upon them and in all the land of Egypt. 12 And the Lord hardened Pharaoh's heart, and he hearkened not unto them, as the Lord had spoken to Moses. 13 And the Lord said to Moses, "Arise in the morning, and stand before Pharaoh, and thou shalt say to him, 'Thus saith the Lord, the God of the Hebrews: "Let my people go to sacrifice to me. 14 For I will at this time send all my plagues upon thy heart and upon thy servants and upon thy people that thou mayst know there is none like me in all the earth. 15 For now *I will stretch out my hand to* strike thee and thy people with pestilence, and thou shalt perish from the earth. 16 And therefore have I raised thee that I may shew my power in thee, and my name may be spoken of throughout all the earth. 17 Dost thou yet hold back my people, and wilt thou not let them go? 18 Behold! I will cause it to rain tomorrow at this same hour an exceeding great hail such as hath not been in Egypt from the day that it was founded until this present time. 19 Send therefore now presently, and gather together thy cattle and all that thou hast in the field, for men and beasts and all things that shall be found abroad and not gathered together out of the fields *which the hail shall fall upon* shall die."'"

20 He that feared the word of the Lord among Pharaoh's servants made his servants and his cattle flee into houses, 21 but he that regarded not the word of the Lord left his servants and his cattle in the fields. 22 And the Lord said to Mo-

in caelum ut fiat grando in universa terra Aegypti, super homines et super iumenta et super omnem herbam agri in
terra Aegypti." 23 Extenditque Moses virgam in caelum, et
Dominus dedit tonitrua et grandinem ac discurrentia fulgura super terram, pluitque Dominus grandinem super terram Aegypti. 24 Et grando et ignis inmixta pariter ferebantur, tantaeque fuit magnitudinis quanta ante numquam
apparuit in universa terra Aegypti ex quo gens illa condita
est. 25 Et percussit grando in omni terra Aegypti cuncta quae
fuerunt in agris, ab homine usque ad iumentum, cunctamque herbam agri percussit grando, et omne lignum regionis
confregit.

26 Tantum in terra Gessen, ubi erant filii Israhel, grando
non cecidit. 27 Misitque Pharao et vocavit Mosen et Aaron,
dicens ad eos, "Peccavi etiam nunc. Dominus iustus; ego et
populus meus impii. 28 Orate Dominum ut desinant tonitrua Dei et grando ut dimittam vos et nequaquam hic ultra
maneatis."

29 Ait Moses, "Cum egressus fuero de urbe, extendam pal-
mas meas ad Dominum, et cessabunt tonitrua, et grando
non erit, ut scias quia Domini est terra. 30 Novi autem quod
et tu et servi tui necdum timeatis Dominum Deum."

31 Linum, ergo, et hordeum laesum est eo quod hordeum
esset virens et linum iam folliculos germinaret, 32 triticum
autem et far non sunt laesa, quia serotina erant. 33 Egressusque Moses a Pharaone ex urbe, tetendit manus ad Dominum, et cessaverunt tonitrua et grando, nec ultra stillavit

ses, "Stretch forth thy hand towards heaven that there may be hail in the whole land of Egypt, upon men and upon beasts and upon every herb of the field in the land of Egypt." 23 And Moses stretched forth his rod towards heaven, and the Lord sent thunder and hail and lightning running along the ground, and the Lord rained hail upon the land of Egypt. 24 And the hail and fire mixed with it drove on together, and it was of so great bigness as never before *was seen* in the whole land of Egypt since that nation was founded. 25 And the hail destroyed through all the land of Egypt all things that were in the fields, *both* man *and* beast, and the hail smote every herb of the field, and it broke every tree of the country.

26 Only in the land of Goshen, where the children of Israel were, the hail fell not. 27 And Pharaoh sent and called Moses and Aaron, saying to them, "I have sinned this time also. The Lord is just; I and my people are wicked. 28 Pray ye to the Lord that the thunderings of God and the hail may cease that I may let you go and that you may stay here no longer."

29 Moses said, "As soon as I am gone out of the city, I will stretch forth my hands to the Lord, and the thunders shall cease, and the hail shall be no more, that thou mayst know that the earth is the Lord's. 30 But I know that neither thou nor thy servants do yet fear the Lord God."

31 The flax, therefore, and the barley were hurt because the barley was green and the flax was now boiled, 32 but the wheat and *other winter* corn were not hurt, because they were lateward. 33 And when Moses was gone from Pharaoh out of the city, he stretched forth his hands to the Lord, and the thunders and the hail ceased, neither did there drop any

pluvia super terram. 34 Videns autem Pharao quod cessasset pluvia et grando et tonitrua, auxit peccatum. 35 Et ingravatum est cor eius et servorum illius, et induratum nimis, nec dimisit filios Israhel, sicut praeceperat Dominus per manum Mosi.

Caput 10

Et dixit Dominus ad Mosen, "Ingredere ad Pharao, ego enim induravi cor eius et servorum illius ut faciam signa mea haec in eo. 2 Et narres in auribus filii tui et nepotum tuorum quotiens contriverim Aegyptios et signa mea fecerim in eis, et sciatis quia ego Dominus."

3 Introierunt ergo Moses et Aaron ad Pharaonem et dixerunt ad eum, "Haec dicit Dominus, Deus Hebraeorum: 'Usquequo non vis subici mihi? Dimitte populum meum ut sacrificet mihi. 4 Sin autem resistis et non vis dimittere eum, ecce: ego inducam cras lucustam in fines tuos 5 quae operiat superficiem terrae ne quicquam eius appareat, sed comedatur quod residuum fuit grandini, conrodet enim omnia ligna

more rain upon the earth. 34 And Pharaoh, seeing that the rain and the hail and the thunders were ceased, increased his sin. 35 And his heart was hardened and the heart of his servants, and it was made exceeding hard, neither did he let the children of Israel go, as the Lord had commanded by the hand of Moses.

Chapter 10

The eighth plague of the locusts, the ninth of darkness. Pharaoh is still hardened.

And the Lord said to Moses, "Go in to Pharaoh, for I have hardened his heart and the heart of his servants that I may work these my signs in him. 2 And thou mayest tell in the ears of thy sons and of thy grandsons how often I have plagued the Egyptians and wrought my signs amongst them, and you may know that I am the Lord."

3 Therefore Moses and Aaron went in to Pharaoh and said to him, "Thus saith the Lord, God of the Hebrews: 'How long refusest thou to submit to me? Let my people go to sacrifice to me. 4 But if thou resist and wilt not let them go, behold: I will bring in tomorrow the locust into thy coasts 5 to cover the face of the earth that nothing thereof may appear, but that which the hail hath left may be eaten, for they shall feed upon all the trees that spring

quae germinant in agris. 6 Et implebunt domos tuas et servorum tuorum et omnium Aegyptiorum, quantam non viderunt patres tui et avi ex quo orti sunt super terram usque in praesentem diem.'"

Avertitque se et egressus est a Pharaone. 7 Dixerunt autem servi Pharaonis ad eum, "Usquequo patiemur hoc scandalum? Dimitte homines ut sacrificent Domino, Deo suo. Nonne vides quod perierit Aegyptus?

8 Revocaveruntque Mosen et Aaron ad Pharaonem, qui dixit eis, "Ite; sacrificate Domino, Deo vestro. Quinam sunt qui ituri sunt?"

9 Ait Moses, "Cum parvulis nostris et senibus pergemus, cum filiis et filiabus, cum ovibus et armentis, est enim sollemnitas Domini, Dei nostri."

10 Et respondit Pharao, "Sic Dominus sit vobiscum quomodo ego dimittam vos et parvulos vestros. Cui dubium est quod pessime cogitetis? 11 Non fiet ita, sed ite tantum viri et sacrificate Domino, hoc enim et ipsi petistis."

Statimque eiecti sunt de conspectu Pharaonis. 12 Dixit autem Dominus ad Mosen, "Extende manum tuam super terram Aegypti ad lucustam ut ascendat super eam et devoret omnem herbam quae residua fuit grandini." 13 Et extendit Moses virgam super terram Aegypti, et Dominus induxit ventum urentem tota illa die ac nocte, et mane facto, ventus urens levavit lucustas, 14 quae ascenderunt super universam terram Aegypti et sederunt in cunctis finibus Aegyptiorum, innumerabiles, quales ante illud tempus non fuerant nec postea futurae sunt. 15 Operueruntque universam superficiem terrae, vastantes omnia. Devorata est igitur herba

in the fields. 6 And they shall fill thy houses and the houses of thy servants and of all the Egyptians, such a number as thy fathers have not seen nor thy grandfathers from the time they were first upon the earth until this present day.'"

And he turned himself away and went forth from Pharaoh. 7 And Pharaoh's servants said to him, "How long shall we endure this scandal? Let the men go to sacrifice to the Lord, their God. Dost thou not see that Egypt is undone?"

8 And they called back Moses and Aaron to Pharaoh, and he said to them, "Go; sacrifice to the Lord, your God. Who are they that shall go?"

9 Moses said, "We will go with our young and old, with our sons and daughters, with our sheep and herds, for it is the solemnity of the Lord, our God."

10 And Pharaoh answered, "So be the Lord with you as I shall let you and your children go. Who can doubt but that you intend *some great evil?* 11 It shall not be so, but go ye men only and sacrifice to the Lord, for this yourselves also desired."

And immediately they were cast out from Pharaoh's presence. 12 And the Lord said to Moses, "Stretch forth thy hand upon the land of Egypt unto the locust that it may come upon it and devour every herb that is left after the hail." 13 And Moses stretched forth his rod upon the land of Egypt, and the Lord brought a burning wind all that day and night, and when it was morning, the burning wind raised the locusts, 14 and they came up over the whole land of Egypt and rested in all the coasts of the Egyptians, innumerable, the like as had not been before that time nor shall be hereafter. 15 And they covered the whole face of the earth, wasting all things. And the grass of the earth was devoured and what

terrae et quicquid pomorum in arboribus fuit quae grando dimiserat. Nihilque omnino virens relictum est in lignis et in herbis terrae in cuncta Aegypto.

16 Quam ob rem festinus Pharao vocavit Mosen et Aaron et dixit eis, "Peccavi in Dominum, Deum vestrum, et in vos. 17 Sed nunc dimittite peccatum mihi etiam hac vice, et rogate Dominum, Deum vestrum, ut auferat a me mortem istam."

18 Egressusque de conspectu Pharaonis oravit ad Dominum. 19 Qui flare fecit ventum ab occidente vehementissimum, et arreptam lucustam proiecit in Mare Rubrum. Non remansit ne una quidem in cunctis finibus Aegypti. 20 Et induravit Dominus cor Pharaonis, nec dimisit filios Israhel.

21 Dixit autem Dominus ad Mosen, "Extende manum tuam in caelum, et sint tenebrae super terram Aegypti, tam densae ut palpari queant." 22 Extenditque Moses manum in caelum, et factae sunt tenebrae horribiles in universa terra Aegypti tribus diebus. 23 Nemo vidit fratrem suum nec movit se de loco in quo erat, ubicumque autem habitabant filii Israhel, lux erat. 24 Vocavitque Pharao Mosen et Aaron et dixit eis, "Ite; sacrificate Domino. Oves tantum vestrae et armenta remaneant; parvuli vestri eant vobiscum.

25 Ait Moses, "Hostias quoque et holocausta dabis nobis quae offeramus Domino, Deo nostro. 26 Cuncti greges pergent nobiscum. Non remanebit ex eis ungula, quae necessaria sunt in cultum Domini, Dei nostri, praesertim cum ignoremus quid debeat immolari donec ad ipsum locum perveniamus."

fruits soever were on the trees which the hail had left. And there remained not any thing that was green on the trees or in the herbs of the earth in all Egypt.

16 Wherefore Pharaoh in haste called Moses and Aaron and said to them, "I have sinned against the Lord, your God, and against you. 17 But now forgive me my sin this time also, and pray to the Lord, your God, that he take away from me this death."

18 And Moses going forth from the presence of Pharaoh prayed to the Lord. 19 And he made a very strong wind to blow from the west, and it took the locusts and cast them into the Red Sea. There remained not so much as one in all the coasts of Egypt. 20 And the Lord hardened Pharaoh's heart, neither did he let the children of Israel go.

21 And the Lord said to Moses, "Stretch out thy hand towards heaven, and may there be darkness upon the land of Egypt, so thick that it may be felt." 22 And Moses stretched forth his hand towards heaven, and there came horrible darkness in all the land of Egypt for three days. 23 No man saw his brother nor moved himself out of the place where he was, but wheresoever the children of Israel dwelt, there was light. 24 And Pharaoh called Moses and Aaron, and said to them, "Go; sacrifice to the Lord. Let your sheep only and herds remain; let your children go with you."

25 Moses said, "Thou shalt give us also sacrifices and burnt offerings to the Lord, our God. 26 All the flocks shall go with us. There shall not a hoof remain of them, for they are necessary for the service of the Lord, our God, especially as we know not what must be offered till we come to the very place."

27 Induravit autem Dominus cor Pharaonis, et noluit dimittere eos. 28 Dixitque Pharao ad Mosen, "Recede a me, et cave ne ultra videas faciem meam. Quocumque die apparueris mihi morieris."

29 Respondit Moses, "Ita fiet ut locutus es: non videbo ultra faciem tuam."

Caput 11

Et dixit Dominus ad Mosen, "Adhuc una plaga tangam Pharaonem et Aegyptum, et post haec dimittet vos et exire conpellet. 2 Dices ergo omni plebi ut postulet unusquisque ab amico suo, et mulier a vicina sua, vasa argentea et aurea. 3 Dabit autem Dominus gratiam populo suo coram Aegyptiis."

Fuitque Moses vir magnus valde in terra Aegypti coram servis Pharao et omni populo. 4 Et ait, "Haec dicit Dominus: 'Media nocte egrediar in Aegyptum. 5 Et morietur omne primogenitum in terra Aegyptiorum, a primogenito Pharaonis qui sedet in solio eius usque ad primogenitum ancillae quae est ad molam et omnia primogenita iumentorum. 6 Eritque

27 And the Lord hardened Pharaoh's heart, and he would not let them go. 28 And Pharaoh said to Moses, "Get thee from me, and beware thou see not my face any more. In what day soever thou shalt come in my sight, thou shalt die."

29 Moses answered, "So shall it be as thou hast spoken: I will not see thy face any more."

Chapter 11

Pharaoh and his people are threatened with the death of their firstborn.

And the Lord said to Moses, "Yet one plague more will I bring upon Pharaoh and Egypt, and after that he shall let you go and thrust you out. 2 Therefore thou shalt tell all the people that every man ask of his friend, and every woman of her neighbour, vessels of silver and of gold. 3 And the Lord will give favour to his people in the sight of the Egyptians."

And Moses was a very great man in the land of Egypt in the sight of Pharaoh's servants and of all the people. 4 And he said, "Thus said the Lord: 'At midnight I will enter into Egypt. 5 And every firstborn in the land of the Egyptians shall die, from the firstborn of Pharaoh who sitteth on his throne even to the firstborn of the handmaid that is at the mill and all the firstborn of beasts. 6 And there shall be a

clamor magnus in universa terra Aegypti qualis nec ante fuit nec postea futurus est. 7 Apud omnes autem filios Israhel non muttiet canis, ab homine usque ad pecus, ut sciatis quanto miraculo dividat Dominus Aegyptios et Israhel. 8 Descendentque omnes servi tui, isti, ad me et adorabunt me, dicentes, "Egredere tu et omnis populus qui subiectus est tibi.'" Post haec egrediemur."

9 Et exivit a Pharaone iratus nimis. Dixit autem Dominus ad Mosen, "Non audiet vos Pharao ut multa signa fiant in terra Aegypti." 10 Moses autem et Aaron fecerunt omnia ostenta quae scripta sunt coram Pharaone. Et induravit Dominus cor Pharaonis, nec dimisit filios Israhel de terra sua.

Caput 12

Dixit quoque Dominus ad Mosen et Aaron in terra Aegypti, 2 "Mensis iste vobis principium mensuum; primus erit in mensibus anni. 3 Loquimini ad universum coetum filiorum Israhel, et dicite eis, 'Decima die mensis huius, tollat unusquisque agnum per familias et domos suas, 4 sin autem

great cry in all the land of Egypt such as neither hath been before nor shall be hereafter. 7 But with all the children of Israel there shall not a dog make the least noise, from man even to beast, that you may know how wonderful a difference the Lord maketh between the Egyptians and Israel. 8 And all these, thy servants, shall come down to me and shall worship me, saying, "Go forth thou and all the people that is under thee."' After that we will go out."

9 And he went out from Pharaoh exceeding angry. But the Lord said to Moses, "Pharaoh will not hear you that many signs may be done in the land of Egypt." 10 And Moses and Aaron did all the wonders that are written before Pharaoh. And the Lord hardened Pharaoh's heart, neither did he let the children of Israel go out of his land.

Chapter 12

The manner of preparing and eating the paschal lamb. The firstborn of Egypt are all slain. The Israelites depart.

And the Lord said to Moses and Aaron in the land of Egypt, 2 "This month shall be to you the beginning of months; it shall be the first in the months of the year. 3 Speak ye to the whole assembly of the children of Israel, and say to them, 'On the tenth day of this month, let every man take a lamb by their families and houses, 4 but if the number be less

minor est numerus ut sufficere possit ad vescendum agnum, adsumet vicinum suum qui iunctus est domui eius, iuxta numerum animarum quae sufficere possunt ad esum agni. 5 Erit autem agnus absque macula, masculus anniculus, iuxta quem ritum tolletis et hedum. 6 Et servabitis eum usque ad quartamdecimam diem mensis huius, immolabitque eum universa multitudo filiorum Israhel ad vesperam. 7 Et sument de sanguine eius ac ponent super utrumque postem et in superliminaribus domorum, in quibus comedent illum. 8 Et edent carnes nocte illa assas igni et azymos panes cum lactucis agrestibus. 9 Non comedetis ex eo crudum quid, nec coctum aqua, sed assum tantum igni. Caput cum pedibus eius et intestinis vorabitis. 10 Nec remanebit ex eo quicquam usque mane. Si quid residuum fuerit, igne conburetis.

11 "'Sic autem comedetis illum: renes vestros accingetis, et calciamenta habebitis in pedibus, tenentes baculos in manibus, et comedetis festinanter, est enim phase (id est transitus) Domini. 12 Et transibo per terram Aegypti nocte illa percutiamque omne primogenitum in terra Aegypti ab homine usque ad pecus, et in cunctis diis Aegypti faciam iudicia. Ego Dominus. 13 Erit autem sanguis vobis in signum in aedibus in quibus eritis, et videbo sanguinem ac transibo vos, nec erit in vobis plaga disperdens quando percussero terram Aegypti. 14 Habebitis autem hanc diem in monumentum, et celebrabitis eam sollemnem Domino in generationibus vestris cultu sempiterno. 15 Septem diebus azyma comedetis. In die primo non erit fermentum in domibus vestris.

than may suffice to eat the lamb, he shall take unto him his neighbour that joineth to his house, according to the number of souls which may be enough to eat the lamb. 5 And it shall be a lamb without blemish, a male of one year, according to which rite also you shall take a kid. 6 And you shall keep it until the fourteenth day of this month, and the whole multitude of the children of Israel shall sacrifice it in the evening. 7 And they shall take of the blood thereof and put it upon both the side-posts and on the upper door-posts of the houses, wherein they shall eat it. 8 And they shall eat the flesh that night roasted at the fire and unleavened bread with wild lettuce. 9 You shall not eat thereof any thing raw, nor boiled in water, but only roasted at the fire. You shall eat the head with the feet and entrails thereof. 10 Neither shall there remain any thing of it until morning. If there be any thing left, you shall burn it with fire.

11 "And thus you shall eat it: you shall gird your reins, and you shall have shoes on your feet, holding staves in your hands, and you shall eat in haste, for it is the phase (that is the passage) of the Lord. 12 And I will pass through the land of Egypt that night and will kill every firstborn in the land of Egypt *both* man *and* beast, and against all the gods of Egypt I will execute judgments. I am the Lord. 13 And the blood shall be unto you for a sign in the houses where you shall be, and I shall see the blood and shall pass over you, and the plague shall not be upon you to destroy you when I shall strike the land of Egypt. 14 *And this day shall be for a memorial to you,* and you shall keep it a feast to the Lord in your generations with an everlasting observance. 15 Seven days shall you eat unleavened bread. In the first day there shall be no leaven in your houses. Whosoever shall eat any thing leav-

Quicumque comederit fermentatum, peribit anima illa de Israhel, a primo die usque ad diem septimum.

16 "'Dies prima erit sancta atque sollemnis, et dies septima eadem festivitate venerabilis: nihil operis facietis in eis exceptis his quae ad vescendum pertinent. 17 Et observabitis azyma, in eadem enim ipsa die educam exercitum vestrum de terra Aegypti, et custodietis diem istum in generationes vestras ritu perpetuo. 18 Primo mense, quartadecima die mensis, ad vesperam, comedetis azyma, usque ad diem vicesimam primam eiusdem mensis, ad vesperam. 19 Septem diebus fermentum non invenietur in domibus vestris. Qui comederit fermentatum, peribit anima eius de coetu Israhel, tam de advenis quam de indigenis terrae. 20 Omne fermentatum non comedetis. In cunctis habitaculis vestris edetis azyma.'"

21 Vocavit autem Moses omnes seniores filiorum Israhel et dixit ad eos, "Ite tollentes animal per familias vestras, et immolate phase. 22 Fasciculumque hysopi tinguite in sanguine qui est in limine et aspergite ex eo superliminare et utrumque postem. Nullus vestrum egrediatur ostium domus suae usque mane, 23 transibit enim Dominus percutiens Aegyptios, cumque viderit sanguinem in superliminari et in utroque poste, transcendet ostium domus et non sinet percussorem ingredi domos vestras et laedere. 24 Custodi verbum istud legitimum tibi et filiis tuis usque in aeternum. 25 Cumque introieritis terram quam Dominus daturus est vobis ut pollicitus est, observabitis caerimonias istas.

ened from the first day until the seventh day, that soul shall perish out of Israel.

16 "'The first day shall be holy and solemn, and the seventh day shall be *kept with the like solemnity:* you shall do no work in them except those things that belong to eating. 17 And you shall observe the *feast of the* unleavened bread, for in this same day I will bring forth your army out of the land of Egypt, and you shall keep this day in your generations by a perpetual observance. 18 The first month, the fourteenth day of the month, in the evening, you shall eat unleavened bread, until the one and twentieth day of the same month, in the evening. 19 Seven days there shall not be found any leaven in your houses. He that shall eat leavened bread, his soul shall perish out of the assembly of Israel, whether he be a stranger or born in the land. 20 You shall not eat any thing leavened. In all your habitations you shall eat unleavened bread.'"

21 And Moses called all the ancients of the children of Israel and said to them, "Go, take a lamb by your families, and sacrifice the phase. 22 And dip a bunch of hyssop in the blood that is at the door and sprinkle the transom of the door therewith and both the door cheeks. Let none of you go out of the door of his house till morning, 23 for the Lord will pass through striking the Egyptians, and when he shall see the blood on the transom and on both the posts, he will pass over the door of the house and not suffer the destroyer to come into your houses and to hurt you. 24 *Thou shalt keep* this thing as a law for thee and thy children for ever. 25 And when you have entered into the land which the Lord will give you as he hath promised, you shall observe these ceremonies.

26 "Et cum dixerint vobis filii vestri, 'Quae est ista religio?' 27 dicetis eis, 'Victima transitus Domini est quando transivit super domos filiorum Israhel in Aegypto, percutiens Aegyptios et domos nostras liberans.'"

Incurvatusque populus adoravit. 28 Et egressi filii Israhel fecerunt sicut praeceperat Dominus Mosi et Aaron. 29 Factum est autem in noctis medio percussit Dominus omne primogenitum in terra Aegypti, a primogenito Pharaonis qui sedebat in solio eius usque ad primogenitum captivae quae erat in carcere et omne primogenitum iumentorum. 30 Surrexitque Pharao nocte et omnes servi eius cunctaque Aegyptus, et ortus est clamor magnus in Aegypto, neque enim erat domus in qua non iaceret mortuus.

31 Vocatisque Pharao Mosen et Aaron nocte ait, "Surgite, et egredimini a populo meo. Vos et filii Israhel, ite; immolate Domino sicut dicitis. 32 Oves vestras et armenta adsumite ut petieratis, et, abeuntes, benedicite mihi."

33 Urguebantque Aegyptii populum de terra exire velociter, dicentes, "Omnes moriemur." 34 Tulit igitur populus conspersam farinam antequam fermentaretur et ligans in palliis posuit super umeros suos. 35 Feceruntque filii Israhel sicut praeceperat Moses, et petierunt ab Aegyptiis vasa argentea et aurea vestemque plurimam.

36 Dedit autem Dominus gratiam populo coram Aegyptiis ut commodarent eis, et spoliaverunt Aegyptios. 37 Profectique sunt filii Israhel de Ramesse in Soccoth, sescenta ferme milia peditum virorum, absque parvulis. 38 Sed et vul-

26 "And when your children shall say to you, 'What is the meaning of this service?' 27 you shall say to them, 'It is the victim of the passage of the Lord when he passed over the houses of the children of Israel in Egypt, striking the Egyptians and saving our houses.'"

And the people bowing themselves adored. 28 And the children of Israel going forth did as the Lord had commanded Moses and Aaron. 29 And it came to pass at midnight the Lord slew every firstborn in the land of Egypt, from the firstborn of Pharaoh who sat on his throne unto the firstborn of the captive woman that was in the prison and all the firstborn of cattle. 30 And Pharaoh arose in the night and all his servants and all Egypt, and there arose a great cry in Egypt, for there was not a house wherein there lay not one dead.

31 And Pharaoh calling Moses and Aaron in the night said, "Arise, and go forth from among my people. You and the children of Israel, go; sacrifice to the Lord as you say. 32 Your sheep and herds take along with you as you demanded, and, departing, bless me."

33 And the Egyptians pressed the people to go forth out of the land speedily, saying, "We shall all die." 34 The people therefore took dough before it was leavened and tying it in their cloaks put it on their shoulders. 35 And the children of Israel did as Moses had commanded, and they asked of the Egyptians vessels of silver and gold and very much raiment.

36 And the Lord gave favour to the people in the sight of the Egyptians so that they lent unto them, and they stripped the Egyptians. 37 And the children of Israel set forward from Rameses to Succoth, being about six hundred thousand men on foot, beside children. 38 And a mixed multitude without

gus promiscuum innumerabile ascendit cum eis, oves et armenta et animantia diversi generis, multa nimis. 39 Coxeruntque farinam quam dudum conspersam de Aegypto tulerant, et fecerunt subcinericios panes azymos, neque enim poterant fermentari, cogentibus exire Aegyptiis, et nullam facere sinentibus moram, nec pulmenti quicquam occurrerat praeparare. 40 Habitatio autem filiorum Israhel qua manserunt in Aegypto fuit quadringentorum triginta annorum, 41 quibus expletis, eadem die egressus est omnis exercitus Domini de terra Aegypti. 42 Nox est ista observabilis Domini quando eduxit eos de terra Aegypti; hanc observare debent omnes filii Israhel in generationibus suis.

43 Dixitque Dominus ad Mosen et Aaron, "Haec est religio phase. Omnis alienigena non comedet ex eo. 44 Omnis autem servus empticius circumcidetur, et sic comedet. 45 Advena et mercennarius non edent ex eo. 46 In una domo comedetur, nec efferetis de carnibus eius foras, nec os illius confringetis. 47 Omnis coetus filiorum Israhel faciet illud. 48 Quod si quis peregrinorum in vestram voluerit transire coloniam et facere phase Domini, circumcidetur prius omne masculinum eius, et tunc rite celebrabit, eritque sicut indigena terrae, si quis autem circumcisus non fuerit, non vescetur ex eo. 49 Eadem lex erit indigenae et colono qui peregrinatur apud vos." 50 Feceruntque omnes filii Israhel sicut praeceperat Dominus Mosi et Aaron. 51 Et eadem die eduxit Dominus filios Israhel de terra Aegypti per turmas suas.

number went up also with them, sheep and herds and beasts of divers kinds, exceeding many. 39 And they baked the meal which a little before they had brought out of Egypt in dough, and they made earth cakes unleavened, for it could not be leavened, the Egyptians pressing them to depart, and not suffering them to make any stay, neither did they think of preparing any meat. 40 And the abode of the children of Israel that they made in Egypt was four hundred and thirty years, 41 which being expired, the same day all the army of the Lord went forth out of the land of Egypt. 42 This is the observable night of the Lord when he brought them forth out of the land of Egypt; this night all the children of Israel must observe in their generations.

43 And the Lord said to Moses and Aaron, "This is the service of the phase. No foreigner shall eat of it. 44 But every bought servant shall be circumcised, and so shall eat. 45 The stranger and the hireling shall not eat thereof. 46 In one house shall it be eaten, neither shall you carry forth of the flesh thereof out of the house, neither shall you break a bone thereof. 47 All the assembly of the children of Israel shall keep it. 48 And if any stranger be willing to dwell among you and to keep the phase of the Lord, all his males shall first be circumcised, and then shall he celebrate it according to the manner, and he shall be as he that is born in the land, but if any man be uncircumcised, he shall not eat thereof. 49 The same law shall be to him that is born in the land and to the proselyte that sojourneth with you." 50 And all the children of Israel did as the Lord had commanded Moses and Aaron. 51 And the same day the Lord brought forth the children of Israel out of the land of Egypt by their companies.

Caput 13

Locutusque est Dominus ad Mosen, dicens, 2 "Sanctifica mihi omne primogenitum quod aperit vulvam in filiis Israhel, tam de hominibus quam de iumentis, mea sunt enim omnia."

3 Et ait Moses ad populum, "Mementote diei huius in qua egressi estis de Aegypto et de domo servitutis (quoniam in manu forti eduxit vos Dominus de loco isto) ut non comedatis fermentatum panem. 4 Hodie egredimini mense novarum frugum. 5 Cumque te introduxerit Dominus in terram Chananei et Hetthei et Amorrei et Evei et Iebusei, quam iuravit patribus tuis ut daret tibi, terram fluentem lacte et melle, celebrabis hunc morem sacrorum mense isto. 6 Septem diebus vesceris azymis, et in die septimo erit sollemnitas Domini. 7 Azyma comedetis septem diebus; non apparebit apud te aliquid fermentatum nec in cunctis finibus tuis. 8 Narrabisque filio tuo in die illo, dicens, 'Hoc est quod fecit Dominus mihi quando egressus sum de Aegypto.' 9 Et erit

Chapter 13

The paschal solemnity is to be observed, and the firstborn
are to be consecrated to God. The people are conducted
through the desert by a pillar of fire in the night and a cloud
in the day.

And the Lord spoke to Moses, saying, 2 "Sanctify unto
me every firstborn that openeth the womb among the children of Israel, as well of men as of beasts, for they are all
mine."

3 And Moses said to the people, "Remember this day in
which you came forth out of Egypt and out of the house of
bondage (for with a strong hand hath the Lord brought you
forth out of this place) that you eat no leavened bread. 4 This
day you go forth in the month of new corn. 5 And when the
Lord shall have brought thee into the land of the Canaanite
and the Hittite and the Amorite and the Hivite and the Jebusite, which he swore to thy fathers that he would give
thee, a land that floweth with milk and honey, thou shalt celebrate this manner of sacred rites in this month. 6 Seven
days shalt thou eat unleavened bread, and on the seventh
day shall be the solemnity of the Lord. 7 Unleavened bread
shall you eat seven days; there shall not be seen any thing
leavened with thee nor in all thy coasts. 8 And thou shalt tell
thy son in that day, saying, 'This is what the Lord did to me
when I came forth out of Egypt.' 9 And it shall be as a sign in

quasi signum in manu tua et quasi monumentum ante oculos tuos et ut lex Domini semper in ore tuo, in manu enim forti eduxit te Dominus de Aegypto. 10 Custodies huiuscemodi cultum statuto tempore a diebus in dies.

11 "Cumque introduxerit te Dominus in terram Chananei, sicut iuravit tibi et patribus tuis, et dederit eam tibi, 12 separabis omne quod aperit vulvam Domino et quod primitivum est in pecoribus tuis. Quicquid habueris masculini sexus consecrabis Domino. 13 Primogenitum asini mutabis ove, quod si non redemeris, interficies. Omne autem primogenitum hominis de filiis tuis pretio redimes. 14 Cumque interrogaverit te filius tuus cras, dicens, 'Quid est hoc?' respondebis ei, 'In manu forti eduxit nos Dominus de terra Aegypti, de domo servitutis, 15 nam cum induratus esset Pharao et nollet nos dimittere occidit Dominus omne primogenitum in terra Aegypti, a primogenito hominis usque ad primogenitum iumentorum. Idcirco, immolo Domino omne quod aperit vulvam masculini sexus, et omnia primogenita filiorum meorum redimo.' 16 Erit igitur quasi signum in manu tua et quasi adpensum quid ob recordationem inter oculos tuos, eo quod in manu forti eduxerit nos Dominus de Aegypto."

17 Igitur cum emisisset Pharao populum, non eos duxit Dominus per viam terrae Philisthim quae vicina est, reputans ne forte paeniteret eum si vidisset adversum se bella consurgere et reverteretur in Aegyptum, 18 sed circumduxit per viam deserti, quae est iuxta Mare Rubrum, et armati ascenderunt filii Israhel de terra Aegypti. 19 Tulit quoque Mo-

thy hand and as a memorial before thy eyes and that the law of the Lord be always in thy mouth, for with a strong hand the Lord hath brought thee out of *the land of* Egypt. 10 Thou shalt keep this observance at the set time from days to days.

11 "And when the Lord shall have brought thee into the land of the Canaanite, as he swore to thee and thy fathers, and shall give it thee, 12 thou shalt set apart all that openeth the womb for the Lord and all that is first brought forth of thy cattle. Whatsoever thou shalt have of the male sex thou shalt consecrate to the Lord. 13 The firstborn of an ass thou shalt change for a sheep, and if thou do not redeem it, thou shalt kill it. And every firstborn of *men* thou shalt redeem with a price. 14 And when thy son shall ask thee tomorrow, saying, 'What is this?' thou shalt answer him, 'With a strong hand did the Lord bring us forth out of the land of Egypt, out of the house of bondage, 15 for when Pharaoh was hardened and would not let us go the Lord slew every firstborn in the land of Egypt, from the firstborn of man to the firstborn of beasts. Therefore, I sacrifice to the Lord all that openeth the womb of the male sex, and all the firstborn of my sons I redeem.' 16 And it shall be as a sign in thy hand and as a thing hung between thy eyes for a remembrance, because the Lord hath brought us forth out of Egypt by a strong hand."

17 And when Pharaoh had sent out the people, the Lord led them not by the way of the land of the Philistines which is near, thinking lest perhaps they would repent if they should see wars arise against them and would return into Egypt, 18 but he led them about by the way of the desert, which is by the Red Sea, and the children of Israel went up armed out of the land of Egypt. 19 And Moses took Joseph's

ses ossa Ioseph secum, eo quod adiurasset filios Israhel, dicens, "Visitabit vos Deus; efferte ossa mea hinc vobiscum." 20 Profectique de Soccoth castrametati sunt in Etham in extremis finibus solitudinis.

21 Dominus autem praecedebat eos ad ostendendam viam per diem in columna nubis, et per noctem in columna ignis ut dux esset itineris utroque tempore. 22 Numquam defuit columna nubis per diem nec columna ignis per noctem coram populo.

Caput 14

Locutus est autem Dominus ad Mosen, dicens, 2 "Loquere filiis Israhel. Reversi castrametentur e regione Phiahiroth quae est inter Magdolum et mare contra Beelsephon; in conspectu eius castra ponetis super mare. 3 Dicturusque est Pharao super filiis Israhel, 'Coartati sunt in terra; conclusit eos desertum.' 4 Et indurabo cor eius, ac persequetur vos, et glorificabor in Pharao et in omni exercitu eius, scientque Aegyptii quia ego sum Dominus." Feceruntque ita.

bones with him, because he had adjured the children of Israel, saying, "God shall visit you; carry out my bones from hence with you." 20 And marching from Succoth they encamped in Etham in the utmost coasts of the wilderness.

21 And the Lord went before them to shew the way by day in a pillar of a cloud, and by night in a pillar of fire that he might be the guide of their journey at both times. 22 There never failed the pillar of the cloud by day nor the pillar of fire by night before the people.

Chapter 14

Pharaoh pursueth the children of Israel. They murmur
against Moses but are encouraged by him and pass through
the Red Sea. Pharaoh and his army following them are
drowned.

And the Lord spoke to Moses, saying, 2 "Speak to the children of Israel. Let them turn and encamp over against Pi-hahiroth which is between Migdol and the sea over against Baal-zephon; you shall encamp before it upon the sea. 3 And Pharaoh will say of the children of Israel, 'They are straitened in the land; the desert hath shut them in.' 4 And I shall harden his heart, and he will pursue you, and I shall be glorified in Pharaoh and in all his army, and the Egyptians shall know that I am the Lord." And they did so.

5 Et nuntiatum est regi Aegyptiorum quod fugisset populus, inmutatumque est cor Pharaonis et servorum eius super populo, et dixerunt, "Quid voluimus facere, ut dimitteremus Israhel ne serviret nobis?"

6 Iunxit ergo currum et omnem populum suum adsumpsit secum. 7 Tulitque sescentos currus electos et quicquid in Aegypto curruum fuit et duces totius exercitus. 8 Induravitque Dominus cor Pharaonis, regis Aegypti, et persecutus est filios Israhel, at illi egressi erant in manu excelsa. 9 Cumque persequerentur Aegyptii vestigia praecedentium, reppererunt eos in castris super mare; omnis equitatus et currus Pharaonis et universus exercitus erant in Ahiroth contra Beelsephon.

10 Cumque adpropinquasset Pharao, levantes filii Israhel oculos viderunt Aegyptios post se, et timuerunt valde clamaveruntque ad Dominum. 11 Et dixerunt ad Mosen, "Forsitan non erant sepulchra in Aegypto; ideo tulisti nos ut moreremur in solitudine. Quid hoc facere voluisti, ut educeres nos ex Aegypto? 12 Nonne iste est sermo quem loquebamur ad te in Aegypto, dicentes, 'Recede a nobis ut serviamus Aegyptiis'? Multo enim melius erat servire eis quam mori in solitudine."

13 Et ait Moses ad populum, "Nolite timere. State, et videte magnalia Domini quae facturus est hodie, Aegyptios enim, quos nunc videtis, nequaquam ultra videbitis usque in sempiternum. 14 Dominus pugnabit pro vobis, et vos tacebitis."

15 Dixitque Dominus ad Mosen, "Quid clamas ad me? Loquere filiis Israhel ut proficiscantur. 16 Tu autem eleva virgam tuam, et extende manum super mare, et divide illud

5 And it was told the king of the Egyptians that the people was fled, and the heart of Pharaoh and of his servants was changed with regard to the people, and they said, "What meant we to do, that we let Israel go from serving us?"

6 So he made ready his chariot and took all his people with him. 7 And he took six hundred chosen chariots and all the chariots that were in Egypt and the captains of the whole army. 8 And the Lord hardened the heart of Pharaoh, king of Egypt, and he pursued the children of Israel, but they were gone forth in a mighty hand. 9 And when the Egyptians followed the steps of them who were gone before, they found them encamped at the sea side; all Pharaoh's horse and chariots and the whole army were in Pi-hahiroth before Baal-zephon.

10 And when Pharaoh drew near, the children of Israel lifting up their eyes saw the Egyptians behind them, and they feared exceedingly and cried to the Lord. 11 And they said to Moses, "Perhaps there were no graves in Egypt; therefore thou hast brought us to die in the wilderness. Why wouldst thou do this, to lead us out of Egypt? 12 Is not this the word that we spoke to thee in Egypt, saying, 'Depart from us that we may serve the Egyptians'? For it was much better to serve them than to die in the wilderness."

13 And Moses said to the people, "Fear not. Stand, and see the great wonders of the Lord which he will do this day, for the Egyptians, whom you see now, you shall see no more for ever. 14 The Lord will fight for you, and you shall hold your peace."

15 And the Lord said to Moses, "Why criest thou to me? Speak to the children of Israel to go forward. 16 But lift thou up thy rod, and stretch forth thy hand over the sea, and di-

ut gradiantur filii Israhel in medio mari per siccum. 17 Ego autem indurabo cor Aegyptiorum ut persequantur vos, et glorificabor in Pharaone et in omni exercitu eius et in curribus et in equitibus illius. 18 Et scient Aegyptii quia ego sum Dominus cum glorificatus fuero in Pharaone et in curribus atque in equitibus eius."

19 Tollensque se angelus Dei qui praecedebat castra Israhel abiit post eos, et cum eo pariter columna nubis priora dimittens post tergum 20 stetit, inter castra Aegyptiorum et castra Israhel, et erat nubes tenebrosa et inluminans noctem ita ut ad se invicem toto noctis tempore accedere non valerent.

21 Cumque extendisset Moses manum super mare, abstulit illud Dominus flante vento vehementi et urente tota nocte, et vertit in siccum, divisaque est aqua. 22 Et ingressi sunt filii Israhel per medium maris sicci, erat enim aqua quasi murus a dextra eorum et leva. 23 Persequentesque Aegyptii ingressi sunt post eos, et omnis equitatus Pharaonis, currus eius et equites per medium maris. 24 Iamque advenerat vigilia matutina, et ecce: respiciens Dominus super castra Aegyptiorum per columnam ignis et nubis interfecit exercitum eorum 25 et subvertit rotas curruum, ferebanturque in profundum. Dixerunt ergo Aegyptii, "Fugiamus Israhelem, Dominus enim pugnat pro eis contra nos."

26 Et ait Dominus ad Mosen, "Extende manum tuam super mare ut revertantur aquae ad Aegyptios, super currus et equites eorum." 27 Cumque extendisset Moses manum contra mare, reversum est primo diluculo ad priorem locum,

vide it that the children of Israel may go through the midst of the sea on dry ground. 17 And I will harden the heart of the Egyptians to pursue you, and I will be glorified in Pharaoh and in all his host and in his chariots and in his horsemen. 18 And the Egyptians shall know that I am the Lord when I shall be glorified in Pharaoh and in his chariots and in his horsemen."

19 And the angel of God who went before the camp of Israel removing went behind them, and together with him the pillar of the cloud leaving the forepart 20 stood behind, between the Egyptians' camp and the camp of Israel, and it was a dark cloud and enlightening the night so that they could not come at one another all the night.

21 And when Moses had stretched forth his hand over the sea, the Lord took it away by a strong and burning wind blowing all the night, and turned it into dry ground, and the water was divided. 22 And the children of Israel went in through the midst of the sea dried up, for the water was as a wall on their right hand and on their left. 23 And the Egyptians pursuing went in after them, and all Pharaoh's horses, his chariots and horsemen through the midst of the sea. 24 And now the morning watch was come, and behold: the Lord, looking upon the Egyptian army through the pillar of fire and of the cloud, slew their host 25 and overthrew the wheels of the chariots, and they were carried into the deep. And the Egyptians said, "Let us flee from Israel, for the Lord fighteth for them against us."

26 And the Lord said to Moses, "Stretch forth thy hand over the sea that the waters may come again upon the Egyptians, upon their chariots and horsemen." 27 And when Moses had stretched forth his hand towards the sea, it returned

fugientibusque Aegyptiis, occurrerunt aquae, et involvit eos Dominus in mediis fluctibus. 28 Reversaeque sunt aquae et operuerunt currus et equites cuncti exercitus Pharaonis qui sequentes ingressi fuerant mare, nec unus quidem superfuit ex eis. 29 Filii autem Israhel perrexerunt per medium sicci maris, et aquae eis erant quasi pro muro a dextris et a sinistris, 30 liberavitque Dominus in die illo Israhel de manu Aegyptiorum. 31 Et viderunt Aegyptios mortuos super litus maris et manum magnam quam exercuerat Dominus contra eos, timuitque populus Dominum, et crediderunt Domino et Mosi, servo eius.

Caput 15

Tunc cecinit Moses et filii Israhel carmen hoc Domino et dixerunt:

"Cantemus Domino, gloriose enim magnificatus est. Equum et ascensorem deiecit in mare. 2 Fortitudo mea et laus mea Dominus, et factus est mihi in salutem. Iste Deus meus, et glorificabo eum, Deus patris mei, et exaltabo

at the first break of day to the former place, and as the Egyptians were fleeing away, the waters came upon them, and the Lord shut them up in the middle of the waves. 28 And the waters returned and covered the chariots and the horsemen of all the army of Pharaoh who had come into the sea after them, neither did there so much as one of them remain. 29 But the children of Israel marched through the midst of the *sea upon dry land,* and the waters were to them as a wall on the right hand and on the left, 30 and the Lord delivered Israel on that day out of the hands of the Egyptians. 31 And they saw the Egyptians dead upon the sea shore and the mighty hand that the Lord had used against them, and the people feared the Lord, and they believed the Lord and Moses, his servant.

Chapter 15

The canticle of Moses. The bitter waters of Marah are made sweet.

Then Moses and the children of Israel sung this canticle to the Lord and said:

"Let us sing to the Lord, for he is gloriously magnified. The horse and the rider he hath thrown into the sea. 2 The Lord is my strength and my praise, and he is become salvation to me. He is my God, and I will glorify him, the God of

eum. 3 Dominus quasi vir pugnator; Omnipotens nomen eius. 4 Currus Pharaonis et exercitum eius proiecit in mare; electi principes eius submersi sunt in Mari Rubro. 5 Abyssi operuerunt eos; descenderunt in profundum quasi lapis.

6 "Dextera tua, Domine, magnificata est in fortitudine. Dextera tua, Domine, percussit inimicum. 7 Et in multitudine gloriae tuae, deposuisti adversarios tuos. Misisti iram tuam quae devoravit eos ut stipulam.

8 "Et in spiritu furoris tui congregatae sunt aquae. Stetit unda fluens; congregatae sunt abyssi in medio mari. 9 Dixit inimicus, 'Persequar et conprehendam; dividam spolia; implebitur anima mea; evaginabo gladium meum; interficiet eos manus mea.' 10 Flavit spiritus tuus, et operuit eos mare. Submersi sunt quasi plumbum in aquis vehementibus.

11 "Quis similis tui in fortibus, Domine? Quis similis tui, magnificus in sanctitate, terribilis atque laudabilis, faciens mirabilia? 12 Extendisti manum tuam, et devoravit eos terra.

13 "Dux fuisti in misericordia tua populo quem redemisti, et portasti eum in fortitudine tua ad habitaculum sanctum tuum.

14 "Ascenderunt populi et irati sunt. Dolores obtinuerunt habitatores Philisthim. 15 Tunc conturbati sunt principes Edom; robustos Moab obtinuit tremor; obriguerunt omnes habitatores Chanaan. 16 Inruat super eos formido et pavor in magnitudine brachii tui. Fiant inmobiles quasi lapis, donec pertranseat populus tuus, Domine, donec pertranseat populus tuus iste, quem possedisti. 17 Introduces eos et plan-

my father, and I will exalt him. 3 The Lord is as a man of war; Almighty is his name. 4 Pharaoh's chariots and his army he hath cast into the sea; his chosen captains are drowned in the Red Sea. 5 The depths have covered them; they are sunk to the bottom like a stone.

6 "Thy right hand, O Lord, is magnified in strength. Thy right hand, O Lord, hath slain the enemy. 7 And in the multitude of thy glory, thou hast put down thy adversaries. Thou hast sent thy wrath which hath devoured them like stubble.

8 "And with the blast of thy anger the waters were gathered together. The flowing water stood; the depths were gathered together in the midst of the sea. 9 The enemy said, 'I will pursue and overtake; I will divide the spoils; my soul shall have its fill; I will draw my sword; my hand shall slay them.' 10 Thy wind blew, and the sea covered them. They sunk as lead in the mighty waters.

11 "Who is like to thee among the strong, O Lord? Who is like to thee, glorious in holiness, terrible and praiseworthy, doing wonders? 12 Thou stretchedst forth thy hand, and the earth swallowed them.

13 "In thy mercy, thou hast been a leader to the people which thou hast redeemed, and in thy strength thou hast carried them to thy holy habitation.

14 "Nations rose up and were angry. Sorrows took hold on the inhabitants of Philistia. 15 Then were the princes of Edom troubled; trembling seized on the stout men of Moab; all the inhabitants of Canaan became stiff. 16 Let fear and dread fall upon them in the greatness of thy arm. Let them become unmoveable as a stone, until thy people, O Lord, pass by, until this thy people pass by, which thou hast possessed. 17 Thou shalt bring them in and plant them in the

tabis in monte hereditatis tuae, firmissimo habitaculo tuo quod operatus es, Domine, sanctuarium tuum, Domine, quod firmaverunt manus tuae.

18 "Dominus regnabit in aeternum et ultra, 19 ingressus est enim eques Pharao cum curribus et equitibus eius in mare, et reduxit super eos Dominus aquas maris. Filii autem Israhel ambulaverunt per siccum in medio eius."

20 Sumpsit ergo Maria, prophetissa, soror Aaron, tympanum in manu, egressaeque sunt omnes mulieres post eam cum tympanis et choris, 21 quibus praecinebat, dicens, "Cantemus Domino, gloriose enim magnificatus est; equum et ascensorem eius deiecit in mare."

22 Tulit autem Moses Israhel de Mari Rubro, et egressi sunt in desertum Sur, ambulaveruntque tribus diebus per solitudinem et non inveniebant aquam. 23 Et venerunt in Marath, nec poterant bibere aquas de Mara eo quod essent amarae. Unde et congruum loco nomen inposuit, vocans illud Mara, id est, Amaritudinem. 24 Et murmuravit populus contra Mosen, dicens, "Quid bibemus?" 25 At ille clamavit ad Dominum, qui ostendit ei lignum, quod cum misisset in aquas in dulcedinem versae sunt. Ibi constituit ei praecepta atque iudicia, et ibi temptavit eum, 26 dicens, "Si audieris vocem Domini, Dei tui, et quod rectum est coram eo feceris et oboedieris mandatis eius custodierisque omnia praecepta illius, cunctum languorem quem posui in Aegypto non indu-

mountain of thy inheritance, in thy most firm habitation which thou hast made, O Lord, thy sanctuary, O Lord, which thy hands have established.

18 "The Lord shall reign for ever and ever, 19 for Pharaoh went in on horseback with his chariots and horsemen into the sea, and the Lord brought back upon them the waters of the sea. But the children of Israel walked on dry ground in the midst thereof."

20 So Miriam, the prophetess, the sister of Aaron, took a timbrel in her hand, and all the women went forth after her with timbrels and with dances, 21 and she began the song to them, saying, "Let us sing to the Lord, for he is gloriously magnified; the horse and his rider he hath thrown into the sea."

22 And Moses brought Israel from the Red Sea, and they went forth into the wilderness of Shur, and they marched three days through the wilderness and found no water. 23 And they came into Marah, and they could not drink the waters of Marah because they were bitter. Whereupon he gave a name also agreeable to the place, calling it Marah, that is, Bitterness. 24 And the people murmured against Moses, saying, "What shall we drink?" 25 But he cried to the Lord, and he shewed him a tree, which when he had cast into the waters they were turned into sweetness. There he appointed him ordinances and judgments, and there he proved him, 26 saying, "If thou wilt hear the voice of the Lord, thy God, and do what is right before him and obey his commandments and keep all his precepts, none of the evils that I laid upon Egypt will I bring upon thee, for I am the

cam super te, ego enim Dominus, sanator tuus." 27 Venerunt autem in Helim filii Israhel, ubi erant duodecim fontes aquarum et septuaginta palmae, et castrametati sunt iuxta aquas.

Caput 16

Profectique sunt de Helim, et venit omnis multitudo filiorum Israhel in desertum Sin, quod est inter Helim et Sinai, quintodecimo die mensis secundi postquam egressi sunt de terra Aegypti. 2 Et murmuravit omnis congregatio filiorum Israhel contra Mosen et Aaron in solitudine. 3 Dixeruntque ad eos filii Israhel, "Utinam mortui essemus per manum Domini in terra Aegypti quando sedebamus super ollas carnium et comedebamus panem in saturitate. Cur eduxistis nos in desertum istud ut occideretis omnem multitudinem fame?"

4 Dixit autem Dominus ad Mosen, "Ecce: ego pluam vobis panes de caelo. Egrediatur populus et colligat quae sufficiunt per singulos dies ut temptem eum utrum ambulet in lege mea an non. 5 Die autem sexta parent quod inferant, et sit duplum quam colligere solebant per singulos dies."

Lord, thy healer." 27 And the children of Israel came into Elim, where there were twelve fountains of water and seventy palm trees, and they encamped by the waters.

Chapter 16

The people murmur for want of meat. God giveth them quails and manna.

And they set forward from Elim, and all the multitude of the children of Israel came into the desert of Sin, which is between Elim and Sinai, the fifteenth day of the second month after they came out of the land of Egypt. 2 And all the congregation of the children of Israel murmured against Moses and Aaron in the wilderness. 3 And the children of Israel said to them, "Would to God we had died by the hand of the Lord in the land of Egypt when we sat over the flesh pots and ate bread to the full. Why have you brought us into this desert that you might destroy all the multitude with famine?"

4 And the Lord said to Moses, "Behold: I will rain bread from heaven for you. Let the people go forth and gather what is sufficient for every day that I may prove them whether they will walk in my law or not. 5 But the sixth day let them provide for to bring in, and let it be double to that they were wont to gather every day."

6 Dixeruntque Moses et Aaron ad omnes filios Israhel, "Vespere scietis quod Dominus eduxerit vos de terra Aegypti, 7 et mane videbitis gloriam Domini, audivit enim murmur vestrum contra Dominum. Nos vero, quid sumus quia mussitatis contra nos?" 8 Et ait Moses, "Dabit Dominus vobis vespere carnes edere, et mane panes in saturitate, eo quod audierit murmurationes vestras quibus murmurati estis contra eum, nos enim quid sumus? Nec contra nos est murmur vestrum, sed contra Dominum." 9 Dixitque Moses ad Aaron, "Dic universae congregationi filiorum Israhel, 'Accedite coram Domino, audivit enim murmur vestrum.'" 10 Cumque loqueretur Aaron ad omnem coetum filiorum Israhel respexerunt ad solitudinem, et ecce: gloria Domini apparuit in nube.

11 Locutus est autem Dominus ad Mosen, dicens, 12 "Audivi murmurationes filiorum Israhel. Loquere ad eos, 'Vespere comedetis carnes, et mane saturabimini panibus, scietisque quod sim Dominus, Deus vester.'" 13 Factum est ergo vespere et ascendens coturnix operuit castra, mane quoque, ros iacuit per circuitum castrorum. 14 Cumque operuisset superficiem terrae, apparuit in solitudine minutum et quasi pilo tunsum, in similitudinem pruinae super terram. 15 Quod cum vidissent filii Israhel, dixerunt ad invicem, "Man hu?!" quod significat, "Quid est hoc?!" ignorabant enim quid esset. Quibus ait Moses, "Iste est panis quem dedit Dominus vobis ad vescendum. 16 Hic est sermo quem praecepit Dominus: 'Colligat ex eo unusquisque quantum sufficiat ad vescendum: gomor per singula capita, iuxta nu-

6 And Moses and Aaron said to the children of Israel, "In the evening you shall know that the Lord hath brought you forth out of the land of Egypt, 7 and in the morning you shall see the glory of the Lord, for he hath heard your murmuring against the Lord. But as for us, what are we that you mutter against us?" 8 And Moses said, "In the evening the Lord will give you flesh to eat, and in the morning bread to the full, for he hath heard your murmurings with which you have murmured against him, for what are we? Your murmuring is not against us, but against the Lord." 9 Moses also said to Aaron, "Say to the whole congregation of the children of Israel, 'Come before the Lord, for he hath heard your murmuring.'" 10 And when Aaron spoke to all the assembly of the children of Israel they looked towards the wilderness, and behold: the glory of the Lord appeared in a cloud.

11 And the Lord spoke to Moses, saying, 12 "I have heard the murmuring of the children of Israel. Say to them, 'In the evening you shall eat flesh, and in the morning you shall have your fill of bread, and you shall know that I am the Lord, your God.'" 13 So it came to pass in the evening that quails coming up covered the camp, and in the morning, a dew lay round about the camp. 14 And when it had covered the face of the earth, it appeared in the wilderness small and as it were beaten with a pestle, like unto the hoar-frost on the ground. 15 And when the children of Israel saw it, they said one to another, "Manhu?!" which signifieth, "What is this?!" for they knew not what it was. And Moses said to them, "This is the bread which the Lord hath given you to eat. 16 This is the word that the Lord hath commanded: 'Let every one gather of it as much as is enough to eat: a gomor for

merum animarum vestrarum quae habitant in tabernaculo, sic tolletis.'"

17 Feceruntque ita filii Israhel, et collegerunt, alius plus, alius minus. 18 Et mensi sunt ad mensuram gomor, nec qui plus collegerat habuit amplius, nec qui minus paraverat repperit minus, sed singuli iuxta id quod edere poterant congregarunt. 19 Dixitque Moses ad eos, "Nullus relinquat ex eo in mane." 20 Qui non audierunt eum, sed dimiserunt quidam ex eis usque mane, et scatere coepit vermibus, atque conputruit, et iratus est contra eos Moses.

21 Colligebant autem mane singuli quantum sufficere poterat ad vescendum, cumque incaluisset sol, liquefiebat. 22 In die vero sexta, collegerunt cibos duplices, id est, duo gomor per singulos homines, venerunt autem omnes principes multitudinis et narraverunt Mosi. 23 Qui ait eis, "Hoc est quod locutus est Dominus: 'Requies sabbati sanctificata est Domino cras. Quodcumque operandum est, facite, et quae coquenda sunt, coquite, quicquid autem reliquum fuerit, reponite usque in mane." 24 Feceruntque ita ut praeceperat Moses, et non conputruit, neque vermis inventus est in eo. 25 Dixitque Moses, "Comedite illud hodie, quia sabbatum est Domini. Non invenietur hodie in agro. 26 Sex diebus colligite, in die autem septimo sabbatum est Domini, idcirco non invenietur."

27 Venitque septima dies, et egressi de populo ut colligerent non invenerunt. 28 Dixit autem Dominus ad Mosen, "Usquequo non vultis custodire mandata mea et legem meam? 29 Videte quod Dominus dederit vobis sabbatum, et propter hoc tribuerit vobis die sexto cibos duplices. Maneat

every man, according to the number of your souls that dwell in a tent, so shall you take *of it.*'"

17 And the children of Israel did so, and they gathered, one more, another less. 18 And they measured by the measure of a gomor, neither had he more that had gathered more, nor did he find less that had provided less, but every one had gathered according to what they were able to eat. 19 And Moses said to them, "Let no man leave thereof till the morning." 20 And they hearkened not to him, but some of them left until the morning, and it began to be full of worms, and it putrified, and Moses was angry with them.

21 Now every one of them gathered in the morning as much as might suffice to eat, and, after the sun grew hot, it melted. 22 But on the sixth day, they gathered twice as much, that is, two gomors every man, and all the rulers of the multitude came and told Moses. 23 And he said to them, "This is what the Lord hath spoken: 'Tomorrow is the rest of the sabbath sanctified to the Lord. Whatsoever work is to be done, do it, and the meats that are to be dressed, dress them, and whatsoever shall remain, lay it up until the morning.'" 24 And they did so as Moses had commanded, and it did not putrify, neither was there worm found in it. 25 And Moses said, "Eat it today, because it is the sabbath of the Lord. Today it shall not be found in the field. 26 Gather it six days, but on the seventh day is the sabbath of the Lord, therefore it shall not be found."

27 And the seventh day came, and some of the people going forth to gather found none. 28 And the Lord said to Moses, "How long will you refuse to keep my commandments and my law? 29 See that the Lord hath given you the sabbath, and for this reason on the sixth day he giveth you a double

unusquisque apud semet ipsum, et nullus egrediatur de loco suo die septimo." 30 Et sabbatizavit populus die septimo. 31 Appellavitque domus Israhel nomen eius man, quod erat quasi semen coriandri album, gustusque eius quasi similae cum melle. 32 Dixit autem Moses, "Iste est sermo quem praecepit Dominus: 'Imple gomor ex eo, et custodiatur in futuras retro generationes ut noverint panem quo alui vos in solitudine quando educti estis de terra Aegypti.'" 33 Dixitque Moses ad Aaron, "Sume vas unum et mitte ibi man, quantum potest capere gomor, et repone coram Domino ad servandum in generationes vestras, 34 sicut praecepit Dominus Mosi." Posuitque illud Aaron in tabernaculo reservandum. 35 Filii autem Israhel comederunt man quadraginta annis donec venirent in terram habitabilem. Hoc cibo aliti sunt usquequo tangerent fines terrae Chanaan. 36 Gomor autem decima pars est oephi.

provision. Let each man stay at home, and let none go forth out of his place the seventh day." 30 And the people kept the sabbath on the seventh day. 31 And the house of Israel called the name thereof manna, and it was like coriander seed white, and the taste thereof like to flour with honey. 32 And Moses said, "This is the word which the Lord hath commanded: 'Fill a gomor of it, and let it be kept unto generations to come hereafter that they may know the bread wherewith I fed you in the wilderness when you were brought forth out of the land of Egypt.'" 33 And Moses said to Aaron, "Take a vessel and put manna into it, as much as a gomor can hold, and lay it up before the Lord to keep unto your generations, 34 as the Lord commanded Moses." And Aaron put it in the tabernacle to be kept. 35 And the children of Israel ate manna forty years till they came to a habitable land. With this meat were they fed until they reached the borders of the land of Canaan. 36 Now a gomor is the tenth part of an ephi.

Caput 17

Igitur profecta omnis multitudo filiorum Israhel de deserto Sin per mansiones suas, iuxta sermonem Domini, castrametata est in Raphidim, ubi non erat aqua ad bibendum populo. 2 Qui iurgatus contra Mosen ait, "Da nobis aquam, ut bibamus."

Quibus respondit Moses, "Quid iurgamini contra me? Cur temptatis Dominum?"

3 Sitivit ergo populus ibi pro aquae penuria, et murmuravit contra Mosen, dicens, "Cur nos exire fecisti de Aegypto? Ut occideres nos et liberos nostros ac iumenta siti?"

4 Clamavit autem Moses ad Dominum, dicens, "Quid faciam populo huic? Adhuc pauxillum et lapidabunt me."

5 Et ait Dominus ad Mosen, "Antecede populum, et sume tecum de senibus Israhel, et virgam qua percussisti fluvium tolle in manu tua, et vade. 6 En: ego stabo coram te ibi super petram Horeb, percutiesque petram, et exibit ex ea aqua ut bibat populus." Fecit Moses ita coram senibus Israhel, 7 et vocavit nomen loci illius Temptatio, propter iurgium filio-

Chapter 17

The people murmur again for want of drink; the Lord
giveth them water out of a rock. Moses lifting up his hand
in prayer, Amalek is overcome.

Then all the multitude of the children of Israel setting
forward from the desert of Sin by their mansions, according to the word of the Lord, encamped in Rephidim, where
there was no water for the people to drink. 2 And they chode
with Moses and said, "Give us water, that we may drink."

And Moses answered them, "Why chide you with me?
Wherefore do you tempt the Lord?"

3 So the people were thirsty there for want of water, and
murmured against Moses, saying, "Why didst thou make us
go forth out of Egypt? To kill us and our children and our
beasts with thirst?"

4 And Moses cried to the Lord, saying, "What shall I do
to this people? Yet a little more and they will stone me."

5 And the Lord said to Moses, "Go before the people, and
take with thee of the ancients of Israel, and take in thy hand
the rod wherewith thou didst strike the river, and go. 6 Behold: I will stand there before thee upon the rock Horeb,
and thou shalt strike the rock, and water shall come out of
it that the people may drink." Moses did so before the ancients of Israel, 7 and he called the name of that place Temptation, because of the chiding of the children of Israel and

rum Israhel et quia temptaverunt Dominum, dicentes, "Estne Dominus in nobis an non?"

8 Venit autem Amalech et pugnabat contra Israhel in Raphidim. 9 Dixitque Moses ad Iosue, "Elige viros, et egressus pugna contra Amalech. Cras ego stabo in vertice collis habens virgam Dei in manu mea." 10 Fecit Iosue ut locutus erat Moses, et pugnavit contra Amalech, Moses autem et Aaron et Hur ascenderunt super verticem collis.

11 Cumque levaret Moses manus, vincebat Israhel, sin autem paululum remisisset, superabat Amalech. 12 Manus autem Mosi erant graves, sumentes igitur lapidem posuerunt subter eum, in quo sedit, Aaron autem et Hur sustentabant manus eius ex utraque parte. Et factum est ut manus ipsius non lassarentur usque ad occasum solis. 13 Fugavitque Iosue Amalech et populum eius in ore gladii. 14 Dixit autem Dominus ad Mosen, "Scribe hoc ob monumentum in libro, et trade auribus Iosue, delebo enim memoriam Amalech sub caelo."

15 Aedificavitque Moses altare et vocavit nomen eius Dominus, Exaltatio Mea, dicens, 16 "Quia manus solii Domini et bellum Domini erit contra Amalech, a generatione in generationem."

for that they tempted the Lord, saying, "Is the Lord amongst us or not?"

8 And Amalek came and fought against Israel in Rephidim. 9 And Moses said to Joshua, "Choose out men, and go out, and fight against Amalek. Tomorrow I will stand on the top of the hill having the rod of God in my hand." 10 Joshua did as Moses had spoken, and he fought against Amalek, but Moses and Aaron and Hur went up upon the top of the hill.

11 And when Moses lifted up his hands, Israel overcame, but if he let them down a little, Amalek overcame. 12 And Moses' hands were heavy, so they took a stone and put under him, and he sat on it, and Aaron and Hur stayed up his hands on both sides. And it came to pass that his hands were not weary until sunset. 13 And Joshua put Amalek and his people to flight by the edge of the sword. 14 And the Lord said to Moses, "Write this for a memorial in a book, and deliver it to the ears of Joshua, for I will destroy the memory of Amalek from under heaven."

15 And Moses built an altar and called the name thereof The Lord, My Exaltation, saying, 16 "Because the hand of the throne of the Lord and the war of the Lord shall be against Amalek, from generation to generation."

Caput 18

Cumque audisset Iethro, sacerdos Madian, cognatus Mosi, omnia quae fecerat Deus Mosi et Israhel, populo suo, et quod eduxisset Dominus Israhel de Aegypto, 2 tulit Sefforam, uxorem Mosi, quam remiserat, 3 et duos filios eius, quorum unus vocabatur Gersan, dicente patre, "Advena fui in terra aliena," 4 alter vero Eliezer, "Deus enim," ait, "patris mei adiutor meus et eruit me de gladio Pharaonis." 5 Venit ergo Iethro, cognatus Mosi, et filii eius et uxor eius ad Mosen in desertum ubi erat castrametatus iuxta montem Dei. 6 Et mandavit Mosi, dicens, "Ego, cognatus tuus, Iethro, venio ad te, et uxor tua et duo filii tui cum ea."

7 Qui egressus in occursum cognati sui adoravit et osculatus est eum, salutaveruntque se mutuo verbis pacificis. Cumque intrasset tabernaculum, 8 narravit Moses cognato suo cuncta quae fecerat Dominus Pharaoni et Aegyptiis propter Israhel universumque laborem qui accidisset eis in itinere et quod liberarat eos Dominus. 9 Laetatusque est Iethro super omnibus bonis quae fecerat Dominus Israheli eo quod eruisset eum de manu Aegyptiorum. 10 Et ait, "Benedictus Dominus, qui liberavit vos de manu Aegyptiorum et de manu Pha-

Chapter 18

Jethro bringeth to Moses his wife and children. His counsel.

And when Jethro, the priest of Midian, the kinsman of Moses, had heard all the things that God had done to Moses and to Israel, his people, and that the Lord had brought forth Israel out of Egypt, 2 he took Zipporah, the wife of Moses, whom he had sent back, 3 and her two sons, of whom one was called Gershom, his father saying, "I have been a stranger in a foreign country," 4 and the other Eliezer, "For the God of my father," said he, "is my helper and hath delivered me from the sword of Pharaoh." 5 And Jethro, the kinsman of Moses, came with his sons and his wife to Moses into the desert where he was camped by the mountain of God. 6 And he sent word to Moses, saying, "I, Jethro, thy kinsman, come to thee, and thy wife and thy two sons with her."

7 And he went out to meet his kinsman and worshipped and kissed him, and they saluted one another with words of peace. And when he was come into the tent, 8 Moses told his kinsman all that the Lord had done to Pharaoh and the Egyptians in favour of Israel and all the labour which had befallen them in the journey and that the Lord had delivered them. 9 And Jethro rejoiced for all the good things that the Lord had done to Israel because he had delivered them out of the hands of the Egyptians. 10 And he said, "Blessed is the Lord, who hath delivered you out of the hand of Pha-

raonis, qui eruit populum suum de manu Aegypti. 11 Nunc
cognovi quia magnus Dominus super omnes deos eo quod
superbe egerint contra illos."

12 Obtulit ergo Iethro, cognatus Mosi, holocausta et hostias Deo, veneruntque Aaron et omnes senes Israhel ut
comederent panem cum eo coram Deo. 13 Altero autem die
sedit Moses ut iudicaret populum qui adsistebat Mosi de
mane usque ad vesperam. 14 Quod cum vidisset cognatus
eius omnia, scilicet, quae agebat in populo, ait, "Quid est
hoc quod facis in plebe? Cur solus sedes, et omnis populus
praestolatur de mane usque ad vesperam?"

15 Cui respondit Moses, "Venit ad me populus quaerens
sententiam Dei, 16 cumque acciderit eis aliqua disceptatio,
veniunt ad me ut iudicem inter eos et ostendam praecepta
Dei et leges eius."

17 At ille, "Non bonam," inquit, "rem facis. 18 Stulto labore
consumeris, et tu et populus iste qui tecum est. Ultra vires
tuas est negotium; solus illud non poteris sustinere. 19 Sed
audi verba mea atque consilia, et erit Deus tecum. Esto tu
populo in his quae ad Deum pertinent ut referas quae dicun-
tur ad eum 20 ostendasque populo caerimonias et ritum co-
lendi viamque per quam ingredi debeant et opus quod facere
debeant. 21 Provide autem de omni plebe viros potentes et
timentes Deum, in quibus sit veritas et qui oderint avari-
tiam, et constitue ex eis tribunos et centuriones et quinquagenarios et decanos 22 qui iudicent populum omni tempore.
Quicquid autem maius fuerit, referant ad te, et ipsi minora
tantummodo iudicent leviusque tibi sit, partito in alios

raoh and out of the hand of the Egyptians, who hath delivered his people out of the hand of Egypt. 11 Now I know that the Lord is great above all gods because they dealt proudly against them."

12 So Jethro, the kinsman of Moses, offered holocausts and sacrifices to God, and Aaron and all the ancients of Israel came to eat bread with them before God. 13 And the next day Moses sat to judge the people who stood by Moses from morning until night. 14 And when his kinsman had seen *all things* that he did among the people, he said, "What is it that thou dost among the people? Why sittest thou alone, and all the people wait from morning till night?"

15 And Moses answered him, "The people come to me to seek the judgment of God, 16 and when any controversy falleth out among them, they come to me to judge between them and to shew the precepts of God and his laws."

17 But he said, "The thing thou dost is not good. 18 Thou are spent with foolish labour, both thou and this people that is with thee. The business is above thy strength; thou alone canst not bear it. 19 But hear my words and counsels, and God shall be with thee. Be thou to the people in those things that pertain to God to bring their words to him 20 and to shew the people the ceremonies and the manner of worshipping and the way wherein they ought to walk and the work that they ought to do. 21 And provide out of all the people able men such as fear God, in whom there is truth and that hate avarice, and appoint of them rulers of thousands and of hundreds and of fifties and of tens 22 who may judge the people at all times. And when any great matter soever shall fall out, let them refer it to thee, and let them judge the lesser matters only *that* so it may be lighter for thee, the bur-

onere. 23 Si hoc feceris, implebis imperium Dei et praecepta eius poteris sustentare, et omnis hic populus revertetur cum pace ad loca sua."

24 Quibus auditis, Moses fecit omnia quae ille suggesserat. 25 Et electis viris strenuis de cuncto Israhel, constituit eos principes populi, tribunos et centuriones et quinquagenarios et decanos. 26 Qui iudicabant plebem omni tempore, quicquid autem gravius erat referebant ad eum, faciliora tantummodo iudicantes. 27 Dimisitque cognatum, qui reversus abiit in terram suam.

Caput 19

Mense tertio egressionis Israhel de terra Aegypti, in die hac, venerunt in solitudinem Sinai, 2 nam profecti de Raphidim et pervenientes usque in desertum Sinai, castrametati sunt in eodem loco, ibique Israhel fixit tentoria e regione montis. 3 Moses autem ascendit ad Deum, vocavitque eum Dominus de monte et ait, "Haec dices domui Iacob et ad-

den being shared out unto others. 23 If thou dost this, thou shalt fulfill the commandment of God and shalt be able to bear his precepts, and all this people shall return to their places with peace."

24 And when Moses heard this, he did all things that he had suggested unto him. 25 And choosing able men out of all Israel, he appointed them rulers of the people, rulers over thousands and over hundreds and over fifties and over tens. 26 And they judged the people at all times, and whatsoever was of greater difficulty they referred to him, and they judged the easier cases only. 27 And he let his kinsman depart, and he returned and went into his own country.

Chapter 19

They come to Sinai. The people are commanded to be sanctified. The Lord coming in thunder and lightning speaketh with Moses.

In the third month of the departure of Israel out of the land of Egypt, on this day, they came into the wilderness of Sinai, 2 for departing out of Rephidim and coming to the desert of Sinai, they camped in the same place, and there Israel pitched their tents over against the mountain. 3 And Moses went up to God, and the Lord called unto him from the mountain and said, "Thus shalt thou say to the house of

nuntiabis filiis Israhel: 4 'Vos ipsi vidistis quae fecerim Aegyptiis, quomodo portaverim vos super alas aquilarum et adsumpserim mihi. 5 Si ergo audieritis vocem meam et custodieritis pactum meum, eritis mihi in peculium de cunctis populis, mea est enim omnis terra. 6 Et vos eritis mihi regnum sacerdotale et gens sancta.' Haec sunt verba quae loqueris ad filios Israhel."

7 Venit Moses, et, convocatis maioribus natu populi, exposuit omnes sermones quos mandaverat Dominus. 8 Responditque universus populus simul, "Cuncta quae locutus est Dominus, faciemus." Cumque rettulisset Moses verba populi ad Dominum, 9 ait ei Dominus, "Iam nunc veniam ad te in caligine nubis ut audiat me populus loquentem ad te et credat tibi in perpetuum." Nuntiavit ergo Moses verba populi ad Dominum. 10 Qui dixit ei, "Vade ad populum, et sanctifica illos hodie et cras, laventque vestimenta sua. 11 Et sint parati in diem tertium, in die enim tertio descendet Dominus coram omni plebe super Montem Sinai. 12 Constituesque terminos populo per circuitum, et dices ad eos, 'Cavete ne ascendatis in montem nec tangatis fines illius. Omnis qui tetigerit montem morte morietur. 13 Manus non tanget eum, sed lapidibus opprimetur aut confodietur iaculis; sive iumentum fuerit sive homo, non vivet.' Cum coeperit clangere bucina, tunc ascendant in montem."

14 Descenditque Moses de monte ad populum et sanctific-

Jacob and tell the children of Israel: 4 'You have seen what I have done to the Egyptians, how I have carried you upon the wings of eagles and have taken you to myself. 5 If therefore you will hear my voice and keep my covenant, you shall be my peculiar possession above all people, for all the earth is mine. 6 And you shall be to me a priestly kingdom and a holy nation.' Those are the words thou shalt speak to the children of Israel."

7 Moses came, and, calling together the elders of the people, he declared all the words which the Lord had commanded. 8 And all the people answered together, "All that the Lord hath spoken, we will do." And when Moses had related the people's words to the Lord, 9 the Lord said to him, "Lo! Now will I come to thee in the darkness of a cloud that the people may hear me speaking to thee and may believe thee for ever." And Moses told the words of the people to the Lord. 10 And he said to him, "Go to the people, and sanctify them today and tomorrow, and let them wash their garments. 11 And let them be ready against the third day, for on the third day the Lord will come down in the sight of all the people upon Mount Sinai. 12 And thou shalt appoint certain limits to the people round about, and thou shalt say to them, 'Take heed you go not up into the mount and that ye touch not the borders thereof. Every one that toucheth the mount, dying he shall die. 13 No hands shall touch him, but he shall be stoned to death or shall be shot through with arrows; whether it be beast or man, he shall not live.' When the trumpet shall begin to sound, then let them go up into the mount."

14 And Moses came down from the mount to the people and sanctified them. And when they had washed their gar-

avit eum. Cumque lavissent vestimenta sua, 15 ait ad eos, "Estote parati in diem tertium, et ne adpropinquetis uxoribus vestris." 16 Iamque advenerat tertius dies, et mane inclaruerat, et ecce: coeperunt audiri tonitrua ac micare fulgura et nubes densissima operire montem, clangorque bucinae vehementius perstrepebat, et timuit populus qui erat in castris. 17 Cumque eduxisset eos Moses in occursum Dei de loco castrorum, steterunt ad radices montis. 18 Totus autem Mons Sinai fumabat eo quod descendisset Dominus super eum in igne, et ascenderet fumus ex eo quasi de fornace, eratque mons omnis terribilis. 19 Et sonitus bucinae paulatim crescebat in maius et prolixius tendebatur. Moses loquebatur, et Deus respondebat ei. 20 Descenditque Dominus super Montem Sinai in ipso montis vertice, et vocavit Mosen in cacumen eius.

Quo cum ascendisset, 21 dixit ad eum, "Descende, et contestare populum ne forte velint transcendere terminos ad videndum Dominum et pereat ex eis plurima multitudo. 22 Sacerdotes quoque qui accedunt ad Dominum, sanctificentur ne percutiat eos."

23 Dixitque Moses ad Dominum, "Non poterit vulgus ascendere in Montem Sinai, tu enim testificatus es et iussisti, dicens, 'Pone terminos circa montem, et sanctifica illum.'"

24 Cui ait Dominus, "Vade; descende, ascendesque, tu et Aaron tecum, sacerdotes autem et populus ne transeant terminos nec ascendant ad Dominum ne forte interficiat illos." 25 Descenditque Moses ad populum et omnia narravit eis.

ments, 15 he said to them, "Be ready against the third day, and come not near your wives." 16 And now the third day was come, and the morning appeared, and behold: thunders began to be heard and lightning to flash and a very thick cloud to cover the mount, and the noise of the trumpet sounded exceeding loud, and the people that was in the camp feared. 17 And when Moses had brought them forth to meet God from the place of the camp, they stood at the bottom of the mount. 18 And all Mount Sinai was on a smoke because the Lord was come down upon it in fire, and the smoke arose from it as out of a furnace, and all the mount was terrible. 19 And the sound of the trumpet grew by degrees louder and louder and was drawn out to a greater length. Moses spoke, and God answered him. 20 And the Lord came down upon Mount Sinai in the very top of the mount, and he called Moses unto the top thereof.

And when he was gone up thither, 21 he said unto him, "Go down, and charge the people lest they should have a mind to pass the limits to see the Lord and a very great multitude of them should perish. 22 The priests also that come to the Lord, let them be sanctified lest he strike them."

23 And Moses said to the Lord, "The people cannot come up to Mount Sinai, for thou did charge and command, saying, 'Set limits about the mount, and sanctify it.'"

24 And the Lord said to him, "Go; get thee down, and thou shalt come up, thou and Aaron with thee, but let not the priests and the people pass the limits nor come up to the Lord *lest* he kill them." 25 And Moses went down to the people and told them all.

Caput 20

Locutus quoque est Dominus cunctos sermones hos: 2 "Ego sum Dominus, Deus tuus, qui eduxi te de terra Aegypti, de domo servitutis. 3 Non habebis deos alienos coram me.

4 "Non facies tibi sculptile neque omnem similitudinem quae est in caelo desuper et quae in terra deorsum nec eorum quae sunt in aquis sub terra. 5 Non adorabis ea neque coles. Ego sum Dominus, Deus tuus, fortis, zelotes, visitans iniquitatem patrum in filiis in tertiam et quartam generationem eorum qui oderunt me, 6 et faciens misericordiam in milia his qui diligunt me et custodiunt praecepta mea.

7 "Non adsumes nomen Domini, Dei tui, in vanum, nec enim habebit insontem Dominus eum qui adsumpserit nomen Domini, Dei sui, frustra.

8 "Memento ut diem sabbati sanctifices. 9 Sex diebus operaberis et facies omnia opera tua. 10 Septimo autem die sabbatum Domini, Dei tui, est. Non facies omne opus in eo, tu et filius tuus et filia tua, servus tuus et ancilla tua, iumentum tuum et advena qui est intra portas tuas, 11 sex enim diebus fecit Dominus caelum et terram et mare et omnia quae in

Chapter 20

The ten commandments.

And the Lord spoke all these words: 2 "I am the Lord, thy God, who brought thee out of the land of Egypt, out of the house of bondage. 3 Thou shalt not have strange gods before me.

4 "Thou shalt not make to thyself a graven thing nor the likeness *of any thing* that is in heaven above or in the earth beneath nor of those things that are in the waters under the earth. 5 Thou shalt not adore them nor serve them. I am the Lord, thy God, mighty, jealous, visiting the iniquity of the fathers upon the children unto the third and fourth generation of them that hate me, 6 and shewing mercy unto thousands to them that love me and keep my commandments.

7 "Thou shalt not take the name of the Lord, thy God, in vain, for the Lord will not hold him guiltless that shall take the name of the Lord, his God, in vain.

8 "Remember that thou keep holy the sabbath day. 9 Six days shalt thou labour and shalt do all thy works. 10 But on the seventh day is the sabbath of the Lord, thy God. Thou shalt do no work on it, thou nor thy son nor thy daughter *nor* thy manservant nor thy maidservant *nor* thy beast nor the stranger that is within thy gates, 11 for in six days the Lord made heaven and earth and the sea and all things that are

eis sunt et requievit in die septimo. Idcirco benedixit Dominus diei sabbati et sanctificavit eum.

12 "Honora patrem tuum et matrem tuam ut sis longevus super terram quam Dominus, Deus tuus, dabit tibi.

13 "Non occides.

14 "Non moechaberis.

15 "Non furtum facies.

16 "Non loqueris contra proximum tuum falsum testimonium.

17 "Non concupisces domum proximi tui, nec desiderabis uxorem eius non servum non ancillam non bovem non asinum nec omnia quae illius sunt."

18 Cunctus autem populus videbat voces et lampadas et sonitum bucinae montemque fumantem et, perterriti ac pavore concussi, steterunt procul, 19 dicentes Mosi, "Loquere tu nobis, et audiemus. Non loquatur nobis Dominus ne forte moriamur."

20 Et ait Moses ad populum, "Nolite timere, ut enim probaret vos venit Deus et ut terror illius esset in vobis et non peccaretis."

21 Stetitque populus de longe. Moses autem accessit ad caliginem in qua erat Deus; 22 dixit praeterea Dominus ad Mosen, "Haec dices filiis Israhel: 'Vos vidistis quod de caelo locutus sum vobis. 23 Non facietis deos argenteos, nec deos aureos facietis vobis. 24 Altare de terra facietis mihi, et offeretis super eo holocausta et pacifica vestra, oves vestras et boves. In omni loco in quo memoria fuerit nominis mei, ve-

in them and rested on the seventh day. Therefore the Lord blessed the seventh day and sanctified it.

12 "Honour thy father and thy mother that thou mayest be longlived upon the land which the Lord, thy God, will give thee.

13 "Thou shalt not kill.

14 "Thou shalt not commit adultery.

15 "Thou shalt not steal.

16 "Thou shalt not *bear* false witness against thy neighbour.

17 "Thou shalt not covet thy neighbour's house, neither shalt thou desire his wife nor his servant nor his handmaid nor his ox nor his ass nor any thing that is his."

18 And all the people saw the voices and the flames and the sound of the trumpet and the mount smoking and, being terrified and struck with fear, they stood afar off, 19 saying to Moses, "Speak thou to us, and we will hear. Let not the Lord speak to us lest we die."

20 And Moses said to the people, "Fear not, for God is come to prove you and that the dread of him might be in you and you should not sin."

21 And the people stood afar off. But Moses went to the dark cloud wherein God was, 22 *and* the Lord said to Moses "Thus shalt thou say to the children of Israel: 'You have seen that I have spoken to you from heaven. 23 You shall not make gods of silver, nor shall you make to yourselves gods of gold. 24 You shall make an altar of earth unto me, and you shall offer upon it your holocausts and peace offerings, your sheep and oxen. In every place where the memory of my name

niam ad te et benedicam tibi. 25 Quod si altare lapideum feceris mihi, non aedificabis illud de sectis lapidibus, si enim
levaveris cultrum super eo, polluetur. 26 Non ascendes per
gradus ad altare meum, ne reveletur turpitudo tua.'"

Caput 21

"Haec sunt iudicia quae propones eis: 2 'Si emeris servum Hebraeum, sex annis serviet tibi. In septimo egredietur
liber gratis. 3 Cum quali veste intraverit, cum tali exeat. Si
habens uxorem, et uxor egredietur simul. 4 Sin autem dominus dederit illi uxorem, et pepererit filios et filias, mulier et
liberi eius erunt domini sui, ipse vero exibit cum vestitu suo.
5 Quod si dixerit servus, 'Diligo dominum meum et uxorem
ac liberos; non egrediar liber,' 6 offeret eum dominus diis, et
adplicabitur ad ostium et postes, perforabitque aurem eius
subula, et erit ei servus in saeculum.

7 "'Si quis vendiderit filiam suam in famulam, non egredietur sicut ancillae exire consuerunt. 8 Si displicuerit oculis
domini sui cui tradita fuerit, dimittet eam, populo autem

shall be, I will come to thee and will bless thee. 25 And if thou make an altar of stone unto me, thou shalt not build it of hewn stones, for if thou lift up *a tool* upon it, it shall be defiled. 26 Thou shalt not go up by steps unto my altar, lest thy nakedness be discovered.'"

Chapter 21

Laws relating to Justice.

"These are the judgments which thou shalt set before them: 2 'If thou buy a Hebrew servant, six years shall he serve thee. In the seventh he shall go out free for nothing. 3 With what raiment he came in, with the like let him go out. If having a wife, his wife also shall go out with him. 4 But if his master gave him a wife, and she hath borne sons and daughters, the woman and her children shall be her master's, but he himself shall go out with his raiment. 5 And if the servant shall say, 'I love my master and my wife and children; I will not go out free,' 6 his master shall bring him to the gods, and he shall be set to the door and the posts, and he shall bore his ear through with an awl, and he shall be his servant for ever.

7 "'If any man sell his daughter to be a servant, she shall not go out as bondwomen are wont to go out. 8 If she displease the eyes of her master to whom she was delivered, he

alieno vendendi non habebit potestatem si spreverit eam. 9 Sin autem filio suo desponderit eam, iuxta morem filiarum faciet illi. 10 Quod si alteram ei acceperit, providebit puellae nuptias et vestimenta, et pretium pudicitiae non negabit. 11 Si tria ista non fecerit, egredietur gratis absque pecunia.

12 "Qui percusserit hominem volens occidere morte moriatur. 13 Qui autem non est insidiatus, sed Deus illum tradidit in manu eius, constituam tibi locum quo fugere debeat. 14 Si quis de industria occiderit proximum suum et per insidias, ab altari meo evelles eum ut moriatur.

15 "Qui percusserit patrem suum aut matrem morte moriatur.

16 "Qui furatus fuerit hominem et vendiderit eum, convictus noxae, morte moriatur.

17 "Qui maledixerit patri suo vel matri morte moriatur.

18 "Si rixati fuerint viri et percusserit alter proximum suum lapide vel pugno et ille mortuus non fuerit sed iacuerit in lectulo, 19 si surrexerit et ambulaverit foris super baculum suum, innocens erit qui percussit, ita tamen ut operas eius et inpensas in medicos restituat.

20 "Qui percusserit servum suum vel ancillam virga, et mortui fuerint in manibus eius, criminis reus erit. 21 Sin autem uno die supervixerit vel duobus, non subiacebit poenae, quia pecunia illius est.

22 "Si rixati fuerint viri et percusserit quis mulierem praegnantem et abortivum quidem fecerit sed ipsa vixerit, subiacebit damno quantum expetierit maritus mulieris et

shall let her go, but he shall have no power to sell her to a foreign nation if he despise her. 9 But if he have betrothed her to his son, he shall deal with her after the manner of daughters. 10 And if he take another wife for him, he shall provide *her* a marriage and raiment, neither shall he refuse the price of her chastity. 11 If he do not these three things, she shall go out free without money.

12 "He that striketh a man with a will to kill him shall be put to death. 13 But he that did not lie in wait for him, but God delivered him into his hands, I will appoint thee a place to which he must flee. 14 If a man kill his neighbour on set purpose and by lying in wait for him, thou shalt take him away from my altar that he may die.

15 "He that striketh his father or mother shall be put to death.

16 "He that shall steal a man and sell him, being convicted of guilt, shall be put to death.

17 "He that curseth his father or mother shall die the death.

18 "If men quarrel and the one strike his neighbour with a stone or with his fist and he die not but *keepeth* his bed, 19 if he rise again and walk abroad upon his staff, he that struck him shall be quit, yet so that he make restitution for his work and for his expenses upon the physicians.

20 "He that striketh his bondman or bondwoman with a rod, and they die under his hands, shall be guilty of the crime. 21 But if the party remain alive a day or two, he shall not be subject to the punishment, because it is his money.

22 "If men quarrel and one strike a woman with child and she miscarry indeed but live herself, he shall be answerable for so much damage as the woman's husband shall re-

arbitri iudicarint. 23 Sin autem mors eius fuerit subsecuta, reddet animam pro anima, 24 oculum pro oculo, dentem pro dente, manum pro manu, pedem pro pede, 25 adustionem pro adustione, vulnus pro vulnere, livorem pro livore.

26 "'Si percusserit quispiam oculum servi sui aut ancillae et luscos eos fecerit, dimittet liberos pro oculo quem eruit. 27 Dentem quoque si excusserit servo vel ancillae suae, similiter dimittet eos liberos.

28 "'Si bos cornu percusserit virum aut mulierem et mortui fuerint, lapidibus obruetur, et non comedentur carnes eius, dominusque bovis innocens erit. 29 Quod si bos cornipeta fuerit ab heri et nudius tertius et contestati sunt dominum eius nec reclusit eum occideritque virum aut mulierem, et bos lapidibus obruetur, et dominum illius occident. 30 Quod si pretium ei fuerit inpositum, dabit pro anima sua quicquid fuerit postulatus. 31 Filium quoque et filiam si cornu percusserit, simili sententiae subiacebit. 32 Si servum ancillamque invaserit, triginta siclos argenti dabit domino, bos vero lapidibus opprimetur.

33 "'Si quis aperuerit cisternam et foderit et non operuerit eam, cecideritque bos vel asinus in eam, 34 dominus cisternae reddet pretium iumentorum, quod autem mortuum est ipsius erit. 35 Si bos alienus bovem alterius vulnerarit et ille mortuus fuerit, vendent bovem vivum et dividend pretium, cadaver autem mortui inter se dispertient, 36 sin autem sciebat quod bos cornipeta esset ab heri et nudius tertius et non custodivit eum dominus suus, reddet bovem pro bove et cadaver integrum accipiet.'"

quire and as arbiters shall award. 23 But if her death ensue thereupon, he shall render life for life, 24 eye for eye, tooth for tooth, hand for hand, foot for foot, 25 burning for burning, wound for wound, stripe for stripe.

26 "'If any man strike the eye of his manservant or maidservant and leave them but one eye, he shall let them go free for the eye which he put out. 27 Also, if he strike out a tooth of his manservant or maidservant, he shall in like manner make them free.

28 "'If an ox *gore* a man or a woman and they die, he shall be stoned, and his flesh shall not be eaten, but the owner of the ox shall be quit. 29 But if the ox was wont to push with his horn yesterday and the day before and they warned his master and he did not shut him up and he shall kill a man or a woman, then the ox shall be stoned, and his owner also *shall be put to death.* 30 And if they set a price upon him, he shall give for his life whatsoever is laid upon him. 31 If he have *gored* a son or a daughter, he shall fall under the like sentence. 32 If he assault a bondman or a bondwoman, he shall give thirty sicles of silver to their master, and the ox shall be stoned.

33 "'If a man open a pit and dig one and cover it not, and an ox or an ass fall into it, 34 the owner of the pit shall pay the price of the beasts, and that which is dead shall be his own. 35 If one man's ox gore another man's ox and he die, they shall sell the live ox and shall divide the price, and the carcass of that which died they shall part between them, 36 but if he knew that his ox was wont to push yesterday and the day before and his master did not keep him in, he shall pay ox for ox and shall take the whole carcass.'"

Caput 22

"Si quis furatus fuerit bovem aut ovem et occiderit vel vendiderit, quinque boves pro uno bove restituet et quattuor oves pro una ove.

2 "'Si effringens fur domum sive suffodiens fuerit inventus et accepto vulnere mortuus fuerit, percussor non erit reus sanguinis. 3 Quod si orto sole hoc fecerit, homicidium perpetravit, et ipse morietur. Si non habuerit quod pro furto reddat, venundabitur. 4 Si inventum fuerit apud eum quod furatus est vivens, sive bos sive asinus sive ovis, duplum restituet.

5 "'Si laeserit quispiam agrum vel vineam et dimiserit iumentum suum ut depascatur aliena, quicquid optimum habuerit in agro suo vel in vinea pro damni aestimatione restituet.

6 "'Si egressus ignis invenerit spinas et conprehenderit acervos frugum sive stantes segetes in agris, reddet damnum qui ignem succenderit.

7 "'Si quis commendaverit amico pecuniam aut vas in custodiam et ab eo qui susceperat furto ablata fuerint, si invenitur fur, duplum reddet. 8 Si latet fur, dominus domus adpli-

Chapter 22

The punishment of theft and other trespasses. The law of lending without usury, of taking pledges of reverences to superiors and of paying tithes.

"If any man steal an ox or a sheep and kill or sell it, he shall restore five oxen for one ox and four sheep for one sheep.

2 "'If a thief be found breaking open a house or undermining it and be wounded so as to die, he that slew him shall not be guilty of blood. 3 But if he did this when the sun is risen, he hath committed murder, and he shall die. If he have not wherewith to make restitution for the theft, he shall be sold. 4 If that which he stole be found with him alive, either ox or ass or sheep, he shall restore double.

5 "'If any man hurt a field or a vineyard and put in his beast to feed upon that which is other men's, he shall restore the best of whatsoever he hath in his own field or in his vineyard according to the estimation of the damage.

6 "'If a fire breaking out light upon thorns and catch stacks of corn or corn standing in the fields, he that kindled the fire shall make good the loss.

7 "'If a man deliver money or *any* vessel unto his friend to keep and they be stolen away from him that received them, if the thief be found, he shall restore double. 8 If the thief be not known, the master of the house shall be brought to the

cabitur ad deos et iurabit quod non extenderit manum in rem proximi sui 9 ad perpetrandam fraudem tam in bove quam in asino et ove ac vestimento et quicquid damnum inferre potest. Ad deos utriusque causa perveniet, et si illi iudicaverint, duplum restituet proximo suo.

10 "'Si quis commendaverit proximo suo asinum, bovem, ovem et omne iumentum ad custodiam, et mortuum fuerit aut debilitatum vel captum ab hostibus nullusque hoc viderit, 11 iusiurandum erit in medio quod non extenderit manum ad rem proximi sui, suscipietque dominus iuramentum, et ille reddere non cogetur. 12 Quod si furto ablatum fuerit, restituet damnum domino. 13 Si comestum a bestia, deferat ad eum quod occisum est, et non restituet. 14 Qui a proximo suo quicquam horum mutuo postularit et debilitatum aut mortuum fuerit, domino non praesente, reddere conpelletur. 15 Quod si inpraesentiarum fuit dominus, non restituet, maxime si conductum venerat pro mercede operis sui.

16 "'Si seduxerit quis virginem necdum desponsatam et dormierit cum ea, dotabit eam et habebit eam uxorem. 17 Si pater virginis dare noluerit, reddet pecuniam iuxta modum dotis quam virgines accipere consuerunt.

18 "'Maleficos non patieris vivere.

19 "'Qui coierit cum iumento morte moriatur.

20 "'Qui immolat diis occidetur, praeter Domino soli.

21 "'Advenam non contristabis neque adfliges eum, advenae enim et ipsi fuistis in terra Aegypti.

22 "'Viduae et pupillo non nocebitis. 23 Si laeseritis eos,

gods and shall swear that he did not lay his hand upon his neighbour's goods 9 to do any fraud either in ox or in ass or sheep or raiment or any thing that may bring damage. The cause of both parties shall come to the gods, and if they give judgment, he shall restore double to his neighbour.

10 "'If a man deliver ass, ox, sheep or any beast to his neighbour's custody, and it die or be hurt or be taken by enemies and no man saw it, 11 there shall be an oath between them that he did not put forth his hand to his neighbour's goods, and the owner shall accept of the oath, and he shall not be compelled to make restitution. 12 But if it were taken away by stealth, he shall make the loss good to the owner. 13 If it were eaten by a beast, let him bring to him that which was slain, and he shall not make restitution. 14 If a man borrow of his neighbour any of these things and it be hurt or die, the owner not being present, he shall be obliged to make restitution. 15 But if the owner be present, he shall not make restitution, especially if it were hired and came for the hire of his work.

16 "'If a man seduce a virgin not yet espoused and lie with her, he shall endow her and have her to wife. 17 If the maid's father will not give her to him, he shall give money according to the dowry which virgins are wont to receive.

18 "'Wizards thou shalt not suffer to live.

19 "'Whosoever copulateth with a beast shall be put to death.

20 "'He that sacrificeth to gods shall be put to death, save only to the Lord.

21 "'Thou shalt not molest a stranger nor afflict him, for yourselves also were strangers in the land of Egypt.

22 "'You shall not hurt a widow or an orphan. 23 If you hurt

vociferabuntur ad me, et ego audiam clamorem eorum, 24 et indignabitur furor meus, percutiamque vos gladio, et erunt uxores vestrae viduae, et filii vestri pupilli.

25 "'Si pecuniam mutuam dederis populo meo pauperi qui habitat tecum, non urguebis eum quasi exactor nec usuris opprimes.

26 "'Si pignus a proximo tuo acceperis vestimentum, ante solis occasum reddes ei, 27 ipsum enim est solum quo operitur, indumentum carnis eius, nec habet aliud in quo dormiat. Si clamaverit ad me exaudiam eum quia misericors sum.

28 "'Diis non detrahes, et principi populi tui non maledices.

29 "'Decimas tuas et primitias non tardabis reddere; primogenitum filiorum tuorum dabis mihi. 30 De bubus quoque et ovibus similiter facies: septem diebus sit cum matre sua; die octavo reddes illum mihi.

31 "'Viri sancti eritis mihi.

"'Carnem quae a bestiis fuerit praegustata, non comedetis, sed proicietis canibus.'"

them, they will cry out to me, and I will hear their cry, 24 and my rage shall be enkindled, and I will strike you with the sword, and your wives shall be widows, and your children fatherless.

25 "'If thou lend money to any of my people that is poor that dwelleth with thee, thou shalt not be hard upon them as an extortioner nor oppress them with usuries.

26 "'If thou take of thy neighbour a garment in pledge, thou shalt give it him again before sunset, 27 for that same is the only thing wherewith he is covered, the clothing of his body, neither hath he any other to sleep in. If he cry to me, I will hear him, because I am compassionate.

28 "'Thou shalt not speak ill of the gods, and the prince of thy people thou shalt not curse.

29 "'Thou shalt not delay to pay thy tithes and thy first-fruits; thou shalt give the firstborn of thy sons to me. 30 Thou shalt do the same with the firstborn of thy oxen also and sheep: seven days let it be with its dam; the eighth day thou shalt give it to me.

31 "'You shall be holy men to me.

"'The flesh that beasts have tasted of before, you shall not eat, but shall cast it to the dogs.'"

Caput 23

"Non suscipies vocem mendacii, nec iunges manum tuam ut pro impio dicas falsum testimonium.

2 "Non sequeris turbam ad faciendum malum, nec in iudicio plurimorum adquiesces sententiae ut a vero devies, 3 pauperis quoque non misereberis in iudicio.

4 "Si occurreris bovi inimici tui aut asino erranti, reduc ad eum. 5 Si videris asinum odientis te iacere sub onere, non pertransibis sed sublevabis cum eo.

6 "Non declinabis in iudicio pauperis.

7 "Mendacium fugies.

"Insontem et iustum non occides, quia aversor impium.

8 "Nec accipies munera, quae excaecant etiam prudentes et subvertunt verba iustorum.

9 "Peregrino molestus non eris, scitis enim advenarum animas, quia et ipsi peregrini fuistis in terra Aegypti.

10 "Sex annis seminabis terram tuam et congregabis fru-

Chapter 23

Laws for judges. The rest of the seventh year and day. Three principal feasts to be solemnized every year. The promise of an angel to conduct and protect them. Idols are to be destroyed.

"Thou shalt not receive the voice of a lie, neither shalt thou join thy hand to *bear* false witness for a wicked person.

2 "'Thou shalt not follow the multitude to do evil, neither shalt thou yield in judgment to the opinion of the most part to stray from the truth, 3 neither shalt thou favour a poor man in judgment.

4 "'If thou meet thy enemy's ox or ass going astray, bring it back to him. 5 If thou see the ass of him that hateth thee lie underneath his burden, thou shalt not pass by but shalt lift him up with him.

6 "'Thou shalt not go aside in the poor man's judgment.

7 "'Thou shalt fly lying.

"'The innocent and just person thou shalt not put to death, because I abhor the wicked.

8 "'Neither shalt thou take bribes, which even blind the wise and pervert the words of the just.

9 "'Thou shalt not molest a stranger, for you know the hearts of strangers, for you also were strangers in the land of Egypt.

10 "'Six years thou shalt sow thy ground and shalt gather

ges eius, 11 anno autem septimo dimittes eam et requiescere facies, ut comedant pauperes populi tui, et quicquid reliquum fuerit, edant bestiae agri. Ita facies in vinea et in oliveto tuo. 12 Sex diebus operaberis. Septima die cessabis ut requiescat bos et asinus tuus et refrigeretur filius ancillae tuae et advena.

13 "Omnia quae dixi vobis custodite, et per nomen externorum deorum non iurabitis, neque audietur ex ore vestro.

14 "Tribus vicibus per singulos annos mihi festa celebrabitis. 15 Sollemnitatem azymorum custodies—septem diebus comedes azyma, sicut praecepi tibi, tempore mensis novarum frugum, quando egressus es de Aegypto; non apparebis in conspectu meo vacuus—16 et sollemnitatem messis primitivorum operis tui, quaecumque seminaveris in agro, sollemnitatem quoque in exitu anni, quando congregaveris omnes fruges tuas de agro. 17 Ter in anno apparebit omne masculinum tuum coram Domino, Deo tuo. 18 Non immolabis super fermento sanguinem victimae meae, nec remanebit adeps sollemnitatis meae usque mane. 19 Primitias frugum terrae tuae deferes in domum Domini, Dei tui. Non coques hedum in lacte matris suae.

20 "Ecce: ego mittam angelum meum, qui praecedat te et custodiat in via et introducat in locum quem paravi. 21 Observa eum, et audi vocem eius, nec contemnendum putes, quia non dimittet cum peccaveris, et est nomen meum in illo. 22 Quod si audieris vocem eius et feceris omnia quae lo-

the corn thereof, 11 but the seventh year thou shalt let it alone and suffer it to rest, that the poor of thy people may eat, and whatsoever shall be left, let the beasts of the field eat it. So shalt thou do with thy vineyard and thy oliveyard. 12 Six days thou shalt work. The seventh day thou shalt cease, that thy ox and thy ass may rest and the son of thy handmaid and the stranger may be refreshed.

13 "Keep all things that I have said to you, and by the name of strange gods you shall not swear, neither shall it be heard out of your mouth.

14 "Three times every year you shall celebrate feasts to me. 15 Thou shalt keep the feast of unleavened bread—seven days shalt thou eat unleavened bread, as I commanded thee, in the time of the month of new corn, when thou didst come forth out of Egypt; thou shalt not appear empty before me—16 and the feast of the harvest of the firstfruits of thy work, whatsoever thou hast sown in the field, the feast also in the end of the year, when thou hast gathered in all thy corn out of the field. 17 Thrice a year shall all thy males appear before the Lord, thy God. 18 Thou shalt not sacrifice the blood of my victim upon leaven, neither shall the fat of my solemnity remain until the morning. 19 Thou shalt carry the firstfruits of the corn of thy ground to the house of the Lord, thy God. Thou shalt not boil a kid in the milk of his dam.

20 "Behold: I will send my angel, who shall go before thee and keep thee in thy journey and bring thee into the place that I have prepared. 21 Take notice of him, and hear his voice, and do not think him one to be contemned, for he will not forgive when thou hast sinned, and my name is in him. 22 But if thou wilt hear his voice and do all that I speak,

quor, inimicus ero inimicis tuis et adfligam adfligentes te. 23 Praecedetque te angelus meus et introducet te ad Amorreum et Hettheum et Ferezeum Chananeumque et Eveum et Iebuseum, quos ego contribo. 24 Non adorabis deos eorum nec coles eos. Non facies opera eorum sed destrues eos et confringes statuas eorum. 25 Servietisque Domino, Deo vestro, ut benedicam panibus tuis et aquis et auferam infirmitatem de medio tui.

26 "'Non erit infecunda nec sterilis in terra tua. Numerum dierum tuorum implebo. 27 Terrorem meum mittam in praecursum tuum et occidam omnem populum ad quem ingredieris cunctorumque inimicorum tuorum coram te terga vertam, 28 emittens crabrones prius qui fugabunt Eveum et Chananeum et Hettheum antequam introeas. 29 Non eiciam eos a facie tua anno uno ne terra in solitudinem redigatur et crescant contra te bestiae. 30 Paulatim expellam eos de conspectu tuo donec augearis et possideas terram.

31 "'Ponam autem terminos tuos a Mari Rubro usque ad mare Palestinorum et a deserto usque ad fluvium. Tradam in manibus vestris habitatores terrae et eiciam eos de conspectu vestro. 32 Non inibis cum eis foedus nec cum diis eorum. 33 Non habitent in terra tua ne forte peccare te faciant in me si servieris diis eorum, quod tibi certo erit in scandalum.'"

I will be an enemy to thy enemies and will afflict them that afflict thee. 23 And my angel shall go before thee and shall bring thee in unto the Amorite and the Hittite and the Perizzite and the Canaanite and the Hivite and the Jebusite, whom I will destroy. 24 Thou shalt not adore their gods nor serve them. Thou shalt not do their works but shalt destroy them and break their statues. 25 And you shall serve the Lord, your God, that I may bless your bread and your waters and may take away sickness from the midst of thee.

26 "'There shall not be one fruitless nor barren in thy land. I will fill the number of thy days. 27 I will send my fear before thee and will destroy all the people to whom thou shalt come and will turn the backs of all thy enemies before thee, 28 sending out hornets before that shall drive away the Hivite and the Canaanite and the Hittite before thou come in. 29 I will not cast them out from thy face in one year lest the land be brought into a wilderness and the beasts multiply against thee. 30 By little and little I will drive them out from before thee till thou be increased and dost possess the land.

31 "'And I will set thy bounds from the Red Sea to the sea of the Philistines and from the desert to the river. I will deliver the inhabitants of the land into your hands and will drive them out from before you. 32 Thou shalt not enter into league with them nor with their gods. 33 Let them not dwell in thy land lest perhaps they make thee sin against me if thou serve their gods, which undoubtedly will be a scandal to thee.'"

Caput 24

Mosi quoque dixit, "Ascende ad Dominum, tu et Aaron, Nadab et Abiu et septuaginta senes ex Israhel, et adorabitis procul. 2 Solusque Moses ascendet ad Dominum, et illi non adpropinquabunt, nec populus ascendet cum eo."

3 Venit ergo Moses et narravit plebi omnia verba Domini atque iudicia, responditque cunctus populus una voce, "Omnia verba Domini quae locutus est faciemus." 4 Scripsit autem Moses universos sermones Domini, et mane consurgens aedificavit altare ad radices montis et duodecim titulos per duodecim tribus Israhel. 5 Misitque iuvenes de filiis Israhel, et obtulerunt holocausta immolaveruntque victimas pacificas Domino vitulos. 6 Tulit itaque Moses dimidiam partem sanguinis et misit in crateras, partem autem residuam fudit super altare. 7 Adsumensque volumen foederis, legit audiente populo, qui dixerunt, "Omnia quae locutus est Dominus faciemus, et erimus oboedientes."

8 Ille vero sumptum sanguinem respersit in populum, et ait, "Hic est sanguis foederis quod pepigit Dominus vobis-

Chapter 24

Moses writeth his law and after offering sacrifices sprinkleth the blood of the testament upon the people, then goeth up the mountain which God covereth with a fiery cloud.

And he said to Moses, "Come up to the Lord, thou and Aaron, Nadab and Abihu and seventy of the ancients of Israel, and you shall adore afar off. 2 And Moses alone shall come up to the Lord, but they shall not come nigh, neither shall the people come up with him."

3 So Moses came and told the people all the words of the Lord and all the judgments, and all the people answered with one voice, "We will do all the words of the Lord which he hath spoken." 4 And Moses wrote all the words of the Lord, and rising in the morning he built an altar at the foot of the mount and twelve titles according to the twelve tribes of Israel. 5 And he sent young men of the children of Israel, and they offered holocausts and sacrificed pacific victims of calves to the Lord. 6 Then Moses took half of the blood and put it into bowls, and the rest he poured upon the altar. 7 And taking the book of the covenant, he read it in the hearing of the people, and they said, "All things that the Lord hath spoken we will do; *we* will be obedient."

8 And he took the blood and sprinkled it upon the people, and he said, "This is the blood of the covenant which the Lord hath made with you concerning all these

cum super cunctis sermonibus his." 9 Ascenderuntque Moses et Aaron, Nadab et Abiu et septuaginta de senioribus Israhel, 10 et viderunt Deum Israhel et sub pedibus eius quasi opus lapidis sapphirini et quasi caelum cum serenum est. 11 Nec super eos qui procul recesserant de filiis Israhel misit manum suam, videruntque Deum, et comederunt ac biberunt.

12 Dixit autem Dominus ad Mosen, "Ascende ad me in montem, et esto ibi, daboque tibi tabulas lapideas et legem ac mandata quae scripsi ut doceas eos." 13 Surrexerunt Moses et Iosue, minister eius, ascendensque Moses in montem Dei 14 senioribus ait, "Expectate hic donec revertamur ad vos. Habetis Aaron et Hur vobiscum. Si quid natum fuerit quaestionis, referetis ad eos."

15 Cumque ascendisset Moses, operuit nubes montem. 16 Et habitavit gloria Domini super Sinai, tegens illum nube sex diebus, septimo autem die vocavit eum de medio caliginis. 17 Erat autem species gloriae Domini quasi ignis ardens super verticem montis in conspectu filiorum Israhel. 18 Ingressusque Moses medium nebulae ascendit in montem, et fuit ibi quadraginta diebus et quadraginta noctibus.

words." 9 Then Moses and Aaron, Nadab and Abihu and seventy of the ancients of Israel went up, 10 and they saw the God of Israel and under his feet, as it were, a work of sapphire stone and as the heaven when clear. 11 Neither did he lay his hand upon those of the children of Israel that retired afar off, and they saw God, and they did eat and drink.

12 And the Lord said to Moses, "Come up to me into the mount, and be there, and I will give thee tables of stone and the law and the commandments which I have written that thou mayst teach them." 13 Moses rose up and his minister, Joshua, and Moses going up into the mount of God 14 said to the ancients, "Wait ye here till we return to you. You have Aaron and Hur with you. If any question shall arise, you shall refer it to them."

15 And when Moses was gone up, a cloud covered the mount. 16 And the glory of the Lord dwelt upon Sinai, covering it with a cloud six days, and the seventh day he called him out of the midst of the cloud. 17 And the sight of the glory of the Lord was like a burning fire upon the top of the mount in the eyes of the children of Israel. 18 And Moses, entering into the midst of the cloud, went up into the mountain, and he was there forty days and forty nights.

Caput 25

Locutusque est Dominus ad Mosen, dicens, 2 "Loquere filiis Israhel, ut tollant mihi primitias. Ab omni homine qui offert ultroneus accipietis eas. 3 Haec sunt autem quae accipere debetis: aurum et argentum et aes, 4 hyacinthum et purpuram coccumque bis tinctum et byssum, pilos caprarum 5 et pelles arietum rubricatas pellesque ianthinas et ligna setthim, 6 oleum ad luminaria concinnanda, aromata in unguentum et thymiama boni odoris, 7 lapides onychinos et gemmas ad ornandum ephod ac rationale.

8 "Facientque mihi sanctuarium, et habitabo in medio eorum, 9 iuxta omnem similitudinem tabernaculi quod ostendam tibi et omnium vasorum in cultum eius, sicque facietis illud: 10 arcam de lignis setthim conpingite, cuius longitudo habeat duos et semis cubitos, latitudo cubitum et dimidium, altitudo cubitum, similiter, ac semissem. 11 Et deaurabis eam auro mundissimo intus et foris, faciesque supra coronam auream per circuitum 12 et quattuor circulos aureos quos pones per quattuor arcae angulos. Duo circuli sint in latere uno et duo in altero. 13 Facies quoque vectes de lignis setthim et operies eos auro, 14 inducesque per circulos qui sunt

Chapter 25

Offerings prescribed for making the tabernacle, the ark, the candlestick, etc.

And the Lord spoke to Moses, saying, 2 "Speak to the children of Israel, that they bring firstfruits to me. Of every man that offereth of his own accord you shall take them. 3 And these are the things you must take: gold and silver and brass, 4 violet and purple and scarlet twice dyed and fine linen and goats' hair 5 and rams' skins dyed red and violet skins and setim wood, 6 oil to make lights, spices for ointment and for sweet-smelling incense, 7 onyx stones and precious stones to adorn the ephod and the rational.

8 "And they shall make me a sanctuary, and I will dwell in the midst of them, 9 according to all the likeness of the tabernacle which I will shew thee and of all the vessels for the service thereof, and thus you shall make it: 10 frame an ark of setim wood, the length whereof shall be of two cubits and a half, the breadth a cubit and a half, the height, likewise, a cubit and a half. 11 And thou shalt overlay it with the purest gold within and without, and over it thou shalt make a golden crown round about 12 and four golden rings which thou shall put at the four corners of the ark. Let two rings be on the one side and two on the other. 13 Thou shalt make bars also of setim wood and shalt overlay them with gold, 14 and thou shalt put them in through the rings that are in

in arcae lateribus ut portetur in eis. 15 Qui semper erunt in circulis, nec umquam extrahentur ab eis. 16 Ponesque in arcam testificationem quam dabo tibi. 17 Facies et propitiatorium de auro mundissimo: duos cubitos et dimidium tenebit longitudo eius et cubitum ac semissem latitudo. 18 Duos quoque cherubin aureos et productiles facies ex utraque parte oraculi. 19 Cherub unus sit in latere uno et alter in altero. 20 Utrumque latus propitiatorii tegant, expandentes alas et operientes oraculum, respiciantque se mutuo, versis vultibus in propitiatorium quo operienda est arca, 21 in qua pones testimonium quod dabo tibi. 22 Inde praecipiam et loquar ad te supra propitiatorio ac de medio duorum cherubin qui erunt super Arcam Testimonii cuncta quae mandabo per te filiis Israhel.

23 "Facies et mensam de lignis setthim, habentem duos cubitos longitudinis et in latitudine cubitum et in altitudine cubitum ac semissem. 24 Et inaurabis eam auro purissimo, faciesque illi labium aureum per circuitum 25 et ipsi labio, coronam interrasilem, altam quattuor digitis, et super illam alteram coronam aureolam. 26 Quattuor quoque circulos aureos praeparabis et pones eos in quattuor angulis eiusdem mensae per singulos pedes. 27 Subter coronam erunt circuli aurei, ut mittantur vectes per eos et possit mensa portari. 28 Ipsosque vectes facies de lignis setthim, et circumdabis auro ad subvehendam mensam.

the sides of the ark that it may be carried on them. 15 And they shall be always in the rings, neither shall they at any time be drawn out of them. 16 And thou shalt put in the ark the testimony which I will give thee. 17 Thou shalt make also a propitiatory of the purest gold: the length thereof shall be two cubits and a half and the breadth a cubit and a half. 18 Thou shalt make also two cherubims of beaten gold on the two sides of the oracle. 19 Let one cherub be on the one side and the other on the other. 20 Let them cover both sides of the propitiatory, spreading their wings and covering the oracle, and let them look one towards the other, their faces being turned towards the propitiatory wherewith the ark is to be covered, 21 in which thou shalt put the testimony that I will give thee. 22 Thence will I give orders and will speak to thee over the propitiatory and from the midst of the two cherubims which shall be upon the Ark of the Testimony all things which I will command the children of Israel by thee.

23 "Thou shalt make a table also of setim wood, of two cubits in length and a cubit in breadth and a cubit and half in height. 24 And thou shalt overlay it with the purest gold, and thou shalt make to it a golden ledge round about 25 and to the ledge itself, a polished crown, four inches high, and over the same another little golden crown. 26 Thou shalt prepare also four golden rings and shalt put them in the four corners of the same table over each foot. 27 Under the crown shall the golden rings be, that the bars may be put through them and the table may be carried. 28 The bars also themselves thou shalt make of setim wood, and shalt overlay them with gold to bear up the table.

29 "Parabis et acetabula ac fialas, turibula et cyatos, in quibus offerenda sunt libamina, ex auro purissimo. 30 Et pones super mensam panes propositionis in conspectu meo semper.

31 "Facies et candelabrum ductile de auro mundissimo, hastile eius et calamos, scyphos et spherulas ac lilia ex ipso procedentia. 32 Sex calami egredientur de lateribus, tres ex uno latere et tres ex altero, 33 tres scyphi, quasi in nucis modum, per calamos singulos spherulaque simul et lilium, et tres similiter scyphi instar nucis in calamo altero spherulaque simul et lilium. Hoc erit opus sex calamorum qui producendi sunt de hastili, 34 in ipso autem candelabro erunt quattuor scyphi in nucis modum, spherulaeque per singulos et lilia, 35 spherulae sub duobus calamis per tria loca, qui simul sex fiunt procedentes de hastili uno. 36 Et spherulae igitur et calami ex ipso erunt universa ductilia de auro purissimo. 37 Facies et lucernas septem et pones eas super candelabrum ut luceant ex adverso. 38 Emunctoria quoque et ubi quae emuncta sunt extinguantur fiant de auro purissimo. 39 Omne pondus candelabri cum universis vasis suis habebit talentum auri purissimi. 40 Inspice, et fac secundum exemplar quod tibi in monte monstratum est."

29 "Thou shalt prepare also dishes and bowls, censers and cups, wherein the libations are to be offered, of the purest gold. 30 And thou shalt set upon the table loaves of proposition in my sight always.

31 "Thou shalt make also a candlestick of beaten work of the finest gold, the shaft thereof and the branches, the cups and the *bowls* and the lilies going forth from it. 32 Six branches shall come out of the sides, three out of the one side and three out of the other, 33 three cups, as it were nuts, to every branch and a *bowl* withal and a lily, and three cups likewise of the fashion of nuts in the other branch and a *bowl* withal and a lily. Such shall be the work of the six branches that are to come out from the shaft, 34 and in the candlestick itself shall be four cups in the manner of a nut, and at every one *bowls* and lilies, 35 *bowls* under two branches in three places, which together make six coming forth out of one shaft. 36 And both the *bowls* and the branches shall be *of the same beaten work* of the purest gold. 37 Thou shalt make also seven lamps and shalt set them upon the candlestick to give light over against. 38 The snuffers also and where the snuffings shall be put out *shall be* made of the purest gold. 39 The whole weight of the candlestick with all the furniture thereof shall be a talent of the purest gold. 40 Look, and make it according to the pattern that was shewn thee in the mount."

Caput 26

"Tabernaculum vero ita facies: decem cortinas de bysso retorta et hyacintho ac purpura coccoque bis tincto, variatas opere plumario facies. 2 Longitudo cortinae unius habebit viginti octo cubitos; latitudo quattuor cubitorum erit. Unius mensurae fient universa tentoria. 3 Quinque cortinae sibi iungentur mutuo, et aliae quinque nexu simili coherebunt. 4 Ansulas hyacinthinas in lateribus ac summitatibus facies cortinarum ut possint invicem copulari. 5 Quinquagenas ansulas cortina habebit in utraque parte, ita insertas ut ansa contra ansam veniat et altera alteri possit aptari. 6 Facies et quinquaginta circulos aureos quibus cortinarum vela iungenda sunt ut unum tabernaculum fiat.

7 "Facies et saga cilicina undecim ad operiendum tectum tabernaculi. 8 Longitudo sagi unius habebit triginta cubitos, et latitudo quattuor; aequa erit mensura sagorum omnium. 9 E quibus quinque iunges seorsum, et sex sibi mutuo copulabis ita ut sextum sagum in fronte tecti duplices. 10 Facies et quinquaginta ansas in ora sagi unius ut coniungi cum al-

Chapter 26

The form of the tabernacle with its appurtenances.

"And nd thou shalt make the tabernacle in this manner: thou shalt make ten curtains of fine twisted linen and violet and purple and scarlet twice dyed, diversified with embroidery. 2 The length of one curtain shall be twenty-eight cubits; the breadth shall be four cubits. All the curtains shall be of one measure. 3 Five curtains shall be joined one to another, and the other five shall be coupled together in like manner. 4 Thou shalt make loops of violet in the sides and tops of the curtains that they may be joined one to another. 5 *Every* curtain shall have fifty loops on both sides, so set on that one loop may be against another loop and one may be fitted to the other. 6 Thou shalt make also fifty rings of gold wherewith the veils of the curtains are to be joined that it may be made one tabernacle.

7 "Thou shalt make also eleven curtains of goats' hair to cover the top of the tabernacle. 8 The length of one hair curtain shall be thirty cubits, and the breadth four; the measure of all the curtains shall be equal. 9 Five of which thou shalt couple by themselves, and the six others thou shalt couple one to another so as to double the sixth curtain in the front of the roof. 10 Thou shalt make also fifty loops in the edge of one curtain that it may be joined with the other, and fifty

tero queat, et quinquaginta ansas in ora sagi alterius ut cum altero copuletur.

11 "Facies et quinquaginta fibulas aeneas quibus iungantur ansae ut unum ex omnibus operimentum fiat. 12 Quod autem superfuerit in sagis quae parantur tecto, id est, unum sagum quod amplius est, ex medietate eius operies posteriora tabernaculi. 13 Et cubitus ex una parte pendebit et alter ex altera, qui plus est in sagorum longitudine, utrumque latus tabernaculi protegens. 14 Facies et operimentum aliud tecto de pellibus arietum rubricatis, et super hoc rursum aliud operimentum de ianthinis pellibus.

15 "Facies et tabulas stantes tabernaculi de lignis setthim. 16 Quae singulae denos cubitos in longitudine habeant, et in latitudine singulos ac semissem. 17 In lateribus tabulae duae incastraturae fient quibus tabula alteri tabulae conectatur, atque in hunc modum cunctae tabulae parabuntur 18 quarum viginti erunt in latere meridiano quod vergit ad austrum, 19 quibus quadraginta bases argenteas fundes, ut binae bases singulis tabulis per duos angulos subiciantur. 20 In latere quoque secundo tabernaculi quod vergit ad aquilonem, viginti tabulae erunt 21 quadraginta habentes bases argenteas; binae bases singulis tabulis subponentur. 22 Ad occidentalem vero plagam tabernaculi, facies sex tabulas 23 et rursum alias duas quae in angulis erigantur post tergum tabernaculi. 24 Eruntque coniunctae a deorsum usque sursum, et una omnes conpago retinebit. Duabus quoque tabulis quae in angulis ponendae sunt similis iunctura servabitur. 25 Et erunt simul tabulae octo, bases earum argenteae sede-

loops in the edge of the other curtain that it may be coupled with its fellow.

11 "Thou shalt make also fifty buckles of brass wherewith the loops may be joined that of all there may be made one covering. 12 And that which shall remain of the curtains that are prepared for the roof, to wit, one curtain that is over and above, with the half thereof thou shalt cover the back parts of the tabernacle. 13 And there shall hang down a cubit on the one side and another on the other side, which is over and above in the length of the curtains, fencing both sides of the tabernacle. 14 Thou shalt make also another cover to the roof of rams' skins dyed red, and over that again another cover of violet coloured skins.

15 "Thou shalt make also the boards of the tabernacle standing upright of setim wood. 16 Let every one of them be ten cubits in length, and in breadth one cubit and a half. 17 In the sides of the boards shall be made two mortises whereby one board may be joined to another board, and after this manner shall all the boards be prepared 18 of which twenty shall be in the south side southward, 19 for which thou shalt cast forty sockets of silver, that under every board may be put two sockets at the two corners. 20 In the second side also of the tabernacle that looketh to the north, there shall be twenty boards 21 having forty sockets of silver; two sockets shall be put under each board. 22 But on the west side of the tabernacle, thou shalt make six boards 23 and again other two which shall be erected in the corners at the back of the tabernacle. 24 And they shall be joined together from beneath unto the top, and one joint shall hold them all. The like joining shall be observed for the two boards also that are to be put in the corners. 25 And they shall be in all eight

cim, duabus basibus per unam tabulam supputatis. 26 Facies et vectes de lignis setthim quinque ad continendas tabulas in uno latere tabernaculi 27 et quinque alios in altero et eiusdem numeri ad occidentalem plagam, 28 qui mittentur per medias tabulas a summo usque ad summum. 29 Ipsasque tabulas deaurabis et fundes eis anulos aureos per quos vectes tabulata contineant, quos operies lamminis aureis. 30 Et eriges tabernaculum iuxta exemplum quod tibi in monte monstratum est.

31 "Facies et velum de hyacintho et purpura coccoque bis tincto et bysso retorta, opere plumario et pulchra varietate contextum, 32 quod adpendes ante quattuor columnas de lignis setthim, quae ipsae quidem deauratae erunt et habebunt capita aurea sed bases argenteas. 33 Inseretur autem velum per circulos, intra quod pones Arcam Testimonii, et quo sanctuarium et sanctuarii sanctuaria dividentur. 34 Pones et propitiatorium super Arcam Testimonii in sancta sanctorum 35 mensamque extra velum et contra mensam candelabrum in latere tabernaculi meridiano, mensa enim stabit in parte aquilonis.

36 "Facies et tentorium in introitu tabernaculi de hyacintho et purpura coccoque bis tincto et bysso retorta opere plumarii. 37 Et quinque columnas deaurabis lignorum setthim, ante quas ducetur tentorium; quarum erunt capita aurea et bases aeneae."

boards and their silver sockets sixteen, reckoning two sockets for each board. 26 Thou shalt make also five bars of setim wood to hold together the boards on one side of the tabernacle 27 and five others on the other side and as many at the west side, 28 and they shall be put along by the midst of the boards from one end to the other. 29 The boards also themselves thou shalt overlay with gold and shall cast rings of gold to be set upon them for places for the bars to hold together boardwork, which bars thou shalt cover with plates of gold. 30 And thou shalt rear up the tabernacle according to the pattern that was shewn thee in the mount.

31 "Thou shalt make also a veil of violet and purple and scarlet twice dyed and fine twisted linen, wrought with embroidered work and goodly variety, 32 and thou shalt hang it up before four pillars of setim wood, which themselves also shall be overlaid with gold and shall have heads of gold but sockets of silver. 33 And the veil shall be hanged on with rings, and within it thou shalt put the Ark of the Testimony, and the sanctuary and the holy of holies shall be divided with it. 34 And thou shalt set the propitiatory upon the Ark of the Testimony in the holy of holies 35 and the table without the veil and over against the table the candlestick in the south side of the tabernacle, for the table shall stand in the north side.

36 "Thou shalt make also a hanging in the entrance of the tabernacle of violet and purple and scarlet twice dyed and fine twisted linen with embroidered work. 37 And thou shalt overlay with gold five pillars of setim wood, before which the hanging shall be drawn; *their* heads shall be of gold and the sockets of brass."

Caput 27

"Facies et altare de lignis setthim, quod habebit quinque cubitos in longitudine et totidem in latitudine, id est, quadrum, et tres cubitos in altitudine. 2 Cornua autem per quattuor angulos ex ipso erunt, et operies illud aere. 3 Faciesque in usus eius lebetas ad suscipiendos cineres et forcipes atque fuscinulas et ignium receptacula. Omnia vasa ex aere fabricabis 4 craticulamque in modum retis aeneam, per cuius quattuor angulos erunt quattuor anuli aenei 5 quos pones subter arulam altaris, eritque craticula usque ad altaris medium.

6 "Facies et vectes altaris de lignis setthim duos quos operies lamminis aeneis, 7 et induces per circulos, eruntque ex utroque latere altaris ad portandum. 8 Non solidum, sed inane et cavum intrinsecus facies illud, sicut tibi in monte monstratum est.

9 "Facies et atrium tabernaculi, in cuius plaga australi contra meridiem erunt tentoria de bysso retorta; centum cubitos unum latus tenebit in longitudine 10 et columnas viginti cum basibus totidem aeneis, quae capita cum celaturis suis habebunt argentea. 11 Similiter et in latere aquilonis per longum erunt tentoria centum cubitorum, columnae viginti

Chapter 27

The altar and the court of the tabernacle with its hangings and pillars. Provision of oil for lamps.

"Thou shalt make also an altar of setim wood, which shall be five cubits long and as many broad, that is, four-square, and three cubits high. 2 And there shall be horns at the four corners of the same, and thou shalt cover it with brass. 3 And thou shalt make for the uses thereof pans to receive the ashes and tongs and fleshhooks and firepans. All its vessels thou shalt make of brass 4 and a grate of brass in manner of a net, at the four corners of which shall be four rings of brass 5 which thou shalt put under the hearth of the altar, and the grate shall be even to the midst of the altar.

6 "Thou shalt make also two bars for the altar of setim wood which thou shalt cover with plates of brass, 7 and thou shalt draw them through rings, and they shall be on both sides of the altar to carry it. 8 Thou shalt not make it solid, but empty and hollow in the inside, as it was shewn thee in the mount.

9 "Thou shalt make also the court of the tabernacle, in the south side whereof southward there shall be hangings of fine twisted linen *of a hundred cubits long for one side* 10 and twenty pillars with as many sockets of brass, *the heads of which with their engraving shall be* of silver. 11 In like manner also on the north side there shall be hangings of a hundred

et bases aeneae eiusdem numeri et capita earum, cum celaturis suis, argentea. 12 In latitudine vero atrii quod respicit
ad occidentem, erunt tentoria per quinquaginta cubitos et
columnae decem basesque totidem. 13 In ea quoque atrii
latitudine quae respicit ad orientem quinquaginta cubiti
erunt 14 in quibus quindecim cubitorum tentoria lateri uno
deputabuntur columnaeque tres et bases totidem, 15 et in latere altero erunt tentoria cubitos obtinentia quindecim, columnae tres et bases totidem.

16 "In introitu vero atrii fiet tentorium cubitorum viginti
ex hyacintho et purpura coccoque bis tincto et bysso retorta
opere plumarii. Columnas habebit quattuor cum basibus totidem. 17 Omnes columnae atrii per circuitum vestitae erunt
argenti lamminis, capitibus argenteis et basibus aeneis. 18 In
longitudine occupabit atrium cubitos centum, in latitudine,
quinquaginta. Altitudo quinque cubitorum erit, fietque de
bysso retorta et habebit bases aeneas. 19 Cuncta vasa tabernaculi in omnes usus et caerimonias tam paxillos eius quam
atrii ex aere facies.

20 "Praecipe filiis Israhel ut adferant tibi oleum de arboribus olivarum purissimum piloque contusum, ut ardeat lu-
cerna semper 21 in Tabernaculo Testimonii extra velum quod
oppansum est testimonio. Et conlocabunt eam Aaron et filii
eius ut usque mane luceat coram Domino. Perpetuus erit
cultus per successiones eorum a filiis Israhel."

cubits long, twenty pillars and as many sockets of brass and their heads, with their engraving, of silver. 12 But in the breadth of the court that looketh to the west, there shall be hangings of fifty cubits and ten pillars and as many sockets. 13 In that breadth also of the court which looketh to the east there shall be fifty cubits 14 in which there shall be for one side hangings of fifteen cubits and three pillars and as many sockets, 15 and in the other side there shall be hangings of fifteen cubits with three pillars and as many sockets.

16 "And in the entrance of the court there shall be made a hanging of twenty cubits of violet and purple and scarlet twice dyed and fine twisted linen with embroidered work. It shall have four pillars with as many sockets. 17 All the pillars of the court round about shall be garnished with plates of silver, silver heads and sockets of brass. 18 In length, the court shall take up a hundred cubits, in breadth, fifty. The height shall be of five cubits, and it shall be made of fine twisted linen and shall have sockets of brass. 19 All the vessels of the tabernacle for all uses and ceremonies and the pins both of it and of the court thou shalt make of brass.

20 "Command the children of Israel that they bring thee the purest oil of the *olives* and beaten with a pestle, that a lamp may burn always 21 in the Tabernacle of the Testimony without the veil that hangs before the testimony. And Aaron and his sons shall order it that it may give light before the Lord until the morning. It shall be a perpetual observance throughout their successions among the children of Israel."

Caput 28

"Adplica quoque ad te Aaron, fratrem tuum, cum filiis suis de medio filiorum Israhel, ut sacerdotio fungantur mihi: Aaron, Nadab et Abiu, Eleazar et Ithamar. 2 Faciesque vestem sanctam Aaron, fratri tuo, in gloriam et decorem. 3 Et loqueris cunctis sapientibus corde quos replevi spiritu prudentiae ut faciant vestes Aaron in quibus sanctificatus ministret mihi. 4 Haec autem erunt vestimenta quae facient: rationale et superumerale, tunicam et lineam strictam, cidarim et balteum. Facient vestimenta sancta Aaron fratri tuo et filiis eius ut sacerdotio fungantur mihi. 5 Accipientque aurum et hyacinthum et purpuram coccumque bis tinctum et byssum.

6 "Facient autem superumerale de auro et hyacintho ac purpura coccoque bis tincto et bysso retorta opere polymito. 7 Duas oras iunctas habebit in utroque latere summitatum ut in unum redeant. 8 Ipsaque textura et cuncta operis varietas erit ex auro et hyacintho et purpura coccoque bis tincto et bysso retorta. 9 Sumesque duos lapides onychinos et sculpes in eis nomina filiorum Israhel: 10 sex nomina in lapide uno et sex reliqua in altero, iuxta ordinem

Chapter 28

The holy vestments for Aaron and his sons.

"Take unto thee also Aaron, thy brother, with his sons from among the children of Israel, that they may *minister* to me *in the* priest's office: Aaron, Nadab and Abihu, Eleazar and Ithamar. 2 And thou shalt make a holy vesture for Aaron, thy brother, for glory and for beauty. 3 And thou shalt speak to all the wise of heart whom I have filled with the spirit of wisdom that they may make Aaron's vestments in which he, being consecrated, may minister to me. 4 And these shall be the vestments that they shall make: a rational and an ephod, a tunick and a strait linen garment, a mitre and a girdle. They shall make the holy vestments for thy brother Aaron and his sons that they may do the office of priesthood unto me. 5 And they shall take gold and violet and purple and scarlet twice dyed and fine linen.

6 "And they shall make the ephod of gold and violet and purple and scarlet twice dyed and fine twisted linen embroidered with divers colours. 7 It shall have the two edges joined in the top on both sides that they may be closed together. 8 The very workmanship also and all the variety of the work shall be of gold and violet and purple and scarlet twice dyed and fine twisted linen. 9 And thou shalt take two onyx stones and shalt grave on them the names of the children of Israel: 10 six names on one stone and the other six on the other, ac-

nativitatis eorum. 11 Opere sculptoris et celatura gemmarii sculpes eos nominibus filiorum Israhel inclusos auro atque circumdatos, 12 et pones in utroque latere superumeralis, memoriale filiis Israhel. Portabitque Aaron nomina eorum coram Domino super utrumque umerum ob recordationem. 13 Facies et uncinos ex auro 14 et duas catenulas auri purissimi sibi invicem coherentes, quas inseres uncinis.

15 "Rationale quoque iudicii facies opere polymito, iuxta texturam superumeralis, ex auro, hyacintho et purpura coccoque bis tincto et bysso retorta. 16 Quadrangulum erit et duplex. Mensuram palmi habebit tam in longitudine quam in latitudine. 17 Ponesque in eo quattuor ordines lapidum. In primo versu erit lapis sardius et topazius et zmaragdus, 18 in secundo, carbunculus, sapphyrus et iaspis, 19 in tertio, ligyrius, achates et amethistus, 20 in quarto, chrysolitus, onychinus et berillus. Inclusi auro erunt per ordines suos. 21 Habebuntque nomina filiorum Israhel. Duodecim nominibus celabuntur, singuli lapides nominibus singulorum per duodecim tribus.

22 "Facies in rationali catenas sibi invicem coherentes ex auro purissimo 23 et duos anulos aureos, quos pones in utraque rationalis summitate. 24 Catenasque aureas iunges anulis qui sunt in marginibus eius, 25 et ipsarum catenarum extrema duobus copulabis uncinis in utroque latere superumeralis, quod rationale respicit. 26 Facies et duos anulos aureos quos pones in summitatibus rationalis in oris quae

cording to the order of their birth. 11 With the work of an engraver and the graving of a jeweller thou shalt engrave them with the names of the children of Israel set in gold and compassed about, 12 and thou shalt put them in both sides of the ephod, a memorial for the children of Israel. And Aaron shall bear their names before the Lord upon both shoulders for a remembrance. 13 Thou shalt make also hooks of gold 14 and two little chains of the purest gold linked one to another, which thou shalt put into the hooks.

15 "And thou shalt make the rational of judgment with embroidered work of divers colours, according to the workmanship of the ephod, of gold, violet and purple and scarlet twice dyed and fine twisted linen. 16 It shall be foursquare and doubled. It shall be the measure of a span both in length and in breadth. 17 And thou shalt set in it four rows of stones. In the first row shall be a sardius stone and a topaz and an emerald, 18 in the second, a carbuncle, a sapphire and a jasper, 19 in the third, a ligurius, an agate and an amethyst, 20 in the fourth, a chrysolite, an onyx and a beryl. They shall be set in gold by their rows. 21 And they shall have the names of the children of Israel. With twelve names shall they be engraved, each stone with the name of one according to the twelve tribes.

22 "And thou shalt make on the rational chains linked one to another of the purest gold 23 and two rings of gold, which thou shalt put in the two ends at the top of the rational. 24 And the golden chains thou shalt join to the rings that are in the ends thereof, 25 and the ends of the chains themselves thou shalt join together with two hooks on both sides of the ephod, which is towards the rational. 26 Thou shalt make also two rings of gold which thou shalt put in the top parts

e regione sunt superumeralis et posteriora eius aspiciunt, 27 nec non et alios duos anulos aureos, qui ponendi sunt in utroque latere superumeralis deorsum quod respicit contra faciem iuncturae inferioris, ut aptari possit cum superumerali 28 et stringatur rationale anulis suis cum anulis superumeralis vitta hyacinthina, ut maneat iunctura fabrefacta et a se invicem rationale et superumerale nequeant separari. 29 Portabitque Aaron nomina filiorum Israhel in rationali iudicii super pectus suum quando ingredietur sanctuarium, memoriale coram Domino in aeternum. 30 Pones autem in rationali iudicii Doctrinam et Veritatem, quae erunt in pectore Aaron quando ingredietur coram Domino, et gestabit iudicium filiorum Israhel in pectore suo in conspectu Domini semper.

31 "Facies et tunicam superumeralis totam hyacinthinam, 32 in cuius medio supra erit capitium et ora per gyrum eius textilis, sicut fieri solet in extremis vestium partibus, ne facile rumpatur. 33 Deorsum vero ad pedes eiusdem tunicae per circuitum quasi mala punica facies ex hyacintho et purpura et cocco bis tincto mixtis in medio tintinabulis, 34 ita ut tintinabulum sit aureum et malum punicum rursumque tintinabulum aliud aureum et malum punicum. 35 Et vestietur ea Aaron in officio ministerii, ut audiatur sonitus quando ingreditur et egreditur sanctuarium in conspectu Domini et non moriatur.

of the rational in the borders that are over against the ephod and look towards the back parts thereof, 27 moreover also other two rings of gold, which are to be set on each side of the ephod beneath that looketh towards the nether joining, that the rational may be fitted with the ephod 28 and may be fastened by the rings thereof unto the rings of the ephod with a violet fillet, that the joining artificially wrought may continue and the rational and the ephod may not be loosed one from the other. 29 And Aaron shall bear the names of the children of Israel in the rational of judgment upon his breast when he shall enter into the sanctuary, a memorial before the Lord for ever. 30 And thou shalt put in the rational of judgment Doctrine and Truth, which shall be on Aaron's breast when he shall go in before the Lord, and he shall bear the judgment of the children of Israel on his breast in the sight of the Lord always.

31 "And thou shalt make the tunick of the ephod all of violet, 32 in the midst whereof above shall be a hole for the head and a border round about it woven, as is wont to be made in the outmost parts of garments, that it may not easily be broken. 33 And beneath at the feet of the same tunick round about, thou shalt make, as it were, pomegranates of violet and purple and scarlet twice dyed with little bells set between, 34 so that there shall be a golden bell and a pomegranate and again another golden bell and a pomegranate. 35 And Aaron shall be vested with it in the office of his ministry, that the sound may be heard when he goeth in and cometh out of the sanctuary in the sight of the Lord and that he may not die.

36 "Facies et lamminam de auro purissimo in qua sculpes opere celatoris, 'Sanctum Domino.' 37 Ligabisque eam vitta hyacinthina, et erit super tiaram 38 inminens fronti pontificis. Portabitque Aaron iniquitates eorum quae obtulerint et sanctificaverint filii Israhel in cunctis muneribus et donariis suis. Erit autem lammina semper in fronte eius, ut placatus eis sit Dominus. 39 Stringesque tunicam bysso, et tiaram byssinam facies et balteum opere plumarii. 40 Porro, filiis Aaron tunicas lineas parabis et balteos ac tiaras in gloriam et decorem. 41 Vestiesque his omnibus Aaron, fratrem tuum, et filios eius cum eo. Et cunctorum consecrabis manus sanctificabisque illos ut sacerdotio fungantur mihi. 42 Facies et feminalia linea ut operiant carnem turpitudinis suae a renibus usque ad femora, 43 et utentur eis Aaron et filii eius quando ingredientur Tabernaculum Testimonii, vel quando adpropinquant ad altare ut ministrent in sanctuario, ne, iniquitatis rei, moriantur. Legitimum sempiternum erit Aaron et semini eius post eum."

36 "Thou shalt make also a plate of the purest gold wherein thou shalt grave with engraver's work, 'Holy to the Lord.' 37 And thou shalt tie it with a violet fillet, and it shall be upon the mitre 38 hanging over the forehead of the high priest. And Aaron shall bear the iniquities of those things which the children of Israel have offered and sanctified in all their gifts and offerings. And the plate shall be always on his forehead, that the Lord may be well pleased with them. 39 And thou shalt gird the tunick with fine linen, and thou shalt make a fine linen mitre and a girdle of embroidered work. 40 Moreover, for the sons of Aaron thou shalt prepare linen tunicks and girdles and mitres for glory and beauty. 41 And with all these things thou shalt vest Aaron, thy brother, and his sons with him. And thou shalt consecrate the hands of them all and shalt sanctify them that they may do the office of priesthood unto me. 42 Thou shalt make also linen breeches to cover the flesh of their nakedness from the reins to the thighs, 43 and Aaron and his sons shall use them when they shall go in to the Tabernacle of the Testimony, or when they approach the altar to minister in the sanctuary, lest, being guilty of iniquity, they die. It shall be a law for ever to Aaron and to his seed after him."

Caput 29

"Sed et hoc facies ut mihi in sacerdotio consecrentur. Tolle vitulum de armento et arietes duos inmaculatos 2 panesque azymos et crustulam absque fermento quae conspersa sit oleo, lagana quoque azyma oleo lita; de simila triticea cuncta facies. 3 Et posita in canistro offeres vitulum autem et duos arietes. 4 Et Aaron ac filios eius adplicabis ad ostium Tabernaculi Testimonii. Cumque laveris patrem cum filiis suis aqua, 5 indues Aaron vestimentis suis, id est, linea et tunica et superumerali et rationali quod constringes balteo. 6 Et pones tiaram in capite eius et lamminam sanctam super tiaram, 7 et oleum unctionis fundes super caput eius, atque hoc ritu consecrabitur. 8 Filios quoque illius adplicabis et indues tunicis lineis cingesque balteo, 9 Aaron, scilicet, et liberos eius, et inpones eis mitras, eruntque sacerdotes mihi religione perpetua.

"Postquam initiaveris manus eorum, 10 adplicabis et vitulum coram Tabernaculo Testimonii. Inponentque Aaron et

Chapter 29

The manner of consecrating Aaron and other priests. The institution of the daily sacrifice of two lambs, one in the morning, the other at evening.

"And thou shalt also do this that they may be consecrated to me in priesthood. Take a calf from the herd and two rams without blemish 2 and unleavened bread and a cake without leaven tempered with oil, wafers also unleavened anointed with oil; thou shalt make them all of wheaten flour. 3 And thou shalt put them in a basket and offer them and the calf and the two rams. 4 And thou shalt bring Aaron and his sons to the door of the Tabernacle of the Testimony. And when thou hast washed the father and his sons with water, 5 thou shalt clothe Aaron with his vestments, that is, with the linen garment and the tunick and the ephod and the rational which thou shalt gird with the girdle. 6 And thou shalt put the mitre upon his head and the holy plate upon the mitre, 7 and thou shalt pour the oil of unction upon his head, and by this rite shall he be consecrated. 8 Thou shalt bring his sons also and shalt put on them the linen tunicks and gird them with a girdle, 9 to wit, Aaron and his children, and thou shalt put mitres upon them, and they shall be priests to me by a perpetual ordinance.

"After thou shalt have consecrated their hands, 10 thou shalt present also the calf before the Tabernacle of the Testi-

filii eius manus super caput illius, 11 et mactabis eum in conspectu Domini iuxta ostium Tabernaculi Testimonii. 12 Sumptumque de sanguine vituli pones super cornua altaris digito tuo, reliquum autem sanguinem fundes iuxta basim eius. 13 Sumes et adipem totum qui operit intestina et reticulum iecoris ac duos renes et adipem qui super eos est, et offeres incensum super altare, 14 carnes vero vituli et corium et fimum conbures foris extra castra eo quod pro peccato sit.

15 "Unum quoque arietem sumes super cuius caput ponent Aaron et filii eius manus. 16 Quem cum mactaveris, tolles de sanguine eius et fundes circa altare. 17 Ipsum autem arietem secabis in frusta, lotaque intestina eius ac pedes pones super concisas carnes et super caput illius. 18 Et offeres totum arietem in incensum super altare. Oblatio est Domino, odor suavissimus victimae Donimi. 19 Tolles quoque arietem alterum super cuius caput Aaron et filii eius ponent manus. 20 Quem cum immolaveris, sumes de sanguine ipsius et pones super extremum dextrae auriculae Aaron et filiorum eius et super pollices manus eorum et pedis dextri, fundesque sanguinem super altare per circuitum. 21 Cumque tuleris de sanguine qui est super altare et de oleo unctionis, asperges Aaron et vestes eius, filios et vestimenta eorum. Consecratisque ipsis et vestibus, 22 tolles adipem de ariete et caudam et arvinam quae operit vitalia ac reticulum iecoris

mony. And Aaron and his sons shall lay their hands upon his head, 11 and thou shalt kill him in the sight of the Lord beside the door of the Tabernacle of the Testimony. 12 And taking some of the blood of the calf, thou shalt put it upon the horns of the altar with thy finger, and the rest of the blood thou shalt pour at the bottom thereof. 13 Thou shalt take also all the fat that covereth the entrails and the caul of the liver and the two kidneys and the fat that is upon them, and shalt offer a burnt offering upon the altar, 14 but the flesh of the calf and the hide and the dung thou shalt burn abroad without the camp because it is for sin.

15 "Thou shalt take also one ram upon the head whereof Aaron and his sons shall lay their hands. 16 And when thou hast killed him, thou shalt take of the blood thereof and pour round about the altar. 17 And thou shalt cut the ram in pieces, and, having washed his entrails and feet, thou shalt put them upon the flesh that is cut in pieces and upon his head. 18 And thou shalt offer the whole ram for a burnt offering upon the altar. It is an oblation to the Lord, a most sweet savour of the victim of the Lord. 19 Thou shalt take also the other ram upon whose head Aaron and his sons shall lay their hands. 20 And when thou hast sacrificed him, thou shalt take of his blood and put upon the tip of the right ear of Aaron and of his sons and upon the thumbs and great toes of their right hand and foot, and thou shalt pour the blood upon the altar round about. 21 And when thou hast taken of the blood that is upon the altar and of the oil of unction, thou shalt sprinkle Aaron and his vesture, his sons and their vestments. And after they and their vestments are consecrated, 22 thou shalt take the fat of the ram and the rump and the fat that covereth the lungs and the caul of the liver

et duos renes atque adipem qui super eos est armumque dextrum, eo quod sit aries consecrationis, 23 tortamque panis unius, crustulum conspersum oleo, laganum de canistro azymorum quod positum est in conspectu Domini, 24 ponesque omnia super manus Aaron et filiorum eius et sanctificabis eos, elevans coram Domino. 25 Suscipiesque universa de manibus eorum et incendes super altare in holocaustum, odorem suavissimum in conspectu Domini, quia oblatio eius est.

26 "Sumes quoque pectusculum de ariete quo initiatus est Aaron, sanctificabisque illud elevatum coram Domino, et cedet in partem tuam. 27 Sanctificabisque et pectusculum consecratum et armum quem de ariete separasti 28 quo initiatus est Aaron et filii eius, cedentque in partem Aaron et filiorum eius iure perpetuo a filiis Israhel, quia primitiva sunt et initia de victimis eorum pacificis quae offerunt Domino. 29 Vestem autem sanctam, qua utetur Aaron, habebunt filii eius post eum ut unguantur in ea et consecrentur manus eorum. 30 Septem diebus utetur illa qui pontifex pro eo fuerit constitutus de filiis eius et qui ingredietur Tabernaculum Testimonii ut ministret in sanctuario.

31 "Arietem autem consecrationis tolles et coques carnes eius in loco sancto, 32 quibus vescetur Aaron et filii eius. Panes quoque qui sunt in canistro, in vestibulo Tabernaculi Testimonii comedent 33 ut sit placabile sacrificium et sanctificentur offerentium manus. Alienigena non vescetur ex eis quia sancti sunt. 34 Quod si remanserit de carnibus conse-

and the two kidneys and the fat that is upon them and the right shoulder, because it is the ram of consecration, 23 and one roll of bread, a cake tempered with oil, a wafer out of the basket of unleavened bread which is set in the sight of the Lord, 24 and thou shalt put all upon the hands of Aaron and of his sons and shalt sanctify them, elevating before the Lord. 25 And thou shalt take all from their hands and shalt burn them upon the altar for a holocaust, a most sweet savour in the sight of the Lord, because it is his oblation.

26 "Thou shalt take also the breast of the ram wherewith Aaron was consecrated, and, elevating it, thou shalt sanctify it before the Lord, and it shall fall to thy share. 27 And thou shalt sanctify both the consecrated breast and the shoulder that thou didst separate of the ram 28 wherewith Aaron was consecrated and his sons, and they shall fall to Aaron's share and his sons' by a perpetual right from the children of Israel, because they are the choicest and the beginnings of their peace-victims which they offer to the Lord. 29 And the holy vesture, which Aaron shall use, his sons shall have after him that they may be anointed and their hands consecrated to it. 30 He of his sons that shall be appointed high priest in his stead and that shall enter into the Tabernacle of the Testimony to minister in the sanctuary shall wear it seven days.

31 "And thou shalt take the ram of the consecration and shalt boil the flesh thereof in the holy place, 32 and Aaron and his sons shall eat it. The loaves also that are in the basket, they shall eat in the entry of the Tabernacle of the Testimony 33 that it may be an atoning sacrifice and the hands of the offerers may be sanctified. A stranger shall not eat of them because they are holy. 34 And if there remain of the consecrated flesh or of the bread till the morning, thou shalt

cratis sive de panibus usque mane, conbures reliquias igni. Non comedentur, quia sanctificata sunt. 35 Omnia quae praecepi tibi facies super Aaron et filiis eius. Septem diebus consecrabis manus eorum, 36 et vitulum pro peccato offeres per singulos dies ad expiandum. Mundabisque altare cum immolaris expiationis hostiam et ungues illud in sanctificationem. 37 Septem diebus expiabis altare et sanctificabis, et erit sanctum sanctorum. Omnis qui tetigerit illud sanctificabitur. 38 Hoc est quod facies in altari: agnos anniculos duos per singulos dies iugiter, 39 unum agnum mane et alterum vespere, 40 decimam partem similae conspersae oleo tunso quod habeat mensuram quartam partem hin et vinum ad libandum eiusdem mensurae in agno uno, 41 alterum vero agnum offeres ad vesperam, iuxta ritum matutinae oblationis et iuxta ea quae diximus in odorem suavitatis. 42 Sacrificium Domino oblatione perpetua in generationes vestras ad ostium Tabernaculi Testimonii coram Domino, ubi constituam ut loquar ad te. 43 Ibique praecipiam filiis Israhel, et sanctificabitur altare in gloria mea. 44 Sanctificabo et Tabernaculum Testimonii cum altari et Aaron cum filiis eius ut sacerdotio fungantur mihi. 45 Et habitabo in medio filiorum Israhel eroque eis Deus, 46 et scient quia ego Dominus, Deus eorum, qui eduxi eos de terra Aegypti ut manerem inter illos, ego, Dominus, Deus ipsorum."

burn the remainder with fire. They shall not be eaten, because they are sanctified. 35 All that I have commanded thee thou shalt do unto Aaron and his sons. Seven days shalt thou consecrate their hands, 36 and thou shalt offer a calf for sin every day for expiation. And thou shalt cleanse the altar when thou hast offered the victim of expiation and shalt anoint it to sanctify it. 37 Seven days shalt thou expiate the altar and sanctify it, and it shall be most holy. Every one that shall touch it shall be holy. 38 This is what thou shalt *sacrifice* upon the altar: two lambs of a year old every day continually, 39 one lamb in the morning and another in the evening, 40 with one lamb, a tenth part of flour tempered with beaten oil of the fourth part of a hin and wine for libation of the same measure, 41 and the other lamb thou shalt offer in the evening, according to the rite of the morning oblation and according to what we have said for a savour of sweetness. 42 It is a sacrifice to the Lord by perpetual oblation unto your generations at the door of the Tabernacle of the Testimony before the Lord, where I will appoint to speak unto thee. 43 And there will I command the children of Israel, and the altar shall be sanctified by my glory. 44 I will sanctify also the Tabernacle of the Testimony with the altar and Aaron with his sons to do the office of priesthood unto me. 45 And I will dwell in the midst of the children of Israel and will be their God, 46 and they shall know that I am the Lord, their God, who have brought them out of the land of Egypt that I might abide among them, I, the Lord, their God."

Caput 30

"Facies quoque altare, in adolendum thymiama, de lignis setthim, 2 habens cubitum longitudinis et alterum latitudinis, id est, quadrangulum, et duos cubitos in altitudine. Cornua ex ipso procedent. 3 Vestiesque illud auro purissimo tam craticulam eius quam parietes per circuitum et cornua. Faciesque ei coronam aureolam per gyrum 4 et duos anulos aureos sub corona per singula latera ut mittantur in eos vectes et altare portetur. 5 Ipsos quoque vectes facies de lignis setthim et inaurabis. 6 Ponesque altare contra velum quod ante Arcam pendet Testimonii coram propitiatorio quo tegitur testimonium, ubi loquar tibi. 7 Et adolebit incensum super eo Aaron suave fragrans mane. Quando conponet lucernas, incendet illud. 8 Et quando conlocabit eas ad vesperum, uret thymiama sempiternum coram Domino in generationes vestras. 9 Non offeretis super eo thymiama conpositionis alterius nec oblationem et victimam, nec libamina libabitis. 10 Et deprecabitur Aaron super cornua eius semel per annum in sanguine quod oblatum est pro peccato

Chapter 30

The altar of incense, money to be gathered for the use of the tabernacle, the brazen laver, the holy oil of unction and the composition of the perfume.

"Thou shalt make also an altar, to burn incense, of setim wood. 2 It shall be a cubit in length and another in breadth, that is, foursquare, and two in height. Horns shall go out of the same. 3 And thou shalt overlay it with the purest gold as well the grate thereof as the walls round about and the horns. And thou shalt make to it a crown of gold round about 4 and two golden rings under the crown on either side that the bars may be put into them and the altar be carried. 5 And thou shalt make the bars also of setim wood and shalt overlay them with gold. 6 And thou shalt set the altar over against the veil that hangeth before the Ark of the Testimony before the propitiatory wherewith the testimony is covered, where I will speak to thee. 7 And Aaron shall burn sweet smelling incense upon it in the morning. When he shall dress the lamps, he shall burn it. 8 And when he shall place them in the evening, he shall burn an everlasting incense before the Lord throughout your generations. 9 You shall not offer upon it incense of another composition nor oblation and victim, neither shall you offer libations. 10 And Aaron shall pray upon the horns thereof once a year with the blood *of that* which was offered for sin and shall make

et placabit super eo in generationibus vestris. Sanctum sanctorum erit Domino."

11 Locutusque est Dominus ad Mosen, dicens, 12 "Quando tuleris summam filiorum Israhel iuxta numerum, dabunt singuli pretium pro animabus suis Domino, et non erit plaga in eis cum fuerint recensiti. 13 Hoc autem dabit omnis qui transit ad nomen: dimidium sicli iuxta mensuram templi. Siclus viginti obolos habet. Media pars sicli offeretur Domino. 14 Qui habetur in numero a viginti annis et supra dabit pretium. 15 Dives non addet ad medium sicli, et pauper nihil minuet. 16 Susceptamque pecuniam quae conlata est a filiis Israhel trades in usus Tabernaculi Testimonii ut sit monumentum eorum coram Domino et propitietur animabus illorum."

17 Locutusque est Dominus ad Mosen, dicens, 18 "Facies et labrum aeneum cum basi sua ad lavandum, ponesque illud inter Tabernaculum Testimonii et altare. Et missa aqua, 19 lavabunt in eo Aaron et filii eius manus suas ac pedes 20 quando ingressuri sunt Tabernaculum Testimonii et quando accessuri ad altare ut offerant in eo thymiama Domino, 21 ne forte moriantur. Legitimum sempiternum erit ipsi et semini eius per successiones."

22 Locutusque est Dominus ad Mosen, 23 dicens, "Sume tibi aromata: primae zmyrnae et electae, quingentos siclos, et cinnamomi, medium, id est, ducentos quinquaginta siclos, calami, similiter ducentos quinquaginta, 24 cassiae autem, quingentos siclos in pondere sanctuarii, olei de olive-

atonement upon it in your generations. It shall be most holy to the Lord."

11 And the Lord spoke to Moses, saying, 12 "When thou shalt take the sum of the children of Israel according to their number, every one of them shall give a price for their souls to the Lord, and there shall be no scourge among them when they shall be reckoned. 13 And this shall every one give that passeth at the naming: half a sicle according to the standard of the temple. A sicle hath twenty obols. Half a sicle shall be offered to the Lord. 14 He that is counted in the number from twenty years and upwards shall give the price. 15 The rich man shall not add to half a sicle, and the poor man shall diminish nothing. 16 And the money received which was contributed by the children of Israel thou shalt deliver unto the uses of the Tabernacle of the Testimony that it may be a memorial of them before the Lord and he may be merciful to their souls."

17 And the Lord spoke to Moses, saying, 18 "Thou shalt make also a brazen laver with its foot to wash in, and thou shalt set it between the Tabernacle of the Testimony and the altar. And water being put into it, 19 Aaron and his sons shall wash their hands and feet in it 20 when they are going into the Tabernacle of the Testimony and when they are to come to the altar to offer on it incense to the Lord, 21 lest perhaps they die. It shall be an everlasting law to him and to his seed by successions."

22 And the Lord spoke to Moses, 23 saying, "Take spices: of principal and chosen myrrh, five hundred sicles, and of cinnamon, half so much, that is, two hundred and fifty sicles, of calamus, in like manner two hundred and fifty, 24 and of cassia, five hundred sicles by the weight of the sanctuary,

tis mensuram hin, 25 faciesque unctionis oleum sanctum, unguentum conpositum opere unguentarii, 26 et ungues ex eo Tabernaculum Testimonii et Arcam Testamenti 27 mensamque cum vasis suis, candelabrum et utensilia eius, altaria thymiamatis 28 et holocausti et universam supellectilem quae ad cultum eorum pertinent. 29 Sanctificabisque omnia, et erunt sancta sanctorum. Qui tetigerit ea sanctificabitur. 30 Aaron et filios eius ungues sanctificabisque eos ut sacerdotio fungantur mihi.

31 "Filiis quoque Israhel dices, 'Hoc oleum unctionis sanctum erit mihi in generationes vestras. 32 Caro hominis non unguetur ex eo, et iuxta conpositionem eius non facietis aliud, quia sanctificatum est et sanctum erit vobis. 33 Homo quicumque tale conposuerit et dederit ex eo alieno, exterminabitur de populo suo.'"

34 Dixitque Dominus ad Mosen, "Sume tibi aromata, stacten et onycha, galbanen boni odoris et tus lucidissimum. Aequalis ponderis erunt omnia, 35 faciesque thymiama conpositum opere unguentarii, mixtum diligenter et purum et sanctificatione dignissimum. 36 Cumque in tenuissimum pulverem universa contuderis, pones ex eo coram Testimonii Tabernaculo in quo loco apparebo tibi. Sanctum sanctorum erit vobis thymiama. 37 Talem conpositionem non facietis in usus vestros, quia sanctum est Domino. 38 Homo quicumque fecerit simile ut odore illius perfruatur, peribit de populis suis."

of oil of olives the measure hin, 25 and thou shalt make the holy oil of unction, an ointment compounded after the art of the perfumer, 26 and therewith thou shalt anoint the Tabernacle of the Testimony and the Ark of the Testament 27 and the table with the vessels thereof, the candlestick and furniture thereof, the altars of incense 28 and of holocaust and all the furniture that belongeth to the service of them. 29 And thou shalt sanctify all, and they shall be most holy. He that shall touch them shall be sanctified. 30 Thou shalt anoint Aaron and his sons and shalt sanctify them that they may do the office of priesthood unto me.

31 "And thou shalt say to the children of Israel, 'This oil of unction shall be holy unto me throughout your generations. 32 The flesh of man shall not be anointed therewith, and you shall make none other of the same composition, because it is sanctified and shall be holy unto you. 33 What man soever shall compound such and shall give thereof to a stranger, he shall be cut off from his people.'"

34 And the Lord said to Moses, "Take unto thee spices, stacte and onycha, galbanum of sweet savour and the clearest frankincense. All shall be of equal weight, 35 and thou shalt make incense compounded by the work of the perfumer, well tempered together and pure and most worthy of sanctification. 36 And when thou has beaten all into very small powder, thou shalt set of it before the Tabernacle of the Testimony in the place where I will appear to thee. Most holy shall this incense be to you. 37 You shall not make such a composition for your own uses, because it is holy to the Lord. 38 What man soever shall make the like to enjoy the smell thereof, he shall perish out of his people."

Caput 31

Locutusque est Dominus ad Mosen, dicens, 2 "Ecce: vocavi ex nomine Beselehel, filium Uri, filii Hur de tribu Iuda, 3 et implevi eum spiritu Dei, sapientia et intellegentia et scientia in omni opere 4 ad excogitandum fabre quicquid fieri potest ex auro et argento et aere, 5 marmore et gemmis et diversitate lignorum, 6 dedique ei socium Hooliab, filium Achisamech de tribu Dan. Et in corde omnis eruditi posui sapientiam ut faciant cuncta quae praecepi tibi: 7 Tabernaculum Foederis et Arcam Testimonii et propitiatorium quod super eam est et cuncta vasa tabernaculi 8 mensamque et vasa eius, candelabrum purissimum cum vasis suis et altaria thymiamatis 9 et holocausti et omnia vasa eorum, labrum cum basi sua, 10 vestes sanctas in ministerio Aaron, sacerdoti, et filiis eius ut fungantur officio suo in sacris, 11 oleum

Chapter 31

Bezalel and Oholiab are appointed by the Lord to make the tabernacle and the things belonging thereto. The observation of the sabbath day is again commanded, and the Lord delivereth to Moses two tables written with the finger of God.

And the Lord spoke to Moses, saying, 2 "Behold: I have called by name Bezalel, the son of Uri, the son of Hur of the tribe of Judah, 3 and I have filled him with the spirit of God, with wisdom and understanding and knowledge in all manner of work 4 to devise whatsoever may be artificially made of gold and silver and brass, 5 of marble and precious stones and variety of wood. 6 And I have given him for his companion Oholiab, the son of Ahisamach of the tribe of Dan. And I have put wisdom in the heart of every skillful man that they may make all things which I have commanded thee: 7 the Tabernacle of the Covenant and the Ark of the Testimony and the propitiatory that is over it and all the vessels of the tabernacle 8 and the table and the vessels thereof, the most pure candlestick with the vessels thereof and the altars of incense 9 and of holocaust and all their vessels, the laver with its foot, 10 the holy vestments in the ministry for Aaron, the priest, and for his sons that they may execute their office about the sacred things, 11 the oil of unction and the in-

unctionis et thymiama aromatum in sanctuario; omnia quae praecepi tibi facient."

12 Et locutus est Dominus ad Mosen, dicens, 13 "Loquere filiis Israhel, et dices ad eos, 'Videte ut sabbatum meum custodiatis quia signum est inter me et vos in generationibus vestris ut sciatis quia ego Dominus qui sanctifico vos. 14 Custodite sabbatum meum, sanctum est enim vobis. Qui polluerit illud morte morietur. Qui fecerit in eo opus, peribit anima illius de medio populi sui. 15 Sex diebus facietis opus. In die septimo sabbatum est, requies sancta Domino. Omnis qui fecerit opus in hac die morietur. 16 Custodiant filii Israhel sabbatum et celebrent illud in generationibus suis. Pactum est sempiternum 17 inter me et filios Israhel signumque perpetuum, sex enim diebus fecit Dominus caelum et terram, et in septimo ab opere cessavit.'" 18 Deditque Dominus Mosi, conpletis huiuscemodi sermonibus in Monte Sinai, duas tabulas testimonii lapideas scriptas digito Dei.

cense of spices in the sanctuary; all things which I have commanded thee shall they make."

12 And the Lord spoke to Moses, saying, 13 "Speak to the children of Israel, and thou shalt say to them, 'See that thou keep my sabbath because it is a sign between me and you in your generations that you may know that I am the Lord who sanctify you. 14 Keep you my sabbath, for it is holy unto you. He that shall profane it shall be put to death. He that shall do any work in it, his soul shall perish out of the midst of his people. 15 Six days shall you do work. In the seventh day is the sabbath, the rest holy to the Lord. Every one that shall do any work on this day shall die. 16 Let the children of Israel keep the sabbath and celebrate it in their generations. It is an everlasting covenant 17 between me and the children of Israel and a perpetual sign, for in six days the Lord made heaven and earth, and in the seventh he ceased from work.'" 18 And the Lord, when he had ended these words in Mount Sinai, gave to Moses two stone tables of testimony written with the finger of God.

Caput 32

Videns autem populus quod moram faceret descendendi de monte Moses, congregatus adversus Aaron ait, "Surge; fac nobis deos qui nos praecedant, Mosi enim huic, viro qui nos eduxit de terra Aegypti, ignoramus quid acciderit."

2 Dixitque ad eos Aaron, "Tollite inaures aureas de uxorum filiorumque et filiarum vestrarum auribus, et adferte ad me." 3 Fecitque populus quae iusserat, deferens inaures ad Aaron. 4 Quas cum ille accepisset, formavit opere fusorio et fecit ex eis vitulum conflatilem.

Dixeruntque, "Hii sunt dii tui, Israhel, qui te eduxerunt de terra Aegypti."

5 Quod cum vidisset Aaron, aedificavit altare coram eo et praeconis voce clamavit, dicens, "Cras sollemnitas Domini est."

6 Surgentesque mane, obtulerunt holocausta et hostias pacificas, et sedit populus comedere ac bibere, et surrexerunt ludere. 7 Locutus est autem Dominus ad Mosen, dicens, "Vade; descende. Peccavit populus tuus quem eduxisti de terra Aegypti. 8 Recesserunt cito de via quam ostendisti

Chapter 32

The people fall into idolatry. Moses prayeth for them. He breaketh the tables, destroyeth the idol, blameth Aaron and causeth many of the idolaters to be slain.

And the people, seeing that Moses delayed to come down from the mount, gathering together against Aaron, said, "Arise; make us gods that may go before us, for as to this Moses, the man that brought us out of the land of Egypt, we know not what has befallen him."

2 And Aaron said to them, "Take the golden earrings from the ears of your wives and your sons and daughters, and bring them to me." 3 And the people did what he had commanded, bringing the earrings to Aaron. 4 And when he had received them, he fashioned them by founders' work and made of them a molten calf.

And they said, "These are thy gods, O Israel, that have brought thee out of the land of Egypt."

5 And when Aaron saw this, he built an altar before it and made proclamation by a crier's voice, saying, "Tomorrow is the solemnity of the Lord."

6 And rising in the morning, they offered holocausts and peace-victims, and the people sat down to eat and drink, and they rose up to play. 7 And the Lord spoke to Moses, saying, "Go; get thee down. Thy people which thou hast brought out of the land of Egypt hath sinned. 8 They have

eis feceruntque sibi vitulum conflatilem et adoraverunt atque, immolantes ei hostias, dixerunt, 'Isti sunt dii tui, Israhel, qui te eduxerunt de terra Aegypti.'" 9 Rursumque ait Dominus ad Mosen, "Cerno quod populus iste durae cervicis sit. 10 Dimitte me ut irascatur furor meus contra eos et deleam eos, faciamque te in gentem magnam."

11 Moses autem orabat Dominum, Deum suum, dicens, "Cur, Domine, irascitur furor tuus contra populum tuum quem eduxisti de terra Aegypti in fortitudine magna et in manu robusta? 12 Ne, quaeso, dicant Aegyptii, 'Callide eduxit eos ut interficeret in montibus et deleret e terra.' Quiescat ira tua, et esto placabilis super nequitia populi tui. 13 Recordare Abraham, Isaac et Israhel, servorum tuorum, quibus iurasti per temet ipsum, dicens, 'Multiplicabo semen vestrum sicut stellas caeli, et universam terram hanc de qua locutus sum dabo semini vestro, et possidebitis eam semper.'" 14 Placatusque est Dominus ne faceret malum quod locutus fuerat adversus populum suum.

15 Et reversus est Moses de monte portans duas tabulas testimonii in manu sua, scriptas ex utraque parte 16 et factas opere Dei. Scriptura quoque Dei erat sculpta in tabulis. 17 Audiens autem Iosue tumultum populi vociferantis, dixit ad Mosen, "Ululatus pugnae auditur in castris."

18 Qui respondit, "Non est clamor adhortantium ad pugnam neque vociferatio conpellentium ad fugam, sed vocem cantantium ego audio." 19 Cumque adpropinquasset ad castra, vidit vitulum et choros, iratusque valde proiecit de manu

quickly strayed from the way which thou didst shew them, and they have made to themselves a molten calf and have adored it and, sacrificing victims to it, have said, 'These are thy gods, O Israel, that have brought thee out of the land of Egypt.'" 9 And again the Lord said to Moses, "I see that this people is stiffnecked. 10 Let me alone that my wrath may be kindled against them and that I may destroy them, and I will make of thee a great nation."

11 But Moses besought the Lord, his God, saying, "Why, O Lord, is thy indignation kindled against thy people whom thou hast brought out of the land of Egypt with great power and with a mighty hand? 12 Let not the Egyptians say, I beseech thee, 'He craftily brought them out that he might kill them in the mountains and destroy them from the earth.' Let thy anger cease, and be appeased upon the wickedness of thy people. 13 Remember Abraham, Isaac and Israel, thy servants, to whom thou sworest by thy own self, saying, 'I will multiply your seed as the stars of heaven, and this whole land that I have spoken of I will give to your seed, and you shall possess it for ever.'" 14 And the Lord was appeased from doing the evil which he had spoken against his people.

15 And Moses returned from the mount carrying the two tables of the testimony in his hand, written on both sides 16 and made by the work of God. The writing also of God was graven in the tables. 17 And Joshua hearing the noise of the people shouting, said to Moses, "The noise of battle is heard in the camp."

18 But he answered, "It is not the cry of men encouraging to fight nor the shout of men compelling to flee, but I hear the voice of singers." 19 And when he came nigh to the camp, he saw the calf and the dances, and, being very angry, he

tabulas et confregit eas ad radicem montis, 20 arripiens-
que vitulum quem fecerant, conbusit et contrivit usque ad
pulverem, quem sparsit in aqua et dedit ex eo potum filiis
Israhel.

21 Dixitque ad Aaron, "Quid tibi fecit hic populus ut in-
duceres super eum peccatum maximum?"

22 Cui ille respondit, "Ne indignetur dominus meus, tu
enim nosti populum istum quod pronus sit ad malum.
23 Dixerunt mihi, 'Fac nobis deos qui praecedant nos, huic
enim Mosi, qui nos eduxit de terra Aegypti, nescimus quid
acciderit.' 24 Quibus ego dixi, 'Quis vestrum habet aurum?'
Tulerunt et dederunt mihi, et proieci illud in ignem, egressusque est hic vitulus."

25 Videns ergo Moses populum quod esset nudatus (spo-
liaverat enim eum Aaron propter ignominiam sordis et inter
hostes nudum constituerat), 26 et stans in porta castrorum,
ait, "Si quis est Domini, iungatur mihi." Congregatique sunt
ad eum omnes filii Levi, 27 quibus ait, "Haec dicit Dominus,
Deus Israhel: 'Ponat vir gladium super femur suum. Ite, et
redite de porta usque ad portam per medium castrorum,
et occidat unusquisque fratrem et amicum et proximum
suum.'" 28 Feceruntque filii Levi iuxta sermonem Mosi, cecideruntque in die illo quasi tria milia hominum. 29 Et ait Moses, "Consecrastis manus vestras hodie Domino, unusquisque in filio et in fratre suo, ut detur vobis benedictio."

threw the tables out of his hand and broke them at the foot of the mount, 20 and laying hold of the calf which they had made, he burnt it and beat it to powder, which he strowed into water and gave thereof to the children of Israel to drink.

21 And he said to Aaron, "What has this people done to thee that thou shouldst bring upon them a most heinous sin?"

22 And he answered him, "Let not my lord be offended, for thou knowest this people that they are prone to evil. 23 They said to me, 'Make us gods that may go before us, for as to this Moses, who brought us forth out of the land of Egypt, we know not what is befallen him.' 24 And I said to them, 'Which of you hath any gold?' And they took and brought it to me, and I cast it into the fire, and this calf came out."

25 And when Moses saw that the people were naked (for Aaron had stripped them by occasion of the shame of the filth and had set them naked among their enemies), 26 then, standing in the gate of the camp, he said, "If any man be on the Lord's side, let him join with me." And all the sons of Levi gathered themselves together unto him, 27 and he said to them, "Thus saith the Lord, God of Israel: 'Put, every man, his sword upon his thigh. Go, and return from gate to gate through the midst of the camp, and let every man kill his brother and friend and neighbour.'" 28 And the sons of Levi did according to the words of Moses, and there were slain that day about three *and twenty* thousand men. 29 And Moses said, "You have consecrated your hands this day to the Lord, every man in his son and in his brother, that a blessing may be given to you."

30 Facto autem die altero, locutus est Moses ad populum, "Peccastis peccatum maximum. Ascendam ad Dominum, si quo modo eum quivero deprecari pro scelere vestro." 31 Reversusque ad Dominum, ait, "Obsecro, peccavit populus iste peccatum magnum, feceruntque sibi deos aureos. Aut dimitte eis hanc noxam, 32 aut, si non facis, dele me de libro tuo quem scripsisti."

33 Cui respondit Dominus, "Qui peccaverit mihi, delebo eum de libro meo. 34 Tu autem vade, et duc populum istum quo locutus sum tibi. Angelus meus praecedet te. Ego autem in die ultionis visitabo et hoc peccatum eorum." 35 Percussit ergo Dominus populum pro reatu vituli quem fecerat Aaron.

Caput 33

Locutusque est Dominus ad Mosen, dicens, "Vade; ascende de loco isto, tu et populus tuus quem eduxisti de terra Aegypti in terram quam iuravi Abraham, Isaac et Iacob, dicens, 'Semini tuo dabo eam.' 2 Et mittam praecursorem tui

30 And when the next day was come, Moses spoke to the people: "You have sinned a very great sin. I will go up to the Lord, if by any means I may be able to entreat him for your crime." 31 And, returning to the Lord, he said, "I beseech thee, this people hath sinned a heinous sin, and they have made to themselves gods of gold. Either forgive them this trespass, 32 or, if thou do not, strike me out of the book that thou hast written."

33 And the Lord answered him, "He that hath sinned against me, him will I strike out of my book. 34 But go thou, and lead this people whither I have told thee. My angel shall go before thee. And I in the day of revenge will visit this sin also of theirs." 35 The Lord therefore struck the people for the guilt on occasion of the calf which Aaron had made.

Chapter 33

The people mourn for their sin. Moses pitcheth the tabernacle without the camp. He converseth familiarly with God, desireth to see his glory.

And the Lord spoke to Moses, saying, "Go; get thee up from this place, thou and thy people which thou has brought out of the land of Egypt into the land concerning which I swore to Abraham, Isaac and Jacob, saying, 'To thy seed I will give it.' 2 And I will send an angel before thee, that I may

angelum, ut eiciam Chananeum et Amorreum et Hettheum et Ferezeum et Eveum et Iebuseum 3 et intres in terram fluentem lacte et melle, non enim ascendam tecum, quia populus durae cervicis es, ne forte disperdam te in via. 4 Audiensque populus sermonem hunc pessimum luxit, et nullus ex more indutus est cultu suo. 5 Dixitque Dominus ad Mosen, "Loquere filiis Israhel: 'Populus durae cervicis es. Semel ascendam in medio tui et delebo te. Iam nunc depone ornatum tuum ut sciam quid faciam tibi.'"

6 Deposuerunt ergo filii Israhel ornatum suum a Monte Horeb. 7 Moses quoque tollens tabernaculum, tetendit extra castra procul vocavitque nomen eius Tabernaculum Foederis. Et omnis populus qui habebat aliquam quaestionem egrediebatur ad Tabernaculum Foederis extra castra. 8 Cumque egrederetur Moses ad tabernaculum, surgebat universa plebs, et stabat unusquisque in ostio papilionis sui, aspiciebantque tergum Mosi donec ingrederetur tentorium. 9 Ingresso autem illo Tabernaculum Foederis, descendebat columna nubis et stabat ad ostium, loquebaturque cum Mosi. 10 Cernentibus universis quod columna nubis staret ad ostium tabernaculi, stabantque ipsi et adorabant per fores tabernaculorum suorum.

11 Loquebatur autem Dominus ad Mosen facie ad faciem sicut loqui solet homo ad amicum suum. Cumque ille reverteretur in castra, minister eius Iosue, filius Nun, puer, non recedebat de tabernaculo. 12 Dixit autem Moses ad Dominum, "Praecipis ut educam populum istum, et non indicas mihi quem missurus es mecum, praesertim cum dixeris,

cast out the Canaanite and the Amorite and the Hittite and the Perizzite and the Hivite and the Jebusite 3 *that* thou mayst enter into the land that floweth with milk and honey, for I will not go up with thee, because thou art a stiffnecked people, lest I destroy thee in the way." 4 And the people hearing these very bad tidings mourned, and no man put on his ornaments according to custom. 5 And the Lord said to Moses, "Say to the children of Israel: 'Thou are a stiffnecked people. Once I shall come up in the midst of thee and shall destroy thee. Now presently lay aside thy ornaments that I may know what to do with thee.'"

6 So the children of Israel laid aside their ornaments by Mount Horeb. 7 Moses also taking the tabernacle, pitched it without the camp afar off and called the name thereof the Tabernacle of the Covenant. And all the people that had any question went forth to the Tabernacle of the Covenant without the camp. 8 And when Moses went forth to the tabernacle, all the people rose up, and every one stood in the door of his pavilion, and they beheld the back of Moses till he went into the tabernacle. 9 And when he was gone into the Tabernacle of the Covenant, the pillar of the cloud came down and stood at the door, and he spoke with Moses. 10 And all saw that the pillar of the cloud stood at the door of the tabernacle, and they stood and worshipped at the doors of their *tents.*

11 And the Lord spoke to Moses face to face as a man is wont to speak to his friend. And when he returned into the camp, his servant Joshua, the son of Nun, a young man, departed not from the tabernacle. 12 And Moses said to the Lord, "Thou commandest me to lead forth this people, and thou dost not let me know whom thou wilt send with me,

'Novi te ex nomine, et invenisti gratiam coram me.' 13 Si ergo inveni gratiam in conspectu tuo, ostende mihi faciem tuam, ut sciam te et inveniam gratiam ante oculos tuos. Respice populum tuum, gentem hanc."

14 Dixitque Dominus, "Facies mea praecedet te, et requiem dabo tibi."

15 Et ait Moses, "Si non tu ipse praecedas, ne educas nos de loco isto, 16 in quo enim scire poterimus, ego et populus tuus, invenisse nos gratiam in conspectu tuo nisi ambulaveris nobiscum ut glorificemur ab omnibus populis qui habitant super terram?"

17 Dixit autem Dominus ad Mosen, "Et verbum istud quod locutus es faciam, invenisti enim gratiam coram me, et te ipsum novi ex nomine."

18 Qui ait, "Ostende mihi gloriam tuam."

19 Respondit, "Ego ostendam omne bonum tibi, et vocabo in nomine Domini coram te, et miserebor cui voluero, et clemens ero in quem mihi placuerit." 20 Rursumque ait, "Non poteris videre faciem meam, non enim videbit me homo et vivet." 21 Et iterum, "Ecce," inquit, "est locus apud me, et stabis super petram. 22 Cumque transibit gloria mea, ponam te in foramine petrae et protegam dextera mea donec transeam. 23 Tollamque manum meam, et videbis posteriora mea, faciem autem meam videre non poteris."

especially whereas thou hast said, 'I know thee by name, and thou hast found favour in my sight.' 13 If therefore I have found favour in thy sight, show me thy face, that I may know thee and may find grace before thy eyes. Look upon thy people, this nation."

14 And the Lord said, "My face shall go before thee, and I will give thee rest."

15 And Moses said, "If thou thyself dost not go before, bring us not out of this place, 16 for how shall we be able to know, I and thy people, that we have found grace in thy sight unless thou walk with us that we may be glorified by all people that dwell upon the earth?"

17 And the Lord said to Moses, "This word also which thou hast spoken will I do, for thou hast found grace before me, and thee I have known by name."

18 And he said, "Shew me thy glory."

19 He answered, "I will shew thee all good, and I will proclaim in the name of the Lord before thee, and I will have mercy on whom I will, and I will be merciful to whom it shall please me." 20 And again he said, "Thou canst not see my face, for man shall not see me and live." 21 And again he said, "Behold: there is a place with me, and thou shalt stand upon the rock. 22 And when my glory shall pass, I will set thee in a hole of the rock and protect thee with my right hand till I pass. 23 And I will take away my hand, and thou shalt see my back parts, but my face thou canst not see."

Caput 34

Ac deinceps, "Praecide," ait, "tibi duas tabulas lapideas instar priorum, et scribam super eas verba quae habuerunt tabulae quas fregisti. 2 Esto paratus mane ut ascendas statim in Montem Sinai, stabisque mecum super verticem montis. 3 Nullus ascendat tecum, nec videatur quispiam per totum montem, boves quoque et oves non pascantur e contra."

4 Excidit ergo duas tabulas lapideas quales ante fuerant, et de nocte consurgens, ascendit in montem Sinai sicut ei praeceperat Dominus, portans secum tabulas. 5 Cumque descendisset Dominus per nubem, stetit Moses cum eo, invocans nomen Domini.

6 Quo transeunte coram eo, ait, "Dominator, Domine, Deus, misericors et clemens, patiens et multae miserationis ac verus, 7 qui custodis misericordiam in milia, qui aufers iniquitatem et scelera atque peccata nullusque apud te per

Chapter 34

The tables are renewed. All society with the Canaanites is forbid. Some precepts concerning the firstborn, the sabbath, and other feasts. After forty days' fast, Moses returneth to the people with the commandments, and his face appearing horned with rays of light, he covereth it whensoever he speaketh to the people.

And after this he said, "Hew thee two tables of stone like unto the former, and I will write upon them the words which were in the tables which thou brokest. 2 Be ready in the morning that thou mayst forthwith go up into Mount Sinai, and thou shalt stand with me upon the top of the mount. 3 Let no man go up with thee, and let not any man be seen throughout all the mount, neither let the oxen nor the sheep feed over against it."

4 Then he cut out two tables of stone such as had been before, and rising very early, he went up into the mount Sinai as the Lord had commanded him, carrying with him the tables. 5 And when the Lord was come down in a cloud, Moses stood with him, calling upon the name of the Lord.

6 And when he passed before him, he said, "O the Lord, the Lord, God, merciful and gracious, patient and of much compassion and true, 7 who keepest mercy unto thousands, who takest away iniquity and wickedness and sin and no man of himself is innocent before thee, who renderest the

se innocens est, qui reddis iniquitatem patrum filiis ac nepotibus in tertiam et quartam progeniem." 8 Festinusque Moses curvatus est pronus in terram et adorans 9 ait, "Si inveni gratiam in conspectu tuo, Domine, obsecro ut gradiaris nobiscum, populus enim durae cervicis est, et auferas iniquitates nostras atque peccata nosque possideas."

10 Respondit Dominus, "Ego inibo pactum videntibus cunctis. Signa faciam quae numquam sunt visa super terram nec in ullis gentibus ut cernat populus iste in cuius es medio opus Domini terribile quod facturus sum. 11 Observa cuncta quae hodie mando tibi. Ego ipse eiciam ante faciem tuam Amorreum et Chananeum et Hettheum, Ferezeum quoque et Eveum et Iebuseum. 12 Cave ne umquam cum habitatoribus terrae illius iungas amicitias, quae tibi sint in ruinam, 13 sed aras eorum destrue, confringe statuas, lucosque succide.

14 "Noli adorare deum alienum. Dominus, Zelotes nomen eius, Deus est aemulator. 15 Ne ineas pactum cum hominibus illarum regionum ne, cum fornicati fuerint cum diis suis et adoraverint simulacra eorum, vocet te quispiam ut comedas de immolatis. 16 Nec uxorem de filiabus eorum accipies filiis tuis, ne postquam ipsae fuerint fornicatae, fornicari faciant et filios tuos in deos suos.

17 "Deos conflatiles non facies tibi.

18 "Sollemnitatem azymorum custodies. Septem diebus vesceris azymis, sicut praecepi tibi, in tempore mensis novorum, mense enim verni temporis egressus es de Aegypto.

19 "Omne quod aperit vulvam generis masculini meum

462

iniquity of the fathers to the children and to the grandchildren unto the third and fourth generation." 8 And Moses
making haste bowed down prostrate unto the earth and
adoring 9 said, "If I have found grace in thy sight, O Lord, I
beseech thee that thou wilt go with us, for it is a stiffnecked
people, and take away our iniquities and sin and possess us."

10 The Lord answered, "I will make a covenant in the sight
of all. I will do signs such as were never seen upon the earth
nor in any nation that this people in the midst of whom thou
art may see the terrible work of the Lord which I will do.
11 Observe all things which this day I command thee. I myself will drive out before thy face the Amorite and the Canaanite and the Hittite and the Perizzite and the Hivite and
the Jebusite. 12 Beware thou never join in friendship with
the inhabitants of that land, which may be thy ruin, 13 but
destroy their altars, break their statues, and cut down their
groves.

14 "Adore not *any* strange god. The Lord, his name is Jealous, *he is a jealous God.* 15 Make no covenant with the men
of those countries lest, when they have committed fornication with their gods and have adored their idols, some
one call thee to eat of the things sacrificed. 16 Neither shalt
thou take of their daughters a wife for thy *son,* lest after they
themselves have committed fornication, they make thy sons
also to commit fornication with their gods.

17 "Thou shalt not make to thyself any molten gods.

18 "Thou shalt keep the feast of the unleavened bread.
Seven days shalt thou eat unleavened bread, as I commanded
thee, in the time of the month of the new corn, for in the
month of the springtime thou camest out from Egypt.

19 "All of the male kind that openeth the womb shall be

erit. De cunctis animantibus, tam de bubus quam de ovibus, meum erit. 20 Primogenitum asini redimes ove, sin autem nec pretium pro eo dederis, occidetur. Primogenitum filiorum tuorum redimes, nec apparebis in conspectu meo vacuus.

21 "Sex diebus operaberis; die septimo cessabis arare et metere. 22 Sollemnitatem ebdomadarum facies tibi in primitiis frugum messis tuae triticeae et sollemnitatem quando redeunte anni tempore cuncta conduntur.

23 "Tribus temporibus anni apparebit omne masculinum tuum in conspectu omnipotentis Domini, Dei Israhel, 24 cum enim tulero gentes a facie tua et dilatavero terminos tuos, nullus insidiabitur terrae tuae ascendente te et apparente in conspectu Domini, Dei tui, ter in anno.

25 "Non immolabis super fermento sanguinem hostiae meae, neque residebit mane de victima sollemnitatis phase.

26 "Primitias frugum terrae tuae offeres in domum Domini, Dei tui. Non coques hedum in lacte matris suae."

27 Dixitque Dominus ad Mosen, "Scribe tibi verba haec quibus et tecum et cum Israhel pepigi foedus." 28 Fuit ergo ibi cum Domino quadraginta dies et quadraginta noctes. Panem non comedit et aquam non bibit, et scripsit in tabulis verba foederis decem. 29 Cumque descenderet Moses de monte Sinai, tenebat duas tabulas testimonii, et ignorabat quod cornuta esset facies sua ex consortio sermonis Domini. 30 Videntes autem Aaron et filii Israhel cornutam Mosi

mine. Of all beasts, both of oxen and of sheep, it shall be mine. 20 The firstling of an ass thou shalt redeem with a sheep, but if thou wilt not give a price for it, it shall be slain. The firstborn of thy sons thou shalt redeem, neither shalt thou appear before me empty.

21 "Six days shalt thou work; the seventh day thou shalt cease to plough and to reap. 22 Thou shalt *keep* the feast of weeks with the firstfruits of the corn of thy wheat harvest and the feast when the time of the year returneth that all things are laid in.

23 "Three times in a year, all thy males shall appear in the sight of the almighty Lord, the God of Israel, 24 for when I shall have taken away the nations from thy face and shall have enlarged thy borders, no man shall lie in wait against thy land when thou shalt go up and appear in the sight of the Lord, thy God, thrice in a year.

25 "Thou shalt not offer the blood of my sacrifice upon leaven, neither shall there remain in the morning any thing of the victim of the solemnity of the phase.

26 "The first of the fruits of thy ground thou shalt offer in the house of the Lord, thy God. Thou shalt not boil a kid in the milk of his dam."

27 And the Lord said to Moses, *"Write* these words by which I have made a covenant both with thee and with Israel." 28 And he was there with the Lord forty days and forty nights. He neither ate bread nor drank water, and he wrote upon the tables the ten words of the covenant. 29 And when Moses came down from the mount Sinai, he held the two tables of the testimony, and he knew not that his face was horned from the conversation of the Lord. 30 And Aaron and the children of Israel seeing the face of Moses horned

faciem timuerunt prope accedere. 31 Vocatique ab eo, reversi sunt, tam Aaron quam principes synagogae. Et postquam locutus est ad eos, 32 venerunt ad eum etiam omnes filii Israhel, quibus praecepit cuncta quae audierat a Domino in Monte Sinai. 33 Impletisque sermonibus, posuit velamen super faciem suam. 34 Quod ingressus ad Dominum et loquens cum eo, auferebat donec exiret, et tunc loquebatur ad filios Israhel omnia quae sibi fuerant imperata. 35 Qui videbant faciem egredientis Mosi esse cornutam, sed operiebat rursus ille faciem suam si quando loquebatur ad eos.

Caput 35

Igitur congregata omni turba filiorum Israhel, dixit ad eos, "Haec sunt quae iussit Dominus fieri. 2 Sex diebus facietis opus; septimus dies erit vobis sanctus, sabbatum et requies Domini. Qui fecerit opus in eo occidetur. 3 Non succendetis ignem in omnibus habitaculis vestris per diem sabbati."

4 Et ait Moses ad omnem catervam filiorum Israhel, "Iste est sermo quem praecepit Dominus, dicens, 5 'Separate apud vos primitias Domino. Omnis voluntarius et proni animi of-

were afraid to come near. 31 And being called by him, they returned, both Aaron and the rulers of the congregation. And after that he spoke to them, 32 *and* all the children of Israel came to him, and he gave them in commandment all that he had heard of the Lord in Mount Sinai. 33 And having done speaking, he put a veil upon his face. 34 *But* when he went in to the Lord and spoke with him, he took it away until he came forth, and then he spoke to the children of Israel all things that had been commanded him. 35 And they saw that the face of Moses when he came out was horned, but he covered his face again if at any time he spoke to them.

Chapter 35

The sabbath. Offerings for making the tabernacle. Bezalel and Oholiab are called to the work.

And all the multitude of the children of Israel being gathered together, he said to them, "These are the things which the Lord hath commanded to be done. 2 Six days you shall do work; the seventh day shall be holy unto you, the sabbath and the rest of the Lord. He that shall do any work on it shall be put to death. 3 You shall kindle no fire in any of your habitations on the sabbath day."

4 And Moses said to all the assembly of the children of Israel, "This is the word the Lord hath commanded, saying, 5 'Set aside with you firstfruits to the Lord. Let every

ferat eas Domino: aurum et argentum et aes, 6 hyacinthum et purpuram coccumque bis tinctum et byssum, pilos caprarum 7 et pelles arietum rubricatas et ianthinas, ligna setthim 8 et oleum ad luminaria concinnanda et ut conficiatur unguentum et thymiama suavissimum, 9 lapides onychinos et gemmas ad ornatum superumeralis et rationalis.

10 "'Quisquis vestrum est sapiens, veniat et faciat quod Dominus imperavit, 11 tabernaculum, scilicet, et tectum eius atque operimentum, anulos et tabulata cum vectibus, paxillos et bases, 12 arcam et vectes, propitiatorium et velum quod ante illud oppanditur, 13 mensam cum vectibus et vasis et propositionis panibus, 14 candelabrum ad luminaria sustentanda, vasa illius et lucernas et oleum ad nutrimenta ignium, 15 altare thymiamatis et vectes et oleum unctionis et thymiama ex aromatibus, tentorium ad ostium tabernaculi, 16 altare holocausti et craticulam eius aeneam cum vectibus et vasis suis, labrum et basim eius, 17 cortinas atrii cum columnis et basibus, tentorium in foribus vestibuli, 18 paxillos tabernaculi et atrii cum funiculis suis, 19 vestimenta quorum usus est in ministerio sanctuarii, vestes Aaron, pontificis, ac filiorum eius ut sacerdotio fungantur mihi.'"

20 Egressaque omnis multitudo filiorum Israhel de conspectu Mosi 21 obtulit mente promptissima atque devota primitias Domino ad faciendum opus Tabernaculi Testimonii. Quicquid ad cultum et ad vestes sanctas necessarium erat 22 viri cum mulieribus praebuerunt: armillas et inaures,

one that is willing and hath a ready heart offer them to the Lord: gold and silver and brass, 6 violet and purple and scarlet twice dyed and fine linen, goats' hair 7 and rams' skins dyed red and violet coloured skins, setim wood 8 and oil to maintain lights and to make ointment and most sweet incense, 9 onyx stones and precious stones for the adorning of the ephod and the rational.

10 "'Whosoever of you is wise, let him come and make that which the Lord hath commanded, 11 to wit, the tabernacle and the roof thereof and the cover, the rings and the board work with the oars, the pillars and the sockets, 12 the ark and the staves, the propitiatory and the veil that is drawn before it, 13 the table with the bars and the vessels and the loaves of proposition, 14 the candlestick to bear up the lights, the vessels thereof and the lamps and the oil for the nourishing of fires, 15 the altar of incense and the bars and the oil of unction and the incense of spices, the hanging at the door of the tabernacle, 16 the altar of holocaust and its grate of brass with the bars and vessels thereof, the laver and its foot, 17 the curtains of the court with the pillars and the sockets, the hanging in the doors of the entry, 18 the pins of the tabernacle and of the court with their little cords, 19 the vestments that are to be used in the ministry of the sanctuary, the vesture of Aaron, the high priest, and of his sons to do the office of priesthood to me.'"

20 And all the multitude of the children of Israel going out from the presence of Moses 21 offered firstfruits to the Lord with a most ready and devout mind to make the work of the Tabernacle of the Testimony. Whatsoever was necessary to the service and to the holy vestments 22 both men and women gave: bracelets and earrings, rings and tablets. Every

anulos et dextralia. Omne vas aureum in donaria Domini separatum est. 23 Si quis habuit hyacinthum et purpuram coccumque bis tinctum, byssum et pilos caprarum, pelles arietum rubricatas et ianthinas, 24 argenti et aeris metalla, obtulerunt Domino, lignaque setthim in varios usus. 25 Sed et mulieres doctae dederunt quae neverant: hyacinthum, purpuram et vermiculum ac byssum 26 et pilos caprarum, sponte propria cuncta tribuentes. 27 Principes vero obtulerunt lapides onychinos et gemmas ad superumerale et rationale 28 aromataque et oleum ad luminaria concinnanda et ad praeparandum unguentum ac thymiama odoris suavissimi conponendum. 29 Omnes viri et mulieres mente devota obtulerunt donaria ut fierent opera quae iusserat Dominus per manum Mosi. Cuncti filii Israhel voluntaria Domino dedicaverunt.

30 Dixitque Moses ad filios Israhel, "Ecce: vocavit Dominus ex nomine Beselehel, filium Uri, filii Hur de tribu Iuda, 31 implevitque eum spiritu Dei, sapientia et intellegentia et scientia et omni doctrina, 32 ad excogitandum et faciendum opus in auro et argento et aere 33 sculpendisque lapidibus et opere carpentario. Quicquid fabre adinveniri potest, 34 dedit in corde eius, Hooliab quoque, filium Achisamech de tribu Dan. 35 Ambos erudivit sapientia ut faciant opera abietarii, polymitarii, plumarii de hyacintho et purpura coccoque bis tincto et bysso et texant omnia ac nova quaeque repperiant.

vessel of gold was set aside to be offered to the Lord. 23 If any man had violet and purple and scarlet twice dyed, fine linen and goats' hair, rams' skins dyed red and violet-coloured skins, 24 metal of silver and brass, they offered it to the Lord, and setim wood for divers uses. 25 The skillful women also gave such things as they had spun: violet, purple and scarlet and fine linen 26 and goats' hair, giving all of their own accord. 27 But the princes offered onyx stone and precious stones for the ephod and the rational 28 and spices and oil for the *lights* and for the preparing of ointment and to make the incense of most sweet savour. 29 *All, both* men and women, with devout mind offered gifts that the works might be done which the Lord had commanded by the hand of Moses. All the children of Israel dedicated voluntary offerings to the Lord.

30 And Moses said to the children of Israel, "Behold: the Lord hath called by name Bezalel, the son of Uri, the son of Hur of the tribe of Judah, 31 and hath filled him with the spirit of God, with wisdom and understanding and knowledge and all learning, 32 to devise and to work in gold and silver and brass 33 and in engraving stones and in carpenters' work. Whatsoever can be devised artificially, 34 he hath given in his heart, Oholiab also, the son of Ahisamach of the tribe of Dan. 35 Both of them hath he instructed with wisdom to do *carpenters' work and tapestry and embroidery* in *blue* and purple and scarlet twice dyed and fine linen and to weave all things and to invent all new things.

Caput 36

Fecit, ergo, Beselehel et Hooliab et omnis vir sapiens quibus dedit Dominus sapientiam et intellectum ut scirent fabre operari quae in usus sanctuarii necessaria sunt et quae praecepit Dominus. 2 Cumque vocasset eos Moses et omnem eruditum virum cui dederat Dominus sapientiam et qui sponte sua obtulerant se ad faciendum opus, 3 tradidit eis universa donaria filiorum Israhel. Qui cum instarent operi, cotidie mane vota populus offerebat. 4 Unde artifices venire conpulsi 5 dixerunt Mosi, "Plus offert populus quam necessarium est."

6 Iussit ergo Moses praeconis voce cantari: "Nec vir nec mulier quicquam ultra offerat in opere sanctuarii." Sicque cessatum est a muneribus offerendis, 7 eo quod oblata sufficerent et superabundarent.

8 Feceruntque omnes corde sapientes ad explendum opus tabernaculi cortinas decem de bysso retorta et hyacintho et purpura coccoque bis tincto opere vario et arte polymita, 9 quarum una habebat in longitudine viginti octo cubitos, et

Chapter 36

The offerings are delivered to the workmen. The curtains,
coverings, boards, bars, veil, pillars and hanging are made.

Bezalel, therefore, and Oholiab and every wise man to
whom the Lord gave wisdom and understanding to know
how to work artificially made the things that are necessary for the uses of the sanctuary and which the Lord commanded. 2 And when Moses had called them and every skillful man to whom the Lord had given wisdom and such as of
their own accord had offered themselves to the making of
the work, 3 he delivered all the offerings of the children of
Israel unto them. And while they were earnest about the
work, the people daily in the morning offered their vows.
4 Whereupon the workmen being constrained to come
5 said to Moses, "The people offereth more than is necessary."

6 Moses therefore commanded proclamation to be made
by the crier's voice: "Let neither man nor woman offer any
more for the work of the sanctuary." And so they ceased
from offering gifts, 7 because the things that were offered
did suffice and were too much.

8 And all the men that were wise of heart to accomplish
the work of the tabernacle made ten curtains of twisted fine
linen and violet and purple and scarlet twice dyed with varied work and the art of embroidering. 9 The length of one

in latitudine quattuor. Una mensura erat omnium cortinarum. 10 Coniunxitque cortinas quinque, alteram alteri, et
alias quinque sibi invicem copulavit. 11 Fecit et ansas hyacinthinas in ora cortinae unius ex utroque latere et in ora cortinae alterius similiter 12 ut contra se invicem venirent ansae
et mutuo iungerentur. 13 Unde et quinquaginta fudit circulos aureos qui morderent cortinarum ansas, et fieret unum
tabernaculum. 14 Fecit et saga undecim de pilis caprarum ad
operiendum tectum tabernaculi. 15 Unum sagum habebat in
longitudine cubitos triginta et in latitudine cubitos quattuor; unius mensurae erant omnia saga, 16 quorum quinque
iunxit seorsum, et sex alia separatim. 17 Fecitque ansas quinquaginta in ora sagi unius et quinquaginta in ora sagi alterius
ut sibi invicem iungerentur 18 et fibulas aeneas quinquaginta
quibus necteretur tectum ut unum pallium ex omnibus sagis
fieret. 19 Fecit et opertorium tabernaculi de pellibus arietum
rubricatis aliudque desuper velamentum de pellibus ianthinis. 20 Fecit et tabulas tabernaculi de lignis setthim stantes.
21 Decem cubitorum erat longitudo tabulae unius, et unum
ac semis cubitum latitudo retinebat. 22 Binae incastraturae
erant per singulas tabulas ut altera alteri iungeretur. Sic fecit
in omnibus tabulis tabernaculi, 23 e quibus viginti ad plagam
meridianam erant contra austrum 24 cum quadraginta basibus argenteis; duae bases sub una tabula ponebantur ex utraque angulorum parte ubi incastraturae laterum in angulis
terminantur. 25 Ad plagam quoque tabernaculi quae respicit
ad aquilonem fecit viginti tabulas 26 cum quadraginta argenteis basibus, duas bases per singulas tabulas. 27 Contra occi-

curtain was twenty-eight cubits, and the breadth four. All the curtains were of the same size. 10 And he joined five curtains, one to another, and the other five he coupled one to another. 11 He made also loops of violet in the edge of the curtain on both sides and in the edge of the other curtain in like manner 12 that the loops might meet one against another and might be joined each with the other. 13 Whereupon also he cast fifty rings of gold that might catch the loops of the curtains, and they might be made one tabernacle. 14 He made also eleven curtains of goats' hair to cover the roof of the tabernacle. 15 One curtain was thirty cubits long and four cubits broad; all the curtains were of one measure, 16 five of which he joined apart, and the other six apart. 17 And he made fifty loops in the edge of one curtain and fifty in the edge of another curtain that they might be joined one to another 18 and fifty buckles of brass wherewith the roof might be knit together that of all the curtains there might be made one covering. 19 He made also a cover for the tabernacle of rams' skins dyed red and another cover over that of violet skins. 20 He made also the boards of the tabernacle of setim wood standing. 21 The length of one board was ten cubits, and the breadth was one cubit and a half. 22 There were two mortises throughout every board that one might be joined to the other. And in this manner he made for all the boards of the tabernacle, 23 of which twenty were at the south side southward 24 with forty sockets of silver; two sockets were put under one board on the two sides of the corners where the mortises of the sides end in the corners. 25 At that side also of the tabernacle that looketh toward the north he made twenty boards 26 with forty sockets of silver, two sockets for every board. 27 But against the

dentem vero, id est, ad eam partem tabernaculi quae mare respicit, fecit sex tabulas 28 et duas alias per singulos angulos tabernaculi retro, 29 quae iunctae erant deorsum usque sursum et in unam conpagem pariter ferebantur. Ita fecit ex utraque parte per angulos, 30 ut octo essent simul tabulae et haberent bases argenteas sedecim, binas, scilicet, bases sub singulis tabulis.

31 Fecit et vectes de lignis setthim, quinque ad continendas tabulas unius lateris tabernaculi 32 et quinque alios ad alterius lateris tabulas coaptandas et, extra hos, quinque alios vectes ad occidentalem plagam tabernaculi contra mare. 33 Fecit quoque vectem alium qui per medias tabulas ab angulo usque ad angulum perveniret. 34 Ipsa autem tabulata deauravit. Et circulos eorum fecit aureos per quos vectes induci possint, quos et ipsos aureis lamminis operuit. 35 Fecit et velum de hyacintho et purpura, vermiculo ac bysso retorta opere polymitario varium atque distinctum, 36 et quattuor columnas de lignis setthim, quas cum capitibus deauravit, fusis basibus earum argenteis. 37 Fecit et tentorium in introitu tabernaculi ex hyacintho, purpura, vermiculo byssoque retorta opere plumarii 38 et columnas quinque cum capitibus suis, quas operuit auro, basesque earum fudit aeneas.

west, to wit, at that side of the tabernacle which looketh to the sea, he made six boards 28 and two others at each corner of the tabernacle behind, 29 which were also joined from beneath unto the top and went together into one joint. Thus he did on both sides at the corners, 30 so there were in all eight boards and they had sixteen sockets of silver, to wit, two sockets under every board.

31 He made also bars of setim wood, five to hold together the boards of one side of the tabernacle 32 and five others to join together the boards of the other side and, besides these, five other bars at the west side of the tabernacle towards the sea. 33 He made also another bar that might come by the midst of the boards from corner to corner. 34 And the board works themselves he overlaid with gold. And their rings he made of gold through which the bars might be drawn, and he covered the bars themselves with plates of gold. 35 He made also a veil of violet and purple, scarlet and fine twisted linen, varied and distinguished with embroidery, 36 and four pillars of setim wood, which with their heads he overlaid with gold, casting for them sockets of silver. 37 He made also a hanging in the entry of the tabernacle of violet, purple, scarlet and fine twisted linen with the work of an embroiderer 38 and five pillars with their heads, which he covered with gold, and their sockets he cast of brass.

Caput 37

Fecit autem Beselehel et arcam de lignis setthim habentem duos semis cubitos in longitudinem et cubitum ac semissem in latitudinem, altitudo quoque unius cubiti fuit et dimidii, vestivitque eam auro purissimo intus ac foris. 2 Et fecit illi coronam auream per gyrum, 3 conflans quattuor anulos aureos per quattuor angulos eius: duos anulos in latere uno et duos in altero. 4 Vectes quoque fecit de lignis setthim quos vestivit auro, 5 et quos misit in anulos qui erant in lateribus arcae ad portandum eam.

6 Fecit et propitiatorium, id est, oraculum, de auro mundissimo, duo cubiti et dimidium in longitudine et cubito ac semisse in latitudine, 7 duos etiam cherubin ex auro ductili, quos posuit ex utraque parte propitiatorii, 8 cherub unum in summitate unius partis et cherub alterum in summitate partis alterius, duos cherubin in singulis summitatibus propitiatorii, 9 extendentes alas et tegentes propitiatorium seque mutuo et illud respectantes.

10 Fecit et mensam de lignis setthim, in longitudine duorum cubitorum et in latitudine unius cubiti, quae habebat in altitudine cubitum ac semissem. 11 Circumdeditque eam auro mundissimo, et fecit illi labium aureum per gy-

Chapter 37

Bezalel maketh the ark, the propitiatory and cherubims, the table, the candlestick, the lamps and the altar of incense and compoundeth the incense.

And Bezalel made also the ark of setim wood. It was two cubits and a half in length and a cubit and a half in breadth, and the height was of one cubit and a half, and he overlaid it with the purest gold within and without. 2 And he made to it a crown of gold round about, 3 casting four rings of gold at the four corners thereof: two rings in one side and two in the other. 4 And he made bars of setim wood which he overlaid with gold, 5 and he put them into the rings that were at the sides of the ark to carry it.

6 He made also the propitiatory, that is, the oracle, of the purest gold, two cubits and a half in length and a cubit and a half in breadth, 7 two cherubims also of beaten gold, which he set on the two sides of the propitiatory, 8 one cherub in the top of one side and the other cherub in the top of the other side, two cherubims at the two ends of the propitiatory, 9 spreading their wings and covering the propitiatory and looking one towards the other and towards it.

10 He made also the table of setim wood, in length two cubits and in breadth one cubit, and in height it was a cubit and a half. 11 And he overlaid it with the finest gold, and he

rum. 12 Ipsique labio coronam auream interrasilem quattuor digitorum, et super eandem alteram coronam auream. 13 Fudit et quattuor circulos aureos, quos posuit in quattuor angulis per singulos pedes mensae 14 contra coronam, misitque in eos vectes ut possit mensa portari. 15 Ipsos quoque vectes fecit de lignis setthim et circumdedit eos auro, 16 et vasa ad diversos usus mensae, acetabula, fialas et cyatos et turibula ex auro puro, in quibus offerenda sunt libamina.

17 Fecit et candelabrum ductile de auro mundissimo. De cuius vecte calami, scyphi spherulaeque ac lilia procedebant, 18 sex in utroque latere, tres calami ex parte una et tres ex altera, 19 tres scyphi in nucis modum per calamos singulos spherulaeque simul et lilia et tres scyphi instar nucis in calamo altero spherulaeque simul et lilia. Aequum erat opus sex calamorum qui procedebant de stipite candelabri. 20 In ipso autem vecte erant quattuor scyphi in nucis modum spherulaeque per singulos simul et lilia 21 et spherulae sub duobus calamis per loca tria, qui simul sex fiunt calami procedentes de vecte uno. 22 Et spherulae igitur et calami ex ipso erant, universa ductilia de auro purissimo. 23 Fecit et lucernas septem cum emunctoriis suis et vasa ubi quae emuncta sunt extinguantur de auro mundissimo. 24 Talentum auri adpendebat candelabrum cum omnibus vasis suis.

25 Fecit et altare thymiamatis de lignis setthim, habens per quadrum singulos cubitos et in altitudine duos, e cuius angulis procedebant cornua. 26 Vestivitque illud auro puris-

made to it a golden ledge round about. 12 And to the ledge itself he made a polished crown of gold of four fingers' breadth, and upon the same another golden crown. 13 And he cast four rings of gold, which he put in the four corners at each foot of the table 14 over against the crown, and he put the bars into them that the table might be carried. 15 And the bars also themselves he made of setim wood and overlaid them with gold, 16 and the vessels for the divers uses of the table, dishes, bowls and cups and censers of pure gold, wherein the libations are to be offered.

17 He made also the candlestick of beaten work of the finest gold. From the shaft whereof its branches, its cups and *bowls* and lilies came out, 18 six on the two sides, three branches on one side and three on the other, 19 three cups in manner of a nut on each branch and *bowls* withal and lilies and three cups of the fashion of a nut in another branch and *bowls* withal and lilies. The work of the six branches that went out from the shaft of the candlestick was equal. 20 And in the shaft itself were four cups after the manner of a nut and *bowls* withal at every one and lilies 21 and *bowls* under two branches in three places, which together make six branches going out from one shaft. 22 So both the *bowls* and the branches were of the same, all beaten work of the purest gold. 23 He made also the seven lamps with their snuffers and the vessels where the snuffings were to be put out of the purest gold. 24 The candlestick with all the vessels thereof weighed a talent of gold.

25 He made also the altar of incense of setim wood, being a cubit on every side, foursquare, and in height two cubits, from the corners of which went out horns. 26 And he overlaid it with the purest gold with its grate and the sides and

simo cum craticula ac parietibus et cornibus. [27] Fecitque ei coronam aureolam per gyrum et duos anulos aureos sub corona per singula latera ut mittantur in eos vectes et possit altare portari. [28] Ipsos autem vectes fecit de lignis setthim et operuit lamminis aureis. [29] Conposuit et oleum ad sanctificationis unguentum et thymiama de aromatibus mundissimis opere pigmentarii.

Caput 38

Fecit et altare holocausti de lignis setthim, quinque cubitorum per quadrum et trium in altitudine, [2] cuius cornua de angulis procedebant, operuitque illud aeneis lamminis. [3] Et in usus eius paravit ex aere vasa diversa: lebetas, forcipes, fuscinulas, uncinos et ignium receptacula. [4] Craticulamque eius in modum retis fecit aeneam et subter eam in altaris medio arulam, [5] fusis quattuor anulis per totidem retiaculi summitates ad inmittendos vectes ad portandum. [6] Quos et ipsos fecit de lignis setthim et operuit lamminis aeneis, [7] induxitque in circulos qui in altaris lateribus eminebant, ipsum autem altare non erat solidum, sed cavum, ex tabulis, et

the horns. 27 And he made to it a crown of gold round about and two golden rings under the crown at each side that the bars might be put into them and the altar be carried. 28 And the bars themselves he made also of setim wood and overlaid them with plates of gold. 29 He compounded also the oil for the ointment of sanctification and incense of the purest spices, according to the work of a perfumer.

Chapter 38

He maketh the altar of holocaust, the brazen laver, the court with its pillars and hangings. The sum of what the people offered.

He made also the altar of holocaust of setim wood, five cubits square and three in height, 2 the horns whereof went out from the corners, and he overlaid it with plates of brass. 3 And for the uses thereof he prepared divers vessels of brass: cauldrons, tongs, fleshhooks, pothooks and firepans. 4 And he made the grate thereof of brass, in manner of a net, and under it in the midst of the altar a hearth, 5 casting four rings at the four ends of the net at the top to put in bars to carry it. 6 And he made *the bars* of setim wood and overlaid them with plates of brass, 7 and he drew them through the rings that stood out in the sides of the altar, and the altar itself was not solid, but hollow, of boards, and empty

intus vacuum. 8 Fecit et labrum aeneum cum base sua de speculis mulierum quae excubabant in ostio tabernaculi. 9 Fecit et atrium in cuius australi plaga erant tentoria de bysso retorta cubitorum centum, 10 columnae aeneae viginti cum basibus suis, capita columnarum et tota operis celatura argentea.

11 Aeque ad septentrionalem plagam, tentoria, columnae basesque et capita columnarum eiusdem mensurae et operis ac metalli erant. 12 In ea vero plaga quae ad occidentem respicit, fuere tentoria cubitorum quinquaginta, columnae decem cum basibus suis aeneae et capita columnarum et tota operis celatura argentea. 13 Porro, contra orientem quinquaginta cubitorum paravit tentoria, 14 e quibus quindecim cubitos columnarum trium cum basibus suis unum tenebat latus. 15 Et in parte altera (quia inter utraque introitum tabernaculi fecit) quindecim aeque cubitorum erant tentoria columnaeque tres et bases totidem.

16 Cuncta atrii tentoria byssus torta texuerat. 17 Bases columnarum fuere aeneae capita autem earum cum cunctis celaturis suis argentea, sed et ipsas columnas atrii vestivit argento. 18 Et in introitu eius opere plumario fecit tentorium ex hyacintho, purpura, vermiculo ac bysso retorta quod habebat viginti cubitos in longitudine, altitudo vero quinque cubitorum erat, iuxta mensuram quam cuncta atrii habebant tentoria. 19 Columnae autem in ingressu fuere quattuor cum basibus aeneis capitaque earum et celaturae argenteae. 20 Paxillos quoque tabernaculi et atrii per gyrum fecit aeneos.

21 Haec sunt instrumenta Tabernaculi Testimonii quae numerata sunt iuxta praeceptum Mosi in caerimonias Levi-

within. 8 He made also the laver of brass with the foot thereof of the mirrors of the women that watch at the door of the tabernacle. 9 He made also the court in the south side whereof were hangings of fine twisted linen of a hundred cubits, 10 twenty pillars of brass with their sockets, the heads of the pillars and the whole graving of the work of silver.

11 In like manner at the north side, the hangings, the pillars and the sockets and heads of the pillars were of the same measure and work and metal. 12 But on that side that looketh to the west, there were hangings of fifty cubits, ten pillars of brass with their sockets and the heads of the pillars and all the graving of the work of silver. 13 Moreover, towards the east he prepared hangings of fifty cubits, 14 fifteen cubits of which were on one side with three pillars and their sockets. 15 And on the other side (for between the two he made the entry of the tabernacle) there were hangings equally of fifteen cubits and three pillars and as many sockets.

16 All the hangings of the court were woven with twisted linen. 17 The sockets of the pillars were of brass and their heads with all their gravings of silver, and he overlaid the pillars of the court also with silver. 18 And he made in the entry thereof an embroidered hanging of violet, purple, scarlet and fine twisted linen that was twenty cubits long and *five cubits high,* according to the measure of all the hangings of the court. 19 And the pillars in the entry were four with sockets of brass and their heads and gravings of silver. 20 The pins also of the tabernacle and of the court round about he made of brass.

21 These are the instruments of the Tabernacle of the Testimony which were counted according to the commandment of Moses in the ceremonies of the Levites by the hand

tarum per manum Ithamar, filii Aaron, sacerdotis, 22 quas Beselehel, filius Uri, filii Hur de tribu Iuda, Domino per Mosen iubente conpleverat, 23 iuncto sibi socio Hooliab, filio Achisamech de tribu Dan, qui et ipse artifex lignorum egregius fuit et polymitarius atque plumarius ex hyacintho, purpura, vermiculo et bysso.

24 Omne aurum quod expensum est in opere sanctuarii et quod oblatum in donariis viginti novem talentorum fuit et septingentorum triginta siclorum ad mensuram sanctuarii. 25 Oblatum est autem ab his qui transierunt ad numerum a viginti annis et supra de sescentis tribus milibus et quingentis quinquaginta armatorum.

26 Fuerunt, praeterea, centum talenta argenti e quibus conflatae sunt bases sanctuarii et introitus ubi velum pendet. 27 Centum bases factae sunt de talentis centum, singulis talentis per bases singulas supputatis. 28 De mille autem septingentis et septuaginta quinque fecit capita columnarum, quas et ipsas vestivit argento. 29 Aeris quoque oblata sunt talenta septuaginta duo milia et quadringenti supra sicli, 30 ex quibus fusae sunt bases in introitu Tabernaculi Testimonii et altare aeneum cum craticula sua omniaque vasa quae ad usum eius pertinent 31 et bases atrii tam in circuitu quam in ingressu eius et paxilli tabernaculi atque atrii per gyrum.

of Ithamar, son of Aaron, the priest, 22 which Bezalel, the son of Uri, the son of Hur of the tribe of Judah, had made as the Lord commanded by Moses, 23 having for his companion Oholiab, the son of Ahisamach of the tribe of Dan, who also was an excellent artificer in wood and worker in tapestry and embroidery in violet, purple, scarlet and fine linen.

24 All the gold that was spent in the work of the sanctuary and that was offered in gifts was nine and twenty talents and seven hundred and thirty sicles according to the standard of the sanctuary. 25 And it was offered by them that went to be numbered from twenty years old and upwards of six hundred and three thousand five hundred and fifty men able to bear arms.

26 There were, moreover, a hundred talents of silver whereof were cast the sockets of the sanctuary and of the entry where the veil hangeth. 27 A hundred sockets were made of a hundred talents, one talent being reckoned for every socket. 28 And of the thousand seven hundred and seventy-five he made the heads of the pillars, which also he overlaid with silver. 29 And there were offered of brass also seventy-two thousand talents and four hundred sicles besides, 30 of which were cast the sockets in the entry of the Tabernacle of the Testimony and the altar of brass with the grate thereof and all the vessels that belong to the use thereof 31 and the sockets of the court as well round about as in the entry thereof and the pins of the tabernacle and of the court round about.

Caput 39

De hyacintho vero et purpura, vermiculo ac bysso fecit vestes quibus indueretur Aaron quando ministrabat in sanctis, sicut praecepit Dominus Mosi. 2 Fecit igitur superumerale de auro, hyacintho et purpura coccoque bis tincto et bysso retorta 3 opere polymitario, inciditque bratteas aureas et extenuavit in fila ut possint torqueri cum priorum colorum subtemine 4 duasque oras sibi invicem copulatas in utroque latere summitatum 5 et balteum ex hisdem coloribus, sicut praeceperat Dominus Mosi.

6 Paravit et duos lapides onychinos adstrictos et inclusos auro et sculptos arte gemmaria nominibus filiorum Israhel, 7 posuitque eos in lateribus superumeralis in monumentum filiorum Israhel, sicut praeceperat Dominus Mosi. 8 Fecit et rationale opere polymito iuxta opus superumeralis ex auro, hyacintho, purpura coccoque bis tincto et bysso retorta, 9 quadrangulum, duplex, mensurae palmi, 10 et posuit in eo gemmarum ordines quattuor. In primo versu erat sardius, topazius, zmaragdus, 11 in secundo carbunculus, sapphyrus et iaspis, 12 in tertio ligyrius, achates et amethistus, 13 in quarto chrysolitus, onychinus et berillus, circumdati et in-

Chapter 39

All the ornaments of Aaron and his sons are made, and the whole work of the tabernacle is finished.

And he made of violet and purple, scarlet and fine linen the vestments for Aaron to wear when he ministered in the holy places, as the Lord commanded Moses. 2 So he made an ephod of gold, violet and purple and scarlet twice dyed and fine twisted linen 3 with embroidered work, and he cut thin plates of gold and drew them small into threads that they might be twisted with the woof of the aforesaid colours 4 and two borders coupled one to the other in the top on either side 5 and a girdle of the same colours, as the Lord had commanded Moses.

6 He prepared also two onyx stones fast set and closed in gold and graven by the art of a lapidary with the names of the children of Israel, 7 and he set them in the sides of the ephod for a memorial of the children of Israel, as the Lord had commanded Moses. 8 He made also a rational with embroidered work according to the work of the ephod of gold, violet, purple and scarlet twice dyed and fine twisted linen, 9 foursquare, double, of the measure of a span, 10 and he set four rows of precious stones in it. In the first row was a sardius, a topaz, an emerald, 11 in the second a carbuncle, a sapphire and a jasper, 12 in the third a ligurius, an agate and an amethyst, 13 in the fourth a chrysolite, an onyx and a beryl,

clusi auro per ordines suos. 14 Ipsique lapides duodecim sculpti erant nominibus duodecim tribuum Israhel, singuli per nomina singulorum. 15 Fecerunt in rationali et catenulas sibi invicem coherentes de auro purissimo 16 et duos uncinos totidemque anulos aureos. Porro anulos posuerunt in utroque latere rationalis, 17 e quibus penderent duae catenae aureae, quas inseruerunt uncinis qui in superumeralis angulis eminebant. 18 Haec et ante et retro ita conveniebant sibi ut superumerale et rationale mutuo necterentur 19 stricta ad balteum et anulis fortius copulata quos iungebat vitta hyacinthina ne laxe fluerent et a se invicem moverentur, sicut praecepit Dominus Mosi.

20 Fecerunt quoque tunicam superumeralis totam hyacinthinam 21 et capitium in superiori parte contra medium oramque per gyrum capitii textilem 22 deorsum autem ad pedes mala punica ex hyacintho, purpura, vermiculo ac bysso retorta 23 et tintinabula de auro purissimo quae posuerunt inter mala granata in extrema parte tunicae per gyrum, 24 tintinabulum autem aureum et malum punicum, quibus ornatus incedebat pontifex quando ministerio fungebatur, sicut praeceperat Dominus Mosi.

25 Fecerunt et tunicas byssinas opere textili Aaron et filiis eius 26 et mitras cum coronulis suis ex bysso, 27 feminalia quoque linea byssina, 28 cingulum vero de bysso retorta hyacintho, purpura ac vermiculo bis tincto arte plumaria, sicut praeceperat Dominus Mosi. 29 Fecerunt et lamminam sacrae venerationis de auro purissimo, scripseruntque in ea opere

set and enclosed in gold by their rows. 14 And the twelve stones were engraved with the names of the twelve tribes of Israel, each one with its several name. 15 They made also in the rational little chains linked one to another of the purest gold 16 and two hooks and as many rings of gold. And they set the rings on either side of the rational, 17 on which rings the two golden chains should hang, which they put into the hooks that stood out in the corners of the ephod. 18 These both before and behind so answered one another that the ephod and the rational were bound together 19 being fastened to the girdle and strongly coupled with rings which a violet fillet joined lest they should flag loose and be moved one from the other, as the Lord commanded Moses.

20 They made also the tunick of the ephod all of violet 21 and a hole for the head in the upper part at the middle and a woven border round about the hole 22 and beneath at the feet pomegranates of violet, purple, scarlet and fine twisted linen 23 and little bells of the purest gold which they put between the pomegranates at the bottom of the tunick round about, 24 to wit, a bell of gold, and a pomegranate, wherewith the high priest went adorned when he discharged his ministry, as the Lord had commanded Moses.

25 They made also fine linen tunicks with woven work for Aaron and his sons 26 and mitres with their little crowns of fine linen 27 and linen breeches of fine linen 28 and a girdle of fine twisted linen, violet, purple and scarlet twice dyed of embroidery work, as the Lord had commanded Moses. 29 They made also the plate of sacred veneration of the purest gold, and they wrote on it with the engraving of a lap-

gemmario, "Sanctum Domini," 30 et strinxerunt eam cum mitra vitta hyacinthina, sicut praeceperat Dominus Mosi.

31 Perfectum est igitur omne opus tabernaculi et tecti testimonii, feceruntque filii Israhel cuncta quae praeceperat Dominus Mosi. 32 Et obtulerunt tabernaculum et tectum et universam supellectilem, anulos, tabulas, vectes, columnas ac bases, 33 opertorium de pellibus arietum rubricatis et aliud operimentum de ianthinis pellibus, 34 velum, arcam, vectes, propitiatorium, 35 mensam cum vasis suis et propositionis panibus, 36 candelabrum, lucernas et utensilia eorum cum oleo, 37 altare aureum et unguentum et thymiama ex aromatibus 38 et tentorium in introitu tabernaculi, 39 altare aeneum, retiaculum, vectes et vasa eius omnia, labrum cum basi sua, tentoria atrii et columnas cum basibus suis, 40 tentorium in introitu atrii funiculosque illius et paxillos. Nihil ex vasis defuit quae in ministerium tabernaculi et in tectum foederis iussa sunt fieri. 41 Vestes quoque quibus sacerdotes utuntur in sanctuario, Aaron, scilicet, et filii eius, 42 obtulerunt filii Israhel sicut praeceperat Dominus. 43 Quae postquam Moses cuncta vidit completa, benedixit eis.

idary, "The Holy of the Lord," 30 and they fastened it to the mitre with a violet fillet, as the Lord had commanded Moses.

31 So all the work of the tabernacle and of the roof of the testimony was finished, and the children of Israel did all things which the Lord had commanded Moses. 32 And they offered the tabernacle and the roof and the whole furniture, the rings, the boards, the bars, the pillars and their sockets, 33 the cover of rams' skins dyed red and the other cover of violet skins, 34 the veil, the ark, the bars, the propitiatory, 35 the table with the vessels thereof and the loaves of proposition, 36 the candlestick, the lamps and the furniture of them with the oil, 37 the altar of gold and the ointment and the incense of spices, 38 and the hanging in the entry of the tabernacle, 39 the altar of brass, the grate, the bars and all the vessels thereof, the laver with the foot thereof, the hangings of the court and the pillars with their sockets, 40 the hanging in the entry of the court and the little cords and the pins thereof. Nothing was wanting of the vessels that were commanded to be made for the ministry of the tabernacle and for the roof of the covenant. 41 The vestments also which the priests, to wit, Aaron and his sons, used in the sanctuary, 42 the children of Israel offered as the Lord had commanded. 43 And when Moses saw all things finished, he blessed them.

Caput 40

Locutusque est Dominus ad Mosen, dicens, 2 "Mense primo, die prima mensis, eriges Tabernaculum Testimonii 3 et pones in eo arcam dimittesque ante illam velum, 4 et inlata mensa pones super eam quae rite praecepta sunt. Candelabrum stabit cum lucernis suis 5 et altare aureum in quo adoletur incensum coram Arca Testimonii. Tentorium in introitu tabernaculi pones, 6 et ante illud altare holocausti, 7 labrum, inter altare et tabernaculum, quod implebis aqua. 8 Circumdabisque atrium tentoriis et ingressum eius. 9 Et adsumpto unctionis oleo ungues tabernaculum cum vasis suis ut sanctificentur. 10 Altare holocausti et omnia vasa eius, 11 labrum cum basi sua, omnia unctionis oleo consecrabis ut sint sancta sanctorum. 12 Adplicabisque Aaron et filios eius ad fores Tabernaculi Testimonii, et lotos aqua, 13 indues sanctis vestibus ut ministrent mihi et unctio eorum in sacerdotium proficiat sempiternum."

14 Fecitque Moses omnia quae praeceperat Dominus. 15 Igitur mense primo anni secundi, prima die mensis, conlo-

Chapter 40

The tabernacle is commanded to be set up and anointed.
God filleth it with his majesty.

And the Lord spoke to Moses, saying, 2 "The first month, the first day of the month, thou shalt set up the Tabernacle of the Testimony 3 and shalt put the ark in it and shalt let down the veil before it, 4 and thou shalt bring in the table and set upon it the things that are commanded according to the rite. The candlestick shall stand with its lamps 5 and the altar of gold whereon the incense is burnt before the Ark of the Testimony. Thou shalt put the hanging in the entry of the tabernacle 6 and before it the altar of holocaust, 7 the laver, between the altar and the tabernacle, and thou shalt fill it with water. 8 And thou shalt encompass the court with hangings and the entry thereof. 9 And thou shalt take the oil of unction and anoint the tabernacle with its vessels that they may be sanctified. 10 The altar of holocaust and all its vessels, 11 the laver with its foot, thou shalt consecrate all with the oil of unction that they may be most holy. 12 And thou shalt bring Aaron and his sons to the door of the Tabernacle of the Testimony, and having washed them with water, 13 thou shalt put on them the holy vestments that they may minister to me and that the unction of them may prosper to an everlasting priesthood."

14 And Moses did all that the Lord had commanded. 15 So in the first month of the second year, the first day of

catum est tabernaculum. 16 Erexitque illud Moses et posuit tabulas ac bases et vectes statuitque columnas 17 et expandit tectum super tabernaculum, inposito desuper operimento, sicut Dominus imperarat. 18 Posuit et testimonium in arca, subditis infra vectibus et oraculum desuper. 19 Cumque intulisset arcam in tabernaculum, adpendit ante eam velum ut expleret Domini iussionem. 20 Posuit et mensam in Tabernaculo Testimonii ad plagam septentrionalem extra velum, 21 ordinatis coram propositionis panibus, sicut praeceperat Dominus Mosi. 22 Posuit et candelabrum in Tabernaculum Testimonii e regione mensae in parte australi, 23 locatis per ordinem lucernis, iuxta praeceptum Domini. 24 Posuit et altare aureum sub tecto testimonii contra velum 25 et adolevit super eo incensum aromatum, sicut iusserat Dominus Mosi. 26 Posuit et tentorium in introitu Tabernaculi Testimonii 27 et altare holocausti in vestibulo testimonii, offerens in eo holocaustum et sacrificia ut Dominus imperarat. 28 Labrum quoque statuit inter Tabernaculum Testimonii et altare, implens illud aqua.

29 Laveruntque Moses et Aaron ac filii eius manus suas et pedes 30 cum ingrederentur tectum foederis et accederent ad altare, sicut praeceperat Dominus Mosi.

31 Erexit et atrium per gyrum tabernaculi et altaris, ducto in introitu eius tentorio. Postquam cuncta perfecta sunt, 32 operuit nubes Tabernaculum Testimonii, et gloria Domini implevit illud, 33 nec poterat Moses ingredi tectum foederis,

the month, the tabernacle was set up. 16 And Moses reared it up and placed the boards and the sockets and the bars and set up the pillars 17 and spread the roof over the tabernacle, putting over it a cover, as the Lord had commanded. 18 And he put the testimony in the ark, thrusting bars underneath and the oracle above. 19 And when he had brought the ark into the tabernacle, he drew the veil before it to fulfill the commandment of the Lord. 20 And he set the table in the Tabernacle of the Testimony at the north side without the veil, 21 setting there in order the loaves of proposition, as the Lord had commanded Moses. 22 He set the candlestick also in the Tabernacle of the Testimony over against the table on the south side, 23 placing the lamps in order, according to the precept of the Lord. 24 He set also the altar of gold under the roof of the testimony over against the veil 25 and burnt upon it the incense of spices, as the Lord had commanded Moses. 26 And he put also the hanging in the entry of the Tabernacle of the Testimony 27 and the altar of holocaust of the entry of the testimony, offering the holocaust and the sacrifices upon it as the Lord had commanded. 28 And he set the laver between the Tabernacle of the Testimony and the altar, filling it with water.

29 And Moses and Aaron and his sons washed their hands and feet 30 when they went into the *Tabernacle* of the Covenant and went to the altar, as the Lord had commanded Moses.

31 He set up also the court round about the tabernacle and the altar, drawing the hanging in the entry thereof. After all things were perfected, 32 the cloud covered the Tabernacle of the Testimony, and the glory of the Lord filled it, 33 neither could Moses go into the *Tabernacle* of the Cove-

nube operiente omnia et maiestate Domini coruscante, quia cuncta nubes operuerat. 34 Si quando nubes tabernaculum deserebat, proficiscebantur filii Israhel per turmas suas. 35 Si pendebat desuper, manebant in eodem loco, 36 nubes quippe Domini incubabat per diem tabernaculo et ignis in nocte videntibus cunctis populis Israhel per cunctas mansiones suas.

nant, the cloud covering all things and the majesty of the Lord shining, for the cloud had covered all. 34 If at any time the cloud removed from the tabernacle, the children of Israel went forward by their troops. 35 If it hung over, they remained in the same place, 36 for the cloud of the Lord hung over the tabernacle by day and a fire by night in the sight of all the *children* of Israel throughout all their mansions.

LEVITICUS

Caput 1

Vocavit autem Mosen et locutus est ei Dominus de Tabernaculo Testimonii, dicens, 2 "Loquere filiis Israhel, et dices ad eos, 'Homo qui obtulerit ex vobis hostiam Domino de pecoribus, id est, de bubus et ovibus offerens victimas, 3 si holocaustum fuerit eius oblatio ac de armento, masculum inmaculatum offeret ad ostium Tabernaculi Testimonii ad placandum sibi Dominum. 4 Ponetque manus super caput hostiae, et acceptabilis erit atque in expiationem eius proficiens. 5 Immolabitque vitulum coram Domino, et offerent filii Aaron, sacerdotes, sanguinem eius, fundentes per altaris circuitum quod est ante ostium tabernaculi. 6 Detractaque pelle hostiae, artus in frusta concident 7 et subicient in altari ignem, strue lignorum ante conposita. 8 Et membra quae caesa sunt desuper ordinantes, caput, videlicet, et cunctaque adherent iecori, 9 intestinis et pedibus lotis aqua, adolebitque ea sacerdos super altare in holocaustum et suavem odorem Domino.

Chapter 1

Of holocausts or burnt offerings.

And the Lord called Moses and spoke to him from the Tabernacle of the Testimony, saying, 2 "Speak to the children of Israel, and thou shalt say to them, 'The man among you that shall offer to the Lord a sacrifice of the cattle, that is, offering victims of oxen and sheep, 3 if his offering be a holocaust and of the herd, he shall offer a male without blemish at the door of the *testimony* to make the Lord favourable to him. 4 And he shall put his *hand* upon the head of the victim, and it shall be acceptable and help to its expiation. 5 And he shall immolate the calf before the Lord, and the priests, the sons of Aaron, shall offer the blood thereof, pouring it round about the altar which is before the door of the tabernacle. 6 And when they have flayed the victim, they shall cut the joints into pieces 7 and shall put fire on the altar, having before laid in order a pile of wood. 8 And they shall lay the parts that are cut out in order thereupon, to wit, the head and all things that cleave to the liver, 9 the entrails and feet being washed with water, and the priest shall burn them upon the altar for a holocaust and a sweet savour to the Lord.

10 "'Quod si de pecoribus oblatio est, de ovibus sive de capris holocaustum, agnum anniculum absque macula offeret, 11 immolabitque ad latus altaris quod respicit ad aquilonem coram Domino, sanguinem vero illius fundent super altare filii Aaron per circuitum, 12 dividentque membra, caput et omnia quae adherent iecori et ponent super ligna quibus subiciendus est ignis, 13 intestina vero et pedes lavabunt aqua. Et oblata omnia adolebit sacerdos super altare in holocaustum et odorem suavissimum Domino.

14 "'Sin autem de avibus holocausti oblatio fuerit Domino, de turturibus et pullis columbae, 15 offeret eam sacerdos ad altare, et, retorto ad collum capite ac rupto vulneris loco, decurrere faciet sanguinem super crepidinem altaris. 16 Vesiculam vero gutturis et plumas proiciet propter altare ad orientalem plagam in loco in quo cineres effundi solent, 17 confringetque ascellas eius et non secabit nec ferro dividet eam et adolebit super altare, lignis igne subposito. Holocaustum est et oblatio suavissimi odoris Domino.'"

10 "And if the offering be of the flocks, a holocaust of sheep or of goats, he shall offer a *male* without blemish, 11 and he shall immolate it at the side of the altar that looketh to the north before the Lord, but the sons of Aaron shall pour the blood thereof upon the altar round about, 12 and they shall divide the joints, the head and all that cleave to the liver and shall lay them upon the wood under which the fire is to be put, 13 but the entrails and the feet they shall wash with water. And the priest shall offer it all and burn it all upon the altar for a holocaust and most sweet savour to the Lord.

14 "But if the oblation of a holocaust to the Lord be of birds, of turtles *or* of young pigeons, 15 the priest shall offer it at the altar, and, twisting back the neck and breaking the place of the wound, he shall make the blood run down upon the brim of the altar. 16 But the crop of the throat and the feathers he shall cast beside the altar at the east side in the place where the ashes are wont to be poured out, 17 and he shall break the pinions thereof and shall not cut nor divide it with a knife and shall burn it upon the altar, putting fire under the wood. It is a holocaust and oblation of most sweet savour to the Lord.'"

Caput 2

"Anima cum obtulerit oblationem sacrificii Domino, simila erit eius oblatio, fundetque super eam oleum et ponet tus 2 ac deferet ad filios Aaron, sacerdotes, quorum unus tollet pugillum plenum similae et olei ac totum tus et ponet memoriale super altare in odorem suavissimum Domino. 3 Quod autem reliquum fuerit de sacrificio erit Aaron et filiorum eius, sanctum sanctorum de oblationibus Domini.

4 "'Cum autem obtuleris sacrificium coctum in clibano de simila, panes, scilicet, absque fermento conspersos oleo et lagana azyma oleo lita, 5 si oblatio tua fuerit de sartagine similae conspersae oleo et absque fermento, 6 divides eam minutatim et fundes supra eam oleum.

7 "'Sin autem de craticula sacrificium, aeque simila oleo conspergetur, 8 quam offerens Domino trades manibus sacerdotis. 9 Qui cum obtulerit eam, tollet memoriale de sacrificio et adolebit super altare in odorem suavitatis Domino. 10 Quicquid autem reliquum est erit Aaron et filiorum eius, sanctum sanctorum de oblationibus Domini.

11 "'Omnis oblatio quae offertur Domino absque fermento fiet, nec quicquam fermenti ac mellis adolebitur in

Chapter 2

Of offerings of flour and firstfruits.

"When *any one* shall offer an oblation of sacrifice to the Lord, his offering shall be of fine flour, and he shall pour oil upon it and put frankincense 2 and shall bring it to the sons of Aaron, the priests, and one of them shall take a handful of the flour and oil and all the frankincense and shall put it, a memorial, upon the altar for a most sweet savour to the Lord. 3 And the remnant of the sacrifice shall be Aaron's and his sons', holy of holies of the offerings of the Lord.

4 "But when thou offerest a sacrifice baked in the oven of flour, to wit, loaves without leaven tempered with oil and unleavened wafers anointed with oil, 5 if thy oblation be from the frying pan of flour tempered with oil and without leaven, 6 thou shalt divide it into little pieces and shalt pour oil upon it.

7 "And if the sacrifice be from the gridiron, in like manner the flour shall be tempered with oil, 8 and when thou offerest it to the Lord, thou shalt deliver it to the hands of the priest. 9 And when he hath offered it, he shall take a memorial out of the sacrifice and burn it upon the altar for a sweet savour to the Lord. 10 And whatsoever is left shall be Aaron's and his sons', holy of holies of the offerings of the Lord.

11 "Every oblation that is offered to the Lord shall be made without leaven, neither shall any leaven or honey be

sacrificio Domini. 12 Primitias tantum eorum offeretis et munera, super altare vero non ponentur in odorem suavitatis. 13 Quicquid obtuleris sacrificii, sale condies nec, auferes sal foederis Dei tui de sacrificio tuo. In omni oblatione offeres sal.

14 "'Sin autem obtuleris munus primarum frugum tuarum Domino, de spicis adhuc virentibus, torrebis igni et confringes in morem farris, et sic offeres primitias tuas Domino, 15 fundens supra oleum et tus inponens, quia oblatio Domini est, 16 de qua adolebit sacerdos in memoriam muneris partem farris fracti et olei ac totum tus.'"

Caput 3

"'Quod si hostia pacificorum fuerit eius oblatio et de bubus voluerit offerre, marem sive feminam, inmaculata offeret coram Domino. 2 Ponetque manum super caput victimae suae, quae immolabitur in introitu Tabernaculi Testimonii, fundentque filii Aaron, sacerdotes, sanguinem per circuitum altaris. 3 Et offerent de hostia pacificorum in

burnt in the sacrifice to the Lord. 12 You shall offer only the firstfruits of them and gifts, but they shall not be put upon the altar for a savour of sweetness. 13 Whatsoever sacrifice thou offerest, thou shalt season it with salt, neither shalt thou take away the salt of the covenant of thy God from thy sacrifice. In *all thy oblations* thou shalt offer salt.

14 "But if thou offer a gift of the firstfruits of thy corn to the Lord, of the ears yet green, thou shalt dry it at the fire and break it small like meal, and so shalt thou offer thy firstfruits to the Lord, 15 pouring oil upon it and putting on frankincense, because it is the oblation of the Lord, 16 whereof the priest shall burn for a memorial of the gift part of the corn broken small and of the oil and all the frankincense.'"

Chapter 3

Of peace offerings.

"And if his oblation be a sacrifice of peace offerings and he will offer of the herd, whether male or female, he shall offer them without blemish before the Lord. 2 And he shall lay his hand upon the head of his victim, which shall be slain in the entry of the Tabernacle of the Testimony, and the sons of Aaron, the priests, shall pour the blood round about upon the altar. 3 And they shall offer of the sacrifice of

oblationem Domino adipem qui operit vitalia et quicquid pinguedinis intrinsecus est, 4 duos renes cum adipe quo teguntur ilia et reticulum iecoris cum renunculis. 5 Adolebuntque ea super altare in holocaustum, lignis igne subposito, in oblationem suavissimi odoris Domino.

6 "'Si vero de ovibus fuerit eius oblatio et pacificorum hostia, sive masculum sive feminam, obtulerit inmaculata erunt. 7 Si agnum obtulerit coram Domino, 8 ponet manum super caput victimae suae, quae immolabitur in vestibulo Tabernaculi Testimonii, fundentque filii Aaron sanguinem eius per altaris circuitum. 9 Et offerent de pacificorum hostia sacrificium Domino: adipem et caudam totam 10 cum renibus et pinguedinem quae operit ventrem atque universa vitalia et utrumque renunculum cum adipe qui est iuxta ilia reticulumque iecoris cum renunculis. 11 Et adolebit ea sacerdos super altare in pabulum ignis et oblationis Domini.

12 "'Si capra fuerit eius oblatio et obtulerit eam Domino, 13 ponet manum suam super caput eius immolabitque eam in introitu Tabernaculi Testimonii. Et fundent filii Aaron sanguinem eius per altaris circuitum. 14 Tollentque ex ea in pastum ignis dominici adipem qui operit ventrem et qui tegit universa vitalia, 15 duos renunculos cum reticulo qui est super eos iuxta ilia et arvinam iecoris cum renunculis. 16 Adolebitque ea sacerdos super altare in alimoniam ignis et suavissimi odoris. Omnis adeps Domini erit 17 iure perpetuo in generationibus et cunctis habitaculis vestris; nec adipem omnino nec sanguinem omnino comedetis.'"

peace offerings for an oblation to the Lord the fat that covereth the entrails and all the fat that is within, 4 the two kidneys with the fat wherewith the flanks are covered and the caul of the liver with the *two* little kidneys. 5 And they shall burn them upon the altar for a holocaust, putting fire under the wood, for an oblation of most sweet savour to the Lord.

6 "But if his oblation and the sacrifice of peace offering be of the flock, whether he offer male or female, they shall be without blemish. 7 If he offer a lamb before the Lord, 8 he shall put his hand upon the head of his victim, and it shall be slain in the entry of the Tabernacle of the Testimony, and the sons of Aaron shall pour the blood thereof round about upon the altar. 9 And they shall offer of the victim of peace offerings a sacrifice to the Lord: the fat and the whole rump 10 with the kidneys and the fat that covereth the belly and all the vitals and both the little kidneys with the fat that is about the flanks and the caul of the liver with the little kidneys. 11 And the priest shall burn them upon the altar for the food of the fire and of the oblation of the Lord.

12 "If his offering be a goat and he offer it to the Lord, 13 he shall put his hand upon the head thereof and shall immolate it in the entry of the Tabernacle of the Testimony. And the sons of Aaron shall pour the blood thereof round about upon the altar. 14 And they shall take of it for the food of the Lord's fire the fat that covereth the belly and that covereth all the vital parts, 15 the two little kidneys with the caul that is upon them which is by the flanks and the fat of the liver with the little kidneys. 16 And the priest shall burn them upon the altar for the food of the fire and of a most sweet savour. All the fat shall be the Lord's 17 by a perpetual law for your generations and in all your habitations; neither blood nor fat shall you eat at all.'"

Caput 4

Locutusque est Dominus ad Mosen, dicens, 2 "Loquere filiis Israhel, 'Anima quae peccaverit per ignorantiam et de universis mandatis Domini quae praecepit ut non fierent quippiam fecerit, 3 si sacerdos qui est unctus peccaverit, delinquere faciens populum, offeret pro peccato suo vitulum inmaculatum Domino. 4 Et adducet illum ad ostium Tabernaculi Testimonii coram Domino ponetque manum super caput eius et immolabit eum Domino. 5 Hauriet quoque de sanguine vituli inferens illud in Tabernaculum Testimonii. 6 Cumque intinxerit digitum in sanguinem, asperget eo septies coram Domino, contra velum sanctuarii. 7 Ponetque de eodem sanguine super cornua altaris thymiamatis gratissimi Domino quod est in Tabernaculo Testimonii. Omnem autem reliquum sanguinem fundet in basim altaris holocausti in introitu tabernaculi. 8 Et adipem vituli auferet pro peccato, tam eum qui operit vitalia quam omnia quae intrinsecus sunt, 9 duos renunculos et reticulum quod est super eos iuxta ilia et adipem iecoris cum renunculis 10 sicut aufertur de vitulo hostiae pacificorum, et adolebit ea super altare holocausti. 11 Pellem vero et omnes carnes cum capite et

Chapter 4

Of offerings for sins of ignorance.

And the Lord spoke to Moses, saying, 2 "Say to the children of Israel, 'The soul that sinneth through ignorance and doth any thing concerning any of the commandments of the Lord which he commanded not to be done, 3 if the priest that is anointed shall sin, making the people to offend, he shall offer to the Lord for his sin a calf without blemish. 4 And he shall bring it to the door of the *testimony* before the Lord and shall put his hand upon the head thereof and shall sacrifice it to the Lord. 5 He shall take also of the blood of the calf and carry it into the Tabernacle of the Testimony. 6 And, having dipped his finger in the blood, he shall sprinkle with it seven times before the Lord, before the veil of the sanctuary. 7 And he shall put some of the same blood upon the horns of the altar of the sweet incense most acceptable to the Lord which is in the Tabernacle of the Testimony. And he shall pour all the rest of the blood at the foot of the altar of holocaust in the entry of the tabernacle. 8 And he shall take off the fat of the calf for the sin *offering,* as well that which covereth the entrails as all the inwards, 9 the two little kidneys and the caul that is upon them, which is by the flanks, and the fat of the liver with the little kidneys 10 as it is taken off from the calf of the sacrifice of peace offerings, and he shall burn them upon the altar of holocaust. 11 But

pedibus et intestinis et fimo 12 et reliquo corpore efferet extra castra in locum mundum ubi cineres effundi solent, incendetque ea super lignorum struem, quae in loco effusorum cinerum cremabuntur.

13 "'Quod si omnis turba Israhel ignoraverit et per inperitiam fecerit quod contra mandatum Domini est 14 et postea intellexerit peccatum suum, offeret vitulum pro peccato suo adducetque eum ad ostium tabernaculi. 15 Et ponent seniores populi manus super caput eius coram Domino. Immolatoque vitulo in conspectu Domini, 16 inferet sacerdos qui unctus est de sanguine eius in Tabernaculum Testimonii, 17 tincto digito aspergens septies contra velum. 18 Ponetque de eodem sanguine in cornibus altaris quod est coram Domino in Tabernaculo Testimonii, reliquum autem sanguinem fundet iuxta basim altaris holocaustorum, quod est in ostio Tabernaculi Testimonii. 19 Omnemque eius adipem tollet et adolebit super altare, 20 sic faciens et de hoc vitulo quomodo fecit et prius, et, rogante pro eis sacerdote, propitius erit eis Dominus. 21 Ipsum autem vitulum efferet extra castra atque conburet sicut et priorem vitulum, quia pro peccato est multitudinis.

22 "'Si peccaverit princeps et fecerit unum e pluribus per ignorantiam quod Domini lege prohibetur 23 et postea intellexerit peccatum suum, offeret hostiam Domino, hircum de capris inmaculatum. 24 Ponetque manum suam super caput

the skin and all the flesh with the head and the feet and the bowels and the dung 12 and the rest of the body he shall carry forth without the camp into a clean place where the ashes are wont to be poured out, and he shall burn them upon a pile of wood; *they* shall be burnt in the place where the ashes are poured out.

13 "'And if all the multitude of Israel shall be ignorant and through ignorance shall do that which is against the commandment of the Lord 14 and afterwards shall understand their sin, they shall offer for their sin a calf and shall bring it to the door of the tabernacle. 15 And the ancients of the people shall put their hands upon the head thereof before the Lord. And the calf being immolated in the sight of the Lord, 16 the priest that is anointed shall carry of the blood into the Tabernacle of the Testimony 17 and shall dip his finger in it and sprinkle it seven times before the veil. 18 And he shall put of the same blood on the horns of the altar that is before the Lord in the Tabernacle of the Testimony, and the rest of the blood he shall pour at the foot of the altar of holocaust, which is at the door of the Tabernacle of the Testimony. 19 And all the fat thereof he shall take off and shall burn it upon the altar, 20 doing so with this calf as he did also with that before, and, the priest praying for them, the Lord will be merciful unto them. 21 But the calf itself he shall carry forth without the camp and shall burn it as he did the former calf, because it is for the sin of the multitude.

22 "'If a prince shall sin and through ignorance do any one of the things that the law of the Lord forbiddeth 23 and afterwards shall come to know his sin, he shall offer a buck-goat without blemish, a sacrifice to the Lord. 24 And he shall put his hand upon the head thereof, and when he hath im-

eius, cumque immolaverit eum in loco ubi solet mactari holocaustum coram Domino, quia pro peccato est, 25 tinguet
sacerdos digitum in sanguine hostiae pro peccato, tangens
cornua altaris holocausti et reliquum fundens ad basim eius.
26 Adipem vero adolebit supra, sicut in victimis pacificorum
fieri solet, rogabitque pro eo sacerdos et pro peccato eius, ac
dimittetur ei.

27 "'Quod si peccaverit anima per ignorantiam de populo
terrae, ut faciat quicquam de his quae Domini lege prohibentur atque delinquat 28 et cognoverit peccatum suum, offeret capram inmaculatam. 29 Ponetque manum super caput
hostiae quae pro peccato est et immolabit eam in loco holocausti. 30 Tolletque sacerdos de sanguine in digito suo et tangens cornua altaris holocausti reliquum fundet ad basim
eius. 31 Omnem autem auferens adipem sicut auferri solet
de victimis pacificorum, adolebit super altare in odorem
suavitatis Domino, rogabitque pro eo, et dimittetur ei. 32 Sin
autem de pecoribus obtulerit victimam pro peccato, ovem,
scilicet, inmaculatam, 33 ponet manum super caput eius et
immolabit eam in loco ubi solent holocaustorum caedi hostiae. 34 Sumetque sacerdos de sanguine eius digito suo et
tangens cornua altaris holocausti reliquum fundet ad basim
eius. 35 Omnem quoque auferens adipem, sicut auferri solet
adeps arietis qui immolatur pro pacificis, et cremabit super
altare in incensum Domini, rogabitque pro eo et pro peccato eius et dimittetur illi.'"

molated it in the place where the holocaust is wont to be slain before the Lord, because it is for sin, 25 the priest shall dip his finger in the blood of the victim for sin, touching therewith the horns of the altar of holocaust and pouring out the rest at the foot thereof. 26 But the fat he shall burn upon it, as is wont to be done with the victims of peace offerings, and the priest shall pray for him and for his sin, and it shall be forgiven him.

27 "And if any one of the people of the land shall sin through ignorance, *doing* any of those things that by the law of the Lord are forbidden and *offending* 28 and shall come to know his sin, he shall offer a she-goat without blemish. 29 And he shall put his hand upon the head of the victim that is for sin and shall immolate it in the place of the holocaust. 30 And the priest shall take of the blood with his finger and shall touch the horns of the altar of holocaust and shall pour out the rest at the foot thereof. 31 But, taking off all the fat as is wont to be taken away of the victims of peace offerings, he shall burn it upon the altar for a sweet savour to the Lord, and he shall pray for him, and it shall be forgiven him. 32 But if he offer of the flock a victim for his sin, to wit, an ewe without blemish, 33 he shall put his hand upon the head thereof and shall immolate it in the place where the victims of holocausts are wont to be slain. 34 And the priest shall take of the blood thereof with his finger and shall touch the horns of the altar of holocaust and the rest he shall pour out at the foot thereof. 35 All the fat also he shall take off, as the fat of the ram that is offered for peace offerings is wont to be taken away, and shall burn it upon the altar for a burnt sacrifice of the Lord, and he shall pray for him and for his sin and it shall be forgiven him.'"

Caput 5

"Si peccaverit anima et audierit vocem iurantis testisque fuerit quod aut ipse vidit aut conscius est, nisi indicaverit, portabit iniquitatem suam.

2 "'Anima quae tetigerit aliquid inmundum, sive quod occisum a bestia est aut per se mortuum vel quodlibet aliud reptile, et oblita fuerit inmunditiae suae, rea est et deliquit, 3 et si tetigerit quicquam de inmunditia hominis iuxta omnem inpuritatem qua pollui solet oblitaque cognoverit postea, subiacebit delicto.

4 "'Anima quae iuraverit et protulerit labiis suis ut vel male quid faceret vel bene et id ipsum iuramento et sermone firmaverit oblitaque postea intellexerit delictum suum, 5 agat paenitentiam pro peccato 6 et offerat agnam de gregibus sive capram, orabitque pro eo sacerdos et pro peccato eius. 7 Sin autem non potuerit offerre pecus, offerat duos turtures vel duos pullos columbarum Domino, unum pro peccato et alterum in holocaustum, 8 dabitque eos sacerdoti qui primum offerens pro peccato retorquebit caput eius ad pinnulas ita ut collo hereat et non penitus abrumpatur. 9 Et asperget de sanguine eius parietem altaris, quicquid autem reliquum fuerit faciet destillare ad fundamentum eius quia

Chapter 5

Of other sacrifices for sins.

"If any one sin and hear the voice of one swearing and is a witness either because he himself hath seen or is privy to it, if he do not utter it, he shall bear his iniquity.

2 "'Whosoever toucheth any unclean thing, either that which hath been killed by a beast or died of itself or any other creeping thing, and forgetteth his uncleanness, he is guilty and hath offended, 3 and if he touch any thing of the uncleanness of man according to any uncleanness wherewith he is wont to be defiled and having forgotten it come afterwards to know it, he shall be guilty of an offence.

4 "'The person that sweareth and uttereth with his lips that he would do either evil or good and bindeth the same with an oath and his word and having forgotten it afterwards understandeth his offence, 5 let him do penance for his sin 6 and offer of the flocks an ewe-lamb or a she-goat, and the priest shall pray for him and for his sin. 7 But if he be not able to offer a beast, let him offer two turtles or two young pigeons to the Lord, one for sin and the other for a holocaust, 8 and he shall give them to the priest who shall offer the first for sin and twist back the head of it to the little pinions so that it stick to the neck and be not altogether broken off. 9 And of its blood he shall sprinkle the side of the altar, and whatsoever is left he shall let it drop at the bottom

pro peccato est. 10 Alterum vero adolebit in holocaustum, ut fieri solet, rogabitque pro eo sacerdos et pro peccato eius, et dimittetur ei.

11 "'Quod si non quiverit manus eius offerre duos turtures vel duos pullos columbae, offeret pro peccato suo similae partem oephi decimam. Non mittet in eam oleum nec turis aliquid inponet, quia pro peccato est, 12 tradetque eam sacerdoti qui plenum ex ea pugillum hauriens cremabit super altare in monumentum eius qui obtulit, 13 rogans pro illo et expians. Reliquam vero partem ipse habebit in munere.'"

14 Locutusque est Dominus ad Mosen, dicens, 15 "Anima si praevaricans caerimonias per errorem in his quae Domino sunt sanctificata peccaverit, offeret pro delicto suo arietem inmaculatum de gregibus qui emi potest duobus siclis, iuxta pondus sanctuarii, 16 ipsumque quod intulit damni restituet et quintam partem ponet supra, tradens sacerdoti, qui rogabit pro eo offerens arietem, et dimittetur ei.

17 "Anima si peccaverit per ignorantiam feceritque unum ex his quae Domini lege prohibentur et peccati rea intellexerit iniquitatem suam, 18 offeret arietem inmaculatum de gregibus sacerdoti iuxta mensuram aestimationemque peccati, qui orabit pro eo quod nesciens fecerit, et dimittetur ei 19 quia per errorem deliquit in Dominum."

thereof because it is for sin. 10 And the other he shall burn for a holocaust, as is wont to be done, and the priest shall pray for him and for his sin, and it shall be forgiven him.

11 "'And if his hand be not able to offer two turtles or two young pigeons, he shall offer for his sin the tenth part of an ephi of flour. He shall not put oil upon it nor put any frankincense thereon, because it is for sin, 12 and he shall deliver it to the priest who shall take a handful thereof and shall burn it upon the altar for a memorial of him that offered it, 13 praying for him and making atonement. But the part that is left he himself shall have for a gift.'"

14 And the Lord spoke to Moses, saying, 15 "If any one shall sin through mistake, transgressing the ceremonies in those things that are sacrificed to the Lord, he shall offer for his offence a ram without blemish out of the flocks that may be bought for two sicles, according to the weight of the sanctuary, 16 and he shall make good the damage itself which he hath done and shall add the fifth part besides, delivering it to the priest, who shall pray for him offering the ram, and it shall be forgiven him.

17 "If any one sin through ignorance and do one of those things which by the law of the Lord are forbidden and being guilty of sin understand his iniquity, 18 he shall offer of the flocks a ram without blemish to the priest according to the measure and estimation of the sin, and the priest shall pray for him because he did it ignorantly, and it shall be forgiven him 19 because by mistake he trespassed against the Lord."

Caput 6

Locutus est Dominus ad Mosen, dicens, 2 "Anima quae peccaverit et contempto Domino negaverit depositum proximo suo quod fidei eius creditum fuerat vel vi aliquid extorserit aut calumniam fecerit 3 sive rem perditam invenerit et infitians insuper peierarit et quodlibet aliud ex pluribus fecerit in quibus peccare solent homines, 4 convicta delicti, reddet 5 omnia quae per fraudem voluit obtinere integra et quintam insuper partem domino cui damnum intulerat. 6 Pro peccato autem suo offeret arietem inmaculatum de grege et dabit eum sacerdoti iuxta aestimationem mensuramque delicti, 7 qui rogabit pro eo coram Domino, et dimittetur illi pro singulis quae faciendo peccaverit."

8 Locutusque est Dominus ad Mosen, dicens, 9 "Praecipe Aaron et filiis eius: 'Haec est lex holocausti: cremabitur in altari tota nocte usque mane; ignis ex eodem altari erit. 10 Vestietur sacerdos tunica et feminalibus lineis, tolletque cineres quos vorans ignis exusit et ponens iuxta altare 11 spo-

Chapter 6

Oblation for sins of injustice, ordinances concerning the holocausts and the perpetual fire, the sacrifices of the priests and the sin offerings.

The Lord spoke to Moses, saying, 2 "Whosoever shall sin and despising the Lord shall deny to his neighbour the thing delivered to his keeping which was committed to his trust or shall by force extort any thing or commit oppression 3 or shall find a thing lost and denying it shall also swear falsely or shall do any other of the many things wherein men are wont to sin, 4 being convicted of the offence, he shall restore 5 all that he would have gotten by fraud in the principal and the fifth part besides to the owner whom he wronged. 6 Moreover, for his sin he shall offer a ram without blemish out of the flock and shall give it to the priest according to the estimation and measure of the offence, 7 and he shall pray for him before the Lord, and he shall have forgiveness for every thing in doing of which he hath sinned."

8 And the Lord spoke to Moses, saying, 9 "Command Aaron and his sons: 'This is the law of a holocaust: it shall be burnt upon the altar all night until morning; the fire shall be of the same altar. 10 The priest shall be vested with the tunick and the linen breeches, and he shall take up the ashes *of that* which the devouring fire hath burnt and putting them beside the altar 11 shall put off his former vestments and be-

liabitur prioribus vestimentis indutusque aliis efferet eos extra castra et in loco mundissimo usque ad favillam consumi faciet. 12 Ignis autem in altari semper ardebit, quem nutriet sacerdos, subiciens ligna mane per singulos dies et inposito holocausto desuper adolebit adipes pacificorum. 13 Ignis est iste perpetuus qui numquam deficiet in altari.

14 "'Haec est lex sacrificii et libamentorum quae offerent filii Aaron coram Domino et coram altari: 15 tollet sacerdos pugillum similae quae conspersa est oleo et totum tus quod super similam positum est, adolebitque illud in altari in monumentum odoris suavissimi Domino. 16 Reliquam autem partem similae, comedet Aaron cum filiis suis absque fermento, et comedet in loco sancto atrii tabernaculi. 17 Ideo autem non fermentabitur, quia pars eius in Domini offertur incensum. Sanctum sanctorum erit sicut pro peccato atque delicto. 18 Mares tantum stirpis Aaron comedent illud. Legitimum ac sempiternum erit in generationibus vestris de sacrificiis Domini. Omnis qui tetigerit illa sanctificabitur.'"

19 Et locutus est Dominus ad Mosen, dicens, 20 "Haec est oblatio Aaron et filiorum eius quam offerre debent Domino in die unctionis suae: decimam partem oephi offerent similae in sacrificio sempiterno, medium eius mane et medium eius vespere, 21 quae in sartagine oleo conspersa frigetur. Offeret autem eam calidam in odorem suavissimum Domino 22 sacerdos qui patri iure successerit, et tota cremabi-

ing clothed with others shall carry them forth without the camp and shall cause them to be consumed to dust in a very clean place. 12 And the fire on the altar shall always burn, and the priest shall feed it, putting wood on it every day in the morning and laying on the holocaust shall burn thereupon the fat of the peace offerings. 13 This is the perpetual fire which shall never go out on the altar.

14 "'This is the law of the sacrifice and libations which the children of Aaron shall offer before the Lord and before the altar: 15 the priest shall take a handful of the flour that is tempered with oil and all the frankincense that is put upon the flour, and he shall burn it on the altar for a memorial of most sweet odour to the Lord. 16 And the part of the flour that is left, Aaron and his sons shall eat without leaven, and he shall eat it in the holy place of the court of the tabernacle. 17 And therefore it shall not be leavened, because part thereof is offered for the burnt sacrifice of the Lord. It shall be most holy as that which is offered for sin and for trespass. 18 The males only of the race of Aaron shall eat it. It shall be an *ordinance everlasting* in your generations concerning the sacrifices of the Lord. Every one that toucheth them shall be sanctified.'"

19 And the Lord spoke to Moses, saying, 20 "This is the oblation of Aaron and of his sons which they must offer to the Lord in the day of their anointing: they shall offer the tenth part of an ephi of flour for a perpetual sacrifice, half of it in the morning and half of it in the evening. 21 *It shall be* tempered with oil and shall be fried in a frying pan. 22 And the priest that rightfully succeedeth his father shall offer it hot for a most sweet odour to the Lord, and it shall be

tur in altari. 23 Omne enim sacrificium sacerdotum igne consumetur, nec quisquam comedet ex eo."

24 Locutus est autem Dominus ad Mosen, dicens, 25 "Loquere Aaron et filiis eius, 'Ista est lex hostiae pro peccato: in loco ubi offertur holocaustum, immolabitur coram Domino. Sanctum sanctorum est. 26 Sacerdos qui offert comedet eam in loco sancto, in atrio tabernaculi. 27 Quicquid tetigerit carnes eius sanctificabitur. Si de sanguine illius vestis fuerit aspersa, lavabitur in loco sancto. 28 Vas autem fictile in quo cocta est confringetur, quod si vas aeneum fuerit, defricabitur et lavabitur aqua. 29 Omnis masculus de genere sacerdotali vescetur de carnibus eius quia sanctum sanctorum est. 30 Hostia enim quae caeditur pro peccato, cuius sanguis infertur in Tabernaculum Testimonii ad expiandum in sanctuario, non comedetur sed conburetur igni.'"

Caput 7

"Haec quoque est lex hostiae pro delicto; sancta sanctorum est. 2 Idcirco, ubi immolatur holocaustum, mactabitur et victima pro delicto; sanguis eius per gyrum fundetur

wholly burnt on the altar. 23 For every sacrifice of the priest shall be consumed with fire, neither shall any man eat thereof."

24 And the Lord spoke to Moses, saying, 25 "Say to Aaron and his sons, 'This is the law of the victim for sin: in the place where the holocaust is offered, it shall be immolated before the Lord. It is holy of holies. 26 The priest that offereth it shall eat it in a holy place, in the court of the tabernacle. 27 Whatsoever shall touch the flesh thereof shall be sanctified. If a garment be sprinkled with the blood thereof, it shall be washed in a holy place. 28 And the earthen vessel wherein it was sodden shall be broken, but if the vessel be of brass, it shall be scoured and washed with water. 29 Every male of the priestly race shall eat of the flesh thereof because it is holy of holies. 30 For the victim that is slain for sin, the blood of which is carried into the Tabernacle of the Testimony to make atonement in the sanctuary, shall not be eaten but shall be burnt with fire.'"

Chapter 7

Of sacrifices for trespasses and thanks offerings. No fat nor blood is to be eaten.

"This also is the law of the sacrifice for a trespass; it is most holy. 2 Therefore, where the holocaust is immolated, the victim also for a trespass shall be slain; the blood thereof

altaris. 3 Offerent ex ea caudam et adipem qui operit vitalia, 4 duos renunculos et pinguedinem quae iuxta ilia est reticulumque iecoris cum renunculis. 5 Et adolebit ea sacerdos super altare; incensum est Domini pro delicto.

6 "'Omnis masculus de sacerdotali genere in loco sancto vescetur his carnibus quia sanctum sanctorum est. 7 Sicut pro peccato offertur hostia, ita et pro delicto. Utriusque hostiae lex una erit; ad sacerdotem qui eam obtulerit pertinebit. 8 Sacerdos qui offert holocausti victimam habebit pellem eius. 9 Et omne sacrificium similae quod coquitur in clibano et quicquid in craticula vel in sartagine praeparatur eius erit sacerdotis a quo offertur; 10 sive oleo conspersa sive arida fuerint, cunctis filiis Aaron aequa mensura per singulos dividetur.

11 "'Haec est lex hostiae pacificorum quae offertur Domino. 12 Si pro gratiarum actione fuerit oblatio, offerent panes absque fermento conspersos oleo et lagana azyma uncta oleo coctamque similam et collyridas olei admixtione conspersas, 13 panes quoque fermentatos cum hostia gratiarum quae immolatur pro pacificis 14 ex quibus unus pro primitiis offeretur Domino et erit sacerdotis qui fundet hostiae sanguinem. 15 Cuius carnes eadem comedentur die, nec remanebit ex eis quicquam usque mane.

16 "'Si voto vel sponte quisquam obtulerit hostiam, eadem similiter edetur die, sed et si quid in crastinum remanserit, vesci licitum est, 17 quicquid autem tertius invenerit dies

shall be poured round about the altar. 3 They shall offer thereof the rump and the fat that covereth the entrails, 4 the two little kidneys and the fat which is by the flanks and the caul of the liver with the little kidneys. 5 And the priest shall burn them upon the altar; it is the burnt sacrifice of the Lord for a trespass.

6 "'Every male of the priestly race shall eat this flesh in a holy place because it is most holy. 7 As the sacrifice for sin is offered, so is also that for a trespass. The same shall be the law of both these sacrifices; it shall belong to the priest that offereth it. 8 The priest that offereth the victim of holocaust shall have the skin thereof. 9 And every sacrifice of flour that is baked in the oven and whatsoever is dressed on the gridiron or in the frying pan shall be the priest's that offereth it; 10 whether they be tempered with oil or dry, all the sons of Aaron shall have one as much as another.

11 "'This is the law of the sacrifice of peace offerings that is offered to the Lord. 12 If the oblation be for thanksgiving, they shall offer loaves without leaven tempered with oil and unleavened wafers anointed with oil and *fine* flour fried and cakes tempered *and mingled with* oil, 13 moreover, loaves of leavened bread with the sacrifice of thanks which is offered for peace offerings 14 of which one shall be offered to the Lord for firstfruits and shall be the priest's that shall pour out the blood of the victim. 15 And the flesh of it shall be eaten the same day, neither shall any of it remain until the morning.

16 "'If any man by vow or of his own accord offer a sacrifice, it shall in like manner be eaten the same day, and if any of it remain until the morrow, it is lawful to eat it, 17 but whatsoever *shall be found on the third day shall be consumed with*

ignis absumet. 18 Si quis de carnibus victimae pacificorum die tertio comederit, irrita fiet oblatio, nec proderit offerenti. Quin potius, quaecumque anima tali se edulio contaminarit praevaricationis rea erit.

19 "'Caro quae aliquid tetigerit inmundum non comedetur, sed conburetur igni. Qui fuerit mundus vescetur ex ea. 20 Anima polluta quae ederit de carnibus hostiae pacificorum quae oblata est Domino, peribit de populis suis. 21 Et quae tetigerit inmunditiam hominis vel iumenti sive omnis rei quae polluere potest et comederit de huiuscemodi carnibus interibit de populis suis.'"

22 Locutusque est Dominus ad Mosen, dicens, 23 "Loquere filiis Israhel, 'Adipem bovis et ovis et caprae non comedetis. 24 Adipem cadaveris morticini et eius animalis quod a bestia captum est, habebitis in usus varios. 25 Si quis adipem qui offerri debet in incensum Domini comederit, peribit de populo suo. 26 Sanguinem quoque omnis animalis non sumetis in cibo, tam de avibus quam de pecoribus. 27 Omnis anima quae ederit sanguinem peribit de populis suis.'"

28 Locutusque est Dominus ad Mosen, dicens, 29 "Loquere filiis Israhel, dicens, 'Qui offert victimam pacificorum Domino, offerat simul et sacrificium, id est, libamenta eius. 30 Tenebit manibus adipem hostiae et pectusculum, cumque ambo oblata Domino consecrarit, tradet sacerdoti 31 qui adolebit adipem super altare, pectusculum autem erit Aaron et filiorum eius. 32 Armus quoque dexter de pacificorum

fire. 18 If any man eat of the flesh of the victim of peace offerings on the third day, the oblation shall be of no effect, neither shall it profit the offerer. Yea rather, whatsoever soul shall defile itself with such meat shall be guilty of transgression.

19 "'The flesh that hath touched any unclean thing shall not be eaten, but shall be burnt with fire. He that is clean shall eat of it. 20 If any one that is defiled shall eat of the flesh of the sacrifice of peace offerings which is offered to the Lord, he shall be cut off from his people. 21 And he that hath touched the uncleanness of man or of beast or of any thing that can defile and shall eat of such kind of flesh shall be cut off from his people.'"

22 And the Lord spoke to Moses, saying, 23 "Say to the children of Israel, 'The fat of a sheep and of an ox and of a goat you shall not eat. 24 The fat of a carcass that hath died of itself and of a beast that was caught by another beast, you shall have for divers uses. 25 If any man eat the fat that should be offered for the burnt sacrifice of the Lord, he shall perish out of his people. 26 Moreover, you shall not eat the blood of any creature whatsoever, whether of birds or beasts. 27 Every one that eateth blood shall perish from among the people.'"

28 And the Lord spoke to Moses, saying, 29 "Speak to the children of Israel, saying, 'He that offereth a victim of peace offerings to the Lord, let him offer therewith a sacrifice also, that is, the libations thereof. 30 He shall hold in his hands the fat of the victim and the breast, and when he hath offered and consecrated both to the Lord, he shall deliver them to the priest 31 who shall burn the fat upon the altar, but the breast shall be Aaron's and his sons'. 32 The right

hostiis cedet in primitias sacerdotis. 33 Qui obtulerit sanguinem et adipem filiorum Aaron, ipse habebit et armum dextrum in portione sua, 34 pectusculum enim elevationis et armum separationis tuli a filiis Israhel de hostiis eorum pacificis et dedi Aaron, sacerdoti, ac filiis eius lege perpetua, ab omni populo Israhel.'"

35 Haec est unctio Aaron et filiorum eius in caerimoniis Domini die qua obtulit eos Moses ut sacerdotio fungerentur 36 et quae praecepit dari eis Dominus a filiis Israhel religione perpetua in generationibus suis. 37 Ista est lex holocausti et sacrificii pro peccato atque delicto et pro consecratione et pacificorum victimis 38 quam constituit Dominus Mosi in Monte Sinai quando mandavit filiis Israhel ut offerrent oblationes suas Domino in deserto Sinai.

Caput 8

Locutusque est Dominus ad Mosen, dicens, 2 "Tolle Aaron cum filiis suis, vestes eorum et unctionis oleum, vitulum pro peccato, duos arietes, canistrum cum azymis, 3 et

shoulder also of the victims of peace offerings shall fall *to the priest for firstfruits*. 33 He among the sons of Aaron that offereth the blood and the fat, he shall have the right shoulder also for his portion, 34 for the breast *that is elevated* and the shoulder that is separated I have taken of the children of Israel from off their victims of peace offerings and have given them to Aaron, the priest, and to his sons by a law for ever, from all the people of Israel.'"

35 This is the anointing of Aaron and his sons in the ceremonies of the Lord in the day when Moses offered them that they might do the office of priesthood 36 and the things that the Lord commanded to be given them by the children of Israel by a perpetual observance in their generations. 37 This is the law of holocaust and of the sacrifice for sin and for trespass and for consecration and the victims of peace offerings 38 which the Lord appointed to Moses in Mount Sinai when he commanded the children of Israel that they should offer their oblations to the Lord in the desert of Sinai.

Chapter 8

Moses consecrateth Aaron and his sons.

And the Lord spoke to Moses, saying, 2 "Take Aaron with his sons, their vestments and the oil of unction, a calf for sin, two rams, a basket with unleavened bread, 3 and thou

congregabis omnem coetum ad ostium tabernaculi." 4 Fecitque Moses ut Dominus imperarat. Congregataque omni
turba ante fores tabernaculi, 5 ait, "Iste est sermo quem iussit Dominus fieri."

6 Statimque obtulit Aaron et filios eius, cumque lavisset
eos, 7 vestivit pontificem subucula linea, accingens eum balteo et induens eum tunica hyacinthina, et desuper umerale
inposuit, 8 quod adstringens cingulo, aptavit rationali in quo
erat Doctrina et Veritas. 9 Cidarim quoque texit caput, et
super eam contra frontem posuit lamminam auream conse-
cratam in sanctificationem, sicut praeceperat ei Dominus.
10 Tulit et unctionis oleum quo levit tabernaculum cum omni
supellectili sua.

11 Cumque sanctificans aspersisset altare septem vicibus,
unxit illud et omnia vasa eius, labrumque cum basi sua sanctificavit oleo. 12 Quod fundens super caput Aaron, unxit
eum et consecravit. 13 Filios quoque eius oblatos vestivit tunicis lineis et cinxit balteis inposuitque mitras, ut iusserat
Dominus. 14 Obtulit et vitulum pro peccato, cumque super
caput eius posuissent Aaron et filii eius manus suas, 15 immolavit eum hauriens sanguinem, et, tincto digito, tetigit
cornua altaris per gyrum, quo expiato et sanctificato, fudit
reliquum sanguinem ad fundamenta eius. 16 Adipem autem
qui erat super vitalia et reticulum iecoris duosque renunculos cum arvinulis suis adolevit super altare. 17 Vitulum cum

shalt gather together all the congregation to the door of the tabernacle." 4 And Moses did as the Lord had commanded. And all the multitude being gathered together before the door of the tabernacle, 5 he said, "This is the word that the Lord hath commanded to be done."

6 And immediately he offered Aaron and his sons, and when he had washed them, 7 he vested the high priest with the strait linen garment, girding him with the girdle and putting on him the violet tunick, and over it he put the ephod, 8 and binding it with the girdle, he fitted it to the rational on which was Doctrine and Truth. 9 He put also the mitre upon his head, and upon the mitre over the forehead he put the plate of gold consecrated with sanctification, as the Lord had commanded him. 10 He took also the oil of unction with which he anointed the tabernacle with all the furniture thereof.

11 And when he had sanctified and sprinkled the altar seven times, he anointed it and all the vessels thereof, and the laver with the foot thereof he sanctified with the oil. 12 And he poured it upon Aaron's head, and he anointed and consecrated him. 13 And after he had offered his sons, he vested them with linen tunicks and girded them with girdles and put mitres on them, as the Lord had commanded. 14 He offered also the calf for sin, and when Aaron and his sons had put their hands upon the head thereof, 15 he immolated it and took the blood, and, dipping his finger in it, he touched the horns of the altar round about, which being expiated and sanctified, he poured the rest of the blood at the bottom thereof. 16 But the fat that was upon the entrails and the caul of the liver and the two little kidneys with their fat he burnt upon the altar. 17 And the calf with the skin and the

pelle et carnibus et fimo cremans extra castra, sicut praeceperat Dominus.

18 Obtulit et arietem in holocaustum, super cuius caput cum inposuissent Aaron et filii eius manus suas, 19 immolavit eum et fudit sanguinem eius per altaris circuitum. 20 Ipsumque arietem in frusta concidens caput eius et artus et adipem adolevit igni, 21 lotis prius intestinis et pedibus. Totumque simul arietem incendit super altare eo quod esset holocaustum suavissimi odoris Domino, sicut praeceperat ei.

22 Obtulit et arietem secundum in consecrationem sacerdotum, posueruntque super caput illius Aaron et filii eius manus suas, 23 quem cum immolasset Moses, sumens de sanguine eius tetigit extremum auriculae dextrae Aaron et pollicem manus eius dextrae similiter et pedis. 24 Obtulit et filios Aaron, cumque de sanguine arietis immolati tetigisset extremum auriculae singulorum dextrae et pollices manus ac pedis dextri, reliquum fudit super altare per circuitum. 25 Adipem vero et caudam omnemque pinguedinem quae operit intestina reticulumque iecoris et duos renes cum adipibus suis et armo dextro separavit.

26 Tollens autem de canistro azymorum quod erat coram Domino panem absque fermento et collyridam conspersam oleo laganumque posuit super adipes et armum dextrum, 27 tradens simul omnia Aaron et filiis eius, qui, postquam levaverunt ea coram Domino, 28 rursum suscepta de manibus eorum adolevit super altare holocausti eo quod consecrationis esset oblatio in odorem suavitatis sacrificii Domino. 29 Tulitque pectusculum, elevans illud coram Domino, de

flesh and the dung he burnt without the camp, as the Lord had commanded.

18 He offered also a ram for a holocaust, and when Aaron and his sons had put their hands upon its head, 19 he immolated it and poured the blood thereof round about *upon* the altar. 20 And cutting the ram into pieces the head thereof and the joints and the fat he burnt in the fire, 21 having first washed the entrails and the feet. And the whole ram together he burnt upon the altar because it was a holocaust of most sweet odour to the Lord, as he had commanded him.

22 He offered also the second ram in the consecration of priests, and Aaron and his sons put their hands upon the head thereof, 23 and when Moses had immolated it, he took of the blood thereof and touched the tip of Aaron's right ear and the thumb of his right hand and in like manner also the great toe of his right foot. 24 He offered also the sons of Aaron, and when with the blood of the ram that was immolated he had touched the tip of the right ear of every one of them and the thumbs of their right hands and the great toes of their right feet, the rest he poured on the altar round about. 25 But the fat and the rump and all the fat that covereth the entrails and the caul of the liver and the two kidneys with their fat and with the right shoulder he separated.

26 And taking out of the basket of unleavened bread which was before the Lord a loaf without leaven and a cake tempered with oil and a wafer he put them upon the fat and the right shoulder, 27 delivering all to Aaron and to his sons, who, having lifted them up before the Lord, 28 took them again from their hands and burnt them upon the altar of holocaust because it was the oblation of consecration for a sweet odour of sacrifice to the Lord. 29 And he took of the

ariete consecrationis in partem suam, sicut praeceperat ei Dominus.

30 Adsumensque unguentum et sanguinem qui erat in altari, aspersit super Aaron et vestimenta eius et super filios illius ac vestes eorum. 31 Cumque sanctificasset eos in vestitu suo, praecepit eis, dicens, "Coquite carnes ante fores tabernaculi, et ibi comedite eas. Panes quoque consecrationis edite qui positi sunt in canistro, sicut praecepit mihi Dominus, dicens, 'Aaron et filii eius comedent eos.' 32 Quicquid autem reliquum fuerit de carne et panibus ignis absumet. 33 De ostio quoque tabernaculi non exibitis septem diebus, usque ad diem quo conplebitur tempus consecrationis vestrae, septem enim diebus finitur consecratio, 34 sicut et inpraesentiarum factum est, ut ritus sacrificii conpleretur. 35 die ac nocte manebitis in tabernaculo observantes custodias Domini ne moriamini, sic enim mihi praeceptum est." 36 Feceruntque Aaron et filii eius cuncta quae locutus est Dominus per manum Mosi.

ram of consecration the breast for his portion, elevating it before the Lord, as the Lord had commanded him.

30 And, taking the ointment and the blood that was upon the altar, he sprinkled Aaron and his vestments and his sons and their vestments with it. 31 And when he had sanctified them in their vestments, he commanded them, saying, "Boil the flesh before the door of the tabernacle, and there eat it. Eat ye also the loaves of consecration that are laid in the basket, as the Lord commanded me, saying, 'Aaron and his sons shall eat them.' 32 And whatsoever shall be left of the flesh and the loaves shall be consumed with fire. 33 And you shall not go out of the door of the tabernacle for seven days, until the day wherein the time of your consecration shall be expired, for in seven days the consecration is finished, 34 as at this present it hath been done, that the rite of the sacrifice might be accomplished. 35 Day and night shall you remain in the tabernacle observing the watches of the Lord lest you die, for so it hath been commanded me." 36 And Aaron and his sons did all things which the Lord spoke by the hand of Moses.

Caput 9

Facto autem octavo die, vocavit Moses Aaron et filios eius ac maiores natu Israhel dixitque ad Aaron, 2 "Tolle de armento vitulum pro peccato et arietem in holocaustum, utrumque inmaculatos, et offer illos coram Domino. 3 Et ad filios Israhel loqueris, 'Tollite hircum pro peccato et vitulum atque agnum, anniculos et sine macula, in holocaustum, 4 bovem et arietem pro pacificis, et immolate eos coram Domino, in sacrificio singulorum similam oleo conspersam offerentes, hodie enim Dominus apparebit vobis.'" 5 Tulerunt ergo cuncta quae iusserat Moses ad ostium tabernaculi ubi cum omnis staret multitudo 6 ait Moses, "Iste est sermo quem praecepit Dominus. Facite, et apparebit vobis gloria eius."

7 Et dixit ad Aaron, "Accede ad altare, et immola pro peccato tuo. Offer holocaustum et deprecare pro te et pro populo, cumque mactaveris hostiam populi, ora pro eo sicut praecepit Dominus." 8 Statimque Aaron, accedens ad altare, immolavit vitulum pro peccato suo, 9 cuius sanguinem obtulerunt ei filii sui, in quo tinguens digitum tetigit cornua altaris et fudit residuum ad basim eius. 10 Adipemque et re-

Chapter 9

Aaron offereth sacrifice for himself and the people. Fire
cometh from the Lord upon the altar.

And when the eighth day was come, Moses called Aaron
and his sons and the ancients of Israel and said to Aaron,
2 "Take of the herd a calf for sin and a ram for a holocaust,
both without blemish, and offer them before the Lord.
3 And to the children of Israel thou shalt say, 'Take ye a he-
goat for sin and a calf and a lamb, both of a year old and
without blemish, for a holocaust, 4 also a bullock and a ram
for peace offerings, and immolate them before the Lord,
offering for the sacrifice of every one of them flour tempered with oil, for today the Lord will appear to you.'" 5 They
brought therefore all things that Moses had commanded
before the door of the tabernacle where when all the multitude stood 6 Moses said, "This is the word which the Lord
hath commanded. Do it, and his glory will appear to you."

7 And he said to Aaron, "Approach to the altar, and offer
sacrifice for thy sin. Offer the holocaust and pray for thyself
and for the people, and when thou hast slain the people's
victim, pray for them as the Lord hath commanded." 8 And
forthwith Aaron, approaching to the altar, immolated the
calf for his sin, 9 and his sons brought him the blood of it,
and he dipped his finger therein and touched the horns of
the altar and poured the rest at the foot thereof. 10 And the

nunculos ac reticulum iecoris, quae sunt pro peccato, adolevit super altare sicut praeceperat Dominus Mosi, 11 carnes vero et pellem eius extra castra conbusit igni. 12 Immolavit et holocausti victimam, obtuleruntque ei filii sui sanguinem eius, quem fudit per altaris circuitum. 13 Ipsam etiam hostiam in frusta concisam cum capite et membris singulis obtulerunt, quae omnia super altare cremavit igni, 14 lotis prius aqua intestinis et pedibus. 15 Et pro peccato populi offerens, mactavit hircum, expiatoque altari 16 fecit holocaustum, 17 addens in sacrificio libamenta quae pariter offeruntur et adolens ea super altare, absque caerimoniis holocausti matutini. 18 Immolavit et bovem atque arietem, hostias pacificas populi, obtuleruntque ei filii sui sanguinem, quem fudit super altare in circuitu. 19 Adipem autem bovis et caudam arietis renunculosque cum adipibus suis et reticulum iecoris 20 posuerunt super pectora. Cumque cremati essent adipes super altare 21 pectora eorum et armos dextros separavit Aaron, elevans coram Domino, sicut praeceperat Moses. 22 Et tendens manum ad populum, benedixit eis. Sicque conpletis hostiis pro peccato et holocaustis et pacificis, descendit.

23 Ingressi autem Moses et Aaron Tabernaculum Testimonii et deinceps egressi benedixerunt populo. Apparuitque gloria Domini omni multitudini, 24 et ecce: egressus ignis a Domino devoravit holocaustum et adipes qui erant super altare, quod cum vidissent turbae, laudaverunt Dominum, ruentes in facies suas.

fat and the little kidneys and the caul of the liver, which are for sin, he burnt upon the altar as the Lord had commanded Moses, 11 but the flesh and skin thereof he burnt with fire without the camp. 12 He immolated also the victim of holocaust, and his sons brought him the blood thereof, which he poured round about on the altar. 13 And the victim being cut into pieces, they brought to him the head and all the members, all which he burnt with fire upon the altar, 14 having first washed the entrails and the feet with water. 15 Then offering for the sin of the people, he slew the he-goat, and expiating the altar 16 he offered the holocaust, 17 adding in the sacrifice the libations which are offered withal and burning them upon the altar, besides the ceremonies of the morning holocaust. 18 He immolated also the bullock and the ram, the peace offerings of the people, and his sons brought him the blood, which he poured upon the altar round about. 19 The fat also of the bullock and the rump of the ram and the *two* little kidneys with their fat and the caul of the liver 20 they put upon the breasts. And after the fat was burnt upon the altar 21 Aaron separated their breasts and the right shoulders, elevating them before the Lord, as Moses had commanded. 22 And stretching forth his *hands* to the people, he blessed them. And so the victims for sin and the holocausts and the peace offerings being finished, he came down.

23 And Moses and Aaron went into the Tabernacle of the Testimony and afterwards came forth and blessed the people. And the glory of the Lord appeared to all the multitude, 24 and behold: a fire coming forth from the Lord devoured the holocaust and the fat that was upon the altar, which when the multitude saw, they praised the Lord, falling on their faces.

Caput 10

Arreptisque Nadab et Abiu, filii Aaron, turibulis, posuerunt ignem et incensum desuper, offerentes coram Domino ignem alienum quod eis praeceptum non erat. 2 Egressusque ignis a Domino devoravit eos, et mortui sunt coram Domino. 3 Dixitque Moses ad Aaron, "Hoc est quod locutus est Dominus: 'Sanctificabor in his qui adpropinquant mihi, et in conspectu omnis populi glorificabor.'" Quod audiens tacuit Aaron. 4 Vocatis autem Moses Misahel et Elsaphan, filios Ozihel, patrui Aaron, ait ad eos, "Ite, et tollite fratres vestros de conspectu sanctuarii, et asportate extra castra." 5 Confestimque pergentes tulerunt eos sicut iacebant, vestitos lineis tunicis, et eiecerunt foras, ut sibi fuerat imperatum.

6 Locutusque est Moses ad Aaron et ad Eleazar atque Ithamar, filios eius, "Capita vestra nolite nudare, et vestimenta nolite scindere, ne forte moriamini et super omnem coetum oriatur indignatio. Fratres vestri et omnis domus Israhel plangant incendium quod Dominus suscitavit, 7 vos autem non egrediemini fores tabernaculi, alioquin peribitis, oleum quippe sanctae unctionis est super vos." Qui fecerunt omnia iuxta praeceptum Mosi.

Chapter 10

Nadab and Abihu for offering strange fire are burnt by fire.
Priests are forbidden to drink wine when they enter into the
tabernacle. The law of eating the holy things.

Ａnd Nadab and Abihu, the sons of Aaron, taking their
censers, put fire therein and incense on it, offering before
the Lord strange fire which was not commanded them.
2 And fire coming out from the Lord destroyed them, and
they died before the Lord. 3 And Moses said to Aaron, "This
is what the Lord hath spoken: 'I will be sanctified in them
that approach to me, and I will be glorified in the sight of all
the people.'" And when Aaron heard this, he held his peace.
4 And Moses called Mishael and Elzaphan, the sons of Uzziel, the uncle of Aaron, and said to them, "Go, and take away
your brethren from before the sanctuary, and carry them
without the camp." 5 And they went forthwith and took
them as they lay, vested with linen tunicks, and cast them
forth, as had been commanded them.

6 And Moses said to Aaron and to Eleazar and Ithamar,
his sons, "Uncover not your heads, and rend not your garments, lest perhaps you die and indignation come upon all
the congregation. Let your brethren and all the house of Israel bewail the burning which the Lord has kindled, 7 but
you shall not go out of the door of the tabernacle, otherwise
you shall perish, for the oil of the holy unction is on you."
And they did all things according to the precept of Moses.

8 Dixit quoque Dominus ad Aaron, 9 "Vinum et omne quod inebriare potest non bibetis, tu et filii tui, quando intratis in Tabernaculum Testimonii, ne moriamini, quia praeceptum est sempiternum in generationes vestras, 10 et ut habeatis scientiam discernendi inter sanctum et profanum, inter pollutum et mundum, 11 doceatisque filios Israhel omnia legitima mea quae locutus est Dominus ad eos per manum Mosi."

12 Locutusque est Moses ad Aaron et ad Eleazar atque Ithamar, filios eius qui residui erant: "Tollite sacrificium quod remansit de oblatione Domini, et comedite illud absque fermento iuxta altare quia sanctum sanctorum est. 13 Comedetis autem in loco sancto quod datum est tibi et filiis tuis de oblationibus Domini, sicut praeceptum est mihi. 14 Pectusculum quoque quod oblatum est et armum qui separatus est edetis in loco mundissimo, tu et filii tui ac filiae tuae tecum, tibi enim ac liberis tuis reposita sunt de hostiis salutaribus filiorum Israhel 15 eo quod armum et pectus et adipes qui cremantur in altari elevaverint coram Domino et pertineant ad te et ad filios tuos lege perpetua, sicut praecepit Dominus."

16 Inter haec, hircum qui oblatus fuerat pro peccato cum quaereret Moses exustum repperit, iratusque contra Eleazar et Ithamar, filios Aaron qui remanserant, ait, 17 "Cur non comedistis hostiam pro peccato in loco sancto, quae sancta sanctorum est et data vobis ut portetis iniquitatem multitudinis et rogetis pro ea in conspectu Domini, 18 praesertim cum de sanguine illius non sit inlatum intra sancta, et come-

8 The Lord also said to Aaron, 9 "You shall not drink wine nor any thing that may make drunk, thou nor thy sons, when you enter into the Tabernacle of the Testimony, lest you die, because it is an everlasting precept through your generations, 10 and that you may have knowledge to discern between holy and unholy, between unclean and clean, 11 and may teach the children of Israel all my ordinances which the Lord hath spoken to them by the hand of Moses."

12 And Moses spoke to Aaron and to Eleazar and Ithamar, his sons that were left: "Take the sacrifice that is remaining of the oblation of the Lord, and eat it without leaven beside the altar because it is holy of holies. 13 And you shall eat it in a holy place which is given to thee and thy sons of the oblations of the Lord, as it hath been commanded me. 14 The breast also that is offered and the shoulder that is separated you shall eat in a most clean place, thou and thy sons and thy daughters with thee, for they are set aside for thee and thy children of the victims of peace offerings of the children of Israel 15 because they have elevated before the Lord the shoulder and the breast and the fat that is burnt on the altar and they belong to thee and to thy sons by a perpetual law, as the Lord hath commanded."

16 *While these things were a-doing*, when Moses sought for the buck-goat that had been offered for sin he found it burnt, and being angry with Eleazar and Ithamar, the sons of Aaron that were left, he said, 17 "Why did you not eat in the holy place the sacrifice for sin, which is most holy and given to you that you may bear the iniquity of the people and may pray for them in the sight of the Lord, 18 especially whereas none of the blood thereof hath been carried within

dere eam debueritis in sanctuario sicut praeceptum est mihi?"

19 Respondit Aaron, "Oblata est hodie victima pro peccato et holocaustum coram Domino, mihi autem accidit quod vides. Quomodo potui comedere eam aut placere Domino in caerimoniis, mente lugubri?" 20 Quod cum audisset Moses, recepit satisfactionem.

Caput 11

Locutusque est Dominus ad Mosen et Aaron, dicens, 2 "Dicite filiis Israhel, 'Haec sunt animalia quae comedere debetis de cunctis animantibus terrae. 3 Omne quod habet divisam ungulam et ruminat in pecoribus comedetis. 4 Quicquid autem ruminat quidem et habet ungulam sed non dividit eam, sicut camelus et cetera, non comedetis illud, et inter inmunda reputabitis. 5 Chyrogryllius, qui ruminat ungulamque non dividit, inmundus est, 6 lepus quoque, nam et ipse ruminat sed ungulam non dividit, 7 et sus, qui, cum ungulam dividat, non ruminat. 8 Horum carnibus non vescemini, nec cadavera contingetis quia inmunda sunt vobis.

the holy places, and you ought to have eaten it in the sanctuary as was commanded me?"

19 Aaron answered, "This day hath been offered the victim for sin and the holocaust before the Lord, and to me what thou seest has happened. How could I eat it or please the Lord in the ceremonies, having a sorrowful heart?" 20 Which when Moses had heard, he was satisfied.

Chapter 11

The distinction of clean and unclean animals.

And the Lord spoke to Moses and Aaron, saying, 2 "Say to the children of Israel, 'These are the animals which you are to eat of all the living things of the earth. 3 Whatsoever hath the hoof divided and cheweth the cud among the beasts you shall eat. 4 But whatsoever cheweth indeed the cud and hath a hoof but divideth it not, as the camel and others, that you shall not eat, but shall reckon it among the unclean. 5 The cherogrillus, which cheweth the cud but divideth not the hoof, is unclean, 6 the hare also, for that too cheweth the cud but divideth not the hoof, 7 and the swine, which, though it divideth the hoof, cheweth not the cud. 8 The flesh of these you shall not eat, nor shall you touch their carcasses because they are unclean to you.

9 "'Haec sunt quae gignuntur in aquis et vesci licitum est: omne quod habet pinnulas et squamas, tam in mari quam in fluminibus et stagnis, comedetis. 10 Quicquid autem pinnulas et squamas non habet eorum quae in aquis moventur et vivunt abominabile vobis 11 et execrandum erit. Carnes eorum non comedetis, et morticina vitabitis. 12 Cuncta quae non habent pinnulas et squamas in aquis polluta erunt.

13 "'Haec sunt quae de avibus comedere non debetis et vitanda sunt vobis: aquilam et grypem et alietum 14 et milvum ac vulturem iuxta genus suum 15 et omne corvini generis in similitudinem suam, 16 strutionem et noctuam et larum et accipitrem iuxta genus suum, 17 bubonem et mergulum et ibin 18 et cycnum et onocrotalum et porphirionem, 19 erodionem et charadrion iuxta genus suum, opupam quoque et vespertilionem.

20 "'Omne de volucribus quod graditur super quattuor pedes abominabile erit vobis. 21 Quicquid autem ambulat quidem super quattuor pedes sed habet longiora retro crura per quae salit super terram, 22 comedere debetis, ut est brucus in genere suo et attacus atque ophiomachus ac lucusta, singula iuxta genus suum. 23 Quicquid autem ex volucribus quattuor tantum habet pedes execrabile erit vobis, 24 et quicumque morticina eorum tetigerit polluetur et erit inmundus usque ad vesperum, 25 et si necesse fuerit ut portet quippiam horum mortuum, lavabit vestimenta sua et inmundus erit usque ad solis occasum.

26 "'Omne animal quod habet quidem ungulam sed non dividit eam nec ruminat inmundum erit, et quicquid tetige-

9 "'These are the things that breed in the waters and which it is lawful to eat: all that hath fins and scales, as well in the sea as in the rivers and the pools, you shall eat. 10 But whatsoever hath not fins and scales of those things that move and live in the waters shall be an abomination to you 11 and detestable. Their flesh you shall not eat, and their carcasses you shall avoid. 12 All that have not fins and scales in the waters shall be unclean.

13 "'Of birds these are they which you must not eat and which are to be avoided by you: the eagle and the griffon and the osprey 14 and the kite and the vulture according to their kind 15 and all that is of the raven kind according to their likeness, 16 the ostrich and the owl and the larus and the hawk according to its kind, 17 the screech owl and the cormorant and the ibis 18 and the swan and the bittern and the porphyrion, 19 the heron and the charadrion according to its kind, the houp also and the bat.

20 "'Of things that fly whatsoever goeth upon four feet shall be abominable to you. 21 But whatsoever walketh upon four feet but hath the legs behind longer wherewith it hoppeth upon the earth, 22 that you shall eat, as the bruchus in its kind, the attacus and ophiomachus and the locust, every one according to their kind. 23 But of flying things whatsoever hath four feet only shall be an abomination to you, 24 and whosoever shall touch the carcasses of them shall be defiled and shall be unclean until the evening, 25 and if it be necessary that he carry any of these things when they are dead, he shall wash his clothes and shall be unclean until the sun set.

26 "'Every beast that hath a hoof but divideth it not nor cheweth the cud shall be unclean, and *he that* toucheth it

rit illud contaminabitur. 27 Quod ambulat super manus ex cunctis animantibus quae incedunt quadrupedia inmundum erit. Qui tetigerit morticina eorum polluetur usque ad vesperum. 28 Et qui portaverit huiuscemodi cadavera lavabit vestimenta sua et inmundus erit usque ad vesperum quia omnia haec inmunda sunt vobis. 29 Haec quoque inter polluta reputabuntur de his quae moventur in terra: mustela et mus et corcodillus, singula iuxta genus suum, 30 migale et cameleon et stelio ac lacerta et talpa. 31 Omnia haec inmunda sunt. Qui tetigerit morticina eorum inmundus erit usque ad vesperum. 32 Et super quod ceciderit quicquam de morticinis eorum, polluetur, tam vas ligneum et vestimentum quam pelles et cilicia et in quocumque fit opus. Tinguentur aqua et polluta erunt usque ad vesperum, et sic postea mundabuntur. 33 Vas autem fictile in quod horum quicquam intro ceciderit polluetur, et idcirco frangendum est. 34 Omnis cibus quem comedetis, si fusa fuerit super eum aqua, inmundus erit, et omne liquens quod bibitur de universo vase inmundum erit.

35 "'Et quicquid de morticinis huiuscemodi ceciderit super illud, inmundum erit, sive clibani sive cytropodes, destruentur et inmundi erunt, 36 fontes vero et cisternae et omnis aquarum congregatio munda erit. Qui morticinum eorum tetigerit polluetur. 37 Si ceciderit super sementem, non polluet eam. 38 Sin autem quispiam aqua sementem perfuderit et postea morticinis tacta fuerit, ilico polluetur. 39 Si mortuum fuerit animal quod licet vobis comedere, qui

shall be defiled. 27 That which walketh upon hands of all animals which go on all four shall be unclean. He that shall touch their carcasses shall be defiled until evening. 28 And he that shall carry such carcasses shall wash his clothes and shall be unclean until evening because all these things are unclean to you. 29 These also shall be reckoned among unclean things of all that move upon the earth: the weasel and the mouse and the crocodile, every one according to their kind, 30 the shrew and the chameleon and the stello and the lizard and the mole. 31 All these are unclean. He that toucheth their carcasses shall be unclean until the evening. 32 And upon what thing soever any of their carcasses shall fall, it shall be defiled, whether it be a vessel of wood or a garment or skins or haircloths or any thing in which work is done. They shall be dipped in water and shall be unclean until the evening, and so afterwards shall be clean. 33 But an earthen vessel into which any of these shall fall shall be defiled, and therefore is to be broken. 34 Any meat which you *eat,* if water from such a vessel be poured upon it, shall be unclean, and every liquor that is drunk out of any such vessel shall be unclean.

35 "And upon whatsoever thing any of these dead beasts shall fall, it shall be unclean, whether it be *oven* or pots with feet, they shall be destroyed and shall be unclean, 36 but fountains and cisterns and all gatherings together of waters shall be clean. He that toucheth their carcasses shall be defiled. 37 If it fall upon seed corn, it shall not defile it. 38 But if any man pour water upon the seed and afterwards it be touched by the carcasses, it shall be forthwith defiled. 39 If any beast die of which it is lawful for you to eat, he that toucheth the carcass thereof shall be unclean until the eve-

cadaver eius tetigerit inmundus erit usque ad vesperum, 40 et qui comederit ex eo quippiam sive portaverit lavabit vestimenta sua et inmundus erit usque ad vesperum.

41 "'Omne quod reptat super terram abominabile erit, nec adsumetur in cibum. 42 Quicquid super pectus quadrupes graditur et multos habet pedes sive per humum trahitur non comedetis quia abominabile est. 43 Nolite contaminare animas vestras nec tangatis quicquam eorum ne inmundi sitis, 44 ego enim sum Dominus, Deus vester: sancti estote quoniam ego sanctus sum. Ne polluatis animas vestras in omni reptili quod movetur super terram, 45 ego enim sum Dominus qui eduxi vos de terra Aegypti ut essem vobis in Deum. Sancti eritis, quia ego sanctus sum.

46 "'Ista est lex animantium et volucrum et omnis animae viventis quae movetur in aqua et reptat in terra 47 ut differentias noveritis mundi et inmundi et sciatis quid comedere et quid respuere debeatis.'"

Caput 12

Locutusque est Dominus ad Mosen, dicens, 2 "Loquere filiis Israhel, et dices ad eos, 'Mulier si suscepto semine pepererit masculum, inmunda erit septem diebus iuxta dies

ning, 40 and he that eateth or carrieth any thing thereof shall wash his clothes and shall be unclean until the evening.

41 "'All that creepeth upon the earth shall be abominable, neither shall it be taken for meat. 42 Whatsoever goeth upon the breast on four feet or hath many feet or traileth on the earth you shall not eat because it is abominable. 43 Do not defile your souls nor touch aught thereof lest you be unclean, 44 for I am the Lord, your God: be holy because I am holy. Defile not your souls by any creeping thing that moveth upon the earth, 45 for I am the Lord who brought you out of the land of Egypt that I might be your God. You shall be holy because I am holy.

46 "'This is the law of beasts and fowls and of every living creature that moveth in the waters and creepeth on the earth 47 that you may know the differences of the clean and unclean and know what you ought to eat and what to refuse.'"

Chapter 12

The purification of women after childbirth.

And the Lord spoke to Moses, saying, 2 "Speak to the children of Israel, and thou shalt say to them, 'If a woman having received seed shall bear a man-child, she shall be unclean seven days according to the days of the separation of

separationis menstruae. 3 Et die octavo circumcidetur infantulus, 4 ipsa vero triginta tribus diebus manebit in sanguine purificationis suae. Omne sanctum non tanget, nec ingredietur in sanctuarium donec impleantur dies purificationis eius. 5 Sin autem feminam pepererit, inmunda erit duabus ebdomadibus iuxta ritum fluxus menstrui, et sexaginta sex diebus manebit in sanguine purificationis suae.

6 "'Cumque expleti fuerint dies purificationis eius pro filio sive pro filia, deferet agnum anniculum in holocaustum et pullum columbae sive turturem pro peccato ad ostium Tabernaculi Testimonii et tradet sacerdoti, 7 qui offeret illa coram Domino et orabit pro ea, et sic mundabitur a profluvio sanguinis sui. Ista est lex parientis masculum aut feminam. 8 Quod si non invenerit manus eius nec potuerit offerre agnum, sumet duos turtures vel duos pullos columbae, unum in holocaustum et alterum pro peccato, orabitque pro ea sacerdos, et sic mundabitur.'"

Caput 13

Locutusque est Dominus ad Mosen et Aaron, dicens, 2 "Homo in cuius carne et cute ortus fuerit diversus color sive pustula aut quasi lucens quippiam, id est, plaga leprae,

her flowers. 3 And on the eighth day the infant shall be circumcised, 4 but she shall remain three and thirty days in the blood of her purification. She shall touch no holy thing, neither shall she enter into the sanctuary until the days of her purification be fulfilled. 5 But if she shall bear a maid-child, she shall be unclean two weeks according to the custom of her monthly courses, and she shall remain in the blood of her purification sixty-six days.

6 "And when the days of her purification are expired for a son or for a daughter, she shall bring to the door of the Tabernacle of the Testimony a lamb of a year old for a holocaust and a young pigeon or a turtle for sin and shall deliver them to the priest, 7 who shall offer them before the Lord and shall pray for her, and so she shall be cleansed from the issue of her blood. This is the law for her that beareth a man-child or a maid-child. 8 And if her hand find not *sufficiency* and she is not able to offer a lamb, she shall take two turtles or two young pigeons, one for a holocaust and another for sin, and the priest shall pray for her, and so she shall be cleansed.'"

Chapter 13

The law concerning leprosy in men and in garments.

And the Lord spoke to Moses and Aaron, saying, 2 "The man in whose skin or flesh shalt arise a different colour or a blister or as it were something shining, that is, the stroke of

adducetur ad Aaron, sacerdotem, vel ad unum quemlibet filiorum eius. 3 Qui cum viderit lepram in cute et pilos in album mutatos colorem ipsamque speciem leprae humiliorem cute et carne reliqua, plaga leprae est, et ad arbitrium eius separabitur. 4 Sin autem lucens candor fuerit in cute nec humilior carne reliqua et pili coloris pristini, recludet eum sacerdos septem diebus. 5 Et considerabit die septimo, et siquidem lepra ultra non creverit nec transierit in cute priores terminos, rursum recludet eum septem diebus aliis. 6 Et die septimo contemplabitur. Si obscurior fuerit lepra et non creverit in cute, mundabit eum quia scabies est, lavabitque homo vestimenta sua et mundus erit. 7 Quod si postquam a sacerdote visus est et redditus munditiae iterum lepra creverit, adducetur ad eum 8 et inmunditiae condemnabitur.

9 "Plaga leprae si fuerit in homine, adducetur ad sacerdotem, 10 et videbit eum. Cumque color albus in cute fuerit et capillorum mutarit aspectum ipsa quoque caro viva apparuerit, 11 lepra vetustissima iudicabitur atque inolita cuti. Contaminabit itaque eum sacerdos et non recludet, quia perspicue inmunditia est. 12 Sin autem effloruerit discurrens lepra in cute et operuerit omnem carnem a capite usque ad pedes, quicquid sub aspectu oculorum cadit, 13 considerabit eum sacerdos et teneri lepra mundissima iudicabit eo quod omnis in candorem versa sit, et idcirco homo mundus erit. 14 Quando vero caro vivens in eo apparuerit, 15 tunc sacer-

the leprosy, shall be brought to Aaron, the priest, or any one of his sons. 3 And if he see the leprosy in his skin and the hair turned white and the place where the leprosy appears lower than the skin and the rest of the flesh, it is the stroke of the leprosy, and upon his judgment he shall be separated. 4 But if there be a shining whiteness in the skin and not lower than the other flesh and the hair be of the former colour, the priest shall shut him up seven days. 5 And the seventh day he shall look on him, and if the leprosy be grown no farther and hath not *spread itself* in the skin, he shall shut him up again other seven days. 6 And on the seventh day he shall look on him. If the leprosy be somewhat obscure and not spread in the skin, he shall *declare him clean* because it is *but* a scab, and the man shall wash his clothes and shall be clean. 7 But if the leprosy grow again after he was seen by the priest and re- stored to cleanness, he shall be brought to him 8 and shall be condemned of uncleanness.

9 "If the stroke of the leprosy be in a man, he shall be brought to the priest, 10 and he shall view him. And when there shall be a white colour in the skin and it shall have changed the look of the hair and the living flesh itself shall appear, 11 it shall be judged an inveterate leprosy and grown into the skin. The priest therefore shall *declare him unclean* and shall not shut him up, because he is evidently unclean. 12 But if the leprosy spring out running about in the skin and cover all the *skin* from the head to the feet, whatsoever fall- eth under the sight of the eyes, 13 the priest shall view him and shall judge that *the leprosy which he has is very clean* be- cause it is all turned into whiteness, and therefore the man shall be clean. 14 But when the live flesh shall appear in him, 15 then by the judgment of the priest he shall be defiled and

dotis iudicio polluetur et inter inmundos reputabitur, caro enim viva si lepra aspergatur inmunda est. 16 Quod si rursum versa fuerit in alborem et totum hominem operuerit, 17 considerabit eum sacerdos et mundum esse decernet.

18 "Caro autem et cutis in qua ulcus natum est et sanatum 19 et in loco ulceris cicatrix apparuerit alba sive subrufa, adducetur homo ad sacerdotem. 20 Qui cum viderit locum leprae humiliorem carne reliqua et pilos versos in candorem, contaminabit eum, plaga enim leprae orta est in ulcere. 21 Quod si pilus coloris est pristini et cicatrix subobscura et vicina carne non est humilior, recludet eum septem diebus. 22 Et siquidem creverit, adiudicabit eum leprae, 23 sin autem steterit in loco suo, ulceris est cicatrix et homo mundus erit.

24 "Caro et cutis quam ignis exuserit et sanata albam sive rufam habuerit cicatricem, 25 considerabit eam sacerdos, et ecce: versa est in alborem et locus eius reliqua cute humilior; contaminabit eum quia plaga leprae in cicatrice orta est. 26 Quod si pilorum color non fuerit inmutatus nec humilior plaga carne reliqua et ipsa leprae species fuerit subobscura, recludet eum septem diebus, 27 et die septimo contemplabitur. Si creverit in cute lepra, contaminabit eum. 28 Sin autem in loco suo candor steterit non satis clarus, plaga conbustionis est et idcirco mundabitur quia cicatrix est conbusturae.

29 "Vir sive mulier in cuius capite vel barba germinarit lepra, videbit eos sacerdos, 30 et siquidem humilior fuerit lo-

shall be reckoned among the unclean, for live flesh if it be spotted with leprosy is unclean. 16 And if again it be turned into whiteness and cover all the man, 17 the priest shall view him and shall judge him to be clean.

18 "When also there has been an ulcer in the flesh and the skin and it has been healed 19 and in the place of the ulcer there appeareth a white scar or somewhat red, the man shall be brought to the priest. 20 And when he shall see the place of the leprosy lower than the other flesh and the hair turned white, he shall declare him unclean, for the plague of leprosy is broken out in the ulcer. 21 But if the hair be of the former colour and the scar somewhat obscure and be not lower than the flesh that is near it, he shall shut him up seven days. 22 And if it spread, he shall judge him to have the leprosy, 23 but if it stay in its place, it is but the scar of an ulcer and the man shall be clean.

24 "The flesh also and skin that *hath been burnt* and after it is healed hath a white or a red scar, 25 the priest shall view it, and *if he see it turned white* and the place thereof is lower than the other skin, he shall *declare him unclean* because the evil of leprosy is broken out in the scar. 26 But if the colour of the hair be not changed nor the blemish lower than the other flesh and the appearance of the leprosy be somewhat obscure, he shall shut him up seven days, 27 and on the seventh day he shall view him. If the leprosy be grown farther in the skin, he shall *declare him unclean.* 28 But if the whiteness stay in its place and be not very clear, it is the sore of a burning, and therefore he shall be cleansed because it is only the scar of a burning.

29 "If the leprosy break out in the head or the beard of a man or woman, the priest shall see them, 30 and if the place

cus carne reliqua et capillus flavus solitoque subtilior, contaminabit eos quia lepra capitis ac barbae est. 31 Sin autem
viderit locum maculae aequalem vicinae carni et capillum
nigrum, recludet eum septem diebus, 32 et die septimo intuebitur. Si non creverit macula et capillus sui coloris est et
locus plagae carni reliquae aequalis, 33 radetur homo absque
loco maculae, et includetur septem diebus aliis. 34 Si die septimo visa fuerit stetisse plaga in loco suo nec humilior carne
reliqua, mundabit eum, lotisque vestibus suis, mundus erit.
35 Sin autem post emundationem rursus creverit macula in
cute, 36 non quaeret amplius utrum capillus in flavum colorem sit commutatus, quia aperte inmundus est. 37 Porro si
steterit macula et capilli nigri fuerint, noverit hominem esse
sanatum, et confidenter eum pronuntiet mundum.

38 "Vir sive mulier in cuius cute candor apparuerit, 39 intuebitur eos sacerdos. Si deprehenderit subobscurum alborem lucere in cute, sciat non esse lepram sed maculam coloris candidi et hominem mundum.

40 "Vir de cuius capite capilli fluunt, calvus ac mundus est,
41 et si a fronte ceciderint pili, recalvaster et mundus est.
42 Sin autem in calvitio sive in recalvatione albus vel rufus
color fuerit exortus 43 et hoc sacerdos viderit, condemnabit
eum haut dubie leprae quae orta est in calvitio.

44 "Quicumque ergo maculatus fuerit lepra et separatus
est ad arbitrium sacerdotis 45 habebit vestimenta dissuta,
caput nudum, os veste contectum, contaminatum ac sordi-

be lower than the other flesh and the hair yellow and thinner than usual, he shall *declare them unclean* because it is the leprosy of the head and the beard. 31 But if he perceive the place of the spot is equal with the flesh that is near it and the hair black, he shall shut him up seven days, 32 and on the seventh day he shall look upon it. If the spot be not grown and the hair keep its colour and the place of the blemish be even with the other flesh, 33 the man shall be shaven all but the place of the spot, and he shall be shut up other seven days. 34 If on the seventh day the *evil* seem to have stayed in its place and not lower than the other flesh, he shall cleanse him, and, his clothes being washed, he shall be clean. 35 But if after his cleansing the spot spread again in the skin, 36 he shall seek no more whether the hair be turned yellow, because he is evidently unclean. 37 But if the spot be stayed and the hair be black, let him know that the man is healed, and let him confidently pronounce him clean.

38 "If a whiteness appear in the skin of a man or a woman, 39 the priest shall view them. If he find that a darkish whiteness shineth in the skin, let him know that it is not the leprosy but a white blemish and that the man is clean.

40 "The man whose hair falleth off from his head, he is bald and clean, 41 and if the hair fall from his forehead, he is bald before and clean. 42 But if in the bald head or in the bald forehead there be risen a white or reddish colour 43 and the priest perceive this, he shall condemn him undoubtedly of leprosy which is risen in the bald part.

44 "Now whosoever shall be defiled with the leprosy and is separated by the judgment of the priest 45 shall have his clothes hanging loose, his head bare, his mouth covered with a cloth, and he shall cry out that he is defiled and un-

dum se clamabit. 46 Omni tempore quo leprosus est et inmundus, solus habitabit extra castra.

47 "Vestis lanea sive linea quae lepram habuerit 48 in stamine atque subtemine aut certe pellis vel quicquid ex pelle confectum est, 49 si alba aut rufa macula fuerit infecta, lepra reputabitur ostendeturque sacerdoti, 50 qui consideratam recludet septem diebus. 51 Et die septimo rursus aspiciens, si crevisse deprehenderit, lepra perseverans est. Pollutum iudicabit vestimentum et omne in quo fuerit inventa, 52 et idcirco conburetur flammis. 53 Quod si eam viderit non crevisse, 54 praecipiet, et lavabunt id in quo lepra est, recludetque illud septem diebus aliis. 55 Et cum viderit faciem quidem pristinam non reversam nec tamen crevisse lepram, inmundum iudicabit et igne conburet, eo quod infusa sit in superficie vestimenti vel per totum lepra. 56 Sin autem obscurior fuerit locus leprae postquam vestis est lota, abrumpet eum et a solido dividet. 57 Quod si ultra apparuerit in his locis quae prius inmaculata erant lepra volatilis et vaga, debet igne conburi. 58 Si cessaverit, lavabit aqua ea quae pura sunt secundo, et munda erunt. 59 Ista est lex leprae vestimenti lanei et linei, staminis atque subteminis, omnisque supellectilis pelliciae, quomodo mundari debeat vel contaminari."

clean. 46 All the time that he is a leper and unclean, he shall dwell alone without the camp.

47 "A woollen or linen garment that shall have the leprosy 48 in the warp and the woof or a skin or whatsoever is made of a skin, 49 if it be infected with a white or red spot, it shall be accounted the leprosy and shall be shewn to the priest, 50 and he shall look upon it and shall shut it up seven days. 51 And on the seventh day when he looketh on it again, if he find that it is grown, it is a fixed leprosy. He shall judge the garment unclean and every thing wherein it shall be found, 52 and therefore it shall be burnt with fire. 53 But if he see that it is not grown, 54 he shall give orders, and they shall wash that part wherein the leprosy is, and he shall shut it up other seven days. 55 And when he shall see that the former *colour* is not returned nor yet the leprosy spread, he shall judge it unclean and shall burn it with fire, for the leprosy *has taken hold of* the outside of the garment or through the whole. 56 But if the place of the leprosy be somewhat dark after the garment is washed, he shall tear it off and divide it from that which is sound. 57 And if after this there appear in those places that before were without spot a flying and wandering leprosy, it must be burnt with fire. 58 If it cease, he shall wash with water the parts that are pure the second time, and they shall be clean. 59 This is the law touching the leprosy of any woollen or linen garment, either in the warp or woof, or any thing of skins, how it ought to be cleansed or *pronounced unclean*."

Caput 14

Locutusque est Dominus ad Mosen, dicens, 2 "Hic est ritus leprosi quando mundandus est: adducetur ad sacerdotem, 3 qui, egressus e castris cum invenerit lepram esse mundatam, 4 praecipiet ei qui purificatur ut offerat pro se duos passeres vivos, quos vesci licitum est, et lignum cedrinum vermiculumque et hysopum. 5 Et unum e passeribus immolari iubebit in vase fictili super aquas viventes, 6 alium autem vivum cum ligno cedrino et cocco et hysopo tinguet in sanguine passeris immolati, 7 quo asperget illum qui mundandus est septies ut iure purgetur. Et dimittet passerem vivum ut in agrum avolet. 8 Cumque laverit homo vestimenta sua, radet omnes pilos corporis et lavabitur aqua. Purificatusque ingredietur castra, ita dumtaxat ut maneat extra tabernaculum suum septem diebus, 9 et die septimo radet capillos capitis barbamque et supercilia ac totius corporis pilos. Et lotis rursum vestibus et corpore, 10 die octavo adsumet duos agnos inmaculatos et ovem anniculam absque macula et tres

Chapter 14

The rites of sacrifices in cleansing the leprosy. Leprosy in houses.

And the Lord spoke to Moses, saying, 2 "This is the rite of a leper when he is to be cleansed: he shall be brought to the priest, 3 who, going out of the camp when he shall find that the leprosy is cleansed, 4 shall command him that is to be purified to offer for himself two living sparrows, which it is lawful to eat, and cedar wood and scarlet and hyssop. 5 And he shall command one of the sparrows to be immolated in an earthen vessel over living waters, 6 but the other that is alive he shall dip with the cedar wood and the scarlet and the hyssop in the blood of the sparrow that is immolated, 7 wherewith he shall sprinkle him that is to be cleansed seven times that he may be rightly purified. And he shall let go the living sparrow that it may fly into the field. 8 And when the man hath washed his clothes, he shall shave all the hair of his body and shall be washed with water. And being purified he shall enter into the camp, yet so that he tarry without his own tent seven days, 9 and on the seventh day he shall shave the hair of his head and his beard and his eyebrows and the hair of all his body. And having washed again his clothes and his body, 10 on the eighth day he shall take two lambs without blemish and an ewe of a year old

decimas similae in sacrificium quae conspersa sit oleo et seorsum olei sextarium.

11 "Cumque sacerdos purificans hominem statuerit eum et haec omnia coram Domino in ostio Tabernaculi Testimonii, 12 tollet agnum et offeret eum pro delicto oleique sextarium, et, oblatis ante Dominum omnibus, 13 immolabit agnum ubi immolari solet hostia pro peccato et holocaustum, id est, in loco sancto, sicut enim pro peccato, ita et pro delicto ad sacerdotem pertinet hostia: sancta sanctorum est. 14 Adsumensque sacerdos de sanguine hostiae quae immolata est pro delicto ponet super extremum auriculae dextrae eius qui mundatur et super pollices manus dextrae et pedis, 15 et de olei sextario mittet in manum suam sinistram 16 tinguetque digitum dextrum in eo et asperget septies coram Domino. 17 Quod autem reliquum est olei in leva manu fundet super extremum auriculae dextrae eius qui mundatur et super pollices manus ac pedis dextri et super sanguinem qui fusus est pro delicto 18 et super caput eius. 19 Rogabitque pro eo coram Domino et faciet sacrificium pro peccato, tunc immolabit holocaustum 20 et ponet illud in altari cum libamentis suis, et homo rite mundabitur.

21 "Quod si pauper est et non potest manus eius invenire quae dicta sunt, adsumet agnum pro delicto ad oblationem, ut roget pro eo sacerdos, decimamque partem similae conspersae oleo in sacrificium et olei sextarium 22 duosque turtures sive duos pullos columbae, quorum sit unus pro peccato et alter in holocaustum, 23 offeretque ea die octavo

without blemish and three tenths of flour tempered with oil for a sacrifice and a sextary of oil apart.

11 "And when the priest that purifieth the man hath presented him and all these things before the Lord at the door of the Tabernacle of the Testimony, 12 he shall take a lamb and offer it for a trespass offering with the sextary of oil, and, having offered all before the Lord, 13 he shall immolate the lamb where the victim for sin is wont to be immolated and the holocaust, that is, in the holy place, for as that which is for sin, so also the victim for a trespass offering pertaineth to the priest: it is holy of holies. 14 And the priest taking of the blood of the victim that was immolated for trespass shall put it upon the tip of the right ear of him that is cleansed and upon the thumb of his right hand and the great toe of his right foot, 15 and he shall pour of the sextary of oil into his own left hand 16 and shall dip his right finger in it and sprinkle it before the Lord seven times. 17 And the rest of the oil in his left hand he shall pour upon the tip of the right ear of him that is cleansed and upon the thumb of his right hand and the great toe of his right foot and upon the blood that was shed for trespass 18 and upon his head. 19 And he shall pray for him before the Lord and shall offer the sacrifice for sin, then shall he immolate the holocaust 20 and put it on the altar with the libations thereof, and the man shall be rightly cleansed.

21 "But if he be poor and his hand cannot find the things aforesaid, he shall take a lamb for an offering for trespass, that the priest may pray for him, and a tenth part of flour tempered with oil for a sacrifice and a sextary of oil 22 and two turtles or two young pigeons, of which one may be for sin and the other for a holocaust, 23 and he shall offer them

purificationis suae sacerdoti ad ostium Tabernaculi Testimonii coram Domino. 24 Qui suscipiens agnum pro delicto et sextarium olei levabit simul. 25 Immolatoque agno, de sanguine eius ponet super extremum auriculae dextrae illius qui mundatur et super pollices manus eius ac pedis dextri. 26 Olei vero partem mittet in manum suam sinistram, 27 in quo tinguens digitum dextrae manus, asperget septies coram Domino, 28 tangetque extremum dextrae auriculae illius qui mundatur et pollices manus ac pedis dextri in loco sanguinis qui effusus est pro delicto. 29 Reliquam autem partem olei quae est in sinistra manu mittet super caput purificati ut placet pro eo Dominum. 30 Et turturem sive pullum columbae offeret, 31 unum pro delicto et alterum in holocaustum, cum libamentis suis. 32 Hoc est sacrificium leprosi qui habere non potest omnia in emundationem sui."

33 Locutusque est Dominus ad Mosen et Aaron, dicens, 34 "Cum ingressi fueritis terram Chanaan, quam ego dabo vobis in possessionem, si fuerit plaga leprae in aedibus, 35 ibit cuius est domus et referet sacerdoti, dicens, 'Quasi plaga leprae videtur mihi esse in domo mea,' 36 at ille praecipiet ut efferant universa de domo priusquam ingrediatur eam et videat utrum leprosa sit ne inmunda fiant omnia quae in domo sunt. Intrabitque postea ut consideret domus lepram. 37 Et si viderit in parietibus illius quasi valliculas, pallore sive rubore deformes et humiliores superficie reliqua, 38 egredietur ostium domus et statim claudet eam septem

on the eighth day of his purification to the priest at the door of the Tabernacle of the Testimony before the Lord. 24 And the priest receiving the lamb for trespass and the sextary of oil shall elevate them together. 25 And the lamb being immolated, he shall put of the blood thereof upon the tip of the right ear of him that is cleansed and upon the thumb of his right hand and the great toe of his right foot. 26 But he shall pour part of the oil into his own left hand, 27 and, dipping the finger of his right hand in it, he shall sprinkle it seven times before the Lord, 28 and he shall touch the tip of the right ear of him that is cleansed and the thumb of his right hand and the great toe of his right foot in the place of the blood that was shed for trespass. 29 And the other part of the oil that is in his left hand he shall pour upon the head of the purified person that he may appease the Lord for him. 30 And he shall offer a turtle or young pigeon, 31 one for trespass and the other for a holocaust, with their libations. 32 This is the sacrifice of a leper that is not able to have all things that appertain to his cleansing."

33 And the Lord spoke to Moses and Aaron, saying, 34 "When you shall be come into the land of Canaan, which I will give you for a possession, if there be the plague of leprosy in a house, 35 he whose house it is shall go and tell the priest, saying, 'It seemeth to me that there is the plague of leprosy in my house,' 36 and he shall command that they carry forth all things out of the house before he go into it and see whether it have the leprosy lest all things become unclean that are in the house. And afterwards he shall go in to view the leprosy of the house. 37 And if he see in the walls thereof as it were little dints, disfigured with paleness or redness and lower than *all the rest,* 38 he shall go out of the

diebus. 39 Reversusque die septimo considerabit eam. Si invenerit crevisse lepram, 40 iubebit erui lapides in quibus lepra est et proici eos extra civitatem in locum inmundum 41 domum autem ipsam radi intrinsecus per circuitum et spargi pulverem rasurae extra urbem in locum inmundum 42 lapidesque alios reponi pro his qui ablati fuerint et luto alio liniri domum. 43 Sin autem, postquam eruti sunt lapides et pulvis erasus et alia terra lita, 44 ingressus sacerdos viderit reversam lepram et parietes aspersos maculis, lepra est perseverans, et inmunda domus. 45 Quam statim destruent et lapides eius ac ligna atque universum pulverem proicient extra oppidum in locum inmundum. 46 Qui intraverit domum quando clausa est inmundus erit usque ad vesperum, 47 et qui dormierit in ea et comederit quippiam lavabit vestimenta sua.

48 "Quod si introiens sacerdos viderit lepram non crevisse in domo postquam denuo lita est, purificabit eam, reddita sanitate, 49 et in purificationem eius sumet duos passeres lignumque cedrinum et vermiculum atque hysopum. 50 Et immolato uno passere in vase fictili super aquas vivas, 51 tollet lignum cedrinum et hysopum et coccum et passerem vivum et intinguet omnia in sanguine passeris immolati atque in aquis viventibus, et asperget domum septies 52 purificabitque eam tam in sanguine passeris quam in aquis viventibus et in passere vivo lignoque cedrino et hysopo atque vermiculo. 53 Cumque dimiserit passerem avolare in agrum libere,

door of the house and forthwith shut it up seven days.
39 And, returning on the seventh day, he shall look upon it. If
he find that the leprosy is spread, 40 he shall command that
the stones wherein the leprosy is be taken out and cast without the city into an unclean place 41 and that the house
be scraped on the inside round about and the dust of the
scraping be scattered without the city into an unclean place
42 and that other stones be laid in the place of them that
were taken away and the house be plastered with other mortar. 43 But if, after the stones be taken out and the dust
scraped off and it be plastered with other earth, 44 the priest
going in perceive that the leprosy is returned and the walls
full of spots, it is a lasting leprosy, and the house is unclean.
45 And they shall destroy it forthwith and shall cast the
stones and timber thereof and all the dust without the town
into an unclean place. 46 He that entereth into the house
when it is shut shall be unclean until evening, 47 and he that
sleepeth in it and eateth any thing shall wash his clothes.

48 "But if the priest going in perceive that the leprosy is
not spread in the house after it was plastered again, he shall
purify it, it being cured, 49 and for the purification thereof
he shall take two sparrows and cedar wood and scarlet and
hyssop. 50 And having immolated one sparrow in an earthen
vessel over living waters, 51 he shall take the cedar wood and
the hyssop and the scarlet and the living sparrow and shall
dip all in the blood of the sparrow that is immolated and in
the living water, and he shall sprinkle the house seven times
52 and shall purify it as well with the blood of the sparrow as
with the living water and with the living sparrow and with
the cedar wood and the hyssop and the scarlet. 53 And when
he hath let go the sparrow to fly freely away into the field,

orabit pro domo, et iure mundabitur. 54 Ista est lex omnis leprae et percussurae, 55 leprae vestium et domorum, 56 cicatricis et erumpentium papularum, lucentis maculae et in varias species coloribus inmutatis, 57 ut possit sciri quo tempore mundum quid vel inmundum sit."

Caput 15

Locutusque est Dominus ad Mosen et Aaron, dicens, 2 "Loquimini filiis Israhel, et dicite eis, 'Vir qui patitur fluxum seminis inmundus erit. 3 Et tunc iudicabitur huic vitio subiacere cum per momenta singula adheserit carni illius atque concreverit foedus humor. 4 Omne stratum in quo dormierit inmundum erit et ubicumque sederit. 5 Si quis hominum tetigerit lectum eius, lavabit vestimenta sua, et ipse lotus aqua inmundus erit usque ad vesperum. 6 Si sederit ubi ille sederat, et ipse lavabit vestimenta sua et lotus aqua inmundus erit usque ad vesperum. 7 Qui tetigerit carnem eius lavabit vestimenta sua et ipse lotus aqua inmundus erit usque ad vesperum.

8 "'Si salivam huiuscemodi homo iecerit super eum qui mundus est, lavabit vestimenta sua, et lotus aqua inmundus

he shall pray for the house, and it shall be rightly cleansed. 54 This is the law of every kind of leprosy and stroke, 55 of the leprosy of garments and houses, 56 of a scar and of blisters breaking out, of a shining spot and when the colours are diversely changed, 57 that it may be known when a thing is clean or unclean."

Chapter 15

Other legal uncleannesses.

And the Lord spoke to Moses and Aaron, saying, 2 "Speak to the children of Israel, and say to them, 'The man that hath an issue of seed shall be unclean. 3 And then shall he be judged subject to this evil when a filthy humour at every moment cleaveth to his flesh and *gathereth there.* 4 Every bed on which he sleepeth shall be unclean and every place on which he sitteth. 5 If any man touch his bed, he shall wash his clothes, and being washed with water he shall be unclean until the evening. 6 If a man sit where that man hath sitten, he also shall wash his clothes and being washed with water shall be unclean until the evening. 7 He that toucheth his flesh shall wash his clothes and being himself washed with water shall be unclean until the evening.

8 "'If such a man cast his spittle upon him that is clean, he shall wash his clothes, and being washed with water he shall

erit usque ad vesperum. 9 Sagma super quo sederit inmundum erit, 10 et quicquid sub eo fuerit qui fluxum seminis patitur pollutum erit usque ad vesperum. Qui portaverit horum aliquid lavabit vestimenta sua, et ipse lotus aqua inmundus erit usque ad vesperum.

11 "'Omnis quem tetigerit qui talis est non lotis ante manibus lavabit vestimenta sua et lotus aqua inmundus erit usque ad vesperum. 12 Vas fictile quod tetigerit confringetur, vas autem ligneum lavabitur aqua. 13 Si sanatus fuerit qui huiuscemodi sustinet passionem, numerabit septem dies post emundationem sui, et, lotis vestibus ac toto corpore in aquis viventibus, erit mundus. 14 Die autem octavo sumet duos turtures aut duos pullos columbae, et veniet in conspectum Domini ad ostium Tabernaculi Testimonii dabitque eos sacerdoti, 15 qui faciet unum pro peccato et alterum in holocaustum. Rogabitque pro eo coram Domino ut emundetur a fluxu seminis sui.

16 "'Vir de quo egreditur semen coitus lavabit aqua omne corpus suum, et inmundus erit usque ad vesperum. 17 Vestem et pellem quam habuerit lavabit aqua, et inmunda erit usque ad vesperum. 18 Mulier cum qua coierit lavabitur aqua et inmunda erit usque ad vesperum.

19 "'Mulier quae redeunte mense patitur fluxum sanguinis septem diebus separabitur. 20 Omnis qui tetigerit eam inmundus erit usque ad vesperum, 21 et in quo dormierit vel

be unclean until the evening. 9 The saddle on which he hath sitten shall be unclean, 10 and whatsoever has been under him that hath the issue of seed shall be unclean until the evening. He that carrieth any of these things shall wash his clothes, and being washed with water he shall be unclean until the evening.

11 "'Every person whom such a one shall touch not having washed his hands before shall wash his clothes and being washed with water shall be unclean until the evening. 12 If he touch a vessel of earth, it shall be broken, but if a vessel of wood, it shall be washed with water. 13 If he who suffereth this disease be healed, he shall number seven days after his cleansing, and, having washed his clothes and all his body in living water, he shall be clean. 14 And on the eighth day he shall take two turtles or two young pigeons, and he shall come *before* the Lord to the door of the Tabernacle of the Testimony and shall give them to the priest, 15 who shall offer one for sin and the other for a holocaust. And he shall pray for him before the Lord that he may be cleansed of the issue of his seed.

16 "'The man from whom the seed of copulation goeth out shall wash all his body with water, and he shall be unclean until the evening. 17 The garment or skin that he weareth he shall wash with water, and it shall be unclean until the evening. 18 The woman with whom he copulateth shall be washed with water and shall be unclean until the evening.

19 "'The woman who at the return of the month hath her issue of blood shall be separated seven days. 20 Every one that toucheth her shall be unclean until the evening, 21 and every thing that she sleepeth on or that she sitteth on in

sederit diebus separationis suae polluetur. 22 Qui tetigerit lectum eius lavabit vestimenta sua et ipse lotus aqua inmundus erit usque ad vesperum. 23 Omne vas super quo illa sederit quisquis adtigerit lavabit vestimenta sua et ipse lotus aqua pollutus erit usque ad vesperum.

24 "'Si coierit cum ea vir tempore sanguinis menstrualis, inmundus erit septem diebus, et omne stratum in quo dormierit polluetur. 25 Mulier quae patitur multis diebus fluxum sanguinis non in tempore menstruali vel quae post menstruum sanguinem fluere non cessat, quamdiu huic subiacet passioni inmunda erit quasi sit in tempore menstruo. 26 Omne stratum in quo dormierit et vas in quo sederit pollutum erit. 27 Quicumque tetigerit ea lavabit vestimenta sua et ipse lotus aqua inmundus erit usque ad vesperum. 28 Si steterit sanguis et fluere cessarit, numerabit septem dies purificationis suae, 29 et octavo die offeret pro se sacerdoti duos turtures vel duos pullos columbae ad ostium Tabernaculi Testimonii, 30 qui unum faciet pro peccato et alterum in holocaustum, rogabitque pro ea coram Domino et pro fluxu inmunditiae eius.

31 "'Docebitis ergo filios Israhel ut caveant inmunditiam et non moriantur in sordibus suis cum polluerint tabernaculum meum quod est inter eos. 32 Ista est lex eius qui patitur fluxum seminis et qui polluitur coitu 33 et quae menstruis temporibus separatur vel quae iugi fluit sanguine et hominis qui dormierit cum ea.'"

the days of her separation shall be defiled. 22 He that toucheth her bed shall wash his clothes and being himself washed with water shall be unclean until the evening. 23 Whosoever shall touch any vessel on which she sitteth shall wash his clothes and himself being washed with water shall be defiled until the evening.

24 "'If a man copulateth with her in the time of her *flowers,* he shall be unclean seven days, and every bed on which he shall sleep shall be defiled. 25 The woman that hath an issue of blood many days out of her *ordinary* time or that ceaseth not to flow after the monthly courses, as long as she is subject to this disease shall be unclean in the same manner as if she were in her flowers. 26 Every bed on which she sleepeth and every vessel on which she sitteth shall be defiled. 27 Whosoever toucheth them shall wash his clothes and himself being washed with water shall be unclean until the evening. 28 If the blood stop and cease to run, she shall count seven days of her purification, 29 and on the eighth day she shall offer for herself to the priest two turtles or two young pigeons at the door of the Tabernacle of the Testimony, 30 and he shall offer one for sin and the other for a holocaust, and he shall pray for her before the Lord and for the issue of her uncleanness.

31 "'You shall teach therefore the children of Israel to take heed of uncleanness that they may not die in their filth when they shall have defiled my tabernacle that is among them. 32 This is the law of him that hath the issue of seed and that is defiled by copulation 33 and of the woman that is separated in her monthly times or that hath a continual issue of blood and of the man that sleepeth with her.'"

Caput 16

Locutusque est Dominus ad Mosen post mortem duum filiorum Aaron quando offerentes ignem alienum interfecti sunt, 2 et praecepit ei, dicens, "Loquere ad Aaron, fratrem tuum, ne omni tempore ingrediatur sanctuarium quod est intra velum coram propitiatorio quo tegitur arca, ut non moriatur (quia in nube apparebo super oraculum), 3 nisi haec ante fecerit: vitulum offeret pro peccato et arietem in holocaustum; 4 tunica linea vestietur; feminalibus lineis verecunda celabit; accingetur zona linea; cidarim lineam inponet capiti, haec enim vestimenta sunt sancta, quibus cunctis cum lotus fuerit induetur.

5 "Suscipietque ab universa multitudine filiorum Israhel duos hircos pro peccato et unum arietem in holocaustum. 6 Cumque obtulerit vitulum et oraverit pro se et pro domo sua, 7 duos hircos stare faciet coram Domino in ostio Tabernaculi Testimonii, 8 mittensque super utrumque sortem, unam Domino et alteram capro emissario, 9 cuius sors exierit Domino offeret illum pro peccato, 10 cuius autem in

Chapter 16

When and how the high priest must enter into the sanctuary. The feast of expiation.

And the Lord spoke to Moses after the death of the two sons of Aaron when they were slain upon their offering strange fire, 2 and he commanded him, saying, "Speak to Aaron, thy brother, that he enter not at all into the sanctuary which is within the veil before the propitiatory with which the ark is covered, lest he die (for I will appear in a cloud over the oracle), 3 unless he first do these things: he shall offer a calf for sin and a ram for a holocaust; 4 he shall be vested with a linen tunick; he shall cover his nakedness with linen breeches; he shall be girded with a linen girdle; and he shall put a linen mitre upon his head, for these are holy vestments, all which he shall put on after he is washed.

5 "And he shall receive from the whole multitude of the children of Israel two buck-goats for sin and one ram for a holocaust. 6 And when he hath offered the calf and prayed for himself and for his own house, 7 he shall make the two buck-goats to stand before the Lord in the door of the Tabernacle of the Testimony, 8 and casting lots upon them both, one to be offered to the Lord and the other to be the emissary-goat, 9 that whose lot fell *to be offered* to the Lord he shall offer for sin, 10 but that whose lot was to be the

caprum emissarium, statuet eum vivum coram Domino ut fundat preces super eo et emittat illum in solitudinem.

11 "His rite celebratis, offeret vitulum, et, rogans pro se et pro domo sua, immolabit eum. 12 Adsumptoque turibulo quod de prunis altaris impleverit et hauriens manu conpositum thymiama in incensum, ultra velum intrabit in sancta 13 ut positis super ignem aromatibus, nebula eorum et vapor operiat oraculum quod est super testimonium et non moriatur. 14 Tollet quoque de sanguine vituli et asperget digito septies contra propitiatorium ad orientem. 15 Cumque mactaverit hircum pro peccato populi, inferet sanguinem eius intra velum, sicut praeceptum est de sanguine vituli, ut aspergat e regione oraculi 16 et expiet sanctuarium ab inmunditiis filiorum Israhel et a praevaricationibus eorum cunctisque peccatis. Iuxta hunc ritum faciet Tabernaculo Testimonii quod fixum est inter eos in medio sordium habitationis eorum.

17 "Nullus hominum sit in tabernaculo quando pontifex ingreditur sanctuarium ut roget pro se et pro domo sua et pro universo coetu Israhel donec egrediatur. 18 Cum autem exierit ad altare quod coram Domino est, oret pro se, et, sumptum sanguinem vituli atque hirci, fundat super cornua eius per gyrum, 19 aspergensque digito septies expiet et sanctificet illud ab inmunditiis filiorum Israhel. 20 Postquam

emissary-goat, he shall present alive before the Lord that he may pour out prayers upon him and let him go into the wilderness.

11 "After these things are duly celebrated, he shall offer the calf, and, praying for himself and for his own house, he shall immolate it. 12 And, taking the censer which he hath filled with the burning coals of the altar and taking up with his hand the compounded perfume for incense, he shall go in within the veil into the holy place 13 that when the perfumes are put upon the fire, the cloud and vapour thereof may cover the oracle which is over the testimony and he may not die. 14 He shall take also of the blood of the calf and sprinkle with his finger seven times towards the propitiatory to the east. 15 And when he hath killed the buck-goat for the sin of the people, he shall carry in the blood thereof within the veil, as he was commanded to do with the blood of the calf, that he may sprinkle it over against the oracle 16 and may expiate the sanctuary from the uncleanness of the children of Israel and from their transgressions and all their sins. According to this rite shall he do to the Tabernacle of the Testimony which is fixed among them in the midst of the filth of their habitation.

17 "Let no man be in the tabernacle when the high priest goeth into the sanctuary to pray for himself and his house and for the whole congregation of Israel until he come out. 18 And when he is come out to the altar that is before the Lord, let him pray for himself, and, taking the blood of the calf and of the buck-goat, let him pour it upon the horns thereof round about, 19 and, sprinkling with his finger seven times, let him expiate and sanctify it from the uncleanness of the children of Israel. 20 After he hath cleansed the sanc-

emundarit sanctuarium et tabernaculum et altare, tunc offerat hircum viventem, 21 et, posita utraque manu super caput eius, confiteatur omnes iniquitates filiorum Israhel et universa delicta atque peccata eorum, quae inprecans capiti eius, emittet illum per hominem paratum in desertum. 22 Cumque portaverit hircus omnes iniquitates eorum in terram solitariam et dimissus fuerit in deserto, 23 revertetur Aaron in Tabernaculum Testimonii, et, depositis vestibus quibus prius indutus erat cum intraret sanctuarium relictisque ibi, 24 lavabit carnem suam in loco sancto indueturque vestimentis suis. Et postquam egressus obtulerit holocaustum suum ac plebis, rogabit tam pro se quam pro populo, 25 et adipem qui oblatus est pro peccatis adolebit super altare. 26 Ille vero qui dimiserit caprum emissarium lavabit vestimenta sua et corpus aqua et sic ingredietur in castra.

27 "Vitulum autem et hircum qui pro peccato fuerant immolati et quorum sanguis inlatus est in sanctuarium ut expiatio conpleretur asportabunt foras castra et conburent igni tam pelles quam carnes eorum et fimum, 28 et quicumque conbuserit ea lavabit vestimenta sua et carnem aqua et sic ingredietur in castra.

29 "Eritque hoc vobis legitimum sempiternum: mense septimo, decima die mensis, adfligetis animas vestras nullumque facietis opus, sive indigena sive advena qui peregrinatur inter vos. 30 In hac die expiatio erit vestri atque mundatio ab omnibus peccatis vestris. Coram Domino mundabimini. 31 Sabbatum enim requietionis est, et adfligetis animas ves-

tuary and the tabernacle and the altar, then let him offer the living goat, 21 and, putting both hands upon his head, let him confess all the iniquities of the children of Israel and all their offences and sins, and, praying that they may light on his head, he shall turn him out by a man ready for it into the desert. 22 And when the goat hath carried all their iniquities into an uninhabited land and shall be let go into the desert, 23 Aaron shall return into the Tabernacle of the Testimony, and, putting off the vestments which he had on him before when he entered into the sanctuary and leaving them there, 24 he shall wash his flesh in the holy place and shall put on his own garments. And after that he has come out and hath offered his own holocaust and that of the people, he shall pray both for himself and for the people, 25 and the fat that is offered for sins he shall burn upon the altar. 26 But he that hath let go the emissary-goat shall wash his clothes and his body with water and so shall enter into the camp.

27 "But the calf and the buck-goat that were sacrificed for sin and whose blood was carried into the sanctuary to accomplish the atonement they shall carry forth without the camp and shall burn with fire their skins and their flesh and their dung, 28 and whosoever burneth them shall wash his clothes and flesh with water and so shall enter into the camp.

29 "And this shall be to you an everlasting ordinance: the seventh month, the tenth day of the month, you shall afflict your souls and shall do no work, whether it be one of your own country or a stranger that sojourneth among you. 30 Upon this day shall be the expiation for you and the cleansing from all your sins. You shall be cleansed before the Lord. 31 For it is a sabbath of rest, and you shall afflict

tras religione perpetua. 32 Expiabit autem sacerdos qui unctus fuerit et cuius initiatae manus ut sacerdotio fungatur pro patre suo, indueturque stola linea et vestibus sanctis, 33 et expiabit sanctuarium et Tabernaculum Testimonii atque altare, sacerdotes quoque et universum populum. 34 Eritque hoc vobis legitimum sempiternum ut oretis pro filiis Israhel et pro cunctis peccatis eorum semel in anno."

Fecit igitur sicut praeceperat Dominus Mosi.

Caput 17

Et locutus est Dominus ad Mosen, dicens, 2 "Loquere Aaron et filiis eius et cunctis filiis Israhel, dicens ad eos, 'Iste est sermo quem mandavit Dominus, dicens, 3 "Homo quilibet de domo Israhel, si occiderit bovem aut ovem sive capram in castris vel extra castra 4 et non obtulerit ad ostium tabernaculi oblationem Domino, sanguinis reus erit. Quasi sanguinem fuderit, sic peribit de medio populi sui. 5 Ideo offerre debent sacerdoti filii Israhel hostias suas quas occidunt in agro ut sanctificentur Domino ante ostium Taber-

your souls by a perpetual religion. 32 And the priest that is anointed and whose hands are consecrated to do the office of the priesthood in his father's stead shall make atonement, and he shall be vested with the linen robe and the holy vestments, 33 and he shall expiate the sanctuary and the Tabernacle of the Testimony and the altar, the priests also and all the people. 34 And this shall be an ordinance for ever that you pray for the children of Israel and for all their sins once in a year."

He did therefore as the Lord had commanded Moses.

Chapter 17

No sacrifices to be offered but at the door of the tabernacle.
A prohibition of blood.

And the Lord spoke to Moses, saying, 2 "Speak to Aaron and his sons and to all the children of Israel, saying to them, 'This is the word which the Lord hath commanded, saying, 3 "Any man whosoever of the house of Israel, if he kill an ox or a sheep or a goat in the camp or without the camp 4 and offer it not at the door of the tabernacle, an oblation to the Lord, shall be guilty of blood. As if he had shed blood, so shall he perish from the midst of his people. 5 Therefore the children of Israel shall bring to the priest their victims which they kill in the field that they may be sanctified to the Lord

naculi Testimonii et immolent eas hostias pacificas Domino.
6 Fundetque sacerdos sanguinem super altare Domini ad ostium Tabernaculi Testimonii et adolebit adipem in odorem
suavitatis Domino. 7 Et nequaquam ultra immolabunt hostias suas daemonibus cum quibus fornicati sunt. Legitimum
sempiternum erit illis et posteris eorum.'"

8 "Et ad ipsos dices, 'Homo de domo Israhel et de advenis
qui peregrinantur apud vos qui obtulerit holocaustum sive
victimam 9 et ad ostium Tabernaculi Testimonii non adduxerit eam ut offeratur Domino interibit de populo suo.
10 Homo quilibet de domo Israhel et de advenis qui peregrinantur inter eos si comederit sanguinem, obfirmabo faciem
meam contra animam illius et disperdam eam de populo suo
11 quia anima carnis in sanguine est et ego dedi illum vobis
ut super altare in eo expietis pro animabus vestris et sanguis
pro animae piaculo sit. 12 Idcirco dixi filiis Israhel, "Omnis
anima ex vobis non comedet sanguinem nec ex advenis qui
peregrinantur apud vos."

13 "'Homo quicumque de filiis Israhel et de advenis qui
peregrinantur apud vos, si venatione atque aucupio ceperit
feram vel avem quibus vesci licitum est, fundat sanguinem
eius et operiat illum terra, 14 anima enim omnis carnis in
sanguine est. Unde dixi filiis Israhel, "Sanguinem universae
carnis non comedetis quia anima carnis in sanguine est, et
quicumque comederit illum interibit."

15 "'Anima quae comederit morticinum vel captum a bes-

before the door of the Tabernacle of the Testimony and they may sacrifice them for peace offerings to the Lord. 6 And the priest shall pour the blood upon the altar of the Lord at the door of the Tabernacle of the Testimony and shall burn the fat for a sweet odour to the Lord. 7 And they shall no more sacrifice their victims to devils with whom they have committed fornication. It shall be an ordinance for ever to them and to their posterity.'"

8 "And thou shalt say to them, 'The man of the house of Israel and of the strangers who sojourn among you that offereth a holocaust or a victim 9 and bringeth it not to the door of the Tabernacle of the Testimony that it may be offered to the Lord shall perish from among his people. 10 If any man whosoever of the house of Israel and of the strangers that sojourn among them eat blood, I will set my face against his soul and will *cut him off* from among his people 11 because the life of the flesh is in the blood and I have given it to you that you may make atonement with it upon the altar for your souls and the blood may be for an expiation of the soul. 12 Therefore I have said to the children of Israel, "No soul of you nor of the strangers that sojourn among you shall eat blood."

13 "'Any man whosoever of the children of Israel and of the strangers that sojourn among you, if by hunting or fowling he take a wild beast or a bird which is lawful to eat, let him pour out its blood and cover it with earth, 14 for the life of all flesh is in the blood. Therefore I said to the children of Israel, "You shall not eat the blood of any flesh at all because the life of the flesh is in the blood, and whosoever eateth it shall *be cut off.*"

15 "'The soul that eateth that which died of itself or has

tia, tam de indigenis quam de advenis, lavabit vestes suas et semet ipsum aqua et contaminatus erit usque ad vesperum, et hoc ordine mundus fiet. 16 Quod si non laverit vestimenta sua et corpus, portabit iniquitatem suam.'"

Caput 18

Locutusque est Dominus ad Mosen, dicens, 2 "Loquere filiis Israhel, et dices ad eos, 'Ego Dominus, Deus vester. 3 Iuxta consuetudinem terrae Aegypti in qua habitastis non facietis, et iuxta morem regionis Chanaan ad quam ego introducturus sum vos non agetis, nec in legitimis eorum ambulabitis. 4 Facietis iudicia mea et praecepta mea servabitis et ambulabitis in eis. Ego Dominus, Deus vester. 5 Custodite leges meas atque iudicia, quae faciens homo vivet in eis. Ego Dominus.

6 "'Omnis homo ad proximam sanguinis sui non accedet ut revelet turpitudinem eius. Ego Dominus. 7 Turpitudinem patris et turpitudinem matris tuae non discoperies: mater tua est; non revelabis turpitudinem eius. 8 Turpitudinem uxoris patris tui non discoperies, turpitudo enim patris tui

been caught by a beast, whether he be one of your own country or a stranger, shall wash his clothes and himself with water and shall be defiled until the evening, and in this manner he shall be made clean. 16 But if he do not wash his clothes and his body, he shall bear his iniquity.'"

Chapter 18

Marriage is prohibited in certain degrees of kindred and all unnatural lusts.

And the Lord spoke to Moses, saying, 2 "Speak to the children of Israel, and thou shalt say to them, 'I am the Lord, your God. 3 You shall not do according to the custom of the land of Egypt in which you dwelt, neither shall you act according to the manner of the country of Canaan into which I will bring you, nor shall you walk in their ordinances. 4 You shall do my judgments and shall observe my precepts and shall walk in them. I am the Lord, your God. 5 Keep my laws and my judgments, which *if a man do,* he shall live in them. I am the Lord.

6 "'No man shall approach to her that is near of kin to him to uncover her nakedness. I am the Lord. 7 Thou shalt not uncover the nakedness of thy father or the nakedness of thy mother: she is thy mother; thou shalt not uncover her nakedness. 8 Thou shalt not uncover the nakedness of thy fa-

est. 9 Turpitudinem sororis tuae ex patre sive ex matre, quae domi vel foris genita est, non revelabis. 10 Turpitudinem filiae filii tui vel neptis ex filia non revelabis, quia turpitudo tua est. 11 Turpitudinem filiae uxoris patris tui quam peperit patri tuo et est soror tua non revelabis. 12 Turpitudinem sororis patris tui non discoperies, quia caro est patris tui. 13 Turpitudinem sororis matris tuae non revelabis, eo quod caro sit matris tuae. 14 Turpitudinem patrui tui non revelabis, nec accedes ad uxorem eius, quae tibi adfinitate coniungitur. 15 Turpitudinem nurus tuae non revelabis, quia uxor filii tui est, nec discoperies ignominiam eius. 16 Turpitudinem uxoris fratris tui non revelabis, quia turpitudo fratris tui est. 17 Turpitudinem uxoris tuae et filiae eius non revelabis. Filiam filii eius et filiam filiae illius non sumes ut reveles ignominiam eius, quia caro illius sunt et talis coitus incestus est. 18 Sororem uxoris tuae in pelicatum illius non accipies, nec revelabis turpitudinem eius adhuc illa vivente. 19 Ad mulierem quae patitur menstrua non accedes, nec revelabis foeditatem eius. 20 Cum uxore proximi tui non coibis nec seminis commixtione maculaberis.

21 "'De semine tuo non dabis ut consecretur idolo Moloch nec pollues nomen Dei tui. Ego Dominus.

22 "'Cum masculo non commiscearis coitu femineo, quia abominatio est. 23 Cum omni pecore non coibis, nec maculaberis cum eo. Mulier non subcumbet iumento nec misce-

ther's wife, for it is the nakedness of thy father. 9 Thou shalt not uncover the nakedness of thy sister by father or by mother, whether born at home or abroad. 10 Thou shalt not uncover the nakedness of thy son's daughter or thy daughter's daughter, because it is thy own nakedness. 11 Thou shalt not uncover the nakedness of thy father's wife's daughter whom she bore to thy father and who is thy sister. 12 Thou shalt not uncover the nakedness of thy father's sister, because she is the flesh of thy father. 13 Thou shalt not uncover the nakedness of thy mother's sister, because she is thy mother's flesh. 14 Thou shalt not uncover the nakedness of thy father's brother, neither shalt thou approach to his wife, who is joined to thee by affinity. 15 Thou shalt not uncover the nakedness of thy daughter-in-law, because she is thy son's wife, neither shalt thou discover her shame. 16 Thou shalt not uncover the nakedness of thy brother's wife, because it is the nakedness of thy brother. 17 Thou shalt not uncover the nakedness of thy wife and her daughter. Thou shalt not take her son's daughter or her daughter's daughter to discover her shame, because they are her flesh and such copulation is incest. 18 Thou shalt not take thy wife's sister for a harlot to rival her, neither shalt thou discover her nakedness while she *[the wife]* is yet living. 19 Thou shalt not approach to a woman having her flowers, neither shalt thou uncover her nakedness. 20 Thou shalt not lie with thy neighbour's wife nor be defiled with mingling of seed.

21 "'Thou shalt not give any of thy seed to be consecrated to the idol Molech nor defile the name of thy God. I am the Lord.

22 "'*Thou shalt not lie* with mankind as with womankind, because it is an abomination. 23 Thou shalt not copulate with any beast, neither shalt thou be defiled with it. A

bitur ei, quia scelus est. 24 Ne polluamini in omnibus his quibus contaminatae sunt universae gentes quas ego eiciam ante conspectum vestrum 25 et quibus polluta est terra, cuius ego scelera visitabo ut evomat habitatores suos.

26 "'Custodite legitima mea atque iudicia, et non faciatis ex omnibus abominationibus istis, tam indigena quam colonus qui peregrinatur apud vos, 27 omnes enim execrationes istas fecerunt accolae terrae qui fuerunt ante vos et polluerunt eam. 28 Cavete ergo ne et vos similiter evomat cum paria feceritis, sicut evomuit gentem quae fuit ante vos. 29 Omnis anima quae fecerit de abominationibus his quippiam peribit de medio populi sui. 30 Custodite mandata mea. Nolite facere quae fecerunt hii qui fuerunt ante vos, et ne polluamini in eis. Ego Dominus, Deus vester.'"

Caput 19

Locutus est Dominus ad Mosen, dicens, 2 "Loquere ad omnem coetum filiorum Israhel, et dices ad eos, 'Sancti estote quia ego sanctus sum, Dominus, Deus vester.

woman shall not lie down to a beast nor copulate with it, because it is a heinous crime. 24 Defile not yourselves with any of these things with which all the nations have been defiled which I will cast out before you 25 and with which the land is defiled, the abominations of which I will visit that it may vomit out its inhabitants.

26 "Keep ye my ordinances and my judgments, and do not any of these abominations, neither any of your own nation nor any stranger that sojourneth among you, 27 for all these detestable things the inhabitants of the land have done that were before you and have defiled it. 28 Beware then lest in like manner it vomit you also out *if* you do the like things, as it vomited out the nation that was before you. 29 Every soul that shall commit any of these abominations shall perish from the midst of his people. 30 Keep my commandments. Do not the things which they have done that have been before you, and be not defiled therein. I am the Lord, your God.'"

Chapter 19

Divers ordinances, partly moral, partly ceremonial or judicial.

The Lord spoke to Moses, saying, 2 "Speak to all the congregation of the children of Israel, and thou shalt say to them, 'Be ye holy because I, the Lord, your God, am holy.

3 "'Unusquisque patrem suum et matrem suam timeat.

"'Sabbata mea custodite. Ego Dominus, Deus vester.

4 "'Nolite converti ad idola, nec deos conflatiles faciatis vobis. Ego Dominus, Deus vester.

5 "'Si immolaveritis hostiam pacificorum Domino ut sit placabilis, 6 eo die quo fuerit immolata comedetis eam et die altero, quicquid autem residuum fuerit in diem tertium igne conburetis. 7 Si quis post biduum comederit ex ea, profanus erit et impietatis reus 8 portabitque iniquitatem suam quia sanctum Domini polluit, et peribit anima illa de populo suo.

9 "'Cum messueris segetes terrae tuae, non tondebis usque ad solum superficiem terrae, nec remanentes spicas colliges. 10 Neque in vinea tua racemos et grana decidentia congregabis, sed pauperibus et peregrinis carpenda dimittes. Ego Dominus, Deus vester.

11 "'Non facietis furtum.

"'Non mentiemini, nec decipiet unusquisque proximum suum.

12 "'Non peierabis in nomine meo nec pollues nomen Dei tui. Ego Dominus.

13 "'Non facies calumniam proximo tuo, nec vi opprimes eum.

"'Non morabitur opus mercennarii tui apud te usque mane.

14 "'Non maledices surdo nec coram caeco pones offendiculum, sed timebis Dominum, Deum tuum, quia ego sum Dominus.

15 "'Non facies quod iniquum est nec iniuste iudicabis.

3 "'Let every one fear his father and his mother.

"'Keep my sabbaths. I am the Lord, your God.

4 "'Turn ye not to idols, nor make to yourselves molten gods. I am the Lord, your God.

5 "'If ye offer in sacrifice a peace offering to the Lord that he may be favourable, 6 you shall eat it on the same day it was offered and the next day, and whatsoever shall be left until the third day you shall burn with fire. 7 If after two days any man eat thereof, he shall be profane and guilty of impiety 8 and shall bear his iniquity because he hath defiled the holy thing of the Lord, and that soul shall perish from among his people.

9 "'When thou reapest the corn of thy land, thou shalt not cut down all that is on the face of the earth to the very ground, nor shalt thou gather the ears that remain. 10 Neither shalt thou gather the bunches and grapes that fall down in thy vineyard, but shalt leave them to the poor and the strangers to take. I am the Lord, your God.

11 "'You shall not steal.

"'You shall not lie, neither shall any man deceive his neighbour.

12 "'Thou shalt not swear falsely by my name nor profane the name of thy God. I am the Lord.

13 "'Thou shalt not calumniate thy neighbour, nor oppress him by violence.

"'The wages of him that hath been hired by thee shall not abide with thee until the morning.

14 "'Thou shalt not speak evil of the deaf nor put a stumblingblock before the blind, but thou shalt fear the Lord, thy God, because I am the Lord.

15 "'Thou shalt not do that which is unjust nor judge un-

Non consideres personam pauperis, nec honores vultum potentis; iuste iudica proximo tuo.

16 "'Non eris criminator nec susurro in populo.

"'Non stabis contra sanguinem proximi tui. Ego Dominus.

17 "'Non oderis fratrem tuum in corde tuo, sed publice argue eum ne habeas super illo peccatum. 18 Non quaeras ultionem, nec memor eris iniuriae civium tuorum. Diliges amicum tuum sicut temet ipsum. Ego Dominus.

19 "'Leges meas custodite.

"'Iumenta tua non facies coire cum alterius generis animantibus. Agrum tuum non seres diverso semine. Veste quae ex duobus texta est non indueris.

20 "'Homo si dormierit cum muliere coitu seminis quae sit ancilla etiam nubilis et tamen pretio non redempta nec libertate donata, vapulabunt ambo et non morientur, quia non fuit libera. 21 Pro delicto autem suo offeret Domino ad ostium Tabernaculi Testimonii arietem, 22 orabitque pro eo sacerdos et pro peccato eius coram Domino, et repropitiabitur ei, dimitteturque peccatum.

23 "'Quando ingressi fueritis terram et plantaveritis in ea ligna pomifera, auferetis praeputia eorum. Poma quae germinant inmunda erunt vobis, nec edetis ex eis. 24 Quarto autem anno, omnis fructus eorum sanctificabitur laudabilis Domino. 25 Quinto autem anno comedetis fructus, congregantes poma quae proferunt. Ego Dominus, Deus vester.

justly. Respect not the person of the poor, nor honour the countenance of the mighty, *but* judge thy neighbour according to justice.

16 "'Thou shalt not be a detractor nor a whisperer among the people.

"'Thou shalt not stand against the blood of thy neighbour. I am the Lord.

17 "'Thou shalt not hate thy brother in thy heart, but reprove him openly lest thou incur sin through him. 18 Seek not revenge, nor be mindful of the injury of thy citizens. Thou shalt love thy friend as thyself. I am the Lord.

19 "'Keep ye my laws.

"'Thou shalt not make thy cattle to gender with beasts of any other kind. Thou shalt not sow thy field with different seeds. Thou shalt not wear a garment that is woven of two sorts.

20 "'If a man carnally lie with a woman that is a bondservant and marriageable and yet not redeemed with a price nor made free, they both shall be scourged, and they shall not be put to death, because she was not a free woman. 21 And for his trespass he shall offer a ram to the Lord at the door of the Tabernacle of the Testimony, 22 and the priest shall pray for him and for his sin before the Lord, and he shall have mercy on him, and the sin shall be forgiven.

23 "'When you shall be come into the land and shall have planted in it fruit trees, you shall take away the *firstfruits* of them. The fruit that comes forth shall be unclean to you, neither shall you eat of them. 24 But in the fourth year, all their fruit shall be sanctified to the praise of the Lord. 25 And in the fifth year you shall eat the fruits thereof, gathering the increase thereof. I am the Lord, your God.

26 "'Non comedetis cum sanguine.

"'Non augurabimini nec observabitis somnia.

27 "'Neque in rotundum adtondebitis comam, nec radatis barbam. 28 Et super mortuo non incidetis carnem vestram, neque figuras aliquas aut stigmata facietis vobis. Ego Dominus.

29 "'Ne prostituas filiam tuam ne contaminetur terra et impleatur piaculo.

30 "'Sabbata mea custodite, et sanctuarium meum metuite. Ego Dominus.

31 "'Ne declinetis ad magos, nec ab ariolis aliquid sciscitemini ut polluamini per eos. Ego Dominus, Deus vester.

32 "'Coram cano capite consurge, et honora personam senis, et time Dominum, Deum tuum. Ego sum Dominus.

33 "'Si habitaverit advena in terra vestra et moratus fuerit inter vos, ne exprobretis ei, 34 sed sit inter vos quasi indigena, et diligetis eum quasi vosmet ipsos, fuistis enim et vos advenae in terra Aegypti. Ego Dominus, Deus vester.

35 "'Nolite facere iniquum aliquid in iudicio, in regula, in pondere, in mensura. 36 Statera iusta et aequa sint pondera, iustus modius aequusque sextarius. Ego Dominus, Deus vester, qui eduxi vos de terra Aegypti.

37 "'Custodite omnia praecepta mea et universa iudicia, et facite ea. Ego Dominus.'"

26 "'You shall not eat with blood.

"'You shall not divine nor observe dreams.

27 "'Nor shall you cut your hair roundwise, nor shave your beard. 28 You shall not make any cuttings in your flesh for the dead, neither shall you make in yourselves any figures or marks. I am the Lord.

29 "'Make not thy daughter a common strumpet lest the land be defiled and filled with wickedness.

30 "'Keep ye my sabbaths, and reverence my sanctuary. I am the Lord.

31 "'Go not aside after wizards, neither ask any thing of soothsayers to be defiled by them. I am the Lord, your God.

32 "'Rise up before the hoary head, and honour the person of the aged man, and fear the Lord, thy God. I am the Lord.

33 "'If a stranger dwell in your land and abide among you, do not upbraid him, 34 but let him be among you as one of the same country, and you shall love him as yourselves, for you were strangers in the land of Egypt. I am the Lord, your God.

35 "'Do not any unjust thing in judgment, in rule, in weight or in measure. 36 Let the balance be just and the weights equal, the bushel just and the sextary equal. I am the Lord, your God, that brought you out of the land of Egypt.

37 "'Keep all my precepts and all my judgments, and do them. I am the Lord.'"

Caput 20

Locutusque est Dominus ad Mosen, dicens, 2 "Haec loqueris filiis Israhel: 'Homo de filiis Israhel et de advenis qui habitant in Israhel si quis dederit de semine suo idolo Moloch, morte moriatur: populus terrae lapidabit eum. 3 Et ego ponam faciem meam contra illum, succidamque eum de medio populi sui eo quod dederit de semine suo Moloch et contaminaverit sanctuarium meum ac polluerit nomen sanctum meum. 4 Quod si neglegens populus terrae et quasi parvipendens imperium meum dimiserit hominem qui dederit de semine suo Moloch nec voluerit eum occidere, 5 ponam faciem meam super hominem illum et cognationem eius succidamque et ipsum et omnes qui consenserunt ei ut fornicarentur cum Moloch de medio populi sui.

6 "'Anima quae declinaverit ad magos et ariolos et fornicata fuerit cum eis, ponam faciem meam contra eam et interficiam illam de medio populi sui.

7 "'Sanctificamini, et estote sancti, quia ego Dominus, Deus vester. 8 Custodite praecepta mea, et facite ea. Ego Dominus qui sanctifico vos.

9 "'Qui maledixerit patri suo aut matri, morte moriatur. Patri matrique maledixit; sanguis eius sit super eum.

Chapter 20

Divers crimes to be punished with death.

And the Lord spoke to Moses, saying, 2 "Thus shalt thou say to the children of Israel: 'If any man of the children of Israel or of the strangers that dwell in Israel give of his seed to the idol Molech, dying let him die: the people of the land shall stone him. 3 And I will set my face against him, and I will cut him off from the midst of his people because he hath given of his seed to Molech and hath defiled my sanctuary and profaned my holy name. 4 And if the people of the land neglecting and as it were little regarding my commandment let alone the man that hath given of his seed to Molech and will not kill him, 5 I will set my face against that man and his kindred and will cut off both him and all that consented with him to commit fornication with Molech out of the midst of their people.

6 "'The soul that shall go aside after magicians and soothsayers and shall commit fornication with them, I will set my face against that soul and destroy it out of the midst of its people.

7 "'Sanctify yourselves, and be ye holy, because I am the Lord, your God. 8 Keep my precepts, and do them. I am the Lord that sanctify you.

9 "'He that curseth his father or mother, dying let him die. He hath cursed his father and mother; let his blood be upon him.

10 "'Si moechatus quis fuerit cum uxore alterius et adulterium perpetrarit cum coniuge proximi sui, morte moriantur, et moechus et adultera.

11 "'Qui dormierit cum noverca sua et revelaverit ignominiam patris sui, morte moriantur ambo. Sanguis eorum sit super eos. 12 Si quis dormierit cum nuru sua, uterque moriantur, quia scelus operati sunt. Sanguis eorum sit super eos.

13 "'Qui dormierit cum masculo coitu femineo, uterque operati sunt nefas; morte moriantur. Sit sanguis eorum super eos.

14 "'Qui supra uxorem filiam duxerit matrem eius, scelus operatus est. Vivus ardebit cum eis, nec permanebit tantum nefas in medio vestri.

15 "'Qui cum iumento et pecore coierit, morte moriatur; pecus quoque occidite. 16 Mulier quae subcubuerit cuilibet iumento simul interficietur cum eo. Sanguis eorum sit super eos.

17 "'Qui acceperit sororem suam, filiam patris sui vel filiam matris suae, et viderit turpitudinem eius illaque conspexerit fratris ignominiam, nefariam rem operati sunt; occidentur in conspectu populi sui eo quod turpitudinem suam mutuo revelarint, et portabunt iniquitatem suam.

18 "'Qui coierit cum muliere in fluxu menstruo et revelaverit turpitudinem eius ipsaque aperuerit fontem sanguinis sui, interficientur ambo de medio populi sui.

19 "'Turpitudinem materterae tuae et amitae tuae non discoperies. Qui hoc fecerit ignominiam carnis suae nudavit;

10 "'If any man commit adultery with the wife of another and *defile* his neighbour's wife, let them be put to death, both the adulterer and the adulteress.

11 "'*If a man* lie with his stepmother and discover the nakedness of his father, let them both be put to death. Their blood be upon them. 12 If any man lie with his daughter-in-law, let both die, because they have done a heinous crime. Their blood be upon them.

13 "'*If any one* lie with a man as with a woman, both have committed an abomination; let them be put to death. Their blood be upon them.

14 "'*If any man after marrying the daughter* marry her mother, he hath done a heinous crime. He shall be burnt alive with them, neither shall so great an abomination remain in the midst of you.

15 "'He that shall copulate with any beast or cattle, dying let him die; the beast also ye shall kill. 16 The woman that shall lie under any beast shall be killed together with the same. Their blood be upon them.

17 "'*If any man take* his sister, the daughter of his father or the daughter of his mother, and see her nakedness and she behold her brother's shame, they have committed a crime; they shall be slain in the sight of their people because they have discovered one another's nakedness, and they shall bear their iniquity.

18 "'*If any man lie* with a woman in her *flowers* and uncover her nakedness and she open the fountain of her blood, both shall be destroyed out of the midst of their people.

19 "'Thou shalt not uncover the nakedness of thy aunt by thy mother and of thy aunt by thy father. He that doth this hath uncovered the shame of his own flesh; both shall bear

portabunt ambo iniquitatem suam. 20 Qui coierit cum uxore patrui vel avunculi sui et revelaverit ignominiam cognationis suae, portabunt ambo peccatum suum. Absque liberis morientur.

21 "'Qui duxerit uxorem fratris sui rem facit inlicitam. Turpitudinem fratris sui revelavit; absque liberis erunt.

22 "'Custodite leges meas atque iudicia, et facite ea ne et vos evomat terra quam intraturi estis et habitaturi. 23 Nolite ambulare in legitimis nationum quas ego expulsurus sum ante vos, omnia enim haec fecerunt et abominatus sum eos. 24 Vobis autem loquor, "Possidete terram eorum quam dabo vobis in hereditatem, terram fluentem lacte et melle."

"'Ego Dominus, Deus vester, qui separavi vos a ceteris populis. 25 Separate ergo et vos iumentum mundum ab inmundo et avem mundam ab inmunda. Ne polluatis animas vestras in pecore et avibus et cunctis quae moventur in terra et quae vobis ostendi esse polluta. 26 Eritis sancti mihi, quia sanctus ego sum, Dominus, et separavi vos a ceteris populis ut essetis mei.

27 "'Vir sive mulier in quibus pythonicus vel divinationis fuerit spiritus, morte moriantur. Lapidibus obruent eos. Sanguis eorum sit super illos.'"

their iniquity. 20 *If any man lie* with the wife of his uncle by the father or of his uncle by the mother and uncover the shame of his near akin, both shall bear their sin. They shall die without children.

21 "'He that marrieth his brother's wife doth an unlawful thing. He hath uncovered his brother's nakedness; they shall be without children.

22 "'Keep my laws and my judgments, and do them lest the land into which you are to enter *to dwell therein* vomit you also out. 23 Walk not after the laws of the nations which I will cast out before you, for they have done all these things and *therefore* I abhorred them. 24 But to you I say, "Possess their land which I will give you for an inheritance, a land flowing with milk and honey."

"'I am the Lord, your God, who have separated you from other people. 25 Therefore do you also separate the clean beast from the unclean and the clean fowl from the unclean. Defile not your souls with beasts or birds or any things that move on the earth and which I have shewn you to be unclean. 26 You shall be holy unto me because I, the Lord, am holy, and I have separated you from other people that you should be mine.

27 "'A man or woman in whom there is a pythonical or divining spirit, dying let them die. They shall stone them. Their blood be upon them.'"

Caput 21

Dixit quoque Dominus ad Mosen, "Loquere ad sacerdotes, filios Aaron, et dices eis, 'Ne contaminetur sacerdos in mortibus civium suorum, 2 nisi tantum in consanguineis ac propinquis, id est, super matre et patre et filio ac filia, fratre quoque 3 et sorore virgine quae non est nupta viro. 4 Sed nec in principe populi sui contaminabitur. 5 Non radent caput nec barbam neque in carnibus suis facient incisuras. 6 Sancti erunt Deo suo et non polluent nomen eius, incensum enim Domini et panes Dei sui offerunt, et ideo sancti erunt.

7 "'Scortum et vile prostibulum non ducet uxorem nec eam quae repudiata est a marito, quia consecrati sunt Deo suo 8 et panes propositionis offerunt. Sint ergo sancti quia et ego sanctus sum, Dominus qui sanctifico eos.

9 "'Sacerdotis filia si deprehensa fuerit in stupro et violaverit nomen patris sui, flammis exuretur.

10 "'Pontifex, id est, sacerdos maximus inter fratres suos, super cuius caput fusum est unctionis oleum et cuius manus

Chapter 21

Ordinances relating to the priests.

The Lord said also to Moses, "Speak to the priests, the sons of Aaron, and thou shalt say to them, 'Let not a priest incur an uncleanness at the death of his citizens, 2 but only for his kin such as are near in blood, that is to say, for his father and for his mother and for his son and for his daughter, for his brother also 3 and for a maiden sister who hath had no husband. 4 But not even for the prince of his people shall he do any thing that may make him unclean. 5 Neither shall they shave their head nor their beard nor make incisions in their flesh. 6 They shall be holy to their God and shall not profane his name, for they offer the burnt offering of the Lord and the bread of their God, and therefore they shall be holy.

7 "'*They* shall not take to wife a harlot or a vile prostitute nor one that has been *put away from* her husband, because they are consecrated to their God 8 and offer the loaves of proposition. Let them therefore be holy because I also am holy, the Lord who sanctify them.

9 "'If the daughter of a priest be taken in whoredom and dishonour the name of her father, she shall be burnt with fire.

10 "'The high priest, that is to say, the priest that is the greatest among his brethren, upon whose head the oil of

in sacerdotio consecratae sunt vestitusque est sanctis vestibus, caput suum non discoperiet; vestimenta non scindet, 11 et ad omnem mortuum non ingredietur omnino. Super patre quoque suo et matre non contaminabitur, 12 nec egredietur de sanctis ne polluat sanctuarium Domini, quia oleum sanctae unctionis Dei sui super eum est. Ego Dominus.

13 "'Virginem ducet uxorem 14 viduam autem et repudiatam et sordidam atque meretricem non accipiet, sed puellam de populo suo. 15 Ne commisceat stirpem generis sui vulgo gentis suae, quia ego Dominus qui sanctifico eum.'"

16 Locutusque est Dominus ad Mosen, dicens, 17 "Loquere ad Aaron, 'Homo de semine tuo per familias qui habuerit maculam, non offeret panes Deo suo. 18 Nec accedet ad ministerium eius. Si caecus fuerit, si claudus, si parvo vel grandi vel torto naso, 19 si fracto pede, si manu, 20 si gibbus, si lippus, si albuginem habens in oculo, si iugem scabiem, si inpetiginem in corpore vel hirniosus, 21 omnis qui habuerit maculam de semine Aaron, sacerdotis, non accedet offerre hostias Domino nec panes Deo suo. 22 Vescetur tamen panibus qui offeruntur in sanctuario, 23 ita dumtaxat ut intra velum non ingrediatur nec accedat ad altare, quia maculam habet et contaminare non debet sanctuarium meum. Ego Dominus qui sanctifico eos.'"

24 Locutus est ergo Moses ad Aaron et ad filios eius et ad omnem Israhel cuncta quae sibi fuerant imperata.

unction hath been poured and whose hands have been consecrated for the priesthood and who hath been vested with the holy vestments, shall not uncover his head; he shall not rend his garments, 11 nor shall he go in at all to any dead person. Not even for his father or his mother shall he be defiled, 12 neither shall he go out of the holy places lest he defile the sanctuary of the Lord, because the oil of the holy unction of his God is upon him. I am the Lord.

13 "'He shall take a virgin unto his wife, 14 but a widow or one that is divorced or defiled or a harlot he shall not take, but a maid of his own people. 15 He shall not mingle the stock of his kindred with the common people of his nation, for I am the Lord who sanctify him.'"

16 And the Lord spoke to Moses, saying, 17 "Say to Aaron, *'Whosoever* of thy seed throughout their families hath a blemish, he shall not offer bread to his God. 18 Neither shall he approach to minister to him. If he be blind, if he be lame, if he have a little or a great or a crooked nose, 19 if his foot or if his hand be broken, 20 if he be crookbacked or blear-eyed or have a pearl in his eye or a continual scab or a dry scurf in his body or a rupture, 21 whosoever of the seed of Aaron, the priest, hath a blemish, he shall not approach to offer sacrifices to the Lord nor bread to his God. 22 He shall eat nevertheless of the loaves that are offered in the sanctuary, 23 yet so that he enter not within the veil nor approach to the altar, because he hath a blemish and he must not defile my sanctuary. I am the Lord who sanctify them.'"

24 Moses therefore spoke to Aaron and to his sons and to all Israel all the things that had been commanded him.

Caput 22

Locutus quoque est Dominus ad Mosen, dicens, 2 "Loquere ad Aaron et ad filios eius ut caveant ab his quae consecrata sunt filiorum Israhel et non contaminent nomen sanctificatorum mihi quae ipsi offerunt. Ego Dominus. 3 Dic ad eos et ad posteros eorum, 'Omnis homo qui accesserit de stirpe vestra ad ea quae consecrata sunt et quae obtulerunt filii Israhel Domino in quo est inmunditia peribit coram Domino. Ego sum Dominus.

4 "'Homo de semine Aaron qui fuerit leprosus aut patiens fluxum seminis non vescetur de his quae sanctificata sunt mihi donec sanetur. Qui tetigerit inmundum super mortuo et ex quo egreditur semen quasi coitus 5 et qui tangit reptile et quodlibet inmundum cuius tactus est sordidus 6 inmundus erit usque ad vesperum et non vescetur his quae sanctificata sunt. Sed cum laverit carnem suam aqua 7 et occubuerit sol, tunc mundatus vescetur de sanctificatis quia cibus illius est. 8 Morticinum et captum a bestia non comedent nec polluentur in eis. Ego sum Dominus.

Chapter 22

Who may eat the holy things and what things may be offered.

And the Lord spoke to Moses, saying, 2 "Speak to Aaron and to his sons that they beware of those things that are consecrated of the children of Israel and defile not the name of the things sanctified to me which they offer. I am the Lord. 3 Say to them and to their posterity, 'Every man of your race that approacheth to those things that are consecrated and which the children of Israel have offered to the Lord in whom there is uncleanness shall perish before the Lord. I am the Lord.

4 "'The man of the seed of Aaron that is a leper or that suffereth a running of the seed shall not eat of those things that are sanctified to me until he be healed. He that toucheth any thing unclean by occasion of the dead and he whose seed goeth from him as in generation 5 and he that toucheth a creeping thing or any unclean thing the touching of which is defiling 6 shall be unclean until the evening and shall not eat those things that are sanctified. But when he hath washed his flesh with water 7 and the sun is down, then being purified he shall eat of the sanctified things because it is his meat. 8 That which dieth of itself and that which was taken by a beast they shall not eat nor be defiled therewith. I am the Lord.

9 "'Custodiant praecepta mea ut non subiaceant peccato et moriantur in sanctuario cum polluerint illud. Ego Dominus qui sanctifico eos.

10 "'Omnis alienigena non comedet de sanctificatis. Inquilinus sacerdotis et mercennarius non vescentur ex eis. 11 Quem autem sacerdos emerit et qui vernaculus domus eius fuerit, hii comedent ex eis. 12 Si filia sacerdotis cuilibet ex populo nupta fuerit, de his quae sanctificata sunt et de primitiis non vescetur. 13 Sin autem vidua vel repudiata et absque liberis reversa fuerit ad domum patris sui, sicut puella consuerat aletur cibis patris sui. Omnis alienigena comedendi ex eis non habet potestatem.

14 "'Qui comederit de sanctificatis per ignorantiam addet quintam partem cum eo quod comedit et dabit sacerdoti in sanctuarium, 15 nec contaminabunt sanctificata filiorum Israhel quae offerunt Domino 16 ne forte sustineant iniquitatem delicti sui cum sanctificata comederint. Ego Dominus qui sanctifico eos.'"

17 Locutusque est Dominus ad Mosen, dicens, 18 "Loquere ad Aaron et ad filios eius et ad omnes filios Israhel, dicesque ad eos, 'Homo de domo Israhel et de advenis qui habitant apud vos qui obtulerit oblationem suam, vel vota solvens vel sponte offerens, quicquid illud obtulerit in holocaustum Domini 19 ut offeratur per vos, masculus inmaculatus erit ex bubus et ovibus et ex capris. 20 Si maculam habuerit non offeretis, neque erit acceptabile.

21 "'Homo qui obtulerit victimam pacificorum Domino, vel vota solvens vel sponte offerens, tam de bubus quam de

9 "'Let them keep my precepts that they may not fall into sin and die in the sanctuary when they shall have defiled it. I am the Lord who sanctify them.

10 "'No stranger shall eat of the sanctified things. A sojourner of the *priests* or a hired servant shall not eat of them. 11 But he whom the priest hath bought and he that is his servant born in his house, these shall eat of them. 12 If the daughter of a priest be married to any of the people, she shall not eat of those things that are sanctified nor of the firstfruits. 13 But if she be a widow or divorced and having no children return to her father's house, she shall eat of her father's meats as she was wont to do when she was a maid. No stranger hath leave to eat of them.

14 "'He that eateth of the sanctified things through ignorance shall add the fifth part with that which he ate and shall give it to the priest into the sanctuary, 15 and they shall not profane the sanctified things of the children of Israel which they offer to the Lord 16 lest perhaps they bear the iniquity of their trespass when they shall have eaten the sanctified things. I am the Lord who sanctify them.'"

17 And the Lord spoke to Moses, saying, 18 "Speak to Aaron and to his sons and to all the children of Israel, and thou shalt say to them, 'The man of the house of Israel and of the strangers who dwell with you that offereth his oblation, either paying his vows or offering of his own accord, whatsoever it be which he presenteth for a holocaust of the Lord 19 to be offered by you, it shall be a male without blemish of the beeves or *of* the sheep or of the goats. 20 If it have a blemish you shall not offer it, neither shall it be acceptable.

21 "'The man that offereth a victim of peace offerings to the Lord, either paying his vows or offering of his own ac-

ovibus, inmaculatum offeret ut acceptabile sit. Omnis macula non erit in eo. 22 Si caecum fuerit, si fractum, si cicatricem habens, si papulas aut scabiem vel inpetiginem, non offeretis ea Domino neque adolebitis ex eis super altare Domini. 23 Bovem et ovem aure et cauda amputatis voluntarie offerre potes, votum autem ex his solvi non potest. 24 Omne animal quod vel contritis vel tunsis vel sectis ablatisque testiculis est non offeretis Domino, et in terra vestra hoc omnino ne faciatis. 25 De manu alienigenae non offeretis panes Deo vestro et quicquid aliud dare voluerit, quia corrupta et maculata sunt omnia. Non suscipietis ea.'"

26 Locutusque est Dominus ad Mosen, dicens, 27 "Bos, ovis et capra, cum genita fuerint, septem diebus erunt sub ubere matris suae, die autem octavo et deinceps, offerri poterunt Domino. 28 Sive illa bos sive ovis, non immolabuntur una die cum fetibus suis. 29 Si immolaveritis hostiam pro gratiarum actione Domino ut possit esse placabilis, 30 eodem die comedetis eam; non remanebit quicquam in mane alterius diei. Ego Dominus.

31 "Custodite mandata mea, et facite ea. Ego Dominus. 32 Ne polluatis nomen meum sanctum ut sanctificer in medio filiorum Israhel. Ego Dominus qui sanctifico vos 33 et eduxi de terra Aegypti ut essem vobis in Deum. Ego Dominus."

cord, whether of beeves or of sheep, shall offer it without blemish that it may be acceptable. There shall be no blemish in it. 22 If it be blind or broken or have a scar or blisters or a scab or a dry scurf, you shall not offer them to the Lord nor burn any thing of them upon the Lord's altar. 23 An ox or a sheep that hath the ear and the tail cut off thou mayst offer voluntarily, but a vow may not be paid with them. 24 You shall not offer to the Lord any beast that hath the testicles bruised or crushed or cut and taken away, neither shall you do any such thing in your land. 25 You shall not offer bread to your God from the hand of a stranger nor any other thing that he would give, because they are all corrupted and defiled. You shall not receive them.'"

26 And the Lord spoke to Moses, saying, 27 "When a bullock or a sheep or a goat is brought forth, they shall be seven days under the udder of their dam, but the eighth day and thenceforth, they may be offered to the Lord. 28 Whether it be a cow or a sheep, they shall not be sacrificed the same day with their young ones. 29 If you immolate a victim for thanksgiving to the Lord that he may be favourable, 30 you shall eat it the same day; there shall not any of it remain until the morning of the next day. I am the Lord.

31 "Keep my commandments, and do them. I am the Lord. 32 Profane not my holy name that I may be sanctified in the midst of the children of Israel. I am the Lord who sanctify you 33 and who brought you out of the land of Egypt that I might be your God. I am the Lord."

Caput 23

Locutusque est Dominus ad Mosen, dicens, 2 "Loquere filiis Israhel, et dices ad eos, 'Hae sunt feriae Domini quas vocabitis sanctas. 3 Sex diebus facietis opus; dies septimus, quia sabbati requies est, vocabitur sanctus. Omne opus non facietis in eo; sabbatum Domini est in cunctis habitationibus vestris.

4 "'Hae sunt ergo feriae Domini sanctae quas celebrare debetis temporibus suis. 5 Mense primo, quartadecima die mensis, ad vesperum, Phase Domini est, 6 et quintadecima die mensis huius sollemnitas azymorum Domini est. Septem diebus azyma comedetis. 7 Dies primus erit vobis celeberrimus sanctusque. Omne opus servile non facietis in eo, 8 sed offeretis sacrificium in igne Domino septem diebus. Dies autem septimus erit celebrior et sanctior, nullumque servile opus facietis in eo.'"

9 Locutusque est Dominus ad Mosen, dicens, 10 "Loquere filiis Israhel, et dices ad eos, 'Cum ingressi fueritis terram quam ego dabo vobis et messueritis segetem, feretis manipulos spicarum, primitias messis vestrae, ad sacerdotem, 11 qui elevabit fasciculum coram Domino ut acceptabile sit pro vobis altero die sabbati et sanctificabit illum. 12 Atque in

Chapter 23

Holy days to be kept.

And the Lord spoke to Moses, saying, 2 "Speak to the children of Israel, and thou shalt say to them, 'These are the feasts of the Lord which you shall call holy. 3 Six days shall ye do work; the seventh day, because it is the rest of the sabbath, shall be called holy. You shall do no work on that day; it is the sabbath of the Lord in all your habitations.

4 "'These also are the holy days of the Lord which you must celebrate in their seasons. 5 The first month, the fourteenth day of the month, at evening, is the Phase of the Lord, 6 and the fifteenth day of the same month is the solemnity of the unleavened bread of the Lord. Seven days shall you eat unleavened bread. 7 The first day shall be most solemn unto you and holy. You shall do no servile work therein, 8 but you shall offer sacrifice in fire to the Lord seven days. And the seventh day shall be more solemn and more holy, and you shall do no servile work therein.'"

9 And the Lord spoke to Moses, saying, 10 "Speak to the children of Israel, and thou shalt say to them, 'When you shall have entered into the land which I will give you and shall reap your corn, you shall bring sheaves of ears, the firstfruits of your harvest, to the priest, 11 who shall lift up the shed before the Lord the next day after the sabbath that it may be acceptable for you and shall sanctify it. 12 And on the

eodem die quo manipulus consecratur, caedetur agnus inmaculatus anniculus in holocaustum Domini. 13 Et libamenta offerentur cum eo, duae decimae similae conspersae
oleo in incensum Domini odoremque suavissimum, liba
quoque vini, quarta pars hin. 14 Panem et pulentam et pultes
non comedetis ex segete usque ad diem qua offeratis ex ea
Deo vestro. Praeceptum est sempiternum in generationibus
cunctisque habitaculis vestris. 15 Numerabitis ergo ab altero
die sabbati in quo obtulistis manipulum primitiarum septem ebdomadas plenas, 16 usque ad alteram diem expletionis
ebdomadae septimae, id est, quinquaginta dies, et sic offeretis sacrificium novum Domino 17 ex omnibus habitaculis
vestris, panes primitiarum duos de duabus decimis similae
fermentatae quos coquetis in primitias Domini. 18 Offeretisque cum panibus septem agnos inmaculatos anniculos et
vitulum de armento unum et arietes duos, et erunt in holocausto cum libamentis suis in odorem suavissimum Domino. 19 Facietis et hircum pro peccato duosque agnos anniculos hostias pacificorum. 20 Cumque elevaverit eos sacerdos
cum panibus primitiarum coram Domino cedent in usum
eius. 21 Et vocabitis hunc diem celeberrimum atque sanctis-
simum. Omne opus servile non facietis in eo. Legitimum
sempiternum erit in cunctis habitaculis et generationibus
vestris.

22 "'Postquam autem messueritis segetem terrae vestrae,
non secabitis eam usque ad solum, nec remanentes spicas
colligetis, sed pauperibus et peregrinis dimittetis eas. Ego
Dominus, Deus vester.'"

23 Locutusque est Dominus ad Mosen, dicens, 24 "Lo-

same day that the sheaf is consecrated, a lamb without blemish of the first year shall be killed for a holocaust of the Lord. 13 And the libations shall be offered with it, two tenths of flour tempered with oil for a burnt offering of the Lord and a most sweet odour, libations also of wine, the fourth part of a hin. 14 You shall not eat either bread or parched corn or frumenty of the harvest until the day that you *shall* offer thereof to your God. It is a precept for ever throughout your generations and all your dwellings. 15 You shall count therefore from the morrow after the sabbath wherein you offered the sheaf of the firstfruits seven full weeks, 16 even unto the morrow after the seventh week be expired, that is to say, fifty days, and so you shall offer a new sacrifice to the Lord 17 out of all your dwellings, two loaves of the firstfruits of two tenths of flour leavened which you shall bake for the firstfruits of the Lord. 18 And you shall offer with the loaves seven lambs without blemish of the first year and one calf from the herd and two rams, and they shall be for a holocaust with their libations for a most sweet odour to the Lord. 19 You shall offer also a buck-goat for sin and two lambs of the first year for sacrifices of peace offerings. 20 And when the priest hath lifted them up with the loaves of the firstfruits before the Lord they shall fall to his use. 21 And you shall call this day most solemn and most holy. You shall do no servile work therein. It shall be an everlasting ordinance in all your dwellings and generations.

22 "'And when you reap the corn of your land, you shall not cut it to the very ground, neither shall you gather the ears that remain, but you shall leave them for the poor and for the strangers. I am the Lord, your God.'"

23 And the Lord spoke to Moses, saying, 24 "Say to the

quere filiis Israhel, 'Mense septimo, prima die mensis, erit vobis sabbatum, memoriale, clangentibus tubis, et vocabitur sanctum. 25 Omne opus servile non facietis in eo, et offeretis holocaustum Domino.'"

26 Locutusque est Dominus ad Mosen, dicens, 27 "Decimo die mensis huius septimi dies expiationum erit celeberrimus, et vocabitur sanctus, adfligetisque animas vestras in eo et offeretis holocaustum Domino. 28 Omne opus servile non facietis in tempore diei huius, quia dies propitiationis est ut propitietur vobis Dominus, Deus vester. 29 Omnis anima quae adflicta non fuerit die hoc peribit de populis suis, 30 et quae operis quippiam fecerit, delebo eam de populo suo. 31 Nihil ergo operis facietis in eo. Legitimum sempiternum erit vobis in cunctis generationibus et habitationibus vestris. 32 Sabbatum requietionis est, et adfligetis animas vestras; die nono mensis, a vespero usque ad vesperum celebrabitis sabbata vestra."

33 Et locutus est Dominus ad Mosen, dicens, 34 "Loquere filiis Israhel, 'A quintodecimo die mensis huius septimi erunt feriae tabernaculorum septem diebus Domino. 35 Dies primus vocabitur celeberrimus atque sanctissimus: omne opus servile non facietis in eo. Et septem diebus offeretis holocausta Domino. 36 Dies quoque octavus erit celeberrimus atque sanctissimus, et offeretis holocaustum Domino, est enim coetus atque collectae. Omne opus servile non facietis in eo.

37 "'Hae sunt feriae Domini quas vocabitis celeberrimas et sanctissimas offeretisque in eis oblationes Domino, holo-

children of Israel, 'The seventh month, on the first day of the month, you shall keep a sabbath, a memorial, with the sound of trumpets, and it shall be called holy. 25 You shall do no servile work therein, and you shall offer a holocaust to the Lord.'"

26 And the Lord spoke to Moses, saying, 27 "Upon the tenth day of this seventh month shall be the day of atonement; *it shall be* most solemn and shall be called holy, and you shall afflict your souls on that day and shall offer a holocaust to the Lord. 28 You shall do no servile work in the time of this day, because it is a day of propitiation that the Lord, your God, may be merciful unto you. 29 Every soul that is not afflicted on this day shall perish from among his people, 30 and every soul that shall do any work, the same will I destroy from among his people. 31 You shall do no work therefore on that day. It shall be an everlasting ordinance unto you in all your generations and dwellings. 32 It is a sabbath of rest, and you shall afflict your souls; beginning on the ninth day of the month, from evening until evening you shall celebrate your sabbaths."

33 And the Lord spoke to Moses, saying, 34 "Say to the children of Israel, 'From the fifteenth day of this *same* seventh month shall be *kept* the feast of tabernacles seven days to the Lord. 35 The first day shall be called most solemn and most holy: you shall do no servile work therein. And seven days you shall offer holocausts to the Lord. 36 The eighth day also shall be most solemn and most holy, and you shall offer holocausts to the Lord, for it is the day of assembly and congregation. You shall do no servile work therein.

37 "'These are the feasts of the Lord which you shall call most solemn and most holy and shall offer on them obla-

causta et libamenta iuxta ritum uniuscuiusque diei, 38 exceptis sabbatis Domini donisque vestris et quae offeretis ex voto vel quae sponte tribuetis Domino.

39 "A quintodecimo ergo die mensis septimi quando congregaveritis omnes fructus terrae vestrae celebrabitis ferias Domini septem diebus. Die primo et die octavo erit sabbatum, id est, requies. 40 Sumetisque vobis die primo fructus arboris pulcherrimae spatulasque palmarum et ramos ligni densarum frondium et salices de torrente, et laetabimini coram Domino, Deo vestro, 41 celebrabitisque sollemnitatem eius septem diebus per annum. Legitimum sempiternum erit in generationibus vestris. Mense septimo festa celebrabitis. 42 Et habitabitis in umbraculis septem diebus. Omnis qui de genere est Israhel manebit in tabernaculis 43 ut discant posteri vestri quod in tabernaculis habitare fecerim filios Israhel cum educerem eos de terra Aegypti. Ego Dominus, Deus vester.'"

44 Locutusque est Moses super sollemnitatibus Domini ad filios Israhel.

tions to the Lord, holocausts and libations according to the rite of every day, 38 besides the sabbaths of the Lord and your gifts and those things that you shall offer by vow or which you shall give to the Lord voluntarily.

39 "'So from the fifteenth day of the seventh month when you shall have gathered in all the fruits of your land you shall celebrate the feast of the Lord seven days. On the first day and the eighth shall be a sabbath, that is, a *day of* rest. 40 And you shall take to you on the first day the fruits of the fairest tree and branches of palm trees and boughs of *thick trees* and willows of the brook, and you shall rejoice before the Lord, your God, 41 and you shall keep the solemnity thereof seven days in the year. It shall be an everlasting ordinance in your generations. In the seventh month shall you celebrate this feast. 42 And you shall dwell in bowers seven days. Every one that is of the race of Israel shall dwell in tabernacles 43 that your posterity may know that I made the children of Israel to dwell in tabernacles when I brought them out of the land of Egypt. I am the Lord, your God.'"

44 And Moses spoke concerning the feasts of the Lord to the children of Israel.

Caput 24

Et locutus est Dominus ad Mosen, dicens, 2 "Praecipe filiis Israhel ut adferant tibi oleum de olivis purissimum ac lucidum ad concinnandas lucernas iugiter 3 extra velum testimonii in Tabernaculo Foederis. Ponetque eas Aaron a vespere usque in mane coram Domino cultu rituque perpetuo in generationibus vestris. 4 Super candelabro mundissimo ponentur semper in conspectu Domini. 5 Accipies quoque similam et coques ex ea duodecim panes; qui singuli habebunt duas decimas, 6 quorum senos altrinsecus super mensam purissimam coram Domino statues. 7 Et pones super eos tus lucidissimum ut sit panis in monumentum oblationis Domini. 8 Per singula sabbata mutabuntur coram Domino, suscepti a filiis Israhel foedere sempiterno. 9 Eruntque Aaron et filiorum eius ut comedant eos in loco sancto, quia sanctum sanctorum est de sacrificiis Domini iure perpetuo."

10 Ecce autem: egressus filius mulieris Israhelitis, quem pepererat de viro Aegyptio, inter filios Israhel iurgatus est in castris cum viro Israhelite. 11 Cumque blasphemasset no-

Chapter 24

The oil for the lamps. The loaves of proposition. The punishment of blasphemy.

And the Lord spoke to Moses, saying, 2 "Command the children of Israel that they bring unto thee the finest and clearest oil of olives to furnish the lamps continually 3 without the veil of the testimony in the Tabernacle of the Covenant. And Aaron shall set them from evening until morning before the Lord by a perpetual service and rite in your generations. 4 They shall be set upon the most pure candlestick before the Lord continually. 5 Thou shalt take also fine flour and shalt bake twelve loaves thereof; two tenths shall be in every loaf, 6 and thou shalt set them six and six, one against another, upon the most clean table before the Lord. 7 And thou shalt put upon them the clearest frankincense that the bread may be for a memorial of the oblation of the Lord. 8 Every sabbath they shall be changed before the Lord, being received of the children of Israel by an everlasting covenant. 9 And they shall be Aaron's and his sons' that they may eat them in the holy place, because it is most holy of the sacrifices of the Lord by a perpetual right."

10 And behold: there went out the son of a woman of Israel, whom she had of an Egyptian, among the children of Israel and fell at words in the camp with a man of Israel. 11 And when he had blasphemed the name and had cursed it,

men et maledixisset ei, adductus est ad Mosen (vocabatur autem mater eius Salumith, filia Dabri de tribu Dan), 12 miseruntque eum in carcerem donec nossent quid iuberet Dominus. 13 Qui locutus est ad Mosen, 14 dicens, "Educ blasphemum extra castra, et ponant omnes qui audierunt manus suas super caput eius, et lapidet eum populus universus. 15 Et ad filios Israhel loqueris: 'Homo qui maledixerit Deo suo portabit peccatum suum, 16 et qui blasphemaverit nomen Domini, morte moriatur. Lapidibus opprimet eum omnis multitudo, sive ille civis seu peregrinus fuerit. Qui blasphemaverit nomen Domini, morte moriatur.

17 "'Qui percusserit et occiderit hominem, morte moriatur.

18 "'Qui percusserit animal reddet vicarium, id est, animam pro anima.

19 "'Qui inrogaverit maculam cuilibet civium suorum, sicut fecit, sic fiet ei: 20 fracturam pro fractura, oculum pro oculo, dentem pro dente restituet. Qualem inflixerit maculam, talem sustinere cogetur.

21 "'Qui percusserit iumentum reddet aliud.

"'Qui percusserit hominem punietur.

22 "Aequum iudicium sit inter vos, sive peregrinus sive civis peccaverit, quia ego sum Dominus, Deus vester.'"

23 Locutusque est Moses ad filios Israhel, et eduxerunt eum qui blasphemaverat extra castra, ac lapidibus oppresserunt. Feceruntque filii Israhel sicut praeceperat Dominus Mosi.

he was brought to Moses (now his mother was called Shelomith, the daughter of Dibri of the tribe of Dan), 12 and they put him into prison till they might know what the Lord would command. 13 And the Lord spoke to Moses, 14 saying, "Bring forth the blasphemer without the camp, and let them that heard him put their hands upon his head, and let all the people stone him. 15 And thou shalt speak to the children of Israel: 'The man that curseth his God shall bear his sin, 16 and he that blasphemeth the name of the Lord, dying let him die. All the multitude shall stone him, whether he be a native or a stranger. He that blasphemeth the name of the Lord, dying let him die.

17 "'He that striketh and killeth a man, dying let him die.

18 "'He that *killeth* a beast shall *make it good,* that is to say, *shall give beast for beast.*

19 "'He that giveth a blemish to any of his neighbours, as he hath done, so shall it be done to him: 20 breach for breach, eye for eye, tooth for tooth shall he restore. What blemish he gave, the like shall he be compelled to suffer.

21 "'He that striketh a beast shall render another.

"'He that striketh a man shall be punished.

22 "'Let there be equal judgment among you, whether he be a stranger or a native that offends, because I am the Lord, your God.'"

23 And Moses spoke to the children of Israel, and they brought forth him that had blasphemed without the camp, and they stoned him. And the children of Israel did as the Lord had commanded Moses.

Caput 25

Locutusque est Dominus ad Mosen in Monte Sinai, dicens, 2 "Loquere filiis Israhel, et dices ad eos, 'Quando ingressi fueritis terram quam ego dabo vobis, sabbatizes sabbatum Domino. 3 Sex annis seres agrum tuum et sex annis putabis vineam tuam colligesque fructus eius. 4 Septimo autem anno sabbatum erit terrae requietionis Domini. Agrum non seres et vineam non putabis. 5 Quae sponte gignet humus non metes, et uvas primitiarum tuarum non colliges quasi vindemiam, annus enim requietionis terrae est, 6 sed erunt vobis in cibum tibi et servo tuo, ancillae et mercennario tuo et advenae qui peregrinatur apud te. 7 Iumentis tuis et pecoribus omnia quae nascuntur praebebunt cibum. 8 Numerabis quoque tibi septem ebdomades annorum, id est, septem septies, quae simul faciunt annos quadraginta novem, 9 et clanges bucina mense septimo, decima die mensis, propitiationis tempore in universa terra vestra. 10 Sanctificabisque annum quinquagesimum et vocabis remissionem cunctis habitatoribus terrae tuae, ipse est enim iobeleus. Revertetur homo ad possessionem suam, et unusquisque rediet ad familiam pristinam 11 quia iobeleus est et quinqua-

Chapter 25

The law of the seventh and of the fiftieth year of jubilee.

And the Lord spoke to Moses in Mount Sinai, saying, 2 "Speak to the children of Israel, and thou shalt say to them, 'When you shall have entered into the land which I will give you, observe the rest of the sabbath to the Lord. 3 Six years thou shalt sow thy field and six years thou shalt prune thy vineyard and shalt gather the fruits thereof. 4 But in the seventh year there shall be a sabbath to the land of the resting of the Lord. Thou shalt not sow thy field nor prune thy vineyard. 5 What the ground shall bring forth of itself thou shalt not reap, neither shalt thou gather the grapes of *the* firstfruits as a vintage, for it is a year of rest to the land, 6 but they shall be unto you for meat to thee and to thy manservant, to thy maidservant and to thy hireling and to the *strangers that sojourn* with thee. 7 All things that grow shall be meat to thy beasts and to thy cattle. 8 Thou shalt also number to thee seven weeks of years, that is to say, seven times seven, which together make forty-nine years, 9 and thou shalt sound the trumpet in the seventh month, the tenth day of the month, in the time of the expiation in all your land. 10 And thou shalt sanctify the fiftieth year and shalt proclaim remission to all the inhabitants of thy land, for it is the year of jubilee. Every man shall return to his possession, and every one shall go back to his former family 11 because it is the jubilee and

gesimus annus. Non seretis neque metetis sponte in agro nascentia, et primitias vindemiae non colligetis, 12 ob sanctificationem iobelei. Sed statim oblata comedetis. 13 Anno iobelei redient omnes ad possessiones suas. 14 Quando vendes quippiam civi tuo vel emes ab eo, ne contristes fratrem tuum, sed iuxta numerum annorum iobelei emes ab eo. 15 Et iuxta supputationem frugum vendet tibi. 16 Quanto plus anni remanserint post iobeleum, tanto crescet et pretium, et quanto minus temporis numeraveris, tanto minoris et emptio constabit, tempus enim frugum vendet tibi.

17 "'Nolite adfligere contribules vestros, sed timeat unusquisque Deum suum, quia ego Dominus, Deus vester. 18 Facite praecepta mea, et iudicia custodite, et implete ea ut habitare possitis in terra absque ullo pavore 19 et gignat vobis humus fructus suos quibus vescamini usque ad saturitatem, nullius impetum formidantes. 20 Quod si dixeritis, "Quid comedemus anno septimo, si non severimus neque collegerimus fruges nostras?" 21 dabo benedictionem meam vobis anno sexto, et faciet fructus trium annorum. 22 Seretisque anno octavo et comedetis veteres fruges usque ad nonum annum. Donec nova nascantur, edetis vetera.

23 "'Terra quoque non veniet in perpetuum, quia mea est et vos advenae et coloni mei estis. 24 Unde cuncta regio possessionis vestrae sub redemptionis condicione vendetur. 25 Si adtenuatus frater tuus vendiderit possessiunculam suam et voluerit propinquus eius, potest redimere quod ille vendiderat. 26 Sin autem non habuerit proximum et ipse pretium ad redimendum potuerit invenire, 27 conputabun-

the fiftieth year. You shall not sow nor reap the things that grow in the field of their own accord, neither shall you gather the firstfruits of the vines, 12 because of the sanctification of the jubilee. But as they grow you shall presently eat them. 13 In the year of the jubilee all shall return to their possessions. 14 When thou shalt sell any thing to thy neighbour or shalt buy of him, grieve not thy brother, but thou shalt buy of him according to the number of years from the jubilee. 15 And he shall sell to thee according to the computation of the fruits. 16 The more years remain after the jubilee, the more shall the price increase, and the less time is *counted,* so much the less shall the purchase cost, for he shall sell to thee the time of the fruits.

17 "'Do not afflict your countrymen, but let every one fear his God, because I am the Lord, your God. 18 Do my precepts, and keep my judgments, and fulfill them that you may dwell in the land without any fear 19 and the ground may yield you its fruits of which you may eat your fill, fearing no man's invasion. 20 But if you say, "What shall we eat the seventh year, if we sow not nor gather our fruits?" 21 I will give you my blessing the sixth year, and it shall yield the fruits of three years. 22 And the eighth year you shall sow and shall eat of the old fruits until the ninth year. Till new grow up, you shall eat the old store.

23 "'The land also shall not be sold for ever, because it is mine and you are strangers and sojourners *with me.* 24 For which cause all the country of your possession shall *be* under the condition of redemption. 25 If thy brother being impoverished sell his little possession and his kinsman will, he may redeem what he had sold. 26 But if he have no kinsman and he himself can find the price to redeem it, 27 the value of the

tur fructus ex eo tempore quo vendidit, et quod reliquum est reddet emptori sicque recipiet possessionem suam. 28 Quod si non invenerit manus eius ut reddat pretium, habebit emptor quod emerat usque ad annum iobeleum, in ipso enim omnis venditio redibit ad dominum et ad possessorem pristinum.

29 "'Qui vendiderit domum intra urbis muros habebit licentiam redimendi donec unus impleatur annus. 30 Si non redemerit et anni circulus fuerit evolutus, emptor possidebit eam et posteri eius in perpetuum, et redimi non poterit, etiam in iobeleo. 31 Sin autem in villa fuerit domus quae muros non habet, agrorum iure vendetur: si ante redempta non fuerit, in iobeleo revertetur ad dominum.

32 "'Aedes Levitarum quae in urbibus sunt semper possunt redimi. 33 Si redemptae non fuerint, in iobeleo revertentur ad dominos quia domus urbium Levitarum pro possessionibus sunt inter filios Israhel. 34 Suburbana autem eorum non venient, quia possessio sempiterna est.

35 "'Si adtenuatus fuerit frater tuus et infirmus manu et susceperis eum quasi advenam et peregrinum et vixerit tecum, 36 ne accipias usuras ab eo nec amplius quam dedisti. Time Deum tuum ut vivere possit frater tuus apud te. 37 Pecuniam tuam non dabis ei ad usuram et frugum superabundantiam non exiges. 38 Ego Dominus, Deus vester, qui eduxi vos de terra Aegypti ut darem vobis terram Chanaan et essem vester Deus. 39 Si paupertate conpulsus vendiderit se tibi frater tuus, non eum opprimes servitute famulorum, 40 sed quasi mercennarius et colonus erit. Usque ad annum

fruits shall be counted from that time when he sold it, and the overplus he shall restore to the buyer and so shall receive his possession again. 28 But if his hands find not the means to repay the price, the buyer shall have what he bought until the year of the jubilee, for in that year all that is sold shall return to the owner and to the ancient possessor.

29 "'He that selleth a house within the walls of a city shall have the liberty to redeem it until one year be expired. 30 If he redeem it not and the whole year be fully out, the buyer shall possess it and his posterity for ever, and it cannot be redeemed, not even in the jubilee. 31 But if the house be in a village that hath no walls, it shall be sold according to the same law as the fields: if it be not redeemed before, in the jubilee it shall return to the owner.

32 "'The houses of Levites which are in cities may always be redeemed. 33 If they be not redeemed, in the jubilee they shall all return to the owners because the houses of the cities of the Levites are for their possessions among the children of Israel. 34 But let not their suburbs be sold, because it is a perpetual possession.

35 "'If thy brother be impoverished and weak of hand and thou receive him as a stranger and sojourner and he live with thee, 36 take not usury of him nor more than thou gavest. Fear thy God that thy brother may live with thee. 37 Thou shalt not give him thy money upon usury nor exact of him any increase of fruits. 38 I am the Lord, your God, who brought you out of the land of Egypt that I might give you the land of Canaan and might be your God. 39 If thy brother constrained by poverty sell himself to thee, thou shalt not oppress him with the service of bondservants, 40 but he shall be as a hireling and a sojourner. He shall work with thee un-

iobeleum operabitur apud te, 41 et postea egredietur cum liberis suis et revertetur ad cognationem et ad possessionem patrum suorum, 42 mei enim servi sunt et ego eduxi eos de terra Aegypti. Non veneant condicione servorum; 43 ne adfligas eum per potentiam, sed metuito Deum tuum.

44 "'Servus et ancilla sint vobis de nationibus quae in circuitu vestro sunt 45 et de advenis qui peregrinantur apud vos vel qui ex his nati fuerint in terra vestra; hos habebitis famulos 46 et hereditario iure transmittetis ad posteros ac possidebitis in aeternum. Fratres autem vestros, filios Israhel, ne opprimatis per potentiam. 47 Si invaluerit apud vos manus advenae atque peregrini et adtenuatus frater tuus vendiderit se ei aut cuiquam de stirpe eius, 48 post venditionem potest redimi. Qui voluerit ex fratribus suis redimet eum, 49 et patruus et patruelis et consanguineus et adfinis. Sin autem et ipse potuerit, redimet se, 50 supputatis dumtaxat annis a tempore venditionis suae usque ad annum iobeleum et pecunia qua venditus fuerat, iuxta annorum numerum et rationem mercennarii, supputata. 51 Si plures fuerint anni qui remanent usque ad iobeleum, secundum hos reddet et pretium. 52 Si pauci, ponet rationem cum eo iuxta annorum numerum et reddet emptori quod reliquum est annorum, 53 quibus ante servivit mercedibus inputatis. Non adfliget eum violenter in conspectu tuo. 54 Quod si per haec redimi non potuerit, anno iobeleo egredietur cum liberis suis, 55 mei sunt enim servi filii Israhel quos eduxi de terra Aegypti.'"

til the year of the jubilee, 41 and afterwards he shall go out with his children and shall return to his kindred and to the possession of his fathers, 42 for they are my servants and I brought them out of the land of Egypt. Let them not be sold as bondmen; 43 afflict him not by might, but fear thy God.

44 "'Let your *bondmen and your bondwomen* be of the nations that are round about you 45 and of the strangers that sojourn among you or that were born of them in your land; these you shall have for servants 46 and by right of inheritance shall leave them to your posterity and shall possess them for ever. But oppress not your brethren, the children of Israel, by might. 47 If the hand of a stranger or a sojourner grow strong among you and thy brother being impoverished sell himself to him or to any of his race, 48 after the sale he may be redeemed. He that will of his brethren shall redeem him, 49 either his uncle or his uncle's son or his kinsman by blood or by affinity. But if he himself be able also, he shall redeem himself, 50 counting only the years from the time of his selling unto the year of the jubilee, and counting the money that he was sold for, according to the number of the years and the reckoning of a hired servant. 51 If there be many years that remain until the jubilee, according to them shall he also repay the price. 52 If few, he shall make the reckoning with him according to the number of the years and shall repay to the buyer for what remaineth of the years, 53 his wages being allowed for which he served before. He shall not afflict him violently in thy sight. 54 And if by these means he cannot be redeemed, in the year of the jubilee he shall go out with his children, 55 for the children of Israel are my servants whom I brought forth out of the land of Egypt.'"

Caput 26

""Ego Dominus, Deus vester. Non facietis vobis idolum et sculptile, nec titulos erigetis nec insignem lapidem ponetis in terra vestra ut adoretis eum, ego enim sum Dominus, Deus vester.

2 "'Custodite sabbata mea, et pavete ad sanctuarium meum. Ego Dominus.

3 "'Si in praeceptis meis ambulaveritis et mandata mea custodieritis et feceritis ea, dabo vobis pluvias temporibus suis. 4 Et terra gignet germen suum, et pomis arbores replebuntur. 5 Adprehendet messium tritura vindemiam, et vindemia occupabit sementem, et comedetis panem vestrum in saturitatem et absque pavore habitabitis in terra vestra. 6 Dabo pacem in finibus vestris. Dormietis, et non erit qui exterreat. Auferam malas bestias, et gladius non transibit terminos vestros. 7 Persequemini inimicos vestros, et corruent coram vobis. 8 Persequentur quinque de vestris centum alienos, et centum de vobis, decem milia. Cadent inimici vestri in conspectu vestro gladio. 9 Respiciam vos et crescere faciam. Multiplicabimini, et firmabo pactum meum vobiscum. 10 Comedetis vetustissima veterum, et vetera,

Chapter 26

God's promises to them that keep his commandments and the many punishments with which he threatens transgressors.

"I am the Lord, your God. You shall not make to yourselves any idol or graven thing, neither shall you erect pillars nor set up a remarkable stone in your land to adore it, for I am the Lord, your God.

2 "Keep my sabbaths, and reverence my sanctuary. I am the Lord.

3 "If you walk in my precepts and keep my commandments and do them, I will give you rain in due seasons. 4 And the ground shall bring forth its increase, and the trees shall be filled with fruit. 5 The threshing of your harvest shall reach unto the vintage, and the vintage shall reach unto the sowing time, and you shall eat your bread to the full and dwell in your land without fear. 6 I will give peace in your coasts. You shall sleep, and there shall be none to make you afraid. I will take away evil beasts, and the sword shall not pass through your quarters. 7 You shall pursue your enemies, and they shall fall before you. 8 Five of yours shall pursue a hundred others, and a hundred of you, ten thousand. Your enemies shall fall before you by the sword. 9 I will look on you and make you increase. You shall be multiplied, and I will establish my covenant with you. 10 You shall eat the old-

novis supervenientibus, proicietis. 11 Ponam tabernaculum meum in medio vestri, et non abiciet vos anima mea. 12 Ambulabo inter vos et ero vester Deus, vosque eritis populus meus. 13 Ego Dominus, Deus vester, qui eduxi vos de terra Aegyptiorum ne serviretis eis et qui confregi catenas cervicum vestrarum ut incederetis erecti.

14 "'Quod si non audieritis me nec feceritis omnia mandata mea, 15 si spreveritis leges meas et iudicia mea contempseritis ut non faciatis ea quae a me constituta sunt et ad irritum perducatis pactum meum, 16 ego quoque haec faciam vobis: visitabo vos velociter in egestate et ardore qui conficiat oculos vestros et consumat animas vestras; frustra seretis sementem, quae ab hostibus devorabitur; 17 ponam faciem meam contra vos, et corruetis coram hostibus vestris et subiciemini his qui oderunt vos; fugietis nemine persequente.

18 "'Sin autem nec sic oboedieritis mihi, addam correptiones vestras septuplum propter peccata vestra, 19 et conteram superbiam duritiae vestrae, daboque caelum vobis desuper sicut ferrum et terram aeneam. 20 Consumetur in cassum labor vester; non proferet terra germen, nec arbores poma praebebunt.

21 "'Si ambulaveritis ex adverso mihi nec volueritis audire me, addam plagas vestras usque in septuplum propter peccata vestra, 22 inmittamque in vos bestias agri quae consumant vos et pecora vestra et ad paucitatem cuncta redigant desertaeque fiant viae vestrae.

23 "'Quod si nec sic volueritis recipere disciplinam sed ambulaveritis ex adverso mihi, 24 ego quoque contra vos ad-

est of the old store, and, new coming on, you shall cast away the old. 11 I will set my tabernacle in the midst of you, and my soul shall not cast you off. 12 I will walk among you and will be your God, and you shall be my people. 13 I am the Lord, your God, who have brought you out of the land of the Egyptians that you should not serve them and who have broken the chains of your necks that you might go upright.

14 "'But if you will not hear me nor do all my commandments, 15 if you despise my laws and contemn my judgments so as not to do those things which are appointed by me and to make void my covenant, 16 I also will do these things to you: I will quickly visit you with poverty and burning heat which shall waste your eyes and consume your lives; you shall sow your seed in vain, which shall be devoured by your enemies; 17 I will set my face against you, and you shall fall down before your enemies and shall be made subject to them that hate you; you shall flee when no man pursueth you.

18 "'But if you will not *yet for all this* obey me, I will chastise you seven times more for your sins, 19 and I will break the pride of your stubbornness, and I will make to you the heaven above as iron and the earth as brass. 20 Your labour shall be spent in vain; the ground shall not bring forth her increase, nor the trees yield their fruit.

21 "'If you walk contrary to me and will not hearken to me, I will bring seven times more plagues upon you for your sins, 22 and I will send in upon you the beasts of the field to destroy you and your cattle and *make you few in number* and that your highways may be desolate.

23 "And if even so you will not *amend* but will walk contrary to me, 24 I also will walk contrary to you and will strike

versus incedam et percutiam vos septies propter peccata vestra. 25 Inducamque super vos gladium ultorem foederis mei. Cumque confugeritis in urbes, mittam pestilentiam in medio vestri, et trademini in manibus hostium 26 postquam confregero baculum panis vestri ita ut decem mulieres in uno clibano coquant panes et reddant eos ad pondus et comedetis et non saturabimini.

27 "'Sin autem nec per haec audieritis me sed ambulaveritis contra me, 28 et ego incedam adversum vos in furore contrario, et corripiam vos septem plagis propter peccata vestra 29 ita ut comedatis carnes filiorum vestrorum et filiarum vestrarum. 30 Destruam excelsa vestra et simulacra confringam. Cadetis inter ruinas idolorum vestrorum, et abominabitur vos anima mea, 31 in tantum ut urbes vestras redigam in solitudinem et deserta faciam sanctuaria vestra nec recipiam ultra odorem suavissimum. 32 Disperdamque terram vestram, et stupebunt super ea inimici vestri cum habitatores illius fuerint. 33 Vos autem dispergam in Gentes, et evaginabo post vos gladium, eritque terra vestra deserta et civitates vestrae dirutae. 34 Tunc placebunt terrae sabbata sua cunctis diebus solitudinis suae quando fueritis 35 in terra hostili; sabbatizabit et requiescet in sabbatis solitudinis suae eo quod non requieverit in sabbatis vestris quando habitabatis in ea.

36 "'Et qui de vobis remanserint, dabo pavorem in cordibus eorum in regionibus hostium; terrebit eos sonitus folii volantis, et ita fugient quasi gladium. Cadent nullo persequente, 37 et corruent singuli super fratres suos quasi bella

you seven times for your sins. 25 And I will bring in upon you the sword that shall avenge my covenant. And when you shall flee into the cities, I will send the pestilence in the midst of you, and you shall be delivered into the hands of your enemies 26 after I shall have broken the staff of your bread so that ten women shall bake your bread in one oven and give it out by weight and you shall eat and shall not be filled.

27 "But if you will *not for all this* hearken to me but will walk against me, 28 I will also go against you with opposite fury, and I will chastise you with seven plagues for your sins 29 so that you shall eat the flesh of your sons and of your daughters. 30 I will destroy your high places and break your idols. You shall fall among the ruins of your idols, and my soul shall abhor you, 31 insomuch that I will bring your cities to be a wilderness and I will make your sanctuaries desolate and will receive no more *your sweet odours.* 32 And I will destroy your land, and your enemies shall be astonished at it when they shall be the inhabitants thereof. 33 And I will scatter you among the Gentiles, and I will draw out the sword after you, and your land shall be desert and your cities destroyed. 34 Then shall the land enjoy her sabbaths all the days of her desolation when you shall be 35 in the enemy's land; she shall keep a sabbath and rest in the sabbaths of her desolation because she did not rest in your sabbaths when you dwelt therein.

36 "And *as to them* that shall remain of you, I will send fear in their hearts in the countries of their enemies; the sound of a flying leaf shall terrify them, and they shall flee as it were from the sword. They shall fall when no man pursueth them, 37 and they shall every one fall upon their brethren as fleeing

fugientes. Nemo vestrum inimicis audebit resistere. 38 Peribitis inter Gentes, et hostilis vos terra consumet.

39 "'Quod si et de his aliqui remanserint, tabescent in iniquitatibus suis in terra inimicorum suorum, et propter peccata patrum suorum et sua adfligentur 40 donec confiteantur iniquitates suas et maiorum suorum quibus praevaricati sunt in me et ambulaverunt ex adverso mihi. 41 Ambulabo igitur et ego contra eos et inducam illos in terram hostilem donec erubescat incircumcisa mens eorum; tunc orabunt pro impietatibus suis.

42 "'Et recordabor foederis mei quod pepigi cum Iacob et Isaac et Abraham. Terrae quoque memor ero, 43 quae, cum relicta fuerit ab eis, conplacebit sibi in sabbatis suis, patiens solitudinem propter illos. Ipsi vero rogabunt pro peccatis suis eo quod abiecerint iudicia mea et leges meas despexerint. 44 Et tamen etiam cum essent in terra hostili, non penitus abieci eos, neque sic despexi ut consumerentur et irritum facerem pactum meum cum eis, ego enim sum Dominus, Deus eorum. 45 Et recordabor foederis mei pristini quando eduxi eos de terra Aegypti in conspectu Gentium ut essem Deus eorum. Ego Dominus.'"

Haec sunt praecepta atque iudicia et leges quas dedit Dominus inter se et inter filios Israhel in Monte Sinai per manum Mosi.

from wars. None of you shall dare to resist your enemies. 38 You shall perish among the Gentiles, and an enemy's land shall consume you.

39 "And if of them also some remain, they shall pine away in their iniquities in the land of their enemies, and they shall be afflicted for the sins of their fathers and their own 40 until they confess their iniquities and the iniquities of their ancestors whereby they have transgressed me and walked contrary unto me. 41 Therefore I also will walk against them and bring them into their enemies' land until their uncircumcised mind be ashamed; then shall they pray for their sins.

42 "And I will remember my covenant that I made with Jacob and Isaac and Abraham. I will remember also the land, 43 which, when she shall be left by them, shall enjoy her sabbaths, being desolate for them. But they shall pray for their sins because they rejected my judgments and despised my laws. 44 And *yet for all that* when they were in the land of their enemies, I did not cast them off altogether, neither did I so despise them that they should be quite consumed and I should make void my covenant with them, for I am the Lord, their God. 45 And I will remember my former covenant when I brought them out of the land of Egypt in the sight of the Gentiles to be their God. I am the Lord.'"

These are the judgments and precepts and laws which the Lord gave between him and the children of Israel in Mount Sinai by the hand of Moses.

Caput 27

Locutusque est Dominus ad Mosen, dicens, 2 "Loquere filiis Israhel, et dices ad eos, 'Homo qui votum fecerit et spoponderit Deo animam suam sub aestimatione dabit pretium. 3 Si fuerit masculus a vicesimo anno usque ad sexagesimum annum, dabit quinquaginta siclos argenti ad mensuram sanctuarii, 4 si mulier, triginta. 5 A quinto autem anno usque ad vicesimum, masculus dabit viginti siclos, femina, decem. 6 Ab uno mense usque ad annum quintum, pro masculo dabuntur quinque sicli, pro femina, tres. 7 Sexagenarius et ultra masculus dabit quindecim siclos, femina, decem. 8 Si pauper fuerit et aestimationem reddere non valebit, stabit coram sacerdote, et quantum ille aestimaverit et viderit eum posse reddere, tantum dabit.

9 "'Animal autem quod immolari potest Domino, si quis voverit, sanctum erit 10 et mutari non poterit, id est, nec melius malo, nec peius bono. Quod si mutaverit, et ipsum quod mutatum est et illud pro quo mutatum est consecratum erit Domino.

11 "'Animal inmundum, quod immolari Domino non potest, si quis voverit, adducetur ante sacerdotem, 12 qui, diiu-

Chapter 27

Of vows and tithes.

And the Lord spoke to Moses, saying, 2 "Speak to the children of Israel, and thou shalt say to them, 'The man that shall have made a vow and promised his soul to God shall give the price according to estimation. 3 If it be a man from twenty years old unto sixty years old, he shall give fifty sicles of silver after the weight of the sanctuary, 4 if a woman, thirty. 5 But from the fifth year until the twentieth, a man shall give twenty sicles, a woman, ten. 6 From one month until the fifth year, for a male shall be given five sicles, for a female, three. 7 A man that is sixty years old or upward shall give fifteen sicles, a woman, ten. 8 If he be poor and not able to pay the estimation, he shall stand before the priest, and as much as he shall value him at and see him able to pay, so much shall he give.

9 "But a beast that may be sacrificed to the Lord, if any one shall vow, shall be holy 10 and cannot be changed, that is to say, neither a better for a worse, nor a worse for a better. And if he shall change it, both that which was changed and that for which it was changed shall be consecrated to the Lord.

11 "An unclean beast, which cannot be sacrificed to the Lord, if any man shall vow, shall be brought before the priest, 12 who, judging whether it be good or bad, shall set

dicans utrum bonum an malum sit, statuet pretium, 13 quod, si dare voluerit is qui offert, addet supra aestimationem quintam partem.

14 "'Homo si voverit domum suam et sanctificaverit Domino, considerabit eam sacerdos, utrum bona an mala sit, et iuxta pretium quod ab eo fuerit constitutum venundabitur. 15 Sin autem ille qui voverat voluerit redimere eam, dabit quintam partem aestimationis supra et habebit domum.

16 "'Quod si agrum possessionis suae voverit et consecraverit Domino, iuxta mensuram sementis aestimabitur pretium. Si triginta modiis hordei seritur terra, quinquaginta siclis venundetur argenti. 17 Si statim ab anno incipientis iobelei voverit agrum, quanto valere potest, tanto aestimabitur. 18 Sin autem post aliquantum temporis, supputabit sacerdos pecuniam iuxta annorum qui reliqui sunt numerum usque ad iobeleum, et detrahetur ex pretio. 19 Quod si voluerit redimere agrum ille qui voverat, addet quintam partem aestimatae pecuniae et possidebit eum. 20 Sin autem noluerit redimere sed alteri cuilibet fuerit venundatus, ultra eum qui voverat redimere non poterit, 21 quia cum iobelei venerit dies, sanctificatus erit Domino, et possessio consecrata ad ius pertinet sacerdotum. 22 Si ager emptus est et non de possessione maiorum sanctificatus fuerit Domino, 23 supputabit sacerdos iuxta annorum numerum usque ad iobeleum pretium, et dabit ille qui voverat eum Domino. 24 In iobeleo autem, revertetur ad priorem dominum qui vendiderat eum et habuerat in sortem possessionis suae. 25 Omnis aestimatio siclo sanctuarii ponderabitur. Siclus viginti obolos habet.

the price, 13 which, if he that offereth it will give, he shall add above the estimation the fifth part.

14 "'If a man shall vow his house and sanctify it to the Lord, the priest shall consider it, whether it be good or bad, and it shall be sold according to the price which he shall appoint. 15 But if he that vowed will redeem it, he shall give the fifth part of the estimation over and above and shall have the house.

16 "'And if he vow the field of his possession and consecrate it to the Lord, the price shall be rated according to the measure of the seed. If the ground be sowed with thirty bushels of barley, let it be sold for fifty sicles of silver. 17 If he vow his field immediately from the year of jubilee that is beginning, as much as it may be worth, at so much it shall be rated. 18 But if some time after, the priest shall reckon the money according to the number of years that remain until the jubilee, and *the price shall be abated.* 19 And if he that had vowed will redeem his field, he shall add the fifth part of the money of the estimation and shall possess it. 20 And if he will not redeem it but it be sold to any other man, he that vowed it may not redeem it any more, 21 for when the day of jubilee cometh, it shall be sanctified to the Lord, and *as* a possession consecrated pertaineth to the right of the priests. 22 If a field *that was* bought and not of a man's ancestors' possession be sanctified to the Lord, 23 the priest shall reckon the price according to the number of years unto the jubilee, and he that had vowed shall give that to the Lord. 24 But in the jubilee, it shall return to the former owner who had sold it and had it in the lot of his possession. 25 All estimation shall be made according to the sicle of the sanctuary. A sicle hath twenty obols.

26 "'Primogenita, quae ad Dominum pertinent, nemo sanctificare poterit et vovere; sive bos sive ovis fuerit, Domini sunt. 27 Quod si inmundum est animal, redimet qui obtulit iuxta aestimationem tuam et addet quintam partem pretii. Si redimere noluerit, vendetur alteri quantocumque a te fuerit aestimatum.

28 "'Omne quod Domino consecratur, sive homo fuerit sive animal sive ager, non veniet, nec redimi poterit. Quicquid semel fuerit consecratum sanctum sanctorum erit Domino. 29 Et omnis consecratio quae offertur ab homine non redimetur sed morte morietur.

30 "'Omnes decimae terrae, sive de frugibus sive de pomis arborum, Domini sunt et illi sanctificantur. 31 Si quis autem voluerit redimere decimas suas, addet quintam partem earum. 32 Omnium decimarum bovis et ovis et caprae quae sub pastoris virga transeunt, quicquid decimum venerit sanctificabitur Domino. 33 Non eligetur nec bonum nec malum, nec altero commutabitur. Si quis mutaverit, et quod mutatum est et pro quo mutatum est sanctificabitur Domino et non redimetur.'"

34 Haec sunt praecepta quae mandavit Dominus Mosi ad filios Israhel in Monte Sinai.

26 "'The firstborn, which belong to the Lord, no man may sanctify and vow; whether it be bullock or sheep, they are the Lord's. 27 And if it be an unclean beast, he that offereth it shall redeem it according to thy estimation and shall add the fifth part of the price. If he will not redeem it, it shall be sold to another for how much soever it was estimated by thee.

28 "Any thing that is devoted to the Lord, whether it be man or beast or field, shall not be sold, neither may it be redeemed. Whatsoever is once consecrated shall be holy of holies to the Lord. 29 And any consecration that is offered by man shall not be redeemed but dying shall die.

30 "All tithes of the land, whether of corn or of the fruits of trees, are the Lord's and are sanctified to him. 31 And if any man will redeem his tithes, he shall add the fifth part of them. 32 Of all the tithes of *oxen* and *sheep* and *goats* that pass under the shepherd's rod, every tenth that cometh shall be sanctified to the Lord. 33 It shall not be chosen neither good nor bad, neither shall it be changed for another. If any man change it, both that which was changed and that for which it was changed shall be sanctified to the Lord and shall not be redeemed.'"

34 These are the precepts which the Lord commanded Moses for the children of Israel in Mount Sinai.

NUMBERS

Caput 1

Locutusque est Dominus ad Mosen in deserto Sinai in Tabernaculo Foederis prima die mensis secundi, anno altero egressionis eorum ex Aegypto, dicens, 2 "Tollite summam universae congregationis filiorum Israhel per cognationes et domos suas et nomina singulorum, quicquid sexus est masculini 3 a vicesimo anno et supra, omnium virorum fortium ex Israhel, et numerabitis eos per turmas suas, tu et Aaron. 4 Eruntque vobiscum principes tribuum ac domorum in cognationibus suis, 5 quorum ista sunt nomina: de Ruben, Elisur, filius Sedeur; 6 de Symeon, Salamihel, filius Surisaddai; 7 de Iuda, Naasson, filius Aminadab; 8 de Isachar, Nathanahel, filius Suar; 9 de Zabulon, Heliab, filius Helon. 10 Filiorum autem Ioseph: de Ephraim, Helisama, filius Ammiud; de Manasse, Gamalihel, filius Phadassur; 11 de Beniamin, Abidan, filius Gedeonis; 12 de Dan, Ahiezer, filius Amisaddai; 13 de Aser, Phegihel, filius Ochran; 14 de Gad, Heliasaph, filius Duhel; 15 de Nepthali, Ahira, filius Henan."

16 Hii nobilissimi principes multitudinis per tribus et co-

Chapter 1

The children of Israel are numbered. The Levites are designed to serve the tabernacle.

And the Lord spoke to Moses in the desert of Sinai in the Tabernacle of the Covenant the first day of the second month, the second year of their going out of Egypt, saying, 2 "Take the sum of all the congregation of the children of Israel by their families and houses and the names of every one, as many as are of the male sex 3 from twenty years old and upwards, of all the men of Israel fit for war, and you shall number them by their troops, thou and Aaron. 4 And there shall be with you the princes of the tribes and of the houses in their kindreds, 5 whose names are these: of Reuben, Elizur, the son of Shedeur; 6 of Simeon, Shelumiel, the son of Zurishaddai; 7 of Judah, Nahshon, the son of Amminadab; 8 of Issachar, Nethanel, the son of Zuar; 9 of Zebulun, Eliab, the son of Helon. 10 And of the sons of Joseph: of Ephraim, Elishama, the son of Ammihud; of Manasseh, Gamaliel, the son of Pedahzur; 11 of Benjamin, Abidan, the son of Gideoni; 12 of Dan, Ahiezer, the son of Ammishaddai; 13 of Asher, Pagiel, the son of Ochran; 14 of Gad, Eliasaph, the son of Deuel; 15 of Naphtali, Ahira, the son of Enan."

16 These are the most noble princes of the multitude by

gnationes suas et capita exercitus Israhel, 17 quos tulerunt Moses et Aaron cum omni vulgi multitudine 18 et congregaverunt primo die mensis secundi, recensentes eos per cognationes et domos ac familias et capita et nomina singulorum a vicesimo anno et supra, 19 sicut praeceperat Dominus Mosi. Numeratique sunt in deserto Sinai.

20 De Ruben, primogenito Israhelis, per generationes et familias ac domos suas et nomina capitum singulorum omne quod sexus est masculini a vicesimo anno et supra procedentium ad bellum 21 quadraginta sex milia quingenti.

22 De filiis Symeon per generationes et familias ac domos cognationum suarum recensiti sunt per nomina et capita singulorum omne quod sexus est masculini a vicesimo anno et supra procedentium ad bellum, 23 quinquaginta novem milia trecenti.

24 De filiis Gad per generationes et familias ac domos cognationum suarum recensiti sunt per nomina singulorum a viginti annis et supra omnes qui ad bella procederent, 25 quadraginta quinque milia sescenti quinquaginta.

26 De filiis Iuda per generationes et familias ac domos cognationum suarum, per nomina singulorum a vicesimo anno et supra omnes qui poterant ad bella procedere 27 recensiti sunt, septuaginta quattuor milia sescenti.

28 De filiis Isachar per generationes et familias ac domos cognationum suarum, per nomina singulorum a vicesimo anno et supra omnes qui ad bella procederent 29 recensiti sunt, quinquaginta quattuor milia quadringenti.

their tribes and kindreds and the chiefs of the army of Israel, 17 whom Moses and Aaron took with all the multitude of the common people 18 and assembled them on the first day of the second month, reckoning them up by the kindreds and houses and families and heads and names of every one from twenty years old and upward, 19 as the Lord had commanded Moses. And they were numbered in the desert of Sinai.

20 Of Reuben, the *eldest son* of Israel, by their generations and families and houses and names of every head all that were of the male sex from twenty years old and upward *that were able to* go forth to war 21 were forty-six thousand five hundred.

22 Of the sons of Simeon by their generations and families and houses of their kindreds were reckoned up by the names and heads of every one all that were of the male sex from twenty years old and upward *that were able to* go forth to war, 23 fifty-nine thousand three hundred.

24 Of the sons of Gad by their generations and families and houses of their kindreds were reckoned up by the names of every one from twenty years old and upward all that *were able to go* forth to war, 25 forty-five thousand six hundred and fifty.

26 Of the sons of Judah by their generations and families and houses of their kindreds, by the names of every one from twenty years old and upward all that were able to go forth to war 27 were reckoned up, seventy-four thousand six hundred.

28 Of the sons of Issachar by their generations and families and houses of their kindreds, by the names of every one from twenty years old and upward all that could go forth to war 29 were reckoned up, fifty-four thousand four hundred.

30 De filiis Zabulon per generationes et familias ac domos cognationum suarum recensiti sunt per nomina singulorum a vicesimo anno et supra omnes qui poterant ad bella procedere, 31 quinquaginta septem milia quadringenti.

32 De filiis Ioseph, filiorum Ephraim per generationes et familias ac domos cognationum suarum recensiti sunt per nomina singulorum a vicesimo anno et supra omnes qui poterant ad bella procedere, 33 quadraginta milia quingenti. 34 Porro, filiorum Manasse per generationes et familias ac domos cognationum suarum recensiti sunt per nomina singulorum a viginti annis et supra omnes qui poterant ad bella procedere, 35 triginta duo milia ducenti.

36 De filiis Beniamin per generationes et familias ac domos cognationum suarum recensiti sunt nominibus singulorum a vicesimo anno et supra omnes qui poterant ad bella procedere, 37 triginta quinque milia quadringenti.

38 De filiis Dan per generationes et familias ac domos cognationum suarum recensiti sunt nominibus singulorum a vicesimo anno et supra omnes qui poterant ad bella procedere, 39 sexaginta duo milia septingenti.

40 De filiis Aser per generationes et familias ac domos cognationum suarum recensiti sunt per nomina singulorum a vicesimo anno et supra omnes qui poterant ad bella procedere, 41 quadraginta milia et mille quingenti.

42 De filiis Nepthali per generationes et familias ac domos cognationum suarum recensiti sunt nominibus singulorum

30 Of the sons of Zebulun by the generations and families and houses of their kindreds were reckoned up by the names of every one from twenty years old and upward all that were able to go forth to war, 31 fifty-seven thousand four hundred.

32 Of the sons of Joseph, namely, of the sons of Ephraim by the generations and families and houses of their kindreds were reckoned up by the names of every one from twenty years old and upward all that were able to go forth to war, 33 forty thousand five hundred. 34 Moreover, of the sons of Manasseh by the generations and families and houses of their kindreds were reckoned up by the names of every one from twenty years old and upward all that could go forth to war, 35 thirty-two thousand two hundred.

36 Of the sons of Benjamin by their generations and families and houses of their kindreds were reckoned up by the names of every one from twenty years old and upward all that were able to go forth to war, 37 thirty-five thousand four hundred.

38 Of the sons of Dan by their generations and families and houses of their kindreds were reckoned up by the names of every one from twenty years old and upward all that were able to go forth to war, 39 sixty-two thousand seven hundred.

40 Of the sons of Asher by their generations and families and houses of their kindreds were reckoned up by the names of every one from twenty years old and upward all that were able to go forth to war, 41 forty-one thousand and five hundred.

42 Of the sons of Naphtali by their generations and families and houses of their kindreds were reckoned up by the

a vicesimo anno et supra omnes qui poterant ad bella procedere, 43 quinquaginta tria milia quadringenti.

44 Hii sunt quos numeraverunt Moses et Aaron et duodecim principes Israhel, singulos per domos cognationum suarum. 45 Fueruntque omnis numerus filiorum Israhel per domos et familias suas a vicesimo anno et supra qui poterant ad bella procedere 46 sescenta tria milia virorum quingenti quinquaginta.

47 Levitae autem in tribu familiarum suarum non sunt numerati cum eis. 48 Locutusque est Dominus ad Mosen, dicens, 49 "Tribum Levi noli numerare, neque pones summam eorum cum filiis Israhel, 50 sed constitue eos super Tabernaculum Testimonii et cuncta vasa eius et quicquid ad caerimonias pertinet. Ipsi portabunt tabernaculum et omnia utensilia eius, et erunt in ministerio ac per gyrum tabernaculi metabuntur.

51 "Cum proficiscendum fuerit, deponent Levitae tabernaculum; cum castra metanda, erigent. Quisquis externorum accesserit occidetur. 52 Metabuntur autem castra filii Israhel unusquisque per turmas et cuneos atque exercitum suum, 53 porro Levitae per gyrum tabernaculi figent tentoria ne fiat indignatio super multitudinem filiorum Israhel, et excubabunt in custodiis Tabernaculi Testimonii."

54 Fecerunt ergo filii Israhel iuxta omnia quae praeceperat Dominus Mosi.

names of every one from twenty years old and upward all that were able to go forth to war, 43 fifty-three thousand four hundred.

44 These are they *who were numbered by Moses and Aaron* and the twelve princes of Israel, every one by the houses of their kindreds. 45 And the whole number of the children of Israel by their houses and families from twenty years old and upward that were able to go to war 46 were six hundred and three thousand five hundred and fifty men.

47 But the Levites in the tribe of their families were not numbered with them. 48 And the Lord spoke to Moses, saying, 49 "Number not the tribe of Levi, neither shalt thou put down the sum of them with the children of Israel, 50 but appoint them over the Tabernacle of the Testimony and all the vessels thereof and whatsoever pertaineth to the ceremonies. They shall carry the tabernacle and all the furniture thereof, and they shall *minister* and shall encamp round about the tabernacle.

51 "When you are to go forward, the Levites shall take down the tabernacle; when you are to camp, they shall set it up. What stranger soever cometh to it shall be slain. 52 And the children of Israel shall camp every man by his troops and bands and army, 53 but the Levites shall pitch their tents round about the tabernacle lest there come indignation upon the multitude of the children of Israel, and they shall keep watch *and guard* the Tabernacle of the Testimony."

54 And the children of Israel did according to all things which the Lord had commanded Moses.

Caput 2

Locutusque est Dominus ad Mosen et Aaron, dicens, 2 "Singuli per turmas, signa atque vexilla et domos cognationum suarum castrametabuntur filiorum Israhel per gyrum Tabernaculi Foederis. 3 Ad orientem, Iudas figet tentoria per turmas exercitus sui, eritque princeps filiorum eius Naasson, filius Aminadab. 4 Et omnis de stirpe eius summa pugnantium septuaginta quattuor milia sescentorum. 5 Iuxta eum, castrametati sunt de tribu Isachar, quorum princeps fuit Nathanahel, filius Suar. 6 Et omnis numerus pugnatorum eius quinquaginta quattuor milia quadringenti. 7 In tribu Zabulon, princeps fuit Heliab, filius Helon. 8 Omnis de stirpe eius exercitus pugnatorum quinquaginta septem milia quadringenti. 9 Universi qui in castris Iudae adnumerati sunt fuerunt centum octoginta sex milia quadringenti, et per turmas suas primi egredientur.

10 "In castris filiorum Ruben, ad meridianam plagam, erit princeps Elisur, filius Sedeur. 11 Et cunctus exercitus pugnatorum eius qui numerati sunt quadraginta sex milia quingenti. 12 Iuxta eum castrametati sunt de tribu Symeon, quorum princeps fuit Salamihel, filius Surisaddai. 13 Et cunctus exercitus pugnatorum eius qui numerati sunt quinquaginta

Chapter 2

The order of the tribes in their camp.

And the Lord spoke to Moses and Aaron, saying, 2 *"All the children* of Israel shall camp by their troops, ensigns and standards and the houses of their kindreds round about the Tabernacle of the Covenant. 3 On the east, Judah shall pitch his tents by the bands of his army, and the prince of his sons shall be Nahshon, the son of Amminadab. 4 And the whole sum of the fighting men of his stock were seventy-four thousand six hundred. 5 Next unto him, they of the tribe of Issachar encamped, whose prince was Nethanel, the son of Zuar. 6 And the whole number of his fighting men were fifty-four thousand four hundred. 7 In the tribe of Zebulun, the prince was Eliab, the son of Helon. 8 And all the army of fighting men of his stock were fifty-seven thousand four hundred. 9 All that were numbered in the camp of Judah were a hundred and eighty-six thousand four hundred, and they by their troops shall march first.

10 "In the camp of the sons of Reuben, on the south side, the prince shall be Elizur, the son of Shedeur. 11 And the whole army of his fighting men that were numbered were forty-six thousand five hundred. 12 Beside him camped they of the tribe of Simeon, whose prince was Shelumiel, the son of Zurishaddai. 13 And the whole army of his fighting men that were numbered were fifty-nine thousand three hun-

novem milia trecenti. 14 In tribu Gad, princeps fuit Heliasaph, filius Duhel. 15 Et cunctus exercitus pugnatorum eius
qui numerati sunt quadraginta quinque milia sescenti quinquaginta. 16 Omnes qui recensiti sunt in castris Ruben centum quinquaginta milia et mille quadringenti quinquaginta
per turmas suas. In secundo loco proficiscentur.

17 "Levabitur autem Tabernaculum Testimonii per officia
Levitarum et turmas eorum. Quomodo erigetur, ita et depo-
netur. Singuli per loca et ordines suos proficiscentur.

18 "Ad occidentalem plagam erunt castra filiorum
Ephraim, quorum princeps fuit Helisama, filius Ammiud
—19 cunctus exercitus pugnatorum eius qui numerati sunt
quadraginta milia quingenti—20 et cum eis, tribus filiorum
Manasse, quorum princeps fuit Gamalihel, filius Phadassur.
21 Cunctusque exercitus pugnatorum eius qui numerati sunt
triginta duo milia ducenti. 22 In tribu filiorum Beniamin,
princeps fuit Abidan, filius Gedeonis. 23 Et cunctus exercitus pugnatorum eius qui recensiti sunt triginta quinque
milia quadringenti. 24 Omnes qui numerati sunt in castris
Ephraim centum octo milia centum per turmas suas. Tertii
proficiscentur.

25 "Ad aquilonis partem castrametati sunt filii Dan, quorum princeps fuit Ahiezer, filius Amisaddai. 26 Cunctus exercitus pugnatorum eius qui numerati sunt sexaginta duo milia septingenti. 27 Iuxta eum, fixere tentoria de tribu Aser,
quorum princeps fuit Phegihel, filius Ochran. 28 Cunctus
exercitus pugnatorum eius qui numerati sunt quadraginta
milia et mille quingenti. 29 De tribu filiorum Nepthalim,

dred. 14 In the tribe of Gad, the prince was Eliasaph, the son of Deuel. 15 And the whole army of his fighting men that were numbered were forty-five thousand six hundred and fifty. 16 All that were reckoned up in the camp of Reuben were a hundred and fifty-one thousand four hundred and fifty by their troops. They shall march in the second place.

17 "And the Tabernacle of the Testimony shall be carried by the officers of the Levites and their troops. As it shall be set up, so shall it be taken down. Every one shall march according to their places and ranks.

18 "On the west side shall be the camp of the sons of Ephraim, whose prince was Elishama, the son of Ammihud — 19 the whole army of his fighting men that were numbered were forty thousand five hundred — 20 and with them, the tribe of the sons of Manasseh, whose prince was Gamaliel, the son of Pedahzur. 21 And the whole army of his fighting men that were numbered were thirty-two thousand two hundred. 22 In the tribe of the sons of Benjamin, the prince was Abidan, the son of Gideoni. 23 And the whole army of fighting men that were reckoned up were thirty-five thousand four hundred. 24 All that were numbered in the camp of Ephraim were a hundred and eight-thousand one hundred by their troops. They shall march in the third place.

25 "On the north side camped the sons of Dan, whose prince was Ahiezar, the son of Ammishaddai. 26 The whole army of his fighting men that were numbered were sixty-two thousand seven hundred. 27 Beside him, they of the tribe of Asher pitched their tents, whose prince was Pagiel, the son of Ochran. 28 The whole army of his fighting men that were numbered were forty-one thousand five hundred. 29 Of the tribe of the sons of Naphtali, the prince was Ahira,

princeps fuit Ahira, filius Henan. 30 Cunctus exercitus pugnatorum eius quinquaginta tria milia quadringenti. 31 Omnes qui numerati sunt in castris Dan fuerunt centum quinquaginta septem milia sescenti. Et novissimi proficiscentur."

32 Hic numerus filiorum Israhel, per domos cognationum suarum et turmas divisi exercitus: sescenta tria milia quingenti quinquaginta.

33 Levitae autem non sunt numerati inter filios Israhel, sic enim praeceperat Dominus Mosi. 34 Feceruntque filii Israhel iuxta omnia quae mandaverat Dominus. Castrametati sunt per turmas suas et profecti per familias ac domos patrum suorum.

Caput 3

Haec sunt generationes Aaron et Mosi in die qua locutus est Dominus ad Mosen in Monte Sinai 2 et haec nomina filiorum Aaron: primogenitus eius Nadab, dein Abiu et Eleazar et Ithamar, 3 haec nomina filiorum Aaron, sacerdotum qui uncti sunt et quorum repletae et consecratae manus ut sacerdotio fungerentur.

the son of Enan. 30 The whole army of his fighting men were fifty-three thousand four hundred. 31 All that were numbered in the camp of Dan were a hundred and fifty-seven thousand six hundred. And they shall march last."

32 This is the number of the children of Israel, of their army divided according to the houses of their kindreds and their troops: six hundred and three thousand five hundred and fifty.

33 And the Levites were not numbered among the children of Israel, for so the Lord had commanded Moses. 34 And the children of Israel did according to all things that the Lord had commanded. They camped by their troops and marched by the families and houses of their fathers.

Chapter 3

The Levites are numbered and their offices distinguished.
They are taken in the place of the firstborn of the children
of Israel.

These are the generations of Aaron and Moses in the day that the Lord spoke to Moses in Mount Sinai 2 and these the names of the sons of Aaron: his firstborn Nadab, then Abihu and Eleazar and Ithamar, 3 these the names of the sons of Aaron, the priests that were anointed and whose hands were filled and consecrated to do the functions of priesthood.

4 Mortui sunt enim Nadab et Abiu cum offerrent ignem alienum in conspectu Domini in deserto Sinai absque liberis, functique sunt sacerdotio Eleazar et Ithamar coram Aaron, patre suo.

5 Locutusque est Dominus ad Mosen, dicens, 6 "Adplica tribum Levi, et fac stare in conspectu Aaron, sacerdotis, ut ministrent ei, et excubent 7 et observent quicquid ad cultum pertinet multitudinis coram Tabernaculo Testimonii. 8 Et custodiant vasa tabernaculi, servientes in ministerio eius. 9 Dabisque dono Levitas 10 Aaron et filiis eius, quibus traditi sunt a filiis Israhel. Aaron autem et filios eius constitues super cultum sacerdotii. Externus qui ad ministrandum acceserit morietur."

11 Locutusque est Dominus ad Mosen, dicens, 12 "Ego tuli Levitas a filiis Israhel pro omni primogenito qui aperit vulvam in filiis Israhel, eruntque Levitae mei, 13 meum est enim omne primogenitum. Ex quo percussi primogenitos in terra Aegypti, sanctificavi mihi quicquid primum nascitur in Israhel ab homine usque ad pecus; mei sunt. Ego Dominus."

14 Locutusque est Dominus ad Mosen in deserto Sinai, dicens, 15 "Numera filios Levi per domos patrum suorum et familias, omnem masculum ab uno mense et supra."

16 Numeravit Moses ut praeceperat Dominus, 17 et inventi sunt filii Levi, per nomina sua Gerson et Caath et Merari. 18 Filii Gerson: Lebni et Semei; 19 filii Caath: Amram et Iessaar, Hebron et Ozihel; 20 filii Merari: Mooli et Musi.

4 Now Nadab and Abihu died without children when they offered strange fire before the Lord in the desert of Sinai, and Eleazar and Ithamar performed the priestly office in the presence of Aaron, their father.

5 And the Lord spoke to Moses, saying, 6 "Bring the tribe of Levi, and make them stand in the sight of Aaron, the priest, to minister to him, and let them watch 7 and observe whatsoever appertaineth to the service of the multitude before the Tabernacle of the Testimony. 8 And let them keep the vessels of the tabernacle, serving in the ministry thereof. 9 And thou shalt give the Levites for a gift 10 to Aaron and to his sons, to whom they are delivered by the children of Israel. But thou shalt appoint Aaron and his sons over the service of priesthood. The stranger that approacheth to minister shall be put to death."

11 And the Lord spoke to Moses, saying, 12 "I have taken the Levites from the children of Israel for every firstborn that openeth the womb among the children of Israel, and the Levites shall be mine, 13 for every firstborn is mine. Since I struck the firstborn in the land of Egypt, I have sanctified to myself whatsoever is firstborn in Israel both of man and beast; they are mine. I am the Lord."

14 And the Lord spoke to Moses in the desert of Sinai, saying, 15 "Number the sons of Levi by the houses of their fathers and their families, every male from one month and upward."

16 Moses numbered them as the Lord had commanded, 17 and there were found sons of Levi, by their names Gershon and Kohath and Merari. 18 The sons of Gershon: Libni and Shimei; 19 the sons of Kohath: Amram and Izhar, Hebron and Uzziel; 20 the sons of Merari: Mahli and Mushi.

21 De Gerson fuere familiae duae: Lebnitica et Semeitica, 22 quarum numeratus est populus sexus masculini ab uno mense et supra septem milia quingentorum.

23 "Hii post tabernaculum metabuntur ad occidentem 24 sub principe, Eliasaph, filio Lahel, 25 et habebunt excubias in Tabernaculo Foederis: 26 ipsum tabernaculum et operimentum eius, tentorium quod trahitur ante fores Tecti Foederis et cortinas atrii, tentorium quoque quod adpenditur in introitu atrii tabernaculi et quicquid ad ritum altaris pertinet, funes tabernaculi et omnia utensilia eius.

27 "Cognatio Caath habebit populos Amramitas et Iessaaritas et Hebronitas et Ozihelitas; hae sunt familiae Caathitarum recensitae per nomina sua: 28 omnes generis masculini ab uno mense et supra, octo milia sescenti. Habebunt excubias sanctuarii 29 et castrametabuntur ad meridianam plagam, 30 principesque eorum erit Elisaphan, filius Ozihel. 31 Et custodient arcam mensamque et candelabrum, altaria et vasa sanctuarii in quibus ministratur et velum cunctamque huiuscemodi supellectilem. 32 Princeps autem principum Levitarum, Eleazar, filius Aaron, sacerdotis, erit super excubitores custodiae sanctuarii.

33 "At vero de Merari erunt populi Moolitae et Musitae, recensiti per nomina sua: 34 omnes generis masculini ab uno mense et supra, sex milia ducenti; 35 princeps eorum, Surihel, filius Abiahihel. In plaga septentrionali castrametabuntur. 36 Erunt sub custodia eorum tabulae tabernaculi et vectes et columnae ac bases earum et omnia quae ad cultum

21 Of Gershon were two families: the Libnites and the Shimeites, 22 of which were numbered people of the male sex from one month and upward seven thousand five hundred.

23 "These shall pitch behind the tabernacle on the west 24 under their prince, Eliasaph, the son of Lael, 25 and their charge shall be in the Tabernacle of the Covenant: 26 the tabernacle itself and the cover thereof, the hanging that is drawn before the doors of the *Tabernacle* of the Covenant and the curtains of the court, the hanging also that is hanged in the entry of the court of the tabernacle and whatsoever belongeth to the rite of the altar, the cords of the tabernacle and all the furniture thereof.

27 *"Of the kindred of Kohath come* the families of the Amramites and Izharites and Hebronites and Uzzielites; these are the families of the Kohathites reckoned up by their names: 28 all of the male sex from one month and upward, eight thousand six hundred. They shall have the guard of the sanctuary 29 and shall camp on the south side, 30 and their prince shall be Elizaphan, the son of Uzziel. 31 And they shall keep the ark and the table and the candlestick, the altars and the vessels of the sanctuary wherewith they minister and the veil and all the furniture of this kind. 32 And the prince of the princes of the Levites, Eleazar, the son of Aaron, the priest, shall be over them that watch for the guard of the sanctuary.

33 "And of Merari are the families of the Mahlites and Mushites, reckoned up by their names: 34 all of the male kind from one month and upward, six thousand two hundred; 35 their prince, Zuriel, the son of Abihail. They shall camp on the north side. 36 Under their custody shall be the boards of the tabernacle and the bars and the pillars and

huiuscemodi pertinent 37 columnaeque atrii per circuitum cum basibus suis et paxilli cum funibus.

38 "Castrametabuntur ante Tabernaculum Foederis, id est ad orientalem plagam, Moses et Aaron cum filiis suis, habentes custodiam sanctuarii, in medio filiorum Israhel. Quisquis alienus accesserit morietur."

39 Omnes Levitae quos numeraverunt Moses et Aaron iuxta praeceptum Domini, per familias suas, in genere masculino a mense uno et supra, fuerunt viginti duo milia.

40 Et ait Dominus ad Mosen, dicens, "Numera primogenitos sexus masculini de filiis Israhel a mense uno et supra, et habebis summam eorum. 41 Tollesque Levitas mihi pro omni primogenito filiorum Israhel—ego sum Dominus—et pecora eorum pro universis primogenitis pecorum filiorum Israhel."

42 Recensuit Moses, sicut praeceperat Dominus, primogenitos filiorum Israhel, 43 et fuerunt masculi per nomina sua a mense uno et supra viginti duo milia ducenti septuaginta tres.

44 Locutusque est Dominus ad Mosen, dicens, 45 "Tolle Levitas pro primogenitis filiorum Israhel et pecora Levitarum pro pecoribus eorum, eruntque Levitae mei. Ego sum Dominus. 46 In pretio autem ducentorum septuaginta trium qui excedunt numerum Levitarum de primogenitis filiorum Israhel, 47 accipies quinque siclos per singula capita, ad mensuram sanctuarii. Siclus habet obolos viginti. 48 Dabisque pecuniam Aaron et filiis eius, pretium eorum qui supra sunt."

their sockets and all things that pertain to this kind of service 37 and the pillars of the court round about with their sockets and the pins with their cords.

38 "Before the Tabernacle of the Covenant, that is to say on the east side, shall Moses and Aaron camp with their sons, having the custody of the sanctuary, in the midst of the children of Israel. What stranger soever cometh unto it shall be put to death."

39 All the Levites that Moses and Aaron numbered according to the precept of the Lord, by their families, of the male kind from one month and upward, were twenty-two thousand.

40 And the Lord said to Moses, "Number the firstborn of the male sex of the children of Israel from one month and upward, and thou shalt take the sum of them. 41 And thou shalt take the Levites to me for all the firstborn of the children of Israel—I am the Lord—and their cattle for all the firstborn of the cattle of the children of Israel."

42 Moses reckoned up, as the Lord had commanded, the firstborn of the children of Israel, 43 and the males by their names from one month and upward were twenty-two thousand two hundred and seventy-three.

44 And the Lord spoke to Moses, saying, 45 "Take the Levites for the firstborn of the children of Israel and the cattle of the Levites for their cattle, and the Levites shall be mine. I am the Lord. 46 But for the price of the two hundred and seventy-three of the firstborn of the children of Israel that exceed the number of the Levites, 47 thou shalt take five sicles for every head, according to the weight of the sanctuary. A sicle hath twenty obols. 48 And thou shalt give the money to Aaron and his sons, the price of them that are above."

49 Tulit igitur Moses pecuniam eorum qui fuerant amplius et quos redemerant a Levitis 50 pro primogenitis filiorum Israhel, mille trecentorum sexaginta quinque siclorum iuxta pondus sanctuarii, 51 et dedit eam Aaroni et filiis eius iuxta verbum quod praeceperat sibi Dominus.

Caput 4

Locutusque est Dominus ad Mosen et Aaron, dicens, 2 "Tolle summam filiorum Caath de medio Levitarum per domos et familias suas 3 a tricesimo anno et supra usque ad quinquagesimum annum omnium qui ingrediuntur ut stent et ministrent in Tabernaculo Foederis; 4 hic est cultus filiorum Caath. Tabernaculum Foederis et Sanctum Sanctorum 5 ingredientur Aaron et filii eius quando movenda sunt castra et deponent velum quod pendet ante fores involventque eo Arcam Testimonii 6 et operient rursum velamine ianthinarum pellium extendentque desuper pallium totum hyacinthinum et inducent vectes. 7 Mensam quoque Propositionis involvent hyacinthino pallio et ponent cum ea turibula et mortariola, cyatos et crateras ad liba fundenda. Panes

49 Moses therefore took the money of them that were above and whom they had redeemed from the Levites 50 for the firstborn of the children of Israel, one thousand three hundred and sixty-five sicles according to the weight of the sanctuary, 51 and gave it to Aaron and his sons according to the word that the Lord had commanded him.

Chapter 4

The age and time of the Levites' service. Their offices and burdens.

And the Lord spoke to Moses and Aaron, saying, 2 "Take the sum of the sons of Kohath from the midst of the Levites by their houses and families 3 from thirty years old and upward to fifty years old of all that go in to stand and to minister in the Tabernacle of the Covenant; 4 this is the service of the sons of Kohath. 5 When the camp is to set forward, Aaron and his sons shall go into the Tabernacle of the Covenant and the Holy of Holies and shall take down the veil that hangeth before the door and shall wrap up the Ark of the Testimony in it 6 and shall cover it again with a cover of violet skins and shall spread over it a cloth all of violet and shall put in the bars. 7 They shall wrap up also the Table of Proposition in a cloth of violet and shall put with it the censers and little mortars, the cups and bowls to pour out the

semper in ea erunt, 8 extendentque desuper pallium cocci-
neum, quod rursum operient velamento ianthinarum pellium et inducent vectes. 9 Sument et pallium hyacinthinum
quo operient candelabrum cum lucernis et forcipibus suis et
emunctoriis et cunctis vasis olei, quae ad concinnandas lucernas necessaria sunt, 10 et super omnia ponent operimentum ianthinarum pellium et inducent vectes. 11 Nec non et
altare aureum involvent hyacinthino vestimento et extendent desuper operimentum ianthinarum pellium inducentque vectes. 12 Omnia vasa quibus ministratur in sanctuario
involvent hyacinthino pallio et extendent desuper operimentum ianthinarum pellium inducentque vectes.

13 "Sed et altare mundabunt cinere et involvent illud pur-
pureo vestimento 14 ponentque cum eo omnia vasa quibus
in ministerio eius utuntur, id est ignium receptacula, fuscinulas ac tridentes, uncinos et vatilla. Cuncta vasa altaris
operient simul velamine ianthinarum pellium et inducent
vectes.

15 "Cumque involverint Aaron et filii eius sanctuarium et
omnia vasa eius in commotione castrorum, tunc intrabunt
filii Caath ut portent involuta. Et non tangent vasa sanctuarii ne moriantur.

"Ista sunt onera filiorum Caath in Tabernaculo Foederis,
16 super quos erit Eleazar, filius Aaron, sacerdotis, ad cuius
pertinet curam oleum ad concinnandas lucernas et conpositionis incensum et sacrificium quod semper offertur et
oleum unctionis et quicquid ad cultum tabernaculi pertinet
omniumque vasorum quae in sanctuario sunt."

libations. The loaves shall be always on it, 8 and they shall spread over it a cloth of scarlet, which again they shall cover with a covering of violet skins and shall put in the bars. 9 They shall take also a cloth of violet wherewith they shall cover the candlestick with the lamps and tongs thereof and the snuffers and all the oil vessels, which are necessary for the dressing of the lamps, 10 and over all they shall put a cover of violet skins and put in the bars. 11 And they shall wrap up the golden altar also in a cloth of violet and shall spread over it a cover of violet skins and put in the bars. 12 All the vessels wherewith they minister in the sanctuary they shall wrap up in a cloth of violet and shall spread over it a cover of violet skins and put in the bars.

13 *"They* shall cleanse the altar also from the ashes and shall wrap it up in a purple cloth 14 and shall put it with all the vessels that they use in the ministry thereof, that is to say firepans, fleshhooks and forks, pothooks and shovels. They shall cover all the vessels of the altar together with a covering of violet skins and shall put in the bars.

15 "And when Aaron and his sons have wrapped up the sanctuary and the vessels thereof at the removing of the camp, then shall the sons of Kohath enter in to carry the things wrapped up. And they shall not touch the vessels of the sanctuary lest they die.

"These are the burdens of the sons of Kohath in the Tabernacle of the Covenant, 16 and over them shall be Eleazar, the son of Aaron, the priest, to whose charge pertaineth the oil to dress the lamps and the *sweet* incense and the sacrifice that is always offered and the oil of unction and whatsoever pertaineth to the service of the tabernacle and of all the vessels that are in the sanctuary."

17 Locutusque est Dominus ad Mosen et Aaron, dicens,
18 "Nolite perdere populum Caath de medio Levitarum,
19 sed hoc facite eis ut vivant et non moriantur si tetigerint
Sancta Sanctorum: Aaron et filii eius intrabunt, ipsique dis-
ponent opera singulorum et dividunt quid portare quis debeat. 20 Alii nulla curiositate videant quae sunt in sanctuario
priusquam involvantur; alioquin morientur."

21 Locutusque est Dominus ad Mosen, dicens, 22 "Tolle
summam etiam filiorum Gerson per domos ac familias et
cognationes suas 23 a triginta annis et supra usque ad annos
quinquaginta. Numera omnes qui ingrediuntur et minis-
trant in Tabernaculo Foederis. 24 Hoc est officium familiae
Gersonitarum: 25 ut portent cortinas tabernaculi et tectum
foederis, operimentum aliud et super omnia velamen ianthi-
num tentoriumque quod pendet in introitu Foederis Tabernaculi, 26 cortinas atrii et velum in introitu quod est ante tabernaculum. Omnia quae ad altare pertinent, funiculos et
vasa ministerii, 27 iubente Aaron et filiis eius portabunt filii
Gerson, et scient singuli cui debeant oneri mancipari. 28 Hic
est cultus familiae Gersonitarum in Tabernaculo Foederis,
eruntque sub manu Ithamar, filii Aaron, sacerdotis.

29 "Filios quoque Merari per familias et domos patrum
suorum recensebis 30 a triginta annis et supra usque ad annos quinquaginta, omnes qui ingrediuntur ad officium ministerii sui et cultum foederis testimonii. 31 Haec sunt onera
eorum: portabunt tabulas tabernaculi et vectes eius, colum-

17 And the Lord spoke to Moses and Aaron, saying, 18 "Destroy not the people of Kohath from the midst of the Levites, 19 but do this to them that they may live and not die by touching the Holies of Holies: Aaron and his sons shall go in, and they shall *appoint every man his work* and shall divide *the burdens that* every man is to carry. 20 Let not others by any curiosity see the things that are in the sanctuary before they be wrapped up; otherwise they shall die."

21 And the Lord spoke to Moses, saying, 22 "Take the sum of the sons of Gershon also by their houses and families and kindreds 23 from thirty years old and upward unto fifty years old. Number them, all that go in and minister in the Tabernacle of the Covenant. 24 This is the office of the family of the Gershonites: 25 to carry the curtains of the tabernacle and the roof of the covenant, the other covering and the violet covering over all and the hanging that hangeth in the entry of the Tabernacle of the Covenant, 26 the curtains of the court and the veil in the entry that is before tabernacle. All things that pertain to the altar, the cords and the vessels of the ministry, 27 the sons of Gershon shall carry by the commandment of Aaron and his sons, and each man shall know to what burden he must be assigned. 28 This is the service of the family of the Gershonites in the Tabernacle of the Covenant, and they shall be under the hand of Ithamar, the son of Aaron, the priest.

29 "Thou shalt reckon up the sons of Merari also by the families and houses of their fathers 30 from thirty years old and upward unto fifty years old, all that go in to the office of their ministry and to the service of the covenant of the testimony. 31 These are their burdens: they shall carry the boards of the tabernacle and the bars thereof, the pillars and

nas et bases earum, 32 columnas quoque atrii per circuitum cum basibus et paxillis et funibus suis. Omnia vasa et supellectilem ad numerum accipient sicque portabunt. 33 Hoc est officium familiae Meraritarum et ministerium in Tabernaculo Foederis, eruntque sub manu Ithamar, filii Aaron, sacerdotis."

34 Recensuerunt igitur Moses et Aaron et principes synagogae filios Caath per cognationes et domos patrum suorum 35 a triginta annis et supra usque ad annum quinquagesimum, omnes qui ingrediuntur ad ministerium Tabernaculi Foederis, 36 et inventi sunt duo milia septingenti quinquaginta. 37 Hic est numerus populi Caath qui intrant Tabernaculum Foederis; hos numeravit Moses et Aaron iuxta sermonem Domini per manum Mosi.

38 Numerati sunt et filii Gerson per cognationes et domos patrum suorum 39 a triginta annis et supra usque ad annum quinquagesimum, omnes qui ingrediuntur ut ministrent in Tabernaculo Foederis, 40 et inventi sunt duo milia sescenti triginta. 41 Hic est populus Gersonitarum, quos numeraverunt Moses et Aaron iuxta verbum Domini.

42 Numerati sunt et filii Merari per cognationes et domos patrum suorum 43 a triginta annis et supra usque ad annum quinquagesimum, omnes qui ingrediuntur ad explendos ritus Tabernaculi Foederis, 44 et inventi sunt tria milia ducenti. 45 Hic est numerus filiorum Merari, quos recensuerunt Moses et Aaron iuxta imperium Domini per manum Mosi.

46 Omnes qui recensiti sunt de Levitis et quos fecit ad no-

their sockets, 32 the pillars also of the court round about with their sockets and pins and cords. They shall receive by account all the vessels and furniture and so shall carry them. 33 This is the office of the family of the Merarites and their ministry in the Tabernacle of the Covenant, and they shall be under the hand of Ithamar, the son of Aaron, the priest."

34 So Moses and Aaron and the princes of the synagogue reckoned up the sons of Kohath by their kindreds and the houses of their fathers 35 from thirty years old and upward unto fifty years old, all that go in to the ministry of the Tabernacle of the Covenant, 36 and they were found two thousand seven hundred and fifty. 37 This is the number of the people of Kohath that go in to the Tabernacle of the Covenant; these did Moses and Aaron number according to the word of the Lord by the hand of Moses.

38 The sons of Gershon also were numbered by the kindreds and houses of their fathers 39 from thirty years old and upward unto fifty years old, all that go in to minister in the Tabernacle of the Covenant, 40 and they were found two thousand six hundred and thirty. 41 This is the people of the Gershonites, whom Moses and Aaron numbered according to the word of the Lord.

42 The sons of Merari also were numbered by the kindreds and houses of their fathers 43 from thirty years old and upward unto fifty years old, all that go in to fulfil the rites of the Tabernacle of the Covenant, 44 and they were found three thousand two hundred. 45 This is the number of the sons of Merari, whom Moses and Aaron reckoned up according to the commandment of the Lord by the hand of Moses.

46 All that were reckoned up of the Levites and whom Moses and Aaron and the princes of Israel took by name, by

men Moses et Aaron et principes Israhel, per cognationes et domos patrum suorum, 47 a triginta annis et supra usque ad annum quinquagesimum ingredientes ad ministerium tabernaculi et onera portanda 48 fuerunt simul octo milia quingenti octoginta. 49 Iuxta verbum Domini recensuit eos Moses, unumquemque iuxta officium et onera sua, sicut praeceperat ei Dominus.

Caput 5

Locutusque est Dominus ad Mosen, dicens, 2 "Praecipe filiis Israhel ut eiciant de castris omnem leprosum et qui semine fluit pollutusque est super mortuo; 3 tam masculum quam feminam, eicite de castris ne contaminent ea cum habitaverim vobiscum."

4 Feceruntque ita filii Israhel, et eiecerunt eos extra castra, sicut locutus erat Dominus Mosi.

5 Locutusque est Dominus ad Mosen, dicens, 6 "Loquere ad filios Israhel, 'Vir sive mulier cum fecerint ex omnibus peccatis quae solent hominibus accidere et per neglegentiam transgressi fuerint mandatum Domini atque delique-

the kindreds and houses of their fathers, 47 from thirty years old and upward until fifty years old that go into the ministry of the tabernacle and to carry the burdens 48 were in all eight thousand five hundred and eighty. 49 Moses reckoned them up according to the word of the Lord, every one according to their office and burdens, as the Lord had commanded him.

Chapter 5

The unclean are removed out of the camp. Confession of sins and satisfaction. Firstfruits and oblations belonging to the priests. Trial of jealousy.

And the Lord spoke to Moses, saying, 2 "Command the children of Israel that they cast out of the camp every leper and whosoever hath an issue of seed or is defiled by the dead; 3 whether it be man or woman, cast ye them out of the camp lest they defile it when I shall dwell with you."

4 And the children of Israel did so, and they cast them forth without the camp, as the Lord had spoken to Moses.

5 And the Lord spoke to Moses, saying, 6 "Say to the children of Israel, 'When a man or woman shall have committed any of all the sins that men are wont to commit and by negligence shall have transgressed the commandment of the

rint, 7 confitebuntur peccatum suum et reddent ipsum caput quintamque partem desuper ei in quem peccaverint. 8 Sin autem non fuerit qui recipiat, dabunt Domino, et erit sacerdotis, excepto ariete qui offertur pro expiatione, ut sit placabilis hostia.

9 "'Omnes quoque primitiae quas offerunt filii Israhel ad sacerdotem pertinent, 10 et quicquid in sanctuarium offertur a singulis et traditur manibus sacerdotis ipsius erit.'"

11 Locutusque est Dominus ad Mosen, dicens, 12 "Loquere ad filios Israhel, et dices ad eos, 'Vir cuius uxor erraverit maritumque contemnens 13 dormierit cum altero viro, et hoc maritus deprehendere non quiverit, sed latet adulterium et testibus argui non potest quia non est inventa in stupro, 14 si spiritus zelotypiae concitaverit virum contra uxorem suam, quae vel polluta est vel falsa suspicione appetitur, 15 adducet eam ad sacerdotem et offeret oblationem pro illa, decimam partem sati farinae hordiaciae. Non fundet super eam oleum nec inponet tus, quia sacrificium zelotypiae est et oblatio investigans adulterium.

16 "'Offeret igitur eam sacerdos et statuet coram Domino. 17 Adsumetque aquam sanctam in vase fictili, et pauxillum terrae de pavimento tabernaculi mittet in eam. 18 Cumque steterit mulier in conspectu Domini, discoperiet caput eius et ponet super manus illius sacrificium recordationis et oblationem zelotypiae, ipse autem tenebit aquas amarissimas, in quibus cum execratione maledicta congessit. 19 Adiurabitque eam et dicet, "Si non dormivit vir alienus tecum et

Lord and offended, 7 they shall confess their sin and restore the principal itself and the fifth part over and above to him against whom they have sinned. 8 But if there be no one to receive it, they shall give it to the Lord, and it shall be the priest's, besides the ram that is offered for expiation, to be an atoning sacrifice.

9 "'All the firstfruits also which the children of Israel offer belong to the priest, 10 and whatsoever is offered into the sanctuary by every one and is delivered into the hands of the priest, it shall be his.'"

11 And the Lord spoke to Moses, saying, 12 "Speak to the children of Israel, and thou shalt say to them, 'The man whose wife shall have gone astray and contemning her husband 13 shall have slept with another man, and her husband cannot discover it, but the adultery is secret and cannot be proved by witnesses because she was not found in the adultery, 14 if the spirit of jealousy stir up the husband against his wife, who either is defiled or is charged with false suspicion, 15 he shall bring her to the priest and shall offer an oblation for her, the tenth part of a measure of barley meal. He shall not pour oil thereon nor put frankincense upon it, because it is a sacrifice of jealousy and an oblation searching out adultery.

16 "'The priest therefore shall offer it and set it before the Lord. 17 And he shall take holy water in an earthen vessel, and he shall cast a little earth of the pavement of the tabernacle into it. 18 And when the woman shall stand before the Lord, he shall uncover her head and shall put on her hands the sacrifice of remembrance and the oblation of jealousy, and he himself shall hold the most bitter waters, whereon he hath heaped curses with execration. 19 And he shall adjure her and shall say, "If another man hath not slept with thee

si non polluta es deserto mariti toro, non te nocebunt aquae istae amarissimae in quas maledicta congessi. 20 Sin autem declinasti a viro tuo atque polluta es et concubuisti cum altero viro, 21 his maledictionibus subiacebis. Det te Dominus in maledictionem exemplumque cunctorum in populo suo. Putrescere faciat femur tuum, et tumens uterus tuus disrumpatur. 22 Ingrediantur aquae maledictae in ventrem tuum, et utero tumescente putrescat femur."

"'Et respondebit mulier, "Amen, amen." 23 Scribetque sacerdos in libello ista maledicta et delebit ea aquis amarissimis in quas maledicta congessit, 24 et dabit ei bibere. Quas cum exhauserit, 25 tollet sacerdos de manu eius sacrificium zelotypiae et elevabit illud coram Domino inponetque illud super altare, ita dumtaxat ut prius 26 pugillum sacrificii tollat de eo quod offertur et incendat super altare et sic potum det mulieri aquas amarissimas.

27 "Quas cum biberit, si polluta est et contempto viro adulterii rea, pertransibunt eam aquae maledictionis, et, inflato ventre, conputrescet femur, eritque mulier in maledictionem et in exemplum omni populo. 28 Quod si polluta non fuerit, erit innoxia et faciet liberos.

29 "Ista est lex zelotypiae. Si declinaverit mulier a viro suo et si polluta fuerit 30 maritusque zelotypiae spiritu concitatus adduxerit eam in conspectu Domini et fecerit ei sacerdos iuxta omnia quae scripta sunt, 31 maritus absque culpa erit, et illa recipiet iniquitatem suam."'

and if thou be not defiled by forsaking thy husband's bed, these most bitter waters on which I have heaped curses shall not hurt thee. 20 But if thou hast gone aside from thy husband and art defiled and hast lain with another man, 21 *these curses shall light upon thee.* The Lord make thee a curse and an example for all among his people. May he make thy thigh to rot, and *may thy belly swell and* burst asunder. 22 Let the cursed waters enter into thy belly, and may thy womb swell and thy thigh rot."

"'And the woman shall answer, "Amen, amen." 23 And the priest shall write these curses in a book and shall wash them out with the most bitter waters upon which he hath heaped the curses, 24 and he shall give them her to drink. And when she hath drunk them up, 25 the priest shall take from her hand the sacrifice of jealousy and shall elevate it before the Lord and shall put it upon the altar, yet so as first 26 to take a handful of the sacrifice of that which is offered and burn it upon the altar and so give the most bitter waters to the woman to drink.

27 "'And when she hath drunk them, if she be defiled and having despised her husband be guilty of adultery, the malediction shall go through her, and, her belly swelling, her thigh shall rot, and the woman shall be a curse and an example to all the people. 28 But if she be not defiled, she shall not be hurt and shall bear children.

29 "'This is the law of jealousy. If a woman hath gone aside from her husband and be defiled 30 and the husband stirred up by the spirit of jealousy bring her before the Lord and the priest do to her according to all things that are here written, 31 the husband shall be blameless, and she shall bear her iniquity.'"

Caput 6

Locutusque est Dominus ad Mosen, dicens, 2 "Loquere ad filios Israhel, et dices ad eos, 'Vir sive mulier cum fecerint votum ut sanctificentur et se voluerint Domino consecrare, 3 vino et omni quod inebriare potest abstinebunt. Acetum ex vino et ex qualibet alia potione et quicquid de uva exprimitur non bibent, uvas recentes siccasque non comedent. 4 Cunctis diebus quibus ex voto Domino consecrantur, quicquid ex vinea esse potest, ab uva passa usque ad acinum, non comedent.

5 "'Omni tempore separationis suae, novacula non transibit super caput eius, usque ad conpletum diem quo Domino consecratur. Sanctus erit crescente caesarie capitis eius.

6 "'Omni tempore consecrationis suae super mortuum non ingredietur, 7 nec super patris quidem et matris et fratris sororisque funere contaminabitur, quia consecratio Dei sui super caput eius est. 8 Omnes dies separationis suae sanctus erit Domino.

9 "'Sin autem mortuus fuerit subito quispiam coram eo, polluetur caput consecrationis eius, quod radet ilico in eadem die purgationis suae et rursum septima. 10 In octavo autem die, offeret duos turtures vel duos pullos columbae

Chapter 6

The law of the Nazirites. The form of blessing the people.

And the Lord spoke to Moses, saying, 2 "Speak to the children of Israel, and thou shalt say to them, 'When *a man or woman shall* make a vow to be sanctified and will consecrate themselves to the Lord, 3 they shall abstain from wine and from every thing that may make a man drunk. They shall not drink vinegar of wine or of any other drink nor any thing that is pressed out of the grape, nor shall they eat grapes either fresh or dried. 4 All the days that they are consecrated to the Lord by vow, they shall eat nothing that cometh of the vineyard, from the raisin even to the kernel.

5 "'All the time of his separation, no razor shall pass over his head, until the day be fulfilled of his consecration to the Lord. He shall be holy and shall let the hair of his head grow.

6 "'All the time of his consecration he shall not go in to any dead, 7 neither shall he make himself unclean even *for his father or for his mother or for his brother or for his sister when they die,* because the consecration of his God is upon his head. 8 All the days of his separation he shall be holy to the Lord.

9 "'But if any man die suddenly before him, the head of his consecration shall be defiled, and he shall shave it forthwith on the same day of his purification and again on the seventh day. 10 And on the eighth day, he shall bring two turtles or two young pigeons to the priest in the entry of the

sacerdoti in introitu foederis testimonii. 11 Facietque sacerdos unum pro peccato et alterum in holocaustum et deprecabitur pro eo quia peccavit super mortuo, sanctificabitque caput eius in die illo 12 et consecrabit Domino dies separationis illius, offerens agnum anniculum pro peccato, ita tamen ut dies priores irriti fiant, quoniam polluta est sanctificatio eius.

13 "'Ista est lex consecrationis. Cum dies quos ex voto decreverat conplebuntur, adducet eum ad ostium Tabernaculi Foederis 14 et offeret oblationem eius Domino: agnum anniculum inmaculatum in holocaustum et ovem anniculam inmaculatam pro peccato et arietem inmaculatum hostiam pacificam, 15 canistrum quoque panum azymorum qui conspersi sunt oleo et lagana absque fermento uncta oleo ac libamina singulorum.

16 "'Quae offeret sacerdos coram Domino et faciet tam pro peccato quam in holocaustum. 17 Arietem vero immolabit hostiam pacificam Domino, offerens simul canistrum azymorum et libamenta quae ex more debentur.

18 "'Tunc radetur Nazareus ante ostium Tabernaculi Foederis caesarie consecrationis suae, tolletque capillos eius et ponet super ignem qui est subpositus sacrificio pacificorum 19 et armum coctum arietis tortamque absque fermento unam de canistro et laganum azymum unum, et tradet in manus Nazarei postquam rasum fuerit caput eius.

20 "'Susceptaque rursum ab eo elevabit in conspectu Domini, et sanctificata sacerdotis erunt, sicut pectusculum

covenant of the testimony. 11 And the priest shall offer one for sin and the other for a holocaust and shall pray for him for that he hath sinned by the dead, and he shall sanctify his head that day 12 and shall consecrate to the Lord the days of his separation, offering a lamb of one year for sin, yet so that the former days be made void, because his sanctification was profaned.

13 "'This is the law of consecration. When the days which he had determined by vow shall be expired, he shall bring him to the door of the Tabernacle of the Covenant 14 and shall offer his oblation to the Lord: *one* he-lamb of a year old without blemish for a holocaust and *one* ewe-lamb of a year old without blemish for a sin-offering and *one* ram without blemish for a victim of peace-offering, 15 a basket also of unleavened bread tempered with oil and wafers without leaven anointed with oil and the libations of each.

16 "And the priest shall present them before the Lord and shall offer both the sin offering and the holocaust. 17 But the ram he shall immolate for a sacrifice of peace-offering to the Lord, offering at the same time the basket of unleavened bread and the libations that are due by custom.

18 "'Then *shall the hair of the consecration of the Nazirite be shaved off* before the door of the Tabernacle of the Covenant, and he shall take his hair and lay it upon the fire which is under the sacrifice of the peace-offerings 19 and shall take the boiled shoulder of the ram and one unleavened cake out of the basket and one unleavened wafer, and he shall deliver them into the hands of the Nazirite after his head is shaven.

20 "And receiving them again from him, he shall elevate them in the sight of the Lord, and they being sanctified shall

quod separari iussum est et femur. Post haec potest bibere Nazareus vinum.

21 "'Ista est lex Nazarei. Cum voverit oblationem suam Domino tempore consecrationis suae, exceptis his quae invenerit manus eius, iuxta quod mente devoverat, ita faciet ad perfectionem sanctificationis suae.'"

22 Locutusque est Dominus ad Mosen, dicens, 23 "Loquere Aaron et filiis eius, 'Sic benedicetis filiis Israhel, et dicetis eis, 24 "Benedicat tibi Dominus et custodiat te. 25 Ostendat Dominus faciem suam tibi et misereatur tui. 26 Convertat Dominus vultum suum ad te et det tibi pacem."

27 "Invocabuntque nomen meum super filios Israhel, et ego benedicam eis.'"

Caput 7

Factum est autem in die qua conplevit Moses tabernaculum et erexit illud unxitque et sanctificavit cum omnibus vasis suis, altare similiter et omnia vasa eius, 2 obtulerunt

belong to the priest, as the breast which was commanded to be separated and the *shoulder.* After this the Nazirite may drink wine.

21 "'This is the law of the Nazirite. When he hath vowed his oblation to the Lord in the time of his consecration, besides those things which his hand shall find, according to that which he had vowed in his mind, so shall he do for the fulfilling of his sanctification.'"

22 And the Lord spoke to Moses, saying, 23 "Say to Aaron and his sons, 'Thus shall you bless the children of Israel, and you shall say to them, 24 "The Lord bless thee and keep thee. 25 The Lord shew his face to thee and have mercy on thee. 26 The Lord turn his countenance to thee and give thee peace."

27 "And they shall invoke my name upon the children of Israel, and I will bless them.'"

Chapter 7

The offerings of the princes at the dedication of the tabernacle. God speaketh to Moses from the propitiatory.

And it came to pass in the day that Moses had finished the tabernacle and set it up and had anointed and sanctified it with all its vessels, the altar likewise and all the vessels thereof, 2 the princes of Israel and the heads of the families

principes Israhel et capita familiarum, qui erant per singulas tribus, praefectique eorum qui numerati fuerant, 3 munera coram Domino, sex plaustra tecta cum duodecim bubus. Unum plaustrum obtulere duo duces, et unum bovem singuli, obtuleruntque ea in conspectu tabernaculi.

4 Ait autem Dominus ad Mosen, 5 "Suscipe ab eis ut serviant in ministerio tabernaculi, et trades ea Levitis iuxta ordinem ministerii sui."

6 Itaque, cum suscepisset Moses plaustra et boves, tradidit eos Levitis. 7 Duo plaustra et quattuor boves dedit filiis Gerson, iuxta id quod habebant necessarium. 8 Quattuor alia plaustra et octo boves dedit filiis Merari, secundum officia et cultum suum, sub manu Ithamar, filii Aaron, sacerdotis. 9 Filiis autem Caath non dedit plaustra et boves, quia in sanctuario serviunt et onera propriis portant umeris. 10 Igitur obtulerunt duces in dedicationem altaris die qua unctum est oblationem suam ante altare.

11 Dixitque Dominus ad Mosen, "Singuli duces, per singulos dies, offerant munera in dedicationem altaris."

12 Primo die, obtulit oblationem suam Naasson, filius Aminadab, de tribu Iuda. 13 Fueruntque in ea acetabulum argenteum pondo centum triginta siclorum, fiala argentea habens septuaginta siclos, iuxta pondus sanctuarii, utrumque plenum simila conspersa oleo in sacrificium; 14 mortariolum ex decem siclis aureis, plenum incenso; 15 bovem de armento et arietem et agnum anniculum in holocaustum; 16 hircumque pro peccato; 17 et in sacrificio pacificorum, bo-

in every tribe, *who were* the rulers of them who had been numbered, offered 3 their gifts before the Lord, six wagons covered and twelve oxen. Two princes offered one wagon, and each one an ox, and they offered them before the tabernacle.

4 And the Lord said to Moses, 5 "Receive them from them to serve in the ministry of the tabernacle, and thou shalt deliver them to the Levites according to the order of their ministry."

6 Moses therefore, receiving the wagons and the oxen, delivered them to the Levites. 7 Two wagons and four oxen he gave to the sons of Gershon, according to their necessity. 8 The other four wagons and eight oxen he gave to the sons of Merari, according to their offices and service, under the hand of Ithamar, the son of Aaron, the priest. 9 But to the sons of Kohath he gave no wagons or oxen, because they serve in the sanctuary and carry their burdens upon their own shoulders. 10 And the princes offered for the dedication of the altar on the day when it was anointed their oblation before the altar.

11 And the Lord said to Moses, "Let each of the princes, one day after another, offer their gifts for the dedication of the altar."

12 The first day, Nahshon, the son of Amminadab of the tribe of Judah, offered his offering. 13 And *his offering was* a silver dish weighing one hundred and thirty sicles, a silver bowl of seventy sicles, according to the weight of the sanctuary, both full of flour tempered with oil for a sacrifice; 14 a little mortar of ten sicles of gold, full of incense; 15 an ox of the herd and a ram and lamb of a year old for a holocaust; 16 and a buck-goat for sin; 17 and for the sacrifice of

ves duos, arietes quinque, hircos quinque, agnos anniculos quinque. Haec est oblatio Naasson, filii Aminadab.

18 Secundo die, obtulit Nathanahel, filius Suar, dux de tribu Isachar: 19 acetabulum argenteum adpendens centum triginta siclos, fialam argenteam habentem septuaginta siclos, iuxta pondus sanctuarii, utrumque plenum simila conspersa oleo in sacrificium; 20 mortariolum aureum habens decem siclos, plenum incenso; 21 bovem de armento et arietem et agnum anniculum in holocaustum; 22 hircumque pro peccato; 23 et in sacrificio pacificorum, boves duos, arietes quinque, hircos quinque, agnos anniculos quinque. Haec fuit oblatio Nathanahel, filii Suar.

24 Tertio die, princeps filiorum Zabulon, Heliab, filius Helon, 25 obtulit acetabulum argenteum adpendens centum triginta siclos, fialam argenteam habentem septuaginta siclos ad pondus sanctuarii, utrumque plenum simila conspersa oleo in sacrificium; 26 mortariolum aureum adpendens decem siclos, plenum incenso; 27 bovem de armento et arietem et agnum anniculum in holocaustum; 28 hircumque pro peccato; 29 et in sacrificio pacificorum, boves duos, arietes quinque, hircos quinque, agnos anniculos quinque. Haec est oblatio Heliab, filii Helon.

30 Die quarto, princeps filiorum Ruben, Helisur, filius Sedeur, 31 obtulit acetabulum argenteum adpendens centum triginta siclos, fialam argenteam habentem septuaginta siclos, ad pondus sanctuarii, utrumque plenum simila conspersa oleo in sacrificium; 32 mortariolum aureum adpendens decem siclos, plenum incenso; 33 bovem de armento et arietem et agnum anniculum in holocaustum; 34 hircumque pro peccato; 35 et in hostias pacificorum, bo-

peace-offerings, two oxen, five rams, five he-goats, five lambs of a year old. This was the offering of Nahshon, the son of Amminadab.

18 The second day, Nethanel, the son of Zuar, prince of the tribe of Issachar, *made his offering:* 19 a silver dish weighing one hundred and thirty sicles, a silver bowl of seventy sicles, according to the weight of the sanctuary, both full of flour tempered with oil for a sacrifice; 20 a little mortar of gold weighing ten sicles, full of incense; 21 an ox of the herd and a ram and a lamb of a year old for a holocaust; 22 and a buck-goat for sin; 23 and for the sacrifice of peace-offerings, two oxen, five rams, five buck-goats, five lambs of a year old. This was the offering of Nethanel, the son of Zuar.

24 The third day, the prince of the sons of Zebulun, Eliab, the son of Helon, 25 offered a silver dish weighing one hundred and thirty sicles, a silver bowl of seventy sicles by the weight of the sanctuary, both full of flour tempered with oil for a sacrifice; 26 a little mortar of gold weighing ten sicles, full of incense; 27 an ox of the herd and a ram and a lamb of a year old for a holocaust; 28 and a buck-goat for sin; 29 and for the sacrifice of peace-offerings, two oxen, five rams, five buck-goats, five lambs of a year old. This is the oblation of Eliab, the son of Helon.

30 The fourth day, the prince of the sons of Reuben, Elizur, the son of Shedeur, 31 offered a silver dish weighing one hundred and thirty sicles, a silver bowl of seventy sicles, according to the weight of the sanctuary, both full of flour tempered with oil for a sacrifice; 32 a little mortar of gold weighing ten sicles, full of incense; 33 an ox of the herd and a ram and a lamb of a year old for a holocaust; 34 and a buck-goat for sin; 35 and for victims of peace-offerings, two oxen,

ves duos, arietes quinque, hircos quinque, agnos anniculos quinque. Haec fuit oblatio Helisur, filii Sedeur.

36 Die quinto, princeps filiorum Symeon, Salamihel, filius Surisaddai, 37 obtulit acetabulum argenteum adpendens centum triginta siclos, fialam argenteam habentem septuaginta siclos, ad pondus sanctuarii, utrumque plenum simila conspersa oleo in sacrificium; 38 mortariolum aureum adpendens decem siclos, plenum incenso; 39 bovem de armento et arietem et agnum anniculum in holocaustum; 40 hircumque pro peccato; 41 et in hostias pacificorum, boves duos, arietes quinque, hircos quinque, agnos anniculos quinque. Haec fuit oblatio Salamihel, filii Surisaddai.

42 Die sexto, princeps filiorum Gad, Heliasaph, filius Duhel, 43 obtulit acetabulum argenteum adpendens centum triginta siclos, fialam argenteam habentem septuaginta siclos, ad pondus sanctuarii, utrumque plenum simila conspersa oleo in sacrificium; 44 mortariolum aureum adpendens siclos decem, plenum incenso; 45 bovem de armento et arietem et agnum anniculum in holocaustum; 46 hircumque pro peccato; 47 et in hostias pacificorum, boves duos, arietes quinque, hircos quinque, agnos anniculos quinque. Haec fuit oblatio Heliasaph, filii Duhel.

48 Die septimo, princeps filiorum Ephraim, Helisama, filius Ammiud, 49 obtulit acetabulum argenteum adpendens centum triginta siclos, fialam argenteam habentem septuaginta siclos, ad pondus sanctuarii, utrumque plenum simila conspersa oleo in sacrificium; 50 mortariolum aureum adpendens decem siclos, plenum incenso; 51 bovem de armento et arietem et agnum anniculum in holocaustum; 52 hircumque pro peccato; 53 et in hostias pacificas, boves

five rams, five buck-goats, five lambs of a year old. This was the offering of Elizur, the son of Shedeur.

36 The fifth day, the prince of the sons of Simeon, Shelumiel, the son of Zurishaddai, 37 offered a silver dish weighing one hundred and thirty sicles, a silver bowl of seventy sicles, after the weight of the sanctuary, both full of flour tempered with oil for a sacrifice; 38 a little mortar of gold weighing ten sicles, full of incense; 39 an ox of the herd and a ram and a lamb of a year old for a holocaust; 40 and a buck-goat for sin; 41 and for sacrifices of peace-offerings, two oxen, five rams, five buck-goats, five lambs of a year old. This was the offering of Shelumiel, the son of Zurishaddai.

42 The sixth day, the prince of the sons of Gad, Eliasaph, the son of Deuel, 43 offered a silver dish weighing a hundred and thirty sicles, a silver bowl of seventy sicles by the weight of the sanctuary, both full of flour tempered with oil for a sacrifice; 44 a little mortar of gold weighing ten sicles, full of incense; 45 an ox of the herd and a ram and a lamb of a year old for a holocaust; 46 and a buck-goat for sin; 47 and for sacrifices of peace-offerings, two oxen, five rams, five buck-goats, five lambs of a year old. This was the offering of Eliasaph, the son of Deuel.

48 The seventh day, the prince of the sons of Ephraim, Elishama, the son of Ammihud, 49 offered a silver dish weighing a hundred and thirty sicles, a silver bowl of seventy sicles, according to the weight of the sanctuary, both full of flour tempered with oil for a sacrifice; 50 a little mortar of gold weighing ten sicles, full of incense; 51 an ox of the herd and a ram and a lamb of a year old for a holocaust; 52 and a buck-goat for sin; 53 and for sacrifices of peace-offerings, two

duos, arietes quinque, hircos quinque, agnos anniculos quinque. Haec fuit oblatio Helisama, filii Ammiud.

54 Die octavo, princeps filiorum Manasse, Gamalihel, filius Phadassur, 55 obtulit acetabulum argenteum adpendens centum triginta siclos, fialam argenteam habentem septuaginta siclos, ad pondus sanctuarii, utrumque plenum simila conspersa oleo in sacrificium; 56 mortariolum aureum adpendens decem siclos plenum incenso; 57 bovem de armento et arietem et agnum anniculum in holocaustum; 58 hircumque pro peccato; 59 et in hostias pacificorum, boves duos, arietes quinque, hircos quinque, agnos anniculos quinque. Haec fuit oblatio Gamalihel, filii Phadassur.

60 Die nono, princeps filiorum Beniamin, Abidan, filius Gedeonis, 61 obtulit acetabulum argenteum adpendens centum triginta siclos, fialam argenteam habentem septuaginta siclos, ad pondus sanctuarii, utrumque plenum simila conspersa oleo in sacrificium; 62 mortariolum aureum adpendens decem siclos, plenum incenso; 63 bovem de armento et arietem et agnum anniculum in holocaustum; 64 hircumque pro peccato; 65 et in hostias pacificorum, boves duos, arietes quinque, hircos quinque, agnos anniculos quinque. Haec fuit oblatio Abidan, filii Gedeonis.

66 Die decimo, princeps filiorum Dan, Ahiezer, filius Amisaddai, 67 obtulit acetabulum argenteum adpendens centum triginta siclos, fialam argenteam habentem septuaginta siclos, ad pondus sanctuarii, utrumque plenum simila conspersa oleo in sacrificium; 68 mortariolum aureum adpendens decem siclos, plenum incenso; 69 bovem de armento et arietem et agnum anniculum in holocaustum; 70 hircumque pro peccato; 71 et in hostias pacificorum, bo-

oxen, five rams, five buck-goats, five lambs of a year old. This was the offering of Elishama, the son of Ammihud.

54 The eighth day, the prince of the sons of Manasseh, Gamaliel, the son of Pedahzur, 55 offered a silver dish weighing a hundred and thirty sicles, a silver bowl of seventy sicles, according to the weight of the sanctuary, both full of flour tempered with oil for a sacrifice; 56 a little mortar of gold weighing ten sicles, full of incense; 57 an ox of the herd and a ram and a lamb of a year old for a holocaust; 58 and a buck-goat for sin; 59 And for sacrifices of peace-offerings, two oxen, five rams, five buck-goats, five lambs of a year old. This was the offering of Gamaliel, the son of Pedahzur.

60 The ninth day, the prince of the sons of Benjamin, Abidan, the son of Gideoni, 61 offered a silver dish weighing a hundred and thirty sicles, a silver bowl of seventy sicles by the weight of the sanctuary, both full of flour tempered with oil for a sacrifice; 62 a little mortar of gold weighing ten sicles, full of incense; 63 an ox of the herd and a ram and a lamb of a year old for a holocaust; 64 and a buck-goat for sin; 65 and for sacrifices of peace-offerings, two oxen, five rams, five buck-goats, five lambs of a year old. This was the offering of Abidan, the son of Gideoni.

66 The tenth day, the prince of the sons of Dan, Ahiezer, the son of Ammishaddai, 67 offered a silver dish weighing a hundred and thirty sicles, a silver bowl of seventy sicles, according to the weight of the sanctuary, both full of flour tempered with oil for a sacrifice; 68 a little mortar of gold weighing ten sicles, full of incense; 69 an ox of the herd and a ram and a lamb of a year old for a holocaust; 70 and a buck-goat for sin; 71 and for sacrifices of peace-offerings, two

ves duos, arietes quinque, hircos quinque, agnos anniculos quinque. Haec fuit oblatio Ahiezer, filii Amisaddai.

72 Die undecimo, princeps filiorum Aser, Phagaihel, filius Ochran, 73 obtulit acetabulum argenteum adpendens centum triginta siclos, fialam argenteam habentem septuaginta siclos, ad pondus sanctuarii, utrumque plenum simila conspersa oleo in sacrificium; 74 mortariolum aureum adpendens decem siclos, plenum incenso; 75 bovem de armento et arietem et agnum anniculum in holocaustum; 76 hircumque pro peccato; 77 et in hostias pacificorum, boves duos, arietes quinque, hircos quinque, agnos anniculos quinque. Haec fuit oblatio Phagaihel, filii Ochran.

78 Die duodecimo, princeps filiorum Nepthalim, Achira, filius Henan, 79 obtulit acetabulum argenteum adpendens centum triginta siclos, fialam argenteam habentem septuaginta siclos, ad pondus sanctuarii, utrumque plenum simila conspersa oleo in sacrificium; 80 mortariolum aureum adpendens decem siclos, plenum incenso; 81 bovem de armento et arietem et agnum anniculum in holocaustum; 82 hircumque pro peccato; 83 et in hostias pacificorum, boves duos, arietes quinque, hircos quinque, agnos anniculos quinque. Haec fuit oblatio Achira, filii Henan.

84 Haec in dedicatione altaris oblata sunt a principibus Israhel in die qua consecratum est: acetabula argentea duodecim, fialae argenteae duodecim, mortariola aurea duodecim, 85 ita ut centum triginta argenti siclos haberet unum acetabulum et septuaginta siclos haberet una fiala, id est, in commune vasorum omnium ex argento, sicli duo milia quadringenti pondere sanctuarii; 86 mortariola aurea duodecim, plena incenso, denos siclos adpendentia pondere sanctuarii,

oxen, five rams, five buck-goats, five lambs of a year old. This was the offering of Ahiezer, the son of Ammishaddai.

72 The eleventh day, the prince of the sons of Asher, Pagiel, the son of Ochran, 73 offered a silver dish weighing a hundred and thirty sicles, a silver bowl of seventy sicles, according to the weight of the sanctuary, both full of flour tempered with oil for a sacrifice; 74 a little mortar of gold weighing ten sicles, full of incense; 75 an ox of the herd and a ram and a lamb of a year old for a holocaust; 76 and a buck-goat for sin; 77 and for sacrifices of peace-offerings, two oxen, five rams, five buck-goats, five lambs of a year old. This was the offering of Pagiel, the son of Ochran.

78 The twelfth day, the prince of the sons of Naphtali, Ahira, the son of Enan, 79 offered a silver dish weighing a hundred and thirty sicles, a silver bowl of seventy sicles, according to the weight of the sanctuary, both full of flour tempered with oil for a sacrifice; 80 a little mortar of gold weighing ten sicles, full of incense; 81 an ox of the herd and a ram and a lamb of a year old for a holocaust; 82 and a buck-goat for sin; 83 and for sacrifices of peace-offerings, two oxen, five rams, five buck-goats, five lambs of a year old. This was the offering of Ahira, the son of Enan.

84 These were the offerings made by the princes of Israel in the dedication of the altar in the day wherein it was consecrated: twelve dishes of silver, twelve silver bowls, twelve little mortars of gold, 85 each dish weighing a hundred and thirty sicles of silver and each *bowl, seventy* sicles, that is, putting all the vessels of silver together, two thousand four hundred sicles by the weight of the sanctuary; 86 twelve little mortars of gold, full of incense, weighing ten sicles apiece by the weight of the sanctuary, that is in all, a hundred and

id est simul, auri sicli centum viginti; 87 boves de armento in holocaustum duodecim, arietes duodecim, agni anniculi duodecim et libamenta eorum; hirci duodecim pro peccato; 88 in hostias pacificorum, boves viginti quattuor, arietes sexaginta, hirci sexaginta, agni anniculi sexaginta. Haec oblata sunt in dedicatione altaris quando unctum est.

89 Cumque ingrederetur Moses Tabernaculum Foederis ut consuleret oraculum, audiebat vocem loquentis ad se de propitiatorio quod erat super Arcam Testimonii inter duos cherubin, unde et loquebatur ei.

Caput 8

Locutusque est Dominus ad Mosen, dicens, 2 "Loquere Aaroni, et dices ad eum, 'Cum posueris septem lucernas, candelabrum in australi parte erigatur contra boream ad mensam panum propositionis; contra eam partem quam candelabrum respicit, lucere debebunt.'" 3 Fecitque Aaron, et inposuit lucernas super candelabrum, ut praeceperat Dominus Mosi.

twenty sicles of gold; 87 twelve oxen out of the herd for a holocaust, twelve rams, twelve lambs of a year old and their libations; twelve buck-goats for sin; 88 *and* for sacrifices of peace-offerings, oxen twenty-four, rams sixty, buck-goats sixty, lambs of a year old sixty. These things were offered in the dedication of the altar when it was anointed.

89 And when Moses entered into the Tabernacle of the Covenant to consult the oracle, he heard the voice of one speaking to him from the propitiatory that is over the *ark* between the two cherubims, and from this place he spoke to him.

Chapter 8

The seven lamps are placed on the golden candlestick to shine towards the loaves of proposition. The ordination of the Levites and to what age they shall serve in the tabernacle.

And the Lord spoke to Moses, saying, 2 "Speak to Aaron, and thou shalt say to him, 'When thou shalt place the seven lamps, let the candlestick be set up on the south side. *Give orders therefore that the lamps look* over against the north, towards the table of the loaves of proposition; over against that part shall they give light towards which the candlestick looketh.'" 3 And Aaron did so, and he put the lamps upon the candlestick, as the Lord had commanded Moses.

4 Haec autem erat factura candelabri: ex auro ductili, tam medius stipes quam cuncta quae ex utroque calamorum latera nascebantur; iuxta exemplum quod ostendit Dominus Mosi, ita operatus est candelabrum.

5 Et locutus est Dominus ad Mosen, dicens, 6 "Tolle Levitas de medio filiorum Israhel, et purificabis eos 7 iuxta hunc ritum: aspergantur aqua lustrationis, et radant omnes pilos carnis suae. Cumque laverint vestimenta sua et mundati fuerint, 8 tollent bovem de armentis et libamentum eius similam oleo conspersam, bovem autem alterum de armento tu accipies pro peccato. 9 Et adplicabis Levitas coram Tabernaculo Foederis, convocata omni multitudine filiorum Israhel. 10 Cumque Levitae fuerint coram Domino, ponent filii Israhel manus suas super eos, 11 et offeret Aaron Levitas munus in conspectu Domini a filiis Israhel ut serviant in ministerio eius.

12 "Levitae quoque ponent manus suas super capita boum, e quibus unum facies pro peccato et alterum in holocaustum Domini, ut depreceris pro eis. 13 Statuesque Levitas in conspectu Aaron et filiorum eius et consecrabis oblatos Domino 14 ac separabis de medio filiorum Israhel, ut sint mei.

15 "Et postea, ingredientur Tabernaculum Foederis ut serviant mihi. Sicque purificabis et consecrabis eos in oblationem Domini, quoniam dono donati sunt mihi a filiis Israhel. 16 Pro primogenitis quae aperiunt omnem vulvam in Israhel

4 Now this was the work of the candlestick: it was of beaten gold, both the shaft in the middle and all that came out of both sides of the branches; according to the pattern which the Lord had shewn to Moses, so he made the candlestick.

5 And the Lord spoke to Moses, saying, 6 "Take the Levites out of the midst of the children of Israel, and thou shalt purify them 7 according to this rite: let them be sprinkled with the water of purification, and let them shave all the hairs of their flesh. And when they shall have washed their garments and are cleansed, 8 they shall take an ox of the herd and for the offering thereof fine flour tempered with oil, and thou shalt take another ox of the herd for a sin-offering. 9 And thou shalt bring the Levites before the Tabernacle of the Covenant, calling together all the multitude of the children of Israel. 10 And when the Levites are before the Lord, the children of Israel shall put their hands upon them, 11 and Aaron shall offer the Levites as a gift in the sight of the Lord from the children of Israel that they may serve in his ministry.

12 "The Levites also shall put their hands upon the heads of the oxen, of which thou shalt *sacrifice* one for sin and the other for a holocaust to the Lord, to pray for them. 13 And thou shalt set the Levites in the sight of Aaron and of his sons and shalt consecrate them being offered to the Lord 14 and shalt separate them from the midst of the children of Israel, to be mine.

15 "And afterwards, they shall enter into the Tabernacle of the Covenant to serve me. And thus shalt thou purify and consecrate them for an oblation of the Lord, for as a gift they were given me by the children of Israel. 16 I have taken

accepi eos, 17 mea sunt enim omnia primogenita filiorum Israhel, tam ex hominibus quam ex iumentis. Ex die quo percussi omnem primogenitum in terra Aegypti sanctificavi eos mihi, 18 et tuli Levitas pro cunctis primogenitis filiorum Israhel 19 tradidique eos dono Aaroni et filiis eius de medio populi, ut serviant mihi pro Israhel in Tabernaculo Foederis et orent pro eis ne sit in populo plaga si ausi fuerint accedere ad sanctuarium."

20 Feceruntque Moses et Aaron et omnis multitudo filiorum Israhel super Levitas quae praeceperat Dominus Mosi, 21 purificatique sunt et laverunt vestimenta sua. Elevavitque eos Aaron in conspectu Domini et oravit pro eis 22 ut purificati ingrederentur ad officia sua in Tabernaculum Foederis coram Aaron et filiis eius. Sicut praeceperat Dominus Mosi de Levitis, ita factum est.

23 Locutusque est Dominus ad Mosen, dicens, 24 "Haec est lex Levitarum: a viginti quinque annis et supra, ingredientur ut ministrent in Tabernaculo Foederis. 25 Cumque quinquagesimum annum aetatis impleverint, servire cessabunt. 26 Eruntque ministri fratrum suorum in Tabernaculo Foederis ut custodiant quae sibi fuerint commendata, opera autem ipsa non faciant. Sic dispones Levitis in custodiis suis."

them instead of the firstborn that open every womb in Israel, 17 for all the firstborn of the children of Israel, both of men and of beasts, are mine. From the day that I slew every firstborn in the land of Egypt have I sanctified them to myself, 18 and I have taken the Levites for all the firstborn of the children of Israel 19 and have delivered them for a gift to Aaron and his sons out of the midst of the people, to serve me for Israel in the Tabernacle of the Covenant and to pray for them lest there should be a plague among the people if they should presume to approach unto my sanctuary."

20 And Moses and Aaron and all the multitude of the children of Israel did with the Levites *all* that the Lord had commanded Moses, 21 and they were purified and washed their garments. And Aaron lifted them up in the sight of the Lord and prayed for them 22 that being purified they might go into the Tabernacle of the Covenant to do their services before Aaron and his sons. As the Lord had commanded Moses touching the Levites, so was it done.

23 And the Lord spoke to Moses, saying, 24 "This is the law of the Levites: from twenty-five years old and upwards, they shall go in to minister in the Tabernacle of the Covenant. 25 And when they shall have accomplished the fiftieth year of their age, they shall cease to serve. 26 And they shall be the ministers of their brethren in the Tabernacle of the Covenant to keep the things that are committed to their care, but not to do the works. Thus shalt thou *order* the Levites touching their charge."

Caput 9

Locutus est Dominus ad Mosen in deserto Sinai anno secundo postquam egressi sunt de terra Aegypti, mense primo, dicens, 2 "Faciant filii Israhel Phase in tempore suo, 3 quartadecima die mensis huius, ad vesperam, iuxta omnes caerimonias et iustificationes eius."

4 Praecepitque Moses filiis Israhel ut facerent Phase. 5 Qui fecerunt tempore suo, quartadecima die mensis, ad vesperam, in Monte Sinai. Iuxta omnia quae mandaverat Dominus Mosi fecerunt filii Israhel.

6 Ecce autem: quidam inmundi super animam hominis, qui non poterant facere Phase in die illo, accedentes ad Mosen et Aaron, 7 dixerunt eis, "Inmundi sumus super animam hominis. Quare fraudamur ut non valeamus offerre oblationem Domino in tempore suo inter filios Israhel?"

8 Quibus respondit Moses, "State ut consulam quid praecipiet Dominus de vobis."

9 Locutusque est Dominus ad Mosen, dicens, 10 "Loquere filiis Israhel, 'Homo qui fuerit inmundus super anima sive in

Chapter 9

The precept of the pasch is renewed. The unclean and travellers are to observe it the second month. The camp is guided by the pillar of the cloud.

The Lord spoke to Moses in the desert of Sinai the second year after they were come out of the land of Egypt, in the first month, saying, 2 "Let the children of Israel make the Phase in its due time, 3 the fourteenth day of this month, in the evening, according to all the ceremonies and justifications thereof."

4 And Moses commanded the children of Israel that they should make the Phase. 5 And they made it in its proper time, the fourteenth day of the month, at evening, in Mount Sinai. The children of Israel did according to all things that the Lord had commanded Moses.

6 But behold: some who were unclean by occasion of the soul of a man, who could not make the Phase on that day, coming to Moses and Aaron, 7 said to them, "We are unclean by occasion of the soul of a man. Why are we kept back that we may not offer in its season the offering to the Lord among the children of Israel?"

8 And Moses answered them, "Stay that I may consult *the Lord what he* will ordain concerning you."

9 And the Lord spoke to Moses, saying, 10 "Say to the children of Israel, 'The man that shall be unclean *by occasion of*

via procul in gente vestra, faciat Phase Domino 11 mense secundo, quartadecima die mensis, ad vesperam; cum azymis
et lactucis agrestibus comedent illud. 12 Non relinquent ex
eo quippiam usque mane et os eius non confringent; omnem
ritum Phase observabunt.

13 "'Si quis autem et mundus est et in itinere non fuit et
tamen non fecit Phase, exterminabitur anima illa de populis
suis, quia sacrificium Domino non obtulit tempore suo. Peccatum suum ipse portabit.

14 "'Peregrinus quoque et advena, si fuerint apud vos, facient Phase Domino iuxta caerimonias et iustificationes
eius. Praeceptum idem erit apud vos, tam advenae quam indigenae.

15 Igitur die qua erectum est tabernaculum, operuit illud
nubes. A vespere autem, super tentorium erat quasi species
ignis usque mane. 16 Sic fiebat iugiter: per diem operiebat illud nubes, et per noctem quasi species ignis.

17 Cumque ablata fuisset nubes quae tabernaculum pro-
tegebat, tunc proficiscebantur filii Israhel. Et in loco ubi
stetisset nubes, ibi castrametabantur. 18 Ad imperium Domini proficiscebantur, et ad imperium illius figebant tabernaculum. Cunctis diebus quibus stabat nubes super tabernaculum manebant in eodem loco. 19 Et si evenisset ut multo
tempore maneret super illud, erant filii Israhel in excubiis
Domini et non proficiscebantur 20 quotquot diebus fuisset
nubes super tabernaculum. Ad imperium Domini erigebant

one that is dead or shall be in a journey afar off in your nation, let him make the Phase to the Lord 11 in the second month, on the fourteenth day of the month, in the evening; they shall eat it with unleavened bread and wild lettuce. 12 They shall not leave any thing thereof until morning nor break a bone thereof; they shall observe all the ceremonies of the Phase.

13 "'But if any man is clean and was not on a journey and did not make the Phase, that soul shall be cut off from among his people, because he offered not sacrifice to the Lord in *due season*. He shall bear his sin.

14 "'The sojourner also and the stranger, if they be among you, shall make the Phase to the Lord according to the ceremonies and justifications thereof. The same ordinance shall be with you, both for the stranger and for him that was born in the land.'"

15 Now on the day that the tabernacle was reared up, a cloud covered it. But from the evening, there was over the tabernacle as it were the appearance of fire until the morning. 16 So it was always: by day the cloud covered it, and by night as it were the appearance of fire.

17 And when the cloud that covered the tabernacle was taken up, then the children of Israel marched forward. And in the place where the cloud stood still, there they camped. 18 At the commandment of the Lord they marched, and at his commandment they pitched the tabernacle. All the days that the cloud abode over the tabernacle they remained in the same place. 19 And if it was so that it continued over it a long time, the children of Israel kept the watches of the Lord and marched not 20 for as many days soever as the cloud stayed over the tabernacle. At the commandment of

tentoria, et ad imperium illius deponebant. 21 Si fuisset nubes a vespere usque mane et statim diluculo tabernaculum reliquisset, proficiscebantur. Et si post diem et noctem recessisset, dissipabant tentoria. 22 Si vero biduo aut uno mense vel longiori tempore fuisset super tabernaculum, manebant filii Israhel in eodem loco et non proficiscebantur, statim autem ut recessisset movebant castra. 23 Per verbum Domini figebant tentoria, et per verbum illius proficiscebantur erantque in excubiis Domini iuxta imperium eius per manum Mosi.

Caput 10

Locutusque est Dominus ad Mosen, dicens, 2 "Fac tibi duas tubas argenteas ductiles quibus convocare possis multitudinem quando movenda sunt castra. 3 Cumque increpueris tubis, congregabitur ad te omnis turba ad ostium Foederis Tabernaculi.

4 "Si semel clangueris, venient ad te principes et capita multitudinis Israhel. 5 Sin autem prolixior atque concisus clangor increpuerit, movebunt castra primi qui sunt ad

the Lord they pitched their tents, and at his commandment they took them down. 21 If the cloud tarried from evening until morning and immediately at break of day left the tabernacle, they marched forward. And if it departed after a day and a night, they took down their tents. 22 But if it *remained* over the tabernacle for two days or a month or a longer time, the children of Israel remained in the same place and marched not, but immediately as soon as it departed they removed the camp. 23 By the word of the Lord they pitched their tents, and by his word they marched and kept the watches of the Lord according to his commandment by the hand of Moses.

Chapter 10

The silver trumpets and their use. They march from Sinai.

And the Lord spoke to Moses, saying, 2 "Make thee two trumpets of beaten silver wherewith thou mayest call together the multitude when the camp is to be removed. 3 And when thou shalt sound the trumpets, all the multitude shall gather unto thee to the door of the Tabernacle of the Covenant.

4 "If thou sound but once, the princes and the heads of the multitude of Israel shall come to thee. 5 But if the *sound of the trumpets be* longer and with interruptions, they that are

orientalem plagam. 6 In secundo autem sonitu et pari ulu-
latu tubae, levabunt tentoria qui habitant ad meridiem. Et
iuxta hunc modum reliqui facient ululantibus tubis in profectione. 7 Quando autem congregandus est populus, simplex tubarum clangor erit, et non concise ululabunt. 8 Filii
autem Aaron, sacerdotes, clangent tubis, eritque hoc legitimum sempiternum in generationibus vestris.

9 "Si exieritis ad bellum de terra vestra contra hostes qui
dimicant adversum vos, clangetis ululantibus tubis, et erit
recordatio vestri coram Domino, Deo vestro, ut eruamini
de manibus inimicorum vestrorum.

10 "Si quando habebitis epulum et dies festos et kalendas,
canetis tubis super holocaustis et pacificis victimis ut sint
vobis in recordationem Dei vestri. Ego Dominus, Deus
vester."

11 Anno secundo, mense secundo, vicesima die mensis,
elevata est nubes de Tabernaculo Foederis. 12 Profectique
sunt filii Israhel per turmas suas de deserto Sinai, et recubuit
nubes in solitudine Pharan.

13 Moveruntque castra primi, iuxta imperium Domini in
manu Mosi: 14 filii Iuda per turmas suas, quorum princeps
erat Naasson, filius Aminadab. 15 In tribu filiorum Isachar
fuit princeps Nathanahel, filius Suar. 16 In tribu Zabulon erat
princeps Heliab, filius Helon.

on the east side shall first go forward. 6 And at the second sounding and like noise of the trumpet, they who lie on the south side shall take up their tents. And after this manner shall the rest do when the trumpets shall sound for a march. 7 But when the people is to be gathered together, the sound of the trumpets shall be plain, and they shall not make a broken sound. 8 And the sons of Aaron, the priests, shall sound the trumpets, and this shall be an ordinance for ever in your generations.

9 "If you go forth to war out of your land against the enemies that fight against you, you shall sound aloud with the trumpets, and there shall be a remembrance of you before the Lord, your God, that you may be delivered out of the hands of your enemies.

10 "If at any time you shall have a banquet and on your festival days and on the first days of your months, you shall sound the trumpets over the holocausts and the sacrifices of peace-offerings that they may be to you for a remembrance of your God. I am the Lord, your God."

11 The second year, in the second month, the twentieth day of the month, the cloud was taken up from the Tabernacle of the Covenant. 12 And the children of Israel marched by their troops from the desert of Sinai, and the cloud rested in the wilderness of Paran.

13 And the first went forward, according to the commandment of the Lord by the hand of Moses: 14 the sons of Judah by their troops, whose prince was Nahshon, the son of Amminadab. 15 In the tribe of the sons of Issachar the prince was Nethanel, the son of Zuar. 16 In the tribe of Zebulun the prince was Eliab, the son of Helon.

17 Depositumque est tabernaculum, quod portantes egressi sunt filii Gerson et Merari.

18 Profectique sunt et filii Ruben, per turmas et ordinem suum, quorum princeps erat Helisur, filius Sedeur. 19 In tribu autem filiorum Symeon princeps fuit Salamihel, filius Surisaddai. 20 Porro in tribu Gad erat princeps Heliasaph, filius Duhel.

21 Profectique sunt et Caathitae portantes sanctuarium. Tamdiu tabernaculum portabatur donec venirent ad erectionis locum.

22 Moverunt castra et filii Ephraim per turmas suas, in quorum exercitu princeps erat Helisama, filius Ammiud. 23 In tribu autem filiorum Manasse princeps fuit Gamalihel, filius Phadassur. 24 Et in tribu Beniamin erat dux Abidan, filius Gedeonis.

25 Novissimi castrorum omnium profecti sunt filii Dan per turmas suas, in quorum exercitu princeps fuit Ahiezer, filius Amisaddai. 26 In tribu autem filiorum Aser erat princeps Phagaihel, filius Ochran. 27 Et in tribu filiorum Nepthalim princeps fuit Achira, filius Henan.

28 Haec sunt castra et profectiones filiorum Israhel per turmas suas quando egrediebantur.

29 Dixitque Moses Hobab, filio Rahuhel, Madianiti, cognato suo, "Proficiscimur ad locum quem Dominus daturus est nobis. Veni nobiscum ut benefaciamus tibi, quia Dominus bona promisit Israheli."

30 Cui ille respondit, "Non vadam tecum, sed revertar in terram meam in qua natus sum."

31 Et ille, "Noli," inquit, "nos relinquere, tu enim nosti in quibus locis per desertum castra ponere debeamus, et eris ductor noster. 32 Cumque nobiscum veneris, quicquid opti-

17 And the tabernacle was taken down, and the sons of Gershon and Merari set forward, bearing it.

18 And the sons of Reuben also marched, by their troops and ranks, whose prince was Elizur, the son of Shedeur. 19 And in the tribe of Simeon the prince was Shelumiel, the son of Zurishaddai. 20 And in the tribe of Gad the prince was Eliasaph, the son of Deuel.

21 Then the Kohathites also marched carrying the sanctuary. So long was the tabernacle carried till they came to the place of setting it up.

22 The sons of Ephraim also moved their camp by their troops, in whose army the prince was Elishama, the son of Ammihud. 23 And in the tribe of the sons of Manasseh the prince was Gamaliel, the son of Pedahzur. 24 And in the tribe of Benjamin, *the prince was* Abidan, the son of Gideoni.

25 The last of all the camp marched the sons of Dan by their troops, in whose army the prince was Ahiezer, the son of Ammishaddai. 26 And in the tribe of the sons of Asher the prince was Pagiel, the son of Ochran. 27 And in the tribe of the sons of Naphtali the prince was Ahira, the son of Enan.

28 This was the order of the camps and marches of the children of Israel by their troops when they set forward.

29 And Moses said to Hobab, the son of Reuel, the Midianite, his kinsman, "We are going towards the place which the Lord will give us. Come with us that we may do thee good, for the Lord hath promised good things to Israel."

30 But he answered him, "I will not go with thee, but I will return to my country wherein I was born."

31 And he said, "Do not leave us, for thou knowest in what places we should encamp in the wilderness, and thou shalt be our guide. 32 And if thou comest with us, we will give thee

mum fuerit ex opibus quas nobis traditurus est Dominus dabimus tibi."

33 Profecti sunt ergo de monte Domini via trium dierum,
Arcaque Foederis Domini praecedebat eos per dies tres pro-
videns castrorum locum. 34 Nubes quoque Domini super eos
erat per diem cum incederent.

35 Cumque elevaretur arca, dicebat Moses, "Surge, Domine, et dissipentur inimici tui, et fugiant qui oderunt te a
facie tua."

36 Cum autem deponeretur, aiebat, "Revertere, Domine,
ad multitudinem exercitus Israhel."

Caput 11

Interea, ortum est murmur populi, quasi dolentium pro
labore, contra Dominum. Quod cum audisset Dominus,
iratus est. Et accensus in eos ignis Domini devoravit extremam castrorum partem. 2 Cumque clamasset populus ad
Mosen, oravit Moses ad Dominum, et absortus est ignis.

what is the best of the riches which the Lord shall deliver to us."

33 So they marched from the mount of the Lord three days' journey, and the Ark of the Covenant of the Lord went before them for three days providing a place for the camp. 34 The cloud also of the Lord was over them by day when they marched.

35 And when the ark was lifted up, Moses said, "Arise, O Lord, and let thy enemies be scattered, and let them that hate thee flee from before thy face."

36 And when it was set down, he said, "Return, O Lord, to the multitude of the host of Israel."

Chapter 11

The people murmur and are punished with fire. God appointeth seventy ancients for assistants to Moses. They prophesy. The people have their fill of flesh, but forthwith many die of the plague.

In the mean time, there arose a murmuring of the people against the Lord, as it were repining at *their fatigue*. And when the Lord heard it, he was angry. And the fire of the Lord being kindled against them devoured them that were at the uttermost part of the camp. 2 And when the people cried to Moses, Moses prayed to the Lord, and the fire was

3 Vocavitque nomen loci illius Incensio, eo quod succensus fuisset contra eos ignis Domini, 4 vulgus quippe promiscuum quod ascenderat cum eis flagravit desiderio, sedens et flens, iunctis sibi pariter filiis Israhel, et ait, "Quis dabit nobis ad vescendum carnes? 5 Recordamur piscium quos comedebamus in Aegypto, gratis. In mentem nobis veniunt cucumeres et pepones porrique et cepae et alia. 6 Anima nostra arida est; nihil aliud respiciunt oculi nostri nisi man."

7 Erat autem man quasi semen coriandri, coloris bdellii. 8 Circuibatque populus et, colligens illud, frangebat mola sive terebat in mortario coquens in olla et faciens ex eo tortulas saporis quasi panis oleati. 9 Cumque descenderet nocte super castra ros, descendebat pariter et man.

10 Audivit ergo Moses flentem populum per familias, singulos per ostia tentorii sui. Iratusque est furor Domini valde; sed et Mosi intoleranda res visa est. 11 Et ait ad Dominum, "Cur adflixisti servum tuum? Quare non invenio gratiam coram te? Et cur inposuisti pondus universi populi huius super me? 12 Numquid ego concepi omnem hanc multitudinem vel genui eam, ut dicas mihi, 'Porta eos in sinu tuo sicut portare solet nutrix infantulum, et defer in terram pro qua iurasti patribus eorum'? 13 Unde mihi carnes ut dem tantae multitudini? Flent contra me, dicentes, 'Da nobis carnes ut comedamus.' 14 Non possum solus sustinere omnem hunc populum quia gravis mihi est. 15 Sin aliter tibi videtur, obsecro ut interficias me, et inveniam gratiam in oculis tuis ne tantis adficiar malis."

swallowed up. 3 And he called the name of that place the Burning, for that the fire of the Lord had been kindled against them, 4 for a mixt multitude of people that came up with them burned with desire, sitting and weeping, the children of Israel also being joined with them, and said, "Who shall give us flesh to eat? 5 We remember the fish that we ate in Egypt, free cost. The cucumbers come into our mind and the melons and the leeks and the onions and the garlic. 6 Our soul is dry; our eyes behold nothing else but manna."

7 Now the manna was like coriander seed, of the colour of bdellium. 8 And the people went about and, gathering it, ground it in a mill or beat it in a mortar and boiled it in a pot and made cakes thereof of the taste of bread tempered with oil. 9 And when the dew fell in the night upon the camp, the manna also fell with it.

10 Now Moses heard the people weeping by their families, every one at the door of his tent. And the wrath of the Lord was exceedingly enkindled; to Moses also the thing seemed insupportable. 11 And he said to the Lord, "Why hast thou afflicted thy servant? Wherefore do I not find favour before thee? And why hast thou laid the weight of all this people upon me? 12 Have I conceived all this multitude or begotten them, that thou shouldst say to me, 'Carry them in thy bosom as the nurse is wont to carry the little infant, and bear them into the land for which thou hast sworn to their fathers'? 13 Whence should I have flesh to give to so great a multitude? They weep against me, saying, 'Give us flesh that we may eat.' 14 I am not able alone to bear all this people because it is too heavy for me. 15 But if it seem unto thee otherwise, I beseech thee to kill me, and let me find grace in thy eyes that I be not afflicted with so great evils."

16 Et dixit Dominus ad Mosen, "Congrega mihi septuaginta viros de senibus Israhel quos tu nosti quod senes populi sint ac magistri, et duces eos ad ostium Tabernaculi Foederis faciesque ibi stare tecum 17 ut descendam et loquar tibi. Et auferam de spiritu tuo tradamque eis ut sustentent tecum onus populi, et non tu solus graveris.

18 "Populo quoque dices, 'Sanctificamini. Cras comedetis carnes, ego enim audivi vos dicere, "Quis dabit nobis escas carnium? Bene nobis erat in Aegypto," ut det vobis Dominus carnes, et comedatis, 19 non uno die nec duobus vel quinque aut decem nec viginti quidem 20 sed usque ad mensem dierum donec exeat per nares vestras et vertatur in nausiam, eo quod reppuleritis Dominum qui in medio vestri est et fleveritis coram eo, dicentes, "Quare egressi sumus ex Aegypto?"'"

21 Et ait Moses, "Sescenta milia peditum huius populi sunt, et tu dicis, 'Dabo eis esum carnium mense integro'? 22 Numquid ovium et boum multitudo caedetur ut possit sufficere ad cibum? Vel omnes pisces maris in unum congregabuntur ut eos satient?"

23 Cui respondit Dominus, "Numquid manus Domini invalida est? Iam nunc videbis utrum meus sermo opere conpleatur."

24 Venit igitur Moses et narravit populo verba Domini congregans septuaginta viros de senibus Israhel quos stare fecit circa tabernaculum. 25 Descenditque Dominus per nubem et locutus est ad eum, auferens de spiritu qui erat in Mosen et dans septuaginta viris. Cumque requievisset in eis spiritus, prophetaverunt, nec ultra cessarunt.

16 And the Lord said to Moses, "Gather unto me seventy men of the ancients of Israel whom thou knowest to be ancients and masters of the people, and thou shalt bring them to the door of the Tabernacle of the Covenant and shalt make them stand there with thee 17 that I may come down and speak with thee. And I will take of thy spirit and will give to them that they may bear with thee the burden of the people, and thou mayest not be burthened alone.

18 "And thou shalt say to the people, 'Be ye sanctified. To-morrow you shall eat flesh, for I have heard you say, "Who will give us flesh to eat? It was well with us in Egypt," that the Lord may give you flesh, and you may eat, 19 not for one day nor two nor five nor ten, no, nor for twenty 20 but even for a month of days till it come out at your nostrils and become loathsome to you, because you have cast off the Lord who is in the midst of you and have wept before him, saying, "Why came we out of Egypt?"'"

21 And Moses said, "There are six hundred thousand footmen of this people, and sayest thou, 'I will give them flesh to eat a whole month'? 22 Shall then a multitude of sheep and oxen be killed that it may suffice for their food? Or shall the fishes of the sea be gathered together to fill them?"

23 And the Lord answered him, "Is the hand of the Lord unable? Thou shalt presently see whether my word shall come to pass *or no.*"

24 Moses therefore came and told the people the words of the Lord and assembled seventy men of the ancients of Israel and made them to stand about the tabernacle. 25 And the Lord came down in a cloud and spoke to him, taking away of the spirit that was in Moses and giving to the seventy men. And when the spirit had rested on them, they prophesied, nor did they cease afterwards.

26 Remanserant autem in castris duo viri, quorum unus vocabatur Heldad, et alter, Medad, super quos requievit spiritus, nam et ipsi descripti fuerant et non exierant ad tabernaculum. 27 Cumque prophetarent in castris, cucurrit puer et nuntiavit Mosi, dicens, "Heldad et Medad prophetant in castris."

28 Statim Iosue, filius Nun, minister Mosi et electus e pluribus, ait, "Domine mi Moses, prohibe eos."

29 At ille, "Quid," inquit, "aemularis pro me? Quis tribuat ut omnis populus prophetet, et det eis Dominus spiritum suum!"

30 Reversusque est Moses et maiores natu Israhel in castra. 31 Ventus autem egrediens a Domino arreptas trans mare coturnices detulit et dimisit in castra itinere quantum uno die confici potest ex omni parte castrorum per circuitum, volabantque in aere duobus cubitis altitudine super terram.

32 Surgens ergo populus toto die illo et nocte ac die altero, congregavit coturnicum; qui parum, decem choros. Et siccaverunt eas per gyrum castrorum. 33 Adhuc carnes erant in dentibus eorum, nec defecerat huiuscemodi cibus, et, ecce, furor Domini concitatus in populum percussit eum plaga magna nimis. 34 Vocatusque est ille locus Sepulchra Concupiscentiae, ibi enim sepelierunt populum qui desideraverat. Egressi autem de Sepulchris Concupiscentiae, venerunt in Aseroth et manserunt ibi.

26 Now there remained in the camp two of the men, of whom one was called Eldad, and the other, Medad, upon whom the spirit rested, for they also had been enrolled but were not gone forth to the tabernacle. 27 And when they prophesied in the camp, there ran a young man and told Moses, saying, "Eldad and Medad prophesy in the camp."

28 Forthwith, Joshua, the son of Nun, the minister of Moses and chosen out of many, said, "My lord Moses, forbid them."

29 But he said, "Why hast thou emulation for me? O that all the people might prophesy, and that the Lord would give them his spirit!"

30 And Moses returned with the ancients of Israel into the camp. 31 And a wind going out from the Lord, taking quails up beyond the sea, brought them and cast them into the camp *for the space of one day's journey* on every side of the camp round about, and they flew in the air two cubits high above the ground.

32 The people therefore rising up all that day and night and the next day, gathered together of quails; he that did least, ten cores. And they dried them round about the camp. 33 As yet the flesh was between their teeth, neither had that kind of meat failed, when, behold, the wrath of the Lord being provoked against the people struck them with an exceeding great plague. 34 And that place was called the Graves of Lust, for there they buried the people that had lusted. And departing from the Graves of Lust, they came unto Hazeroth and abode there.

Caput 12

Locutaque est Maria et Aaron contra Mosen propter uxorem eius, Aethiopissam, 2 et dixerunt, "Num per solum Mosen locutus est Dominus? Nonne et nobis similiter est locutus?"

Quod cum audisset Dominus 3 (erat enim Moses vir mi-
tissimus super omnes homines qui morabantur in terra),
4 statim locutus est ad eum et ad Aaron et Mariam, "Egredimini, vos tantum tres, ad Tabernaculum Foederis." Cumque
fuissent egressi, 5 descendit Dominus in columna nubis et
stetit in introitu tabernaculi vocans Aaron et Mariam.

Qui cum issent, 6 dixit ad eos, "Audite sermones meos: si
quis fuerit inter vos propheta Domini, in visione apparebo
ei vel per somnium loquar ad illum. 7 At non talis servus
meus Moses, qui in omni domo mea fidelissimus est, 8 ore
enim ad os loquor ei et palam, et non per enigmata et figuras
Dominum videt. Quare igitur non timuistis detrahere servo
meo Mosi?"

Chapter 12

Miriam and Aaron murmur against Moses, whom God praiseth above other prophets. Miriam being struck with leprosy, Aaron confesseth his fault. Moses prayeth for her, and after seven days' separation from the camp she is restored.

And Miriam and Aaron spoke against Moses because of his wife, the Ethiopian, 2 and they said, "Hath the Lord spoken by Moses only? Hath he not also spoken to us in like manner?"

And when the Lord heard this 3 (for Moses was a man exceeding meek above all men that dwelt upon earth), 4 immediately he spoke to him and to Aaron and Miriam, "Come out, you three only, to the Tabernacle of the Covenant." And when they were come out, 5 the Lord came down in a pillar of the cloud, and stood in the entry of the tabernacle calling to Aaron and Miriam.

And when they were come, 6 he said to them, "Hear my words: if there be among you a prophet of the Lord, I will appear to him in a vision or I will speak to him in a dream. 7 But it is not so with my servant Moses, who is most faithful in all my house, 8 for I speak to him mouth to mouth and plainly, and not by riddles and figures doth he see the Lord. Why then were you not afraid to speak ill of my servant Moses?"

9 Iratusque contra eos abiit. 10 Nubes quoque recessit quae erat super tabernaculum, et ecce: Maria apparuit candens lepra quasi nix. Cumque respexisset eam Aaron et vidisset perfusam lepra, 11 ait ad Mosen, "Obsecro, domine mi, ne inponas nobis hoc peccatum quod stulte commisimus. 12 Ne fiat haec quasi mortua et ut abortivum quod proicitur de vulva matris suae. Ecce, iam medium carnis eius devoratum est lepra."

13 Clamavitque Moses ad Dominum, dicens, "Deus, obsecro, sana eam."

14 Cui respondit Dominus, "Si pater eius spuisset in faciem illius, nonne debuerat saltem septem dierum rubore suffundi? Separetur septem diebus extra castra, et postea revocabitur."

15 Exclusa est itaque Maria extra castra septem diebus, et populus non est motus de loco illo donec revocata est Maria.

Caput 13

Profectusque est populus de Aseroth fixis tentoriis in deserto Pharan. 2 Ibique locutus est Dominus ad Mosen, dicens, 3 "Mitte viros qui considerent terram Chanaan quam

9 And being angry with them he went away. 10 The cloud also that was over the tabernacle departed, and behold: Miriam appeared white as snow with a leprosy. And when Aaron had looked on her and saw her all covered with leprosy, 11 he said to Moses, "I beseech thee, my lord, lay not upon us this sin which we have foolishly committed. 12 Let her not be as one dead and as an abortive that is cast forth from the mother's womb. Lo, now one half of her flesh is consumed with the leprosy."

13 And Moses cried to the Lord, saying, "O God, I beseech thee, heal her."

14 And the Lord answered him, "If her father had spitten upon her face, ought she not to have been ashamed for seven days at least? Let her be separated seven days without the camp, and afterwards she shall be called again."

15 Miriam therefore was put out of the camp seven days, and the people moved not from that place until Miriam was called again.

Chapter 13

The twelve spies are sent to view the land. The relation they make of it.

And the people marched from Hazeroth and pitched their tents in the desert of Paran. 2 And there the Lord spoke to Moses, saying, 3 "Send men to view the land of Canaan

daturus sum filiis Israhel, singulos de singulis tribubus, ex principibus."

4 Fecit Moses quod Dominus imperarat, de deserto Pharan mittens principes viros quorum ista sunt nomina: 5 de tribu Ruben, Semmua, filium Zecchur; 6 de tribu Symeon, Saphat, filium Huri; 7 de tribu Iuda, Chaleb, filium Iepphonne; 8 de tribu Isachar, Igal, filium Ioseph; 9 de tribu Ephraim, Osee, filium Nun; 10 de tribu Beniamin, Phalti, filium Raphu; 11 de tribu Zabulon, Geddihel, filium Sodi; 12 de tribu Ioseph, sceptri Manasse, Gaddi, filium Susi; 13 de tribu Dan, Ammihel, filium Gemalli; 14 de tribu Aser, Sthur, filium Michahel; 15 de tribu Nepthali, Naabbi, filium Vaphsi; 16 de tribu Gad, Guhel, filium Machi. 17 Haec sunt nomina virorum quos misit Moses ad considerandam terram, vocavitque Osee, filium Nun, Iosue.

18 Misit ergo eos Moses ad considerandam terram Chanaan et dixit ad eos, "Ascendite per meridianam plagam, cumque veneritis ad montes, 19 considerate terram: qualis sit et populum qui habitator est eius, utrum fortis sit an infirmus, pauci numero an plures, 20 ipsa terra, bona an mala, urbes quales, muratae an absque muris, 21 humus, pinguis an sterilis, nemorosa an absque arboribus. Confortamini, et adferte nobis de fructibus terrae." Erat autem tempus quando iam praecoquae uvae vesci possunt.

22 Cumque ascendissent, exploraverunt terram a deserto Sin usque Roob intrantibus Emath. 23 Ascenderuntque ad meridiem et venerunt in Hebron, ubi erant Ahiman et Si-

which I will give to the children of Israel, one of every tribe, of the rulers."

4 Moses did what the Lord had commanded, sending from the desert of Paran principal men whose names are these: 5 of the tribe of Reuben, Shammua, the son of Zaccur; 6 of the tribe of Simeon, Shaphat, the son of Hori; 7 of the tribe of Judah, Caleb, the son of Jephunneh; 8 of the tribe of Issachar, Igal, the son of Joseph; 9 of the tribe of Ephraim, Hoshea, the son of Nun; 10 of the tribe of Benjamin, Palti, the son of Raphu; 11 of the tribe of Zebulun, Gaddiel, the son of Sodi; 12 of the tribe of Joseph, of the sceptre of Manasseh, Gaddi, the son of Susi; 13 of the tribe of Dan, Ammiel, the son of Gemalli; 14 of the tribe of Asher, Sethur, the son of Michael; 15 of the tribe of Naphtali, Nahbi, the son of Vophsi; 16 of the tribe of Gad, Geuel, the son of Machi. 17 These are the names of the men whom Moses sent to view the land, and he called Hoshea, the son of Nun, Joshua.

18 And Moses sent them to view the land of Canaan and said to them, "Go you up by the south side, and when you shall come to the mountains, 19 view the land: of what sort it is and the people that are the inhabitants thereof, whether they be strong or weak, few in number or many, 20 the land itself, whether it be good or bad, what manner of cities, walled or without walls, 21 the ground, fat or barren, woody or without trees. Be of good courage, and bring us of the fruits of the land." Now it was the time when the firstripe grapes are fit to be eaten.

22 And when they were gone up, they viewed the land from the desert of Zin unto Rehob as you enter into Hamath. 23 And they went up at the south side and came to Hebron, where were Ahiman and Sheshai and Talmai, the sons of

sai et Tholmai, filii Enach, nam Hebron septem annis ante Tanim, urbem Aegypti, condita est. 24 Pergentesque usque ad Torrentem Botri, absciderunt palmitem cum uva sua, quem portaverunt in vecte duo viri. De malis quoque granatis et de ficis loci illius tulerunt, 25 qui appellatus est Neelescol, id est, Torrens Botri, eo quod botrum inde portassent filii Israhel.

26 Reversique exploratores terrae post quadraginta dies, omni regione circuita, 27 venerunt ad Mosen et Aaron et ad omnem coetum filiorum Israhel in desertum Pharan, quod est in Cades, locutique eis et omni multitudini, ostenderunt fructus terrae. 28 Et narraverunt, dicentes, "Venimus in terram ad quam misisti nos, quae re vera fluit lacte et melle ut ex his fructibus cognosci potest, 29 sed cultores fortissimos habet, et urbes grandes atque muratas. Stirpem Enach vidimus ibi. 30 Amalech habitat in meridie, Hettheus et Iebuseus et Amorreus in montanis, Chananeus vero moratur iuxta mare et circa fluenta Iordanis."

31 Inter haec, Chaleb, conpescens murmur populi qui oriebatur contra Mosen, ait, "Ascendamus et possideamus terram, quoniam poterimus obtinere eam."

32 Alii vero qui fuerant cum eo dicebant, "Nequaquam ad hunc populum valemus ascendere quia fortior nobis est." 33 Detraxeruntque terrae quam inspexerant apud filios Israhel, dicentes, "Terram quam lustravimus devorat habitatores suos; populum quem aspeximus procerae staturae est. 34 Ibi vidimus monstra quaedam filiorum Enach, de genere giganteo, quibus conparati quasi lucustae videbamur."

Anak, for Hebron was built seven years before Tanis, the city of Egypt. 24 And forward as far as the Torrent of the Cluster of Grapes, they cut off a branch with its cluster of grapes, which two men carried upon a lever. They took also of the pomegranates and of the figs of that place, 25 which was called Nehelescol, that is to say, the Torrent of the Cluster of Grapes, because from thence the children of Israel had carried a cluster of grapes.

26 And they that went to spy out the land returned after forty days, having gone round all the country, 27 and came to Moses and Aaron and to all the assembly of the children of Israel to the desert of Paran, which is in Kadesh, and, speaking to them and to all the multitude, they shewed them the fruits of the land. 28 And they related and said, "We came into the land to which thou sentest us, which in very deed floweth with milk and honey as may be known by these fruits, 29 but it hath very strong inhabitants, and the cities are great and walled. We saw there the race of Anak. 30 Amalek dwelleth in the south, the Hittite and the Jebusite and the Amorite in the mountains, but the Canaanite abideth by the sea and near the streams of the Jordan."

31 In the mean time, Caleb, to still the murmuring of the people that rose against Moses, said, "Let us go up and possess the land, for we shall be able to conquer it."

32 But the others that had been with him said, "No, we are not able to go up to this people because they are stronger than we." 33 And they spoke ill of the land which they had viewed before the children of Israel, saying, "The land which we have viewed devoureth its inhabitants; the people that we beheld are of a tall stature. 34 There we saw certain monsters of the sons of Anak, of the giant kind, in comparison of whom we seemed like locusts."

Caput 14

Igitur vociferans omnis turba flevit nocte illa. 2 Et murmurati sunt contra Mosen et Aaron cuncti filii Israhel, dicentes, 3 "Utinam mortui essemus in Aegypto, et in hac vasta solitudine utinam pereamus, et non inducat nos Dominus in terram istam ne cadamus gladio et uxores ac liberi nostri ducantur captivi! Nonne melius est reverti in Aegyptum?"

4 Dixeruntque alter ad alterum, "Constituamus nobis ducem, et revertamur in Aegyptum."

5 Quo audito Moses et Aaron ceciderunt proni in terram coram omni multitudine filiorum Israhel. 6 At vero Iosue, filius Nun, et Chaleb, filius Iepphonne, qui et ipsi lustraverant terram, sciderunt vestimenta sua 7 et ad omnem multitudinem filiorum Israhel locuti sunt, "Terram quam circuivimus valde bona est. 8 Si propitius fuerit Dominus, inducet nos in eam et tradet humum lacte et melle manantem. 9 Nolite rebelles esse contra Dominum, neque timeatis populum terrae huius, quia sicut panem ita eos possumus devorare. Recessit ab illis omne praesidium. Dominus nobiscum est; nolite metuere."

Chapter 14

The people murmur. God threateneth to destroy them. He is appeased by Moses, yet so as to exclude the murmurers from entering the promised land. The authors of the sedition are struck dead. The rest going to fight against the will of God are beaten.

Therefore the whole multitude crying wept that night. 2 And all the children of Israel murmured against Moses and Aaron, saying, 3 "Would God that we had died in Egypt, and would God we may die in this vast wilderness, and that the Lord may not bring us into this land lest we fall by the sword and our wives and children be led away captives! Is it not better to return into Egypt?"

4 And they said one to another, "Let us appoint a captain, and let us return into Egypt."

5 And when Moses and Aaron heard this, they fell down flat upon the ground before the multitude of the children of Israel. 6 But Joshua, the son of Nun, and Caleb, the son of Jephunneh, who themselves also had viewed the land, rent their garments 7 and said to all the multitude of the children of Israel, "The land which we have gone round is very good. 8 If the Lord be favourable, he will bring us into it and give us a land flowing with milk and honey. 9 Be not rebellious against the Lord, and fear ye not the people of this land, for we are able to eat them up as bread. All aid is gone from them. The Lord is with us; fear ye not."

10 Cumque clamaret omnis multitudo et lapidibus eos vellet opprimere, apparuit gloria Domini super Tectum Foederis cunctis filiis Israhel. 11 Et dixit Dominus ad Mosen, "Usquequo detrahet mihi populus iste? Quousque non credent mihi in omnibus signis quae feci coram eis? 12 Feriam igitur eos pestilentia atque consumam. Te autem faciam principem super gentem magnam et fortiorem quam haec est."

13 Et ait Moses ad Dominum, "Ut audiant Aegyptii, de quorum medio eduxisti populum istum, 14 et habitatores terrae huius, qui audierunt quod tu, Domine, in populo isto sis et facie videaris ad faciem et nubes tua protegat illos et in columna nubis praecedas eos per diem et in columna ignis per noctem, 15 quod occideris tantam multitudinem quasi unum hominem et dicant, 16 'Non poterat introducere populum in terram pro qua iuraverat, idcirco occidit eos in solitudine'! 17 Magnificetur ergo fortitudo Domini, sicut iurasti, dicens, 18 'Dominus patiens et multae misericordiae auferens iniquitatem et scelera nullumque innoxium derelinquens, qui visitas peccata patrum in filios in tertiam et quartam generationem.' 19 Dimitte, obsecro, peccatum populi tui huius secundum magnitudinem misericordiae tuae, sicut propitius fuisti egredientibus de Aegypto usque ad locum istum."

20 Dixitque Dominus, "Dimisi iuxta verbum tuum. 21 Vivo ego, et implebitur gloria Domini universa terra. 22 Attamen omnes homines qui viderunt maiestatem meam et signa quae feci in Aegypto et in solitudine et temptaverunt me

10 And when all the multitude cried out and would have stoned them, the glory of the Lord appeared over the *Tabernacle* of the Covenant to all the children of Israel. 11 And the Lord said to Moses, "How long will this people detract me? How long will they not believe me for all the signs that I have wrought before them? 12 I will strike them therefore with pestilence and will consume them. But thee I will make a ruler over a great nation and a mightier than this is."

13 And Moses said to the Lord, "That the Egyptians, from the midst of whom thou hast brought forth this people, 14 and the inhabitants of this land, who have heard that thou, O Lord, art among this people and art seen face to face and thy cloud protecteth them and thou goest before them in a pillar of a cloud by day and in a pillar of fire by night, 15 may hear that thou hast killed so great a multitude as it were one man and may say, 16 'He could not bring the people into the land for which he had sworn, therefore did he kill them in the wilderness'! 17 Let then the strength of the Lord be magnified, as thou hast sworn, saying, 18 'The Lord is patient and full of mercy by taking away iniquity and wickedness and leaving no man clear, who visitest the sins of the fathers upon the children unto the third and fourth generation.' 19 Forgive, I beseech thee, the sins of *this* people according to the greatness of thy mercy, as thou hast been merciful to them from their going out of Egypt unto this place."

20 And the Lord said, "I have forgiven according to thy word. 21 As I live, and the whole earth shall be filled with the glory of the Lord. 22 But yet all the men that have seen my majesty and the signs that I have done in Egypt and in the wilderness and have tempted me now ten times and have

iam per decem vices nec oboedierunt voci meae 23 non videbunt terram pro qua iuravi patribus eorum, nec quisquam ex
illis qui detraxit mihi intuebitur eam. 24 Servum meum Chaleb, qui plenus alio spiritu secutus est me, inducam in terram
hanc quam circuivit, et semen eius possidebit eam, 25 quoniam Amalechites et Chananeus habitant in vallibus. Cras
movete castra, et revertimini in solitudinem per viam Maris
Rubri."

26 Locutusque est Dominus ad Mosen et Aaron, dicens,
27 "Usquequo multitudo haec pessima murmurat contra me?
Querellas filiorum Israhel audivi. 28 Dic ergo eis, "'Vivo ego,"
ait Dominus, "sicut locuti estis audiente me, sic faciam vobis. 29 In solitudine hac iacebunt cadavera vestra. Omnes qui
numerati estis a viginti annis et supra et murmurastis contra
me 30 non intrabitis terram super quam levavi manum meam
ut habitare vos facerem, praeter Chaleb, filium Iepphonne,
et Iosue, filium Nun. 31 Parvulos autem vestros de quibus
dixistis quod praedae hostibus forent introducam ut videant
terram quae vobis displicuit. 32 Vestra cadavera iacebunt in
solitudine. 33 Filii vestri erunt vagi in deserto annis quadraginta et portabunt fornicationem vestram donec consuman-
tur cadavera patrum in deserto 34 iuxta numerum quadraginta dierum quibus considerastis terram: annus pro die
inputabitur. Et quadraginta annis recipietis iniquitates vestras et scietis ultionem meam, 35 quoniam sicut locutus sum,
ita faciam omni multitudini huic pessimae quae consurrexit
adversum me. In solitudine hac deficiet et morietur.""

not obeyed my voice 23 shall not see the land for which I swore to their fathers, neither shall any one of them that hath detracted me behold it. 24 My servant Caleb, who being full of another spirit hath followed me, I will bring into this land which he hath gone round, and his seed shall possess it, 25 for the Amalekite and the Canaanite dwell in the valleys. Tomorrow remove the camp, and return into the wilderness by the way of the Red Sea."

26 And the Lord spoke to Moses and Aaron, saying, 27 "How long doth this wicked multitude murmur against me? I have heard the murmurings of the children of Israel. 28 Say therefore to them, '"As I live," saith the Lord, "according as you have spoken in my hearing, so will I do to you. 29 In *the* wilderness shall your carcasses lie. All you that were numbered from twenty years old and upward and have murmured against me 30 shall not enter into the land over which I lifted up my hand to make you dwell therein, except Caleb, the son of Jephunneh, and Joshua, the son of Nun. 31 But your children of whom you said that they should be a prey to the enemies will I bring in that they may see the land which you have despised. 32 Your carcasses shall lie in the wilderness. 33 Your children shall wander in the desert forty years and shall bear your fornication until the carcasses of their fathers be consumed in the desert 34 according to the number of the forty days wherein you viewed the land: a year shall be counted for a day. And forty years you shall receive your iniquities and shall know my revenge, 35 for as I have spoken, so will I do to all this wicked multitude that hath risen up together against me. In this wilderness shall it faint away and die."'"

741

36 Igitur omnes viri quos miserat Moses ad contemplandam terram et qui reversi murmurare fecerant contra eum omnem multitudinem, detrahentes terrae quod esset mala, 37 mortui sunt atque percussi in conspectu Domini. 38 Iosue autem, filius Nun, et Chaleb, filius Iepphonne, vixerunt ex omnibus qui perrexerant ad considerandam terram. 39 Locutusque est Moses universa verba haec ad omnes filios Israhel, et luxit populus nimis.

40 Et ecce: mane primo surgentes, ascenderunt verticem montis atque dixerunt, "Parati sumus ascendere ad locum de quo Dominus locutus est, quia peccavimus."

41 Quibus Moses, "Cur," inquit, "transgredimini verbum Domini quod vobis non cedet in prosperum? 42 Nolite ascendere, non enim est Dominus vobiscum, ne corruatis coram inimicis vestris. 43 Amalechites et Chananeus ante vos sunt, quorum gladio corruetis eo quod nolueritis adquiescere Domino, nec erit Dominus vobiscum."

44 At illi contenebrati ascenderunt in verticem montis. Arca autem Testamenti Domini et Moses non recesserunt de castris. 45 Descenditque Amalechites et Chananeus qui habitabat in monte et percutiens eos atque concidens persecutus est eos usque Horma.

36 Therefore all the men whom Moses had sent to view the land and who at their return had made the whole multitude to murmur against him, speaking ill of the land that it was naught, 37 died and were struck in the sight of the Lord. 38 But Joshua, the son of Nun, and Caleb, the son of Jephunneh, lived of all them that had gone to view the land. 39 And Moses spoke all these words to all the children of Israel, and the people mourned exceedingly.

40 And behold: rising up very early in the morning, they went up to the top of the mountain and said, "We are ready to go up to the place of which the Lord hath spoken, for we have sinned."

41 And Moses said to them, "Why transgress you the word of the Lord which shall not succeed prosperously with you? 42 Go not up, for the Lord is not with you, lest you fall before your enemies. 43 The Amalekite and the Canaanite are before you, and by their sword you shall fall because you would not consent to the Lord, neither will the Lord be with you."

44 But they being blinded went up to the top of the mountain. But the Ark of the Testament of the Lord and Moses departed not from the camp. 45 And the Amalekite came down and the Canaanite that dwelt in the mountain and smiting and slaying them pursued them as far as Hormah.

Caput 15

Locutusque est Dominus ad Mosen, dicens, 2 "Loquere ad filios Israhel, et dices ad eos, 'Cum ingressi fueritis terram habitationis vestrae quam ego dabo vobis 3 et feceritis oblationem Domino in holocaustum aut victimam vota solventes vel sponte offerentes munera aut in sollemnitatibus vestris adolentes odorem suavitatis Domino de bubus sive de ovibus, 4 offeret quicumque immolaverit victimam sacrificium similae decimam partem oephi conspersae oleo quod mensuram habebit quartam partem hin, 5 et vinum ad liba fundenda eiusdem mensurae dabit in holocausto sive in victima. Per agnos singulos 6 et arietes erit sacrificium similae duarum decimarum, quae conspersa sit oleo tertiae partis hin, 7 et vinum ad libamentum tertiae partis eiusdem mensurae offeret in odorem suavitatis Domino. 8 Quando vero de bubus feceris holocaustum aut hostiam ut impleas votum vel pacificas victimas, 9 dabis per singulos boves similae tres decimas conspersae oleo quod habeat medium mensurae hin 10 et vinum ad liba fundenda eiusdem mensurae in oblationem suavissimi odoris Domino. 11 Sic facies 12 per singulos boves et arietes et agnos et hedos. 13 Tam indigenae quam

Chapter 15

Certain laws concerning sacrifices. Sabbath-breaking is punished with death. The law of fringes on their garments.

And the Lord spoke to Moses, saying, 2 "Speak to the children of Israel, and thou shalt say to them, 'When you shall be come unto the land of your habitation which I will give you 3 and shall make an offering to the Lord for a holocaust or a victim paying your vows or voluntarily offering gifts or in your solemnities burning a sweet savour unto the Lord of oxen or of sheep, 4 whosoever immolateth the victim shall offer a sacrifice of fine flour the tenth part of an ephi tempered with the fourth part of a hin of oil, 5 and he shall give the same measure of wine to pour out in libations for the holocaust or for the victim. For every lamb 6 and for every ram there shall be a sacrifice of flour of two tenths, which shall be tempered with the third part of a hin of oil, 7 and he shall offer the third part the same measure of wine for the libation for a sweet savour to the Lord. 8 But when thou offerest a holocaust or sacrifice of oxen to fulfil thy vow or for victims of peace-offerings, 9 thou shalt give for every ox three tenths of flour tempered with half a hin of oil 10 and wine for libations of the same measure for an offering of most sweet savour to the Lord. 11 Thus shalt thou do 12 for every ox and ram and lamb and kid. 13 Both they that

peregrini 14 eodem ritu offerent sacrificia. 15 Unum praeceptum erit atque iudicium tam vobis quam advenis terrae.'"

16 Locutus est Dominus ad Mosen, dicens, 17 "Loquere filiis Israhel, et dices ad eos, 18 'Cum veneritis in terram quam
dabo vobis 19 et comederitis de panibus regionis illius, separabitis primitias Domino 20 de cibis vestris. Sicut de areis
primitias separatis, 21 ita et de pulmentis dabitis primitiva
Domino.

22 "'Quod si per ignorantiam praeterieritis quicquam horum quae locutus est Dominus ad Mosen 23 et mandavit per
eum ad vos a die qua coepit iubere et ultra 24 oblitaque fuerit
facere multitudo, offeret vitulum de armento, holocaustum
in odorem suavissimum Domino, et sacrificium eius ac liba
ut caerimoniae postulant hircumque pro peccato. 25 Et rogabit sacerdos pro omni multitudine filiorum Israhel, et dimittetur eis quoniam non sponte peccaverunt, nihilominus
offerentes incensum Domino pro se et pro peccato atque
errore suo. 26 Et dimittetur universae plebi filiorum Israhel
et advenis qui peregrinantur inter eos quoniam culpa est
omnis populi per ignorantiam.

27 "'Quod si anima una nesciens peccaverit, offeret capram anniculam pro peccato suo. 28 Et deprecabitur pro ea
sacerdos quod inscia peccaverit coram Domino, inpetrabit-
que ei veniam, et dimittetur illi. 29 Tam indigenis quam advenis, una lex erit omnium qui peccaverint ignorantes.

are born in the land and the strangers 14 shall offer sacrifices after the same rite. 15 There shall be all one law and judgment both for you and for them who are strangers in the land.'"

16 And the Lord spoke to Moses, saying, 17 "Speak to the children of Israel, and thou shalt say to them, 18 'When you are come into the land which I will give you 19 and shall eat of the bread of that country, you shall separate firstfruits to the Lord 20 of the things you eat. As you separate firstfruits of your barnfloors, 21 so also shall you give firstfruits of your dough to the Lord.

22 "'And if through ignorance you omit any of these things which the Lord hath spoken to Moses 23 and by him hath commanded you from the day that he began to command and thenceforward 24 and the multitude have forgotten to do it, they shall offer a calf out of the herd, a holocaust for a most sweet savour to the Lord, and the sacrifice and libations thereof as the ceremonies require and a buck-goat for sin. 25 And the priest shall pray for all the multitude of the children of Israel, and it shall be forgiven them because they sinned ignorantly, offering notwithstanding a burnt offering to the Lord for themselves and for their sin and their ignorance. 26 And it shall be forgiven all the people of the children of Israel and the strangers that sojourn among them because it is the fault of all the people through ignorance.

27 "'But if one soul shall sin ignorantly, he shall offer a she-goat of a year old for his sin. 28 And the priest shall pray for him because he sinned ignorantly before the Lord, and he shall obtain his pardon, and it shall be forgiven him. 29 The same law shall be for all that sin by ignorance, whether they be natives or strangers.

30 "Anima vero quae per superbiam aliquid commiserit, sive civis sit ille sive peregrinus, quoniam adversum Dominum rebellis fuit peribit de populo suo, 31 verbum enim Domini contempsit et praeceptum illius fecit irritum. Idcirco delebitur et portabit iniquitatem suam.'"

32 Factum est autem cum essent filii Israhel in solitudine et invenissent hominem colligentem ligna in die sabbati 33 obtulerunt eum Mosi et Aaron et universae multitudini. 34 Qui recluserunt eum in carcerem nescientes quid super eo facere deberent.

35 Dixitque Dominus ad Mosen, "Morte moriatur homo iste; obruat eum lapidibus omnis turba extra castra."

36 Cumque eduxissent eum foras, obruerunt lapidibus, et mortuus est sicut praeceperat Dominus.

37 Dixit quoque Dominus ad Mosen, 38 "Loquere filiis Israhel, et dices ad eos ut faciant sibi fimbrias per angulos palliorum, ponentes in eis vittas hyacinthinas, 39 quas cum viderint, recordentur omnium mandatorum Domini nec sequantur cogitationes suas et oculos per res varias fornicantes 40 sed magis, memores praeceptorum Domini, faciant ea sintque sancti Deo suo. 41 Ego Dominus, Deus vester, qui eduxi vos de terra Aegypti ut essem vester Deus."

30 "'But the soul that committeth any thing through pride, whether he be born in the land or a stranger, because he hath been rebellious against the Lord shall be cut off from among his people, 31 for he hath contemned the word of the Lord and made void his precept. Therefore shall he be destroyed and shall bear his iniquity.'"

32 And it came to pass when the children of Israel were in the wilderness and had found a man gathering sticks on the sabbath day 33 that they brought him to Moses and Aaron and the whole multitude. 34 And they put him into prison, not knowing what they should do with him.

35 And the Lord said to Moses, "Let that man die; let all the multitude stone him without the camp."

36 And when they had brought him out, they stoned him, and he died as the Lord had commanded.

37 The Lord also said to Moses, 38 "Speak to the children of Israel, and thou shalt tell them to make to themselves fringes in the corners of their garments, putting in them ribands of blue, 39 that when they shall see them, they may remember all the commandments of the Lord and not follow their own thoughts and eyes going astray after divers things 40 but rather, being mindful of the precepts of the Lord, may do them and be holy to their God. 41 I am the Lord, your God, who brought you out of the land of Egypt that I might be your God."

Caput 16

Ecce autem: Core, filius Isaar, filii Caath, filii Levi, et Dathan atque Abiram, filii Heliab, Hon quoque, filius Pheleth, de filiis Ruben, 2 surrexerunt contra Mosen, aliique filiorum Israhel ducenti quinquaginta, viri proceres synagogae et qui tempore concilii per nomina vocabantur. 3 Cumque stetissent adversum Mosen et Aaron, dixerunt, "Sufficiat vobis quia omnis multitudo sanctorum est et in ipsis est Dominus. Cur elevamini super populum Domini?"

4 Quod cum audisset Moses, cecidit pronus in faciem, 5 locutusque ad Core et ad omnem multitudinem, "Mane," inquit, "notum faciet Dominus qui ad se pertineant, et sanctos adplicabit sibi, et quos elegerit, adpropinquabunt ei. 6 Hoc igitur facite: tollat unusquisque turibula sua, tu, Core, et omne concilium tuum. 7 Et hausto cras igne, ponite desuper thymiama coram Domino, et quemcumque elegerit, ipse erit sanctus. Multum erigimini, filii Levi."

8 Dixitque rursum ad Core, "Audite, filii Levi. 9 Num parum vobis est quod separavit vos Deus Israhel ab omni populo et iunxit sibi ut serviretis ei in cultu tabernaculi et sta-

Chapter 16

The schism of Korah and his adherents. Their punishment.

And behold: Korah, the son of Izhar, the son of Kohath, the son of Levi, and Dathan and Abiram, the sons of Eliab, and On, the son of Peleth, of the children of Reuben, 2 rose up against Moses, and with them two hundred and fifty others of the children of Israel, leading men of the synagogue and who in the time of assembly were called by name. 3 And when they had stood up against Moses and Aaron, they said, "Let it be enough for you that all the multitude consisteth of holy ones and the Lord is among them. Why lift you up yourselves above the people of the Lord?"

4 When Moses heard this, he fell flat on his face, 5 and, speaking to Korah and all the multitude, he said, "In the morning, the Lord will make known who belong to him, and the holy he will join to himself, and whom he shall choose, they shall approach to him. 6 Do this therefore: take, every man *of you, your* censers, thou, Korah, and all thy company. 7 And putting fire in them tomorrow, put incense upon it before the Lord, and whomsoever he shall choose, the same shall be holy. You take too much upon you, ye sons of Levi."

8 And he said again to Korah, "Hear ye, sons of Levi. 9 Is it a small thing unto you that the God of Israel hath separated you from all the people and joined you to himself that you should serve him in the service of the tabernacle and should

retis coram frequentia populi et ministraretis ei? 10 Idcirco ad se fecit accedere te et omnes fratres tuos, filios Levi, ut vobis etiam sacerdotium vindicetis 11 et omnis globus tuus stet contra Dominum? Quid est enim Aaron ut murmuretis contra eum?"

12 Misit ergo Moses ut vocaret Dathan et Abiram, filios Heliab. Qui responderunt, "Non venimus. 13 Numquid parum est tibi quod eduxisti nos de terra quae lacte et melle manabat ut occideres in deserto, nisi et dominatus fueris nostri? 14 Re vera induxisti nos in terram quae fluit rivis lactis et mellis et dedisti nobis possessiones agrorum et vinearum; an et oculos nostros vis eruere? Non venimus."

15 Iratusque Moses valde ait ad Dominum, "Ne respicias sacrificia eorum. Tu scis quod ne asellum quidem umquam acceperim ab eis nec adflixerim quempiam eorum."

16 Dixitque ad Core, "Tu et omnis congregatio tua, state seorsum coram Domino et Aaron die crastino separatim. 17 Tollite singuli turibula vestra, et ponite super ea incensum, offerentes Domino ducenta quinquaginta turibula; Aaron quoque teneat turibulum suum."

18 Quod cum fecissent, stantibus Mose et Aaron, 19 et coacervassent adversum eos omnem multitudinem ad ostium tabernaculi, apparuit cunctis gloria Domini. 20 Locutusque Dominus ad Mosen et Aaron, ait, 21 "Separamini de medio congregationis huius ut eos repente disperdam."

22 Qui ceciderunt proni in faciem atque dixerunt, "Fortis-

stand before the congregation of the people and should minister to him? 10 Did he therefore make thee and all thy brethren, the sons of Levi, to approach unto him that you should challenge to yourselves the priesthood also 11 and that all thy company should stand against the Lord? For what is Aaron that you murmur against him?"

12 Then Moses sent to call Dathan and Abiram, the sons of Eliab. But they answered, "We *will not come.* 13 Is it a small matter to thee that thou hast brought us out of a land that flowed with milk and honey to kill us in the desert, except thou rule also like a lord over us? 14 Thou hast brought us indeed into a land that floweth with rivers of milk and honey and hast given us possessions of fields and vineyards; wilt thou also pull out our eyes? We *will not come."*

15 Moses therefore being very angry said to the Lord, "Respect not their sacrifices. Thou knowest that I have not taken of them so much as a young ass at any time nor have injured any of them."

16 And he said to Korah, "Do thou and thy congregation stand apart before the Lord tomorrow, and Aaron apart. 17 Take, every one *of you,* censers, and put incense upon them, offering to the Lord two hundred and fifty censers; let Aaron also hold his censer."

18 When they had done this, Moses and Aaron standing, 19 and had drawn up all the multitude against them to the door of the tabernacle, the glory of the Lord appeared to them all. 20 And the Lord, speaking to Moses and Aaron, said, 21 "Separate yourselves from among this congregation that I may presently destroy them."

22 They fell flat on their face and said, "O most mighty,

sime, Deus spirituum universae carnis, num uno peccante contra omnes tua ira desaeviet?"

23 Et ait Dominus ad Mosen, 24 "Praecipe universo populo ut separetur a tabernaculis Core et Dathan et Abiram."

25 Surrexitque Moses et abiit ad Dathan et Abiram, et, sequentibus eum senioribus Israhel, 26 dixit ad turbam, "Recedite a tabernaculis hominum impiorum, et nolite tangere quae ad eos pertinent ne involvamini in peccatis eorum."

27 Cumque recessissent a tentoriis eorum per circuitum, Dathan et Abiram egressi stabant in introitu papilionum suorum cum uxoribus et liberis omnique frequentia. 28 Et ait Moses, "In hoc scietis quod Dominus miserit me ut facerem universa quae cernitis et non ex proprio ea corde protulerim: 29 si consueta hominum morte interierint et visitaverit eos plaga qua et ceteri visitari solent, non misit me Dominus. 30 Sin autem novam rem fecerit Dominus ut aperiens terra os suum degluttiat eos et omnia quae ad illos pertinent descenderintque viventes in infernum, scietis quod blasphemaverint Dominum."

31 Confestim igitur ut cessavit loqui, disrupta est terra sub pedibus eorum 32 et aperiens os suum devoravit illos cum tabernaculis suis et universa substantia eorum. 33 Descenderuntque vivi in infernum, operti humo, et perierunt de medio multitudinis.

34 At vero omnis Israhel qui stabat per gyrum fugit ad clamorem pereuntium, dicens, "Ne forte et nos terra degluttiat!"

the God of the spirits of all flesh, for one man's sin shall thy wrath rage against all?"

23 And the Lord said to Moses, 24 "Command the whole people to separate themselves from the tents of Korah and Dathan and Abiram."

25 And Moses arose and went to Dathan and Abiram, and, the ancients of Israel following him, 26 he said to the multitude, "Depart from the tents of these wicked men, and touch nothing of theirs lest you be involved in their sins."

27 And when they were departed from their tents round about, Dathan and Abiram coming out stood in the entry of their pavilions with their wives and children and all the people. 28 And Moses said, "By this you shall know that the Lord hath sent me to do all things that you see and that I have not forged them of my own *head:* 29 if these men die the common death of men and if *they be visited with a plague* wherewith others also are wont to be visited, the Lord did not send me. 30 But if the Lord do a new thing and the earth opening her mouth swallow them down and all things that belong to them and they go down alive into hell, you shall know that they have blasphemed the Lord."

31 And immediately as he had made an end of speaking, the earth broke asunder under their feet 32 and opening her mouth devoured them with their tents and all their substance. 33 And they went down alive into hell, the ground closing upon them, and they perished from among the people.

34 But all Israel that was standing round about fled at the cry of them that were perishing, saying, "Lest perhaps the earth swallow us up also!"

35 Sed et ignis egressus a Domino interfecit ducentos quinquaginta viros qui offerebant incensum.

36 Locutusque est Dominus ad Mosen, dicens, 37 "Praecipe Eleazaro, filio Aaron, sacerdotis, ut tollat turibula quae iacent in incendio et ignem huc illucque dispergat, quoniam sanctificata sunt 38 in mortibus peccatorum, producatque ea in lamminas et adfigat altari, eo quod oblatum sit in eis incensum Domino et sanctificata sint, ut cernant ea pro signo et monumento filii Israhel."

39 Tulit ergo Eleazar, sacerdos, turibula aenea in quibus obtulerant hii quos incendium devoravit et produxit ea in lamminas, adfigens altari 40 ut haberent postea filii Israhel quibus commonerentur, ne quis accedat alienigena et qui non est de semine Aaron ad offerendum incensum Domino ne patiatur sicut passus est Core et omnis congregatio eius, loquente Domino ad Mosen.

41 Murmuravit autem omnis multitudo filiorum Israhel sequenti die contra Mosen et Aaron, dicens, "Vos interfecistis populum Domini." 42 Cumque oreretur seditio et tumultus incresceret, 43 Moses et Aaron fugerunt ad Tabernaculum Foederis.

Quod postquam ingressi sunt, operuit nubes et apparuit gloria Domini. 44 Dixitque Dominus ad Mosen, 45 "Recedite de medio huius multitudinis; etiam nunc delebo eos."

Cumque iacerent in terra, 46 dixit Moses ad Aaron, "Tolle turibulum, et hausto igne de altari mitte incensum desuper,

³⁵ And a fire coming out from the Lord destroyed the two hundred and fifty men that offered the incense.

³⁶ And the Lord spoke to Moses, saying, ³⁷ "Command Eleazar, the son of Aaron, the priest, to take up the censers that lie in the burning and to scatter the fire of one side and the other, because they are sanctified ³⁸ in the deaths of the sinners, and let him beat them into plates and fasten them to the altar, because incense hath been offered in them to the Lord and they are sanctified, that the children of Israel may see them for a sign and a memorial."

³⁹ Then Eleazar, the priest, took the brazen censers wherein they had offered whom the burning fire had devoured and beat them into plates, fastening them to the altar ⁴⁰ that the children of Israel might have for the time to come wherewith they should be admonished, that no stranger or any one that is not of the seed of Aaron should come near to offer incense to the Lord lest he should suffer as Korah suffered and all his congregation, according as the Lord spoke to Moses.

⁴¹ The following day, all the multitude of the children of Israel murmured against Moses and Aaron, saying, "You have killed the people of the Lord." ⁴² And when there arose a sedition and the tumult increased, ⁴³ Moses and Aaron fled to the Tabernacle of the Covenant.

And when they were gone into it, the cloud covered it and the glory of the Lord appeared. ⁴⁴ And the Lord said to Moses, ⁴⁵ "Get you out from the midst of this multitude; this moment will I destroy them."

And as they were lying on the ground, ⁴⁶ Moses said to Aaron, "Take the censer, and putting fire in it from the altar put incense upon it, and go quickly to the people to pray for

pergens cito ad populum ut roges pro eis, iam enim egressa est ira a Domino et plaga desaevit."

47 Quod cum fecisset Aaron et cucurrisset ad mediam multitudinem quam iam vastabat incendium, obtulit thymiama. 48 Et, stans inter mortuos ac viventes, pro populo deprecatus est, et plaga cessavit. 49 Fuerunt autem qui percussi sunt quattuordecim milia hominum et septingenti, absque his qui perierant in seditione Core. 50 Reversusque est Aaron ad Mosen ad ostium Tabernaculi Foederis postquam quievit interitus.

Caput 17

Et locutus est Dominus ad Mosen, dicens, 2 "Loquere ad filios Israhel, et accipe ab eis virgas singulas per cognationes suas a cunctis principibus tribuum, virgas duodecim, et uniuscuiusque nomen superscribes virgae suae. 3 Nomen autem Aaron erit in tribu Levi, et una virga cunctas eorum familias continebit. 4 Ponesque eas in Tabernaculo Foederis coram testimonio, ubi loquar ad te. 5 Quem ex his elegero,

them, for already wrath is gone out from the Lord and the plague rageth."

47 When Aaron had done this and had run to the midst of the multitude which the burning fire was now destroying, he offered the incense. 48 And, standing between the dead and the living, he prayed for the people, and the plague ceased. 49 And the number of them that were slain was fourteen thousand and seven hundred men, besides them that had perished in the sedition of Korah. 50 And Aaron returned to Moses to the door of the Tabernacle of the Covenant after the destruction was over.

Chapter 17

The priesthood is confirmed to Aaron by the miracle of the blooming of his rod, which is kept for a monument in the tabernacle.

And the Lord spoke to Moses, saying, 2 "Speak to the children of Israel, and take of every one of them a rod by their kindreds of all the princes of the tribes, twelve rods, and write the name of every man upon his rod. 3 And the name of Aaron shall be for the tribe of Levi, and one rod shall contain all their families. 4 And thou shalt lay them up in the Tabernacle of the Covenant before the testimony, where I will speak to thee. 5 Whomsoever of these I shall

germinabit virga eius, et cohibebo a me querimonias filiorum Israhel quibus contra vos murmurant."

6 Locutusque est Moses ad filios Israhel, et dederunt ei omnes principes virgas, per singulas tribus, fueruntque virgae duodecim absque virga Aaron. 7 Quas cum posuisset Moses coram Domino in Tabernaculo Testimonii, 8 sequenti die regressus invenit germinasse virgam Aaron in domo Levi et turgentibus gemmis eruperant flores, qui, foliis dilatatis, in amigdalas deformati sunt. 9 Protulit ergo Moses omnes virgas de conspectu Domini ad cunctos filios Israhel, videruntque, et receperunt singuli virgas suas.

10 Dixitque Dominus ad Mosen, "Refer virgam Aaron in Tabernaculum Testimonii ut servetur ibi in signum rebellium filiorum Israhel et quiescant querellae eorum a me ne moriantur." 11 Fecitque Moses sicut praeceperat Dominus.

12 Dixerunt autem filii Israhel ad Mosen, "Ecce: consumpti sumus; omnes perivimus. 13 Quicumque accedit ad tabernaculum Domini moritur. Num usque ad internicionem cuncti delendi sumus?"

choose, his rod shall blossom, and I will make to cease from me the murmurings of the children of Israel wherewith they murmur against you."

6 And Moses spoke to the children of Israel, and all the princes gave him rods, one for every tribe, and there were twelve rods besides the rod of Aaron. 7 And when Moses had laid them up before the Lord in the Tabernacle of the Testimony, 8 he returned on the following day and found that the rod of Aaron for the house of Levi was budded and that, the buds swelling, *it had bloomed blossoms* which, spreading the leaves, were formed into almonds. 9 Moses therefore brought out all the rods from before the Lord to all the children of Israel, and they saw, and every one received their rods.

10 And the Lord said to Moses, "Carry back the rod of Aaron into the Tabernacle of the Testimony that it may be kept there for a token of the rebellious children of Israel and that their complaints may cease from me lest they die." 11 And Moses did as the Lord had commanded.

12 And the children of Israel said to Moses, "Behold: we are consumed; we all perish. 13 Whosoever approacheth to the tabernacle of the Lord, he dieth. Are we all to a man to be utterly destroyed?"

Caput 18

Dixitque Dominus ad Aaron, "Tu et filii tui et domus patris tui tecum portabitis iniquitatem sanctuarii, et tu et filii tui simul sustinebitis peccata sacerdotii vestri. 2 Sed et fratres tuos de tribu Levi et sceptro patris tui sume tecum, praestoque sint et ministrent tibi, tu autem et filii tui ministrabitis in Tabernaculo Testimonii. 3 Excubabuntque Levitae ad praecepta tua et ad cuncta opera tabernaculi, ita dumtaxat ut ad vasa sanctuarii et ad altare non accedant ne et illi moriantur et vos pereatis simul. 4 Sint autem tecum et excubent in custodiis tabernaculi et in omnibus caerimoniis eius. Alienigena non miscebitur vobis. 5 Excubate in custodia sanctuarii et in ministerio altaris ne oriatur indignatio super filios Israhel.

6 "Ego dedi vobis fratres vestros, Levitas, de medio filiorum Israhel et tradidi donum Domino ut serviant in ministeriis tabernaculi eius. 7 Tu autem et filii tui, custodite sacerdotium vestrum, et omnia quae ad cultum altaris pertinent et intra velum sunt per sacerdotes administrabuntur. Si quis externus accesserit, occidetur."

Chapter 18

The charge of the priests and of the Levites and their portion.

And the Lord said to Aaron, "Thou and thy sons and thy father's house with thee shall bear the iniquity of the sanctuary, and thou and thy sons with thee shall bear the sins of your priesthood. 2 And take with thee thy brethren also of the tribe of Levi and the sceptre of thy father, and let them be ready at hand and minister to thee, but thou and thy sons shall minister in the Tabernacle of the Testimony. 3 And the Levites shall watch *to do* thy commands and about all the works of the tabernacle, only they shall not come nigh the vessels of the sanctuary *nor* the altar lest both they die and you also perish with them. 4 But let them be with thee and watch in the charge of the tabernacle and in all the ceremonies thereof. A stranger shall not join himself with you. 5 Watch ye in the charge of the sanctuary and in the ministry of the altar lest indignation rise upon the children of Israel.

6 "I have given you your brethren, the Levites, from among the children of Israel and have delivered them for a gift to the Lord to serve in the ministries of *the* tabernacle. 7 But thou and thy sons, look ye to *the* priesthood, and all things that pertain to the service of the altar and that are within the veil shall be executed by the priests. If any stranger shall approach, he shall be slain."

8 Locutusque est Dominus ad Aaron, "Ecce: dedi tibi custodiam primitiarum mearum. Omnia quae sanctificantur a filiis Israhel, tibi tradidi et filiis tuis pro officio sacerdotali legitima sempiterna. 9 Haec ergo accipies de his quae sanctificantur et oblata sunt Domino: omnis oblatio et sacrificium et quicquid pro peccato atque delicto redditur mihi et cedit in sancta sanctorum tuum erit et filiorum tuorum. 10 In sanctuario comedes illud; mares tantum edent ex eo, quia consecratum est tibi.

11 "Primitias autem quas voverint et obtulerint filii Israhel tibi dedi et filiis tuis ac filiabus tuis iure perpetuo. Qui mundus est in domo tua vescetur eis. 12 Omnem medullam olei et vini ac frumenti, quicquid offerunt primitiarum Domino, tibi dedi. 13 Universa frugum initia quas gignit humus et Domino deportantur cedent in usus tuos. Qui mundus est in domo tua vescetur eis.

14 "Omne quod ex voto reddiderint filii Israhel tuum erit. 15 Quicquid primum erumpit e vulva cunctae carnis quam offerunt Domino, sive ex hominibus sive de pecoribus fuerit, tui iuris erit. Ita dumtaxat ut pro hominis primogenito pretium accipias, et omne animal quod inmundum est redimi facias. 16 Cuius redemptio erit post unum mensem siclis argenti quinque, pondere sanctuarii. Siclus viginti obolos habet.

17 "Primogenitum autem bovis et ovis et caprae non facies redimi, quia sanctificata sunt Domino. Sanguinem tantum eorum fundes super altare, et adipes adolebis in sua-

8 And the Lord said to Aaron, "Behold: I have given thee the charge of my firstfruits. All things that are sanctified by the children of Israel, I have delivered to thee and to thy sons for the priestly office *by* everlasting ordinances. 9 These therefore shalt thou take of the things that are sanctified and are offered to the Lord: every offering and sacrifice and whatsoever is rendered to me for sin and for trespass and becometh Holy of Holies shall be for thee and thy sons. 10 Thou shalt eat it in the sanctuary; the males only shall eat thereof, because it is a consecrated thing to thee.

11 "But the firstfruits which the children of Israel shall vow and offer I have given to thee and to thy sons and to thy daughters by a perpetual law. He that is clean in thy house shall eat them. 12 All the best of the oil and of the wine and of the corn, whatsoever firstfruits they offer to the Lord, I have given them to thee. 13 All the firstripe of the fruits that the ground bringeth forth and which are brought to the Lord shall be for thy use. He that is clean in thy house shall eat them.

14 "Every thing that the children of Israel shall give by vow shall be thine. 15 Whatsoever *is firstborn* of all flesh which they offer to the Lord, whether it be of men or of beasts, shall belong to thee. Only for the firstborn of man thou shalt take a price, and every beast that is unclean thou *shalt* cause to be redeemed. 16 And the redemption of it shall be after one month for five sicles of silver, by the weight of the sanctuary. A sicle hath twenty obols.

17 "But the firstling of a cow and of a sheep and of a goat thou shalt not cause to be redeemed, because they are sanctified to the Lord. Their blood only thou shalt pour upon the altar, and their fat thou shalt burn for a most sweet

vissimum odorem Domino. 18 Carnes vero in usum tuum cedent sicut pectusculum consecratum, et armus dexter tua erunt.

19 "Omnes primitias sanctuarii quas offerunt filii Israhel Domino tibi dedi et filiis ac filiabus tuis iure perpetuo. Pactum salis est sempiternum coram Domino, tibi ac filiis tuis."

20 Dixitque Dominus ad Aaron, "In terra eorum nihil possidebitis, nec habebitis partem inter eos. Ego pars et hereditas tua in medio filiorum Israhel. 21 Filiis autem Levi dedi omnes decimas Israhelis in possessionem pro ministerio quo serviunt mihi in Tabernaculo Foederis 22 ut non accedant ultra filii Israhel ad tabernaculum nec committant peccatum mortiferum, 23 solis filiis Levi mihi in tabernaculo servientibus et portantibus peccata populi. Legitimum sempiternum erit in generationibus vestris. Nihil aliud possidebunt 24 decimarum oblatione contenti quas in usus eorum et necessaria separavi."

25 Locutusque est Dominus ad Mosen, dicens, 26 "Praecipe Levitis, atque denuntia ad eos, 'Cum acceperitis a filiis Israhel decimas quas dedi vobis, primitias earum offerte Domino, id est, decimam partem decimae, 27 ut reputetur vobis in oblationem primitivorum tam de areis quam de torcularibus. 28 Et universis quorum accipitis, primitias offerte Domino, et date Aaron, sacerdoti. 29 Omnia quae offeretis ex decimis et in donaria Domini separabitis optima et electa erunt.'

30 "Dicesque ad eos, 'Si praeclara et meliora quaeque ob-

odour to the Lord. 18 But the flesh shall fall to thy use as the consecrated breast, and the right shoulder shall be thine.

19 "All the firstfruits of the sanctuary which the children of Israel offer to the Lord I have given to thee and to thy sons and daughters by a perpetual ordinance. It is a covenant of salt for ever before the Lord, to thee and to thy sons."

20 And the Lord said to Aaron, "You shall possess nothing in their land, neither shall you have a portion among them. I am thy portion and inheritance in the midst of the children of Israel. 21 And I have given to the sons of Levi all the tithes of Israel for a possession for the ministry wherewith they serve me in the Tabernacle of the Covenant 22 that the children of Israel may not approach any more to the tabernacle nor commit deadly sin, 23 but only the sons of Levi may serve me in the tabernacle and bear the sins of the people. It shall be an everlasting ordinance in your generations. They shall not possess any other thing 24 but be content with the oblation of tithes which I have separated for their uses and necessities."

25 And the Lord spoke to Moses, saying, 26 "Command the Levites, and declare unto them, 'When you shall receive of the children of Israel the tithes which I have given you, offer the firstfruits of them to the Lord, that is to say, the tenth part of the tenth, 27 that it may be reckoned to you as an oblation of firstfruits as well of the barnfloors as of the winepresses. 28 And of all the things of which you receive *tithes,* offer the firstfruits to the Lord, and give them to Aaron, the priest. 29 All the things that you shall offer of the tithes and shall separate for the gifts of the Lord shall be the best and choicest things.'

30 "And thou shalt say to them, 'If you offer all the goodly

tuleritis ex decimis, reputabitur vobis quasi de area et torculari dederitis primitias. 31 Et comedetis eas in omnibus locis vestris, tam vos quam familiae vestrae, quia pretium est pro ministerio quo servitis in Tabernaculo Testimonii. 32 Et non peccabitis super hoc egregia vobis et pinguia reservantes ne polluatis oblationes filiorum Israhel et moriamini.'"

Caput 19

Locutusque est Dominus ad Mosen et Aaron, dicens, 2 "Ista est religio victimae quam constituit Dominus. Praecipe filiis Israhel ut adducant ad te vaccam rufam aetatis integrae in qua nulla sit macula nec portaverit iugum. 3 Tradetisque eam Eleazaro, sacerdoti, qui eductam extra castra immolabit in conspectu omnium 4 et, tinguens digitum in sanguine eius, asperget contra fores tabernaculi septem vicibus 5 conburetque eam cunctis videntibus, tam pelle et carnibus eius quam sanguine et fimo flammae traditis.

6 "Lignum quoque cedrinum et hysopum coccumque bis

and the better things of the tithes, it shall be reckoned to you as if you had given the firstfruits of the barnfloor and the winepress. 31 And you shall eat them in all your places, both you and your families, because it is your reward for the ministry wherewith you serve in the Tabernacle of the Testimony. 32 And you shall not sin in this point by reserving the choicest and fat things to yourselves lest you profane the oblations of the children of Israel and die.'"

Chapter 19

The law of the sacrifice of the red cow and the water of expiation.

And the Lord spoke to Moses and Aaron, saying, 2 "This is the observance of the victim which the Lord hath ordained. Command the children of Israel that they bring unto thee a red cow of full age in which there is no blemish and which hath not carried the yoke. 3 And you shall deliver her to Eleazar, the priest, who shall bring her forth without the camp and shall immolate her in the sight of all 4 and, dipping his finger in her blood, shall sprinkle it over against the door of the tabernacle seven times 5 and shall burn her in the sight of all, delivering up to the fire her skin and her flesh and her blood and her dung.

6 "The priest shall also *take* cedar wood and hyssop and

tinctum sacerdos mittet in flammam quae vaccam vorat. 7 Et tunc demum, lotis vestibus et corpore suo, ingredietur in castra commaculatusque erit usque ad vesperam. 8 Sed et ille qui conbuserit eam lavabit vestimenta sua et corpus et inmundus erit usque ad vesperam.

9 "Colliget autem vir mundus cineres vaccae et effundet eos extra castra in loco purissimo ut sint multitudini filiorum Israhel in custodiam et in aquam aspersionis, quia pro peccato vacca conbusta est. 10 Cumque laverit qui vaccae portaverat cineres vestimenta sua, inmundus erit usque ad vesperum. Habebunt hoc filii Israhel et advenae qui habitant inter eos sanctum iure perpetuo.

11 "Qui tetigerit cadaver hominis et propter hoc septem diebus fuerit inmundus 12 aspergetur ex hac aqua die tertio et septimo et sic mundabitur. Si die tertio aspersus non fuerit, septimo non poterit emundari. 13 Omnis qui tetigerit humanae animae morticinum et aspersus hac commixtione non fuerit polluet tabernaculum Domini et peribit ex Israhel, quia aqua expiationis non est aspersus: inmundus erit, et manebit spurcitia eius super eum.

14 "Ista est lex hominis qui moritur in tabernaculo: omnes qui ingrediuntur tentorium illius et universa vasa quae ibi sunt polluta erunt septem diebus. 15 Vas quod non habuerit operculum nec ligaturam desuper inmundum erit.

scarlet twice dyed *and* cast it into the flame with which the cow is consumed. 7 And then, after washing his garments and body, he shall enter into the camp and shall be unclean until the evening. 8 He also that hath burned her shall wash his garments and his body and shall be unclean until the evening.

9 "And a man that is clean shall gather up the ashes of the cow and shall pour them forth without the camp in a most clean place that they may be reserved for the multitude of the children of Israel and for a water of aspersion, because the cow was burnt for sin. 10 And when he that carried the ashes of the cow hath washed his garments, he shall be unclean until the evening. The children of Israel and the strangers that dwell among them shall observe this for a holy thing by a perpetual ordinance.

11 "He that toucheth the corpse of a man and is therefore unclean seven days 12 shall be sprinkled with this water on the third day and on the seventh and so shall be cleansed. If he were not sprinkled on the third day, he cannot be cleansed on the seventh. 13 Every one that toucheth the corpse of a man and is not sprinkled with this mixture shall profane the tabernacle of the Lord and shall perish out of Israel, because he was not sprinkled with the water of expiation: he shall be unclean, and his uncleanness shall remain upon him.

14 "This is the law of a man that dieth in a *tent:* all that go into his tent and all the vessels that are there shall be unclean seven days. 15 The vessel that hath no cover nor binding over it shall be unclean.

16 "Si quis in agro tetigerit cadaver occisi hominis aut per se mortui sive os illius vel sepulchrum, inmundus erit septem diebus. 17 Tollentque de cineribus conbustionis atque peccati et mittent aquas vivas super eos in vas. 18 In quibus cum homo mundus tinxerit hysopum asperget eo omne tentorium et cunctam supellectilem et homines huiuscemodi contagione pollutos. 19 Atque hoc modo mundus lustrabit inmundum tertio et septimo die. Expiatusque die septimo, lavabit et se et vestimenta sua et inmundus erit usque ad vesperam.

20 "Si quis hoc ritu non fuerit expiatus, peribit anima illius de medio ecclesiae quia sanctuarium Domini polluit et non est aqua lustrationis aspersus. 21 Erit hoc praeceptum legitimum sempiternum. Ipse quoque qui aspergit aquas lavabit vestimenta sua. Omnis qui tetigerit aquas expiationis inmundus erit usque ad vesperam. 22 Quicquid tetigerit inmundus, inmundum faciet, et anima quae horum quippiam tetigerit inmunda erit usque ad vesperum."

16 "If any man in the field touch the corpse of a man that was slain or that died of himself or his bone or his grave, he shall be unclean seven days. 17 And they shall take of the ashes of the burning and of the sin offering and shall pour living waters upon them into a vessel. 18 And a man that is clean shall dip hyssop in them and shall sprinkle therewith all the tent and all the furniture and the men that are defiled with touching any such thing. 19 And in this manner he that is clean shall purify the unclean on the third and on the seventh day. And, being expiated the seventh day, he shall wash both himself and his garments and be unclean until the evening.

20 "If any man be not expiated after this rite, his soul shall perish out of the midst of the church because he hath profaned the sanctuary of the Lord and was not sprinkled with the water of purification. 21 This precept shall be an ordinance for ever. He also that sprinkled the water shall wash his garments. Every one that shall touch the waters of expiation shall be unclean until the evening. 22 Whatsoever a person toucheth who is unclean, he shall make it unclean, and the person that toucheth any of these things shall be unclean until the evening."

Caput 20

Veneruntque filii Israhel et omnis multitudo in desertum Sin mense primo, et mansit populus in Cades. Mortuaque est ibi Maria et sepulta in eodem loco.

2 Cumque indigeret aqua populus coierunt adversum Mosen et Aaron, 3 et, versi in seditionem, dixerunt, "Utinam perissemus inter fratres nostros coram Domino! 4 Cur eduxistis ecclesiam Domini in solitudinem ut et nos et nostra iumenta moriantur? 5 Quare nos fecistis ascendere de Aegypto et adduxistis in locum istum pessimum qui seri non potest, qui nec ficum gignit nec vineas nec mala granata, insuper et aquam non habet ad bibendum?"

6 Ingressusque Moses et Aaron dimissa multitudine Tabernaculum Foederis corruerunt proni in terram clamaveruntque ad Dominum atque dixerunt, "Domine Deus, audi clamorem huius populi, et aperi eis thesaurum tuum, fontem aquae vivae, ut satiati cesset murmuratio eorum."

Et apparuit gloria Domini super eos, 7 locutusque est Dominus ad Mosen, dicens, 8 "Tolle virgam, et congrega populum, tu et Aaron, frater tuus, et loquimini ad petram coram

Chapter 20

The death of Miriam, the sister of Moses. The people murmur for want of water. God giveth it them from the rock. The death of Aaron.

And the children of Israel and all the multitude came into the desert of Zin in the first month, and the people abode in Kadesh. And Miriam died there and was buried in the same place.

2 And the people wanting water came together against Moses and Aaron, 3 and, making a sedition, they said, "Would God we had perished among our brethren before the Lord! 4 Why have you brought out the church of the Lord into the wilderness that both we and our cattle should die? 5 Why have you made us come up out of Egypt and have brought us into this wretched place which cannot be sowed nor bringeth forth figs nor vines nor pomegranates, neither *is there* any water to drink?"

6 And Moses and Aaron leaving the multitude went into the Tabernacle of the Covenant and fell flat upon the ground and cried to the Lord and said, "O Lord God, hear the cry of this people, and open to them thy treasure, a fountain of living water, that being satisfied *they may cease to murmur.*"

And the glory of the Lord appeared over them, 7 and the Lord spoke to Moses, saying, 8 "Take the rod, and assemble the people together, thou and Aaron, thy brother, and speak

eis, et illa dabit aquas. Cumque eduxeris aquam de petra, bibet omnis multitudo et iumenta eius."

9 Tulit igitur Moses virgam quae erat in conspectu Domini, sicut praeceperat ei, 10 congregata multitudine ante petram dixitque eis, "Audite, rebelles et increduli: num de petra hac vobis aquam poterimus eicere?" 11 Cumque elevasset Moses manum, percutiens virga bis silicem, egressae sunt aquae largissimae, ita ut populus biberet et iumenta, 12 dixitque Dominus ad Mosen et Aaron, "Quia non credidistis mihi ut sanctificaretis me coram filiis Israhel, non introducetis hos populos in terram quam dabo eis." 13 Haec est Aqua Contradictionis, ubi iurgati sunt filii Israhel contra Dominum, et sanctificatus est in eis.

14 Misit interea nuntios Moses de Cades ad regem Edom qui dicerent, "Haec mandat frater tuus Israhel, 'Nosti omnem laborem qui adprehendit nos, 15 quomodo descenderint patres nostri in Aegyptum et habitaverimus ibi multo tempore adflixerintque nos Aegyptii et patres nostros 16 et quomodo clamaverimus ad Dominum et exaudierit nos miseritque angelum qui eduxerit nos de Aegypto. Ecce: nunc in urbe Cades quae est in extremis finibus tuis positi, 17 obsecramus ut nobis transire liceat per terram tuam. Non ibimus per agros nec per vineas; non bibemus aquas de puteis tuis, sed gradiemur via publica, nec ad dextram nec ad sinistram declinantes donec transeamus terminos tuos."

18 Cui respondit Edom, "Non transibis per me. Alioquin armatus occurram tibi."

to the rock before them, and it shall yield waters. And when thou hast brought forth water out of the rock, all the multitude and their cattle shall drink."

9 Moses therefore took the rod which was before the Lord, as he had commanded him, 10 and, having gathered together the multitude before the rock, he said to them, "Hear, ye rebellious and incredulous: can we bring you forth water out of this rock?" 11 And when Moses had lifted up his hand, and struck the rock twice with the rod, there came forth water in great abundance, so that the people and their cattle drank, 12 and the Lord said to Moses and Aaron, "Because you have not believed me to sanctify me before the children of Israel, you shall not bring these people into the land which I will give them." 13 This is the Water of Contradiction, where the children of Israel *strove with words* against the Lord, and he was sanctified in them.

14 In the mean time, Moses sent messengers from Kadesh to the king of Edom to say, "Thus saith thy brother Israel, 'Thou knowest all the labour that hath come upon us, 15 in what manner our fathers went down into Egypt and there we dwelt a long time and the Egyptians afflicted us and our fathers 16 and how we cried to the Lord and he heard us and sent an angel who hath brought us out of Egypt. Lo: we are now in the city of Kadesh which is in the uttermost of thy borders, 17 and we beseech thee that we may have leave to pass through thy country. We will not go through the fields nor through the vineyards; we will not drink the waters of thy wells, but we will go by the common highway, neither turning aside to the right hand nor to the left till we are past thy borders."

18 And Edom answered them, "Thou shalt not pass by me. If thou dost, I will come out armed against thee."

19 Dixeruntque filii Israhel, "Per tritam gradiemur viam, et si biberimus aquas tuas nos et pecora nostra, dabimus quod iustum est. Nulla erit in pretio difficultas; tantum velociter transeamus."

20 At ille respondit, "Non transibis." Statimque egressus est obvius cum infinita multitudine et manu forti, 21 nec voluit adquiescere deprecanti ut concederet transitum per fines suos, quam ob rem devertit ab eo Israhel.

22 Cumque castra movissent de Cades, venerunt in Montem Or, qui est in finibus terrae Edom, 23 ubi locutus est Dominus ad Mosen: 24 "Pergat," inquit, "Aaron ad populos suos, non enim intrabit terram quam dedi filiis Israhel eo quod incredulus fuerit ori meo ad Aquas Contradictionis. 25 Tolle Aaron et filium eius cum eo, et duces eos in Montem Or, 26 cumque nudaveris patrem veste sua, indues ea Eleazarum, filium eius. Aaron colligetur et morietur ibi."

27 Fecit Moses ut praeceperat Dominus, et ascenderunt in Montem Or coram omni multitudine. 28 Cumque Aaron spoliasset vestibus suis, induit eis Eleazarum, filium eius. 29 Illo mortuo in montis supercilio, descendit cum Eleazaro. 30 Omnis autem multitudo videns occubuisse Aaron flevit super eo triginta diebus per cunctas familias suas.

19 And the children of Israel said, "We will go by the beaten way, and if we and our cattle drink of thy waters, we will give thee what is just. There shall be no difficulty in the price; only let us pass speedily."

20 But he answered, "Thou shalt not pass." And immediately he came forth to meet them with an infinite multitude and a strong hand, 21 neither would he condescend to their desire to grant them passage through his borders, wherefore Israel turned another way from him.

22 And when they had removed the camp from Kadesh, they came to Mount Hor, which is in the borders of the land of Edom, 23 where the Lord spoke to Moses: 24 "Let Aaron," saith he, "go to his people, for he shall not go into the land which I have given the children of Israel because he was incredulous to my words at the Waters of Contradiction. 25 Take Aaron and his son with him, and *bring* them up into Mount Hor, 26 and when thou hast stripped the father of his vesture, thou shalt vest therewith Eleazar, his son. Aaron shall be gathered *to his people* and die there."

27 Moses did as the Lord had commanded, and they went up into Mount Hor before all the multitude. 28 And when he had stripped Aaron of his vestments, he vested Eleazar, his son, with them. 29 And, Aaron being dead in the top of the mountain, he came down with Eleazar. 30 And all the multitude seeing that Aaron was dead mourned for him thirty days throughout all their families.

Caput 21

Quod cum audisset Chananeus, Rex Arad, qui habitabat ad meridiem, venisse, scilicet, Israhel per exploratorum viam, pugnavit contra illum et victor existens duxit ex eo praedam. 2 At Israhel voto se Domino obligans ait, "Si tradideris populum istum in manu mea, delebo urbes eius."

3 Exaudivitque Dominus preces Israhel et tradidit Chananeum, quem ille interfecit subversis urbibus eius, et vocavit nomen loci illius Horma, id est, Anathema.

4 Profecti sunt autem et de Monte Or per viam quae ducit ad Mare Rubrum ut circumirent terram Edom. Et taedere coepit populum itineris ac laboris, 5 locutusque contra Deum et Mosen, ait, "Cur eduxisti nos de Aegypto ut moreremur in solitudine? Deest panis; non sunt aquae. Anima nostra iam nausiat super cibo isto levissimo." 6 Quam ob rem misit Dominus in populum ignitos serpentes, ad quorum plagas et mortes plurimorum, 7 venerunt ad Mosen atque dixerunt, "Peccavimus quia locuti sumus contra Dominum et te. Ora ut tollat a nobis serpentes." Oravitque Moses pro populo.

Chapter 21

King Arad is overcome. The people murmur and are punished with fiery serpents. They are healed by the brazen serpent. They conquer the kings Sihon and Og.

And when King Arad, the Canaanite, who dwelt towards the south, had heard this, to wit, that Israel was come by the way of the spies, he fought against them and *overcoming them* carried off their spoils. 2 But Israel binding himself by vow to the Lord said, "If thou wilt deliver this people into my hand, I will utterly destroy their cities."

3 And the Lord heard the prayers of Israel and delivered up the Canaanite, *and they cut them off* and destroyed their cities, and they called the name of that place Hormah, that is to say, Anathema.

4 And they marched from Mount Hor by the way that leadeth to the Red Sea to compass the land of Edom. And the people began to be weary of their journey and labour, 5 and speaking against God and Moses, they said, "Why didst thou bring us out of Egypt to die in the wilderness? There is no bread, *nor have we any waters.* Our soul now *loatheth* this very light food." 6 Wherefore the Lord sent among the people fiery serpents *which bit them and killed many of them,* 7 *upon which* they came to Moses and said, "We have sinned because we have spoken against the Lord and thee. Pray that he may take away *these* serpents from us." And Moses prayed for the people.

8 Et locutus est Dominus ad eum, "Fac serpentem aeneum, et pone eum pro signo. Qui percussus aspexerit eum,
vivet."

9 Fecit ergo Moses serpentem aeneum et posuit eum pro
signo, quem cum percussi aspicerent, sanabantur.

10 Profectique filii Israhel castrametati sunt in Oboth;
11 unde egressi fixere tentoria in Hieabarim, in solitudine
quae respicit Moab contra orientalem plagam. 12 Et, inde
moventes, venerunt ad torrentem Zared, 13 quem relinquen-
tes castrametati sunt contra Arnon, quae est in deserto et
prominet in finibus Amorrei, siquidem Arnon terminus est
Moab, dividens Moabitas et Amorreos. 14 Unde dicitur in
Libro Bellorum Domini, "Sicut fecit in Mari Rubro, sic faciet in torrentibus Arnon. 15 Scopuli torrentium inclinati
sunt ut requiescerent in Ar et recumberent in finibus Moabitarum."

16 Ex eo loco, apparuit puteus super quo locutus est Dominus ad Mosen, "Congrega populum, et dabo ei aquam."

17 Tunc cecinit Israhel carmen istud: "Ascendat Puteus."
Concinebant: 18 "Puteus quem foderunt principes et para-
verunt duces multitudinis in datore legis et in baculis suis."

Profectique de solitudine in Matthana, 19 de Matthana in
Nahalihel, de Nahalihel in Bamoth 20 (de Bamoth vallis est
in regione Moab), in vertice Phasga, quod respicit contra
desertum.

21 Misit autem Israhel nuntios ad Seon, regem Amorreorum, dicens, 22 "Obsecro ut transire mihi liceat per terram

8 And the Lord said to him, "Make a brazen serpent, and set it up for a sign. Whosoever being struck shall look on it, shall live."

9 Moses therefore made a brazen serpent and set it up for a sign, which when they that were bitten looked upon, they were healed.

10 And the children of Israel setting forwards camped in Oboth, 11 and departing thence they pitched their tents in Iye-abarim, in the wilderness that faceth Moab toward the east. 12 And, removing from thence, they came to the torrent Zered, 13 which they left and encamped over against Arnon, which is in the desert and standeth out on the borders of the Amorite, for Arnon is the border of Moab, dividing the Moabites and the Amorites. 14 Wherefore it is said in the Book of the Wars of the Lord, "As he did in the Red Sea, so will he do in the streams of Arnon. 15 The rocks of the torrents were bowed down that they might rest in Ar and lie down in the borders of the Moabites."

16 *When they went* from that place, the well appeared whereof the Lord said to Moses, "Gather the people together, and I will give them water."

17 Then Israel sung this song, "Let the Well Spring Up." They sung thereto: 18 "The well which the princes dug and the chiefs of the people prepared by the direction of the lawgiver and with their staves."

And they marched from the wilderness to Mattanah, 19 from Mattanah unto Nahaliel, from Nahaliel unto Bamoth 20 (from Bamoth is a valley in the country of Moab), to the top of Pisgah, which looked towards the desert.

21 And Israel sent messengers to Sihon, king of the Amorites, saying, 22 "I beseech thee that I may have leave to pass

tuam. Non declinabimus in agros et vineas; non bibemus aquas ex puteis; via regia gradiemur donec transeamus terminos tuos."

23 Qui concedere noluit ut transiret Israhel per fines suos quin potius, exercitu congregato, egressus est obviam in desertum et venit in Iasa pugnavitque contra eum. 24 A quo percussus est in ore gladii, et possessa est terra eius ab Arnon usque Iebboc et filios Ammon, quia forti praesidio tenebantur termini Ammanitarum. 25 Tulit ergo Israhel omnes civitates eius et habitavit in urbibus Amorrei, in Esebon, scilicet, et viculis eius.

26 Urbs Esebon fuit Seon, regis Amorrei, qui pugnavit contra regem Moab et tulit omnem terram quae dicionis illius fuerat usque Arnon. 27 Idcirco dicitur in proverbio, "Venite in Esebon; aedificetur et construatur civitas Seon. 28 Ignis egressus est de Esebon, flamma de oppido Seon, et devoravit Ar Moabitarum et habitatores excelsorum Arnon.

29 "Vae tibi, Moab. Peristi, popule Chamos. Dedit filios eius in fugam et filias in captivitatem regi Amorreorum, Seon. 30 Iugum ipsorum disperiit ab Esebon usque Dibon; lassi pervenerunt in Nophe et usque Medaba."

31 Habitavit itaque Israhel in terra Amorrei, 32 misitque Moses qui explorarent Iazer, cuius ceperunt viculos et possederunt habitatores. 33 Verteruntque se et ascenderunt per viam Basan, et occurrit eis Og, rex Basan, cum omni populo suo pugnaturus in Edrai.

through thy land. We will not go aside into the fields or the vineyards; we will not drink waters of the wells; we will go the king's highway till we be past thy borders."

23 And he would not grant that Israel should pass by his borders but rather, gathering an army, went forth to meet them in the desert and came to Jahaz and fought against them. 24 And he was slain by them with the edge of the sword, and they possessed his land from the Arnon unto the Jabbok and to *the confines of* the children of Ammon, for the borders of the Ammonites were kept with a strong garrison. 25 So Israel took all his cities and dwelt in the cities of the Amorite, to wit, in Heshbon and in the villages thereof.

26 Heshbon was the city of Sihon, the king of the *Amorites,* who fought against the king of Moab and took all the land that had been of his dominion as far as the Arnon. 27 Therefore it is said in the proverb, "Come into Heshbon; let the city of Sihon be built and set up. 28 A fire is gone out of Heshbon, a flame from the city of Sihon, and hath consumed Ar of the Moabites and the inhabitants of the high places of the Arnon.

29 "Woe to thee, Moab. Thou art undone, O people of Chemosh. He hath given his sons to flight and his daughters into captivity to Sihon, the king of the Amorites. 30 Their yoke is perished from Heshbon unto Dibon; they came weary to Nophe and unto Medeba."

31 So Israel dwelt in the land of the Amorite, 32 and Moses sent some to take a view of Jazer, and they took the villages of it and conquered the inhabitants. 33 And they turned themselves and went up by the way of Bashan, and Og, the king of Bashan, came against them with all his people to fight in Edrei.

34 Dixitque Dominus ad Mosen, "Ne timeas eum, quia in manu tua tradidi illum et omnem populum ac terram eius, faciesque illi sicut fecisti Seon, regi Amorreorum, habitatori Esebon." 35 Percusserunt igitur et hunc cum filiis suis universumque populum eius, usque ad internicionem, et possederunt terram illius.

Caput 22

Profectique castrametati sunt in campestribus Moab ubi trans Iordanem Hierichus sita est. 2 Videns autem Balac, filius Sepphor, omnia quae fecerat Israhel Amorreo 3 et quod pertimuissent eum Moabitae et impetum eius ferre non possent, 4 dixit ad maiores natu Madian, "Ita delebit hic populus omnes qui in nostris finibus commorantur quomodo solet bos herbas usque ad radices carpere."

Ipse erat eo tempore rex in Moab. 5 Misit ergo nuntios ad Balaam, filium Beor, ariolum qui habitabat super flumen terrae filiorum Ammon, ut vocarent eum et dicerent, "Ecce! Egressus est populus ex Aegypto qui operuit superficiem terrae, sedens contra me. 6 Veni igitur, et maledic populo

34 And the Lord said to Moses, "Fear him not, for I have delivered him and all his people and his country into thy hand, and thou shalt do to him as thou didst to Sihon, the king of the Amorites, the inhabitant of Heshbon." 35 So they slew him also with his sons and all his people, *not letting any one escape,* and they possessed his land.

Chapter 22

Balak, king of Moab, sendeth twice for Balaam to curse Israel. In his way, Balaam is rebuked by an angel.

And they went forward and encamped in the plains of Moab over against where Jericho is situate beyond the Jordan. 2 And Balak, the son of Zippor, seeing all that Israel had done to the Amorite 3 and that the Moabites were in great fear of him and were not able to sustain his assault, 4 he said to the elders of Midian, "So will this people destroy all that dwell in our borders as the ox is wont to eat the grass to the very roots."

Now he was at that time king in Moab. 5 He sent therefore messengers to Balaam, the son of Beor, a soothsayer who dwelt by the river of the land of the children of Ammon, to call him and to say, "Behold! A people is come out of Egypt that hath covered the face of the earth, sitting over against me. 6 Come therefore, and curse this people, be-

huic, quia fortior me est, si quo modo possim percutere et eicere eum de terra mea, novi enim quod benedictus sit cui benedixeris et maledictus in quem maledicta congesseris."

7 Perrexeruntque seniores Moab et maiores natu Madian habentes divinationis pretium in manibus. Cumque venissent ad Balaam et narrassent ei omnia verba Balac, 8 ille respondit, "Manete hic hac nocte et respondebo quicquid mihi dixerit Dominus."

Manentibus illis apud Balaam, venit Deus et ait ad eum, 9 "Quid sibi volunt homines isti apud te?"

10 Respondit, "Balac, filius Sepphor, rex Moabitarum, misit ad me, 11 dicens, 'Ecce! Populus qui egressus est de Aegypto operuit superficiem terrae. Veni, et maledic ei, si quo modo possim pugnans abigere eum.'"

12 Dixitque Deus ad Balaam, "Noli ire cum eis, neque maledicas populo, quia benedictus est."

13 Qui mane consurgens dixit ad principes, "Ite in terram vestram quia prohibuit me Dominus venire vobiscum."

14 Reversi principes dixerunt ad Balac, "Noluit Balaam venire nobiscum."

15 Rursum ille multo plures et nobiliores quam ante miserat misit, 16 qui cum venissent ad Balaam dixerunt, "Sic dicit Balac, filius Sepphor: 'Ne cuncteris venire ad me; 17 paratus sum honorare te et quicquid volueris dabo tibi. Veni, et maledic populo isti.'"

18 Respondit Balaam, "Si dederit mihi Balac plenam domum suam argenti et auri, non potero inmutare verbum Domini, Dei mei, ut vel plus vel minus loquar. 19 Obsecro ut hic

cause it is mightier than I, if by any means I may beat them and drive them out of my land, for I know that he whom thou shalt bless is blessed and *he whom thou shalt curse is cursed.*"

7 And the ancients of Moab and the elders of Midian went with the price of divination in their hands. And where they were come to Balaam and had told him all the words of Balak, 8 he answered, "Tarry here this night and I will answer whatsoever the Lord shall say to me."

And while they stayed with Balaam, God came and said to him, 9 "What mean these men that are with thee?"

10 He answered, "Balak, the son of Zippor, king of the Moabites, hath sent to me, 11 saying, 'Behold! A people that is come out of Egypt hath covered the face of the land. Come, and curse them, if by any means I may fight with them and drive them away.'"

12 And God said to Balaam, "*Thou shalt not go* with them, nor *shalt thou curse* the people, because it is blessed."

13 And he rose in the morning and said to the princes, "Go into your country because the Lord hath forbid me to come with you."

14 The princes returning said to Balak, "Balaam would not come with us."

15 Then he sent many more and more noble than he had sent before, 16 who when they were come to Balaam said, "Thus saith Balak, the son of Zippor: 'Delay not to come to me, 17 *for* I am ready to honour thee and will give thee whatsoever thou wilt. Come, and curse this people.'"

18 Balaam answered, "If Balak would give me his house, full of silver and gold, I cannot alter the word of the Lord, my God, to speak either more or less. 19 I pray you to stay

maneatis etiam hac nocte et scire queam quid mihi rursum respondeat Dominus."

20 Venit ergo Deus ad Balaam nocte et ait ei, "Si vocare te venerunt homines isti, surge, et vade cum eis, ita dumtaxat ut quod tibi praecepero facias."

21 Surrexit Balaam mane et strata asina sua profectus est cum eis. 22 Et iratus est Deus. Stetitque angelus Domini in via contra Balaam, qui sedebat asinae et duos pueros habebat secum. 23 Cernens asina angelum stantem in via evaginato gladio, avertit se de itinere et ibat per agrum.

Quam cum verberaret Balaam et vellet ad semitam reducere, 24 stetit angelus in angustiis duarum maceriarum quibus vineae cingebantur. 25 Quem videns asina iunxit se parieti et adtrivit sedentis pedem.

At ille iterum verberabat eam, 26 et nihilominus angelus, ad locum angustum transiens ubi nec ad dextram nec ad sinistram poterat deviare, obvius stetit. 27 Cumque vidisset asina stantem angelum, concidit sub pedibus sedentis, qui iratus vehementius caedebat fuste latera eius.

28 Aperuitque Dominus os asinae, et locuta est, "Quid feci tibi? Cur percutis me, ecce, iam tertio?"

29 Respondit Balaam, "Quia commeruisti et inlusisti mihi. Utinam haberem gladium ut te percuterem!"

30 Dixit asina, "Nonne animal tuum sum cui semper sedere consuesti usque in praesentem diem? Dic quid simile umquam fecerim tibi."

At ille ait, "Numquam."

here this night also *that* I may know what the Lord will answer me once more."

²⁰ God therefore came to Balaam in the night and said to him, "If these men be come to call thee, arise, and go with them, yet so that thou do what I shall command thee."

²¹ Balaam arose in the morning and saddling his ass went with them. ²² And God was angry. And an angel of the Lord stood in the way against Balaam, who sat on the ass and had two servants with him. ²³ The ass, seeing the angel standing in the way with a drawn sword, turned herself out of the way and went into the field.

And when Balaam beat her and had a mind to bring her again to the way, ²⁴ the angel stood in a narrow place between two walls wherewith the vineyards were enclosed. ²⁵ And the ass seeing him thrust herself close to the wall and bruised the foot of the rider.

But he beat her again, ²⁶ and nevertheless the angel, going on to a narrow place where there was no way to turn aside either to the right hand or to the left, stood to meet him. ²⁷ And when the ass saw the angel standing, she fell under the feet of the rider, who being angry beat her sides more vehemently with a staff.

²⁸ And the Lord opened the mouth of the ass, and she said, "What have I done to thee? Why strikest thou me, lo, now this third time?"

²⁹ Balaam answered, "Because thou hast deserved it and hast *served* me *ill.* I would I had a sword that I might kill thee!"

³⁰ The ass said, "Am not I thy beast on which thou hast been always accustomed to ride until this present day? Tell me if I ever did the like thing to thee."

But he said, "Never."

31 Protinus, aperuit Dominus oculos Balaam, et vidit angelum stantem in via evaginato gladio, adoravitque eum pronus in terram.

32 Cui angelus, "Cur," inquit, "tertio verberas asinam tuam? Ego veni ut adversarer tibi quia perversa est via tua mihique contraria, 33 et nisi asina declinasset de via, dans locum resistenti, te occidissem, et illa viveret."

34 Dixit Balaam, "Peccavi, nesciens quod tu stares contra me. Et nunc, si displicet tibi ut vadam, revertar."

35 Ait angelus, "Vade cum istis, et cave ne aliud quam praecepero tibi loquaris." Ivit igitur cum principibus.

36 Quod cum audisset Balac, egressus est in occursum eius in oppido Moabitarum quod situm est in extremis finibus Arnon. 37 Dixitque ad Balaam, "Misi nuntios ut vocarent te; cur non statim venisti ad me? An quia mercedem adventui tuo reddere nequeo?"

38 Cui ille respondit, "Ecce: adsum. Numquid loqui potero aliud nisi quod Deus posuerit in ore meo?"

39 Perrexerunt ergo simul et venerunt in urbem quae in extremis regni eius finibus erat. 40 Cumque occidisset Balac boves et oves, misit ad Balaam et principes qui cum eo erant munera. 41 Mane autem facto, duxit eum ad excelsa Baal, et intuitus est extremam partem populi.

31 Forthwith, the Lord opened the eyes of Balaam, and he saw the angel standing in the way with a drawn sword, and he worshipped him falling flat on the ground.

32 And the angel said to him, "Why beatest thou thy ass *these three times?* I am come to withstand thee because thy way is perverse and contrary to me, 33 and unless the ass had turned out of the way, giving place to me who stood against thee, I had slain thee, and she should have lived."

34 Balaam said, "I have sinned, not knowing that thou didst stand against me. And now, if it displease thee that I go, I will return."

35 The angel said, "Go with these men, and see thou speak no other thing than what I shall command thee." He went therefore with the princes.

36 And when Balak heard it, he came forth to meet him in a town of the Moabites that is situate in the uttermost borders of Arnon. 37 And he said to Balaam, "I sent messengers to call thee; why didst thou not come immediately to me? Was it because I am not able to reward thy coming?"

38 He answered him, "Lo: here I am. Shall I have power to speak any other thing but that which God shall put in my mouth?"

39 So they went on together and came into a city that was in the uttermost borders of his kingdom. 40 And when Balak had killed oxen and sheep, he sent presents to Balaam and to the princes that were with him. 41 And when morning was come, he brought him to the high places of Baal, and he beheld the uttermost part of the people.

Caput 23

Dixitque Balaam ad Balac, "Aedifica mihi hic septem aras, et para totidem vitulos eiusdemque numeri arietes." 2 Cumque fecisset iuxta sermonem Balaam, inposuerunt simul vitulum et arietem super aram.

3 Dixitque Balaam ad Balac, "Sta paulisper iuxta holocaustum tuum donec vadam si forte occurrat mihi Dominus, et quodcumque imperaverit, loquar tibi."

4 Cumque abisset velociter, occurrit ei Deus. Locutusque ad eum Balaam, "Septem," inquit, "aras erexi et inposui vitulum et arietem desuper."

5 Dominus autem posuit verbum in ore eius et ait, "Revertere ad Balac, et sic loqueris."

6 Reversus invenit stantem Balac iuxta holocaustum suum et omnes principes Moabitarum, 7 adsumptaque parabola sua, dixit, "De Aram adduxit me Balac, rex Moabitarum, de montibus orientis. 'Veni,' inquit, 'et maledic Iacob. Propera, et detestare Israhel.'

8 "Quomodo maledicam cui non maledixit Deus? Qua ratione detester quem Dominus non detestatur?

9 "De summis silicibus videbo eum et de collibus considerabo illum. Populus solus habitabit et inter gentes non reputabitur.

Chapter 23

Balaam, instead of cursing Israel, is obliged to bless them and prophesy good things of them.

And Balaam said to Balak, "Build me here seven altars, and prepare as many calves and the same number of rams." ²And when he had done according to the word of Balaam, they laid together a calf and a ram upon *every* altar.

³And Balaam said to Balak, "Stand a while by thy burnt offering until I go to see if perhaps the Lord will meet me, and whatsoever he shall command, I will speak to thee."

⁴And when he was gone with speed, God met him. And Balaam speaking to him said, "I have erected seven altars and have laid on every one a calf and a ram."

⁵And the Lord put the word in his mouth and said, "Return to Balak, and thus shalt thou speak."

⁶Returning he found Balak standing by his burnt offering with all the princes of the Moabites, ⁷and taking up his parable, he said, "Balak, king of the Moabites, hath brought me from Aram, from the mountains of the east. 'Come,' said he, 'and curse Jacob. Make haste, and detest Israel.'

⁸"How shall I curse him whom God hath not cursed? By what means should I detest him whom the Lord detesteth not?

⁹"I shall see him from the tops of the rocks and shall consider him from the hills. This people shall dwell alone and shall not be reckoned among the nations.

10 "Quis dinumerare possit pulverem Iacob et nosse numerum stirpis Israhel? Moriatur anima mea morte iustorum et fiant novissima mea horum similia."

11 Dixitque Balac ad Balaam, "Quid est hoc quod agis? Ut malediceres inimicis meis vocavi te, et tu e contrario benedicis eis."

12 Cui ille respondit, "Num aliud possum loqui nisi quod iusserit Dominus?"

13 Dixit ergo Balac, "Veni mecum in alterum locum unde partem Israhelis videas et totum videre non possis. Inde maledicito ei."

14 Cumque duxisset eum in locum sublimem super verticem Montis Phasga, aedificavit Balaam septem aras, et, inpositis supra vitulo atque ariete, 15 dixit ad Balac, "Sta hic iuxta holocaustum tuum donec ego pergam obvius."

16 Cui cum Dominus occurrisset posuissetque verbum in ore eius, ait, "Revertere ad Balac, et haec loqueris ei."

17 Reversus invenit eum stantem iuxta holocaustum suum et principes Moabitarum cum eo. Ad quem Balac, "Quid," inquit, "locutus est Dominus?"

18 At ille adsumpta parabola sua ait, "Sta, Balac, et ausculta. Audi, fili Sepphor: 19 non est Deus quasi homo ut mentiatur, nec ut filius hominis ut mutetur. Dixit ergo, et non faciet? Locutus est, et non implebit?

20 "Ad benedicendum adductus sum; benedictionem prohibere non valeo.

21 "Non est idolum in Iacob, nec videtur simulacrum in Israhel. Dominus, Deus eius, cum eo est, et clangor victoriae regis in illo.

10 "Who can count the dust of Jacob and know the number of the stock of Israel? Let my soul die the death of the just and my last *end be* like to them."

11 And Balak said to Balaam, "What is this that thou dost? I *sent for* thee to curse my enemies, and thou contrariwise blessest them."

12 He answered him, "Can I speak any thing else but what the Lord commandeth?"

13 Balak therefore said, "Come with me to another place from whence thou mayest see part of Israel and canst not see them all. Curse them from thence."

14 And when he had brought him to a high place upon the top of Mount Pisgah, Balaam built seven altars, and, laying on every one a calf and a ram, 15 he said to Balak, "Stand here by thy burnt offering while I go to meet him."

16 And when the Lord had met him and had put the word in his mouth, he said, "Return to Balak, and thus shalt thou say to him."

17 Returning he found him standing by his burnt sacrifice and the princes of the Moabites with him. And Balak said to him, "What hath the Lord spoken?"

18 But he taking up his parable said, "Stand, O Balak, and give ear. Hear thou, son of Zippor: 19 God is not a man that he should lie, nor is the son of man that he should be changed. Hath he said then, and will he not do? Hath he spoken, and will he not fulfil?

20 "I was brought to bless; the blessing I am not able to hinder.

21 "There is no idol in Jacob, neither is there an image-god to be seen in Israel. The Lord, his God, is with him, and the sound of the victory of the king in him.

22 "Deus eduxit eum de Aegypto, cuius fortitudo similis est rinocerotis.

23 "Non est augurium in Iacob, nec divinatio in Israhel. Temporibus suis dicetur Iacob et Israheli quid operatus sit Deus.

24 "Ecce! Populus ut leaena consurget et quasi leo erigetur. Non accubabit donec devoret praedam et occisorum sanguinem bibat."

25 Dixitque Balac ad Balaam, "Nec maledicas ei nec benedicas."

26 Et ille, "Nonne," ait, "dixi tibi quod quicquid mihi Deus imperaret, hoc facerem?"

27 Et ait Balac ad eum, "Veni, et ducam te ad alium locum, si forte placeat Deo ut inde maledicas eis."

28 Cumque duxisset eum super verticem Montis Phogor, qui respicit solitudinem, 29 dixit ei Balaam, "Aedifica mihi hic septem aras, et para totidem vitulos eiusdemque numeri arietes." 30 Fecit Balac ut Balaam dixerat, inposuitque vitulos et arietes per singulas aras.

²² "God hath brought him out of Egypt, whose strength is like to the rhinoceros.

²³ "There is no soothsaying in Jacob, nor divination in Israel. In their times it shall be told to Jacob and to Israel what God hath wrought.

²⁴ "Behold! The people shall rise up as a lioness and shall lift itself up as a lion. It shall not lie down till it devour the prey and drink the blood of the slain."

²⁵ And Balak said to Balaam, "Neither curse nor bless him."

²⁶ And he said, "Did I not tell thee that whatsoever God should command me, that I would do?"

²⁷ And Balak said to him, "Come, and I will bring thee to another place, if peradventure it please God that thou mayest curse them from thence."

²⁸ And when he had brought him upon the top of Mount Peor, which looketh towards the wilderness, ²⁹ Balaam said to him, "Build me here seven altars, and prepare as many calves and the same number of rams." ³⁰ Balak did as Balaam had said, and he laid on every altar *a calf and a ram.*

Caput 24

Cumque vidisset Balaam quod placeret Domino ut benediceret Israheli, nequaquam abiit ut ante perrexerat ut augurium quaereret, sed dirigens contra desertum vultum suum 2 et elevans oculos, vidit Israhel in tentoriis commorantem per tribus suas, et, inruente in se spiritu Dei, 3 adsumpta parabola ait, "Dixit Balaam, filius Beor; dixit homo cuius obturatus est oculus; 4 dixit auditor sermonum Dei, qui visionem Omnipotentis intuitus est, qui cadit et sic aperiuntur oculi eius, 5 'Quam pulchra tabernacula tua, Iacob, et tentoria tua, Israhel!

6 "Ut valles nemorosae, ut horti iuxta fluvios inrigui, ut tabernacula quae fixit Dominus, quasi cedri propter aquas.

7 "Fluet aqua de situla eius, et semen illius erit in aquas multas, tolletur, propter Agag, rex eius, et auferetur regnum illius.

8 "Deus eduxit illum de Aegypto, cuius fortitudo similis est rinocerotis. Devorabunt gentes hostes illius ossaque eorum confringent et perforabunt sagittis.

9 "Accubans dormivit ut leo et quasi leaena quam susci-

Chapter 24

Balaam still continues to prophesy good things in favour of Israel.

And when Balaam saw that it pleased the Lord that he should bless Israel, he went not as he had gone before to seek divination, but setting his face towards the desert 2 and lifting up his eyes, he saw Israel abiding in their tents by their tribes, and, the spirit of God rushing upon him, 3 he took up his parable and said, "Balaam, the son of Beor hath said; the man hath said whose eye is stopped up; 4 the bearer of the words of God hath said, he that hath beheld the vision of the Almighty, he that falleth and so his eyes are opened, 5 'How beautiful are thy tabernacles, O Jacob, and thy tents, O Israel!

6 "As woody valleys, as watered gardens near the rivers, as tabernacles which the Lord hath pitched, as cedars by the waterside.

7 "'Water shall flow out of his bucket, and his seed shall be in many waters, for Agag, his king shall be removed, and his kingdom shall be taken away.

8 "'God hath brought him out of Egypt, whose strength is like to the rhinoceros. They shall devour the nations that are his enemies and break their bones and pierce them with arrows.

9 "'Lying down he hath slept as a lion and as a lioness whom none shall dare to rouse. He that blesseth thee shall

tare nullus audebit. Qui benedixerit tibi erit et ipse benedictus; qui maledixerit in maledictione reputabitur.'"

10 Iratusque Balac contra Balaam conplosis manibus ait, "Ad maledicendum inimicis meis vocavi te, quibus e contrario tertio benedixisti. 11 Revertere ad locum tuum. Decreveram quidem magnifice honorare te, sed Dominus privavit te honore disposito.'"

12 Respondit Balaam ad Balac, "Nonne nuntiis tuis quos misisti ad me dixi, 13 'Si dederit mihi Balac plenam domum suam argenti et auri, non potero praeterire sermonem Domini, Dei mei, ut vel boni quid vel mali proferam ex corde meo, sed quicquid Dominus dixerit, hoc loquar'? 14 Verumtamen, pergens ad populum meum, dabo consilium quid populus tuus huic populo faciet extremo tempore."

15 Sumpta igitur parabola, rursum ait, "Dixit Balaam, filius Beor; dixit homo cuius obturatus est oculus; 16 dixit auditor sermonum Dei, qui novit doctrinam Altissimi et visiones Omnipotentis videt, qui cadens apertos habet oculos, 17 'Videbo eum, sed non modo; intuebor illum, sed non prope. Orietur stella ex Iacob, et consurget virga de Israhel et percutiet duces Moab vastabitque omnes filios Seth. 18 Et erit Idumea possessio eius; hereditas Seir cedet inimicis suis, Israhel vero fortiter aget.

19 "'De Iacob erit qui dominetur et perdat reliquias civitatis.'"

20 Cumque vidisset Amalech, adsumens parabolam ait, "Principium gentium, Amalech, cuius extrema perdentur."

also himself be blessed; he that curseth thee shall be reckoned accursed.'"

10 And Balak being angry against Balaam clapped his hands together and said, "I called thee to curse my enemies, and thou on the contrary hast blessed them *three times*. 11 Return to thy place. I had determined indeed greatly to honour thee, but the Lord hath deprived thee of the honour designed for thee."

12 Balaam made answer to Balak, "Did I not say to thy messengers whom thou sentest to me, 13 'If Balak would give me his house full of silver and gold, I cannot go beyond the word of the Lord, my God, to utter any thing of my own *head* either good or evil, but whatsoever the Lord shall say, that I will speak'? 14 But yet, going to my people, I will give thee counsel what thy people shall do to this people in the latter days."

15 Therefore, taking up his parable, again he said, "Balaam, the son of Beor, hath said; the man whose eye is stopped up hath said; 16 the hearer of the words of God hath said, who knoweth the doctrine of the Highest and seeth the visions of the Almighty, who falling hath his eyes opened, 17 'I shall see him, but not now; I shall behold him, but not near. A star shall rise out of Jacob, and a sceptre shall spring up from Israel and shall strike the chiefs of Moab and shall waste all the children of Sheth. 18 And *he shall possess Edom;* the inheritance of Seir shall come to their enemies, but Israel shall do manfully.

19 "'Out of Jacob shall he come that shall rule and shall destroy the remains of the city.'"

20 And when he saw Amalek, he took up his parable and said, "Amalek, the beginning of nations, whose latter ends shall be destroyed."

21 Vidit quoque Cineum et adsumpta parabola ait, "Robustum est quidem habitaculum tuum, sed si in petra posueris nidum tuum 22 et fueris electus de stirpe Cain, quamdiu poteris permanere? Assur enim capiet te."

23 Adsumptaque parabola, iterum locutus est, "Heu, quis victurus est quando ista faciet Deus? 24 Venient in trieribus de Italia; superabunt Assyrios vastabuntque Hebraeos, et ad extremum etiam ipsi peribunt."

25 Surrexitque Balaam et reversus est in locum suum; Balac quoque via qua venerat rediit.

Caput 25

Morabatur autem eo tempore Israhel in Setthim, et fornicatus est populus cum filiabus Moab, 2 quae vocaverunt eos ad sacrificia sua. At illi comederunt et adoraverunt deos earum. 3 Initiatusque est Israhel Beelphegor, et iratus Dominus 4 ait ad Mosen, "Tolle cunctos principes populi, et suspende eos contra solem in patibulis ut avertatur furor meus ab Israhel."

21 He saw also the Kenite and took up his parable and said, "Thy habitation indeed is strong, but *though* thou build thy nest in a rock 22 and thou be chosen of the stock of Kain, how long shalt thou be able to continue? For Asshur shall take thee captive."

23 And, taking up his parable, again he said, "Alas, who shall live when God shall do these things? 24 They shall come in galleys from Italy; they shall overcome the Assyrians and shall waste the Hebrews, and at the last they themselves also shall perish."

25 And Balaam rose and returned to his place; Balak also returned the way that he came.

Chapter 25

The people fall into fornication and idolatry for which twenty-four thousand are slain. The zeal of Phinehas.

And Israel at that time abode in Shittim, and the people committed fornication with the daughters of Moab, 2 who called them to their sacrifices. And they ate of them and adored their gods. 3 And Israel was initiated to Baal of Peor, upon which the Lord being angry 4 said to Moses, "Take all the princes of the people, and hang them up on gibbets against the sun that my fury may be turned away from Israel."

5 Dixitque Moses ad iudices Israhel, "Occidat unusquisque proximos suos qui initiati sunt Beelphegor."

6 Et ecce: unus de filiis Israhel intravit coram fratribus suis ad scortum Madianitin vidente Mose et omni turba filiorum Israhel, qui flebant ante fores tabernaculi. 7 Quod cum vidisset Finees, filius Eleazari, filii Aaron, sacerdotis, surrexit de medio multitudinis et arrepto pugione 8 ingressus est post virum Israhelitem in lupanar et perfodit ambos simul, virum, scilicet, et mulierem, in locis genitalibus. Cessavitque plaga a filiis Israhel.

9 Et occisi sunt viginti quattuor milia homines.

10 Dixitque Dominus ad Mosen, 11 "Finees, filius Eleazari, filii Aaron, sacerdotis, avertit iram meam a filiis Israhel quia zelo meo commotus est contra eos ut non ipse delerem filios Israhel in zelo meo. 12 Idcirco loquere ad eum, 'Ecce: do ei pacem foederis mei, 13 et erit tam ipsi quam semini illius pactum sacerdotii sempiternum, quia zelatus est pro Deo suo et expiavit scelus filiorum Israhel.'"

14 Erat autem nomen viri Israhelitae qui occisus est cum Madianitide Zambri, filius Salu, dux de cognatione et tribu Symeonis. 15 Porro mulier Madianitis quae pariter interfecta est vocabatur Chozbi, filia Sur, principis nobilissimi Madianitarum.

16 Locutusque est Dominus ad Mosen, dicens, 17 "Hostes vos sentiant Madianitae, et percutite eos 18 quia et ipsi hostiliter egerunt contra vos et decepere insidiis per idolum

5 And Moses said to the judges of Israel, "Let every man kill his neighbours that have been initiated to Baal of Peor."

6 And behold: one of the children of Israel went in before his brethren to a harlot of Midian in the sight of Moses and of all the children of Israel, who were weeping before the door of the tabernacle. 7 And when Phinehas, the son of Eleazar, the son of Aaron, the priest, saw it, he rose up from the midst of the multitude and taking a dagger 8 went in after the Israelite into the brothel-house and thrust both of them through together, to wit, the man and the woman, in the genital parts. And the scourge ceased from the children of Israel.

9 And there were slain four and twenty thousand men.

10 And the Lord said to Moses, 11 "Phinehas, the son of Eleazar, the son of Aaron, the priest, hath turned away my wrath from the children of Israel because he was moved with my zeal against them that I myself might not destroy the children of Israel in my zeal. 12 Therefore say to him, 'Behold: I give him the peace of my covenant, 13 and the covenant of the priesthood for ever shall be both to him and his seed, because he hath been zealous for his God and hath made atonement for the wickedness of the children of Israel.'"

14 And the name of the Israelite that was slain with the woman of Midian was Zimri, the son of Salu, a prince of the kindred and tribe of Simeon. 15 And the Midianite woman that was slain with him was called Cozbi, the daughter of Zur, a most noble prince among the Midianites.

16 And the Lord spoke to Moses, saying, 17 "Let the Midianites find you their enemies, and slay you them 18 because they also have acted like enemies against you and have guile-

Phogor et Chozbi, filiam ducis Madian, sororem suam, quae percussa est in die plagae pro sacrilegio Phogor."

Caput 26

Postquam noxiorum sanguis effusus est, dixit Dominus ad Mosen et Eleazarum, filium Aaron, sacerdotem, 2 "Numerate omnem summam filiorum Israhel a viginti annis et supra per domos et cognationes suas, cunctos qui possunt ad bella procedere."

3 Locuti sunt itaque Moses et Eleazar, sacerdos, in campestribus Moab super Iordanem contra Hierichum, ad eos qui erant 4 a viginti annis et supra sicut Dominus imperarat, quorum iste est numerus:

5 Ruben, primogenitus Israhel, huius filius Enoch, a quo familia Enochitarum, et Phallu, a quo familia Phalluitarum, 6 et Esrom, a quo familia Esromitarum, et Charmi, a quo familia Charmitarum. 7 Hae sunt familiae de stirpe Ruben, quarum numerus inventus est quadraginta tria milia et septingenti triginta. 8 Filius Phallu Heliab. 9 Huius filii Namuhel et Dathan et Abiram. Isti sunt Dathan et Abiram, prin-

fully deceived you by the idol Peor and Cozbi, their sister, a daughter of a prince of Midian, who was slain in the day of the plague for the sacrilege of Peor."

Chapter 26

The people are again numbered by their tribes and families.

After the blood of the guilty was shed, the Lord said to Moses and to Eleazar, the son of Aaron, the priest, 2 "Number the whole sum of the children of Israel from twenty years old and upward by their houses and kindreds, all that are able to go forth to war."

3 Moses therefore and Eleazar, the priest, being in the plains of Moab upon the Jordan over against Jericho, spoke to them that were 4 from twenty years old and upward as the Lord had commanded, and this is the number of them:

5 Reuben, the firstborn of Israel, his *sons were* Hanoch, of whom is the family of the Hanochites, and Pallu, of whom is the family of the Palluites, 6 and Hezron, of whom is the family of the Hezronites, and Carmi, of whom is the family of the Carmites. 7 These are the families of the stock of Reuben, whose number was found to be forty-three thousand seven hundred and thirty. 8 The son of Pallu was Eliab. 9 His sons were Nemuel and Dathan and Abiram. These are Dathan and Abiram, the princes of the people that rose against

cipes populi qui surrexerunt contra Mosen et Aaron in seditione Core, quando adversum Dominum rebellaverunt, 10 et aperiens terra os suum devoravit Core, morientibus plurimis, quando conbusit ignis ducentos quinquaginta viros. Et factum est grande miraculum 11 ut Core pereunte filii illius non perirent.

12 Filii Symeon per cognationes suas: Namuhel, ab hoc familia Namuhelitarum; Iamin, ab hoc familia Iaminitarum; Iachin, ab hoc familia Iachinitarum; 13 Zare, ab hoc familia Zareitarum; Saul, ab hoc familia Saulitarum. 14 Hae sunt familiae de stirpe Symeon, quarum omnis numerus fuit viginti duo milia ducentorum.

15 Filii Gad per cognationes suas: Sephon, ab hoc familia Sephonitarum; Aggi, ab hoc familia Aggitarum; Suni, ab hoc familia Sunitarum; 16 Ozni, ab hoc familia Oznitarum; Heri, ab hoc familia Heritarum; 17 Arod, ab hoc familia Aroditarum; Arihel, ab hoc familia Arihelitarum. 18 Istae sunt familiae Gad, quarum omnis numerus fuit quadraginta milia quingentorum.

19 Filii Iuda: Her et Onan, qui ambo mortui sunt in terra Chanaan. 20 Fueruntque filii Iuda per cognationes suas Sela, a quo familia Selanitarum; Phares, a quo familia Pharesitarum; Zare, a quo familia Zareitarum. 21 Porro, filii Phares: Esrom, a quo familia Esromitarum, et Amul, a quo familia Amulitarum. 22 Istae sunt familiae Iuda, quarum omnis numerus fuit septuaginta milia quingentorum.

23 Filii Isachar, per cognationes suas: Thola, a quo familia

Moses and Aaron in the sedition of Korah, when they rebelled against the Lord, 10 and the earth opening her mouth swallowed up Korah, many others dying, when the fire burned two hundred and fifty men. And there was a great miracle wrought 11 that when Korah perished his sons did not perish.

12 The sons of Simeon by their kindreds: Nemuel, of him is the family of the Nemuelites; Jamin, of him is the family of the Jaminites; Jachin, of him is the family of the Jachinites; 13 Zerah, of him is the family of the Zerahites; Shaul, of him is the family of the Shaulites. 14 These are the families of the stock of Simeon, of which the whole number was twenty-two thousand two hundred.

15 The sons of Gad by their kindreds: Zephon, of him is the family of the Zephonites; Haggi, of him is the family of the Haggites; Shuni, of him is the family of the Shunites; 16 Ozni, of him is the family of the Oznites; Eri, of him is the family of the Erites; 17 Arod, of him is the family of the Arodites; Areli, of him is the family of the Arelites. 18 These are the families of Gad, of which the whole number was forty thousand five hundred.

19 The sons of Judah: Er and Onan, who both died in the land of Canaan. 20 And the sons of Judah by their kindreds were Shelah, of whom is the family of the Shelanites; Perez, of whom is the family of the Perezites; Zerah, of whom is the family of the Zerahites. 21 Moreover, the sons of Perez were Hezron, of whom is the family of the Hezronites, and Hamul, of whom is the family of the Hamulites. 22 These are the families of Judah, of which the whole number was seventy-six thousand five hundred.

23 The sons of Issachar, by their kindreds: Tola, of whom

Tholaitarum; Phua, a quo familia Phuaitarum; 24 Iasub, a quo familia Iasubitarum; Semran, a quo familia Semranitarum. 25 Hae sunt cognationes Isachar, quarum numerus fuit sexaginta quattuor milia trecentorum.

26 Filii Zabulon, per cognationes suas: Sared, a quo familia Sareditarum; Helon, a quo familia Helonitarum; Ialel, a quo familia Ialelitarum. 27 Hae sunt cognationes Zabulon, quarum numerus fuit sexaginta milia quingentorum.

28 Filii Ioseph, per cognationes suas: Manasse et Ephraim. 29 De Manasse ortus est Machir, a quo familia Machiritarum; Machir genuit Galaad, a quo familia Galaaditarum; 30 Galaad habuit filios: Hiezer, a quo familia Hiezeritarum, et Elec, a quo familia Elecarum, 31 et Asrihel, a quo familia Asrihelitarum, et Sechem, a quo familia Sechemitarum, 32 et Semida, a quo familia Semidatarum, et Epher, a quo familia Epheritarum. 33 Fuit autem Epher pater Salphaad, qui filios non habebat sed tantum filias, quarum ista sunt nomina: Maala et Noa et Egla et Melcha et Thersa. 34 Hae sunt familiae Manasse, et numerus earum quinquaginta duo milia septingentorum. 35 Filii autem Ephraim, per cognationes suas, fuerunt hii: Suthala, a quo familia Suthalitarum; Becher, a quo familia Becheritarum; Tehen, a quo familia Tehenitarum. 36 Porro filius Suthala fuit Heran, a quo familia Heranitarum. 37 Hae sunt cognationes filiorum Ephraim, quarum numerus fuit triginta duo milia quingentorum. 38 Isti sunt filii Ioseph, per familias suas.

is the family of the Tolaites; Puvah, of whom is the family of the Punites; 24 Jashub, of whom is the family of the Jashubites; Shimron, of whom is the family of the Shimronites. 25 These are the kindreds of Issachar, whose number was sixty-four thousand three hundred.

26 The sons of Zebulun, by their kindreds: Sered, of whom is the family of the Seredites; Elon, of whom is the family of the Elonites; Jahleel, of whom is the family of the Jahleelites. 27 These are the kindreds of Zebulun, whose number was sixty thousand five hundred.

28 The sons of Joseph, by their kindreds: Manasseh and Ephraim. 29 Of Manasseh was born Machir, of whom is the family of the Machirites; Machir begot Gilead, of whom is the family of the Gileadites; 30 Gilead had sons: Iezer, of whom is the family of the Iezerites, and Helek, of whom is the family of the Helekites, 31 and Asriel, of whom is the family of the Asrielites, and Shechem, of whom is the family of the Shechemites, 32 and Shemida, of whom is the family of the Shemidaites, and Hepher, of whom is the family of the Hepherites. 33 And Hepher was the father of Zelophehad, who had no sons but only daughters, whose names are these: Mahlah and Noah and Hoglah and Milcha and Tirza. 34 These are the families of Manasseh, and the number of them fifty-two thousand seven hundred. 35 And the sons of Ephraim, by their kindreds, were these: Shuthelah, of whom is the family of the Shuthelahites; Becher, of whom is the family of the Becherites; Tahan, of whom is the family of the Tahanites. 36 Now the son of Shuthelah was Eran, of whom is the family of the Eranites. 37 These are the kindreds of the sons of Ephraim, whose number was thirty-two thousand five hundred. 38 These are the sons of Joseph, by their families.

Filii Beniamin in cognationibus suis: Bale, a quo familia Baleitarum; Azbel, a quo familia Azbelitarum; Ahiram, a quo familia Ahiramitarum; 39 Supham, a quo familia Suphamitarum; Hupham, a quo familia Huphamitarum. 40 Filii Bale: Hered et Noeman. De Hered familia Hereditarum; de Noeman, familia Noemitarum. 41 Hii sunt filii Beniamin, per cognationes suas, quorum numerus fuit quadraginta quinque milia sescentorum.

42 Filii Dan, per cognationes suas: Suham, a quo familia Suhamitarum. Hae sunt cognationes Dan, per familias suas. 43 Omnes fuere Suhamitae, quorum numerus erat sexaginta quattuor milia quadringentorum.

44 Filii Aser, per cognationes suas: Iemna, a quo familia Iemnaitarum; Iessui, a quo familia Iessuitarum; Brie, a quo familia Brieitarum. 45 Filii Brie: Haber, a quo familia Haberitarum, et Melchihel, a quo familia Melchihelitarum. 46 Nomen autem filiae Aser fuit Sara. 47 Hae cognationes filiorum Aser, et numerus eorum quinquaginta tria milia quadringentorum.

48 Filii Nepthalim, per cognationes suas: Iessihel, a quo familia Iessihelitarum; Guni, a quo familia Gunitarum; 49 Iesser, a quo familia Iesseritarum; Sellem, a quo familia Sellemitarum. 50 Hae sunt cognationes filiorum Nepthalim, per familias suas, quorum numerus quadraginta quinque milia quadringentorum.

51 Ista est summa filiorum Israhel qui recensiti sunt: sescenta milia et mille septingenti triginta.

The sons of Benjamin in their kindreds: Bela, of whom is the family of the Belaites; Ashbel, of whom is the family of the Ashbelites; Ahiram, of whom is the family of the Ahiramites; 39 Shephupham, of whom is the family of the Shuphamites; Hupham, of whom is the family of the Huphamites. 40 The sons of Bela: Ard and Naaman. Of Ard is the family of the Ardites; of Naaman, the family of the Naamites. 41 These are the sons of Benjamin, by their kindreds, whose number was forty-five thousand six hundred.

42 The sons of Dan, by their kindreds: Shuham, of whom is the family of the Shuhamites. These are the kindreds of Dan, by their families. 43 All were Shuhamites, whose number was sixty-four thousand four hundred.

44 The sons of Asher, by their kindreds: Imnah, of whom is the family of the Imnites; Ishvi, of whom is the family of the Ishvites; Beriah, of whom is the family of the Beriites. 45 The sons of Beriah: Heber, of whom is the family of the Heberites, and Malchiel, of whom is the family of the Malchielites. 46 And the name of the daughter of Asher was Serah. 47 These are the kindreds of the sons of Asher, and their number fifty-three thousand four hundred.

48 The sons of Naphtali, by their kindreds: Jahzeel, of whom is the family of the Jahzeelites; Guni, of whom is the family of the Gunites; 49 Jezer, of whom is the family of the Jezerites; Shillem, of whom is the family of the Shillemites. 50 These are the kindreds of the sons of Naphtali, by their families, whose number was forty-five thousand four hundred.

51 This is the sum of the children of Israel that were reckoned up: six hundred and one thousand seven hundred and thirty.

52 Locutusque est Dominus ad Mosen, dicens, 53 "Istis dividetur terra iuxta numerum vocabulorum in possessiones suas. 54 Pluribus maiorem partem dabis, et paucioribus minorem. Singulis, sicut nunc recensiti sunt, tradetur possessio, 55 ita dumtaxat ut sors terram tribubus dividat et familiis. 56 Quicquid sorte contigerit, hoc vel plures accipiant vel pauciores."

57 Hic quoque est numerus filiorum Levi, per familias suas: Gerson, a quo familia Gersonitarum; Caath, a quo familia Caathitarum; Merari, a quo familia Meraritarum. 58 Hae sunt familiae Levi: familia Lobni, familia Hebroni, familia Mooli, familia Musi, familia Cori. At vero Caath genuit Amram, 59 qui habuit uxorem Iochabed, filiam Levi, quae nata est ei in Aegypto. Haec genuit viro suo, Amram, filios, Aaron et Mosen, et Mariam, sororem eorum. 60 De Aaron orti sunt Nadab et Abiu et Eleazar et Ithamar, 61 quorum Nadab et Abiu mortui sunt cum obtulissent ignem alienum coram Domino. 62 Fueruntque omnes qui numerati sunt viginti tria milia generis masculini ab uno mense et supra, quia non sunt recensiti inter filios Israhel, nec eis cum ceteris data possessio est.

63 Hic est numerus filiorum Israhel qui descripti sunt a Mosen et Eleazaro, sacerdote, in campestribus Moab supra Iordanem, contra Hiericho. 64 Inter quos nullus fuit eorum qui ante numerati sunt a Mose et Aaron in deserto Sinai, 65 praedixerat enim Dominus quod omnes morerentur in solitudine, nullusque remansit ex eis nisi Chaleb, filius Iepphonne, et Iosue, filius Nun.

52 And the Lord spoke to Moses, saying, 53 "To these shall the land be divided for their possessions according to the number of names. 54 To the greater number thou shalt give a greater portion, and to the fewer a less. To every one, as they have now been reckoned up, shall a possession be delivered, 55 yet so that *by lot the land be divided* to the tribes and families. 56 Whatsoever shall fall by lot, that *shall be taken by* the more or the fewer."

57 This also is the number of the sons of Levi, by their families: Gershon, of whom is the family of the Gershonites; Kohath, of whom is the family of the Kohathites; Merari, of whom is the family of the Merarites. 58 These are the families of Levi: the family of Libni, the family of Hebroni, the family of Mahli, the family of Mushi, the family of Korah. Now Kohath begot Amram, 59 who had to wife Jochebed, the daughter of Levi, who was born to him in Egypt. She bore to her husband, Amram, sons, Aaron and Moses, and Miriam, their sister. 60 Of Aaron were born Nadab and Abihu and Eleazar and Ithamar, 61 of whom Nadab and Abihu died when they had offered the strange fire before the Lord. 62 And all that were numbered were twenty-three thousand males from one month old and upward, for they were not reckoned up among the children of Israel, neither was a possession given to them with the rest.

63 This is the number of the children of Israel that were enrolled by Moses and Eleazar, the priest, in the plains of Moab upon the Jordan, over against Jericho. 64 Among whom there was not one of them that were numbered before by Moses and Aaron in the desert of Sinai, 65 for the Lord had foretold that they should die in the wilderness, and none remained of them but Caleb, the son of Jephunneh, and Joshua, the son of Nun.

Caput 27

Accesserunt autem filiae Salphaad, filii Epher, filii Galaad, filii Machir, filii Manasse, qui fuit filius Ioseph, quarum sunt nomina Maala et Noa et Egla et Melcha et Thersa. 2 Steteruntque coram Mosen et Eleazaro, sacerdote, et cunctis principibus populi ad ostium Tabernaculi Foederis atque dixerunt, 3 "Pater noster mortuus est in deserto nec fuit in seditione quae concitata est contra Dominum sub Core, sed in peccato suo mortuus est; hic non habuit mares filios. Cur tollitur nomen illius de familia sua quia non habet filium? Date nobis possessionem inter cognatos patris nostri."

4 Rettulitque Moses causam earum ad iudicium Domini. 5 Qui dixit ad eum, 6 "Iustam rem postulant filiae Salphaad. Da eis possessionem inter cognatos patris sui, et ei in hereditate succedant. 7 Ad filios autem Israhel loqueris haec: 8 'Homo cum mortuus fuerit absque filio, ad filiam eius transibit hereditas. 9 Si filiam non habuerit, habebit successores fratres suos, 10 quod si et fratres non fuerint, dabitis hereditatem fratribus patris eius, 11 sin autem nec patruos habue-

Chapter 27

The law of inheritance. Joshua is appointed to succeed
Moses.

Then came the daughters of Zelophehad, the son of Hepher, the son of Gilead, the son of Machir, the son of Manasseh, who was the son of Joseph, and their names are Mahlah and Noah and Hoglah and Milcha and Tirzah. 2 And they stood before Moses and Eleazar, the priest, and all the princes of the people at the door of the Tabernacle of the Covenant and said, 3 "Our father died in the desert and was not in the sedition that was raised against the Lord under Korah, but he died in his own sin, *and* he had no male children. Why is his name taken away out of his family because he had no son? Give us a possession among the kinsmen of our father."

4 And Moses referred their cause to the judgment of the Lord. 5 And the Lord said to him, 6 "The daughters of Zelophehad demand a just thing. Give them a possession among their father's kindred, and let them succeed him in his inheritance. 7 And to the children of Israel thou shalt speak these things: 8 'When a man dieth without a son, his inheritance shall pass to his daughter. 9 If he have no daughter, his brethren shall succeed him, 10 and if he have no brethren, you shall give the inheritance to his father's brethren, 11 but if he have no uncles by the father, the inheritance

rit, dabitur hereditas his qui ei proximi sunt. Eritque hoc filiis Israhel sanctum lege perpetua, sicut praecepit Dominus Mosi.'"

12 Dixit quoque Dominus ad Mosen, "Ascende in montem istum, Abarim, et contemplare inde terram quam daturus sum filiis Israhel. 13 Cumque videris eam, ibis et tu ad populum tuum, sicut ivit frater tuus Aaron, 14 quia offendistis me in deserto Sin in contradictione multitudinis, nec sanctificare me voluistis coram ea super aquas." Hae sunt Aquae Contradictionis in Cades deserti Sin.

15 Cui respondit Moses, 16 "Provideat Dominus, Deus spirituum omnis carnis, hominem qui sit super multitudinem hanc 17 et possit exire et intrare ante eos et educere illos vel introducere ne sit populus Domini sicut oves absque pastore."

18 Dixitque Dominus ad eum, "Tolle Iosue, filium Nun, virum in quo est spiritus, et pone manum tuam super eum. 19 Qui stabit coram Eleazaro, sacerdote, et omni multitudine, 20 et dabis ei praecepta cunctis videntibus et partem gloriae tuae ut audiat eum omnis synagoga filiorum Israhel. 21 Pro hoc si quid agendum erit Eleazar, sacerdos, consulet Dominum. Ad verbum eius egredietur et ingredietur ipse et omnes filii Israhel cum eo et cetera multitudo."

22 Fecit Moses ut praeceperat Dominus, cumque tulisset Iosue, statuit eum coram Eleazaro, sacerdote, et omni frequentia populi, 23 et, inpositis capiti eius manibus, cuncta replicavit quae mandaverat Dominus.

shall be given to them that are the next akin. And this shall be to the children of Israel sacred by a perpetual law, as the Lord hath commanded Moses.'"

12 The Lord also said to Moses, "Go up into this mountain, Abarim, and view from thence the land which I will give to the children of Israel. 13 And when thou shalt have seen it, thou also shalt go to thy people, as thy brother Aaron is gone, 14 because you offended me in the desert of Zin in the contradiction of the multitude, neither would you sanctify me before them at the waters." These are the Waters of Contradiction in Kadesh of the desert of Zin.

15 And Moses answered him, 16 "May the Lord, the God of the spirits of all flesh, provide a man that may be over this multitude 17 and may go out and in before them and may lead them out or bring them in lest the people of the Lord be as sheep without a shepherd."

18 And the Lord said to him, "Take Joshua, the son of Nun, a man in whom is the spirit, and put thy hand upon him. 19 And he shall stand before Eleazar, the priest, and all the multitude, 20 and thou shalt give him precepts in the sight of all and part of thy glory that all the congregation of the children of Israel may hear him. 21 If any thing be to be done, Eleazar, the priest, shall consult the Lord for him. He and all the children of Israel with him and the rest of the multitude shall go out and go in at his word."

22 Moses did as the Lord had commanded, and, when he had taken Joshua, he set him before Eleazar, the priest, and all the assembly of the people, 23 and, laying his hands on his head, he repeated all things that the Lord had commanded.

Caput 28

Dixit quoque Dominus ad Mosen, 2 "Praecipe filiis Israhel, et dices ad eos, "Oblationem meam et panes et incensum odoris suavissimi offerte per tempora sua. 3 Haec sunt sacrificia quae offerre debetis: agnos anniculos inmaculatos duos cotidie in holocaustum sempiternum—4 unum offeretis mane et alterum ad vesperam—5 decimam partem oephi similae, quae conspersa sit oleo purissimo et habeat quartam partem hin. 6 Holocaustum iuge est quod obtulistis in Monte Sinai in odorem suavissimum incensi Domini. 7 Et libabitis vini quartam partem hin per agnos singulos in sanctuario Domini. 8 Alterumque agnum similiter offeretis ad vesperam iuxta omnem ritum sacrificii matutini et libamentorum eius, oblationem suavissimi odoris Domino.

9 "Die autem sabbati, offeretis duos agnos anniculos inmaculatos et duas decimas similae oleo conspersae in sacrificio et liba, 10 quae rite funduntur per singula sabbata in holocausto sempiterno.

11 "'In kalendis autem offeretis holocaustum Domino: vitulos de armento duos, arietem unum, agnos anniculos septem inmaculatos, 12 et tres decimas similae oleo conspersae

Chapter 28

Sacrifices are appointed as well for every day as for sabbaths and other festivals.

The Lord also said to Moses, 2 "Command the children of Israel, and thou shalt say to them, 'Offer ye my oblation and *my bread* and burnt sacrifice of most sweet odour in their due seasons. 3 These are the sacrifices which you *shall* offer: two lambs of a year old without blemish every day for the perpetual holocaust—4 one you shall offer in the morning, and the other in the evening—5 and the tenth part of an ephi of flour, which shall be tempered with the purest oil, *of the measure of* the fourth part of a hin. 6 It is the continual holocaust which you offered in Mount Sinai for a most sweet odour of a sacrifice by fire to the Lord. 7 And for a libation you shall offer of wine the fourth part of a hin for every lamb in the sanctuary of the Lord. 8 And you shall offer the other lamb in like manner in the evening according to all the rites of the morning sacrifice and of the libations thereof, an oblation of most sweet odour to the Lord.

9 "And on the sabbath day, you shall offer two lambs of a year old without blemish and two tenths of flour tempered with oil in sacrifice and the libations, 10 which *regularly* are poured out every sabbath for the perpetual holocaust.

11 "And on the first day of the month you shall offer a holocaust to the Lord: two calves of the herd, one ram and seven lambs of a year old without blemish, 12 and three tenths of flour tempered with oil in sacrifice for every calf

823

in sacrificio per singulos vitulos et duas decimas similae oleo conspersae per singulos arietes 13 et decimam decimae similae consparsae oleo in sacrificio per agnos singulos. Holocaustum suavissimi odoris atque incensi est Domino. 14 Libamenta autem vini quae per singulas fundenda sunt victimas ista erunt: media pars hin per vitulos singulos, tertia per arietem, quarta per agnum. Hoc erit holocaustum per omnes menses qui sibi anno vertente succedunt.

15 "'Hircus quoque offeretur Domino pro peccatis in holocaustum sempiternum cum libamentis suis.

16 "'Mense autem primo, quartadecima die mensis, Phase Domini erit, 17 et quintadecima die sollemnitas. Septem diebus vescentur azymis. 18 Quarum dies prima venerabilis et sancta erit; omne opus servile non facietis in ea. 19 Offeretisque incensum, holocaustum, Domino: vitulos de armento duos, arietem unum, agnos anniculos inmaculatos septem, 20 et sacrificia singulorum ex simila quae conspersa sit oleo tres decimas per singulos vitulos et duas decimas per arietem 21 et decimam decimae per agnos singulos, id est, per septem agnos, 22 et hircum pro peccato unum ut expietur pro vobis, 23 praeter holocaustum matutinum quod semper offeretis. 24 Ita facietis per singulos dies septem dierum in fomitem ignis et in odorem suavissimum Domino, qui surget de holocausto et de libationibus singulorum. 25 Dies quoque septimus celeberrimus et sanctus erit vobis; omne opus servile non facietis in eo.

26 "'Dies etiam primitivorum, quando offeretis novas fru-

and two tenths of flour tempered with oil for every ram 13 and the tenth of a tenth of flour tempered with oil in sacrifice for every lamb. It is a holocaust of most sweet odour and an offering by fire to the Lord. 14 And these shall be the libations of wine that are to be poured out for every victim: half a hin for every calf, a third for a ram *and* a fourth for a lamb. This shall be the holocaust for every month as they succeed one another in the course of the year.

15 "A buck-goat also shall be offered to the Lord for a sin offering *over and above the* perpetual holocaust with its libations.

16 "And in the first month, on the fourteenth day of the month, shall be the Phase of the Lord, 17 and on the fifteenth day the solemn feast. Seven days shall they eat unleavened bread. 18 And the first day of them shall be venerable and holy; you shall not do any servile work therein. 19 And you shall offer a burnt sacrifice, a holocaust, to the Lord: two calves of the herd, one ram, seven lambs of a year old without blemish, 20 and for the sacrifice of every one three tenths of flour which shall be tempered with oil to every calf and two tenths to every ram 21 and the tenth of a tenth to every lamb, that is to say, to all the seven lambs, 22 and one buck-goat for sin to make atonement for you, 23 besides the morning holocaust which you shall always offer. 24 So shall you do every day of the seven days for the food of the fire and for a most sweet odour to the Lord, which shall rise from the holocaust and from the libations of each. 25 The seventh day also shall be most solemn and holy unto you; you shall do no servile work therein.

26 "The day also of firstfruits, when after the weeks are accomplished you shall offer new fruits to the Lord, shall be

ges Domino expletis ebdomadibus, venerabilis et sancta erit; omne opus servile non facietis in ea. 27 Offeretisque holocaustum in odorem suavissimum Domino: vitulos de armento duos, arietem unum et agnos anniculos inmaculatos septem, 28 atque in sacrificiis eorum similae oleo conspersae tres decimas per singulos vitulos, per arietes duas, 29 per agnos decimam decimae, qui simul sunt agni septem, hircum quoque, 30 qui mactatur pro expiatione praeter holocaustum sempiternum et liba eius. 31 Inmaculata offeretis omnia cum libationibus suis.'"

Caput 29

"'Mensis etiam septimi prima dies venerabilis et sancta erit vobis; omne opus servile non facietis in ea quia dies clangoris est et tubarum. 2 Offeretisque holocaustum in odorem suavissimum Domino: vitulum de armento unum, arietem unum et agnos anniculos inmaculatos septem, 3 et in sacrificiis eorum, similae oleo conspersae tres decimas per singulos vitulos, duas decimas per arietem, 4 unam decimam per agnum, qui simul sunt agni septem, 5 et hircum pro peccato, qui offertur in expiationem populi, 6 praeter holo-

venerable and holy; you shall do no servile work therein.
27 And you shall offer a holocaust for a most sweet odour to
the Lord: two calves of the herd, one ram and seven lambs of
a year old without blemish, 28 and in the sacrifices of them
three tenths of flour tempered with oil to every calf, two to
every ram, 29 the tenth of a tenth to every lamb, which in
all are seven lambs, a buck-goat also, 30 which is slain for
expiation besides the perpetual holocaust and the libations
thereof. 31 You shall offer them all without blemish with
their libations.'"

Chapter 29

Sacrifices for the festivals of the seventh month.

"The first day also of the seventh month shall be venerable and holy unto you; you shall do no servile work therein
because it is the day of the sounding and of trumpets. 2 And
you shall offer a holocaust for a most sweet odour to the
Lord: one calf of the herd, one ram and seven lambs of a year
old without blemish, 3 and for their sacrifices, three tenths
of flour tempered with oil to every calf, two tenths to a ram,
4 one tenth to a lamb, which in all are seven lambs, 5 and a
buck-goat for sin, which is offered for the expiation of the
people, 6 besides the holocaust of the first day of the month

caustum kalendarum cum sacrificiis suis et holocaustum sempiternum cum libationibus solitis. Hisdem caerimoniis offeretis in odorem suavissimum incensum Domino.

7 "'Decima quoque dies mensis huius septimi erit vobis sancta atque venerabilis, et adfligetis animas vestras; omne opus servile non facietis in ea. 8 Offeretisque holocaustum Domino in odorem suavissimum: vitulum de armento unum, arietem unum, agnos anniculos inmaculatos septem, 9 et in sacrificiis eorum, similae oleo conspersae tres decimas per vitulos singulos, duas decimas per arietem, 10 decimam decimae per agnos singulos, qui sunt simul septem agni, 11 et hircum pro peccato, absque his quae offerri pro delicto solent, in expiationem et holocaustum sempiternum cum sacrificio et libaminibus eorum.

12 "'Quintadecima vero die mensis septimi, quae vobis erit sancta atque venerabilis, omne opus servile non facietis in ea, sed celebrabitis sollemnitatem Domino septem diebus. 13 Offeretisque holocaustum in odorem suavissimum Domino, vitulos de armento tredecim, arietes duos, agnos anniculos quattuordecim inmaculatos. 14 Et in libamentis eorum, similae oleo conspersae tres decimas per vitulos singulos, qui sunt simul vituli tredecim, et duas decimas arieti uno, id est simul arietibus duobus, 15 et decimam decimae agnis singulis, qui sunt simul agni quattuordecim, 16 et hircum pro peccato, absque holocausto sempiterno et sacrificio et libamine eius.

17 "'In die altero, offeretis vitulos de armento duodecim, arietes duos agnos anniculos inmaculatos quattuordecim, 18 sacrificiaque et libamina singulorum, per vitulos et arietes

with the sacrifices thereof and the perpetual holocaust with the accustomed libations. With the same ceremonies you shall offer a burnt sacrifice for a most sweet odour to the Lord.

7 "'The tenth day also of this seventh month shall be holy and venerable unto you, and you shall afflict your souls; you shall do no servile work therein. 8 And you shall offer a holocaust to the Lord for a most sweet odour: one calf of the herd, one ram and seven lambs of a year old without blemish, 9 and for their sacrifices, three tenths of flour tempered with oil to every calf, two tenths to a ram, 10 the tenth of a tenth to every lamb, which are in all seven lambs, 11 and a buck-goat for sin, besides the things that are wont to be offered for *sin,* for expiation and for the perpetual holocaust with their sacrifice and libations.

12 "'And on the fifteenth day of the seventh month, which shall be unto you holy and venerable, you shall do no servile work, but shall celebrate a solemnity to the Lord seven days. 13 And you shall offer a holocaust for a most sweet odour to the Lord, thirteen calves of the herd, two rams and fourteen lambs of a year old without blemish, 14 and for their libations, three tenths of flour tempered with oil to every calf, being in all thirteen calves, and two tenths to each ram, being two rams, 15 and the tenth of a tenth to every lamb, being in all fourteen lambs, 16 and a buck-goat for sin, besides the perpetual holocaust and the sacrifice and the libation thereof.

17 "'On the second day, you shall offer twelve calves of the herd, two rams and fourteen lambs of a year old without blemish, 18 and the sacrifices and the libations for every one, for the calves and *for* the rams and *for* the lambs, you shall

et agnos, rite celebrabitis, 19 et hircum pro peccato, absque holocausto sempiterno sacrificioque et libamine eius.

20 "'Die tertio offeretis vitulos undecim, arietes duos, agnos anniculos inmaculatos quattuordecim, 21 sacrificiaque et libamina singulorum, per vitulos et arietes et agnos, rite celebrabitis, 22 et hircum pro peccato, absque holocausto sempiterno et sacrificio et libamine eius.

23 "'Die quarto offeretis vitulos decem, arietes duos, agnos anniculos inmaculatos quattuordecim, 24 sacrificiaque et libamina singulorum, per vitulos et arietes et agnos, rite celebrabitis, 25 et hircum pro peccato, absque holocausto sempiterno sacrificioque eius et libamine.

26 "'Die quinto offeretis vitulos novem, arietes duos, agnos anniculos inmaculatos quattuordecim, 27 sacrificiaque et libamina singulorum, per vitulos et arietes et agnos, rite celebrabitis, 28 et hircum pro peccato, absque holocausto sempiterno sacrificioque eius et libamine.

29 "'Die sexto offeretis vitulos octo, arietes duos, agnos anniculos inmaculatos quattuordecim, 30 sacrificiaque et libamina singulorum, per vitulos et arietes et agnos, rite celebrabitis, 31 et hircum pro peccato, absque holocausto sempiterno sacrificioque eius et libamine.

32 "'Die septimo offeretis vitulos septem et arietes duos, agnos anniculos inmaculatos quattuordecim, 33 sacrificiaque et libamina singulorum, per vitulos et arietes et agnos, rite

duly celebrate, 19 and a buck-goat for a sin offering, besides the perpetual holocaust and the sacrifice and the libation thereof.

20 "'The third day you shall offer eleven calves, two rams *and* fourteen lambs of a year old without blemish, 21 and the sacrifices and the libations of every one, for the calves and for the rams and for the lambs, you shall *offer* according to the rite 22 and a buck-goat for sin, besides the perpetual holocaust and the sacrifice and the libation thereof.

23 "'The fourth day you shall offer ten calves, two rams and fourteen lambs of a year old without blemish, 24 and the sacrifices and the libations of every one, for the calves and for the rams and for the lambs, you shall celebrate in right manner, 25 and a buck-goat for sin, besides the perpetual holocaust and the sacrifice and the libation thereof.

26 "'The fifth day you shall offer nine calves, two rams and fourteen lambs of a year old without blemish, 27 and the sacrifices and the libations of every one, for the calves and for the rams and for the lambs, you shall celebrate according to the rite, 28 and a buck-goat for sin, besides the perpetual holocaust and the sacrifice and the libation thereof.

29 "'The sixth day you shall offer eight calves, two rams *and* fourteen lambs of a year old without blemish, 30 and the sacrifices and the libations of every one, for the calves and the rams and the lambs, you shall celebrate according to the rite, 31 and a buck-goat for sin, besides the perpetual holocaust and the sacrifice and the libation thereof.

32 "'The seventh day you shall offer seven calves and two rams *and* fourteen lambs of a year old without blemish, 33 and the sacrifices and the libations of every one, for the calves and the rams and the lambs, you shall celebrate ac-

celebrabitis, 34 et hircum pro peccato, absque holocausto sempiterno sacrificioque eius et libamine.

35 "'Die octavo, qui est celeberrimus, omne opus servile non facietis, 36 offerentes holocaustum in odorem suavissimum Domino: vitulum unum, arietem unum, agnos anniculos inmaculatos septem, 37 sacrificiaque et libamina singulorum, per vitulos et arietes et agnos, rite celebrabitis, 38 et hircum pro peccato, absque holocausto sempiterno sacrificioque eius et libamine.

39 "'Haec offeretis Domino in sollemnitatibus vestris praeter vota et oblationes spontaneas in holocausto, in sacrificio, in libamine et in hostiis pacificis.'"

Caput 30

Narravitque Moses filiis Israhel omnia quae ei Dominus imperarat, 2 et locutus est ad principes tribuum filiorum Israhel, "Iste est sermo quem praecepit Dominus: 3 'Si quis virorum votum Domino voverit aut se constrinxerit iuramento, non faciet irritum verbum suum sed omne quod promisit implebit.

cording to the rite, 34 and a buck-goat for sin, besides the perpetual holocaust and the sacrifice and the libation thereof.

35 "'On the eighth day, which is most solemn, you shall do no servile work, 36 but you shall offer a holocaust for a most sweet odour to the Lord: one calf, one ram *and* seven lambs of a year old without blemish, 37 and the sacrifices and the libations of every one, for the calves and *for* the rams and *for* the lambs, you shall celebrate according to the rite, 38 and a buck-goat for sin, besides the perpetual holocaust and the sacrifice and the libation thereof.

39 "'These things shall you offer to the Lord in your solemnities besides your vows and voluntary oblations for holocaust, for sacrifice, for libation and for victims of peace-offerings.'"

Chapter 30

Of vows and oaths and their obligation.

And Moses told the children of Israel all that the Lord had commanded him, 2 and he said to the princes of the tribes of the children of Israel, "This is the word that the Lord hath commanded: 3 'If any man make a vow to the Lord or bind himself by an oath, he shall not make his word void but shall fulfil all that he promised.

4 "'Mulier si quippiam voverit et se constrinxerit iuramento, quae est in domo patris sui et in aetate adhuc puellari, si cognoverit pater votum quod pollicita est et iuramentum quo obligavit animam suam et tacuerit, voti rea erit: 5 quicquid pollicita est et iuravit, opere conplebit. 6 Sin autem statim ut audierit contradixerit pater, et vota et iuramenta eius irrita erunt, nec obnoxia tenebitur sponsioni, eo quod contradixerit pater.

7 "'Si maritum habuerit et voverit aliquid et semel verbum de ore eius egrediens animam illius obligaverit iuramento, 8 quo die audierit vir et non contradixerit, voti rea erit reddetque quodcumque promiserat. 9 Sin autem audiens statim contradixerit et irritas fecerit pollicitationes eius verbaque quibus obstrinxerat animam suam, propitius ei erit Dominus.

10 "'Vidua et repudiata quicquid voverint reddent.

11 "'Uxor in domo viri cum se voto constrinxerit et iuramento, 12 si audierit vir et tacuerit nec contradixerit sponsioni, reddet quodcumque promiserat. 13 Sin autem extemplo contradixerit, non tenebitur promissionis rea, quia maritus contradixit, et Dominus ei propitius erit. 14 Si voverit et iuramento se constrinxerit ut per ieiunium vel ceterarum rerum abstinentiam adfligat animam suam, in arbitrio viri erit ut faciat sive non faciat. 15 Quod si audiens vir tacuerit et in alteram diem distulerit sententiam, quicquid voverat atque promiserat reddet quia statim ut audivit tacuit. 16 Sin autem contradixerit postquam rescivit, portabit ipse iniquitatem eius.'"

4 "'If a woman vow any thing and bind herself by an oath, being in her father's house and but yet a girl in age, if her father knew the vow that she hath promised and the oath wherewith she hath bound her soul and held his peace, she shall be bound by the vow: 5 whatsoever she promised and swore, she shall fulfil in deed. 6 But if her father immediately as soon as he heard it gainsaid it, both her vows and her oaths shall be void, neither shall she be bound to what she promised, because her father hath gainsaid it.

7 "'If she have a husband and shall vow any thing and the word once going out of her mouth shall bind her soul by an oath, 8 the day that her husband shall hear it and not gainsay it, she shall be bound to the vow and shall give whatsoever she promised. 9 But if as soon as he heareth he gainsay it and make her promises and the words wherewith she had bound her soul of no effect, the Lord will forgive her.

10 "'The widow and she that is divorced shall *fulfil* whatsoever they vow.

11 "'If the wife in the house of her husband hath bound herself by vow and by oath, 12 if her husband hear and hold his peace and doth not disallow the promise, she shall *accomplish* whatsoever she had promised. 13 But if forthwith he gainsay it, she shall not be *bound* by the promise, because her husband gainsaid it, and the Lord will be merciful to her. 14 If she vow and bind herself by oath to afflict her soul by fasting or abstinence from other things, it shall depend on the will of her husband whether she shall do it or not do it. 15 But if the husband hearing it hold his peace and defer the declaring his mind till another day, whatsoever she had vowed and promised she shall fulfil because immediately as he heard it he held his peace. 16 But if he gainsay it after that he knew it, he shall bear her iniquity.'"

17 Istae sunt leges quas constituit Dominus Mosi inter virum et uxorem, inter patrem et filiam quae in puellari adhuc aetate est vel quae manet in parentis domo.

Caput 31

Locutusque est Dominus ad Mosen, dicens, 2 "Ulciscere prius filios Israhel de Madianitis, et sic colligeris ad populum tuum."

3 Statimque Moses, "Armate," inquit, "ex vobis viros ad pugnam qui possint ultionem Domini expetere de Madianitis. 4 Mille viri de singulis tribubus eligantur Israhel qui mittantur ad bellum."

5 Dederuntque millenos de singulis tribubus, id est, duodecim milia expeditorum ad pugnam. 6 Quos misit Moses cum Finees, filio Eleazari, sacerdotis, vasa quoque sancta et tubas ad clangendum tradidit ei. 7 Cumque pugnassent contra Madianitas atque vicissent, omnes mares occiderunt.

8 Et reges eorum, Evi et Recem et Sur et Ur et Rebe, quinque principes gentis, Balaam quoque, filium Beor, interfecerunt gladio. 9 Ceperuntque mulieres eorum et parvulos om-

17 These are the laws which the Lord appointed to Moses between the husband and the wife, between the father and the daughter that is as yet but a girl in age or that abideth in her father's house.

Chapter 31

The Midianites are slain for having drawn the people of
Israel into sin. The dividing of the booty.

And the Lord spoke to Moses, saying, 2 "Revenge first the children of Israel on the Midianites, and so thou shalt be gathered to thy people."

3 And Moses forthwith said, "Arm of you men to fight who may take the revenge of the Lord on the Midianites. 4 Let a thousand men be chosen out of every tribe of Israel to be sent to the war."

5 And they gave a thousand of every tribe, that is to say, twelve thousand men well appointed for battle. 6 And Moses sent them with Phinehas, the son of Eleazar, the priest, and he delivered to him the holy vessels and the trumpets to sound. 7 And when they had fought against the Midianites and had overcome them, they slew all the men.

8 And their kings, Evi and Rekem and Zur and Hur and Reba, five princes of the nation, Balaam also, the son of Beor, they killed with the sword. 9 And they took their

niaque pecora et cunctam supellectilem; quicquid habere potuerant depopulati sunt; 10 tam urbes quam viculos et castella flamma consumpsit. 11 Et tulerunt praedam et universa quae ceperant tam ex hominibus quam ex iumentis, 12 et adduxerunt ad Mosen et Eleazarum, sacerdotem, et ad omnem multitudinem filiorum Israhel. Reliqua autem utensilia portaverunt ad castra in campestribus Moab, iuxta Iordanem, contra Hiericho.

13 Egressi sunt autem Moses et Eleazar, sacerdos, et omnes principes synagogae in occursum eorum extra castra. 14 Iratusque Moses principibus exercitus, tribunis et centurionibus qui venerant de bello 15 ait, "Cur feminas reservastis? 16 Nonne istae sunt quae deceperunt filios Israhel ad suggestionem Balaam et praevaricari vos fecerunt in Domino super peccato Phogor, unde et percussus est populus? 17 Ergo cunctos interficite quicquid est generis masculini, etiam in parvulis, et mulieres quae noverunt viros in coitu iugulate. 18 Puellas autem et omnes feminas virgines reservate vobis, 19 et manete extra castra septem diebus. Qui occiderit hominem vel occisum tetigerit lustrabitur die tertio et septimo. 20 Et de omni praeda, sive vestimentum fuerit sive vas et aliquid in utensilia praeparatum de caprarum pellibus et pilis et ligno expiabitur."

21 Eleazar quoque, sacerdos, ad viros exercitus qui pugnaverant sic locutus est: "Hoc est praeceptum legis quod mandavit Dominus Mosi: 22 'Aurum et argentum et aes et ferrum et plumbum et stagnum 23 et omne quod potest transire per flammas igne purgabitur, quicquid autem ignem non potest

women and their children captives and all their cattle and all their goods, *and all their possessions* they plundered, 10 and all their cities and their villages and castles they burned. 11 And they carried away the booty and all that they had taken both of men and of beasts, 12 and they brought them to Moses and Eleazar, the priest, and to all the multitude of the children of Israel. But the rest of the things for use they carried to the camp on the plains of Moab, beside the Jordan, over against Jericho.

13 And Moses and Eleazar, the priest, and all the princes of the synagogue went forth to meet them without the camp. 14 And Moses being angry with the chief officers of the army, the tribunes and the centurions that were come from the battle 15 said, "Why have you saved the women? 16 Are not these they that deceived the children of Israel by the counsel of Balaam and made you transgress against the Lord by the sin of Peor, for which also the people was punished? 17 Therefore kill all that are of the male sex, even of the children, and put to death the women that have carnally known men. 18 But the girls and all the women that are virgins save for yourselves, 19 and stay without the camp seven days. He that hath killed a man or touched one that is killed shall be purified the third day and the seventh day. 20 And of all the spoil, every garment or vessel or any thing made for use of the skins or hair of goats or of wood shall be purified."

21 Eleazar also, the priest, spoke to the men of the army that had fought in this manner: "This is the ordinance of the law which the Lord hath commanded Moses: 22 'Gold and silver and brass and iron and lead and tin 23 and all that may pass through the fire shall be purified by fire, but whatso-

sustinere aqua expiationis sanctificabitur. 24 Et lavabitis vestimenta vestra die septimo, et purificati postea castra intrabitis.'"

25 Dixitque Dominus ad Mosen, 26 "Tollite summam eorum quae capta sunt ab homine usque ad pecus, tu et Eleazar, sacerdos, et principes vulgi. 27 Dividesque ex aequo praedam inter eos qui pugnaverunt et egressi sunt ad bellum et inter omnem reliquam multitudinem. 28 Et separabis partem Domino ab his qui pugnaverunt et fuerunt in bello, unam animam de quingentis tam ex hominibus quam ex bubus et asinis et ovibus, 29 et dabis eam Eleazaro, sacerdoti, quia primitiae Domini sunt. 30 Ex media quoque parte filiorum Israhel accipies quinquagesimum caput hominum et boum et asinorum et ovium cunctarumque animantium, et dabis ea Levitis qui excubant in custodiis tabernaculi Domini."

31 Feceruntque Moses et Eleazar sicut praeceperat Dominus. 32 Fuit autem praeda quam exercitus ceperat ovium sescenta septuaginta quinque milia, 33 boum septuaginta duo milia, 34 asinorum sexaginta milia et mille 35 animae hominum sexus feminei quae non cognoverant viros triginta duo milia. 36 Dataque est media pars his qui in proelio fuerant, ovium trecenta triginta septem milia quingenta, 37 e quibus in partem Domini supputatae sunt oves sescentae septuaginta quinque, 38 et de bubus triginta sex milibus, boves septuaginta et duo, 39 de asinis triginta milibus quingentis, asini sexaginta unus, 40 de animabus hominum sedecim milibus, cesserunt in partem Domini triginta duae animae. 41 Tradiditque Moses numerum primitiarum Domini Elea-

ever cannot abide the fire shall be sanctified with the water of expiation. 24 And you shall wash your garments the seventh day, and being purified you shall afterwards enter into the camp.'"

25 And the Lord said to Moses, 26 "Take the sum of the things that were taken both of man and beast, thou and Eleazar, the priest, and the princes of the multitude, 27 and thou shalt divide the spoil equally between them that fought and went out to the war and between the rest of the multitude. 28 And thou shalt separate a portion to the Lord from them that fought and were in the battle, one soul of five hundred as well of persons as of oxen and asses and sheep, 29 and thou shalt give it to Eleazar, the priest, because they are the firstfruits of the Lord. 30 Out of the moiety also of the children of Israel thou shalt take the fiftieth head of persons and of oxen and asses and sheep and of all beasts, and thou shalt give them to the Levites that watch in the charge of the tabernacle of the Lord."

31 And Moses and Eleazar did as the Lord had commanded. 32 And the spoil which the army had taken was six hundred seventy-five thousand sheep, 33 seventy-two thousand oxen, 34 sixty-one thousand asses 35 and thirty-two thousand persons of the female sex that had not known men. 36 And one half was given to them that had been in the battle, to wit, three hundred thirty-seven thousand five hundred sheep, 37 out of which for the portion of the Lord were reckoned six hundred seventy five sheep, 38 and out of the thirty-six thousand oxen, seventy-two oxen, 39 out of the thirty thousand five hundred asses, sixty-one asses, 40 out of the sixteen thousand persons, there fell to the portion of the Lord thirty-two souls. 41 And Moses delivered the number of the firstfruits of the Lord to Eleazar, the priest, as had

zaro, sacerdoti, sicut ei fuerat imperatum, 42 ex media parte filiorum Israhel quam separaverat his qui in proelio fuerant.

43 De media vero parte quae contigerat reliquae multitudini, id est, de ovium trecentis triginta septem milibus quingentis 44 et de bubus triginta sex milibus 45 et de asinis triginta milibus quingentis 46 et de hominibus sedecim milibus, 47 tulit Moses quinquagesimum caput et dedit Levitis qui excubabant in tabernaculo Domini, sicut praeceperat Dominus.

48 Cumque accessissent principes exercitus ad Mosen et tribuni centurionesque, dixerunt, 49 "Nos, servi tui, recensuimus numerum pugnatorum quos habuimus sub manu nostra, et ne unus quidem defuit. 50 Ob hanc causam offerimus in donariis Domini singuli quod in praeda auri potuimus invenire, periscelides et armillas, anulos et dextralia ac murenulas, ut depreceris pro nobis Dominum."

51 Susceperuntque Moses et Eleazar, sacerdos, omne aurum in diversis speciebus. 52 Pondo sedecim milia septingentos quinquaginta siclos, a tribunis et centurionibus, 53 unusquisque enim quod in praeda rapuerat suum erat, 54 et susceptum intulerunt in Tabernaculum Testimonii in monumentum filiorum Israhel coram Domino.

been commanded him, 42 out of the half of the children of Israel which he had separated for them that had been in the battle.

43 But out of the half that fell to the rest of the multitude, that is to say, out of the three hundred thirty-seven thousand five hundred sheep 44 and out of the thirty-six thousand oxen 45 and out of the thirty thousand five hundred asses 46 and out of the sixteen thousand persons, 47 Moses took the fiftieth head and gave it to the Levites that watched in the tabernacle of the Lord, as the Lord had commanded.

48 And when the commanders of the army and the tribunes and centurions were come to Moses, they said, 49 "We, thy servants, have reckoned up the number of the fighting men whom we had under our hand, and not so much as one was wanting. 50 Therefore we offer as gifts to the Lord what gold every one of us could find in the booty, in garters and tablets, rings and bracelets and chains, that thou mayst pray to the Lord for us."

51 And Moses and Eleazar, the priest, received all the gold in divers kinds, 52 in weight sixteen thousand seven hundred and fifty sicles, from the tribunes and from the centurions, 53 for that which every one had taken in the booty was his own, 54 and that which was received they brought into the Tabernacle of the Testimony for a memorial of the children of Israel before the Lord.

Caput 32

Filii autem Ruben et Gad habebant pecora multa, et erat illis in iumentis infinita substantia. Cumque vidissent Iazer et Galaad aptas alendis animalibus terras, 2 venerunt ad Mosen et ad Eleazarum, sacerdotem, et principes multitudinis atque dixerunt, 3 "Atharoth et Dibon et Iazer et Nemra, Esbon et Eleale et Sabam et Nebo et Beon, 4 terram quam percussit Dominus in conspectu filiorum Israhel, regionis uberrimae est ad pastum animalium, et nos, servi tui, habemus iumenta plurima, 5 precamurque, si invenimus gratiam coram te, ut des nobis, famulis tuis, eam in possessionem nec facias nos transire Iordanem."

6 Quibus respondit Moses, "Numquid fratres vestri ibunt ad pugnam, et vos hic sedebitis? 7 Cur subvertitis mentes filiorum Israhel ne transire audeant in locum quem eis daturus est Dominus? 8 Nonne ita egerunt patres vestri, quando misi de Cadesbarne ad explorandam terram? 9 Cumque venissent usque ad Vallem Botri, lustrata omni regione, subverterunt cor filiorum Israhel ut non intrarent fines quos eis Dominus dedit. 10 Qui iratus iuravit, dicens, 11 'Si videbunt

Chapter 32

The tribes of Reuben and Gad and half of the tribe of Manasseh receive their inheritance on the east side of Jordan upon conditions approved of by Moses.

And the sons of Reuben and Gad had many flocks of cattle, and their substance in beasts was infinite. And when they saw the lands of Jazer and Gilead fit for feeding cattle, 2 they came to Moses and Eleazar, the priest, and the princes of the multitude and said, 3 "Ataroth and Dibon and Jazer and Nimrah, Heshbon and Elealeh and Sebam and Nebo and Beon, 4 the land which the Lord hath conquered in the sight of the children of Israel, *is* a very fertile soil for the feeding of beasts, and we, thy servants, have very much cattle, 5 and we pray thee, if we have found favour in thy sight, that thou give it to us, thy servants, in possession and make us not pass over the Jordan."

6 And Moses answered them, "What, shall your brethren go to fight, and will you sit here? 7 Why do ye overturn the minds of the children of Israel that they may not dare to pass into the place which the Lord *hath given* them? 8 Was it not thus your fathers did, when I sent from Kadesh-barnea to view the land? 9 And when they were come as far as the Valley of the Cluster, having viewed all the country, they overturned the hearts of the children of Israel that they should not enter into the coasts which the Lord gave them. 10 And he swore in his anger, saying, 11 'If these men that

homines isti qui ascenderunt ex Aegypto, a viginti annis et supra, terram quam sub iuramento pollicitus sum Abraham, Isaac et Iacob, et noluerunt sequi me—12 praeter Chaleb, filium Iepphonne, Cenezeum, et Iosue, filium Nun: isti impleverunt voluntatem meam.'

13 "Iratusque Dominus adversum Israhel circumduxit eum per desertum quadraginta annis, donec consumeretur universa generatio quae fecerat malum in conspectu eius. 14 Et ecce," inquit, "vos surrexistis pro patribus vestris, incrementa et alumni hominum peccatorum, ut augeretis furorem Domini contra Israhel, 15 quod si nolueritis sequi eum, in solitudine populum derelinquet, et vos causa eritis necis omnium."

16 At illi prope accedentes dixerunt, "Caulas ovium fabricabimus et stabula iumentorum parvulis quoque nostris urbes munitas. 17 Nos autem ipsi armati et accincti pergemus ad proelium ante filios Israhel donec introducamus eos ad loca sua. Parvuli nostri et quicquid habere possumus erunt in urbibus muratis propter habitatorum insidias. 18 Non revertemur in domos nostras usquequo possideant filii Israhel hereditatem suam, 19 nec quicquam quaeremus trans Iordanem, quia iam habemus possessionem nostram in orientali eius plaga."

20 Quibus Moses ait, "Si facitis quod promittitis, expediti pergite coram Domino ad pugnam, 21 et omnis vir bellator armatus Iordanem transeat donec subvertat Dominus inimicos suos 22 et subiciatur ei omnis terra; tunc eritis inculpabiles apud Dominum et apud Israhel, et obtinebitis regiones quas vultis coram Domino. 23 Sin autem quod dicitis non feceritis, nulli dubium quin peccetis in Deum, et scitote

came up out of Egypt, from twenty years old and upward, shall see the land which I promised with an oath to Abraham, Isaac and Jacob, *because* they would not follow me— 12 except Caleb, the son of Jephunneh, the Kenizzite, and Joshua, the son of Nun: these have fulfilled my will.'

13 "And the Lord being angry against Israel led them about through the desert forty years, until the whole generation that had done evil in his sight was consumed. 14 And behold," said he, "you are risen up instead of your fathers, the increase and offspring of sinful men, to augment the fury of the Lord against Israel, 15 for if you will not follow him, he will leave the people in the wilderness, and you shall be the cause of the destruction of all."

16 But they coming near said, "We will make sheepfolds and stalls for our cattle and strong cities for our children. 17 And we ourselves will go armed and ready for battle before the children of Israel until we bring them in unto their places. Our little ones and all we *have* shall be in walled cities for fear of the ambushes of the inhabitants. 18 We will not return into our houses until the children of Israel possess their inheritance, 19 neither will we seek any thing beyond the Jordan, because we have already our possession on the east side thereof."

20 And Moses said to them, "If you do what you promise, go on well appointed for war before the Lord, 21 and let every fighting man pass over the Jordan until the Lord overthrow his enemies 22 and all the land be brought under him; then shall you be blameless before the Lord and before Israel, and you shall obtain the countries that you desire before the Lord. 23 But if you do not what you say, no man can doubt but you sin against God, and know ye that your sin

quoniam peccatum vestrum adprehendet vos. 24 Aedificate ergo urbes parvulis vestris et caulas ac stabula ovibus ac iumentis, et quod polliciti estis implete."

25 Dixeruntque filii Gad et Ruben ad Mosen, "Servi tui sumus; faciemus quod iubet dominus noster. 26 Parvulos nostros et mulieres et pecora ac iumenta relinquemus in urbibus Galaad, 27 nos autem, famuli tui, omnes expediti, pergemus ad bellum, sicut tu, domine, loqueris."

28 Praecepit ergo Moses Eleazaro, sacerdoti, et Iosue, filio Nun, et principibus familiarum per tribus Israhel et dixit ad eos, 29 "Si transierint filii Gad et filii Ruben vobiscum Iordanem, omnes armati ad bellum coram Domino, et vobis fuerit terra subiecta, date eis Galaad in possessionem. 30 Sin autem noluerint transire armati vobiscum in terram Chanaan, inter vos habitandi accipiant loca."

31 Responderuntque filii Gad et filii Ruben, "Sicut locutus est Dominus servis suis, ita faciemus. 32 Ipsi armati pergemus coram Domino in terram Chanaan, et possessionem iam suscepisse nos confitemur trans Iordanem."

33 Dedit itaque Moses filiis Gad et Ruben et dimidiae tribui Manasse, filii Ioseph, regnum Seon, regis Amorrei, et regnum Og, regis Basan, et terram eorum cum urbibus suis per circuitum.

34 Igitur extruxerunt filii Gad Dibon et Atharoth et Aroer 35 et Etroth et Sophan et Iazer et Iecbaa 36 et Bethnemra et Betharan, urbes munitas, et caulas pecoribus suis. 37 Filii vero Ruben aedificaverunt Esbon et Eleale et Cariathaim

shall overtake you. 24 Build therefore cities for your children and folds and stalls for your sheep and beasts, and accomplish what you have promised."

25 And the children of Gad and Reuben said to Moses, "We are thy servants; we will do what my lord commandeth. 26 We will leave our children and our wives and sheep and cattle in the cities of Gilead, 27 and we, thy servants, all well appointed, will march on to the war, as thou, my lord, speakest."

28 Moses therefore commanded Eleazar, the priest, and Joshua, the son of Nun, and the princes of the families *of all* the tribes of Israel and said to them, 29 "If the children of Gad and the children of Reuben pass with you over the Jordan, all armed for war before the Lord, and the land be made subject to you, give them Gilead in possession. 30 But if they will not pass armed with you into the land of Canaan, let them receive places to dwell in among you."

31 And the children of Gad and the children of Reuben answered, "As the Lord hath spoken to his servants, so will we do. 32 We will go armed before the Lord into the land of Canaan, and we confess that we have already received our possession beyond the Jordan."

33 Moses therefore gave to the children of Gad and of Reuben and to the half tribe of Manasseh, the son of Joseph, the kingdom of Sihon, king of the Amorites, and the kingdom of Og, king of Bashan, and their land and the cities thereof round about.

34 And the sons of Gad built Dibon and Ataroth and Aroer 35 and Atroth and Shophan and Jazer and Jogbehah 36 and Beth-nimrah and Beth-haran, fenced cities, and folds for their cattle. 37 But the children of Reuben built Heshbon

38 et Nabo et Baalmeon (versis nominibus), Sabama quoque, inponentes vocabula urbibus quas extruxerant.

39 Porro, filii Machir, filii Manasse, perrexerunt in Galaad et vastaverunt eam, interfecto Amorreo, habitatore eius. 40 Dedit ergo Moses terram Galaad Machir, filio Manasse, qui habitavit in ea. 41 Iair autem, filius Manasse, abiit et occupavit vicos eius, quos appellavit Avoth Iair, id est, villas Iair. 42 Nobe quoque perrexit et adprehendit Canath cum viculis suis, vocavitque eam ex nomine suo, Nobe.

Caput 33

Hae sunt mansiones filiorum Israhel, qui egressi sunt de Aegypto per turmas suas in manu Mosi et Aaron, 2 quas descripsit Moses iuxta castrorum loca quae Domini iussione mutabant.

3 Profecti igitur de Ramesse mense primo, quintadecima die mensis primi, altera die fecerunt Phase, filii Israhel, in manu excelsa videntibus cunctis Aegyptiis 4 et sepelientibus

and Elealeh and Kiriathaim 38 and Nebo and Baal-meon (their names being changed) and Sibmah, giving names to the cities which they had built.

39 Moreover, the children of Machir, the son of Manasseh, went into Gilead and wasted it, cutting off the Amorites, the inhabitants thereof. 40 And Moses gave the land of Gilead to Machir, the son of Manasseh, and he dwelt in it. 41 And Jair, the son of Manasseh, went and took the villages thereof, and he called them Havvoth Jair, that is to say, the villages of Jair. 42 Nobah also went and took Kenath with the villages thereof, and he called it by his own name, Nobah.

Chapter 33

The mansions or journeys of the children of Israel towards the land of promise.

These are the mansions of the children of Israel, who went out of Egypt by their troops *under the conduct* of Moses and Aaron, 2 which Moses wrote down according to the places of their encamping which they changed by the commandment of the Lord.

3 Now the children of Israel departed from Rameses the first month, on the fifteenth day of the first month, the day *after* the Phase, with a mighty hand in the sight of all the Egyptians 4 who were burying their firstborn whom the

primogenitos quos percusserat Dominus; nam et in diis eorum exercuerat ultionem. 5 Castrametati sunt in Soccoth.
6 Et de Soccoth venerunt in Aetham, quae est in extremis
finibus solitudinis. 7 Inde egressi, venerunt contra Phiahiroth quae respicit Beelsephon, et castrametati sunt ante
Magdolum. 8 Profectique de Phiahiroth, transierunt per
medium mare in solitudinem, et, ambulantes tribus diebus
per desertum Aetham, castrametati sunt in Mara. 9 Profectique de Mara, venerunt in Helim, ubi erant duodecim fontes
aquarum et palmae septuaginta, ibique castrametati sunt.
10 Sed et inde egressi, fixere tentoria super Mare Rubrum.
Profectique de Mari Rubro, 11 castrametati sunt in deserto
Sin. 12 Unde egressi venerunt in Dephca. 13 Profectique de
Dephca, castrametati sunt in Alus. 14 Egressique de Alus, in
Raphidim fixere tentoria, ubi aqua populo defuit ad bibendum. 15 Profectique de Raphidim, castrametati sunt in deserto Sinai. 16 Sed et de solitudine Sinai egressi, venerunt ad
Sepulchra Concupiscentiae. 17 Profectique de Sepulchris
Concupiscentiae, castrametati sunt in Aseroth. 18 Et de Aseroth venerunt in Rethma. 19 Profectique de Rethma, castrametati sunt in Remmonphares. 20 Unde egressi venerunt
in Lebna. 21 De Lebna, castrametati sunt in Ressa. 22 Egressique de Ressa, venerunt in Ceelatha. 23 Unde profecti
castrametati sunt in monte Sepher. 24 Egressi de monte
Sepher, venerunt in Arada. 25 Inde, proficiscentes castrametati sunt in Maceloth. 26 Profectique de Maceloth, venerunt in Thaath. 27 De Thaath, castrametati sunt in Thare.

Lord had slain; upon their gods also he had executed vengeance. 5 And they camped in Succoth. 6 And from Succoth they came into Etham, which is in the uttermost borders of the wilderness. 7 Departing from thence, they came over against Pi-hahiroth which looketh towards Baal-zephon, and they camped before Migdol. 8 And departing from Pi-hahiroth, they passed through the midst of the sea into the wilderness, and, having marched three days through the desert of Etham, they camped in Marah. 9 And departing from Marah, they came into Elim, where there were twelve fountains of waters and seventy palm trees, and there they camped. 10 But departing from thence also, they pitched their tents by the Red Sea. And departing from the Red Sea, 11 they camped in the desert of Sin. 12 And they removed from thence and came to Dophkah. 13 And departing from Dophkah, they camped in Alush. 14 And departing from Alush, they pitched their tents in Rephidim, where the people wanted water to drink. 15 And departing from Rephidim, they camped in the desert of Sinai. 16 But departing also from the desert of Sinai, they came to the Graves of Lust. 17 And departing from the Graves of Lust, they camped in Hazeroth. 18 And from Hazeroth they came to Rithmah. 19 And departing from Rithmah, they camped in Rimmon-perez. 20 And they departed from thence and came to Libnah. 21 Removing from Libnah, they camped in Rissah. 22 And departing from Rissah, they came to Kehelathah. 23 And they removed from thence and camped in the mountain Shepher. 24 Departing from the mountain Shepher, they came to Haradah. 25 From thence, they went and camped in Makheloth. 26 And departing from Makheloth, they came to Tahath. 27 *Removing* from Tahath, they camped in Terah.

28 Unde egressi fixerunt tentoria in Methca. 29 Et de Methca, castrametati sunt in Esmona. 30 Profectique de Esmona, venerunt in Moseroth. 31 Et de Moseroth, castrametati sunt in Baneiacan. 32 Egressique de Baneiacan, venerunt in Montem Gadgad. 33 Unde profecti castrametati sunt in Hietebatha. 34 Et de Hietebatha venerunt in Ebrona. 35 Egressique de Ebrona, castrametati sunt in Asiongaber. 36 Inde profecti venerunt in desertum Sin; haec est Cades. 37 Egressique de Cades, castrametati sunt in Monte Hor, in extremis finibus terrae Edom.

38 Ascenditque Aaron, sacerdos, in Montem Hor iubente Domino, et ibi mortuus est anno quadragesimo egressionis filiorum Israhel ex Aegypto, mense quinto, prima die mensis, 39 cum esset annorum centum viginti trium.

40 Audivitque Chananeus Rex Arad, qui habitabat ad meridiem, in terram Chanaan venisse filios Israhel. 41 Et profecti de Monte Hor, castrametati sunt in Salmona. 42 Unde egressi venerunt in Phinon. 43 Profectique de Phinon, castrametati sunt in Oboth. 44 Et de Oboth, venerunt in Ieabarim, quae est in finibus Moabitarum. 45 Profectique de Ieabarim, fixere tentoria in Dibongad. 46 Unde egressi castrametati sunt in Elmondeblathaim. 47 Egressique de Elmondeblathaim, venerunt ad montes Abarim contra Nabo. 48 Profectique de montibus Abarim, transierunt ad campestria Moab, super Iordanem, contra Hiericho, 49 ibique castrametati sunt de Bethsimon usque ad Belsattim in planiori-

28 And they departed from thence and pitched their tents in Mithkah. 29 And *removing* from Mithkah, they camped in Hashmonah. 30 And departing from Hashmonah, they came to Moseroth. 31 And *removing* from Moseroth, they camped in Bene-jaakan. 32 And departing from Bene-jaakan, they came to Mount Gadgad. 33 From thence they went and camped in Jotbathah. 34 And from Jotbathah they came to Abronah. 35 And departing from Abronah, they camped in Ezion-geber. 36 They removed from thence and came into the desert of Zin, *which* is Kadesh. 37 And departing from Kadesh, they camped in Mount Hor, in the uttermost borders of the land of Edom.

38 And Aaron, the priest, went up into Mount Hor at the commandment of the Lord, and there he died in the fortieth year of the coming forth of the children of Israel out of Egypt, the fifth month, the first day of the month, 39 when he was a hundred and twenty-three years old.

40 And King Arad, the Canaanite, who dwelt towards the south, heard that the children of Israel were come to the land of Canaan. 41 And they departed from Mount Hor and camped in Zelmonah. 42 From whence they removed and came to Punon. 43 And departing from Punon, they camped in Oboth. 44 And from Oboth, they came to Iye-abarim, which is in the borders of the Moabites. 45 And departing from Iye-abarim, they pitched their tents in Dibon-gab. 46 From thence they went and camped in Almon-diblathaim. 47 And departing from Almon-diblathaim, they came to the mountains of Abarim over against Nebo. 48 And departing from the mountains of Abarim, they passed to the plains of Moab, *by* the Jordan, over against Jericho, 49 and there they camped from Beth-jeshimoth even to Abel-shittim in the

bus locis Moabitarum, 50 ubi locutus est Dominus ad Mosen, 51 "Praecipe filiis Israhel, et dic ad eos, 'Quando transieritis Iordanem, intrantes terram Chanaan, 52 disperdite cunctos habitatores terrae illius. Confringite titulos, et statuas comminuite, atque omnia excelsa vastate, 53 mundantes terram et habitantes in ea, ego enim dedi vobis illam in possessionem, 54 quam dividetis vobis sorte. Pluribus dabitis latiorem, et paucioribus angustiorem. Singulis ut sors ceciderit, ita tribuetur hereditas. Per tribus et familias possessio dividetur. 55 Sin autem nolueritis interficere habitatores terrae, qui remanserint erunt vobis quasi clavi in oculis et lanceae in lateribus, et adversabuntur vobis in terra habitationis vestrae, 56 et quicquid illis facere cogitaram, vobis faciam.'"

Caput 34

Locutusque est Dominus ad Mosen, dicens, 2 "Praecipe filiis Israhel, et dices ad eos, 'Cum ingressi fueritis terram Chanaan et in possessionem vobis sorte ceciderit, his finibus terminabitur: 3 pars meridiana incipiet a solitudine Sin,

plains of the Moabites, 50 where the Lord said to Moses, 51 "Command the children of Israel, and say to them, 'When you shall have passed over the Jordan, entering into the land of Canaan, 52 destroy all the inhabitants of that land. Beat down their pillars, and break in pieces their statues, and waste all their high places, 53 cleansing the land and dwelling in it, for I have given it you for a possession, 54 and you shall divide it among you by lot. To the more you shall give a larger part, and to the fewer a lesser. To every one as the lot shall fall, so shall the inheritance be given. The possession shall be divided by the tribes and the families. 55 But if you will not kill the inhabitants of the land, they that remain shall be unto you as nails in your eyes and spears in your sides, and they shall be your adversaries in the land of your habitation, 56 and whatsoever I had thought to do to them, I will do to you.'"

Chapter 34

The limits of Canaan with the names of the men that make the division of it.

And the Lord spoke to Moses, saying, 2 "Command the children of Israel, and thou shalt say to them, 'When you are entered into the land of Canaan and it shall be fallen into your possession by lot, it shall be bounded by these limits: 3 the south side shall begin from the wilderness of Zin,

quae est iuxta Edom, et habebit terminos contra orientem Mare Salsissimum, 4 qui circumibunt australem plagam per ascensum Scorpionis ita ut transeant in Senna et perveniant in meridiem usque ad Cadesbarne, unde egredientur confinia ad villam nomine Addar et tendent usque ad Asemona. 5 Ibitque per gyrum terminus ab Asemona usque ad torrentem Aegypti, et Maris Magni litore finietur. 6 Plaga autem occidentalis a Mari Magno incipiet, et ipso fine cludetur. 7 Porro ad septentrionalem plagam, a Mari Magno termini incipient, pervenientes usque ad montem altissimum, 8 a quo venient in Emath usque ad terminos Sedada, 9 ibuntque confinia usque ad Zephrona et villam Henan. Hii erunt termini in parte aquilonis. 10 Inde metabuntur fines contra orientalem plagam de villa Henan usque Sephama. 11 Et de Sephama descendent termini in Rebla contra fontem Daphnim; inde pervenient contra orientem ad mare Chenereth 12 et tendent usque Iordanem et ad ultimum Salsissimo cludentur Mari. Hanc habebitis terram per fines suos in circuitu.'"

13 Praecepitque Moses filiis Israhel, dicens, "Haec erit terra quam possidebitis sorte et quam iussit dari Dominus novem tribubus et dimidiae tribui, 14 tribus enim filiorum Ruben per familias suas et tribus filiorum Gad iuxta cognationum numerum media quoque tribus Manasse, 15 id est, duae semis tribus, acceperunt partem suam trans Iordanem contra Hiericho ad orientalem plagam."

which is by Edom, and shall have the Most Salt Sea for its furthest limits eastward, 4 which limits shall go round on the south side by the ascent of the Scorpion and so into Zin and reach toward the south as far as Kadesh-barnea, from whence the frontiers shall go out to the town called Adar and shall reach as far as Azmon. 5 And the *limits* shall fetch a compass from Azmon to the torrent of Egypt, and shall end in the shore of the Great Sea. 6 And the west side shall begin from the Great Sea, and the same shall be the end thereof. 7 But toward the north side, the borders shall begin from the Great Sea, reaching to the most high mountain, 8 from which they shall come to Hamath as far as the borders of Zedad, 9 and the limits shall go as far as Ziphron and the village of Enan. These shall be the borders on the north side. 10 From thence they shall mark out the bounds towards the east side from the village of Enan unto Shepham. 11 And from Shepham the bounds shall go down to Riblah over against the fountain of Daphnis; from thence they shall come eastward to the sea of Chinnereth 12 and shall reach as far as the Jordan and at the last shall be closed in by the Most Salt Sea. This shall be your land with its borders round about.'"

13 And Moses commanded the children of Israel, saying, "This shall be the land which you shall possess by lot and which the Lord hath commanded to be given to the nine tribes and to the half tribe, 14 for the tribe of the children of Reuben by their families and the tribe of the children of Gad according to the number of their kindreds and half of the tribe of Manasseh, 15 that is, two tribes and a half, have received their portion beyond the Jordan over against Jericho at the east side."

16 Et ait Dominus ad Mosen, 17 "Haec sunt nomina virorum qui terram vobis divident: Eleazar, sacerdos, et Iosue, filius Nun, 18 et singuli principes de tribubus singulis, 19 quorum ista sunt vocabula: de tribu Iuda, Chaleb, filius Iepphonne; 20 de tribu Symeon, Samuhel, filius Ammiud; 21 de tribu Beniamin, Helidad, filius Chaselon; 22 de tribu filiorum Dan, Bocci, filius Iogli; 23 filiorum Ioseph, de tribu Manasse, Hannihel, filius Ephod, 24 de tribu Ephraim, Camuhel, filius Sephtan; 25 de tribu Zabulon, Elisaphan, filius Pharnach; 26 de tribu Isachar, dux Faltihel, filius Ozan; 27 de tribu Aser, Ahiud, filius Salomi; 28 de tribu Nepthali, Phedahel, filius Ameiud. 29 Hii sunt quibus praecepit Dominus ut dividerent filiis Israhel terram Chanaan."

Caput 35

Haec quoque locutus est Dominus ad Mosen in campestribus Moab super Iordanem, contra Hiericho, 2 "Praecipe filiis Israhel ut dent Levitis de possessionibus suis 3 urbes ad habitandum et suburbana earum per circuitum

16 And the Lord said to Moses, 17 "These are the names of the men that shall divide the land unto you: Eleazar, the priest, and Joshua, the son of Nun, 18 and one prince of every tribe, 19 whose names are these: of the tribe of Judah, Caleb, the son of Jephunneh; 20 of the tribe of Simeon, Shemuel, the son of Ammihud; 21 of the tribe of Benjamin, Elidad, the son of Chislon; 22 of the tribe of the children of Dan, Bukki, the son of Jogli; 23 of the children of Joseph, of the tribe of Manasseh, Hanniel, the son of Ephod, 24 of the tribe of Ephraim, Kemuel, the son of Shiphtan; 25 of the tribe of Zebulun, Eli-zaphan, the son of Parnach; 26 of the tribe of Issachar, Paltiel, the prince, the son of Azzan; 27 of the tribe of Asher, Ahihud, the son of Shelomi; 28 of the tribe of Naphtali, Pedahel, the son of Ammihud. 29 These are they whom the Lord hath commanded to divide the land of Canaan to the children of Israel."

Chapter 35

Cities are appointed for the Levites, of which six are to be the cities of refuge.

And the Lord spoke these things also to Moses in the plains of Moab by the Jordan, over against Jericho, 2 "Command the children of Israel that they give to the Levites out of their possessions 3 cities to dwell in and their suburbs

ut ipsi in oppidis maneant et suburbana sint pecoribus eorum ac iumentis, 4 quae a muris civitatum forinsecus per circuitum, mille passuum spatio tendentur. 5 Contra orientem
duo milia erunt cubiti, et contra meridiem similiter erunt
duo milia. Ad mare quoque, quod respicit ad occidentem,
eadem mensura erit, et septentrionalis plaga aequali termino
finietur. Eruntque urbes in medio, et foris suburbana.

6 "De ipsis autem oppidis quae Levitis dabitis, sex erunt
in fugitivorum auxilia separata ut fugiat ad ea qui fuderit
sanguinem, et exceptis his alia quadraginta duo oppida, 7 id
est simul quadraginta octo cum suburbanis suis. 8 Ipsaeque
urbes quae dabuntur de possessionibus filiorum Israhel, ab
his qui plus habent, plures auferentur, et qui minus, pauciores. Singuli iuxta mensuram hereditatis suae dabunt oppida
Levitis."

9 Ait Dominus ad Mosen, 10 "Loquere filiis Israhel, et dices ad eos, 'Quando transgressi fueritis Iordanem in terram
Chanaan, 11 decernite quae urbes esse debeant in praesidia
fugitivorum qui nolentes sanguinem fuderint. 12 In quibus
cum fuerit profugus, cognatus occisi eum non poterit occidere donec stet in conspectu multitudinis et causa illius iudicetur. 13 De ipsis autem urbibus quae ad fugitivorum sub-
sidia separantur, 14 tres erunt trans Iordanem et tres in terra
Chanaan, 15 tam filiis Israhel quam advenis atque peregrinis,
ut confugiat ad eas qui nolens sanguinem fuderit.

16 "'Si quis ferro percusserit et mortuus fuerit qui percus-

round about that they may abide in the towns and the suburbs may be for their cattle and beasts, 4 which suburbs shall reach from the walls of the cities outward, a thousand paces on every side. 5 Toward the east shall be two thousand cubits, and toward the south in like manner shall be two thousand *cubits.* Toward the sea also, which looketh to the west, shall be the same extent, and the north side shall be bounded with the like limits. And the cities shall be in the midst, and the suburbs without.

6 "And among the cities which you shall give to the Levites, six shall be separated for refuge to fugitives that he who hath shed blood may flee to them, and besides these there shall be other forty-two cities, 7 that is, in all forty-eight with their suburbs. 8 And *of* these cities which shall be given out of the possessions of the children of Israel, from them that have more, more shall be taken, and *from them* that have less, fewer. Each shall give towns to the Levites according to the extent of their inheritance."

9 The Lord said to Moses, 10 "Speak to the children of Israel, and thou shalt say to them, 'When you shall have passed over the Jordan into the land of Canaan, 11 determine what cities shall be for the refuge of fugitives who have shed blood against their will. 12 And when the fugitive shall be in them, the kinsman of him that is slain may not have power to kill him until he stand before the multitude and his cause be judged. 13 And of those cities that are separated for the refuge of fugitives, 14 three shall be beyond the Jordan and three in the land of Canaan, 15 as well for the children of Israel as for strangers and sojourners, that he may flee to them who hath shed blood against his will.

16 "'If any man strike with iron and he die that was struck,

sus est, reus erit homicidii, et ipse morietur. 17 Si lapidem iecerit et ictus occubuerit, similiter punietur. 18 Si ligno percussus interierit, percussoris sanguine vindicabitur. 19 Propinquus occisi homicidam interficiet; statim ut adprehenderit eum, interficiet.

20 "'Si per odium quis hominem inpulerit vel iecerit quippiam in eum per insidias 21 aut cum esset inimicus manu percusserit et ille mortuus fuerit, percussor homicidii reus erit; cognatus occisi statim ut invenerit eum iugulabit.

22 "'Quod si fortuito et absque odio 23 et inimicitiis quicquam horum fecerit 24 et hoc audiente populo fuerit conprobatum atque inter percussorem et propinquum sanguinis quaestio ventilata, 25 liberabitur innocens de ultoris manu et reducetur per sententiam in urbem ad quam confugerat, manebitque ibi donec sacerdos magnus qui oleo sancto unctus est moriatur.

26 "'Si interfector extra fines urbium quae exulibus deputatae sunt 27 fuerit inventus et percussus ab eo qui ultor est sanguinis, absque noxa erit qui eum occiderit, 28 debuerat enim profugus usque ad mortem pontificis in urbe residere, postquam autem ille obierit, homicida revertetur in terram suam.

29 "'Haec sempiterna erunt et legitima in cunctis habitationibus vestris.

30 "'Homicida sub testibus punietur; ad unius testimonium nullus condemnabitur. 31 Non accipietis pretium ab eo qui reus est sanguinis, statim et ipse morietur. 32 Exules et

he shall be guilty of murder, and he himself shall die. 17 If he throw a stone and he that is struck die, he shall be punished in the same manner. 18 If he that is struck with wood die, he shall be revenged by the blood of him that struck him. 19 The kinsman of him that was slain shall kill the murderer; as soon as he apprehendeth him, he shall kill him.

20 "'If through hatred any one push a man or fling any thing at him with ill design 21 or being his enemy strike him with his hand and he die, the striker shall be guilty of murder; the kinsman of him that was slain as soon as he findeth him shall kill him.

22 "'But if by chance medley and without hatred 23 and enmity he do any of these things 24 and this be proved in the hearing of the people and the cause be debated between him that struck and the next of kin, 25 the innocent shall be delivered from the hand of the revenger and shall be brought back by sentence into the city to which he had fled, and he shall abide there until the death of the high priest that is anointed with the holy oil.

26 "'If the murderer be found without the limits of the cities that are appointed for the banished 27 and be struck by him that is the avenger of blood, he shall not be guilty that killed him, 28 for the fugitive ought to have stayed in the city until the death of the high priest, and after he is dead, then shall the manslayer return to his own country.

29 "'These things shall be perpetual and for an ordinance in all your dwellings.

30 "'The murderer shall be punished by witnesses; none shall be condemned upon the evidence of one man. 31 You shall not take money of him that is guilty of blood, but he shall die forthwith. 32 The banished and fugitives before the

profugi ante mortem pontificis nullo modo in urbes suas reverti poterunt. 33 Ne polluatis terram habitationis vestrae quae insontium cruore maculatur, nec aliter expiari potest nisi per eius sanguinem qui alterius sanguinem fuderit, 34 atque ita emundabitur vestra possessio, me commorante vobiscum, ego enim sum Dominus qui habito inter filios Israhel.'"

Caput 36

Accesserunt autem et principes familiarum Galaad, filii Machir, filii Manasse, de stirpe filiorum Ioseph, locutique sunt Mosi coram principibus Israhel atque dixerunt, 2 "Tibi, domino nostro, praecepit Dominus ut terram sorte divideres filiis Israhel et ut filiabus Salphaad, fratris nostri, dares possessionem debitam patri. 3 Quas si alterius tribus homines uxores acceperint, sequetur possessio sua et translata ad aliam tribum de nostra hereditate minuetur. 4 Atque ita fiet ut cum iobeleus, id est, quinquagesimus annus remissionis, advenerit, confundatur sortium distributio, et aliorum possessio ad alios transeat."

death of the high priest may by no means return into their own cities. 33 Defile not the land of your habitation which is stained with the blood of the innocent, neither can it otherwise be expiated but by his blood that hath shed the blood of another. 34 And thus shall your possession be cleansed, myself abiding with you, for I am the Lord that dwell among the children of Israel.'"

Chapter 36

That the inheritances may not be alienated from one tribe to another, all are to marry within their own tribes.

And the princes of the families of Gilead, the son of Machir, the son of Manasseh, of the stock of the children of Joseph, came and spoke to Moses before the princes of Israel and said, 2 "The Lord hath commanded thee, my lord, that thou shouldst divide the land by lot to the children of Israel and that thou shouldst give to the daughters of Zelophehad, our brother, the possession due to their father. 3 Now if men of another tribe take them to wives, their possession will follow them and being transferred to another tribe will be a diminishing of our inheritance. 4 And so it shall come to pass that when the jubilee, the is, the fiftieth year of remission, is come, the distribution made by the lots shall be confounded, and the possession of the one shall pass to the others."

5 Respondit Moses filiis Israhel et Domino praecipiente ait, "Recte tribus filiorum Ioseph locuta est. 6 Et haec lex super filiabus Salphaad a Domino promulgata est: 'Nubant quibus volunt, tantum ut suae tribus hominibus 7 ne commisceatur possessio filiorum Israhel de tribu in tribum, omnes enim viri ducent uxores de tribu et cognatione sua, 8 et cunctae feminae maritos de eadem tribu accipient ut hereditas permaneat in familiis 9 nec sibi misceantur tribus sed ita maneant 10 ut a Domino separatae sunt.'"

Feceruntque filiae Salphaad ut fuerat imperatum. 11 Et nupserunt Maala et Thersa et Egla et Melcha et Noa filiis patrui sui 12 de familia Manasse, qui fuit filius Ioseph, et possessio quae illis fuerat adtributa mansit in tribu et familia patris earum.

13 Haec sunt mandata atque iudicia quae praecepit Dominus per manum Mosi ad filios Israhel in campestribus Moab, super Iordanem, contra Hiericho.

5 Moses answered the children of Israel and said by the command of the Lord, "The tribe of the children of Joseph hath spoken rightly. 6 And this is the law promulgated by the Lord touching the daughters of Zelophehad: 'Let them marry to whom they will, only so that it be to men of their own tribe 7 lest the possession of the children of Israel be mingled from tribe to tribe, for all men shall marry wives of their own tribe and kindred, 8 and all women shall take husbands of the same tribe that the inheritance may remain in the families 9 and that the tribes be not mingled one with another but remain so 10 as they were separated by the Lord.'"

And the daughters of Zelophehad did as was commanded. 11 And Mahlah and Tirzah and Hoglah and Milcah and Noah were married to the sons of their uncle by their father 12 of the family of Manasseh, who was the son of Joseph, and the possession that had been allotted to them remained in the tribe and family of their father.

13 These are the commandments and judgments which the Lord commanded by the hand of Moses to the children of Israel in the plains of Moab, upon the Jordan, over against Jericho.

DEUTERONOMY

Caput 1

Haec sunt verba quae locutus est Moses ad omnem Israhel trans Iordanem, in solitudine campestri contra Mare
Rubrum, inter Pharan et Thophel et Laban et Aseroth, ubi
auri est plurimum, 2 undecim diebus de Horeb per viam
Montis Seir usque Cadesbarne.

3 Quadragesimo anno, undecimo mense, prima die mensis, locutus est Moses ad filios Israhel omnia quae praeceperat illi Dominus ut diceret eis 4 postquam percussit Seon,
regem Amorreorum, qui habitavit in Esebon, et Og, regem
Basan, qui mansit in Aseroth et in Edrai, 5 trans Iordanem
in terra Moab. Coepitque Moses explanare legem et dicere,
6 "Dominus, Deus noster, locutus est ad nos in Horeb, dicens, 'Sufficit vobis quod in hoc monte mansistis. 7 Revertimini, et venite ad montem Amorreorum et ad cetera quae ei
proxima sunt, campestria atque montana et humiliora loca
contra meridiem et iuxta litus maris, terram Chananeorum
et Libani, usque ad flumen magnum Eufraten.'

8 "En," inquit, "tradidi vobis; ingredimini, et possidete

Chapter 1

A repetition of what passed at Sinai and Kadesh-barnea and of the people's murmuring and their punishment.

These are the words which Moses spoke to all Israel beyond the Jordan, in the plain wilderness over against the Red Sea, between Paran and Tophel and Laban and Hazeroth, where there is very much gold, 2 eleven days' journey from Horeb by the way of Mount Seir to Kadesh-barnea.

3 In the fortieth year, the eleventh month, the first day of the month, Moses spoke to the children of Israel all that the Lord had commanded him to say to them 4 after that he had slain Sihon, king of the Amorites, who dwelt in Heshbon, and Og, king of Bashan, who abode in Ashtaroth and in Edrei, 5 beyond the Jordan in the land of Moab. And Moses began to expound the law and to say, 6 "The Lord, our God, spoke to us in Horeb, saying, '*You have stayed long enough* in this mountain. 7 Turn you, and come to the mountain of the Amorites and to the other places that are next to it, the plains and the hills and the vales towards the south and by the sea shore, the land of the Canaanites and of Libanus, as far as the great river Euphrates.'

8 "Behold," said he, "I have delivered it to you; go in, and possess it concerning which the Lord swore to your fathers

eam super qua iuravit Dominus patribus vestris Abraham, Isaac et Iacob ut daret illam eis et semini eorum post eos.

9 "Dixique vobis illo in tempore, 10 'Non possum solus sustinere vos, quia Dominus, Deus vester, multiplicavit vos et estis hodie sicut stellae caeli plurimi.' 11 (Dominus, Deus patrum vestrorum, addat ad hunc numerum multa milia et benedicat vobis sicut locutus est.) 12 'Non valeo solus vestra negotia sustinere et pondus ac iurgia. 13 Date e vobis viros sapientes et gnaros et quorum conversatio sit probata in tribubus vestris ut ponam eos vobis principes.'

14 "Tunc respondistis mihi, 'Bona res est quam vis facere.'

15 "Tulique de tribubus vestris viros sapientes et nobiles et constitui eos principes, tribunos et centuriones et quinquagenarios ac decanos, qui docerent vos singula. 16 Praecepique eis, dicens, 'Audite illos, et quod iustum est iudicate, sive civis sit ille sive peregrinus. 17 Nulla erit distantia personarum; ita parvum audietis ut magnum, nec accipietis cuiusquam personam, quia Dei iudicium est. Quod si difficile vobis aliquid visum fuerit, referte ad me, et ego audiam.' 18 Praecepique omnia quae facere deberetis.

19 "Profecti autem de Horeb, transivimus per heremum terribilem et maximam quam vidistis per viam montis Amorrei sicut praeceperat Dominus, Deus noster, nobis. Cumque venissemus in Cadesbarne, 20 dixi vobis, 'Venistis ad montem Amorrei, quem Dominus, Deus noster, daturus est nobis. 21 Vide terram quam Dominus, Deus tuus, dat tibi.

Abraham, Isaac and Jacob that he would give it to them and to their seed after them.

9 "And I said to you at that time, 10 'I alone am not able to bear you, for the Lord, your God, hath multiplied you and you are this day as the stars of heaven for multitude.' 11 (The Lord, God of your fathers, add to this number many thousands and bless you as he hath spoken.) 12 'I alone am not able to bear your business and the charge *of you* and *your* differences. 13 Let me have from among you wise and understanding men and such whose conversation is approved among your tribes that I may appoint them your rulers.'

14 "Then you answered me, 'The thing is good which thou meanest to do.'

15 "And I took out of your tribes men wise and honourable and appointed them rulers, tribunes and centurions and officers over fifties and over tens, who might teach you all things. 16 And I commanded them, saying, 'Hear them, and judge that which is just, whether he be one of your country or a stranger. 17 There shall be no difference of persons; you shall hear the little as well as the great, neither shall you respect any man's person, because it is the judgment of God. And if any thing seem hard to you, refer it to me, and I will hear it.' 18 And I commanded you all things that you were to do.

19 "And, departing from Horeb, we passed through the terrible and vast wilderness which you saw by the way of the mountain of the Amorite as the Lord, our God, had commanded us. And when we were come into Kadesh-barnea, 20 I said to you, 'You are come to the mountain of the Amorite, which the Lord, our God, will give to us. 21 See the land which the Lord, thy God, giveth thee. Go up, and possess it

Ascende, et posside eam sicut locutus est Dominus, Deus noster, patribus tuis. Noli metuere, nec quicquam paveas.'

22 "Et accessistis ad me omnes atque dixistis, 'Mittamus viros qui considerent terram et renuntient per quod iter debeamus ascendere et ad quas pergere civitates.'

23 "Cumque mihi sermo placuisset, misi e vobis duodecim viros, singulos de tribubus suis, 24 qui, cum perrexissent et ascendissent in montana, venerunt usque ad Vallem Botri, et considerata terra, 25 sumentes de fructibus eius ut ostenderent ubertatem, adtulerunt ad nos atque dixerunt, 'Bona est terra quam Dominus, Deus noster, daturus est nobis.'

26 "Et noluistis ascendere, sed increduli ad sermonem Domini, Dei nostri, 27 murmurati estis in tabernaculis vestris atque dixistis, 'Odit nos Dominus, et idcirco eduxit nos de terra Aegypti ut traderet nos in manu Amorrei atque deleret nos. 28 Quo ascendemus? Nuntii terruerunt cor nostrum, dicentes, "Maxima multitudo est et nobis in statura procerior; urbes magnae et ad caelum usque munitae; filios Enacim vidimus ibi."'"

29 "Et dixi vobis, 'Nolite metuere, nec timeatis eos. 30 Dominus Deus, qui ductor est vester, pro vobis ipse pugnabit, sicut fecit in Aegypto videntibus cunctis. 31 Et in solitudine (ipse vidisti) portavit te Dominus, Deus tuus, ut solet homo gestare parvulum filium suum, in omni via per quam ambulastis donec veniretis ad locum istum.' 32 Et nec sic quidem credidistis Domino, Deo vestro, 33 qui praecessit vos in via et metatus est locum in quo tentoria figere deberetis, nocte ostendens vobis iter per ignem et die per columnam nubis.

as the Lord, our God, hath spoken to thy fathers. Fear not, nor *be any way discouraged.'*

22 "And you came all to me and said, 'Let us send men who may view the land and bring us word what way we shall go up and to what cities we shall go.'

23 "And because the saying pleased me, I sent of you twelve men, one of every tribe, 24 who, when they had set forward and had gone up to the mountains, came as far as the Valley of the Cluster, and having viewed the land, 25 taking of the fruits thereof to shew its fertility, they brought them to us and said, 'The land is good which the Lord, our God, will give us.'

26 "And you would not go up, but being incredulous to the word of the Lord, our God, 27 you murmured in your *tents* and said, 'The Lord hateth us, and therefore he hath brought us out of the land of Egypt that he might deliver us into the hand of the Amorite and destroy us. 28 Whither shall we go up? The messengers have terrified our hearts, saying, "The multitude is very great and taller than we; the cities are great and walled up to the sky; we have seen the sons of the Anakim there."'

29 "And I said to you, 'Fear not, neither be ye afraid of them. 30 The Lord God, who is your leader, himself will fight for you, as he did in Egypt in the sight of all. 31 And in the wilderness *(as* thou hast seen) the Lord, thy God, hath carried thee as a man is wont to carry his little son, all the way that you have come until you came to this place.' 32 And *yet for all this* you did not believe the Lord, your God, 33 who went before you in the way and marked out the place wherein you should pitch your tents, in the night shewing you the way by fire and in the day by the pillar of a cloud.

34 "Cumque audisset Dominus vocem sermonum vestrorum, iratus iuravit et ait, 35 'Non videbit quispiam de hominibus generationis huius pessimae terram bonam quam sub iuramento pollicitus sum patribus vestris, 36 praeter Chaleb, filium Iepphonne, ipse enim videbit eam, et ipsi dabo terram quam calcavit et filiis eius quia secutus est Dominum.'

37 "Nec miranda indignatio in populum, cum mihi quoque iratus Dominus propter vos dixerit, 'Nec tu ingredieris illuc, 38 sed Iosue, filius Nun, minister tuus, ipse intrabit pro te. Hunc exhortare et robora, et ipse terram sorte dividet Israheli. 39 Parvuli vestri, de quibus dixistis quod captivi ducerentur, et filii qui hodie boni ac mali ignorant distantiam, ipsi ingredientur, et ipsis dabo terram, et possidebunt eam. 40 Vos autem revertimini, et abite in solitudinem per viam Maris Rubri.'

41 "Et respondistis mihi, 'Peccavimus Domino; ascendemus atque pugnabimus sicut praecepit Dominus, Deus noster.'

"Cumque instructi armis pergeretis in montem, 42 ait mihi Dominus. 'Dic ad eos, "Nolite ascendere, neque pugnetis, non enim sum vobiscum, ne cadatis coram inimicis vestris."'

43 "Locutus sum, et non audistis, sed, adversantes imperio Domini et tumentes superbia, ascendistis in montem. 44 Itaque egressus Amorreus qui habitabat in montibus et obviam veniens persecutus est vos sicut solent apes persequi et cecidit de Seir usque Horma.

34 "And when the Lord had heard the voice of your words, he was angry and swore and said, 35 'Not one of the men of this wicked generation shall see the good land which I promised with an oath to your fathers, 36 except Caleb, the son of Jephunneh, for he shall see it, and to him I will give the land that he hath trodden upon and to his children because he hath followed the Lord.'

37 "Neither is his indignation against the people to be wondered at, since the Lord was angry with me also on your account and said, 'Neither shalt thou go in thither, 38 but Joshua, the son of Nun, thy minister, he shall go in for thee. Exhort and encourage him, and he shall divide the land by lot to Israel. 39 Your children, of whom you said that they should be led away captives, and your sons who know not this day the difference of good and evil, they shall go in, and to them I will give the land, and they shall possess it. 40 But return you, and go into the wilderness by the way of the Red Sea.'

41 "And you answered me, 'We have sinned against the Lord; we will go up and fight as the Lord, our God, hath commanded.'

"And when you went ready armed unto the mountain, 42 the Lord said to me, 'Say to them, "Go not up, and fight not, for I am not with you, lest you fall before your enemies."'

43 "I spoke, and you hearkened not, but, resisting the commandment of the Lord and swelling with pride, you went up into the mountain. 44 And the Amorite that dwelt in the mountains coming out and meeting you chased you as bees *do* and made slaughter of you from Seir as far as Hormah.

⁴⁵ "Cumque reversi ploraretis coram Domino, non audivit vos, nec voci vestrae voluit adquiescere. ⁴⁶ Sedistis ergo in Cadesbarne multo tempore."

Caput 2

"Profectique inde venimus in solitudinem quae ducit ad Mare Rubrum, sicut mihi dixerat Dominus, et circumivimus Montem Seir longo tempore. ² Dixitque Dominus ad me, ³ 'Sufficit vobis circumire montem istum. Ite contra aquilonem, ⁴ et populo praecipe, dicens, "Transibitis per terminos fratrum vestrorum filiorum Esau, qui habitant in Seir, et timebunt vos. ⁵ Videte ergo diligenter ne moveamini contra eos, neque enim dabo vobis de terra eorum quantum potest unius pedis calcare vestigium, quia in possessionem Esau dedi Montem Seir. ⁶ Cibos emetis ab eis pecunia et comedetis; aquam emptam haurietis et bibetis. ⁷ Dominus, Deus tuus, benedixit tibi in omni opere manuum tuarum. Novit iter tuum, quomodo transieris solitudinem hanc magnam per quadraginta annos, habitans tecum Dominus, Deus tuus, et nihil tibi defuit."'

45 "And when you returned and wept before the Lord, he heard you not, neither would he yield to your voice. 46 So you abode in Kadesh-barnea a long time."

Chapter 2

They are forbid to fight against the Edomites, Moabites and Ammonites. Their victory over Sihon, king of Heshbon.

"And departing from thence we came into the wilderness that leadeth to the Red Sea, as the Lord had spoken to me, and we compassed Mount Seir a long time. 2 And the Lord said to me, 3 *You have compassed* this mountain *long enough.* Go toward the north, 4 and command thou the people, saying, "You shall pass by the borders of your brethren the children of Esau, who dwell in Seir, and they will be afraid of you. 5 Take ye then good heed that you stir not against them, for I will not give you of their land so much as the step of one foot can tread upon, because I have given Mount Seir to Esau for a possession. 6 You shall buy meats of them for money and shall eat; you shall draw water *for money* and shall drink. 7 The Lord, thy God, hath blessed thee in every work of thy hands. The Lord, thy God, dwelling with thee knoweth thy journey, how thou hast passed through this great wilderness for forty years and thou hast wanted nothing."'

8 "Cumque transissemus fratres nostros filios Esau qui habitabant in Seir per viam campestrem de Helath et de Asiongaber, venimus ad iter quod ducit in desertum Moab. 9 Dixitque Dominus ad me, 'Non pugnes contra Moabitas, nec ineas adversum eos proelium, non enim dabo tibi quicquam de terra eorum, quia filiis Loth tradidi Ar in possessionem.' 10 Emim primi fuerunt habitatores eius, populus magnus et validus et tam excelsus, ut de Enacim stirpe, 11 quasi gigantes crederentur et essent similes filiorum Enacim. Denique Moabitae appellant eos Emim. 12 In Seir autem prius habitaverunt Horim, quibus expulsis atque deletis, habitaverunt filii Esau, sicut fecit Israhel in terra possessionis suae quam dedit ei Dominus.

13 "Surgentes ergo ut transiremus torrentem Zared, venimus ad eum. 14 Tempus autem quo ambulavimus de Cadesbarne usque ad transitum torrentis Zared triginta et octo annorum fuit donec consumeretur omnis generatio hominum bellatorum de castris, sicut iuraverat Dominus, 15 cuius manus fuit adversum eos ut interirent de castrorum medio.

16 "Postquam autem universi ceciderunt pugnatores, 17 locutus est Dominus ad me, dicens, 18 'Tu transibis hodie terminos Moab, urbem nomine Ar, 19 et accedens in vicina filiorum Ammon, cave ne pugnes contra eos nec movearis ad proelium, non enim dabo tibi de terra filiorum Ammon, quia filiis Loth dedi eam in possessionem.' 20 Terra gigantum reputata est, et in ipsa olim habitaverunt gigantes quos Ammanitae vocant Zomzommim, 21 populus magnus et multus et procerae longitudinis, sicut Enacim quos delevit

8 "And when we had passed by our brethren the children of Esau that dwelt in Seir by the way of the plain from Elath and from Eziongeber, we came to the way that leadeth to the desert of Moab. 9 And the Lord said to me, 'Fight not against the Moabites, neither go to battle against them, for I will not give thee any of their land, because I have given Ar to the children of Lot in possession.' 10 The Emim first were the inhabitants thereof, a people great and strong and so tall that, like the race of the Anakim, 11 they were esteemed as giants and were like the sons of the Anakim. But the Moabites call them Emim. 12 The Horim also formerly dwelt in Seir, who being driven out and destroyed, the children of Esau dwelt there, as Israel did in the land of his possession which the Lord gave him.

13 "Then, rising up to pass the torrent Zered, we came to it. 14 And the time that we journeyed from Kadesh-barnea till *we passed over* the torrent Zered was thirty-eight years until all the generation of the men that were fit for war was consumed out of the camp, as the Lord had sworn, 15 *for his* hand was against them that they should perish from the midst of the camp.

16 "And after all the fighting men were dead, 17 the Lord spoke to me, saying, 18 'Thou shalt pass this day the borders of Moab, the city named Ar, 19 and when thou comest nigh the frontiers of the children of Ammon, take heed thou fight not against them nor once move to battle, for I will not give thee of the land of the children of Ammon, because I have given it to the children of Lot for a possession.' 20 It was accounted a land of giants, and giants formerly dwelt in it whom the Ammonites call Zamzammim, 21 a people great and many and of tall stature, like the Anakim whom the

Dominus a facie eorum, et fecit illos habitare pro eis, 22 sicut fecerat filiis Esau qui habitant in Seir, delens Horreos et terram eorum illis tradens, quam possident usque in praesens. 23 Eveos quoque, qui habitabant in Aserim usque Gazam, Cappadoces expulerunt qui egressi de Cappadocia deleverunt eos et habitaverunt pro illis.

24 "'Surgite, et transite torrentem Arnon. Ecce! Tradidi in manu tua Seon, regem Esebon, Amorreum, et terram eius incipe possidere, et committe adversum eum proelium. 25 Hodie incipiam mittere terrorem atque formidinem tuam in populos qui habitant sub omni caelo, ut audito nomine tuo paveant et in morem parturientium contremescant et dolore teneantur.'

26 "Misi ergo nuntios de solitudine Cademoth ad Seon, regem Esebon, verbis pacificis, dicens, 27 'Transibimus per terram tuam; publica gradiemur via; non declinabimus neque ad dextram neque ad sinistram. 28 Alimenta pretio vende nobis ut vescamur; aquam pecunia tribue, et sic bibemus. Tantum est ut nobis concedas transitum, 29 sicut fecerunt filii Esau qui habitant in Seir et Moabitae qui morantur in Ar, donec veniamus ad Iordanem et transeamus ad terram quam Dominus, Deus noster, daturus est nobis.'

30 "Noluitque Seon, rex Esebon, dare nobis transitum quia induraverat Dominus, Deus tuus, spiritum eius et obfirmaverat cor illius ut traderetur in manus tuas, sicut nunc vides.

31 "Dixitque Dominus ad me, 'Ecce! Coepi tradere tibi Seon et terram eius; incipe possidere eam.' 32 Egressusque est Seon obviam nobis cum omni populo suo ad proelium in

Lord destroyed before their face, and he made them to dwell in their stead, 22 as he had done in favour of the children of Esau that dwell in Seir, destroying the Horim and delivering their land to them, which they possess to this day. 23 The Avvim also, that dwelt in Haserim as far as Gaza, *were expelled by the Cappadocians* who came out of Cappadocia and destroyed them and dwelt in their stead.

24 "'Arise ye, and pass the torrent Arnon. Behold! I have delivered into thy hand Sihon, king of Heshbon, the Amorite, and begin thou to possess his land, and make war against him. 25 This day will I begin to send the dread and fear of thee upon the nations that dwell under the whole heaven, that when they hear thy name they may fear and tremble and be in pain like women in travail.'

26 "So I sent messengers from the wilderness of Kedemoth to Sihon, the king of Heshbon, with peaceable words, saying, 27 'We will pass through thy land; we will go along by the highway; we will not turn aside neither to the right hand nor to the left. 28 Sell us meat for money that we may eat; give us water for money, and so we will drink. *We only ask that thou wilt let us pass through,* 29 as the children of Esau have done that dwell in Seir and the Moabites that abide in Ar, until we come to the Jordan and pass to the land which the Lord, our God, will give us.'

30 "And Sihon, the king of Heshbon, would not let us pass because the Lord, thy God, had hardened his spirit and fixed his heart that he might be delivered into thy hands, as now thou seest.

31 "And the Lord said to me, 'Behold! I have begun to deliver unto thee Sihon and his land; begin to possess it.' 32 And Sihon came out to meet us with all his people to fight at

Iesa, 33 et tradidit eum Dominus, Deus noster, nobis, percussimusque eum cum filiis suis et omni populo suo. 34 Cunc-
tasque urbes in tempore illo cepimus, interfectis habitatoribus earum, viris ac mulieribus et parvulis. Non reliquimus in
eis quicquam 35 absque iumentis quae in partem venere
praedantium et spoliis urbium quas cepimus. 36 Ab Aroer,
quae est super ripam torrentis Arnon, oppido quod in valle
situm est, usque Galaad, non fuit vicus et civitas quae nostras effugeret manus. Omnes tradidit Dominus, Deus noster, nobis 37 absque terra filiorum Ammon ad quam non ac-
cessimus et cunctis quae adiacent torrenti Ieboc et urbibus
montanis universisque locis a quibus nos prohibuit Dominus, Deus noster."

Caput 3

"Itaque conversi ascendimus per iter Basan, egressusque
est Og, rex Basan, in occursum nobis cum populo suo ad
bellandum in Edrai. 2 Dixitque Dominus ad me, 'Ne timeas
eum, quia in manu tua traditus est cum omni populo ac terra
sua, faciesque ei sicut fecisti Seon, regi Amorreorum, qui
habitavit in Esebon.'

Jahaz, 33 and the Lord, our God, delivered him to us, and we slew him with his sons and all his people. 34 And we took all his cities at that time, killing the inhabitants of them, men and women and children. We left nothing of them 35 except the cattle which came to the share of them that took them and the spoils of the cities which we took. 36 From Aroer, which is upon the bank of the torrent Arnon, a town that is situate in a valley, as far as Gilead, there was not a village or city that escaped our hands. The Lord, our God, delivered all unto us 37 except the land of the children of Ammon to which we approached not and all that border upon the torrent Jabbok and the cities in the mountains and all the places which the Lord, our God, forbade us."

Chapter 3

The victory over Og, king of Bashan. Reuben, Gad, and half the tribe of Manasseh receive their possession on the other side of Jordan.

"Then we turned and went by the way of Bashan, and Og, the king of Bashan, came out to meet us with his people to fight in Edrei. 2 And the Lord said to me, 'Fear him not, because he is delivered into thy hand with all his people and his land, and thou shalt do to him as thou hast done to Sihon, king of the Amorites, that dwelt in Heshbon.'

3 "Tradidit ergo Dominus, Deus noster, in manibus nostris etiam Og, regem Basan, et universum populum eius, percussimusque eos usque ad internicionem, 4 vastantes cunctas civitates illius uno tempore. Non fuit oppidum quod nos effugeret: sexaginta urbes, omnem regionem Argob, regni Og, in Basan. 5 Cunctae urbes erant munitae muris altissimis portisque et vectibus, absque oppidis innumeris quae non habebant muros. 6 Et delevimus eos sicut feceramus Seon, regi Esebon, disperdentes omnem civitatem virosque ac mulieres et parvulos. 7 Iumenta autem et spolia urbium diripuimus. 8 Tulimusque illo in tempore terram de manu duorum regum Amorreorum qui erant trans Iordanem, a torrente Arnon usque ad Montem Hermon, 9 quem Sidonii Sarion vocant et Amorrei Sanir, 10 omnes civitates quae sitae sunt in planitie et universam terram Galaad et Basan usque ad Selcha et Edrai, civitates regni Og in Basan, 11 solus quippe Og, rex Basan, restiterat de stirpe gigantum. Monstratur lectus eius ferreus, qui est in Rabbath filiorum Ammon, novem cubitos habens longitudinis et quattuor latitudinis, ad mensuram cubiti virilis manus.

12 "Terramque possedimus tempore illo ab Aroer, quae est super ripam torrentis Arnon, usque ad mediam partem Montis Galaad, et civitates illius dedi Ruben et Gad. 13 Reliquam autem partem Galaad et omnem Basan, regni Og, tradidi mediae tribui Manasse, omnem regionem Argob. Cunctaque Basan vocatur Terra Gigantum.

14 "Iair, filius Manasse, possedit omnem regionem Argob usque ad terminos Gesuri et Machathi. Vocavitque ex no-

3 "So the Lord, our God, delivered into our hands Og also, the king of Bashan, and all his people, and we utterly destroyed them, 4 wasting all his cities at one time. There was not a town that escaped us: sixty cities, all the country of Argob, the kingdom of Og, in Bashan. 5 All the cities were fenced with very high walls and with gates and bars, besides innumerable towns that had no walls. 6 And we utterly destroyed them as we had done to Sihon, the king of Heshbon, destroying every city, men and women and children. 7 But the cattle and the spoils of the cities we took for our prey. 8 And we took at that time the land out of the hand of the two kings of the Amorites that were beyond the Jordan, from the torrent Arnon unto the Mount Hermon, 9 which the Sidonians call Sirion and the Amorites Senir, 10 all the cities that are situate in the plain and all the land of Gilead and Bashan as far as Salecah and Edrei, cities of the kingdom of Og in Bashan, 11 for only Og, king of Bashan, remained of the race of the giants. His bed of iron is shewn, which is in Rabbah of the children of Ammon, being nine cubits long and four broad, after the measure of the cubit of a man's hand.

12 "And we possessed the land at that time from Aroer, which is upon the bank of the torrent Arnon, unto the half of Mount Gilead, and I gave the cities thereof to Reuben and Gad. 13 And I delivered the other part of Gilead and all Bashan, the kingdom of Og, to the half-tribe of Manasseh, all the country of Argob. And all Bashan is called the Land of Giants.

14 "Jair, the son of Manasseh, possessed all the country of Argob unto the borders of Geshur and Maacah. And he

mine suo Basan Avoth Iair, id est, villas Iair, usque in praesentem diem.

15 "Machir quoque dedi Galaad. 16 Et tribubus Ruben et
Gad dedi de terra Galaad usque ad torrentem Arnon, medium torrentis et confinium usque ad torrentem Ieboc, qui
est terminus filiorum Ammon, 17 et planitiem solitudinis atque Iordanem et terminos Chenereth usque ad mare deserti, quod est Salsissimum, ad radices Montis Phasga contra
orientem.

18 "Praecepique vobis in tempore illo, dicens, 'Dominus,
Deus vester, dat vobis terram hanc in hereditatem; expediti
praecedite fratres vestros filios Israhel, omnes viri robusti,
19 absque uxoribus et parvulis ac iumentis, novi enim quod
plura habeatis pecora, et in urbibus remanere debebunt quas
tradidi vobis, 20 donec requiem tribuat Dominus fratribus
vestris sicut vobis tribuit, et possideant etiam ipsi terram
quam daturus est eis trans Iordanem, tunc revertetur unusquisque in possessionem suam quam dedi vobis.'

21 "Iosue quoque in tempore illo praecepi, dicens, 'Oculi
tui viderunt quae fecit Dominus, Deus vester, duobus his
regibus; sic faciet omnibus regnis ad quae transiturus es.
22 Ne timeas eos, Dominus enim, Deus vester, pugnabit pro
vobis.'

23 "Precatusque sum Dominum in tempore illo, dicens,
24 'Domine Deus, tu coepisti ostendere servo tuo magnitudinem tuam manumque fortissimam, neque enim est alius
Deus vel in caelo vel in terra qui possit facere opera tua et
conparari fortitudini tuae. 25 Transibo igitur et videbo terram hanc optimam trans Iordanem et montem istum egre-
gium et Libanum.'

called Bashan by his own name Havvoth Jair, that is to say, the towns of Jair, until this present day.

15 "To Machir also I gave Gilead. 16 And to the tribes of Reuben and Gad I gave of the land of Gilead as far as the torrent Arnon, half the torrent and the confines even unto the torrent Jabbok, which is the border of the children of Ammon, 17 and the plain of the wilderness and the Jordan and the borders of Chinnereth unto the sea of the desert, which is the Most Salt *Sea,* to the foot of Mount Pisgah eastward.

18 "And I commanded you at that time, saying, 'The Lord, your God, giveth you this land for an inheritance; go ye well appointed before your brethren the children of Israel, all the strong men of you, 19 leaving your wives and children and cattle, for I know you have much cattle, and they must remain in the cities which I have delivered to you, 20 until the Lord give rest to your brethren as he hath given to you, and they also possess the land which he will give them beyond the Jordan, then shall every man return to his possession which I have given you.'

21 "I commanded Joshua also at that time, saying, 'Thy eyes have seen what the Lord, your God, hath done to these two kings; so will he do to all the kingdoms to which thou shalt pass. 22 Fear them not, for the Lord, your God, will fight for you.'

23 "And I besought the Lord at that time, saying, 24 'Lord God, thou hast begun to shew unto thy servant thy greatness and most mighty hand, for there is no other God either in heaven or earth that is able to do thy works or to be compared to thy strength. 25 I will pass over therefore and will see this excellent land beyond the Jordan and this goodly mountain and Libanus.'

26 "Iratusque est Dominus mihi propter vos nec exaudivit me sed dixit mihi, 'Sufficit tibi; nequaquam ultra loquaris de hac re ad me. 27 Ascende cacumen Phasgae, et oculos tuos circumfer ad occidentem et ad aquilonem austrumque et orientem, et aspice, nec enim transibis Iordanem istum.

28 "'Praecipe Iosue, et corrobora eum atque conforta, quia ipse praecedet populum istum et dividet eis terram quam visurus es.'

29 "Mansimusque in valle contra fanum Phogor."

Caput 4

"Et nunc, Israhel, audi praecepta et iudicia quae ego doceo te ut faciens ea vivas et ingrediens possideas terram quam Dominus, Deus patrum vestrorum, daturus est vobis. 2 Non addetis ad verbum quod vobis loquor, neque aufere-

26 "And the Lord was angry with me on your account and heard me not but said to me, 'It is enough; speak no more to me of this matter. 27 Go up to the top of Pisgah, and cast thy eyes round about to the west and to the north and *to* the south and *to* the east, and behold it, for thou shalt not pass this Jordan.

28 "'Command Joshua, and encourage and strengthen him, for he shall go before this people and shall divide unto them the land which thou shalt see.'

29 "And we abode in the valley over against the temple of Peor."

Chapter 4

Moses exhorteth the people to keep God's commandments,
particularly to fly idolatry, appointeth three cities of refuge
on that side of the Jordan.

"And now, O Israel, hear the commandments and judgments which I teach thee that doing them thou mayst live and entering in mayst possess the land which the Lord, the God of your fathers, will give you. 2 You shall not add to the word that I speak to you, neither shall you take away from

tis ex eo. Custodite mandata Domini, Dei vestri, quae ego praecipio vobis.

3 "Oculi vestri viderunt omnia quae fecit Dominus contra Beelphegor, quomodo contriverit omnes cultores eius de medio vestri, 4 vos autem qui adheretis Domino, Deo vestro, vivitis universi usque in praesentem diem. 5 Scitis quod docuerim vos praecepta atque iustitias; sicut mandavit mihi Dominus, Deus meus, sic facietis ea in terra quam possessuri estis, 6 et observabitis et implebitis opere, haec est enim vestra sapientia et intellectus coram populis, ut audientes universa praecepta haec dicant, 'En: populus sapiens et intellegens, gens magna.' 7 Nec est alia natio tam grandis quae habeat deos adpropinquantes sibi sicut Deus noster adest cunctis obsecrationibus nostris, 8 quae est enim alia gens sic inclita ut habeat caerimonias iustaque iudicia et universam legem quam ego proponam hodie ante oculos vestros?

9 "Custodi igitur temet ipsum et animam tuam sollicite. Ne obliviscaris verborum quae viderunt oculi tui, et ne excidant de corde tuo cunctis diebus vitae tuae. Docebis ea filios ac nepotes tuos, 10 die in quo stetisti coram Domino, Deo tuo, in Horeb quando Dominus locutus est mihi, dicens, 'Congrega ad me populum ut audiant sermones meos et discant timere me omni tempore quo vivunt in terra doceantque filios suos.' 11 Et accessistis ad radices montis, qui ardebat usque ad caelum, erantque in eo tenebrae et nubes et caligo. 12 Locutusque est Dominus ad vos de medio ignis. Vocem verborum eius audistis, et formam penitus non vidistis. 13 Et ostendit vobis pactum suum quod praecepit ut faceretis et decem verba quae scripsit in duabus tabulis lapi-

it. Keep the commandments of the Lord, your God, which I command you.

3 "Your eyes have seen all that the Lord hath done against Baal of Peor, how he hath destroyed all his worshippers from among you, 4 but you that adhere to the Lord, your God, are all alive until this present day. 5 You know that I have taught you statutes and justices; as the Lord, my God, hath commanded me, so shall you do them in the land which you shall possess, 6 and you shall observe and fulfil them in practice, for this is your wisdom and understanding in the sight of *nations,* that hearing all these precepts they may say, 'Behold: a wise and understanding people, a great nation.' 7 Neither is there any other nation so great that hath gods so nigh them as our God is present to all our petitions, 8 for what other nation is there so renowned that hath ceremonies and just judgments and all the law which I will set forth this day before your eyes?

9 "Keep thyself therefore and thy soul carefully. Forget not the words that thy eyes have seen, and let them not *go* out of thy heart all the days of thy life. Thou shalt teach them to thy sons and to thy grandsons, 10 *from* the day in which thou didst stand before the Lord, thy God, in Horeb, when the Lord spoke to me, saying, 'Call together the people unto me that they may hear my words and may learn to fear me all the time that they live on the earth and may teach their children.' 11 And you came to the foot of the mount, which burned even unto heaven, and there was darkness and a cloud and obscurity in it. 12 And the Lord spoke to you from the midst of the fire. You heard the voice of his words, but you saw not any form at all. 13 And he shewed you his covenant which he commanded you to do and the ten

deis, 14 mihique mandavit in illo tempore ut docerem vos caerimonias et iudicia quae facere deberetis in terra quam possessuri estis.

15 "Custodite igitur sollicite animas vestras. Non vidistis aliquam similitudinem in die qua locutus est Dominus vobis in Horeb de medio ignis 16 ne forte decepti faciatis vobis sculptam similitudinem aut imaginem masculi vel feminae, 17 similitudinem omnium iumentorum quae sunt super terram vel avium sub caelo volantium 18 atque reptilium quae moventur in terra sive piscium qui sub terra morantur in aquis, 19 ne forte oculis elevatis ad caelum videas solem et lunam et omnia astra caeli et errore deceptus adores ea et colas quae creavit Dominus, Deus tuus, in ministerium cunctis gentibus quae sub caelo sunt.

20 "Vos autem tulit Dominus et eduxit de fornace ferrea Aegypti ut haberet populum hereditarium, sicut est in praesenti die. 21 Iratusque est Dominus contra me propter sermones vestros, et iuravit ut non transirem Iordanem nec ingrederer terram optimam quam daturus est vobis. 22 Ecce: morior in hac humo; non transibo Iordanem. Vos transibitis et possidebitis terram egregiam. 23 Cave nequando obliviscaris pacti Domini, Dei tui, quod pepigit tecum et facias tibi sculptam similitudinem eorum quae fieri Dominus prohibuit, 24 quia Dominus, Deus tuus, ignis consumens est, Deus aemulator.

25 "Si genueritis filios ac nepotes et morati fueritis in terra deceptique feceritis vobis aliquam similitudinem, patrantes malum coram Domino, Deo vestro, ut eum ad iracundiam

words that he wrote in two tables of stone, 14 and he commanded me at that time that I should teach you the ceremonies and judgments which you *shall* do in the land that you shall possess.

15 "Keep therefore your souls carefully. You saw not any similitude in the day that the Lord God spoke to you in Horeb from the midst of the fire 16 lest perhaps being deceived you might make you a graven similitude or image of male or female, 17 the similitude of any beasts that are upon the earth or of birds that fly under heaven 18 or of creeping things that move on the earth or of fishes that abide in the waters under the earth, 19 lest perhaps lifting up thy eyes to heaven thou see the sun and the moon and all the stars of heaven and being deceived by error thou adore and serve them which the Lord, thy God, created for the service of all the nations that are under heaven.

20 "But the Lord hath taken you and brought you out of the iron furnace of Egypt to *make* you his people of inheritance, as it is this present day. 21 And the Lord was angry with me for your words, and he swore that I should not pass over the Jordan nor enter into the excellent land which he will give you. 22 Behold: I die in this land; I shall not pass over the Jordan. You shall pass and possess the goodly land. 23 Beware lest thou ever forget the covenant of the Lord, thy God, which he hath made with thee and make to thyself a graven likeness of those things which the Lord hath forbid to be made, 24 because the Lord, thy God, is a consuming fire, a jealous God.

25 "If you shall beget sons and grandsons and abide in the land and being deceived make to yourselves any similitude, committing evil before the Lord, your God, to provoke him

provocetis, 26 testes invoco hodie caelum et terram cito perituros vos esse de terra quam, transito Iordane, possessuri estis. Non habitabitis in ea longo tempore, sed delebit vos Dominus 27 atque disperget in omnes gentes, et remanebitis pauci in nationibus ad quas vos ducturus est Dominus. 28 Ibique servietis diis qui hominum manu fabricati sunt, ligno et lapidi qui non vident nec audiunt nec comedunt nec odorantur.

29 "Cumque quaesieris ibi Dominum, Deum tuum, invenies eum, si tamen toto corde quaesieris et tota tribulatione animae tuae. 30 Postquam te invenerint omnia quae praedicta sunt, novissimo tempore reverteris ad Dominum, Deum tuum, et audies vocem eius, 31 quia Deus misericors Dominus, Deus tuus, est. Non dimittet te nec omnino delebit neque obliviscetur pacti in quo iuravit patribus tuis.

32 "Interroga de diebus antiquis qui fuerunt ante te ex die quo creavit Deus hominem super terram a summo caeli usque ad summum eius si facta est aliquando huiuscemodi res aut umquam cognitum est 33 ut audiret populus vocem Dei loquentis de medio ignis sicut tu audisti et vixisti, 34 si fecit Deus ut ingrederetur et tolleret sibi gentem de medio nationum per temptationes, signa atque portenta, per pugnam et robustam manum extentumque brachium et horribiles visiones iuxta omnia quae fecit pro vobis Dominus, Deus vester, in Aegypto, videntibus oculis tuis 35 ut scires quoniam Dominus, ipse est Deus, et non est alius praeter eum.

36 "De caelo te fecit audire vocem suam ut doceret te. Et in terra ostendit tibi ignem suum maximum, et audisti verba

to wrath, 26 I call this day heaven and earth to witness that you shall quickly perish out of the land which, when you have passed over the Jordan, you shall possess. You shall not dwell therein long, but the Lord will destroy you 27 and scatter you among all nations, and you shall remain a few among the nations to which the Lord shall lead you. 28 And there you shall serve gods that were framed with men's hands, wood and stone that neither see nor hear nor eat nor smell.

29 "And when thou shalt seek there the Lord, thy God, thou shalt find him, yet so if thou seek him with all thy heart and all the affliction of thy soul. 30 After all the things aforesaid shall find thee, in the latter time thou shalt return to the Lord, thy God, and shalt hear his voice, 31 because the Lord, thy God, is a merciful God. He will not leave thee nor altogether destroy thee nor forget the covenant by which he swore to thy fathers.

32 "Ask of the days of old that have been before *thy time* from the day that God created man upon the earth from one end of heaven to the other end thereof if ever there was done the like thing or it hath been known at any time 33 that a people should hear the voice of God speaking out of the midst of fire as thou hast heard and lived, 34 if God ever did so as to go and take to himself a nation out of the midst of nations by temptations, signs and wonders, by fight and a strong hand and stretched out arm and horrible visions according to all the things that the Lord, your God, did for you in Egypt, before thy eyes 35 that thou mightest know that the Lord, he is God, and there is no other besides him.

36 "From heaven he made thee to hear his voice that he might teach thee. And upon earth he shewed thee his exceeding great fire, and thou didst hear his words out of the

illius de medio ignis 37 quia dilexit patres tuos et elegit semen eorum post eos. Eduxitque te, praecedens in virtute sua
magna, ex Aegypto 38 ut deleret nationes maximas et fortiores te in introitu tuo et introduceret te daretque tibi terram
earum in possessionem, sicut cernis in praesenti die.

39 "Scito ergo hodie, et cogitato in corde tuo quod Dominus, ipse sit Deus in caelo sursum et in terra deorsum, et non
sit alius. 40 Custodi praecepta eius atque mandata quae ego
praecipio tibi ut bene sit tibi et filiis tuis post te et perma-
neas multo tempore super terram quam Dominus, Deus
tuus, daturus est tibi."

41 Tunc separavit Moses tres civitates trans Iordanem ad
orientalem plagam 42 ut confugiat ad eas qui occiderit nolens proximum suum nec sibi fuerit inimicus ante unum et
alterum diem et ad harum aliquam urbium possit evadere:
43 Bosor in solitudine, quae sita est in terra campestri de
tribu Ruben, et Ramoth in Galaad, quae est in tribu Gad, et
Golam in Basan, quae est in tribu Manasse.

44 Ista est lex quam proposuit Moses coram filiis Israhel,
45 et haec testimonia et caerimoniae atque iudicia quae locutus est ad filios Israhel quando egressi sunt de Aegypto
46 trans Iordanem in valle contra fanum Phogor, in terra
Seon, regis Amorrei qui habitavit in Esebon quem percussit Moses. Filii quoque Israhel egressi ex Aegypto 47 possederunt terram eius et terram Og, regis Basan, duorum
regum Amorreorum qui erant trans Iordanem ad solis
ortum 48 ab Aroer, quae sita est super ripam torrentis

midst of the fire 37 because he loved thy fathers and chose their seed after them. And he brought thee out of Egypt, going before thee with his great power 38 to destroy at thy coming very great nations and stronger than thou art and to bring thee in and give thee their land for a possession, as thou seest at this present day.

39 "Know therefore this day, and think in thy heart that the Lord, he is God in heaven above and in the earth beneath, and there is no other. 40 Keep his precepts and commandments which I command thee that it may be well with thee and thy children after thee and thou mayst remain a long time upon the land which the Lord, thy God, will give thee."

41 Then Moses set aside three cities beyond the Jordan at the east side 42 that any one might flee to them who should kill his neighbour unwillingly and was not his enemy a day or two before and that he might escape to some one of these cities: 43 Bezer in the wilderness, which is situate in the plains of the tribe of Reuben, and Ramoth in Gilead, which is in the tribe of Gad, and Golan in Bashan, which is in the tribe of Manasseh.

44 This is the law that Moses set before the children of Israel, 45 and these are the testimonies and ceremonies and judgments which he spoke to the children of Israel when they came out of Egypt 46 beyond the Jordan in the valley over against the temple of Peor, in the land of Sihon, king of the Amorites that dwelt in Heshbon whom Moses slew. And the children of Israel coming out of Egypt 47 possessed his land and the land of Og, king of Bashan, of the two kings of the Amorites who were beyond the Jordan towards the rising of the sun 48 from Aroer, which is situate upon the bank

Arnon, usque ad montem Sion, qui est et Hermon, 49 omnem planitiem trans Iordanem ad orientalem plagam usque ad mare solitudinis et usque ad radices Montis Phasga.

Caput 5

Vocavitque Moses omnem Israhelem et dixit ad eum, "Audi, Israhel, caerimonias atque iudicia quae ego loquor in auribus vestris hodie. Discite ea, et opere conplete.

2 "Dominus, Deus noster, pepigit nobiscum foedus in Horeb. 3 Non cum patribus nostris iniit pactum, sed nobiscum qui inpraesentiarum sumus et vivimus. 4 Facie ad faciem locutus est nobis in monte de medio ignis. 5 Ego sequester et medius fui inter Dominum et vos in tempore illo ut adnuntiarem vobis verba eius, timuistis enim ignem et non ascendistis in montem, et ait, 6 'Ego Dominus, Deus tuus, qui eduxi te de terra Aegypti, de domo servitutis; 7 non habebis deos alienos in conspectu meo.

8 "'Non facies tibi sculptile nec similitudinem omnium quae in caelo sunt desuper et quae in terra deorsum et quae versantur in aquis sub terra. 9 Non adorabis ea, et non coles, ego enim sum Dominus, Deus tuus, Deus aemulator, red-

of the torrent Arnon, unto Mount Sion, which is also *called* Hermon, 49 all the plain beyond the Jordan at the east side unto the sea of the wilderness and unto the foot of Mount Pisgah.

Chapter 5

The ten commandments are repeated and explained.

And Moses called all Israel and said to them, "Hear, O Israel, the ceremonies and judgments which I speak in your ears this day. Learn them, and fulfil them in work.

2 "The Lord, our God, made a covenant with us in Horeb. 3 He made not the covenant with our fathers, but with us who are *now present and living.* 4 He spoke to us face to face in the mount out of the midst of fire. 5 I was the mediator and stood between the Lord and you at that time to shew you his words, for you feared the fire and went not up into the mountain, and he said, 6 'I am the Lord, thy God, who brought thee out of the land of Egypt, out of the house of bondage; 7 thou shalt not have strange gods in my sight.

8 "'Thou shalt not make to thy self a graven thing nor the likeness of any things that are in heaven above or that are in the earth beneath or that abide in the waters under the earth. 9 Thou shalt not adore them, and thou shalt not serve them, for I am the Lord, thy God, a jealous God, visiting

dens iniquitatem patrum super filios in tertiam et quartam generationem his qui oderunt me, 10 et faciens misericordiam in multa milia diligentibus me et custodientibus praecepta mea.

11 "Non usurpabis nomen Domini, Dei tui, frustra, quia non erit inpunitus qui super re vana nomen eius adsumpserit.

12 "Observa diem sabbati ut sanctifices eum, sicut praecepit tibi Dominus, Deus tuus. 13 Sex diebus operaberis et facies omnia opera tua. 14 Septimus dies sabbati est, id est, requies Domini, Dei tui. Non facies in eo quicquam operis, tu et filius tuus et filia, servus et ancilla et bos et asinus et omne iumentum tuum et peregrinus qui est intra portas tuas, ut requiescat servus tuus et ancilla tua sicut et tu. 15 Memento quod et ipse servieris in Aegypto, et eduxerit te inde Dominus, Deus tuus, in manu forti et brachio extento. Idcirco praecepit tibi ut observares diem sabbati.

16 "Honora patrem tuum et matrem sicut praecepit tibi Dominus, Deus tuus, ut longo vivas tempore et bene sit tibi in terra quam Dominus, Deus tuus, daturus est tibi.

17 "Non occides.

18 "Neque moechaberis.

19 "Furtumque non facies.

20 "Nec loqueris contra proximum tuum falsum testimonium.

21 "Non concupisces uxorem proximi tui non domum

the iniquity of the fathers upon their children unto the third and fourth generation to them that hate me, 10 and shewing mercy unto many thousands to them that love me and keep my commandments.

11 "'Thou shalt not take the name of the Lord, thy God, in vain, for he shall not be unpunished that taketh his name upon a vain thing.

12 "'Observe the day of the sabbath to sanctify it, as the Lord, thy God, hath commanded thee. 13 Six days shalt thou labour and shalt do all thy works. 14 The seventh is the day of the sabbath, that is, the rest of the Lord, thy God. Thou shalt not do any work therein, thou nor thy son nor *thy* daughter nor *thy* manservant nor *thy* maidservant nor *thy* ox nor *thy* ass nor any of thy beasts nor the stranger that is within thy gates, that thy manservant and thy maidservant may rest even as thyself. 15 Remember that thou also didst serve in Egypt, and the Lord, thy God, brought thee out from thence with a strong hand and a stretched out arm. Therefore hath he commanded thee that thou shouldst observe the sabbath day.

16 "'Honour thy father and mother as the Lord, thy God, hath commanded thee that thou mayst live a long time and it may be well with thee in the land which the Lord, thy God, will give thee.

17 "'Thou shalt not kill.

18 "'Neither shalt thou commit adultery.

19 "'And thou shalt not steal.

20 "'Neither shalt thou bear false witness against thy neighbour.

21 "'Thou shalt not covet thy neighbour's wife nor his

non agrum non servum non ancillam non bovem non asinum et universa quae illius sunt.'

22 "Haec verba locutus est Dominus ad omnem multitudinem vestram in monte de medio ignis et nubis et caliginis voce magna, nihil addens amplius, et scripsit ea in duabus tabulis lapideis quas tradidit mihi. 23 Vos autem, postquam audistis vocem de medio tenebrarum et montem ardere vidistis, accessistis ad me, omnes principes tribuum et maiores natu, atque dixistis, 24 'Ecce! Ostendit nobis Dominus, Deus noster, maiestatem et magnitudinem suam; vocem eius audivimus de medio ignis et probavimus hodie quod, loquente Deo cum homine, vixerit homo. 25 Cur ergo moriemur, et devorabit nos ignis hic maximus? Si enim audierimus ultra vocem Domini, Dei nostri, moriemur. 26 Quid est omnis caro, ut audiat vocem Dei viventis qui de medio ignis loquitur, sicut nos audivimus, et possit vivere? 27 Tu magis accede, et audi cuncta quae dixerit Dominus, Deus noster, tibi. Loquerisque ad nos, et nos audientes faciemus ea.'

28 "Quod cum audisset Dominus, ait ad me, 'Audivi vocem verborum populi huius quae locuti sunt tibi; bene omnia sunt locuti. 29 Quis det talem eos habere mentem ut timeant me et custodiant universa mandata mea in omni tempore ut bene sit eis et filiis eorum in sempiternum? 30 Vade, et dic eis, "Revertimini in tentoria vestra." 31 Tu vero hic sta mecum, et loquar tibi omnia mandata mea et caerimonias atque iudicia, quae docebis eos ut faciant ea in terra quam dabo illis in possessionem.'

house nor his field nor his manservant nor his maidservant nor his ox nor his ass nor any thing that is his.'

22 "These words the Lord spoke to all the multitude of you in the mountain out of the midst of the fire and the cloud and the darkness with a loud voice, adding nothing more, and he wrote them in two tables of stone which he delivered unto me. 23 But you, after you heard the voice out of the midst of the darkness and saw the mountain burn, came to me, all the princes of the tribes and the elders, and you said, 24 'Behold! The Lord, our God, hath shewn us his majesty and his greatness; we have heard his voice out of the midst of the fire and have proved this day that, God speaking with man, man hath lived. 25 Why shall we die therefore, and why shall this exceeding great fire consume us? For if we hear the voice of the Lord, our God, any more, we shall die. 26 What is all flesh, that it should hear the voice of the living God who speaketh out of the midst of the fire, as we have heard, and be able to live? 27 Approach thou rather, and hear all things that the Lord, our God, shall say to thee. And thou shalt speak to us, and we will hear and will do them.'

28 "And when the Lord had heard this, he said to me, 'I have heard the voice of the words of this people which they spoke to thee; they have spoken all things well. 29 Who shall give them to have such a mind to fear me and to keep all my commandments at all times that it may be well with them and with their children for ever? 30 Go, and say to them, "Return into your tents." 31 But stand thou here with me, and I will speak to thee all my commandments and ceremonies and judgments, which thou shalt teach them that they may do them in the land which I will give them for a possession.'

³² "Custodite igitur et facite quae praecepit Dominus Deus vobis; non declinabitis, neque ad dextram neque ad sinistram, ³³ sed per viam quam praecepit Dominus, Deus vester, ambulabitis ut vivatis et bene sit vobis et protelentur dies in terra possessionis vestrae."

Caput 6

"Haec sunt praecepta et caerimoniae atque iudicia quae mandavit Dominus, Deus vester, ut docerem vos et faciatis ea in terra ad quam transgredimini possidendam, 2 ut timeas Dominum, Deum tuum, et custodias omnia mandata et praecepta eius quae ego praecipio tibi et filiis ac nepotibus tuis cunctis diebus vitae tuae, ut prolongentur dies tui.

3 "Audi, Israhel, et observa ut facias quae praecepit tibi Dominus, et bene sit tibi et multipliceris amplius, sicut pollicitus est Dominus, Deus patrum tuorum, tibi terram lacte et melle manantem.

4 "Audi, Israhel, Dominus, Deus noster, Dominus unus est. 5 Diliges Dominum, Deum tuum, ex toto corde tuo et ex tota anima tua et ex tota fortitudine tua. 6 Eruntque

32 "Keep therefore and do the things which the Lord God hath commanded you; you shall not go aside, neither to the right hand nor to the left, 33 but you shall walk in the way that the Lord, your God, hath commanded that you may live and it may be well with you and your days may be long in the land of your possession."

Chapter 6

An exhortation to the love of God and obedience to his law.

"These are the precepts and ceremonies and judgments which the Lord, your God, commanded that I should teach you and that you should do them in the land into which you pass over to possess it, 2 that thou mayst fear the Lord, thy God, and keep all his commandments and precepts which I command thee and thy sons and thy grandsons all the days of thy life, that thy days may be prolonged.

3 "Hear, O Israel, and observe to do the things which the Lord hath commanded thee, *that* it may be well with thee and thou mayst be greatly multiplied, as the Lord, the God of thy fathers, hath promised thee a land flowing with milk and honey.

4 "Hear, O Israel, the Lord, our God, is one Lord. 5 Thou shalt love the Lord, thy God, with thy whole heart and with thy whole soul and with thy whole strength. 6 And these

verba haec quae ego praecipio tibi hodie in corde tuo, 7 et narrabis ea filiis tuis, et meditaberis sedens in domo tua et ambulans in itinere, dormiens atque consurgens. 8 Et ligabis ea quasi signum in manu tua, eruntque et movebuntur inter oculos tuos. 9 Scribesque ea in limine et ostiis domus tuae. 10 Cumque introduxerit te Dominus, Deus tuus, in terram pro qua iuravit patribus tuis Abraham, Isaac et Iacob et dederit tibi civitates magnas et optimas quas non aedificasti, 11 domos plenas cunctarum opum quas non extruxisti, cisternas quas non fodisti, vineta et oliveta quae non plantasti 12 et comederis et saturatus fueris, 13 cave diligenter ne obliviscaris Domini qui eduxit te de terra Aegypti, de domo servitutis. Dominum, Deum tuum, timebis et ipsi soli servies, ac per nomen illius iurabis.

14 "Non ibitis post deos alienos cunctarum gentium quae in circuitu vestro sunt, 15 quoniam Deus aemulator Dominus, Deus tuus, in medio tui, nequando irascatur furor Domini, Dei tui, contra te et auferat te de superficie terrae.

16 "Non temptabis Dominum, Deum tuum, sicut temptasti in Loco Temptationis.

17 "Custodi praecepta Domini, Dei tui, ac testimonia et caerimonias quas praecepit tibi, 18 et fac quod placitum est et bonum in conspectu Domini, ut bene sit tibi et ingressus possideas terram optimam de qua iuravit Dominus patribus tuis 19 ut deleret omnes inimicos tuos coram te, sicut locutus est.

words which I command thee this day shall be in thy heart, 7 and thou shalt tell them to thy children, and thou shalt meditate *upon them* sitting in thy house and walking on thy journey, sleeping and rising. 8 And thou shalt bind them as a sign on thy hand, and they shall be and shall move between thy eyes. 9 And thou shalt write them in the entry and on the doors of thy house. 10 And when the Lord, thy God, shall have brought thee into the land for which he swore to thy fathers Abraham, Isaac and Jacob and shall have given thee great and goodly cities which thou didst not build, 11 houses full of *riches* which thou didst not set up, cisterns which thou didst not dig, vineyards and oliveyards which thou didst not plant 12 and thou shalt have eaten and be full, 13 take heed diligently lest thou forget the Lord who brought thee out of the land of Egypt, out of the house of bondage. Thou shalt fear the Lord, thy God, and shalt serve him only, and thou shalt swear by his name.

14 "You shall not go after the strange gods of all the nations that are round about you, 15 because the Lord, thy God, is a jealous God in the midst of thee, lest at any time the wrath of the Lord, thy God, be kindled against thee and take thee away from the face of the earth.

16 "Thou shalt not tempt the Lord, thy God, as thou temptedst him in the Place of Temptation.

17 "Keep the precepts of the Lord, thy God, and the testimonies and ceremonies which he hath commanded thee, 18 and do that which is pleasing and good in the sight of the Lord, that it may be well with thee and going in thou mayst possess the goodly land concerning which the Lord swore to thy fathers 19 that he would destroy all thy enemies before thee, as he hath spoken.

20 "Cumque interrogaverit te filius tuus cras, dicens, 'Quid sibi volunt testimonia haec et caerimoniae atque iudicia quae praecepit Dominus, Deus noster, nobis?' 21 dices ei, 'Servi eramus Pharaonis in Aegypto, et eduxit nos Dominus de Aegypto in manu forti. 22 Fecitque signa atque prodigia magna et pessima in Aegypto contra Pharaonem et omnem domum illius in conspectu nostro, 23 et eduxit nos inde ut introductis daret terram super qua iuravit patribus nostris. 24 Praecepitque nobis Dominus ut faciamus omnia legitima haec et timeamus Dominum, Deum nostrum, ut bene sit nobis cunctis diebus vitae nostrae, sicut est hodie. 25 Eritque nostri misericors si custodierimus et fecerimus omnia praecepta eius coram Domino, Deo nostro, sicut mandavit nobis.'"

Caput 7

"Cum introduxerit te Dominus, Deus tuus, in terram quam possessurus ingrederis et deleverit gentes multas coram te, Hettheum et Gergeseum et Amorreum et Chana-

20 "And when thy son shall ask thee to-morrow, saying, 'What mean these testimonies and ceremonies and judgments which the Lord, our God, hath commanded us?' 21 thou shalt say to him, 'We were bondmen of Pharaoh in Egypt, and the Lord brought us out of Egypt with a strong hand. 22 And he wrought signs and wonders great and very grievous in Egypt against Pharaoh and all his house in our sight, 23 and he brought us out from thence that he might bring us in and give us the land concerning which he swore to our fathers. 24 And the Lord commanded that we should do all these ordinances and should fear the Lord, our God, that it might be well with us all the days of our life, as it is at this day. 25 And he will be merciful to us if we keep and do all his precepts before the Lord, our God, as he hath commanded us.'"

Chapter 7

No league nor fellowship to be made with the Canaanites. God promiseth his people his blessing and assistance if they keep his commandments.

"When the Lord, thy God, shall have brought thee into the land which thou art going in to possess and shall have destroyed many nations before thee, the Hittite and the Girgashite and the Amorite and the Canaanite and the Per-

neum et Ferezeum et Eveum et Iebuseum, septem gentes
multo maioris numeri quam tu es et robustiores te, 2 tradi-
deritque eas Dominus, Deus tuus, tibi, percuties eas usque
ad internicionem. Non inibis cum eis foedus nec misereberis earum. 3 Neque sociabis cum eis coniugia: filiam tuam
non dabis filio eius nec filiam illius accipies filio tuo, 4 quia
seducet filium tuum ne sequatur me et ut magis serviat diis
alienis irasceturque furor Domini et delebit te cito.

5 "Quin potius haec facietis eis: aras eorum subvertite, et
confringite statuas, lucosque succidite, et sculptilia conburite, 6 quia populus sanctus es Domino, Deo tuo. Te elegit
Dominus, Deus tuus, ut sis ei populus peculiaris de cunctis
populis qui sunt super terram.

7 "Non quia cunctas gentes numero vincebatis vobis iunctus est Dominus et elegit vos, cum omnibus sitis populis
pauciores, 8 sed quia dilexit vos Dominus et custodivit iuramentum quod iuravit patribus vestris eduxitque vos in manu
forti et redemit de domo servitutis de manu Pharaonis, regis Aegypti.

9 "Et scies quia Dominus, Deus tuus, ipse est Deus fortis
et fidelis, custodiens pactum et misericordiam diligentibus
se et his qui custodiunt praecepta eius in mille generationes, 10 et reddens odientibus se statim ita ut disperdat eos
et ultra non differat, protinus eis restituens quod merentur.
11 Custodi ergo praecepta et caerimonias atque iudicia quae
ego mando tibi hodie ut facias.

izzite and the Hivite and the Jebusite, seven nations much more numerous than thou art and stronger than thou, 2 and the Lord, thy God, shall have delivered them to thee, thou shalt utterly destroy them. Thou shalt make no league with them nor shew mercy to them. 3 Neither shalt thou make marriages with them: thou shalt not give thy daughter to his son nor take his daughter for thy son, 4 for she will turn away thy son from following me that he may rather serve strange gods and the wrath of the Lord will be kindled and will quickly destroy thee.

5 "But thus rather shall you deal with them: destroy their altars, and break their statues, and cut down their groves, and burn their graven things, 6 because thou art a holy people to the Lord, thy God. The Lord, thy God, hath chosen thee to be his peculiar people of all peoples that are upon the earth.

7 "Not because you surpass all nations in number is the Lord joined unto you and hath chosen you, for you are *the fewest of any people,* 8 but because the Lord hath loved you and hath kept his oath which he swore to your fathers and hath brought you out with a strong hand and redeemed you from the house of bondage out of the hand of Pharaoh, the king of Egypt.

9 "And thou shalt know that the Lord, thy God, he is a strong and faithful God, keeping his covenant and mercy to them that love him and to them that keep his commandments unto a thousand generations, 10 and repaying forthwith them that hate him so as to destroy them without further delay, immediately rendering to them what they deserve. 11 Keep therefore the precepts and ceremonies and judgments which I command thee this day to do.

12 "Si, postquam audieris haec iudicia, custodieris ea et feceris, custodiet et Dominus, Deus tuus, tibi pactum et misericordiam quam iuravit patribus tuis. 13 Et diliget te ac multiplicabit benedicetque fructui ventris tui et fructui terrae tuae, frumento tuo atque vindemiae, oleo et armentis, gregibus ovium tuarum super terram pro qua iuravit patribus tuis ut daret eam tibi.

14 "Benedictus eris inter omnes populos. Non erit apud te sterilis utriusque sexus, tam in hominibus quam in gregibus tuis. 15 Auferet Dominus a te omnem languorem, et infirmitates Aegypti pessimas quas novisti non inferet tibi, sed cunctis hostibus tuis.

16 "Devorabis omnes populos quos Dominus, Deus tuus, daturus est tibi. Non parcet eis oculus tuus, nec servies diis eorum, ne sint in ruinam tui.

17 "Si dixeris in corde tuo, 'Plures sunt gentes istae quam ego; quomodo potero delere eas?' 18 noli metuere, sed recordare quae fecerit Dominus, Deus tuus, Pharaoni et cunctis Aegyptiis—19 plagas maximas quas viderunt oculi tui et signa atque portenta manumque robustam et extentum brachium ut educeret te Dominus, Deus tuus—sic faciet cunctis populis quos metuis. 20 Insuper et crabrones mittet Dominus, Deus tuus, in eos donec deleat omnes atque disperdat qui te fugerint et latere potuerint. 21 Non timebis eos, quia Dominus, Deus tuus, in medio tui est, Deus magnus et terribilis. 22 Ipse consumet nationes has in conspectu tuo paulatim atque per partes. Non poteris delere eas pariter ne forte multiplicentur contra te bestiae terrae, 23 dabitque eos Dominus, Deus tuus, in conspectu tuo et

12 "If, after thou hast heard these judgments, thou keep and do them, the Lord, thy God, will also keep his covenant to thee and the mercy which he swore to thy fathers. 13 And he will love thee and multiply thee and will bless the fruit of thy womb and the fruit of thy land, thy corn and *thy* vintage, *thy* oil and *thy* herds and the flocks of thy sheep upon the land for which he swore to thy fathers that he would give it thee.

14 "Blessed shalt thou be among all people. No one shall be barren among you of either sex, neither of men nor cattle. 15 The Lord will take away from thee all sickness, and the grievous infirmities of Egypt which thou knowest he will not bring upon thee, but upon thy enemies.

16 "Thou shalt consume all the people which the Lord, thy God, will deliver to thee. Thy eye shall not spare them, neither shalt thou serve their gods, lest they be thy ruin.

17 "If thou say in thy heart, 'These nations are more than I; how shall I be able to destroy them?' 18 fear not, but remember what the Lord, thy God, did to Pharaoh and to all the Egyptians—19 the exceeding great plagues which thy eyes saw and the signs and wonders and the strong hand and the stretched out arm *with which* the Lord, thy God, *brought* thee out—so will he do to all the people whom thou fearest. 20 Moreover the Lord, thy God, will send also hornets among them until he destroy and consume all that have escaped thee and could hide themselves. 21 Thou shalt not fear them, because the Lord, thy God, is in the midst of thee, a God mighty and terrible. 22 He will consume these nations in thy sight by little and little and by degrees. Thou wilt not be able to destroy them altogether lest perhaps the beasts of the earth should increase upon thee, 23 but the Lord, thy God, shall deliver them in thy sight and shall slay them until

interficiet illos donec penitus deleantur, 24 tradetque reges eorum in manus tuas, et disperdes nomina eorum sub caelo. Nullus poterit resistere tibi donec conteras eos.

25 "Sculptilia eorum igne conbures. Non concupisces argentum et aurum de quibus facta sunt, neque adsumes ex eis tibi quicquam ne offendas propter ea, quia abominatio est Domini, Dei tui. 26 Nec inferes quippiam ex idolo in domum tuam ne fias anathema sicut et illud est. Quasi spurcitiam detestaberis et velut inquinamentum ac sordes abominationi habebis, quia anathema est."

Caput 8

"Omne mandatum quod ego praecipio tibi hodie cave diligenter ut facias ut possitis vivere et multiplicemini ingressique possideatis terram pro qua iuravit Dominus patribus vestris. 2 Et recordaberis cuncti itineris per quod adduxit te Dominus, Deus tuus, quadraginta annis per desertum ut adfligeret te atque temptaret et nota fierent quae in tuo animo versabantur, utrum custodires mandata illius an

they be utterly destroyed, 24 and he shall deliver their kings into thy hands, and thou shalt destroy their names from under heaven. No man shall be able to resist thee until thou destroy them.

25 "Their graven things thou shalt burn with fire. Thou shalt not covet the silver and gold of which they are made, neither shalt thou take to thee any thing thereof lest thou offend, because it is an abomination to the Lord, thy God. 26 Neither shalt thou bring any thing of the idol into thy house lest thou become an anathema like it. Thou shalt detest it as dung and shalt utterly abhor it as uncleanness and filth, because it is an anathema."

Chapter 8

The people is put in mind of God's dealings with them to the end that they may love him and serve him.

"*All the commandments* that I command thee this day take great care to observe that you may live and be multiplied and going in may possess the land for which the Lord swore to your fathers. 2 And thou shalt remember all the way through which the Lord, thy God, hath brought thee for forty years through the desert to afflict thee and to prove thee and that the things that were in thy heart might be made known, whether thou wouldst keep his command-

non. 3 Adflixit te penuria et dedit tibi cibum manna, quem ignorabas tu et patres tui, ut ostenderet tibi quod non in solo pane vivat homo, sed in omni verbo quod egreditur de ore Dei.

4 "Vestimentum tuum quo operiebaris nequaquam vetustate defecit, et pes tuus non est subtritus—en, quadragesimus annus est—5 ut recogites in corde tuo quia sicut erudit homo filium suum, sic Dominus, Deus tuus, erudivit te, 6 ut custodias mandata Domini, Dei tui, et ambules in viis eius et timeas eum, 7 Dominus enim, Deus tuus, introducet te in terram bonam, terram rivorum aquarumque et fontium, in cuius campis et montibus erumpunt fluviorum abyssi, 8 terram frumenti, hordei ac vinearum, in qua ficus et mala granata et oliveta nascuntur, terram olei ac mellis 9 ubi absque ulla penuria comedes panem tuum et rerum omnium abundantia perfrueris, cuius lapides ferrum sunt et de montibus eius aeris metalla fodiuntur, 10 ut cum comederis et satiatus fueris, benedicas Domino, Deo tuo, pro terra optima quam dedit tibi.

11 "Observa, et cave nequando obliviscaris Domini, Dei tui, et neglegas mandata eius atque iudicia et caerimonias quas ego praecipio tibi hodie, 12 ne, postquam comederis et satiatus fueris, domos pulchras aedificaveris et habitaveris in eis 13 habuerisque armenta boum et ovium greges et argenti et auri cunctarumque rerum copiam, 14 elevetur cor tuum et non reminiscaris Domini, Dei tui, qui eduxit te de terra Aegypti, de domo servitutis, 15 et ductor tuus fuit in solitudine magna atque terribili in qua erat serpens flatu adurens et scorpio ac dipsas et nullae omnino aquae, qui

ments or no. 3 He afflicted thee with want and gave thee manna for thy food, which neither thou nor thy fathers knew, to shew that not in bread alone doth man live, but in every word that proceedeth from the mouth of God.

4 "Thy raiment with which thou wast covered hath not decayed for age, and thy foot is not worn—lo, this is the fortieth year—5 that thou mayst consider in thy heart that as a man traineth up his son, so the Lord, thy God, hath trained thee up, 6 that thou shouldst keep the commandments of the Lord, thy God, and walk in his ways and fear him, 7 for the Lord, thy God, will bring thee into a good *land* of brooks and of waters and of fountains, in the plains of which and the hills deep rivers break out, 8 a land of wheat *and* barley and vineyards, wherein fig trees and pomegranates and oliveyards grow, a land of oil and honey 9 where without any want thou shalt eat thy bread and enjoy abundance of all things, *where the* stones are iron and out of its hills are dug mines of brass, 10 that when thou hast eaten and art full, thou mayst bless the Lord, thy God, for the excellent land which he hath given thee.

11 "Take heed, and beware lest at any time thou forget the Lord, thy God, and neglect his commandments and judgments and ceremonies which I command thee this day, 12 lest, after thou hast eaten and art filled, hast built goodly houses and dwelt in them 13 and shalt have herds of oxen and flocks of sheep and plenty of gold and of silver and of all things, 14 thy heart be lifted up and thou remember not the Lord, thy God, who brought thee out of the land of Egypt, out of the house of bondage, 15 and was thy leader in the great and terrible wilderness wherein there was the serpent burning with his breath and the scorpion and the dipsas and

eduxit rivos de petra durissima 16 et cibavit te manna in solitudine quod nescierunt patres tui.

"Et postquam adflixit ac probavit, ad extremum misertus
est tui 17 ne diceres in corde tuo, 'Fortitudo mea et robur
manus meae haec mihi omnia praestiterunt.'

18 "Sed recorderis Domini, Dei tui, quod ipse tibi vires
praebuerit ut impleret pactum suum super quo iuravit patribus tuis, sicut praesens indicat dies. 19 Sin autem oblitus Domini, Dei tui, secutus fueris alienos deos coluerisque illos
et adoraveris, ecce: nunc praedico tibi quod omnino dispe-
reas. 20 Sicut gentes quas delevit Dominus in introitu tuo,
ita et vos peribitis si inoboedientes fueritis voci Domini,
Dei vestri."

Caput 9

"Audi, Israhel: tu transgredieris hodie Iordanem ut possideas nationes maximas et fortiores te, civitates ingentes et
ad caelum usque muratas, 2 populum magnum atque subli-

no waters at all, who brought forth streams out of the hardest rock 16 and fed thee in the wilderness with manna which thy fathers knew not.

"And after he had afflicted and proved thee, at the last he had mercy on thee 17 lest thou shouldst say in thy heart, 'My own might and the strength of my own hand have achieved all these things for me.'

18 "But remember the Lord, thy God, that he hath given thee strength that he might fulfil his covenant concerning which he swore to thy fathers, as this present day sheweth. 19 But if thou forget the Lord, thy God, and follow strange gods and serve and adore them, behold: now I foretell thee that thou shalt utterly perish. 20 As the nations which the Lord destroyed at thy entrance, so shall you also perish if you be disobedient to the voice of the Lord, your God."

Chapter 9

Lest they should impute their victories to their own merits, they are put in mind of their manifold rebellions and other sins for which they should have been destroyed, but God spared them for his promise made to Abraham, Isaac and Jacob.

"Hear, O Israel: thou shalt go over the Jordan this day to possess nations very great and stronger than thyself, cities great and walled up to the sky, 2 a people great and tall,

mem, filios Enacim, quos ipse vidisti et audisti, quibus nullus potest ex adverso resistere. 3 Scies ergo hodie quod Dominus, Deus tuus, ipse transibit ante te, ignis devorans atque consumens, qui conterat eos et deleat atque disperdat ante faciem tuam velociter, sicut locutus est tibi.

4 "Ne dicas in corde tuo, cum deleverit eos Dominus, Deus tuus, in conspectu tuo, 'Propter iustitiam meam introduxit me Dominus ut terram hanc possiderem,' cum propter impietates suas istae deletae sint nationes, 5 neque enim propter iustitias tuas et aequitatem cordis tui ingredieris ut possideas terras eorum, sed quia illae egerunt impie te introeunte deletae sunt et ut conpleret verbum suum Dominus quod sub iuramento pollicitus est patribus tuis Abraham, Isaac et Iacob.

6 "Scito igitur quod non propter iustitias tuas Dominus, Deus tuus, dederit tibi terram hanc optimam in possessionem, cum durissimae cervicis sis populus. 7 Memento et ne obliviscaris quomodo ad iracundiam provocaveris Dominum, Deum tuum, in solitudine. Ex eo die quo es egressus ex Aegypto usque ad locum istum, semper adversum Dominum contendisti, 8 nam et in Horeb provocasti eum, et iratus delere te voluit 9 quando ascendi in montem ut acciperem tabulas lapideas, tabulas pacti quod pepigit vobiscum Dominus, et perseveravi in monte quadraginta diebus ac noctibus, panem non comedens et aquam non bibens. 10 Deditque mihi Dominus duas tabulas lapideas scriptas digito Dei et continentes omnia verba quae vobis in monte locutus est de medio ignis quando contio populi congregata est. 11 Cumque transissent quadraginta dies et totidem noctes, dedit mihi Dominus duas tabulas lapideas,

the sons of the Anakim, whom thou hast seen and heard of, against whom no man is able to stand. 3 Thou shalt know therefore this day that the Lord, thy God, himself will pass over before thee, a devouring and consuming fire, to destroy and extirpate and bring them to nothing before thy face quickly, as he hath spoken to thee.

4 "Say not in thy heart, when the Lord, thy God, shall have destroyed them in thy sight, 'For my justice hath the Lord brought me in to possess this land,' whereas these nations are destroyed for their wickedness, 5 for it is not for thy justices and the uprightness of thy heart that thou shalt go in to possess their lands, but because they have done wickedly they are destroyed at thy coming in and that the Lord might accomplish his word which he promised by oath to thy fathers Abraham, Isaac and Jacob.

6 "Know therefore that the Lord, thy God, giveth thee not this excellent land in possession for thy justices, for thou art a very stiffnecked people. 7 Remember and forget not how thou provokedst the Lord, thy God, to wrath in the wilderness. From the day that thou camest out of Egypt unto this place, thou hast always strove against the Lord, 8 for in Horeb also thou didst provoke him, and he was angry and would have destroyed thee 9 when I went up into the mount to receive the tables of stone, the tables of the covenant which the Lord made with you, and I continued in the mount forty days and nights, neither eating bread nor drinking water. 10 And the Lord gave me two tables of stone written with the finger of God and containing all the words that he spoke to you in the mount from the midst of the fire when the people were assembled together. 11 And when forty days were passed and as many nights, the Lord gave me

tabulas foederis, 12 dixitque mihi, 'Surge, et descende hinc cito, quia populus tuus quos eduxisti de Aegypto deseruerunt velociter viam quam demonstrasti eis feceruntque sibi conflatile.'

13 "Rursumque ait Dominus ad me, 'Cerno quod populus iste durae cervicis sit; 14 dimitte me ut conteram eum et deleam nomen eius de sub caelo et constituam te super gentem quae hac maior et fortior sit.'

15 "Cumque de monte ardente descenderem et duas tabulas foederis utraque tenerem manu 16 vidissemque vos peccasse Domino, Deo vestro, et fecisse vobis vitulum conflatilem ac deseruisse velociter viam eius quam vobis ostenderat, 17 proieci tabulas de manibus meis confregique eas in conspectu vestro. 18 Et procidi ante Dominum sicut prius, quadraginta diebus et noctibus panem non comedens et aquam non bibens, propter omnia peccata vestra quae gessistis contra Dominum et eum ad iracundiam provocastis, 19 timui enim indignationem et iram illius qua, adversum vos concitatus, delere vos voluit. Et exaudivit me Dominus etiam hac vice. 20 Adversum Aaron quoque vehementer iratus voluit eum conterere, et pro illo similiter deprecatus sum. 21 Peccatum autem vestrum quod feceratis, id est, vitulum, arripiens igne conbusi, et in frusta comminuens omninoque in pulverem redigens proieci in torrentem qui de monte descendit.

22 "In Incendio quoque, et in Temptatione et in Sepulchris Concupiscentiae, provocastis Dominum, 23 et quando misit vos de Cadesbarne, dicens, 'Ascendite, et possidete terram quam dedi vobis,' et contempsistis imperium Domini, Dei

the two tables of stone, the tables of the covenant, 12 and said to me, 'Arise, and go down from hence quickly, for thy people which thou hast brought out of Egypt have quickly forsaken the way that thou hast shewn them and have made to themselves a molten idol.'

13 "And again the Lord said to me, 'I see that this people is stiffnecked; 14 let me alone that I may destroy them and abolish their name from under heaven and set thee over a nation that is greater and stronger than this.'

15 "And when I came down from the burning mount and held the two tables of the covenant with both hands 16 and saw that you had sinned against the Lord, your God, and had made to yourselves a molten calf and had quickly forsaken his way which he had shewn you, 17 I cast the tables out of my hands and broke them in your sight. 18 And I fell down before the Lord as before, forty days and nights neither eating bread nor drinking water, for all your sins which you had committed against the Lord and had provoked him to wrath, 19 for I feared his indignation and anger wherewith, being moved against you, he would have destroyed you. And the Lord heard me this time also. 20 And he was exceeding angry against Aaron also and would have destroyed him, and I prayed in like manner for him. 21 And your sin that you had committed, that is, the calf, I took and burned it with fire, and breaking it into pieces *until it was as small as* dust I threw it into the torrent which cometh down from the mountain.

22 "At the Burning also, and at the *place of* Temptation and at the Graves of Lust, you provoked the Lord, 23 and when he sent you from Kadesh-barnea, saying, 'Go up, and possess the land that I have given you,' and you slighted the

vestri, et non credidistis ei, neque vocem eius audire voluistis 24 sed semper fuistis rebelles a die qua nosse vos coepi.

25 "Et iacui coram Domino quadraginta diebus ac noctibus, quibus eum suppliciter deprecabar ne deleret vos ut fuerat comminatus. 26 Et orans dixi, 'Domine Deus, ne disperdas populum tuum et hereditatem tuam quam redemisti in magnitudine tua, quos eduxisti de Aegypto in manu forti. 27 Recordare servorum tuorum Abraham, Isaac et Iacob. Ne aspicias duritiam populi huius et impietatem atque peccatum 28 ne forte dicant habitatores terrae de qua eduxisti nos, "Non poterat Dominus introducere eos in terram quam pollicitus est eis, et oderat illos. Idcirco eduxit ut interficeret eos in solitudine," 29 qui sunt populus tuus et hereditas tua quos eduxisti in fortitudine tua magna et in brachio tuo extento.'"

Caput 10

"In tempore illo, dixit Dominus ad me, 'Dola tibi duas tabulas lapideas sicut priores fuerunt, et ascende ad me in montem, faciesque arcam ligneam, 2 et scribam in tabulis

commandment of the Lord, your God, and did not believe him, neither would you hearken to his voice 24 but were always rebellious from the day that I began to know you.

25 "And I lay prostrate before the Lord forty days and nights, in which I humbly besought him that he would not destroy you as he had threatened. 26 And praying I said, 'O Lord God, destroy not thy people and thy inheritance which thou hast redeemed in thy greatness, whom thou hast brought out of Egypt with a strong hand. 27 Remember thy servants Abraham, Isaac and Jacob. Look not on the stubbornness of this people nor on their wickedness and sin 28 lest perhaps the inhabitants of the land out of which thou hast brought us say, "The Lord could not bring them into the land that he promised them, and he hated them. Therefore he brought them out that he might kill them in the wilderness," 29 who are thy people and thy inheritance whom thou hast brought out by thy great strength and in thy stretched out arm.'"

Chapter 10

God giveth the second tables of the law. A further exhortation to fear and serve the Lord.

"At that time, the Lord said to me, 'Hew thee two tables of stone like the former, and come up to me into the mount, and thou shalt make an ark of wood, 2 and I will write on the

verba quae fuerunt in his quas ante confregisti, ponesque eas in arca.'

3 "Feci igitur arcam de lignis setthim. Cumque dolassem duas tabulas lapideas instar priorum, ascendi in montem habens eas in manibus. 4 Scripsitque in tabulis, iuxta id quod prius scripserat, verba decem quae locutus est Dominus ad vos in monte de medio ignis quando populus congregatus est, et dedit eas mihi. 5 Reversusque de monte, descendi et posui tabulas in arcam quam feceram, quae hucusque ibi sunt, sicut mihi praecepit Dominus.

6 "Filii autem Israhel castra moverunt ex Beroth filiorum Iacan in Musera, ubi Aaron mortuus ac sepultus est pro quo sacerdotio functus est filius eius, Eleazar. 7 Inde venerunt in Gadgad, de quo loco profecti castrametati sunt in Ietabatha, in terra aquarum atque torrentium. 8 Eo tempore separavit tribum Levi ut portaret Arcam Foederis Domini et staret coram eo in ministerio ac benediceret in nomine illius usque in praesentem diem. 9 Quam ob rem non habuit Levi partem neque possessionem cum fratribus suis, quia ipse Dominus possessio eius est, sicut promisit ei Dominus, Deus tuus.

10 "Ego autem steti in monte sicut prius, quadraginta diebus ac noctibus, exaudivitque me Dominus etiam hac vice et te perdere noluit. 11 Dixitque mihi, 'Vade, et praecede populum ut ingrediatur et possideat terram quam iuravi patribus eorum ut traderem eis.'

12 "Et nunc, Israhel, quid Dominus, Deus tuus, petit a te nisi ut timeas Dominum, Deum tuum, et ambules in viis eius et diligas eum ac servias Domino, Deo tuo, in toto

tables the words that were in them which thou brokest before, and thou shalt put them in the ark.'

3 "And I made an ark of setim wood. And when I had hewn two tables of stone like the former, I went up into the mount having them in my hands. 4 And he wrote in the tables, according as he had written before, the ten words which the Lord spoke to you in the mount from the midst of the fire when the people were assembled, and he gave them to me. 5 And returning from the mount, I came down and put the tables into the ark that I had made, and they are there till this present, as the Lord commanded me.

6 "And the children of Israel removed their camp from Beeroth of the children of Jakan into Moserah, where Aaron died and was buried, and Eleazar, his son, succeeded him in the priestly office. 7 From thence they came to Gudgodah, from which place they departed and camped in Jotbathah, in a land of waters and torrents. 8 At that time he separated the tribe of Levi to carry the Ark of the Covenant of the Lord and to stand before him in the ministry and to bless in his name until this present day. 9 Wherefore Levi hath no part nor possession with his brethren, because the Lord himself is his possession, as the Lord, thy God, promised him.

10 "And I stood in the mount as before, forty days and nights, and the Lord heard me this time also and would not destroy thee. 11 And he said to me, 'Go, and walk before the people that they may enter and possess the land which I swore to their fathers that I would give them.'

12 "And now, Israel, what doth the Lord, thy God, require of thee but that thou fear the Lord, thy God, and walk in his ways and love him and serve the Lord, thy God, with all thy

corde tuo et in tota anima tua 13 custodiasque mandata Domini et caerimonias eius quas ego hodie praecipio tibi ut bene sit tibi?

14 "En! Domini, Dei tui, caelum est et caelum caeli, terra et omnia quae in ea sunt. 15 Et tamen patribus tuis conglutinatus est Dominus et amavit eos elegitque semen eorum post eos, id est, vos, de cunctis gentibus, sicut hodie conprobatur.

16 "Circumcidite igitur praeputium cordis vestri, et cervicem vestram ne induretis amplius, 17 quia Dominus, Deus vester, ipse est Deus deorum et Dominus dominantium, Deus magnus et potens et terribilis, qui personam non accipit nec munera. 18 Facit iudicium pupillo et viduae, amat peregrinum et dat ei victum atque vestitum. 19 Et vos ergo amate peregrinos, quia et ipsi fuistis advenae in terra Aegypti.

20 "Dominum, Deum tuum, timebis et ei soli servies; ipsi adherebis iurabisque in nomine illius. 21 Ipse est laus tua et Deus tuus qui fecit tibi haec magnalia et terribilia quae viderunt oculi tui. 22 In septuaginta animabus descenderunt patres tui in Aegyptum, et ecce: nunc multiplicavit te Dominus, Deus tuus, sicut astra caeli."

heart and with all thy soul 13 and keep the commandments of the Lord and his ceremonies which I command thee this day that it may be well with thee?

14 "Behold! Heaven is the Lord's, thy God, and the heaven of heaven, the earth and all things that are therein. 15 And yet the Lord hath been closely joined to thy fathers and loved them and chose their seed after them, that is to say, you, out of all nations, as this day it is proved.

16 "Circumcise therefore the foreskin of your heart, and stiffen your neck no more, 17 because the Lord, your God, he is the God of gods and the Lord of lords, a great God and mighty and terrible, who accepteth no person nor *taketh* bribes. 18 He doth judgment to the fatherless and the widow, loveth the stranger and giveth him food and raiment. 19 And do you therefore love strangers, because you also were strangers in the land of Egypt.

20 "Thou shalt fear the Lord, thy God, and serve him only; to him thou shalt adhere and shalt swear by his name. 21 He is thy praise and thy God that hath done for thee these great and terrible things which thy eyes have seen. 22 In seventy souls thy fathers went down into Egypt, and behold: now the Lord, thy God, hath multiplied thee as the stars of heaven."

Caput 11

"Ama, itaque, Dominum, Deum tuum, et observa praecepta eius et caerimonias, iudicia atque mandata omni tempore. 2 Cognoscite hodie quae ignorant filii vestri, qui non viderunt disciplinam Domini, Dei vestri, magnalia eius et robustam manum extentumque brachium, 3 signa et opera quae fecit in medio Aegypti Pharaoni regi et universae terrae eius 4 omnique exercitui Aegyptiorum et equis ac curribus, quomodo operuerint eos aquae Rubri Maris cum vos persequerentur et deleverit eos Dominus usque in praesentem diem 5 vobisque quae fecerit in solitudine donec veniretis ad hunc locum 6 et Dathan atque Abiram, filiis Heliab, qui fuit filius Ruben, quos aperto ore suo terra absorbuit cum domibus et tabernaculis et universa substantia eorum quam habebant in medio Israhelis.

7 "Oculi vestri viderunt omnia opera Domini magna quae fecit 8 ut custodiatis universa mandata illius quae ego hodie praecipio vobis et possitis introire et possidere terram ad quam ingredimini 9 multoque in ea vivatis tempore, quam sub iuramento pollicitus est Dominus patribus vestris et semini eorum, lacte et melle manantem, 10 terra enim ad

Chapter 11

The love and service of God are still inculcated with a blessing to them that serve him and threats of punishment if they forsake his law.

"Therefore, love the Lord, thy God, and observe his precepts and ceremonies, his judgments and commandments at all times. 2 Know this day the things that your children know not, who saw not the chastisements of the Lord, your God, his great doings and strong hand and stretched out arm, 3 the signs and works which he did in the midst of Egypt to King Pharaoh and to all his land 4 and to all the host of the Egyptians and to their horses and chariots, how the waters of the Red Sea covered them when they pursued you and how the Lord destroyed them until this present day 5 and what he hath done to you in the wilderness till you came to this place 6 and to Dathan and Abiram, the sons of Eliab, who was the son of Reuben, whom the earth opening her mouth swallowed up with their households and tents and all their substance which they had in the midst of Israel.

7 "Your eyes have seen all the great works of the Lord that he hath done 8 that you may keep all his commandments which I command you this day and may go in and possess the land to which you are entering 9 and may live in it a long time, which the Lord promised by oath to your fathers and to their seed, *a land which floweth* with milk and honey, 10 for

quam ingrederis possidendam non est sicut terra Aegypti de qua existi ubi, iacto semine, in hortorum morem aquae ducuntur inriguae, 11 sed montuosa est et campestris, de caelo expectans pluvias, 12 quam Dominus, Deus tuus, semper invisit, et oculi illius in ea sunt a principio anni usque ad finem eius.

13 "Si ergo oboedieritis mandatis meis quae hodie praecipio vobis ut diligatis Dominum, Deum vestrum, et serviatis ei in toto corde vestro et in tota anima vestra, 14 dabit pluviam terrae vestrae temporivam et serotinam ut colligatis frumentum et vinum et oleum 15 faenumque ex agris ad pascenda iumenta et ut ipsi comedatis ac saturemini. 16 Cavete ne forte decipiatur cor vestrum et recedatis a Domino serviatisque diis alienis et adoretis eos 17 iratusque Dominus claudat caelum et pluviae non descendant nec terra det germen suum pereatisque velociter de terra optima quam Dominus daturus est vobis.

18 "Ponite haec verba mea in cordibus et in animis vestris, et suspendite ea pro signo in manibus, et inter vestros oculos conlocate. 19 Docete filios vestros ut illa meditentur quando sederis in domo tua et ambulaveris in via et accubueris atque surrexeris. 20 Scribes ea super postes et ianuas domus tuae 21 ut multiplicentur dies tui et filiorum tuorum in terra quam iuravit Dominus patribus tuis ut daret eis quamdiu caelum inminet terrae.

22 "Si enim custodieritis mandata quae ego praecipio vobis et feceritis ea, ut diligatis Dominum, Deum vestrum, et

the land which thou goest to possess is not like the land of Egypt from whence thou camest out where, when the seed is sown, waters are brought in to water it after the manner of gardens, 11 but it is a land of hills and plains, expecting rain from heaven, 12 and the Lord, thy God, doth always visit it, and his eyes are on it from the beginning of the year unto the end thereof.

13 "If then you obey my commandments which I command you this day that you love the Lord, your God, and serve him with all your heart and with all your soul, 14 he will give to your land the early rain and the latter rain that you may gather in your corn and your wine and your oil 15 and your hay out of the fields to feed your cattle and that you may eat and be filled. 16 Beware lest perhaps your heart be deceived and you depart from the Lord and serve strange gods and adore them 17 and the Lord being angry shut up heaven *that* the rain *come* not down nor the earth yield her fruit and you perish quickly from the excellent land which the Lord will give you.

18 "Lay up these words in your hearts and minds, and hang them for a sign on your hands, and place them between your eyes. 19 Teach your children that they meditate on them when thou sittest in thy house and when thou walkest on the way and when thou liest down and risest up. 20 Thou shalt write them upon the posts and the doors of thy house 21 that thy days may be multiplied and the days of thy children in the land which the Lord swore to thy fathers that he would give them as long as the heaven hangeth over the earth.

22 "For if you keep the commandments which I command you and do them, to love the Lord, your God, and walk in all

ambuletis in omnibus viis eius adherentes ei, 23 disperdet Dominus omnes gentes istas ante faciem vestram, et possidebitis eas quae maiores et fortiores vobis sunt. 24 Omnis locus quem calcaverit pes vester vester erit. A deserto et a Libano, a flumine magno Eufraten usque ad mare occidentale erunt termini vestri. 25 Nullus stabit contra vos. Terrorem vestrum et formidinem dabit Dominus, Deus vester, super omnem terram quam calcaturi estis, sicut locutus est vobis.

26 "En! Propono in conspectu vestro hodie benedictionem et maledictionem: 27 benedictionem, si oboedieritis mandatis Domini, Dei vestri, quae ego hodie praecipio vobis, 28 maledictionem, si non oboedieritis mandatis Domini, Dei vestri, sed recesseritis de via quam ego nunc ostendo vobis et ambulaveritis post deos alienos quos ignoratis.

29 "Cum vero introduxerit te Dominus, Deus tuus, in terram ad quam pergis habitandam, pones benedictionem super Montem Garizim, maledictionem super Montem Hebal, 30 qui sunt trans Iordanem, post viam quae vergit ad solis occubitum, in terra Chananei qui habitat in campestribus contra Galgalam, quae est iuxta vallem tendentem et intrantem procul, 31 vos enim transibitis Iordanem ut possideatis terram quam Dominus, Deus vester, daturus est vobis ut habeatis ac possideatis illam. 32 Videte ergo ut impleatis caerimonias atque iudicia quae ego hodie ponam in conspectu vestro."

his ways cleaving unto him, 23 the Lord will destroy all these nations before your face, and you shall possess them which are greater and stronger than you. 24 Every place that your foot shall tread upon shall be yours. From the desert and from Libanus, from the great river Euphrates unto the western sea shall be your borders. 25 None shall stand against you. The Lord, your God, shall lay the dread and fear of you upon all the land that you shall tread upon, as he hath spoken to you.

26 "Behold! I set forth in your sight this day a blessing and a curse: 27 a blessing, if you obey the commandments of the Lord, your God, which I command you this day, 28 a curse, if you obey not the commandments of the Lord, your God, but revolt from the way which now I shew you and walk after strange gods which you know not.

29 "And when the Lord, thy God, shall have brought thee into the land whither thou goest to dwell, thou shalt put the blessing upon Mount Gerizim, the curse upon Mount Ebal, 30 which are beyond the Jordan, behind the way that goeth to the setting of the sun, in the land of the Canaanite who dwelleth in the plain country over against Gilgal, which is near the valley that reacheth and entereth far, 31 for you shall pass over the Jordan to possess the land which the Lord, your God, will give you that you may have it and possess it. 32 See therefore that you fulfil the ceremonies and judgments which I shall set this day before you."

Caput 12

"Haec sunt praecepta atque iudicia quae facere debetis in terra quam Dominus, Deus patrum tuorum, daturus est tibi ut possideas eam cunctis diebus quibus super humum gradieris.

2 "Subvertite omnia loca in quibus coluerunt gentes quas possessuri estis deos suos, super montes excelsos et colles et subter omne lignum frondosum. 3 Dissipate aras earum, et confringite statuas; lucos igne conburite, et idola comminuite. Disperdite nomina eorum de locis illis.

4 "Non facietis ita Domino, Deo vestro, 5 sed ad locum quem elegerit Dominus, Deus vester, de cunctis tribubus vestris ut ponat nomen suum ibi et habitet in eo venietis. 6 Et offeretis in illo loco holocausta et victimas vestras, decimas et primitias manuum vestrarum et vota atque donaria, primogenita boum et ovium. 7 Et comedetis ibi in conspectu Domini, Dei vestri, ac laetabimini in cunctis ad quae miseritis manum, vos et domus vestrae in quibus benedixerit vobis Dominus, Deus vester.

8 "Non facietis ibi quae nos hic facimus hodie, singuli

Chapter 12

All idolatry must be extirpated. Sacrifices, tithes and first-fruits must be offered in one only place. All eating of blood is prohibited.

"These are the precepts and judgments that you must do in the land which the Lord, the God of thy fathers, will give thee to possess it all the days that thou shalt walk upon the earth.

2 "Destroy all the places in which the nations that you shall possess worshipped their gods, upon high mountains and hills and under every shady tree. 3 Overthrow their altars, and break down their statues; burn their groves with fire, and break their idols in pieces. Destroy their names out of those places.

4 "You shall not do so to the Lord, your God, 5 but you shall come to the place which the Lord, your God, shall choose out of all your tribes to put his name there and to dwell in it. 6 And you shall offer in that place your holocausts and victims, the tithes and firstfruits of your hands and your vows and gifts, the firstborn of your *herds* and your sheep. 7 And you shall eat there in the sight of the Lord, your God, and you shall rejoice in all things whereunto you shall put your hand, you and your houses wherein the Lord, your God, hath blessed you.

8 "You shall not do there the things we do here this day,

quod sibi rectum videtur, 9 neque enim usque in praesens tempus venistis ad requiem et possessionem quam Dominus, Deus vester, daturus est vobis. 10 Transibitis Iordanem et habitabitis in terram quam Dominus, Deus vester, daturus est vobis ut requiescatis a cunctis hostibus per circuitum et absque ullo timore habitetis 11 in loco quem elegerit Dominus, Deus vester, ut sit nomen eius in eo. Illuc omnia quae praecipio conferetis, holocausta et hostias ac decimas et primitias manuum vestrarum et quicquid praecipuum est in muneribus quae vovebitis Domino. 12 Ibi epulabimini coram Domino, Deo vestro, vos et filii ac filiae vestrae, famuli et famulae atque Levites qui in vestris urbibus commorantur, neque enim habet aliam partem et possessionem inter vos.

13 "Cave ne offeras holocausta tua in omni loco quem videris, 14 sed in eo quem elegerit Dominus in una tribuum tuarum offeres hostias et facies quaecumque praecipio tibi. 15 Sin autem comedere volueris et te esus carnium delectarit, occide, et comede iuxta benedictionem Domini, Dei tui, quam dedit tibi in urbibus tuis, sive inmundum fuerit, hoc est, maculatum et debile, sive mundum, hoc est, integrum et sine macula, quod offerri licet, sicut capream et cervum, comedes. 16 Absque esu dumtaxat sanguinis, quod super terram quasi aquam effundes.

17 "Non poteris comedere in oppidis tuis decimam frumenti et vini et olei tui, primogenita armentorum et pecorum et omnia quae voveris et sponte offerre volueris et primitias manuum tuarum. 18 Sed coram Domino, Deo tuo, comedes ea in loco quem elegerit Dominus, Deus tuus, tu et

every man that which seemeth good to himself, 9 for until this present time you are not come to rest and to the possession which the Lord, your God, will give you. 10 You shall pass over the Jordan and shall dwell in the land which the Lord, your God, will give you that you may have rest from all enemies round about and may dwell without any fear 11 in the place which the Lord, your God, shall choose that his name may be therein. Thither shall you bring all the things that I command you, holocausts and victims and tithes and the firstfruits of your hands and whatsoever is the choicest in the gifts which you shall vow to the Lord. 12 There shall you feast before the Lord, your God, you and your sons and *your* daughters, *your* menservants and maidservants and the Levite that dwelleth in your cities, for he hath no other part and possession among you.

13 "Beware lest thou offer thy holocausts in every place that thou shalt see, 14 but in the place which the Lord shall choose in one of thy tribes shalt thou offer sacrifices and shalt do all that I command thee. 15 But if thou desirest to eat and the eating of flesh delight thee, kill, and eat according to the blessing of the Lord, thy God, which he hath given thee in thy cities, whether it be unclean, that is to say, having blemish or defect, or clean, that is to say, sound and without blemish, such as may be offered, as the roe and the hart, shalt thou eat it. 16 Only the blood thou shalt not eat, but thou shalt pour it out upon the earth as water.

17 "Thou mayst not eat in thy towns the tithes of thy corn and *thy* wine and *thy* oil, the firstborn of *thy* herds and *thy* cattle nor any thing that thou vowest and that thou wilt offer voluntarily and the firstfruits of thy hands. 18 But thou shalt eat them before the Lord, thy God, in the place which

filius tuus ac filia tua et servus et famula atque Levites qui
manet in urbibus tuis, et laetaberis et reficieris coram Domino, Deo tuo, in cunctis ad quae extenderis manum tuam.
19 Cave ne derelinquas Leviten omni tempore quo versaris
in terra.

20 "Quando dilataverit Dominus, Deus tuus, terminos
tuos, sicut locutus est tibi, et volueris vesci carnibus quas
desiderat anima tua, 21 locus autem quem elegerit Dominus,
Deus tuus, ut sit nomen eius ibi, si procul fuerit, occides
de armentis et pecoribus quae habueris, sicut praecepi tibi,
et comedes in oppidis tuis, ut tibi placet. 22 Sicut comedi-
tur caprea et cervus, ita vesceris eis; et mundus et inmundus in commune vescentur. 23 Hoc solum cave: ne sanguinem comedas, sanguis enim eorum pro anima est, et idcirco
non debes animam comedere cum carnibus, 24 sed super terram fundes quasi aquam 25 ut sit tibi bene et filiis tuis post te
cum feceris quod placet in conspectu Domini.

26 "Quae autem sanctificaveris et voveris Domino tolles
et venies ad locum quem elegerit Dominus 27 et offeres oblationes tuas, carnem et sanguinem super altare Domini, Dei
tui; sanguinem hostiarum fundes in altari, carnibus autem
ipse vesceris.

28 "Observa et audi omnia quae ego praecipio tibi, ut bene
sit tibi et filiis tuis post te in sempiternum cum feceris quod
bonum est et placitum in conspectu Domini, Dei tui.
29 Quando disperderit Dominus, Deus tuus, ante faciem
tuam gentes ad quas ingredieris possidendas et possederis

the Lord, thy God, shall choose, thou and thy son and thy daughter and *thy* manservant and maidservant and the Levite that dwelleth in thy cities, and thou shalt rejoice and be refreshed before the Lord, thy God, in all things whereunto thou shalt put thy hand. 19 Take heed thou forsake not the Levite all the time that thou livest in the land.

20 "When the Lord, thy God, shall have enlarged thy borders, as he hath spoken to thee, and thou wilt eat the flesh that thy soul desireth, 21 and if the place which the Lord, thy God, shall choose that his name should be there be far off, thou shalt kill of thy herds and of thy flocks, as I have commanded thee, and shalt eat in thy towns, as it pleaseth thee. 22 Even as the roe and the hart is eaten, so shalt thou eat them; both the clean and unclean shall eat of them alike. 23 Only beware of this: that thou eat not the blood, for *the* blood is for the soul, and therefore thou must not eat the soul with the flesh, 24 but thou shalt pour it upon the earth as water 25 that it may be well with thee and thy children after thee when thou shalt do that which is pleasing in the sight of the Lord.

26 "But the things which thou hast sanctified and vowed to the Lord thou shalt take and shalt come to the place which the Lord shall choose 27 and shalt offer thy oblations, the flesh and the blood upon the altar of the Lord, thy God; the blood of thy victims thou shalt pour on the altar, and the flesh thou thyself shalt eat.

28 "Observe and hear all the things that I command thee, that it may be well with thee and thy children after thee for ever when thou shalt do what is good and pleasing in the sight of the Lord, thy God. 29 When the Lord, thy God, shall have destroyed before thy face the nations which thou shalt

eas atque habitaveris in terra earum, 30 cave ne imiteris eas postquam te fuerint introeunte subversae et requiras caerimonias earum, dicens, 'Sicut coluerunt gentes istae deos suos, ita et ego colam.' 31 Non facies similiter Domino, Deo tuo, omnes enim abominationes quas aversatur Dominus fecerunt diis suis, offerentes filios et filias et conburentes igne.

32 "Quod praecipio tibi, hoc tantum facito Domino. Nec addas quicquam nec minuas."

Caput 13

"Si surrexerit in medio tui prophetes aut qui somnium vidisse se dicat et praedixerit signum atque portentum 2 et evenerit quod locutus est et dixerit tibi, 'Eamus et sequamur deos alienos,' quos ignoras, et, 'Serviamus eis,' 3 non audies verba prophetae illius aut somniatoris, quia temptat vos Dominus, Deus vester, ut palam fiat utrum diligatis eum an non in toto corde et in tota anima vestra.

4 "Dominum, Deum vestrum, sequimini, et ipsum timete, et mandata illius custodite, et audite vocem eius. Ipsi servietis, et ipsi adherebitis. 5 Propheta autem ille aut fictor som-

go in to possess and when thou shalt possess them and dwell in their land, 30 beware lest thou imitate them after they are destroyed at thy coming in and lest thou seek after their ceremonies, saying, 'As these nations have worshipped their gods, so will I also worship.' 31 Thou shalt not do in like manner to the Lord, thy God, for they have done to their gods all the abominations which the Lord abhorreth, offering their sons and daughters and burning them with fire.

32 "What I command thee, that only do thou to the Lord. Neither add any thing nor diminish."

Chapter 13

False prophets must be slain and idolatrous cities destroyed.

"If there rise in the midst of thee a prophet or one that saith he hath dreamed a dream and he foretell a sign and a wonder 2 and that come to pass which he spoke and he say to thee, 'Let us go and follow strange gods,' which thou knowest not, and, 'Let us serve them,' 3 thou shalt not hear the words of that prophet or dreamer, for the Lord, your God, trieth you that it may appear whether you love him with all your heart and with all your soul or not.

4 "Follow the Lord, your God, and fear him, and keep his commandments, and hear his voice. Him you shall serve, and to him you shall cleave. 5 And that prophet or forger of

niorum interficietur quia locutus est ut vos averteret a Domino, Deo vestro, qui eduxit vos de terra Aegypti et redemit vos de domo servitutis ut errare te faceret de via quam tibi praecepit Dominus, Deus tuus, et auferes malum de medio tui.

6 "Si tibi voluerit persuadere frater tuus, filius matris tuae, aut filius tuus vel filia sive uxor quae est in sinu tuo aut amicus quem diligis ut animam tuam, clam, dicens, 'Eamus et serviamus diis alienis,' quos ignoras tu et patres tui 7 cunctarum in circuitu gentium quae iuxta vel procul sunt ab initio usque ad finem terrae, 8 non adquiescas ei, nec audias, neque parcat ei oculus tuus ut miserearis et occultes eum, 9 sed statim interficies. Sit primum manus tua super eum, et post te omnis populus mittat manum. 10 Lapidibus obrutus necabitur quia voluit te abstrahere a Domino, Deo tuo, qui eduxit te de terra Aegypti, de domo servitutis, 11 ut omnis Israhel audiens timeat et nequaquam ultra faciat quippiam huius rei simile.

12 "Si audieris in una urbium tuarum quas Dominus, Deus tuus, dabit tibi ad habitandum dicentes aliquos, 13 'Egressi sunt filii Belial de medio tui et averterunt habitatores urbis suae atque dixerunt, "Eamus et serviamus diis alienis,"' quos ignoratis, 14 quaere sollicite et diligenter rei veritate perspecta; si inveneris certum esse quod dicitur et abominationem hanc opere perpetratam, 15 statim percuties habitatores urbis illius in ore gladii et delebis eam omniaque quae in illa sunt, usque ad pecora. 16 Quicquid etiam supellectilis

dreams shall be slain because he spoke to draw you away from the Lord, your God, who brought you out of the land of Egypt and redeemed you from the house of bondage to make thee go out of the way which the Lord, thy God, commanded thee, and thou shalt take away the evil out of the midst of thee.

6 "If thy brother, the son of thy mother, or thy son or daughter or thy wife that is in thy bosom or thy friend whom thou lovest as thy own soul, would persuade thee secretly, saying, 'Let us go and serve strange gods,' which thou knowest not nor thy fathers 7 of all the nations round about that are near or afar off from *one end of the earth to the other,* 8 consent not to him; hear him not, neither let thy eye spare him to pity and conceal him, 9 but thou shalt presently put him to death. Let thy hand be first upon him, and *afterwards* the hands of all the people. 10 *With stones shall he be stoned to death* because he would have withdrawn thee from the Lord, thy God, who brought thee out of the land of Egypt, from the house of bondage, 11 that all Israel hearing may fear and may do no more any thing like this.

12 "If in one of thy cities which the Lord, thy God, shall give thee to dwell in thou hear some say, 13 'Children of Belial are gone out of the midst of thee and have withdrawn the inhabitants of their city and have said, "Let us go and serve strange gods,"' which you know not, 14 inquire carefully and diligently *the truth of the thing by looking well into it, and* if thou find that which is said to be certain and that this abomination hath been really committed, 15 thou shalt forthwith kill the inhabitants of that city with the edge of the sword and shalt destroy it and all things that are in it, even the cattle. 16 *And all the household goods that are there*

fuerit congregabis in medium platearum eius et cum ipsa civitate succendes, ita ut universa consumas Domino, Deo tuo, et sit tumulus sempiternus; non aedificabitur amplius. 17 Et non adherebit de illo anathemate quicquam in manu tua ut avertatur Dominus ab ira furoris sui et misereatur tui multiplicetque te sicut iuravit patribus tuis 18 quando audieris vocem Domini, Dei tui, custodiens omnia praecepta eius quae ego praecipio tibi hodie ut facias quod placitum est in conspectu Domini, Dei tui."

Caput 14

"Filii estote Domini, Dei vestri. Non vos incidetis nec facietis calvitium super mortuo, 2 quoniam populus sanctus es Domino, Deo tuo, et te elegit ut sis ei in populum peculiarem de cunctis gentibus quae sunt super terram.

3 "Ne comedatis quae inmunda sunt. 4 Hoc est animal quod comedere debetis: bovem et ovem et capram, 5 cervum et capream, bubalum, tragelaphum, pygargon, orygem, camelopardalum.

thou shalt gather together in the midst of the streets thereof and shall burn them with the city itself, so as to comsume all for the Lord, thy God, and that it be a heap for ever; it shall be built no more. 17 And there shall nothing of that anathema stick to thy hand that the Lord may turn from the wrath of his fury and may have mercy on thee and multiply thee as he swore to thy fathers 18 when thou shalt hear the voice of the Lord, thy God, keeping all his precepts which I command thee this day that thou mayst do what is pleasing in the sight of the Lord, thy God."

Chapter 14

In mourning for the dead they are not to follow the ways of the Gentiles. The distinction of clean and unclean meats. Ordinances concerning tithes and firstfruits.

"Be ye children of the Lord, your God. You shall not cut yourselves nor make any baldness for the dead, 2 because thou art a holy people to the Lord, thy God, and he chose thee to be his peculiar people of all nations that are upon the earth.

3 "Eat not the things that are unclean. 4 These are the beasts that you shall eat: the ox and the sheep and the goat, 5 the hart and the roe, the buffle, the chamois, the pygarg, the wild goat, the camelopardalus.

6 "Omne animal quod in duas partes ungulam findit et ruminat, comedetis. 7 De his autem quae ruminant et ungulam
non findunt, comedere non debetis, ut camelum, leporem,
choerogyllium. Quia ruminant et non dividunt ungulam, inmunda erunt vobis. 8 Sus quoque, quoniam dividit ungulam
et non ruminat, inmunda erit; carnibus eorum non vescemini, et cadavera non tangetis.

9 "Haec comedetis ex omnibus quae morantur in aquis:
quae habent pinnulas et squamas comedite. 10 Quae absque
pinnulis et squamis sunt, ne comedatis, quia inmunda sunt.

11 "Omnes aves mundas comedite. 12 Inmundas ne comedatis, aquilam, scilicet, et grypem et alietum, 13 ixon et vulturem ac milvum, iuxta genus suum, 14 et omne corvini generis 15 et strutionem ac noctuam et larum atque accipitrem,
iuxta genus suum, 16 herodium et cycnum et ibin 17 ac mergulum, porphirionem et nycticoracem, 18 onocrotalum et
charadrium, singula in genere suo, upupam quoque et vespertilionem.

19 "Et omne quod reptat et pinnulas habet inmundum erit
nec comedetur.

20 "Omne quod mundum est, comedite, 21 quicquid autem
morticinum est, ne vescamini ex eo. Peregrino qui intra portas tuas est da ut comedat, aut vende ei, quia tu populus
sanctus Domini, Dei tui es. Non coques hedum in lacte matris suae.

22 "Decimam partem separabis de cunctis frugibus tuis
quae nascuntur in terra per annos singulos, 23 et comedes
in conspectu Domini, Dei tui, in loco quem elegerit ut in
eo nomen illius invocetur decimam frumenti tui et vini et
olei et primogenita de armentis et ovibus tuis ut discas

6 "Every beast that divideth the hoof in two parts and cheweth the cud, you shall eat. 7 But of them that chew the cud but divide not the hoof, *you* shall not eat, such as the camel, the hare and the cherogril. Because they chew the cud but divide not the hoof, they shall be unclean to you. 8 The swine also, because it divideth the hoof but cheweth not the cud, shall be unclean; their flesh you shall not eat, and their carcasses you shall not touch.

9 "These shall you eat of all that abide in the waters: *all that* have fins and scales you shall eat. 10 Such as are without fins and scales, you shall not eat, because they are unclean.

11 "All birds that are clean *you shall eat.* 12 The unclean eat not, to wit, the eagle and the grype and the osprey, 13 the ringtail and the vulture and the kite, according to their kind, 14 and all of the raven's kind 15 and the ostrich and the owl and the larus and the hawk, according to its kind, 16 the heron and the swan and the stork 17 and the cormorant, the porphirion and the night crow, 18 the bittern and the charadrion, every one in their kind, the houp also and the bat.

19 "Every thing that creepeth and hath little wings shall be unclean and shall not be eaten.

20 "All that is clean, *you shall eat,* 21 but whatsoever is dead of itself, eat not thereof. Give it to the stranger that is within thy gates to eat, or sell it to him, because thou art the holy people of the Lord, thy God. Thou shalt not boil a kid in the milk of his dam.

22 "Every year thou shalt set aside the tithes of all thy fruits that *the earth bringeth forth,* 23 and thou shalt eat before the Lord, thy God, in the place which he shall choose that his name may be called upon therein the tithe of thy corn and *thy* wine and *thy* oil and the firstborn of thy herds and

timere Dominum, Deum tuum, omni tempore. 24 Cum autem longior fuerit via et locus quem elegerit Dominus, Deus tuus, tibique benedixerit nec potueris ad eum haec cuncta portare, 25 vendes omnia et in pretium rediges portabisque manu tua et proficisceris ad locum quem elegerit Dominus, Deus tuus, 26 et emes ex eadem pecunia quicquid tibi placuerit sive ex armentis sive ex ovibus, vinum quoque et siceram et omne quod desiderat anima tua, et comedes coram Domino, Deo tuo, et epulaberis, tu et domus tua 27 et Levita qui intra portas tuas est—cave ne derelinquas eum, quia non habet aliam partem in possessione tua.

28 "Anno tertio separabis aliam decimam ex omnibus quae nascuntur tibi eo tempore et repones intra ianuas tuas. 29 Venietque Levites qui aliam non habet partem nec possessionem tecum et peregrinus et pupillus ac vidua qui intra portas tuas sunt et comedent et saturabuntur ut benedicat tibi Dominus, Deus tuus, in cunctis operibus manuum tuarum quae feceris."

thy sheep that thou mayst learn to fear the Lord, thy God, at all times. 24 But when the way and the place which the Lord, thy God, shall choose are far off and he hath blessed thee and thou canst not carry all these things thither, 25 thou shalt sell them all and *turn them into money* and shalt carry it in thy hand and shalt go to the place which the *Lord* shall choose, 26 and thou shalt buy with the same money whatsoever pleaseth thee either of the herds or of sheep, wine also and strong drink and all that thy soul desireth, and thou shalt eat before the Lord, thy God, and shalt feast, thou and thy house 27 and the Levite that is within thy gates—beware thou forsake him not, because he hath no other part in thy possession.

28 "The third year thou shalt separate another tithe of all things that grow to thee at that time and shalt lay it up within thy gates. 29 And the Levite that hath no other part nor possession with thee and the stranger and the fatherless and the widow that are within thy gates *shall come* and shall eat and be filled that the Lord, thy God, may bless thee in all the works of thy hands that thou shalt do."

Caput 15

"Septimo anno facies remissionem 2 quae hoc ordine celebrabitur: cui debetur aliquid ab amico vel proximo ac fratre suo repetere non poterit, quia annus remissionis est Domini. 3 A peregrino et advena exiges; civem et propinquum repetendi non habebis potestatem.

4 "Et omnino indigens et mendicus non erit inter vos ut benedicat tibi Dominus, Deus tuus, in terra quam traditurus est tibi in possessionem. 5 Si tamen audieris vocem Domini, Dei tui, et custodieris universa quae iussit et quae ego hodie praecipio tibi, benedicet tibi ut pollicitus est.

6 "Fenerabis gentibus multis, et ipse a nullo accipies mutuum. Dominaberis nationibus plurimis, et tui nemo dominabitur. 7 Si unus de fratribus tuis qui morantur intra portas civitatis tuae in terra quam Dominus, Deus tuus, daturus est tibi ad paupertatem venerit, non obdurabis cor tuum nec contrahes manum tuam 8 sed aperies eam pauperi; et dabis mutuum quod eum indigere perspexeris. 9 Cave ne forte subrepat tibi impia cogitatio et dicas in corde tuo,

Chapter 15

The law of the seventh year of remission. The firstlings of cattle are to be sanctified to the Lord.

"In the seventh year thou shalt make a remission 2 which shall be celebrated in this order: he to whom any thing is owing from his friend or neighbour or brother cannot demand it again, because it is the year of remission of the Lord. 3 Of the foreigner or stranger thou mayst exact it; of thy countryman and neighbour thou shalt not have power to demand it again.

4 "And there shall be no poor nor beggar among you that the Lord, thy God, may bless thee in the land which he will give thee in possession. 5 Yet so if thou hear the voice of the Lord, thy God, and keep all things that he hath ordained and which I command thee this day, he will bless thee as he hath promised.

6 "Thou shalt lend to many nations, and thou shalt borrow of no man. Thou shalt have dominion over very many nations, and no one shall have dominion over thee. 7 If one of thy brethren that dwelleth within thy gates of thy city in the land which the Lord, thy God, will give thee come to poverty, thou shalt not harden thy heart nor close thy hand 8 but shalt open it to the poor man; *thou* shalt lend him that which thou perceivest he hath need of. 9 Beware lest perhaps a wicked thought steal in upon thee and thou say in

'Adpropinquat septimus annus remissionis,' et avertas oculos tuos a paupere fratre tuo, nolens ei quod postulat mutuum commodare, ne clamet contra te ad Dominum et fiat tibi in peccatum. 10 Sed dabis ei, nec ages quippiam callide in eius necessitatibus sublevandis, ut benedicat tibi Dominus, Deus tuus, in omni tempore et in cunctis ad quae manum miseris.

11 "Non deerunt pauperes in terra habitationis tuae, idcirco ego praecipio tibi ut aperias manum fratri tuo egeno et pauperi qui tecum versatur in terra. 12 Cum tibi venditus fuerit frater tuus, Hebraeus aut Hebraea, et sex annis servierit tibi, in septimo anno dimittes eum liberum. 13 Et quem libertate donaveris, nequaquam vacuum abire patieris 14 sed dabis viaticum de gregibus et de area et torculari tuo quibus Dominus, Deus tuus, benedixerit tibi. 15 Memento quod et ipse servieris in terra Aegypti et liberaverit te Dominus, Deus tuus, et idcirco ego nunc praecipio tibi. 16 Sin autem dixerit, 'Nolo egredi,' eo quod diligat te et domum tuam et bene sibi apud te esse sentiat, 17 adsumes subulam et perforabis aurem eius in ianua domus tuae, et serviet tibi usque in aeternum. Ancillae quoque similiter facies. 18 Non avertas ab eis oculos tuos quando dimiseris eos liberos, quoniam iuxta mercedem mercennarii per sex annos servivit tibi, ut benedicat tibi Dominus, Deus tuus, in cunctis operibus quae agis.

19 "De primogenitis quae nascuntur in armentis et ovibus tuis, quicquid sexus est masculini sanctificabis Domino, Deo tuo. Non operaberis in primogenito bovis, et non ton-

thy heart, 'The seventh year of remission draweth nigh,' and thou turn away thy eyes from thy poor brother, denying to lend him that which he asketh, lest he cry against thee to the Lord and it become a sin unto thee. 10 But thou shalt give to him, neither shalt thou do any thing craftily in relieving his necessities, that the Lord, thy God, may bless thee at all times and in all things to which thou shalt put thy hand.

11 "There will not be wanting poor in the land of thy habitation, therefore I command thee to open thy hand to thy needy and poor brother that liveth in the land. 12 When thy brother, a Hebrew man or Hebrew woman, is sold to thee and hath served thee six years, in the seventh year thou shalt let him go free. 13 And when thou sendest him out free, thou shalt not let him go away empty 14 but shall give him for his way out of *thy* flocks and out of *thy* barnfloor and thy winepress wherewith the Lord, thy God, shall bless thee. 15 Remember that thou also wast a bondservant in the land of Egypt and the Lord, thy God, made thee free, and therefore I now command thee this. 16 But if he say, 'I will not depart,' because he loveth thee and thy house and findeth that he is well with thee, 17 thou shalt take an awl and bore through his ear in the door of thy house, and he shall serve thee for ever. Thou shalt do in like manner to thy womanservant also. 18 Turn not away thy eyes from them when thou makest them free, because he hath served thee six years according to the wages of a hireling, that the Lord, thy God, may bless thee in all the works that thou dost.

19 "Of the firstlings that come of thy herds and thy sheep, thou shalt sanctify to the Lord, thy God, whatsoever is of the male sex. Thou shalt not work with the firstling of a bull-

debis primogenita ovium. 20 In conspectu Domini, Dei tui,
comedes ea per annos singulos in loco quem elegerit Dominus, tu et domus tua. 21 Sin autem habuerit maculam, et vel
claudum fuerit vel caecum aut in aliqua parte deforme vel
debile, non immolabitur Domino, Deo tuo, 22 sed intra portas urbis tuae comedes illud. Tam mundus quam inmundus
similiter vescentur eis, quasi caprea et cervo. 23 Hoc solum
observabis, ut sanguinem eorum non comedas, sed effundas
in terram quasi aquam."

Caput 16

"Observa mensem novarum frugum et verni primum
temporis, ut facias phase Domino, Deo tuo, quoniam in isto
mense eduxit te Dominus, Deus tuus, de Aegypto nocte.
2 Immolabisque phase Domino, Deo tuo, de ovibus et de
bubus in loco quem elegerit Dominus, Deus tuus, ut habitet
nomen eius ibi. 3 Non comedes in eo panem fermentatum.
Septem diebus comedes absque fermento adflictionis panem, quoniam in pavore egressus es de Aegypto, ut memine-
ris diei egressionis tuae de Aegypto omnibus diebus vitae

ock, and thou shalt not shear the firstlings of thy sheep. 20 In the sight of the Lord, thy God, shalt thou eat them every year in the place that the Lord shall choose, thou and thy house. 21 But if it have a blemish *or* be lame or blind or in any part disfigured or feeble, it shall not be sacrificed to the Lord, thy God, 22 but thou shalt eat it within the gates of thy city. The clean and the unclean shall eat them alike, as the roe and as the hart. 23 Only thou shalt take heed not to eat their blood, but pour it out on the earth as water."

Chapter 16

The three principal solemnities to be observed. Just judges to be appointed in every city. All occasions of idolatry to be avoided.

"Observe the month of new corn, *which is* the first of the spring, that thou mayst celebrate the phase to the Lord, thy God, because in this month the Lord, thy God, brought thee out of Egypt by night. 2 And thou shalt sacrifice the phase to the Lord, thy God, of sheep and of oxen in the place which the Lord, thy God, shall choose that his name may dwell there. 3 Thou shalt not eat with it leavened bread. Seven days shalt thou eat without leaven the bread of affliction, because thou camest out of Egypt in fear, that thou mayst remember the day of thy coming out of Egypt all the

tuae. 4 Non apparebit fermentum in omnibus terminis tuis septem diebus, et non manebit de carnibus eius quod immolatum est vesperi in die primo usque mane.

5 "Non poteris immolare phase in qualibet urbium tuarum quas Dominus, Deus tuus, daturus est tibi 6 sed in loco quem elegerit Dominus, Deus tuus, ut habitet nomen eius ibi. Immolabis phase vesperi ad solis occasum, quando egressus es de Aegypto. 7 Et coques et comedes in loco quem elegerit Dominus, Deus tuus, maneque consurgens vades in tabernacula tua. 8 Sex diebus comedes azyma, et in die septimo, quia collecta est Domini, Dei tui, non facies opus.

9 "Septem ebdomadas numerabis tibi ab ea die qua falcem in segetem miseris, 10 et celebrabis diem festum ebdomadarum Domino, Deo tuo, oblationem spontaneam manus tuae quam offeres iuxta benedictionem Domini, Dei tui. 11 Et epulaberis coram Domino, Deo tuo, tu et filius tuus et filia tua et servus tuus et ancilla tua et Levites qui est intra portas tuas et advena ac pupillus et vidua qui morantur vobiscum in loco quem elegerit Dominus, Deus tuus, ut habitet nomen eius ibi, 12 et recordaberis quoniam servus fueris in Aegypto, custodiesque ac facies quae praecepta sunt.

13 "Sollemnitatem quoque tabernaculorum celebrabis per septem dies quando collegeris de area et torculari fruges tuas, 14 et epulaberis in festivitate tua, tu, filius tuus et filia

days of thy life. 4 No leaven shall be seen in all thy coasts for seven days, neither shall any of the flesh of that which was sacrificed the first day in the evening remain until morning.

5 "Thou mayst not immolate the phase in any one of thy cities which the Lord, thy God, will give thee 6 but in the place which the Lord, thy God, shall choose that his name may dwell there. Thou shalt immolate the phase in the evening at the going down of the sun, at which time thou camest out of Egypt. 7 And thou shalt dress and eat it in the place which the Lord, thy God, shall choose, and in the morning rising up thou shalt go into thy dwellings. 8 Six days shalt thou eat unleavened bread, and on the seventh day, because it is the assembly of the Lord, thy God, thou shalt do no work.

9 "Thou shalt number unto thee seven weeks from that day wherein thou didst put the sickle to the corn, 10 and thou shalt celebrate the festival of weeks to the Lord, thy God, a voluntary oblation of thy hand which thou shalt offer according to the blessing of the Lord, thy God. 11 And thou shalt feast before the Lord, thy God, thou and thy son and thy daughter and thy manservant and thy maidservant and the Levite that is within thy gates and the stranger and the fatherless and the widow who abide with you in the place which the Lord, thy God, shall choose that his name may dwell there, 12 and thou shalt remember that thou wast a servant in Egypt, and thou shalt keep and do the things that are commanded.

13 "Thou shalt celebrate the solemnity also of tabernacles seven days when thou hast gathered in thy fruit of the barnfloor and of the winepress, 14 and thou shalt make merry in thy festival time, thou, thy son and thy daughter, thy man-

tua, servus tuus et ancilla, Levites quoque et advena et pupillus ac vidua qui intra portas tuas sunt. 15 Septem diebus
Domino, Deo tuo, festa celebrabis in loco quem elegerit
Dominus, benedicetque tibi Dominus, Deus tuus, in cunctis frugibus tuis et in omni opere manuum tuarum, erisque
in laetitia.

16 "Tribus vicibus per annum apparebit omne masculinum
tuum in conspectu Domini, Dei tui, in loco quem elegerit:
in sollemnitate azymorum, in sollemnitate ebdomadarum et
in sollemnitate tabernaculorum. Non apparebit ante Dominum vacuus, 17 sed offeret unusquisque secundum quod habuerit, iuxta benedictionem Domini, Dei sui, quam dederit ei.

18 "Iudices et magistros constitues in omnibus portis tuis
quas Dominus, Deus tuus, dederit tibi, per singulas tribus
tuas, ut iudicent populum iusto iudicio 19 nec in alteram partem declinent. Non accipies personam nec munera, quia
munera excaecant oculos sapientium et mutant verba iustorum. 20 Iuste quod iustum est persequeris ut vivas et possideas terram quam Dominus, Deus tuus, dederit tibi.

21 "Non plantabis lucum et omnem arborem iuxta altare
Domini, Dei tui, 22 nec facies tibi neque constitues statuam,
quae odit Dominus, Deus tuus."

servant and *thy* maidservant, the Levite also and the stranger and the fatherless and the widow that are within thy gates. 15 Seven days shalt thou celebrate feasts to the Lord, thy God, in the place which the Lord shall choose, and the Lord, thy God, will bless thee in all thy fruits and in every work of thy hands, and thou shalt be in joy.

16 "Three times in a year shall all thy *males* appear before the Lord, thy God, in the place which he shall choose: in the feast of unleavened bread, in the feast of weeks and in the feast of tabernacles. No one shall appear *with his hands* empty before the Lord, 17 but every one shall offer according to what he hath, according to the blessing of the Lord, his God, which he shall give him.

18 "Thou shalt appoint judges and magistrates in all thy gates which the Lord, thy God, shall give thee, in all thy tribes, that they may judge the people with just judgment 19 and not go aside to either part. Thou shalt not accept person nor gifts, for gifts blind the eyes of the wise and change the words of the just. 20 Thou shalt follow justly after that which is just that thou mayst live and possess the land which the Lord, thy God, shall give thee.

21 "Thou shalt plant no grove nor any tree near the altar of the Lord, thy God, 22 neither shalt thou make nor set up to thyself a statue, which things the Lord, thy God, hateth."

Caput 17

"Non immolabis Domino, Deo tuo, ovem et bovem in quo est macula aut quippiam vitii, quia abominatio est Domino, Deo tuo.

2 "Cum repperti fuerint apud te intra unam portarum tuarum quas Dominus, Deus tuus, dabit tibi vir aut mulier qui faciant malum in conspectu Domini, Dei tui, et transgrediantur pactum illius 3 ut vadant et serviant diis alienis et adorent eos, solem et lunam et omnem militiam caeli, quae non praecepi, 4 et hoc tibi fuerit nuntiatum audiensque inquisieris diligenter et verum esse reppereris et abominatio facta est in Israhel, 5 educes virum ac mulierem qui rem sceleratissimam perpetrarunt ad portas civitatis tuae, et lapidibus obruentur. 6 In ore duorum aut trium testium peribit qui interficietur; nemo occidatur uno contra se dicente testimonium. 7 Manus testium prima interficiet eum, et manus reliqui populi extrema mittetur, ut auferas malum de medio tui.

Chapter 17

Victims must be without blemish. Idolaters are to be slain. Controversies are to be decided by the high priest and council, whose sentence must be obeyed under pain of death. The duty of a king, who is to receive the law of God at the priest's hands.

"Thou shalt not sacrifice to the Lord, thy God, a sheep or an ox wherein there is blemish or any fault, for that is an abomination to the Lord, thy God.

2 "When there shall be found among you within any of thy gates which the Lord, thy God, shall give thee man or woman that do evil in the sight of the Lord, thy God, and transgress his covenant 3 so as to go and serve strange gods and adore them, the sun and the moon and all the host of heaven, which I have not commanded, 4 and this is told thee and hearing it thou hast inquired diligently and found it to be true and that the abomination is committed in Israel, 5 thou shalt bring forth the man or the woman who have committed that most wicked thing to the gates of thy city, and they shall be stoned. 6 By the mouth of two or three witnesses shall he die that is to be slain; let no man be put to death when only one beareth witness against him. 7 The hands of the witnesses shall be first *upon him to kill him, and afterwards, the hands of the rest of the people,* that thou mayst take away the evil out of the midst of thee.

8 "Si difficile et ambiguum apud te iudicium esse perspexeris inter sanguinem et sanguinem, causam et causam, lepram et non lepram et iudicum intra portas tuas videris verba variari, surge, et ascende ad locum quem elegerit Dominus, Deus tuus, 9 veniesque ad sacerdotes Levitici generis et ad iudicem qui fuerit illo tempore, quaeresque ab eis, qui indicabunt tibi iudicii veritatem. 10 Et facies quodcumque dixerint qui praesunt loco quem elegerit Dominus et docuerint te 11 iuxta legem eius, sequerisque sententiam eorum; nec declinabis ad dextram neque ad sinistram.

12 "Qui autem superbierit nolens oboedire sacerdotis imperio qui eo tempore ministrat Domino, Deo tuo, et decreto iudicis, morietur homo ille, et auferes malum de Israhel. 13 Cunctusque populus audiens timebit, ut nullus deinceps intumescat superbia.

14 "Cum ingressus fueris terram quam Dominus, Deus tuus, dabit tibi et possederis eam habitaverisque in illa et dixeris, 'Constituam super me regem, sicut habent omnes per circuitum nationes,' 15 eum constitues quem Dominus, Deus tuus, elegerit de numero fratrum tuorum. Non poteris alterius gentis hominem regem facere qui non sit frater tuus. 16 Cumque fuerit constitutus, non multiplicabit sibi equos nec reducet populum in Aegyptum, equitatus numero sublevatus, praesertim cum Dominus praeceperit vobis ut nequaquam amplius per eandem viam revertamini. 17 Non habebit uxores plurimas quae inliciant animum eius neque argenti et

8 "If thou perceive that there be among you a hard and doubtful matter in judgment between blood and blood, cause and cause, leprosy and *leprosy* and thou see that the words of the judges within thy gates do vary, arise, and go up to the place which the Lord, thy God, shall choose, 9 and thou shalt come to the priests of the Levitical race and to the judge that shall be at that time, and thou shalt ask of them, and they shall shew thee the truth of the judgment. 10 And thou shalt do whatsoever they shall say that preside in the place which the Lord shall choose and what they shall teach thee 11 according to his law, and thou shalt follow their sentence; neither shalt thou decline to the right hand nor to the left hand.

12 "But he that will be proud and refuse to obey the commandment of the priest who ministereth at that time to the Lord, thy God, and the decree of the judge, that man shall die, and thou shalt take away the evil from Israel. 13 And all the people hearing it shall fear, that no one afterwards swell with pride.

14 "When thou art come into the land which the Lord, thy God, will give thee and possessest it and dwellest in it and shalt say, 'I will set a king over me, as all nations have that are round about,' 15 thou shalt set him whom the Lord, thy God, shall choose out of the number of thy brethren. Thou mayst not make a man of another nation king that is not thy brother. 16 And when he is made king, he shall not multiply horses to himself nor lead back the people into Egypt, being lifted up with the number of his horsemen, especially since the Lord hath commanded you to return no more the same way. 17 He shall not have many wives that may allure his mind nor immense sums of silver and gold.

auri inmensa pondera. 18 Postquam autem sederit in solio regni sui, describet sibi Deuteronomium legis huius in volumine, accipiens exemplar a sacerdotibus Leviticae tribus, 19 et habebit secum legetque illud omnibus diebus vitae suae ut discat timere Dominum, Deum suum, et custodire verba et caerimonias eius quae in lege praecepta sunt 20 nec elevetur cor eius in superbiam super fratres suos neque declinet in partem dextram vel sinistram, ut longo tempore regnet ipse et filii eius super Israhel."

Caput 18

"Non habebunt sacerdotes et Levitae et omnes qui de eadem tribu sunt partem et hereditatem cum reliquo Israhel quia sacrificia Domini et oblationes eius comedent, 2 et nihil aliud accipient de possessione fratrum suorum, Dominus enim ipse est hereditas eorum, sicut locutus est illis. 3 Hoc erit iudicium sacerdotum a populo et ab his qui offerunt victimas, sive bovem sive ovem immolaverint, dabunt sacerdoti armum ac ventriculum, 4 primitias frumenti, vini et olei et lanarum partem ex ovium ton-

18 But after he *is raised* to the throne of his kingdom, he shall copy out to himself the Deuteronomy of this law in a volume, taking the copy of the priests of the Levitical tribe, 19 and he shall have it with him and shall read it all the days of his life that he may learn to fear the Lord, his God, and keep his words and ceremonies that are commanded in the law 20 and that his heart be not lifted up with pride over his brethren nor decline to the right or to the left, that he and his sons may reign a long time over Israel."

Chapter 18

The Lord is the inheritance of the priests and Levites. Heathenish abominations are to be avoided. The great prophet Christ is promised. False prophets must be slain.

"The priests and Levites and all that are of the same tribe shall have no part nor inheritance with the rest of Israel because they shall eat the sacrifices of the Lord and his oblations, 2 and they shall receive nothing else of the possession of their brethren, for the Lord himself is their inheritance, as he hath said to them. 3 This shall be the *priest's due* from the people and from them that offer victims, whether they sacrifice an ox or a sheep, they shall give to the priest the shoulder and the breast, 4 the firstfruits *also* of corn, of wine and of oil and a part of the wool from the shearing of

sione, 5 ipsum enim elegit Dominus, Deus tuus, de cunctis tribubus tuis ut stet et ministret nomini Domini, ipse et filii eius in sempiternum.

6 "Si exierit Levites de una urbium tuarum ex omni Israhel in qua habitat et voluerit venire desiderans locum quem elegerit Dominus, 7 ministrabit in nomine Domini, Dei sui, sicut omnes fratres eius Levitae qui stabunt eo tempore coram Domino. 8 Partem ciborum eandem accipiet quam et ceteri excepto eo quod in urbe sua ex paterna ei successione debetur.

9 "Quando ingressus fueris terram quam Dominus, Deus tuus, dabit tibi, cave ne imitari velis abominationes illarum gentium. 10 Nec inveniatur in te qui lustret filium suum aut filiam, ducens per ignem, aut qui ariolos sciscitetur et observet somnia atque auguria, nec sit maleficus 11 nec incantator nec qui pythones consulat nec divinos et quaerat a mortuis veritatem, 12 omnia enim haec abominatur Dominus, et propter istiusmodi scelera delebit eos in introitu tuo.

13 "Perfectus eris et absque macula cum Domino, Deo tuo. 14 Gentes istae quarum possidebis terram augures et divinos audiunt, tu autem a Domino, Deo tuo, aliter institutus es.

15 "Prophetam de gente tua et de fratribus tuis sicut me suscitabit tibi Dominus, Deus tuus. Ipsum audies 16 ut petisti a Domino, Deo tuo, in Horeb, quando contio congregata est, atque dixisti, 'Ultra non audiam vocem Domini,

their sheep, 5 for the Lord, thy God, hath chosen him of all thy tribes to stand and to minister to the name of the Lord, him and his sons for ever.

6 "If a Levite go out of any one of the cities throughout all Israel in which he dwelleth and *have a longing mind* to come to the place which the Lord shall choose, 7 he shall minister in the name of the Lord, his God, as all his brethren the Levites do that shall stand at that time before the Lord. 8 He shall receive the same portion of food that the rest do besides that which is due to him in his own city by succession from his fathers.

9 "When thou art come into the land which the Lord, thy God, shall give thee, beware lest thou have a mind to imitate the abominations of those nations. 10 Neither let there be found among you any one that shall expiate his son or daughter, making them to pass through the fire, or that consulteth soothsayers or observeth dreams and omens, neither let there be any wizard 11 nor charmer nor any one that consulteth *pythonic spirits* or fortune tellers *or* that seeketh the truth from the dead, 12 for the Lord abhorreth all these things, and for these abominations he will destroy them at thy coming.

13 "Thou shalt be perfect and without spot *before* the Lord, thy God. 14 These nations whose land thou shalt possess hearken to soothsayers and diviners, but thou art otherwise instructed by the Lord, thy God.

15 "The Lord, thy God, will raise up to thee a prophet of thy nation and of thy brethren like unto me. Him thou shalt hear 16 as thou desiredst of the Lord, thy God, in Horeb, when the assembly was gathered together, and saidst, 'Let me not hear any more the voice of the Lord, my God, nei-

Dei mei, et ignem hunc maximum amplius non videbo ne moriar,' 17 et ait Dominus mihi, 'Bene omnia sunt locuti. 18 Prophetam suscitabo eis de medio fratrum suorum similem tui, et ponam verba mea in ore eius, loqueturque ad eos omnia quae praecepero illi. 19 Qui autem verba eius quae loquetur in nomine meo audire noluerit, ego ultor existam.

20 "'Propheta autem qui arrogantia depravatus voluerit loqui in nomine meo quae ego non praecepi illi ut diceret aut ex nomine alienorum deorum interficietur.'

21 "Quod si tacita cogitatione responderis, 'Quomodo possum intellegere verbum quod non est locutus Dominus?' 22 hoc habebis signum: quod in nomine Domini propheta ille praedixerit et non evenerit, hoc Dominus non locutus est, sed per tumorem animi sui propheta confinxit, et idcirco non timebis eum."

Caput 19

"Cum disperderit Dominus, Deus tuus, gentes quarum tibi traditurus est terram et possederis eam habitaverisque in urbibus eius et in aedibus, 2 tres civitates separabis tibi in medio terrae quam Dominus, Deus tuus, dabit tibi in pos-

ther *let me* see any more this exceeding great fire lest I die,' 17 and the Lord said to me, 'They have spoken all things well. 18 I will raise them up a prophet out of the midst of their brethren like to thee, and I will put my words in his mouth, and he shall speak to them all that I shall command him. 19 And he that will not hear his words which he shall speak in my name, I will be the revenger.

20 "'But the prophet who being corrupted with pride *shall* speak in my name things that I did not command him to say or in the name of strange gods shall be slain.'

21 "And if in silent thought thou answer, 'How shall I know the word that the Lord hath not spoken?' 22 thou shalt have this sign: whatsoever that *same* prophet foretelleth in the name of the Lord and it cometh not to pass, that thing the Lord hath not spoken, but the prophet hath forged it by the pride of his mind, and therefore thou shalt not fear him."

Chapter 19

The cities of refuge. Wilful murder and false witnesses must be punished.

"When the Lord, thy God, hath destroyed the nations whose land he will deliver to thee and thou shalt possess it and shalt dwell in the cities and houses thereof, 2 thou shalt separate to thee three cities in the midst of the land which

sessionem, 3 sternens diligenter viam, et in tres aequaliter partes totam terrae tuae provinciam divides, ut habeat e vicino qui propter homicidium profugus est quo possit evadere.

4 "Haec erit lex homicidae fugientis cuius vita servanda est: qui percusserit proximum suum nesciens et qui heri et nudius tertius nullum contra eum habuisse odium conprobatur 5 sed abisse simpliciter cum eo in silvam ad ligna caedenda et in succisione lignorum securis fugerit manu ferrumque lapsum de manubrio amicum eius percusserit et occiderit, hic ad unam supradictarum urbium confugiet et vivet. 6 Ne forsitan proximus eius cuius effusus est sanguis, dolore stimulatus, persequatur et adprehendat eum, si longior via fuerit, et percutiat animam eius qui non est reus mortis quia nullum contra eum qui occisus est odium prius habuisse monstratur, 7 idcirco praecipio tibi ut tres civitates aequalis inter se spatii dividas.

8 "Cum autem dilataverit Dominus, Deus tuus, terminos tuos sicut iuravit patribus tuis et dederit tibi cunctam terram quam eis pollicitus est, 9 si tamen custodieris mandata eius et feceris quae hodie praecipio tibi, ut diligas Dominum, Deum tuum, et ambules in viis eius omni tempore, addes tibi tres alias civitates et supradictarum trium urbium numerum duplicabis 10 ut non effundatur sanguis innoxius in medio terrae quam Dominus, Deus tuus, dabit tibi possidendam, ne sis sanguinis reus.

11 "Si quis autem odio habens proximum suum insidiatus fuerit vitae eius surgensque percusserit illum et mortuus fuerit fugeritque ad unam de supradictis urbibus, 12 mittent

the *Lord* will give thee in possession, 3 paving diligently the way, and thou shalt divide the whole province of thy land equally into three parts, that he who is forced to flee for manslaughter may have near at hand whither to escape.

4 "This shall be the law of the slayer that fleeth whose life is to be saved: he that killeth his neighbor ignorantly and who is proved to have had no hatred against him yesterday and the day before 5 but to have gone with him to the wood to hew wood and in cutting down the *tree* the axe slipped out of his hand and the iron slipping from the handle struck his friend and killed him, he shall flee to one of the cities aforesaid and live. 6 Lest perhaps the next kinsman of him whose blood was shed, pushed on by his grief, should pursue and apprehend him, if the way be too long, and take away the life of him who is not guilty of death because he is proved to have had no hatred before against him that was slain, 7 therefore I command thee that thou separate three cities at equal distance one from another.

8 "And when the Lord, thy God, shall have enlarged thy borders as he swore to thy fathers and shall give thee all the land that he promised them, 9 yet so, if thou keep his commandments and do the things which I command thee this day, that thou love the Lord, thy God, and walk in his ways at all times, thou shalt add to thee other three cities and shalt double the number of the three cities aforesaid 10 that innocent blood may not be shed in the midst of the land which the Lord, thy God, will give thee to possess, lest thou be guilty of blood.

11 "But if any man hating his neighbour lie in wait for his life and rise and strike him and he die and he flee to one of the cities aforesaid, 12 the ancients of his city shall send and

seniores civitatis illius et arripient eum de loco effugii tradentque in manu proximi cuius sanguis effusus est, et morietur. 13 Non misereberis eius, et auferes innoxium sanguinem de Israhel ut bene sit tibi.

14 "Non adsumes et transferes terminos proximi tui quos fixerunt priores in possessione tua quam Dominus, Deus tuus, dabit tibi in terra quam acceperis possidendam.

15 "Non stabit testis unus contra aliquem, quicquid illud peccati et facinoris fuerit, sed in ore duorum aut trium testium stabit omne verbum.

16 "Si steterit testis mendax contra hominem, accusans eum praevaricationis, 17 stabunt ambo quorum causa est ante Dominum in conspectu sacerdotum et iudicum qui fuerint in diebus illis. 18 Cumque diligentissime perscrutantes invenerint falsum testem dixisse contra fratrem suum mendacium, 19 reddent ei sicut fratri suo facere cogitavit, et auferes malum de medio tui 20 ut audientes ceteri timorem habeant et nequaquam talia audeant facere. 21 Non misereberis eius, sed animam pro anima, oculum pro oculo, dentem pro dente, manum pro manu, pedem pro pede exiges."

take him out of the place of refuge and shall deliver him into the hand of the kinsman of him whose blood was shed, and he shall die. 13 Thou shalt not pity him, and thou shalt take away the guilt of innocent blood out of Israel that it may be well with thee.

14 "Thou shalt not take nor remove thy neighbour's *landmarks* which thy predecessors have set in thy possession which the Lord, thy God, will give thee in the land that thou shalt receive to possess.

15 "One witness shall not rise up against any man, whatsoever the sin or wickedness be, but in the mouth of two or three witnesses every word shall stand.

16 "If a lying witness stand against a man, accusing him of transgression, 17 both of them between whom the controversy is shall stand before the Lord in the sight of the priests and the judges that shall be in those days. 18 And when after most diligent inquisition they shall find that the false witness hath told a lie against his brother, 19 they shall render to him as he meant to do to his brother, and thou shalt take away the evil out of the midst of thee 20 that others hearing may fear and may not dare to do such things. 21 Thou shalt not pity him, but shalt require life for life, eye for eye, tooth for tooth, hand for hand, foot for foot."

Caput 20

"Si exieris ad bellum contra hostes tuos et videris equitatum et currus et maiorem quam tu habes adversarii exercitus multitudinem, non timebis eos, quia Dominus, Deus tuus, tecum est, qui eduxit te de terra Aegypti.

2 "Adpropinquante autem iam proelio, stabit sacerdos ante aciem et sic loquetur ad populum: 3 'Audi, Israhel: vos hodie contra inimicos vestros pugnam committitis; non pertimescat cor vestrum; nolite metuere; nolite cedere, nec formidetis eos, 4 quia Dominus, Deus vester, in medio vestri est et pro vobis contra adversarios dimicabit ut eruat vos de periculo.'

5 "Duces quoque per singulas turmas audiente exercitu proclamabunt, 'Quis est homo qui aedificavit domum novam et non dedicavit eam? Vadat et revertatur in domum suam ne forte moriatur in bello et alius dedicet illam.

6 "'Quis est homo qui plantavit vineam et necdum eam fecit esse communem de qua vesci omnibus liceat? Vadat et revertatur in domum suam ne forte moriatur in bello et alius homo eius fungatur officio.

7 "'Quis est homo qui despondit uxorem et non accepit eam? Vadat et revertatur in domum suam ne forte moriatur in bello et alius homo accipiat eam.'

Chapter 20

Laws relating to war.

"If thou go out to war against thy enemies and see horsemen and chariots and the *numbers* of the enemy's army greater than *thine,* thou shalt not fear them, because the Lord, thy God, is with thee, who brought thee out of the land of Egypt.

2 "And when the battle is now at hand, the priest shall stand before the army and shall speak to the people in this manner: 3 'Hear, O Israel: you join battle this day against your enemies; let not your heart be dismayed; be not afraid; do not give back; fear ye them not, 4 because the Lord, your God, is in the midst of you and will fight for you against your enemies to deliver you from danger.'

5 "And the captains shall proclaim through every band in the hearing of the army, 'What man is there that hath built a new house and hath not dedicated it? Let him go and return to his house lest he die in the battle and another man dedicate it.

6 "'What man is there that hath planted a vineyard and hath not as yet made it to be common whereof all men may eat? Let him go and return to his house lest he die in the battle and another man execute his office.

7 "'What man is there that hath espoused a wife and not taken her? Let him go and return to his house lest he die in the war and another man take her.'

8 "His dictis, addent reliqua et loquentur ad populum, 'Quis est homo formidolosus et corde pavido? Vadat et revertatur in domum suam ne pavere faciat corda fratrum suorum, sicut ipse timore perterritus est.'

9 "Cumque siluerint exercitus duces et finem loquendi fecerint, unusquisque suos ad bellandum cuneos praeparabit.

10 "Si quando accesseris ad expugnandam civitatem, offeres ei primum pacem. 11 Si receperit et aperuerit tibi portas, cunctus populus qui in ea est salvabitur et serviet tibi sub tributo. 12 Sin autem foedus inire noluerint et coeperint contra te bellum, obpugnabis eam. 13 Cumque tradiderit Dominus, Deus tuus, illam in manu tua, percuties omne quod in ea generis masculini est in ore gladii, 14 absque mulieribus et infantibus, iumentis et ceteris quae in civitate sunt; omnem praedam exercitui divides, et comedes de spoliis hostium tuorum quae Dominus, Deus tuus, dederit tibi.

15 "Sic facies cunctis civitatibus quae a te procul valde sunt et non sunt de his urbibus quas in possessionem accepturus es. 16 De his autem civitatibus quae dabuntur tibi, nullum omnino permittes vivere, 17 sed interficies in ore gladii, Hettheum, videlicet, et Amorreum et Chananeum, Ferezeum et Eveum et Iebuseum, sicut praecepit tibi Dominus, Deus tuus, 18 ne forte doceant vos facere cunctas abominationes quas ipsi operati sunt diis suis et peccetis in Dominum, Deum vestrum.

19 "Quando obsederis civitatem multo tempore et muni-

8 "After these things are declared, they shall add the rest and shall speak to the people, 'What man is there that is fearful and faint hearted? Let him go and return to his house lest he make the hearts of his brethren to fear, as he himself is possessed with fear.'

9 "And when the captains of the army shall hold their peace and have made an end of speaking, every man shall prepare their bands to fight.

10 "If at any time thou come to fight against a city, thou shalt first offer it peace. 11 If they receive it and open the gates to thee, all the people that are therein shall be saved and shall serve thee *paying* tribute. 12 But if they will not make peace and shall begin war against thee, thou shalt besiege it. 13 And when the Lord, thy God, shall deliver it into thy hands, thou shalt slay all that are therein of the male sex with the edge of the sword, 14 excepting women and children, cattle and other things that are in the city, *and* thou shalt divide all the prey to the army, and thou shalt eat the spoils of thy enemies which the Lord, thy God, shall give thee.

15 "So shalt thou do to all cities that are at a great distance from thee and are not of these cities which thou shalt receive in possession. 16 But of those cities that shall be given thee, thou shalt suffer none at all to live, 17 but shalt kill them with the edge of the sword, to wit, the Hittite and the Amorite and the Canaanite, the Perizzite and the Hivite and the Jebusite, as the Lord, thy God, hath commanded thee, 18 lest they teach you to do all the abominations which they have done to their gods and you should sin against the Lord, your God.

19 "When thou hast besieged a city a long time and hath

tionibus circumdederis ut expugnes eam, non succides arbores de quibus vesci potest, nec securibus per circuitum
debes vastare regionem, quoniam lignum est et non homo,
nec potest bellantium contra te augere numerum. 20 Si qua
autem ligna non sunt pomifera sed agrestia et in ceteros
apta usus, succide et extrue machinas donec capias civitatem quae contra te dimicat."

Caput 21

"Quando inventum fuerit in terra quam Dominus,
Deus tuus, daturus est tibi hominis cadaver occisi et ignoratur caedis reus, 2 egredientur maiores natu et iudices tui et
metientur a loco cadaveris singularum per circuitum spatia
civitatum, 3 et quam viciniorem ceteris esse perspexerint
seniores civitatis eius tollent vitulam de armento quae non
traxit iugum nec terram scidit vomere, 4 et ducent eam ad
vallem asperam atque saxosam quae numquam arata est nec

compassed it with bulwarks to take it, thou shalt not cut down the trees that may be eaten of, neither shalt thou spoil the country round about with axes, for it is a tree and not a man, neither can it increase the number of them that fight against thee. 20 But if there be any trees that are not fruitful but wild and fit for other uses, cut them down and make engines until thou take the city which fighteth against thee."

Chapter 21

The expiation of a secret murder. The marrying a captive.
The eldest son must not be deprived of his birthright for
hatred of his mother. A stubborn son is to be stoned to
death. When one is hanged on a gibbet, he must be taken
down the same day and buried.

"When there shall be found in the land which the Lord, thy God, will give thee the corpse of a man slain and it is not known who is guilty of the murder, 2 thy ancients and judges shall go out and shall measure from the place *where the body lieth* the distance of every city round about, 3 and the ancients of that city which they shall perceive to be nearer than the rest shall take a heifer of the herd that hath not drawn in the yoke nor ploughed the ground, 4 and they shall bring her into a rough and stony valley that never was ploughed nor sown, and there they shall strike off the head

sementem recepit, et caedent in ea cervices vitulae. 5 Accedentque sacerdotes, filii Levi, quos elegerit Dominus, Deus tuus, ut ministrent ei et benedicant in nomine eius et ad verbum eorum omne negotium pendet et quicquid mundum vel inmundum est iudicetur, 6 et venient maiores natu civitatis illius ad interfectum lavabuntque manus suas super vitulam quae in valle percussa est 7 et dicent, 'Manus nostrae non effuderunt hunc sanguinem, nec oculi viderunt. 8 Propitius esto populo tuo Israhel quem redemisti, Domine, et non reputes sanguinem innocentem in medio populi tui Israhel.' Et auferetur ab eis reatus sanguinis, 9 tu autem alienus eris ab innocentis cruore qui fusus est cum feceris quod praecepit Dominus.

10 "Si egressus fueris ad pugnam contra inimicos tuos et tradiderit eos Dominus, Deus tuus, in manu tua captivosque duxeris 11 et videris in numero captivorum mulierem pulchram et adamaveris eam voluerisque habere uxorem, 12 introduces eam in domum tuam, quae radet caesariem et circumcidet ungues 13 et deponet vestem in qua capta est sedensque in domo tua flebit patrem et matrem suam uno mense, et postea intrabis ad eam dormiesque cum illa, et erit uxor tua. 14 Sin autem postea non sederit animo tuo, dimittes eam liberam, nec vendere poteris pecunia nec opprimere per potentiam quia humiliasti eam.

15 "Si habuerit homo uxores duas, unam dilectam et alteram odiosam, genuerintque ex eo liberos et fuerit filius odiosae primogenitus 16 volueritque substantiam inter filios suos

of the heifer. 5 And the priests, the sons of Levi, shall come, whom the Lord, thy God, hath chosen to minister to him and to bless in his name and that by their word every matter should be decided and whatsoever is clean or unclean should be judged, 6 and the ancients of that city shall come to the person slain and shall wash their hands over the heifer that was killed in the valley 7 and shall say, 'Our hands did not shed this blood, nor did our eyes see it. 8 Be merciful to thy people Israel whom thou hast redeemed, O Lord, and lay not innocent blood to their charge in the midst of thy people Israel.' And the guilt of blood shall be taken from them, 9 and thou shalt be free from the innocent's blood that was shed when thou shalt have done what the Lord hath commanded thee.

10 "If thou go out to fight against thy enemies and the Lord, thy God, deliver them into thy hand and thou lead them away captives 11 and seest in the number of the captives a beautiful woman and lovest her and wilt have her to wife, 12 thou shalt bring her into thy house, and she shall shave her hair and pare her nails 13 and shall put off the raiment wherein she was taken and shall remain in thy house and mourn for her father and mother one month, and after that thou shalt go in unto her and shalt sleep with her, and she shall be thy wife. 14 But if afterwards she please *thee* not, thou shalt let her go free, but thou mayst not sell her for money nor oppress her by might because thou hast humbled her.

15 "If a man have two wives, one beloved and the other hated, and they have had children by him and the son of the hated be the firstborn 16 and he meaneth to divide his substance among his sons, he may not make the son of the

dividere, non poterit filium dilectae facere primogenitum et praeferre filio odiosae, 17 sed filium odiosae agnoscet primogenitum dabitque ei de his quae habuerit cuncta duplicia, iste est enim principium liberorum eius et huic debentur primogenita.

18 "Si genuerit homo filium contumacem et protervum qui non audiat patris aut matris imperium et coercitus oboedire contempserit, 19 adprehendent eum et ducent ad seniores civitatis illius et ad portam iudicii 20 dicentque ad eos, 'Filius noster iste protervus et contumax est; monita nostra audire contemnit; comesationibus vacat et luxuriae atque conviviis.' 21 Lapidibus eum obruet populus civitatis, et morietur ut auferatis malum de medio vestri et universus Israhel audiens pertimescat.

22 "Quando peccaverit homo quod morte plectendum est et adiudicatus morti adpensus fuerit in patibulo, 23 non permanebit cadaver eius in ligno sed in eadem die sepelietur, quia maledictus a Deo est qui pendet in ligno, et nequaquam contaminabis terram tuam quam Dominus, Deus tuus, dederit tibi in possessionem."

beloved the firstborn and prefer him before the son of the hated, 17 but he shall acknowledge the son of the hated for the firstborn and shall give him a double portion of all he hath, for this is the first of his children and to him are due the first birthrights.

18 "If a man have a stubborn and unruly son who will not *hear the commandments* of his father or mother and being corrected slighteth obedience, 19 they shall take him and bring him to the ancients of the city and to the gate of judgment 20 and shall say to them, 'This our son is rebellious and stubborn; he slighteth hearing our admonitions; he giveth himself to revelling and to debauchery and banquetings.' 21 The people of the city shall stone him, and he shall die that you may take away the evil out of the midst of you and all Israel hearing it may be afraid.

22 "When a man hath *committed a crime for which he is to be punished* with death and being condemned to die is hanged on a gibbet, 23 his body shall not remain upon the tree but shall be buried the same day, for he is accursed of God that hangeth on a tree, and thou shalt not defile thy land which the Lord, thy God, shall give thee in possession."

Caput 22

"Non videbis bovem fratris tui aut ovem errantem et praeteribis, sed reduces fratri tuo. 2 Etiam si non est propinquus tuus frater nec nosti eum, duces in domum tuam, et erunt apud te quamdiu quaerat ea frater tuus et recipiat. 3 Similiter facies de asino et de vestimento et de omni re fratris tui quae perierit. Si inveneris eam, ne neglegas quasi alienam.

4 "Si videris asinum fratris tui aut bovem cecidisse in via, non despicies, sed sublevabis cum eo.

5 "Non induetur mulier veste virili, nec vir utetur veste feminea, abominabilis enim apud Deum est qui facit haec.

6 "Si ambulans per viam in arbore vel in terra nidum avis inveneris et matrem pullis vel ovis desuper incubantem, non tenebis eam cum filiis, 7 sed abire patieris, captos tenens filios ut bene sit tibi et longo vivas tempore.

Chapter 22

Humanity towards neighbours. Neither sex may use the apparel of the other. Cruelty to be avoided even to birds. Battlements about the roof of a house. Things of divers kinds not to be mixed. The punishment of him that slandereth his wife, as also of adultery and rape.

"*Thou shalt not pass by if thou seest* thy brother's ox or his sheep go astray, but thou shalt bring them back to thy brother. 2 And if thy brother be not nigh or thou know him not, thou shalt bring them to thy house, and they shall be with thee until thy brother seek them and receive them. 3 Thou shalt do in like manner with his ass and with his raiment and with every thing that is thy brother's which is lost. If thou find it, neglect it not as pertaining to another.

4 "If thou see thy brother's ass or his ox to be fallen down in the way, thou shalt not slight it, but shalt lift it up with him.

5 "A woman shall not be clothed with man's apparel, neither shall a man use woman's apparel, for he that doth these things is abominable before God.

6 "If thou find as thou walkest by the way a bird's nest in a tree or on the ground and the dam sitting upon the young or upon the eggs, thou shalt not take her with her young, 7 but shalt let her go, keeping the young which thou hast caught that it may be well with thee and thou mayst live a long time.

8 "Cum aedificaveris domum novam, facies murum tecti per circuitum ne effundatur sanguis in domo tua et sis reus labente alio et in praeceps ruente.

9 "Non seres vineam tuam altero semine ne et sementis quam sevisti et quae nascuntur ex vinea pariter sanctificentur.

10 "Non arabis in bove simul et asino.

11 "Non indueris vestimento quod ex lana linoque contextum est.

12 "Funiculos in fimbriis facies per quattuor angulos pallii tui quo operieris.

13 "Si duxerit vir uxorem et postea eam odio habuerit 14 quaesieritque occasiones quibus dimittat eam, obiciens ei nomen pessimum, et dixerit, 'Uxorem hanc accepi, et, ingressus ad eam, non inveni virginem,' 15 tollent eam pater et mater eius et ferent secum signa virginitatis eius ad seniores urbis qui in porta sunt, 16 et dicet pater, 'Filiam meam dedi huic uxorem, quam quia odit 17 inponit ei nomen pessimum, ut dicat, "Non inveni filiam tuam virginem," et ecce: haec sunt signa virginitatis filiae meae.' Expandent vestimentum coram senibus civitatis, 18 adprehendentque senes urbis illius virum et verberabunt illum, 19 condemnantes insuper centum siclis argenti quos dabit patri puellae, quoniam diffamavit nomen pessimum super virginem Israhel, habebitque eam uxorem et non poterit dimittere eam omnibus diebus vitae suae. 20 Quod si verum est quod obicit et non est in puella inventa virginitas, 21 eicient eam extra fores domus patris sui, et lapidibus obruent viri civitatis eius, et morietur

8 "When thou buildest a new house, thou shalt make a battlement to the roof round about lest blood be shed in thy house and thou be guilty if any one slip and fall down headlong.

9 "Thou shalt not sow thy vineyard with divers seeds lest both the seed which thou hast sown and the *fruit* of the vineyard be sanctified together.

10 "Thou shalt not plough with an ox and an ass together.

11 "Thou shalt not wear a garment that is woven of woollen and linen together.

12 "Thou shalt make strings in the hem at the four corners of thy cloak wherewith thou shalt be covered.

13 "If a man marry a wife and afterwards hate her 14 and seek occasions to put her away, laying to her charge a very ill name, and say, 'I took this woman to wife, and, going in to her, I found her not a virgin,' 15 her father and mother shall take her and shall bring with them the tokens of her virginity to the ancients of the city that are in the gate, 16 and the father shall say, 'I gave my daughter unto this man to wife, and because he hateth her 17 he layeth to her charge a very ill name, so as to say, "I found not thy daughter a virgin," and behold: these are the tokens of my daughter's virginity.' And they shall spread the cloth before the ancients of the city, 18 and the ancients of that city shall take *that* man and beat him, 19 condemning him besides in a hundred sicles of silver which he shall give to the damsel's father, because he hath defamed by a very ill name a virgin of Israel, and he shall have her to wife and may not put her away all the days of his life. 20 But if what he charged her with be true and virginity be not found in the damsel, 21 they shall cast her out of the doors of her father's house, and the men of the city shall

quoniam fecit nefas in Israhel, ut fornicaretur in domo patris sui, et auferes malum de medio tui.

22 "Si dormierit vir cum uxore alterius, uterque morientur, id est, adulter et adultera, et auferes malum de Israhel.

23 "Si puellam virginem desponderit vir et invenerit eam aliquis in civitate et concubuerit cum illa, 24 educes utrumque ad portam civitatis illius, et lapidibus obruentur, puella quia non clamavit cum esset in civitate, vir quia humiliavit uxorem proximi sui. Et auferes malum de medio tui. 25 Sin autem in agro reppererit vir puellam quae desponsata est, et adprehendens concubuerit cum illa, ipse morietur solus. 26 Puella nihil patietur, nec est rea mortis, quoniam sicut latro consurgit contra fratrem suum et occidit animam eius, ita et puella perpessa est. 27 Sola erat in agro, clamavit, et nullus adfuit qui liberaret eam.

28 "Si invenerit vir puellam virginem quae non habet sponsum et adprehendens concubuerit cum ea et res ad iudicium venerit, 29 dabit qui dormivit cum ea patri puellae quinquaginta siclos argenti et habebit eam uxorem, quia humiliavit illam. Non poterit dimittere eam cunctis diebus vitae suae.

30 "Non accipiet homo uxorem patris sui, nec revelabit operimentum eius."

stone her to death, and she shall die because she hath done a wicked thing in Israel, to play the whore in her father's house, and thou shalt take away the evil out of the midst of thee.

22 "If a man lie with another man's wife, they shall both die, that is to say, the adulterer and the adulteress, and thou shalt take away the evil out of Israel.

23 "If a man have espoused a damsel that is a virgin and some one find her in the city and lie with her, 24 thou shalt bring them both out to the gate of that city, and they shall be stoned, the damsel because she cried not out being in the city, the man because he hath humbled his neighbour's wife. And thou shalt take away the evil from the midst of thee. 25 But if a man find a damsel that is betrothed in the field, and taking hold of her lie with her, he alone shall die. 26 The damsel shall suffer nothing, neither is she guilty of death, for as a robber riseth against his brother and taketh away his life, so also did the damsel suffer. 27 She was alone in the field, she cried, and there was no man to *help* her.

28 "If a man find a damsel that is a virgin who is not espoused and taking her lie with her and the matter come to judgment, 29 he that lay with her shall give to the father of the maid fifty sicles of silver and shall have her to wife, because he hath humbled her. He may not put her away all the days of his life.

30 "No man shall take his father's wife, nor remove his covering."

Caput 23

"Non intrabit eunuchus adtritis vel amputatis testiculis et absciso veretro ecclesiam Domini.

2 "Non ingredietur mamzer, hoc est, de scorto natus, in ecclesiam Domini usque ad decimam generationem.

3 "Ammanites et Moabites, etiam post decimam generationem, non intrabunt ecclesiam Domini in aeternum 4 quia noluerunt vobis occurrere cum pane et aqua in via quando egressi estis de Aegypto et quia conduxerunt contra te Balaam, filium Beor, de Mesopotamiam Syriae, ut malediceret tibi. 5 Et noluit Dominus, Deus tuus, audire Balaam, vertitque maledictionem eius in benedictionem tuam eo quod diligeret te. 6 Non facies cum eis pacem, nec quaeras eis bona cunctis diebus vitae tuae in sempiternum.

7 "Non abominaberis Idumeum, quia frater tuus est, nec Aegyptium, quia advena fuisti in terra eius. 8 Qui nati fuerint ex eis tertia generatione intrabunt ecclesiam Domini.

9 "Quando egressus fueris adversus hostes tuos in pugnam, custodies te ab omni re mala.

Chapter 23

Who may and who may not enter into the church. Uncleanness to be avoided. Other precepts concerning fugitives, fornication, usury, vows and eating other men's grapes and corn.

"An eunuch whose testicles are broken or cut away or yard cut off shall not enter into the church of the Lord.

2 "A mamzer, that is to say, one born of a prostitute, shall not enter into the church of the Lord until the tenth generation.

3 "The Ammonite and the Moabite, even after the tenth generation, shall not enter into the church of the Lord for ever 4 because they would not meet you with bread and water in the way when you came out of Egypt and because they hired against thee Balaam, the son of Beor, from Mesopotamia in Syria, to curse thee. 5 And the Lord, thy God, would not hear Balaam, and he turned his cursing into thy blessing because he loved thee. 6 Thou shalt not make peace with them, neither *shalt* thou seek their prosperity all the days of thy life for ever.

7 "Thou shalt not abhor the Edomite, because he is thy brother, nor the Egyptian, because thou wast a stranger in his land. 8 They that are born of them in the third generation shall enter into the church of the Lord.

9 "When thou goest out to war against thy enemies, thou shalt keep thyself from every evil thing.

10 "Si fuerit inter vos homo qui nocturno pollutus sit somnio, egredietur extra castra 11 et non revertetur priusquam ad vesperam lavetur aqua. Et post solis occasum regredietur in castra.

12 "Habebis locum extra castra ad quem egrediaris ad requisita naturae, 13 gerens paxillum in balteo. Cumque sederis fodies per circuitum, et egesta humo operies 14 quo relevatus es, Dominus enim, Deus tuus, ambulat in medio castrorum ut eruat te et tradat tibi inimicos tuos, et sint castra tua sancta, et nihil in eis appareat foeditatis ne derelinquat te.

15 "Non trades servum domino suo qui ad te confugerit. 16 Habitabit tecum in loco qui ei placuerit et in una urbium tuarum requiescet. Ne contristes eum.

17 "Non erit meretrix de filiabus Israhel, neque scortator de filiis Israhel.

18 "Non offeres mercedem prostibuli nec pretium canis in domum Domini, Dei tui, quicquid illud est quod voveris, quia abominatio est utrumque apud Dominum, Deum tuum.

19 "Non fenerabis fratri tuo ad usuram pecuniam nec fruges nec quamlibet aliam rem, 20 sed alieno. Fratri autem tuo absque usura id quod indiget commodabis ut benedicat tibi Dominus, Deus tuus, in omni opere tuo in terra ad quam ingredieris possidendam.

21 "Cum voveris votum Domino, Deo tuo, non tardabis reddere, quia requiret illud Dominus, Deus tuus. Et si moratus fueris, reputabitur tibi in peccatum.

10 "If there be among you any man that is defiled in a dream by night, he shall go forth out of the camp 11 and shall not return before he be washed with water in the evening. And after sunset he shall return into the camp.

12 "Thou shalt have a place without the camp to which thou mayst go for the necessities of nature, 13 carrying a paddle at thy girdle. And when thou sittest down thou shalt dig round about, and with the earth that is dug up thou shalt cover 14 that which thou art eased of, for the Lord, thy God, walketh in the midst of thy camp to deliver thee and to give up thy enemies to thee, and let thy camp be holy, and let no uncleanness appear therein lest he go away from thee.

15 "Thou shalt not deliver to his master the servant that is fled to thee. 16 He shall dwell with thee in the place that shall please him and shall rest in one of thy cities. Give him no trouble.

17 "There shall be no whore among the daughters of Israel, nor whoremonger among the sons of Israel.

18 "Thou shalt not offer the hire of a strumpet nor the price of a dog in the house of the Lord, thy God, whatsoever it be that thou hast vowed, because both these are an abomination to the Lord, thy God.

19 "Thou shalt not lend to thy brother money to usury nor corn nor any other thing, 20 but to the stranger. To thy brother thou shalt lend that which he wanteth without usury that the Lord, thy God, may bless thee in all thy *works* in the land which thou shalt go in to possess.

21 "When thou hast made a vow to the Lord, thy God, thou shalt not delay to pay it, because the Lord, thy God, will require it. And if thou delay, it shall be imputed to thee for a sin.

22 "Si nolueris polliceri, absque peccato eris. 23 Quod autem semel egressum est de labiis tuis, observabis et facies sicut promisisti Domino, Deo tuo, et propria voluntate et ore tuo locutus es.

24 "Ingressus vineam proximi tui, comede uvas quantum tibi placuerit, foras autem ne efferas tecum.

25 "Si intraveris in segetem amici tui, franges spicas et manu conteres, falce autem non metes."

Caput 24

"Si acceperit homo uxorem et habuerit eam et non invenerit gratiam ante oculos eius propter aliquam foeditatem, scribet libellum repudii et dabit in manu illius et dimittet eam de domo sua. 2 Cumque egressa alterum maritum duxerit 3 et ille quoque oderit eam dederitque ei libellum repudii et dimiserit de domo sua vel certe mortuus fuerit, 4 non poterit prior maritus recipere eam in uxorem, quia polluta est et abominabilis facta est coram Domino, ne peccare facias

22 "If thou wilt not promise, thou shalt be without sin. 23 But that which is once gone out of thy lips, thou shalt observe and shalt do as thou hast promised to the Lord, thy God, and hast spoken with thy own will and with thy own mouth.

24 "Going into thy neighbour's vineyard, *thou mayst eat* as many grapes as thou pleasest, but must carry none out with thee.

25 "If thou go into thy friend's corn, thou mayst break the ears and rub them in thy hand, but not reap them with a sickle."

Chapter 24

Divorce permitted to avoid greater evil. The newly married must not go to war. Of men stealers, of leprosy, of pledges, of labourers' hire, of justice and of charity to the poor.

"If a man take a wife and have her and she find not favour in his eyes for some uncleanness, he shall write a bill of divorce and shall give it in her hand and send her out of his house. 2 And when she is departed and marrieth another husband 3 and he also hateth her and hath given her a bill of divorce and hath sent her out of his house or is dead, 4 the former husband cannot take her again to wife, because she is defiled and is become abominable before the Lord, lest

terram tuam quam Dominus, Deus tuus, tibi tradiderit possidendam.

5 "Cum acceperit homo nuper uxorem, non procedet ad bellum, nec ei quippiam necessitatis iniungetur publicae, sed vacabit absque culpa domui suae ut uno anno laetetur cum uxore sua.

6 "Non accipies loco pignoris inferiorem et superiorem molam, quia animam suam adposuit tibi.

7 "Si deprehensus fuerit homo sollicitans fratrem suum de filiis Israhel et vendito eo acceperit pretium, interficietur, et auferes malum de medio tui.

8 "Observa diligenter ne incurras plagam leprae, sed facies quaecumque docuerint te sacerdotes Levitici generis iuxta id quod praecepi eis, et imple sollicite. 9 Mementote quae fecerit Dominus, Deus vester, Mariae in via cum egrederemini de Aegypto.

10 "Cum repetes a proximo tuo rem aliquam quam debet tibi, non ingredieris domum eius ut pignus auferas, 11 sed stabis foris, et ille tibi proferet quod habuerit, 12 sin autem pauper est, non pernoctabit apud te pignus, 13 sed statim reddes ei ante solis occasum ut dormiens in vestimento suo benedicat tibi et habeas iustitiam coram Domino, Deo tuo.

14 "Non negabis mercedem indigentis et pauperis fratris tui sive advenae qui tecum moratur in terra et intra portas tuas est, 15 sed eadem die reddes ei pretium laboris sui ante solis occasum, quia pauper est et ex eo sustentat animam

thou cause thy land to sin which the Lord, thy God, shall give thee to possess.

⁵ "When a man hath lately taken a wife, he shall not go out to war, neither shall any public business be enjoined him, but he shall *be free at home* without fault that for one year he may rejoice with his wife.

⁶ "Thou shalt not take the nether nor the upper millstone to pledge, for he hath pledged his life to thee.

⁷ "If any man be found soliciting his brother of the children of Israel and selling him shall take a price, he shall be put to death, and thou shalt take away the evil from the midst of thee.

⁸ "Observe diligently that thou incur not the stroke of the leprosy, but thou shalt do whatsoever the priests of the Levitical race shall teach thee according to what I have commanded them, and fulfil thou it carefully. ⁹ Remember what the Lord, your God, did to Miriam in the way when you came out of Egypt.

¹⁰ "When thou shalt demand of thy neighbour any thing that he oweth thee, thou shalt not go into his house to take away a pledge, ¹¹ but thou shalt stand without, and he shall bring out to thee what he hath, ¹² but if he be poor, the pledge shall not lodge with thee that night, ¹³ but thou shalt restore it to him presently before the going down of the sun that he may sleep in his own raiment and bless thee and thou mayst have justice before the Lord, thy God.

¹⁴ "Thou shalt not refuse the hire of the needy and the poor, whether he be thy brother or a stranger that dwelleth with thee in the land and is within thy gates, ¹⁵ but thou shalt pay him the price of his labour the same day before the going down of the sun, because he is poor and with it main-

suam, ne clamet contra te ad Dominum et reputetur tibi in peccatum.

16 "Non occidentur patres pro filiis, nec filii pro patribus, sed unusquisque pro suo peccato morietur.

17 "Non pervertes iudicium advenae et pupilli, nec auferes pignoris loco viduae vestimentum. 18 Memento quod servieris in Aegypto et eruerit te Dominus, Deus tuus inde. Idcirco praecipio tibi ut facias hanc rem.

19 "Quando messueris segetem in agro tuo et oblitus manipulum reliqueris, non reverteris ut tollas eum, sed advenam et pupillum et viduam auferre patieris ut benedicat tibi Dominus, Deus tuus, in omni opere manuum tuarum. 20 Si fruges collegeris olivarum, quicquid remanserit in arboribus non reverteris ut colligas, sed relinques advenae, pupillo ac viduae. 21 Si vindemiaveris vineam tuam, non colliges remanentes racemos, sed cedent in usus advenae, pupilli ac viduae. 22 Memento quod et tu servieris in Aegypto, et idcirco praecipio tibi ut facias hanc rem."

taineth his life, lest he cry against thee to the Lord and it be reputed to thee for a sin.

16 "The fathers shall not be put to death for the children, nor the children for the fathers, but every one shall die for his own sin.

17 "Thou shalt not pervert the judgment of the stranger nor of the fatherless, neither shalt thou take away the widow's raiment for a pledge. 18 Remember that thou wast a slave in Egypt and the Lord, thy God, delivered thee from thence. Therefore I command thee to do this thing.

19 "When thou hast reaped the corn in thy field and hast forgot and left a sheaf, thou shalt not return to take it away, but thou shalt suffer the stranger and the fatherless and the widow to take it away that the Lord, thy God, may bless thee in all the works of thy hands. 20 If thou have gathered the fruit of thy olive trees, thou shalt not return to gather whatsoever remaineth on the trees but shalt leave it for the stranger, for the fatherless and the widow. 21 If thou make the vintage of thy vineyard, thou shalt not gather the clusters that remain, but they shall *be for* the stranger, the fatherless and the widow. 22 Remember that thou also wast a bondman in Egypt, and therefore I command thee to do this thing."

Caput 25

"Si fuerit causa inter aliquos et interpellaverint iudices, quem iustum esse perspexerint illi iustitiae palmam dabunt, quem impium condemnabunt impietatis. 2 Si autem eum qui peccavit dignum viderint plagis, prosternent et coram se facient verberari. Pro mensura peccati erit et plagarum modus, 3 ita dumtaxat ut quadragenarium numerum non excedant ne foede laceratus ante oculos tuos abeat frater tuus.

4 "Non ligabis os bovis terentis in area fruges tuas.

5 "Quando habitaverint fratres simul et unus ex eis absque liberis mortuus fuerit, uxor defuncti non nubet alteri, sed accipiet eam frater eius et suscitabit semen fratris sui, 6 et primogenitum ex ea filium nomine illius appellabit ut non deleatur nomen eius ex Israhel. 7 Sin autem noluerit accipere uxorem fratris sui, quae ei lege debetur, perget mulier ad portam civitatis et interpellabit maiores natu dicetque, 'Non vult frater viri mei suscitare nomen fratris sui in Israhel nec me in coniugium sumere.' 8 Statimque accersiri eum

Chapter 25

Stripes must not exceed forty. The ox is not to be muzzled.
Of raising seed to the brother, of the immodest woman, of
unjust weight, of destroying the Amalekites.

"If there be a controversy between *men* and they call
upon the judges, they shall give the prize of justice to him
whom they perceive to be just, and him whom they find to
be wicked they shall condemn of wickedness. 2 And if they
see that the offender be worthy of stripes, they shall lay him
down and shall cause him to be beaten before them. According
to the measure of the sin shall the measure also of the
stripes be, 3 yet so that they exceed not the number of forty
lest thy brother depart shamefully torn before thy eyes.

4 "Thou shalt not muzzle the ox that treadeth out thy
corn on the floor.

5 "When brethren dwell together and one of them dieth
without children, the wife of the deceased shall not marry
to another, but his brother shall take her and raise up seed
for his brother, 6 and the first son he shall have of her he
shall call by his name that his name be not abolished out of
Israel. 7 But if he will not take his brother's wife, who by law
belongeth to him, the woman shall go to the gate of the city
and call upon the ancients and say, 'My husband's brother refuseth to raise up his brother's name in Israel and will not
take me to wife.' 8 And they shall cause him to be sent for

facient et interrogabunt. Si responderit, 'Nolo eam uxorem accipere,' 9 accedet mulier ad eum coram senioribus et tollet calciamentum de pede eius spuetque in faciem illius et dicet, 'Sic fiet homini qui non aedificat domum fratris sui,' 10 et vocabitur nomen illius in Israhel Domus Disculciati.

11 "Si habuerint inter se iurgium viri duo et unus contra alterum rixari coeperit volensque uxor alterius eruere virum suum de manu fortioris miserit manum et adprehenderit verenda eius, 12 abscides manum illius, nec flecteris super eam ulla misericordia.

13 "Non habebis in sacculo diversa pondera, maius et minus, 14 nec erit in domo tua modius maior et minor. 15 Pondus habebis iustum et verum, et modius aequalis et verus erit tibi ut multo vivas tempore super terram quam Dominus, Deus tuus, dederit tibi, 16 abominatur enim Dominus tuus eum qui facit haec, et aversatur omnem iniustitiam.

17 "Memento quae fecerit tibi Amalech in via quando egrediebaris ex Aegypto, 18 quomodo occurrerit tibi et extremos agminis tui, qui lassi residebant, ceciderit quando tu eras fame et labore confectus, et non timuerit Deum. 19 Cum ergo Dominus, Deus tuus, dederit tibi requiem et subiecerit cunctas per circuitum nationes in terra quam tibi pollicitus est, delebis nomen eius sub caelo. Cave ne obliviscaris."

forthwith and shall ask him. If he answer, 'I will not take her to wife,' 9 the woman shall come to him before the ancients and shall take off his shoe from his foot and spit in his face and say, 'So shall it be done to the man that will not build up his brother's house,' 10 and his name shall be called in Israel the House of the Unshod.

11 "If two men have words together and one begin to fight against the other and the other's wife willing to deliver her husband out of the hand of the stronger shall put forth her hand and take him by the secrets, 12 thou shalt cut off her hand, neither shalt thou be moved with any pity in her regard.

13 "Thou shalt not have divers weights in thy bag, a greater and a less, 14 neither shall there be in thy house a greater bushel and a less. 15 Thou shalt have a just and a true weight, and thy bushel shall be equal and true that thou mayest live a long time upon the land which the Lord, thy God, shall give thee, 16 for *the Lord, thy God,* abhorreth him that doth these things, and he hateth all injustice.

17 "Remember what Amalek did to thee in the way when thou camest out of Egypt, 18 how he met thee and slew the hindmost of the army, who sat down being weary, when thou wast spent with hunger and labour, and he feared not God. 19 Therefore when the Lord, thy God, shall give thee rest and shall have subdued all the nations round about in the land which he hath promised thee, thou shalt blot out his name from under heaven. See thou forget it not."

Caput 26

"Cumque intraveris terram quam Dominus, Deus tuus, tibi daturus est possidendam et obtinueris eam atque habitaveris in illa, 2 tolles de cunctis frugibus tuis primitias et pones in cartallo pergesque ad locum quem Dominus, Deus tuus, elegerit ut ibi invocetur nomen eius, 3 accedesque ad sacerdotem qui fuerit in diebus illis et dices ad eum, 'Profiteor hodie coram Domino, Deo tuo, quod ingressus sim in terram pro qua iuravit patribus nostris ut daret eam nobis.'

4 "Suscipiensque sacerdos cartallum de manu eius ponet ante altare Domini, Dei tui, 5 et loqueris in conspectu Domini, Dei tui, 'Syrus persequebatur patrem meum qui descendit in Aegyptum et ibi peregrinatus est in paucissimo numero crevitque in gentem magnam et robustam et infinitae multitudinis. 6 Adflixeruntque nos Aegyptii et persecuti sunt, inponentes onera gravissima, 7 et clamavimus ad Dominum, Deum patrum nostrorum, qui exaudivit nos et respexit humilitatem nostram et laborem atque angustiam 8 et eduxit nos de Aegypto in manu forti et brachio extento, in ingenti pavore, in signis atque portentis, 9 et introduxit ad locum istum et tradidit nobis terram hanc lacte et melle manantem. 10 Et idcirco nunc offero primitias frugum terrae

Chapter 26

The form of words with which the firstfruits and tithes are to be offered. God's covenant.

"And when thou art come into the land which the Lord, thy God, will give thee to possess and hast conquered it and dwellest in it, 2 thou shalt take the first of all thy fruits and put them in a basket and shalt go to the place which the Lord, thy God, shall choose that his name may be invocated there, 3 and thou shalt go to the priest that shall be in those days and say to him, 'I profess this day before the Lord, thy God, that I am come into the land for which he swore to our fathers that he would give it us.'

4 "And the priest taking the basket at *thy* hand shall set it before the altar of the Lord, thy God, 5 and thou shalt speak *thus* in the sight of the Lord, thy God: 'The Syrian pursued my father who went down into Egypt and sojourned there in a very small number and grew into a nation great and strong and of an infinite multitude. 6 And the Egyptians afflicted us and persecuted us, laying on us most grievous burdens, 7 and we cried to the Lord, God of our fathers, who heard us and looked down upon our affliction and labour and distress 8 and brought us out of Egypt with a strong hand and a stretched out arm, with great terror, with signs and wonders, 9 and brought us into this place and gave us this land flowing with milk and honey. 10 And therefore now

quam dedit Dominus mihi.' Et dimittes eas in conspectu Domini, Dei tui, adorato Domino, Deo tuo. 11 Et epulaberis in omnibus bonis quae Dominus, Deus tuus, dederit tibi et domui tuae, tu et Levites et advena qui tecum est.

12 "Quando conpleveris decimam cunctarum frugum tuarum, anno decimarum tertio dabis Levitae et advenae et pupillo et viduae ut comedant intra portas tuas et saturentur. 13 Loquerisque in conspectu Domini, Dei tui, 'Abstuli quod sanctificatum est de domo mea, et dedi illud Levitae et advenae et pupillo et viduae sicut iussisti mihi. Non praeterivi mandata tua nec sum oblitus imperii tui. 14 Non comedi ex eis in luctu meo nec separavi ea in qualibet inmunditia nec expendi ex his quicquam in re funebri. Oboedivi voci Domini, Dei mei, et feci omnia sicut praecepisti mihi. 15 Respice de sanctuario tuo et de excelso caelorum habitaculo, et benedic populo tuo Israhel et terrae quam dedisti nobis, sicut iurasti patribus nostris, terrae lacte et melle mananti.'

16 "Hodie Dominus, Deus tuus, praecepit tibi ut facias mandata haec atque iudicia et custodias et impleas ex toto corde tuo et ex tota anima tua.

17 "Dominum elegisti hodie ut sit tibi Deus et ambules in viis eius et custodias caerimonias illius et mandata atque iudicia et oboedias eius imperio, 18 et Dominus elegit te hodie ut sis ei populus peculiaris, sicut locutus est tibi, et custo-

I offer the firstfruits of the land which the Lord hath given me.' And thou shalt leave them in the sight of the Lord, thy God, adoring the Lord, thy God. 11 And thou shalt feast in all the good things which the Lord, thy God, hath given thee and thy house, thou and the Levite and the stranger that is with thee.

12 "When thou hast made an end of tithing all thy fruits, in the third year of tithes thou shalt give it to the Levite and to the stranger and to the fatherless and to the widow that they may eat within thy gates and be filled. 13 And thou shalt speak *thus* in the sight of the Lord, thy God: 'I have taken that which was sanctified out of my house, and I have given it to the Levite and to the stranger and to the fatherless and to the widow as thou hast commanded me. I have not transgressed thy commandments nor forgotten thy precepts. 14 I have not eaten of them in my mourning nor separated them for any uncleanness nor spent any thing of them in funerals. I have obeyed the voice of the Lord, my God, and have done all things as thou hast commanded me. 15 Look from thy sanctuary and thy high habitation of heaven, and bless thy people Israel and the land which thou hast given us, as thou didst swear to our fathers, a land flowing with milk and honey.'

16 "This day the Lord, thy God, hath commanded thee to do these commandments and judgments and to keep and fulfil them with all thy heart and with all thy soul.

17 "Thou hast chosen the Lord this day to be thy God and to walk in his ways and keep his ceremonies and precepts and judgments and obey his command, 18 and the Lord hath chosen thee this day to be his peculiar people, as he hath

dias omnia praecepta eius 19 et faciat te excelsiorem cunctis gentibus quas creavit, in laudem et nomen et gloriam suam, ut sis populus sanctus Domini, Dei tui, sicut locutus est."

Caput 27

Praecepit autem Moses et seniores Israhel populo, dicentes, "Custodite omne mandatum quod praecipio vobis hodie. 2 Cumque transieritis Iordanem in terram quam Dominus, Deus tuus, dabit tibi, eriges ingentes lapides et calce levigabis eos 3 ut possis in eis scribere omnia verba legis huius Iordane transmisso, ut introeas terram quam Dominus, Deus tuus, dabit tibi, terram lacte et melle manantem, sicut iuravit patribus tuis.

4 "Quando ergo transieritis Iordanem, erigite lapides quos ego hodie praecipio vobis in Monte Hebal, et levigabis eos calce, 5 et aedificabis ibi altare Domino, Deo tuo, de lapidibus quos ferrum non tetigit 6 et de saxis informibus et inpolitis, et offeres super eo holocausta Domino,

spoken to thee, and to keep all his commandments 19 and to make thee higher than all nations which he hath created, to his own praise and name and glory, that thou mayst be a holy people of the Lord, thy God, as he hath spoken."

Chapter 27

The commandments must be written on stones and an altar erected and sacrifices offered. The observers of the commandments are to be blessed and the transgressors cursed.

And Moses with the ancients of Israel commanded the people, saying, "Keep every commandment that I command you this day. 2 And when you are passed over the Jordan into the land which the Lord, thy God, will give thee, thou shalt set up great stones and shalt *plaster* them over with plaster 3 that thou mayst write on them all the words of this law when thou art passed over the Jordan, that thou mayst enter into the land which the Lord, thy God, will give thee, a land flowing with milk and honey, as he swore to thy fathers.

4 "Therefore when you are passed over the Jordan, set up the stones which I command you this day in Mount Ebal, and thou shalt *plaster* them with plaster, 5 and thou shalt build there an altar to the Lord, thy God, of stones which iron hath not touched 6 and of stones not fashioned nor polished, and thou shalt offer upon it holocausts to the Lord,

Deo tuo. 7 Et immolabis hostias pacificas comedesque ibi et epulaberis coram Domino, Deo tuo. 8 Et scribes super lapides omnia verba legis huius plane et lucide."

9 Dixeruntque Moses et sacerdotes Levitici generis ad omnem Israhelem, "Adtende, et audi, Israhel. Hodie factus es populus Domini, Dei tui. 10 Audies vocem eius et facies mandata atque iustitias quas ego praecipio tibi."

11 Praecepitque Moses populo in die illo, dicens, 12 "Hii stabunt ad benedicendum populo super Montem Garizim Iordane transmisso: Symeon, Levi, Iudas, Isachar, Ioseph et Beniamin. 13 Et e regione isti stabunt ad maledicendum in Monte Hebal: Ruben, Gad et Aser et Zabulon, Dan et Nepthalim.

14 "Et pronuntiabunt Levitae dicentque ad omnes viros Israhel excelsa voce, 15 'Maledictus homo qui facit sculptile et conflatile, abominationem Domini, opus manuum artificum, ponetque illud in abscondito.' Et respondebit omnis populus et dicet, 'Amen.'

16 "'Maledictus qui non honorat patrem suum et matrem.' Et dicet omnis populus, 'Amen.'

17 "'Maledictus qui transfert terminos proximi sui.' Et dicet omnis populus, 'Amen.'

18 "'Maledictus qui errare facit caecum in itinere.' Et dicet omnis populus, 'Amen.'

19 "'Maledictus qui pervertit iudicium advenae, pupilli et viduae.' Et dicet omnis populus, 'Amen.'

20 "'Maledictus qui dormit cum uxore patris sui et revelat operimentum lectuli eius.' Et dicet omnis populus, 'Amen.'

thy God. 7 And shalt immolate peace victims and eat there and feast before the Lord, thy God. 8 And thou shalt write upon the stones all the words of this law plainly and clearly."

9 And Moses and the priests of the race of Levi said to all Israel, "Attend, and hear, O Israel. This day thou art made the people of the Lord, thy God. 10 Thou shalt hear his voice and do the commandments and justices which I command thee."

11 And Moses commanded the people in that day, saying, 12 "These shall stand upon Mount Gerizim to bless the people when you are passed the Jordan: Simeon, Levi, Judah, Issachar, Joseph and Benjamin. 13 And over against them *shall* stand on Mount Hebal to curse: Reuben, Gad and Asher and Zebulun, Dan and Naphtali.

14 "And the Levites shall pronounce and say to all the men of Israel with a loud voice, 15 'Cursed be the man that maketh a graven and molten thing, the abomination of the Lord, the work of the hands of artificers, and shall put it in a secret place.' And all the people shall answer and say, 'Amen.'

16 "'Cursed be he that honoureth not his father and mother.' And all the people shall say, 'Amen.'

17 "'Cursed be he that removeth his neighbour's landmarks.' And all the people shall say, 'Amen.'

18 "'Cursed be he that maketh the blind to wander out of his way.' And all the people shall say, 'Amen.'

19 "'Cursed be he that perverteth the judgment of the stranger, of the fatherless and the widow.' And all the people shall say, 'Amen.'

20 "'Cursed be he that lieth with his father's wife and uncovereth his bed.' And all the people shall say, 'Amen.'

21 "'Maledictus qui dormit cum omni iumento.' Et dicet omnis populus, 'Amen.'

22 "'Maledictus qui dormit cum sorore sua, filia patris sui sive matris suae.' Et dicet omnis populus, 'Amen.'

23 "'Maledictus qui dormit cum socru sua.' Et dicet omnis populus, 'Amen.'

24 "'Maledictus qui clam percusserit proximum suum.' Et dicet omnis populus, 'Amen.'

25 "'Maledictus qui accipit munera ut percutiat animam sanguinis innocentis.' Et dicet omnis populus, 'Amen.'

26 "'Maledictus qui non permanet in sermonibus legis huius nec eos opere perficit.' Et dicet omnis populus, 'Amen.'"

Caput 28

"Sin autem audieris vocem Domini, Dei tui, ut facias atque custodias omnia mandata eius quae ego praecipio tibi hodie, faciet te Dominus, Deus tuus, excelsiorem cunctis gentibus quae versantur in terra. 2 Venientque super te universae benedictiones istae et adprehendent te, si tamen praecepta eius audieris:

21 "'Cursed be he that lieth with any beast.' And all the people shall say, 'Amen.'

22 "'Cursed be he that lieth with his sister, the daughter of his father or of his mother.' And all the people shall say, 'Amen.'

23 "'Cursed be he that lieth with his mother-in-law.' And all the people shall say, 'Amen.'

24 "'Cursed be he that secretly killeth his neighbour.' And all the people shall say, 'Amen.'

25 "'Cursed be he that taketh gifts to slay *an innocent person.*' And all the people shall say, 'Amen.'

26 "'Cursed be he that abideth not in the words of this law and fulfilleth them not in work.' And all the people shall say, 'Amen.'"

Chapter 28

Many blessings are promised to observers of God's commandments, and curses threatened to transgressors.

"Now if thou wilt hear the voice of the Lord, thy God, to do and keep all his commandments which I command thee this day, the Lord, thy God, will make thee higher than all the nations that are on the earth. 2 And all these blessings shall come upon thee and overtake thee, yet so if thou hear his precepts:

3 "Benedictus tu in civitate et benedictus in agro.

4 "Benedictus fructus ventris tui et fructus terrae tuae fructusque iumentorum tuorum, greges armentorum tuorum et caulae ovium tuarum.

5 "Benedicta horrea tua et benedictae reliquiae tuae.

6 "Benedictus eris et ingrediens et egrediens.

7 "Dabit Dominus inimicos tuos qui consurgunt adversum te corruentes in conspectu tuo: per unam viam venient contra te, et per septem fugient a facie tua.

8 "Emittet Dominus benedictionem super cellaria tua et super omnia opera manuum tuarum benedicetque tibi in terra quam acceperis.

9 "Suscitabit te Dominus sibi in populum sanctum, sicut iuravit tibi, si custodieris mandata Domini, Dei tui, et ambulaveris in viis eius. 10 Videbuntque omnes terrarum populi quod nomen Domini invocatum sit super te, et timebunt te.

11 "Abundare te faciet Dominus omnibus bonis, fructu uteri tui et fructu iumentorum tuorum, fructu terrae tuae quam iuravit Dominus patribus tuis ut daret tibi.

12 "Aperiet Dominus thesaurum suum optimum, caelum, ut tribuat pluviam terrae tuae in tempore suo benedicetque cunctis operibus manuum tuarum. Et fenerabis gentibus multis, et ipse a nullo fenus accipies.

13 "Constituet te Dominus in caput et non in caudam, et eris semper supra et non subter, si tamen audieris mandata Domini, Dei tui, quae ego praecipio tibi hodie et custodieris et feceris 14 ac non declinaveris ab eis nec ad dextram nec ad sinistram nec secutus fueris deos alienos neque colueris eos.

3 "Blessed shalt thou be in the city and blessed in the field.

4 "Blessed shall be the fruit of thy womb and the fruit of thy ground and the fruit of thy cattle, the droves of thy herds and the folds of thy sheep.

5 "Blessed shall be thy barns and blessed thy stores.

6 "Blessed shalt thou be coming in and going out.

7 "The Lord shall cause thy enemies that rise up against thee to fall down before thy face: one way shall they come out against thee, and seven ways shall they flee before thee.

8 "The Lord will send forth a blessing upon thy storehouses and upon all the works of thy hands and will bless thee in the land that thou shalt receive.

9 "The Lord will raise thee up to be a holy people to himself, as he swore to thee, if thou keep the commandments of the Lord, thy God, and walk in his ways. 10 And all the people of the earth shall see that the name of the Lord is invocated upon thee, and they shall fear thee.

11 "The Lord will make thee abound with all goods, with the fruit of thy womb and the fruit of thy cattle, with the fruit of thy land which the Lord swore to thy fathers that he would give thee.

12 "The Lord will open his excellent treasure, the heaven, that it may give *rain* in due season, and he will bless all the works of thy hands. And thou shalt lend to many nations and shalt not borrow of any one.

13 "And the Lord shall make thee the head and not the tail, and thou shalt be always above and not beneath, yet so if thou wilt hear the commandments of the Lord, thy God, which I command thee this day and keep and do them 14 and turn not away from them neither to the right hand nor to the left nor follow strange gods nor worship them.

15 "Quod si audire nolueris vocem Domini, Dei tui, ut custodias et facias omnia mandata eius et caerimonias quas ego praecipio tibi hodie, venient super te omnes maledictiones istae et adprehendent te:

16 "Maledictus eris in civitate, maledictus in agro.

17 "Maledictum horreum tuum et maledictae reliquiae tuae.

18 "Maledictus fructus ventris tui et fructus terrae tuae, armenta boum tuorum et greges ovium tuarum.

19 "Maledictus eris ingrediens et maledictus egrediens.

20 "Mittet Dominus super te famem et esuriem et increpationem in omnia opera tua quae facies donec conterat te et perdat velociter propter adinventiones tuas pessimas in quibus reliquisti me.

21 "Adiungat Dominus tibi pestilentiam donec consumat te de terra ad quam ingredieris possidendam.

22 "Percutiat te Dominus egestate, febri et frigore, ardore et aestu et aere corrupto ac robigine et persequatur donec pereas.

23 "Sit caelum quod supra te est aeneum et terra quam calcas ferrea.

24 "Det Dominus imbrem terrae tuae pulverem, et de caelo descendat super te cinis donec conteraris.

25 "Tradat te Dominus corruentem ante hostes tuos; per unam viam egrediaris contra eos et per septem fugias et dispergaris per omnia regna terrae, 26 sitque cadaver tuum in escam cunctis volatilibus caeli et bestiis terrae, et non sit qui abigat.

15 "But if thou wilt not hear the voice of the Lord, thy God, to keep and to do all his commandments and ceremonies which I command thee this day, all these curses shall come upon thee and overtake thee:

16 "Cursed shalt thou be in the city, cursed in the field.

17 "Cursed shall be thy barn and cursed thy stores.

18 "Cursed shall be the fruit of thy womb and the fruit of thy ground, the herds of thy oxen and the flocks of thy sheep.

19 "Cursed shalt thou be coming in and cursed going out.

20 "The Lord shall send upon thee famine and hunger and a rebuke upon all the works which thou shalt do until he consume and destroy thee quickly for thy most wicked inventions by which thou hast forsaken me.

21 "May the Lord set the pestilence upon thee until he consume thee out of the land which thou shalt go in to possess.

22 "May the Lord afflict thee with *miserable* want, with the fever and with cold, with burning and with heat and with corrupted air and with blasting and pursue thee till thou perish.

23 "Be the heaven that is over thee of brass and the ground thou treadest on of iron.

24 "The Lord give thee dust for rain upon thy land, and let ashes come down from heaven upon thee till thou be consumed.

25 "The Lord make thee to fall down before thy enemies; one way mayst thou go out against them and flee seven ways and be scattered throughout all the kingdoms of the earth, 26 and be thy carcass meat for all the fowls of the air and the beasts of the earth, and be there none to drive them away.

27 "Percutiat te Dominus ulcere Aegypti et partem corporis per quam stercora egeruntur scabie quoque et prurigine
ita ut curari nequeas.

28 "Percutiat te Dominus amentia et caecitate ac furore
mentis.

29 "Et palpes in meridie sicut palpare solet caecus in tenebris et non dirigas vias tuas. Omnique tempore calumniam
sustineas et opprimaris violentia nec habeas qui liberet te.

30 "Uxorem accipias et alius dormiat cum ea. Domum ae-
difices et non habites in ea. Plantes vineam et non vindemies
eam.

31 "Bos tuus immoletur coram te et non comedas ex eo.
Asinus tuus rapiatur in conspectu tuo et non reddatur tibi.
Oves tuae dentur inimicis tuis, et non sit qui te adiuvet.

32 "Filii tui et filiae tuae tradantur alteri populo, videntibus oculis tuis et deficientibus ad conspectum eorum tota
die, et non sit fortitudo in manu tua.

33 "Fructus terrae tuae et omnes labores tuos comedat
populus quem ignoras, et sis semper calumniam sustinens et
oppressus cunctis diebus 34 et stupens ad terrorem eorum
quae videbunt oculi tui.

35 "Percutiat te Dominus ulcere pessimo in genibus et in
suris, sanarique non possis a planta pedis usque ad verticem
tuum.

36 "Ducet Dominus te et regem tuum quem constitueris
super te in gentem quam ignoras tu et patres tui, et servies
ibi diis alienis, ligno et lapidi, 37 et eris perditus in proverbium ac fabulam omnibus populis ad quos te introduxerit

27 "The Lord strike thee with the ulcer of Egypt and the part of thy body by which the dung is cast out with the scab and with the itch so that thou canst not be healed.

28 "The Lord strike thee with madness and blindness and fury of mind.

29 "And mayst thou grope at midday as the blind is wont to grope in the dark and not make straight thy ways. And mayst thou at all times suffer wrong and be oppressed with violence, and mayst thou have no one to deliver thee.

30 "Mayst thou take a wife and another sleep with her. Mayst thou build a house and not dwell therein. Mayest thou plant a vineyard and not gather the vintage thereof.

31 "May thy ox be slain before thee and thou not eat thereof. May thy ass be taken away in thy sight and not restored to thee. May thy sheep be given to thy enemies, and may there be none to help thee.

32 "May thy sons and thy daughters be given to another people, thy eyes looking on and languishing at the sight of them all the day, and may there be no strength in thy hand.

33 "May a people which thou knowest not eat the fruits of thy land and all thy labours, and mayst thou always suffer oppression and be crushed at all times 34 and be astonished at the terror of those things which thy eyes shall see.

35 "May the Lord strike thee with a very sore ulcer in the knees and in the legs, and be thou incurable from the sole of the foot to the top of the head.

36 "The Lord shall bring thee and thy king whom thou shalt have appointed over thee into a nation which thou and thy fathers know not, and there thou shalt serve strange gods, wood and stone, 37 and thou shalt be lost as a proverb and a byword to all people among whom the

Dominus. 38 Sementem multam iacies in terram et modicum congregabis, quia lucustae omnia devorabunt. 39 Vineam plantabis et fodies et vinum non bibes nec colliges ex ea quippiam, quoniam vastabitur vermibus. 40 Olivas habebis in omnibus terminis tuis et non ungueris oleo, quia defluent et peribunt. 41 Filios generabis et filias et non frueris eis, quoniam ducentur in captivitatem. 42 Omnes arbores tuas et fruges terrae tuae robigo consumet. 43 Advena qui tecum versatur in terra ascendet super te eritque sublimior, tu autem descendes et eris inferior. 44 Ipse fenerabit tibi, et tu non fenerabis ei. Ipse erit in caput, et tu eris in caudam. 45 Et venient super te omnes maledictiones istae et persequentes adprehendent te donec intereas quia non audisti vocem Domini, Dei tui, nec servasti mandata eius et caerimonias quas praecepit tibi. 46 Et erunt in te signa atque prodigia, et in semine tuo usque in sempiternum, 47 eo quod non servieris Domino, Deo tuo, in gaudio cordisque laetitia propter rerum omnium abundantiam.

48 "Servies inimico tuo quem inmittet Dominus tibi in fame et siti et nuditate et omnium penuria, et ponet iugum ferreum super cervicem tuam donec te conterat. 49 Adducet Dominus super te gentem de longinquo et de extremis finibus terrae, in similitudinem aquilae volantis cum impetu, cuius linguam intellegere non possis, 50 gentem procacissimam quae non deferat seni nec misereatur parvulo 51 et devoret fructum iumentorum tuorum ac fruges terrae tuae donec intereas et non relinquat tibi triticum, vinum et

Lord shall bring thee in. 38 Thou shalt cast much seed into the ground and gather little, because the locusts shall consume all. 39 Thou shalt plant a vineyard and dig it and shalt not drink the wine nor gather any thing thereof, because it shall be wasted with worms. 40 Thou shalt have olive trees in all thy borders and shalt not be anointed with the oil, for the olives shall fall off and perish. 41 Thou shalt beget sons and daughters and shalt not enjoy them, because they shall be led into captivity. 42 The blast shall consume all the trees and the fruits of thy ground. 43 The stranger that liveth with thee in the land shall rise up over thee and shall be higher, and thou shalt go down and be lower. 44 He shall lend to thee, and thou shalt not lend to him. He shall be as the head, and thou shalt be the tail. 45 And all these curses shall come upon thee and shall pursue and overtake thee till thou perish because thou heardst not the voice of the Lord, thy God, and didst not keep his commandments and ceremonies which he commanded thee. 46 And they shall be as signs and wonders on thee, and on thy seed for ever, 47 because thou didst not serve the Lord, thy God, with joy and gladness of heart for the abundance of all things.

48 "Thou shalt serve thy enemy whom the Lord will send upon thee in hunger and thirst and nakedness and in want *of all things,* and he shall put an iron yoke upon thy neck till he consume thee. 49 The Lord will bring upon thee a nation from afar and from the uttermost ends of the earth, like an eagle that flyeth swiftly, whose tongue thou canst not understand, 50 a most insolent nation that will shew no regard to the ancients nor have pity on the infant 51 and will devour the fruit of thy cattle and the fruits of thy land until thou be destroyed and will leave thee no wheat *nor* wine nor oil *nor*

oleum, armenta boum et greges ovium donec te disperdat
52 et conterat in cunctis urbibus tuis et destruantur muri tui
firmi atque sublimes in quibus habebas fiduciam in omni
terra tua. Obsideberis intra portas tuas in omni terra tua
quam dabit tibi Dominus, Deus tuus, 53 et comedes fructum
uteri tui et carnes filiorum tuorum et filiarum tuarum quas
dederit tibi Dominus, Deus tuus, in angustia et vastitate qua
opprimet te hostis tuus. 54 Homo delicatus in te et luxurio-
sus valde invidebit fratri suo et uxori quae cubat in sinu suo
55 ne det eis de carnibus filiorum suorum, quas comedet eo
quod nihil habeat aliud in obsidione et penuria qua vastave-
rint te inimici tui intra omnes portas tuas. 56 Tenera mulier
et delicata quae super terram ingredi non valebat nec pedis
vestigium figere propter mollitiem et teneritudinem nimiam
invidebit viro suo qui cubat in sinu eius super filii et filiae
carnibus 57 et inluvie secundarum quae egrediuntur de medio feminum eius et super liberis qui eadem hora nati sunt,
comedent enim eos clam propter rerum omnium penuriam
in obsidione et vastitate qua opprimet te inimicus tuus intra
portas tuas.

58 "Nisi custodieris et feceris omnia verba legis huius quae
scripta sunt in hoc volumine et timueris nomen eius glorio-
sum et terribile, hoc est, Dominum, Deum tuum, 59 augebit
Dominus plagas tuas et plagas seminis tui, plagas magnas
et perseverantes, infirmitates pessimas et perpetuas. 60 Et
convertet in te omnes adflictiones Aegypti quas timuisti, et
adherebunt tibi. 61 Insuper, et universos languores et plagas
quae non sunt scriptae in volumine legis huius inducet Do-

herds of oxen nor flocks of sheep until he destroy thee 52 and consume thee in all thy cities and thy strong and high walls be brought down wherein thou trustedst in all thy land. Thou shalt be besieged within thy gates in all thy land which the Lord, thy God, will give thee, 53 and thou shalt eat the fruit of thy womb and the flesh of thy sons and of thy daughters which the Lord, thy God, shall give thee in the distress and extremity wherewith thy enemy shall oppress thee. 54 The man that is nice among you and very delicate shall envy his own brother and his wife that lieth in his bosom 55 so that he will not give them of the flesh of his children, which he shall eat because he hath nothing else in the siege and the want wherewith thy enemies shall distress thee within all thy gates. 56 The tender and delicate woman that could not go upon the ground nor set down her foot for over much niceness and tenderness will envy her husband who lieth in her bosom the flesh of her son and of her daughter 57 and the filth of the afterbirths that come forth from between her thighs and the children that are born the same hour, for they shall eat them secretly for the want of all things in the siege and distress wherewith thy enemy shall oppress thee within thy gates.

58 "If thou wilt not keep and fulfil all the words of this law that are written in this volume and fear his glorious and terrible name, that is, the Lord, thy God, 59 the Lord shall increase thy plagues and the plagues of thy seed, plagues great and lasting, infirmities grievous and perpetual. 60 And he shall bring back on thee all the afflictions of Egypt which thou wast afraid of, and they shall stick fast to thee. 61 Moreover, the Lord will bring upon thee all the diseases and plagues that are not written in the volume of this law till he

minus super te donec te conterat, 62 et remanebitis pauci numero qui prius eratis sicut astra caeli prae multitudine, quoniam non audisti vocem Domini, Dei tui. 63 Et sicut ante laetatus est Dominus super vos bene vobis faciens vosque multiplicans, sic laetabitur disperdens vos atque subvertens ut auferamini de terra ad quam ingredieris possidendam.

64 "Disperget te Dominus in omnes populos a summitate terrae usque ad terminos eius, et servies ibi diis alienis quos et tu ignoras et patres tui, lignis et lapidibus. 65 In gentibus quoque illis non quiesces, neque erit requies vestigio pedis tui, dabit enim tibi Dominus ibi cor pavidum et deficientes oculos et animam maerore consumptam, 66 et erit vita tua quasi pendens ante te. Timebis nocte et die, et non credes vitae tuae. 67 Mane dices, 'Quis mihi det vesperum?' et vespere, 'Quis mihi det mane?' propter cordis tui formidinem qua terreberis et propter ea quae tuis videbis oculis.

68 "Reducet te Dominus classibus in Aegyptum per viam de qua dixit tibi ut eam amplius non videres. Ibi venderis inimicis tuis in servos et ancillas, et non erit qui emat."

consume thee, 62 and you shall remain few in number who before were as the stars of heaven for multitude, because thou heardst not the voice of the Lord, thy God. 63 And as the Lord rejoiced upon you before doing good to you and multiplying you, so he shall rejoice destroying and *bringing* you *to nought* so that you shall be taken away from the land which thou shalt go in to possess.

64 "The Lord shall scatter thee among all people from the farthest parts of the earth to the ends thereof, and there thou shalt serve strange gods which both thou art ignorant of and thy fathers, wood and stone. 65 Neither shalt thou be quiet even in those nations, nor shall there be any rest for the sole of thy foot, for the Lord will give thee a fearful heart and languishing eyes and a soul consumed with pensiveness, 66 and thy life shall be as it were hanging before thee. Thou shalt fear night and day, neither shalt thou trust thy life. 67 In the morning thou shalt say, 'Who will grant me evening?' and at evening, 'Who will grant me morning?' for the fearfulness of thy heart wherewith thou shalt be terrified and for those things which thou shalt see with thy eyes.

68 "The Lord shall bring thee again with ships into Egypt by the way whereof he said to thee that thou shouldst see it no more. There shalt thou be set to sale to thy enemies for bondmen and bondwomen, and no man shall buy you."

Caput 29

Haec sunt verba foederis quod praecepit Dominus Mosi ut feriret cum filiis Israhel in terra Moab, praeter illud foedus quod cum eis pepigit in Horeb.

2 Vocavitque Moses omnem Israhelem, et dixit ad eos, "Vos vidistis universa quae fecit Dominus coram vobis in terra Aegypti Pharaoni et omnibus servis eius universaeque terrae illius, 3 temptationes magnas quas viderunt oculi tui, signa illa portentaque ingentia, 4 et non dedit Dominus vobis cor intellegens et oculos videntes et aures quae possint audire, usque in praesentem diem. 5 Adduxit vos quadraginta annis per desertum.

"'Non sunt adtrita vestimenta vestra, nec calciamenta pedum vestrorum vetustate consumpta sunt; 6 panem non comedistis, vinum et siceram non bibistis, ut sciretis quia ego sum Dominus, Deus vester.'

7 "Et venistis ad locum hunc, egressusque est Seon, rex Esebon, et Og, rex Basan, occurrens nobis ad pugnam. Et percussimus eos 8 et tulimus terram eorum ac tradidimus possidendam Ruben et Gad et dimidiae tribui Manasse. 9 Custodite ergo verba pacti huius, et implete ea, ut intellegatis universa quae facitis.

Chapter 29

The covenant is solemnly confirmed between God and his people. Threats against those that shall break it.

These are the words of the covenant which the Lord commanded Moses to make with the children of Israel in the land of Moab, beside that covenant which he made with them in Horeb.

2 And Moses called all Israel, and said to them, "You have seen all the things that the Lord did before you in the land of Egypt to Pharaoh and to all his servants and to his whole land, 3 the great temptations which thy eyes have seen, those mighty signs and wonders, 4 and the Lord hath not given you a heart to understand and eyes to see and ears that may hear, unto this present day. 5 He hath brought you forty years through the desert.

"'Your garments are not worn out, neither are the shoes of your feet consumed with age; 6 you have not eaten bread, nor have you drunk wine or strong drink, that you might know that I am the Lord, your God.'

7 "And you came to this place, and Sihon, king of Heshbon, and Og, king of Bashan, came out against us to fight. And we slew them 8 and took their land and delivered it for a possession to Reuben and Gad and the half-tribe of Manasseh. 9 Keep therefore the words of this covenant, and fulfil them, that you may understand all that you do.

10 "Vos statis hodie cuncti coram Domino, Deo vestro, principes vestri ac tribus et maiores natu atque doctores, omnis populus Israhel, 11 liberi et uxores vestrae et advena qui tecum moratur in castris, exceptis lignorum caesoribus et his qui conportant aquas, 12 ut transeas in foedere Domini, Dei tui, et in iureiurando quod hodie Dominus, Deus tuus, percutit tecum 13 ut suscitet te, sibi in populum, et ipse sit Deus tuus sicut locutus est tibi et sicut iuravit patribus tuis Abraham, Isaac et Iacob. 14 Nec vobis solis ego hoc foedus ferio et haec iuramenta confirmo, 15 sed cunctis praesentibus et absentibus, 16 vos enim nostis quomodo habitaverimus in terra Aegypti et quomodo transierimus per medium nationum, quas transeuntes 17 vidistis abominationes et sordes, id est, idola eorum, lignum et lapidem, argentum et aurum, quae colebant, 18 ne forte sit inter vos vir aut mulier, familia aut tribus, cuius cor aversum est hodie a Domino, Deo nostro, ut vadat et serviat diis illarum gentium et sit inter vos radix germinans fel et amaritudinem. 19 Cumque audierit verba iuramenti huius, benedicat sibi in corde suo, dicens, 'Pax erit mihi et ambulabo in pravitate cordis mei, et adsumat ebria sitientem.' 20 Et Dominus non ignoscat ei, sed tunc quam maxime furor eius fumet et zelus contra hominem illum, et sedeant super eo omnia maledicta quae scripta sunt in hoc volumine, et deleat Dominus nomen eius sub caelo 21 et consumat eum in perditionem ex omnibus tribubus Israhel, iuxta maledictiones quae in libro legis huius ac foederis continentur.

10 "You all stand this day before the Lord, your God, your princes and tribes and ancients and doctors, all the people of Israel, 11 your children and your wives and the stranger that abideth with thee in the camp, besides the hewers of wood and them that bring water, 12 that thou mayst pass in the covenant of the Lord, thy God, and in the oath which this day the Lord, thy God, maketh with thee 13 that he may raise thee up, a people to himself, and he may be thy God as he hath spoken to thee and as he swore to thy fathers Abraham, Isaac and Jacob. 14 Neither with you only do I make this covenant and confirm these oaths, 15 but with all that are present and that are absent, 16 for you know how we dwelt in the land of Egypt and how we have passed through the midst of nations, and passing through them 17 you have seen their abominations and filth, that is to say, their idols, wood and stone, silver and gold, which they worshipped, 18 lest perhaps there should be among you a man or a woman, a family or a tribe, whose heart is turned away this day from the Lord, our God, to go and serve the gods of those nations and there should be among you a root bringing forth gall and bitterness. 19 And when he shall hear the words of this oath, he should bless himself in his heart, saying, 'I shall have peace and will walk on in the naughtiness of my heart, and the drunken may consume the thirsty.' 20 And the Lord should not forgive him, but his wrath and jealousy against that man should be exceedingly enkindled at that time, and all the curses that are written in this volume should light upon him, and the Lord should blot out his name from under heaven 21 and utterly destroy him out of all the tribes of Israel, according to the curses that are contained in the book of this law and covenant.

22 "Dicetque sequens generatio et filii qui nascentur deinceps et peregrini qui de longe venerint, videntes plagas terrae illius et infirmitates quibus eam adflixerit Dominus, 23 sulphure et salis ardore conburens ita ut ultra non seratur nec virens quippiam germinet in exemplum subversionis Sodomae et Gomorrae, Adamae et Seboim, quas subvertit Dominus in ira et furore suo, 24 et dicent omnes gentes, 'Quare sic fecit Dominus terrae huic? Quae est haec ira furoris eius inmensa?'

25 "Et respondebunt, 'Quia dereliquerunt pactum Domini quod pepigit cum patribus eorum quando eduxit eos de terra Aegypti 26 et servierunt diis alienis et adoraverunt eos quos nesciebant et quibus non fuerant adtributi, 27 idcirco iratus est furor Domini contra terram istam, ut induceret super eam omnia maledicta quae in hoc volumine scripta sunt, 28 et eiecit eos de terra sua in ira et furore et in indignatione maxima proiecitque in terram alienam, sicut hodie conprobatur.'

29 "Abscondita Domino, Deo nostro; quae manifesta sunt nobis et filiis nostris usque in aeternum, ut faciamus universa verba legis huius."

22 "And the following generation shall say and the children that shall be born hereafter and the strangers that shall come from afar, seeing the plagues of that land and the evils wherewith the Lord hath afflicted it, 23 burning it with brimstone and the heat of salt so that it cannot be sown any more nor any green thing grow therein after the example of the destruction of Sodom and Gomorrah, Admah and Zeboiim, which the Lord destroyed in his wrath and indignation, 24 and all the nations shall say, 'Why hath the Lord done thus to this land? What meaneth this exceeding *great heat* of his wrath?'

25 "And they shall answer, 'Because they forsook the covenant of the Lord which he made with their fathers when he brought them out of the land of Egypt 26 and they have served strange gods and adored them whom they knew not and for whom they had not been assigned, 27 therefore the wrath of the Lord was kindled against this land, to bring upon it all the curses that are written in this volume, 28 and he hath cast them out of their land in anger and *in* wrath and in very great indignation and hath thrown them into a strange land, as it is seen this day.'

29 "Secret things to the Lord, our God; things that are manifest to us and to our children for ever, that we may do all the words of this law."

Caput 30

"Cum ergo venerint super te omnes sermones isti, bene-dictio sive maledictio quam proposui in conspectu tuo, et ductus paenitudine cordis tui in universis gentibus in quas disperserit te Dominus, Deus tuus, 2 et reversus fueris ad eum et oboedieris eius imperiis sicut ego hodie praecipio tibi, cum filiis tuis, in toto corde tuo et in tota anima tua, 3 reducet Dominus, Deus tuus, captivitatem tuam ac mise-rebitur tui et rursum congregabit te de cunctis populis in quos te ante dispersit. 4 Si ad cardines caeli fueris dissipatus, inde te retrahet Dominus, Deus tuus, 5 et adsumet atque in-troducet in terram quam possederunt patres tui, et obtine-bis eam, et, benedicens tibi, maioris numeri esse te faciet quam fuerunt patres tui. 6 Circumcidet Dominus, Deus tuus, cor tuum et cor seminis tui ut diligas Dominum, Deum tuum, in toto corde tuo et in tota anima tua, ut possis vi-vere. 7 Omnes autem maledictiones has convertet super ini-micos tuos et eos qui oderunt te et persequuntur. 8 Tu autem reverteris et audies vocem Domini, Dei tui, facies-que universa mandata quae ego praecipio tibi hodie, 9 et abundare te faciet Dominus, Deus tuus, in cunctis operibus

Chapter 30

Great mercies are promised to the penitent. God's commandment is feasible. Life and death are set before them.

"Now when all these *things* shall be come upon thee, the blessing or the curse which I have set forth before thee, and thou shalt be touched with repentance of thy heart among all the nations into which the Lord, thy God, shall have scattered thee 2 and shalt return to him and obey his commandments as I command thee this day, *thou and* thy children, with all thy heart and with all thy soul, 3 the Lord, thy God, will bring back again thy captivity and will have mercy on thee and gather thee again out of all the nations into which he scattered thee before. 4 If thou be driven as far as the poles of heaven, the Lord, thy God, will fetch thee back from thence 5 and will take thee *to himself* and bring thee into the land which thy fathers possessed, and thou shalt possess it, and, blessing thee, he will make thee more numerous than were thy fathers. 6 The Lord, thy God, will circumcise thy heart and the heart of thy seed that thou mayst love the Lord, thy God, with all thy heart and with all thy soul, that thou mayst live. 7 And he will turn all these curses upon thy enemies and upon them that hate and persecute thee. 8 But thou shalt return and hear the voice of the Lord, thy God, and shalt do all the commandments which I command thee this day, 9 and the Lord, thy God, will make thee

manuum tuarum, in subole uteri tui et in fructu iumentorum tuorum, in ubertate terrae tuae et in rerum omnium
largitate, revertetur enim Dominus ut gaudeat super te in
omnibus bonis, sicut gavisus est in patribus tuis, 10 si tamen
audieris vocem Domini, Dei tui, et custodieris praecepta
eius et caerimonias quae in hac lege conscriptae sunt et revertaris ad Dominum, Deum tuum, in toto corde tuo et in
tota anima tua.

11 "Mandatum hoc quod ego praecipio tibi hodie non supra te est neque procul positum, 12 nec in caelo situm ut possis dicere, 'Quis nostrum ad caelum valet ascendere ut deferat illud ad nos et audiamus atque opere conpleamus?'
13 Neque trans mare positum ut causeris et dicas, 'Quis e nobis transfretare poterit mare et illud ad nos usque deferre ut
possimus audire et facere quod praeceptum est?' 14 Sed iuxta
te est sermo valde, in ore tuo et in corde tuo, ut facias illum.

15 "Considera quod hodie proposuerim in conspectu tuo
vitam et bonum et e contrario mortem et malum 16 ut diligas
Dominum, Deum tuum, et ambules in viis eius et custodias
mandata illius et caerimonias atque iudicia, et vivas, ac multiplicet te benedicatque tibi in terra ad quam ingredieris
possidendam. 17 Sin autem aversum fuerit cor tuum et audire
nolueris, atque errore deceptus adoraveris deos alienos et
servieris eis, 18 praedico tibi hodie quod pereas et parvo
tempore moreris in terra ad quam Iordane transmisso ingredieris possidendam.

19 "Testes invoco hodie caelum et terram quod proposuerim vobis vitam et mortem, benedictionem et maledictionem. Elige ergo vitam ut et tu vivas et semen tuum 20 et

abound in all the works of thy hands, in the fruit of thy womb and in the fruit of thy cattle, in the fruitfulness of thy land and in the plenty of all things, for the Lord will return to rejoice over thee in all good things, as he rejoiced in thy fathers, 10 yet so if thou hear the voice of the Lord, thy God, and keep his precepts and ceremonies which are written in this law and return to the Lord, thy God, with all thy heart and with all thy soul.

11 "This commandment that I command thee this day is not above thee nor far off *from thee,* 12 nor is it in heaven that thou shouldst say, 'Which of us can go up to heaven to bring it unto us and we may hear and fulfil it in work?' 13 Nor is it beyond the sea that thou mayst excuse thyself and say, 'Which of us can cross the sea and bring it unto us that we may hear and do that which is commanded?' 14 But the word is very nigh unto thee, in thy mouth and in thy heart, that thou mayst do it.

15 "Consider that I have set before thee this day life and good and on the other hand death and evil 16 that thou mayst love the Lord, thy God, and walk in his ways and keep his commandments and ceremonies and judgments, and thou mayst live, and he may multiply thee and bless thee in the land which thou shalt go in to possess. 17 But if thy heart be turned away so that thou wilt not hear, and being deceived with error thou adore strange gods and serve them, 18 I foretell thee this day that thou shalt perish and shalt remain but a short time in the land to which thou shalt pass over the Jordan and shalt go in to possess it.

19 "I call heaven and earth to witness this day that I have set before you life and death, blessing and cursing. Choose therefore life that both thou and thy seed may live 20 and

diligas Dominum, Deum tuum, atque oboedias voci eius et illi adhereas, ipse est enim vita tua et longitudo dierum tuorum, ut habites in terra pro qua iuravit Dominus patribus tuis Abraham, Isaac et Iacob ut daret eam illis."

Caput 31

Abiit itaque Moses et locutus est omnia verba haec ad universum Israhel, 2 et dixit ad eos, "Centum viginti annorum sum hodie; non possum ultra egredi et ingredi, praesertim cum et Dominus dixerit mihi, 'Non transibis Iordanem istum.'

3 "Dominus ergo, Deus tuus, transibit ante te. Ipse delebit omnes gentes has in conspectu tuo, et possidebis eas, et Iosue iste transibit ante te, sicut locutus est Dominus. 4 Facietque Dominus eis sicut fecit Seon et Og, regibus Amorreorum, et terrae eorum delebitque eos.

5 "Cum ergo et hos tradiderit vobis, similiter facietis eis

that thou mayst love the Lord, thy God, and obey his voice and adhere to him, for he is thy life and the length of thy days, that thou mayst dwell in the land for which the Lord swore to thy fathers Abraham, Isaac and Jacob that he would give it them."

Chapter 31

Moses encourageth the people and Joshua, who is appointed to succeed him. He delivereth the law to the priests. God foretelleth that the people will often forsake him and that he will punish them. He commandeth Moses to write a canticle as a constant remembrancer of the law.

And Moses went and spoke all these words to all Israel, 2 and he said to them, "I am this day a hundred and twenty years old; I can no longer go out and come in, especially as the Lord also hath said to me, 'Thou shalt not pass over this Jordan.'

3 "The Lord, thy God, then will pass over before thee. He will destroy all these nations in thy sight, and thou shalt possess them, and this Joshua shall go over before thee, as the Lord hath spoken. 4 And the Lord shall do to them as he did to Sihon and Og, the kings of the Amorites, and to their land and shall destroy them.

5 "Therefore when the Lord shall have delivered these

sicut praecepi vobis. 6 Viriliter agite, et confortamini; nolite timere, nec paveatis ad conspectum eorum, quia Dominus, Deus tuus, ipse est ductor tuus et non dimittet nec derelinquet te."

7 Vocavitque Moses Iosue et dixit ei coram omni Israhel, "Confortare, et esto robustus, tu enim introduces populum istum in terram quam daturum se patribus eorum iuravit Dominus, et tu eam sorte divides. 8 Et Dominus qui ductor vester est, ipse erit tecum. Non dimittet nec derelinquet te. Noli timere, nec paveas."

9 Scripsit itaque Moses legem hanc et tradidit eam sacerdotibus, filiis Levi, qui portabant Arcam Foederis Domini, et cunctis senioribus Israhelis. 10 Praecepitque eis, dicens, "Post septem annos, anno remissionis, in sollemnitate tabernaculorum, 11 convenientibus cunctis ex Israhel ut appareant in conspectu Domini, Dei tui, in loco quem elegerit Dominus, leges verba legis huius coram omni Israhel audientibus eis 12 et in unum omni populo congregato, tam viris quam mulieribus, parvulis et advenis qui sunt intra portas tuas, ut audientes discant et timeant Dominum, Deum vestrum, et custodiant impleantque omnes sermones legis huius, 13 filii quoque eorum, qui nunc ignorant, ut audire possint et timeant Dominum, Deum suum, cunctis diebus quibus versantur in terra ad quam vos Iordane transito pergitis obtinendam."

14 Et ait Dominus ad Mosen, "Ecce: prope sunt dies mortis tuae. Voca Iosue, et state in Tabernaculo Testimonii ut praecipiam ei." Abierunt ergo Moses et Iosue et steterunt in Tabernaculo Testimonii, 15 apparuitque Dominus ibi in co-

also to you, you shall do in like manner to them as I have commanded you. 6 Do manfully, and be of good heart; fear not, nor be ye dismayed at their sight, for the Lord, thy God, he himself is thy leader and will not leave thee nor forsake thee."

7 And Moses called Joshua and said to him before all Israel, "Take courage, and be valiant, for thou shalt bring this people into the land which the Lord swore he would give to their fathers, and thou shalt divide it by lot. 8 And the Lord who is your leader, he himself will be with thee. He will not leave thee nor forsake thee. Fear not, neither be dismayed."

9 And Moses wrote this law and delivered it to the priests, the sons of Levi, who carried the Ark of the Covenant of the Lord, and to all the ancients of Israel. 10 And he commanded them, saying, "After seven years, in the year of remission, in the feast of tabernacles, 11 when all Israel come together to appear in the sight of the Lord, thy God, in the place which the Lord shall choose, thou shalt read the words of this law before all Israel in their hearing 12 and the people being all assembled together, both men and women, children and strangers that are within thy gates, that hearing they may learn and fear the Lord, your God, and keep and fulfil all the words of this law, 13 that their children also, who now are ignorant, may hear and fear the Lord, their God, all the days that they live in the land whither you are going over the Jordan to possess it."

14 And the Lord said to Moses, "Behold: the days of thy death are nigh. Call Joshua, and stand ye in the Tabernacle of the Testimony that I may give him a charge." So Moses and Joshua went and stood in the Tabernacle of the Testimony, 15 and the Lord appeared there in the pillar of a cloud

lumna nubis quae stetit in introitu tabernaculi. 16 Dixitque Dominus ad Mosen, "Ecce! Tu dormies cum patribus tuis, et populus iste consurgens fornicabitur post deos alienos in terra ad quam ingreditur ut habitet in ea. Ibi derelinquet me et irritum faciet foedus quod pepigi cum eo. 17 Et irascetur furor meus contra eum in die illo, et derelinquam eum et abscondam faciem meam ab eo, et erit in devorationem. Invenient eum omnia mala et adflictiones ita ut dicat in illo die, 'Vere quia non est Deus mecum invenerunt me haec mala.' 18 Ego autem abscondam et celabo faciem meam in die illo propter omnia mala quae fecit, quia secutus est deos alienos.

19 "Nunc itaque scribite vobis canticum istud, et docete filios Israhel ut memoriter teneant et ore decantent et sit mihi carmen istud pro testimonio inter filios Israhel, 20 introducam enim eum in terram pro qua iuravi patribus eius lacte et melle manantem. Cumque comederint et saturati crassique fuerint, avertentur ad deos alienos et servient eis et detrahent mihi et irritum facient pactum meum. 21 Postquam invenerint eum mala multa et adflictiones, respondebit ei canticum istud pro testimonio quod nulla delebit oblivio ex ore seminis sui, scio enim cogitationes eius, quae facturus sit hodie antequam introducam eum in terram quam ei pollicitus sum."

22 Scripsit ergo Moses canticum et docuit filios Israhel.

23 Praecepitque Dominus Iosue, filio Nun, et ait, "Confor-

which stood in the entry of the tabernacle. 16 And the Lord said to Moses, "Behold! Thou shalt sleep with thy fathers, and this people rising up will go a-fornicating after strange gods in the land to which it goeth in to dwell. There will they forsake me and will make void the covenant which I have made with them. 17 And my wrath shall be kindled against them in that day, and I will forsake them and will hide my face from them, and they shall be devoured. All evils and afflictions shall find them so that they shall say in that day, 'In truth it is because God is not with me that these evils have found me.' 18 But I will hide and cover my face in that day for all the evils which they have done, because they have followed strange gods.

19 "Now therefore write you this canticle, and teach the children of Israel that they may know it by heart and sing it by mouth and this song may be unto me for a testimony among the children of Israel, 20 for I will bring them into the land for which I swore to their fathers that floweth with milk and honey. And when they have eaten and are full and fat, they will turn away after strange gods and will serve them and will despise me and make void my covenant. 21 *And* after many evils and afflictions shall have come upon them, this canticle shall answer them for a testimony which no oblivion shall take away out of the mouth of their seed, for I know their thoughts *and* what they are about to do this day before that I bring them into the land which I have promised them."

22 Moses therefore wrote the canticle and taught it to the children of Israel.

23 And the Lord commanded Joshua, the son of Nun, and

tare, et esto robustus, tu enim introduces filios Israhel in terram quam pollicitus sum, et ego ero tecum."

24 Postquam ergo scripsit Moses verba legis huius in volumine atque conplevit, 25 praecepit Levitis, qui portabant Arcam Foederis Domini, dicens, 26 "Tollite librum istum, et ponite eum in latere Arcae Foederis Domini, Dei vestri, ut sit ibi contra te in testimonio, 27 ego enim scio contentionem tuam et cervicem tuam durissimam. Adhuc vivente me et ingrediente vobiscum, semper contentiose egistis contra Dominum; quanto magis cum mortuus fuero? 28 Congregate ad me omnes maiores natu per tribus vestras atque doctores, et loquar audientibus eis sermones istos et invocabo contra eos caelum et terram, 29 novi enim quod post mortem meam inique agetis et declinabitis cito de via quam praecepi vobis et occurrent vobis mala in extremo tempore quando feceritis malum in conspectu Domini ut inritetis eum per opera manuum vestrarum."

30 Locutus est ergo Moses audiente universo coetu Israhel verba carminis huius et ad finem usque conplevit.

said, "Take courage, and be valiant, for thou shalt bring the children of Israel into the land which I have promised, and I will be with thee."

24 Therefore after Moses had wrote the words of this law in a volume and finished it, 25 he commanded the Levites, who carried the Ark of the Covenant of the Lord, saying, 26 "Take this book, and put it in the side of the Ark of the Covenant of the Lord, your God, that it may be there for a testimony against thee, 27 for I know thy obstinacy and thy most stiff neck. While I am yet living and going in with you, you have always *been rebellious* against the Lord; how much more when I shall be dead? 28 Gather unto me all the ancients of your tribes and your doctors, and I will speak these words in their hearing and will *call* heaven and earth *to witness* against them, 29 for I know that after my death you will do wickedly and will quickly turn aside form the way that I have commanded you and evils shall come upon you in the latter times when you shall do evil in the sight of the Lord to provoke him by the works of your hands."

30 Moses therefore spoke in the hearing of the whole assembly of Israel the words of this canticle and finished it even to the end.

Caput 32

"Audite, caeli, quae loquor; audiat terra verba oris mei.

2 "Concrescat ut pluvia doctrina mea; fluat ut ros eloquium meum, quasi imber super herbam et quasi stillae super gramina.

3 "Quia nomen Domini invocabo, date magnificentiam Deo nostro.

4 "Dei perfecta sunt opera, et omnes viae eius iudicia. Deus fidelis et absque ulla iniquitate; iustus et rectus.

5 "Peccaverunt ei et non filii eius in sordibus; generatio prava atque perversa.

6 "Haecine reddis Domino, popule stulte et insipiens? Numquid non ipse est pater tuus qui possedit te et fecit et creavit te?

7 "Memento dierum antiquorum; cogita generationes singulas. Interroga patrem tuum, et adnuntiabit tibi, maiores tuos, et dicent tibi.

8 "Quando dividebat Altissimus gentes, quando separabat filios Adam, constituit terminos populorum iuxta numerum filiorum Israhel.

Chapter 32

A canticle for the remembrance of the law. Moses is commanded to go up into a mountain from whence he shall see the promised land but not enter into it.

"Hear, O ye heavens, the things I speak; let the earth give ear to the words of my mouth.

2 "Let my doctrine gather as the rain; let my speech distil as the dew, as a shower upon the herb and as drops upon the grass.

3 "Because I will invoke the name of the Lord, give ye magnificence to our God.

4 "The works of God are perfect, and all his ways are judgments. God is faithful and without any iniquity; he is just and right.

5 "They have sinned against him and *are none of* his children in their filth; they are a wicked and perverse generation.

6 "*Is this the return thou makest* to the Lord, O foolish and senseless people? Is not he thy father that hath possessed thee and made *thee* and created thee?

7 "Remember the days of old; think upon every generation. Ask thy father, and he will declare to thee, thy elders, and they will tell thee.

8 "When the Most High divided the nations, when he separated the sons of Adam, he appointed the bounds of people according to the number of the children of Israel.

9 "Pars autem Domini populus eius, Iacob funiculus hereditatis eius.

10 "Invenit eum in terra deserta, in loco horroris et vastae solitudinis; circumduxit eum et docuit, et custodivit quasi pupillam oculi sui.

11 "Sicut aquila provocans ad volandum pullos suos et super eos volitans, expandit alas suas et adsumpsit eum atque portavit in umeris suis.

12 "Dominus solus dux eius fuit, et non erat cum eo deus alienus.

13 "Constituit eum super excelsam terram ut comederet fructus agrorum, ut sugeret mel de petra oleumque de saxo durissimo, 14 butyrum de armento et lac de ovibus cum adipe agnorum et arietum filiorum Basan et hircos cum medulla tritici et sanguinem uvae biberet meracissimum.

15 "Incrassatus est dilectus et recalcitravit, incrassatus, inpinguatus, dilatatus; dereliquit Deum, factorem suum, et recessit a Deo, salutari suo.

16 "Provocaverunt eum in diis alienis et in abominationibus ad iracundiam concitaverunt.

17 "Immolaverunt daemonibus et non Deo, diis quos ignorabant novi recentesque venerunt, quos non coluerunt patres eorum.

18 "Deum qui te genuit dereliquisti et oblitus es Domini, creatoris tui.

19 "Vidit Dominus et ad iracundiam concitatus est quia provocaverunt eum filii sui et filiae.

20 "Et ait, 'Abscondam faciem meam ab eis et considerabo novissima eorum, generatio enim perversa est et infideles filii.

9 "But the Lord's portion is his people, Jacob the *lot* of his inheritance.

10 "He found him in a desert land, in a place of horror and of vast wilderness; he led him about and taught him, and he kept him as the apple of his eye.

11 "As the eagle enticing her young to fly and hovering over them, he spread his wings and hath taken him and carried him on his shoulders.

12 "The Lord alone was his leader, and there was no strange god with him.

13 "He set him upon high land that he might eat the fruits of the fields, that he might suck honey out of the rock and oil out of the hardest stone, 14 butter of the herd and milk of the sheep with the fat of lambs and of the rams of the breed of Bashan and goats with the marrow of wheat and might drink the purest blood of the grape.

15 "The beloved grew fat and kicked; *he grew* fat and thick and gross; he forsook God who made him and departed from God, his saviour.

16 "They provoked him by strange gods and stirred him up to anger with their abominations.

17 "They sacrificed to devils and not to God, to gods whom they knew not that were newly come up, whom their fathers worshipped not.

18 "Thou hast forsaken the God that begot thee and hast forgotten the Lord that created thee.

19 "The Lord saw and was moved to wrath because his own sons and daughters provoked him.

20 "And he said, 'I will hide my face from them and will consider what their last end shall be, for it is a perverse generation and unfaithful children.

21 "'Ipsi me provocaverunt in eo qui non erat deus et inritaverunt in vanitatibus suis, et ego provocabo eos in eo qui non est populus et in gente stulta inritabo illos.

22 "'Ignis succensus est in furore meo et ardebit usque ad inferni novissima devorabitque terram cum germine suo et montium fundamenta conburet.

23 "'Congregabo super eos mala et sagittas meas conplebo in eis.

24 "'Consumentur fame, et devorabunt eos aves morsu amarissimo. Dentes bestiarum inmittam in eos cum furore trahentium super terram atque serpentium.

25 "'Foris, vastabit eos gladius, et intus pavor, iuvenem simul ac virginem, lactentem cum homine sene.

26 "'Dixi, "Ubinam sunt? Cessare faciam ex hominibus memoriam eorum."

27 "'Sed propter iram inimicorum distuli, ne forte superbirent hostes eorum et dicerent, "Manus nostra excelsa et non Dominus fecit haec omnia."'

28 "Gens absque consilio est et sine prudentia.

29 "Utinam saperent et intellegerent ac novissima providerent!

30 "Quomodo persequatur unus mille et duo fugent decem milia? Nonne ideo quia Deus suus vendidit eos et Dominus conclusit illos?

31 "Non enim est Deus noster ut dii eorum, et inimici nostri sunt iudices.

21 "'They have provoked me with that which was no god and have angered me with their vanities, and I will provoke them with that which is no people and will vex them with a foolish nation.

22 "'A fire is kindled in my wrath and shall burn even to the *lowest hell* and shall devour the earth with her increase and shall burn the foundations of the mountains.

23 "'I will heap evils upon them and will spend my arrows among them.

24 "'They shall be consumed with famine, and birds shall devour them with a most bitter bite. I will send the teeth of beasts upon them with the fury of creatures that trail upon the ground and of serpents.

25 "'Without, the sword shall lay them waste, and terror within, both the young man and the virgin, the sucking child with the man in years.

26 "'I said, "Where are they? I will make the memory of them to cease from among men."

27 "'But for the wrath of the enemies I have deferred it, lest perhaps their enemies might be proud and should say, "Our mighty hand and not the Lord hath done all these things."'

28 "They are a nation without counsel and without wisdom.

29 "O that they would be wise and would understand and would provide for their last end!

30 "How should one pursue after a thousand and two chase ten thousand? Was it not because their God had sold them and the Lord had shut them up?

31 "For our God is not as their gods; our enemies themselves are judges.

³² "'De vinea Sodomorum vinea eorum et de suburbanis Gomorrae; uva eorum uva fellis, et botri amarissimi.

³³ "'Fel draconum vinum eorum et venenum aspidum, insanabile.

³⁴ "'Nonne haec condita sunt apud me et signata in thesauris meis?

³⁵ "'Mea est ultio, et ego retribuam in tempore ut labatur pes eorum; iuxta est dies perditionis, et adesse festinant tempora.'

³⁶ "Iudicabit Dominus populum suum et in servis suis miserebitur; videbit quod infirmata sit manus et clausi quoque defecerint residuique consumpti sint.

³⁷ "Et dicet, 'Ubi sunt dii eorum in quibus habebant fiduciam, ³⁸ de quorum victimis comedebant adipes et bibebant vinum libaminum? Surgant et opitulentur vobis et in necessitate vos protegant.

³⁹ "'Videte quod ego sim solus, et non sit alius deus praeter me. Ego occidam, et ego vivere faciam. Percutiam, et ego sanabo, et non est qui de manu mea possit eruere.

⁴⁰ "'Levabo ad caelum manum meam, et dicam, "Vivo ego in aeternum."

⁴¹ "'Si acuero ut fulgur gladium meum et arripuerit iudicium manus mea, reddam ultionem hostibus meis et his qui oderunt me retribuam.

⁴² "'Inebriabo sagittas meas sanguine, et gladius meus devorabit carnes de cruore occisorum et de captivitate, nudati inimicorum capitis.'

⁴³ "Laudate, gentes, populum eius, quia sanguinem servo-

32 "'Their vines are of the vineyard of Sodom and of the suburbs of Gomorrah; their grapes are grapes of gall, and their clusters most bitter.

33 "'Their wine is the gall of dragons and the venom of asps, *which is* incurable.

34 "Are not these things stored up with me, and sealed up in my treasures?

35 "'Revenge is mine, and I will repay them in due time that their foot may slide; the day of destruction is at hand, and the time makes haste to come.'

36 "The Lord will judge his people and will have mercy on his servants; he shall see that their hand is weakened and that they who were shut up have also failed and they that remained are consumed.

37 "And he shall say, 'Where are their gods in whom they trusted, 38 of whose victims they ate the fat and drank the wine of their drink offerings? Let them arise and help you and protect you in your distress.

39 "'See ye that I alone am, and there is no other God besides me. I will kill, and I will make to live. I will strike, and I will heal, and there is none that can deliver out of my hand.

40 "'I will lift up my hand to heaven, and I will say, "I live for ever."

41 "'If I shall whet my sword as the lightning and my hand take hold on judgment, I will render vengeance to my enemies and repay them that hate me.

42 "'I will make my arrows drunk with blood, and my sword shall devour flesh of the blood of the slain and of the captivity, of the bare head of the enemies.'

43 "Praise his people, ye nations, for he will revenge the

rum suorum ulciscetur et vindictam retribuet in hostes eorum et propitius erit terrae populi sui."

44 Venit ergo Moses et locutus est omnia verba cantici
huius in auribus populi, ipse et Iosue, filius Nun.

45 Conplevitque omnes sermones istos, loquens ad universum Israhel, 46 et dixit ad eos, "Ponite corda vestra in
omnia verba quae ego testificor vobis hodie, ut mandetis
ea filiis vestris custodire et facere et implere universa quae
scripta sunt legis huius, 47 quia non in cassum praecepta sunt
vobis, sed ut singuli in eis viverent quae facientes longo per-
severetis tempore in terra ad quam Iordane transmisso ingredimini possidendam."

48 Locutusque est Dominus ad Mosen in eadem die, dicens, 49 "Ascende in montem istum Abarim," id est Transi-
tuum, "in Montem Nebo, qui est in terra Moab contra Hiericho, et vide terram Chanaan quam ego tradam filiis Israhel
obtinendam, et morere in monte. 50 Quem conscendens,
iungeris populis tuis, sicut mortuus est Aaron, frater tuus, in
Monte Hor et adpositus populis suis, 51 quia praevaricati estis contra me in medio filiorum Israhel ad Aquas Contradictionis, in Cades deserti Sin, et non sanctificastis me inter filios Israhel. 52 E contra videbis terram, et non ingredieris in
eam, quam ego dabo filiis Israhel."

blood of his servants and will render vengeance to their enemies and he will be merciful to the land of his people."

44 So Moses came and spoke all the words of this canticle in the ears of the people *and* Joshua, the son of Nun.

45 And he ended all these words, speaking to all Israel, 46 and he said to them, "Set your hearts on all the words which I testify to you this day, *which* you *shall* command your children to observe and to do and to fulfil all that is written in this law, 47 for they are not commanded you in vain, but that every one should live in them and that doing them you may continue a long time in the land whither you are going over the Jordan to possess it."

48 And the Lord spoke to Moses the same day, saying, 49 "Go up into this mountain Abarim," that is to say, Of Passages, "unto Mount Nebo, which is in the land of Moab over against Jericho, and see the land of Canaan which I will deliver to the children of Israel to possess, and die thou in the mountain. 50 When thou art gone up into it, thou shalt be gathered to thy people, as Aaron, thy brother, died in Mount Hor and was gathered to his people, 51 because you trespassed against me in the midst of the children of Israel at the Waters of Contradiction, in Kadesh of the desert of Zin, and you did not sanctify me among the children of Israel. 52 Thou shalt see the land before thee which I will give to the children of Israel, but thou shalt not enter into it."

Caput 33

Haec est benedictio qua benedixit Moses, homo Dei, filiis Israhel ante mortem suam.

2 Et ait, "Dominus de Sina venit, et de Seir ortus est nobis. Apparuit de Monte Pharan, et cum eo sanctorum milia, in dextera eius ignea lex.

3 "Dilexit populos; omnes sancti in manu illius sunt, et qui adpropinquant pedibus eius accipient de doctrina illius.

4 "Legem praecepit nobis Moses, hereditatem multitudinis Iacob. 5 Erit apud rectissimum rex, congregatis principibus populi cum tribubus Israhel.

6 "Vivat Ruben et non moriatur, et sit parvus in numero."

7 Haec est Iudae benedictio: "Audi, Domine, vocem Iudae, et ad populum suum introduc eum. Manus eius pugnabunt pro eo, et adiutor illius contra adversarios eius erit."

8 Levi quoque ait, "Perfectio tua et doctrina tua viro sancto tuo quem probasti in temptatione et iudicasti ad Aquas Contradictionis, 9 qui dixit patri suo et matri suae, 'Nescio vos,' et fratribus suis, 'Ignoro vos,' et nescierunt filios suos. Hii custodierunt eloquium tuum et pactum tuum

Chapter 33

Moses before his death blesseth the tribes of Israel.

This is the blessing wherewith the man of God, Moses, blessed the children of Israel before his death.

2 And he said, "The Lord came from Sinai, and from Seir he rose up to us. He hath appeared from Mount Paran, and with him thousands of saints, in his right hand a fiery law.

3 "He hath loved the people; all the saints are in his hand, and they that approach to his feet shall receive of his doctrine.

4 "Moses commanded us a law, the inheritance of the multitude of Jacob. 5 He shall be king with the most right, the princes of the people being assembled with the tribes of Israel.

6 "Let Reuben live and not die, and be he small in number."

7 This is the blessing of Judah: "Hear, O Lord, the voice of Judah, and bring him in unto his people. His hands shall fight for him, and he shall be his helper against his enemies."

8 To Levi also he said, "Thy perfection and thy doctrine be to thy holy man whom thou hast proved in the temptation and judged at the Waters of Contradiction, 9 who hath said to his father and to his mother, 'I do not know you,' and to his brethren, 'I know you not,' and their own children they have not known. These have kept thy word and ob-

servaverunt, 10 iudicia tua, o Iacob, et legem tuam, o Israhel. Ponent thymiama in furore tuo et holocaustum super altare tuum. 11 Benedic, Domine, fortitudini eius, et opera manuum illius suscipe. Percute dorsa inimicorum eius, et qui oderunt eum non consurgant."

12 Et Beniamin ait, "Amantissimus Domini habitabit confidenter in eo; quasi in thalamo tota die morabitur, et inter umeros illius requiescet."

13 Ioseph quoque ait, "De benedictione Domini terra eius, de pomis caeli et rore atque abysso subiacente, 14 de pomis fructuum solis ac lunae, 15 de vertice antiquorum montium, de pomis collium aeternorum 16 et de frugibus terrae et de plenitudine eius. Benedictio illius qui apparuit in rubo veniat super caput Ioseph et super verticem Nazarei inter fratres suos. 17 Quasi primogeniti tauri pulchritudo eius, cornua rinocerotis cornua illius, in ipsis ventilabit gentes usque ad terminos terrae. Hae sunt multitudines Ephraim et haec milia Manasse."

18 Et Zabulon ait, "Laetare, Zabulon, in exitu tuo, et Isachar in tabernaculis tuis. 19 Populos ad montem vocabunt; ibi immolabunt victimas iustitiae, qui inundationem maris quasi lac sugent et thesauros absconditos harenarum."

20 Et Gad ait, "Benedictus in latitudine Gad. Quasi leo requievit cepitque brachium et verticem, 21 et vidit principatum suum quod in parte sua doctor esset repositus qui fuit

served thy covenant, 10 thy judgments, O Jacob, and thy law, O Israel. They shall put incense in thy wrath and holocaust upon thy altar. 11 Bless, O Lord, his strength, and receive the works of his hands. Strike the backs of his enemies, and let not them that hate him rise."

12 And to Benjamin he said, "The best beloved of the Lord shall dwell confidently in him; as in a bride chamber shall he abide all the day long, and between his shoulders shall he rest."

13 To Joseph also he said, "Of the blessing of the Lord be his land, of the fruits of heaven and of the dew and of the deep that lieth beneath, 14 of the *fruits* brought forth by the sun and by the moon, 15 of the tops of the ancient mountains, of the fruits of the everlasting hills 16 and of the fruits of the earth and of the fulness thereof. The blessing of him that appeared in the bush come upon the head of Joseph and upon the crown of the Nazirite among his brethren. 17 His beauty as of the firstling of a bullock, his horns as the horns of a rhinoceros, with them shall he push the nations even to the ends of the earth. These are the multitudes of Ephraim and these the thousands of Manasseh."

18 And to Zebulun he said, "Rejoice, O Zebulun, in thy going out, and Issachar in thy tabernacles. 19 They shall call the people to the mountain; there shall they sacrifice the victims of justice, who shall suck as milk the abundance of the sea and the hidden treasures of the sands."

20 And to Gad he said, "Blessed be Gad in his breadth. He hath rested as a lion and hath seized upon the arm and the top of the head, 21 and he saw his pre-eminence that in his portion the teacher was laid up who was with the princes of

cum principibus populi et fecit iustitias Domini et iudicium suum cum Israhel."

22 Dan quoque ait, "Dan catulus leonis; fluet largiter de Basan."

23 Et Nepthalim dixit, "Nepthalim abundantia perfruetur et plenus erit benedictionibus Domini; mare et meridiem possidebit."

24 Aser quoque ait, "Benedictus in filiis Aser sit, placens fratribus suis, et tinguat in oleo pedem suum. 25 Ferrum et aes calciamentum eius. Sicut dies iuventutis tuae, ita et senectus tua.

26 "Non est Deus alius ut Deus rectissimi. Ascensor caeli auxiliator tuus. Magnificentia eius discurrunt nubes.

27 "Habitaculum eius sursum, et subter brachia sempiterna. Eiciet a facie tua inimicum dicetque, 'Conterere.'

28 "Habitabit Israhel confidenter et solus, oculus Iacob in terra frumenti et vini, caelique caligabunt rore.

29 "Beatus tu, Israhel. Quis similis tui, popule qui salvaris in Domino, scutum auxilii tui et gladius gloriae tuae? Negabunt te inimici tui, et tu eorum colla calcabis."

the people and did the justices of the Lord and his judgment with Israel."

22 To Dan also he said, "Dan is a young lion; he shall flow plentifully from Bashan."

23 And to Naphtali he said, "Naphtali shall enjoy abundance and shall be full of the blessings of the Lord; he shall possess the sea and the south."

24 To Asher also he said, "Let Asher be blessed with children; let him be acceptable to his brethren, and let him dip his foot in oil. 25 His shoe shall be iron and brass. As the days of thy youth, so also shall thy old age be.

26 "There is no other God like the God of the rightest. *He that is mounted upon* the heaven is thy helper. By his magnificence the clouds run hither and thither.

27 "His dwelling is above, and underneath are the everlasting arms. He shall cast out the enemy from *before thee* and shall say, 'Be thou brought to nought.'

28 "Israel shall dwell in safety and alone, the eye of Jacob in a land of corn and wine, and the heavens shall be misty with dew.

29 "Blessed art thou, Israel. Who is like to thee, O people that art saved by the Lord, the shield of thy help and the sword of thy glory? Thy enemies shall deny thee, and thou shalt tread upon their necks."

Caput 34

Ascendit ergo Moses de campestribus Moab super Montem Nebo, in verticem Phasga contra Hiericho, ostenditque ei Dominus omnem terram Galaad usque Dan 2 et universum Nepthalim terramque Ephraim et Manasse et omnem terram Iuda usque ad mare novissimum 3 et australem partem et latitudinem campi Hiericho, civitatis palmarum usque Segor.

4 Dixitque Dominus ad eum, "Haec est terra pro qua iuravi Abraham, Isaac et Iacob, dicens, 'Semini tuo dabo eam.' Vidisti eam oculis tuis et non transibis ad illam."

5 Mortuusque est ibi Moses, servus Domini, in terra Moab, iubente Domino. 6 Et sepelivit eum in valle terrae Moab contra Phogor, et non cognovit homo sepulchrum eius usque in praesentem diem.

7 Moses centum et viginti annorum erat quando mortuus

Chapter 34

Moses seeth the promised land but is not suffered to go into it. He dieth at the age of 120 years. God burieth his body secretly, and all Israel mourn for him thirty days. Joshua, replenished by imposition of Moses's hands with the spirit of God, succeedeth. But Moses, for his special familiarity with God and for most wonderful miracles, is commended above all other prophets.

Then Moses went up from the plains of Moab upon Mount Nebo, to the top of Pisgah over against Jericho, and the Lord shewed him all the land of Gilead as far as Dan 2 and all Naphtali and the land of Ephraim and Manasseh and all the land of Judah unto the furthermost sea 3 and the south part and the breadth of the plain of Jericho, the city of palm trees as far as Zoar.

4 And the Lord said to him, "This is the land for which I swore to Abraham, Isaac and Jacob, saying, 'I will give it to thy seed.' Thou hast seen it with thy eyes and shalt not pass over to it."

5 And Moses, the servant of the Lord, died there, in the land of Moab, by the commandment of the Lord. 6 And he buried him in the valley of the land of Moab over against Peor, and no man hath known of his sepulchre until this present day.

7 Moses was a hundred and twenty years old when he

est. Non caligavit oculus eius, nec dentes illius moti sunt. 8 Fleveruntque eum filii Israhel in campestribus Moab triginta diebus, et conpleti sunt dies planctus lugentium Mosen. 9 Iosue vero, filius Nun, repletus est spiritu sapientiae quia Moses posuit super eum manus suas. Et oboedierunt ei filii Israhel feceruntque sicut praecepit Dominus Mosi.

10 Et non surrexit propheta ultra in Israhel sicut Moses, quem nosset Dominus facie ad faciem, 11 in omnibus signis atque portentis quae misit per eum ut faceret in terra Aegypti Pharaoni et omnibus servis eius universaeque terrae illius 12 et cunctam manum robustam magnaque mirabilia quae fecit Moses coram universo Israhel.

died. His eye was not dim, neither were his teeth moved. 8 And the children of Israel mourned for him in the plains of Moab thirty days, and the days of their mourning *in which they* mourned Moses were ended. 9 And Joshua, the son of Nun, was filled with the spirit of wisdom because Moses had laid his hands upon him. And the children of Israel obeyed him and did as the Lord commanded Moses.

10 And there arose no more a prophet in Israel like unto Moses, whom the Lord knew face to face, 11 in all the signs and wonders which he sent by him to do in the land of Egypt to Pharaoh and to all his servants and to his whole land 12 and all the mighty hand and great miracles which Moses did before all Israel.

Note on the Text

This edition is meant to present a Latin text close to what the Douay-Rheims translators saw. Therefore the readings in this edition are not necessarily preferred in the sense that they are thought to be "original"; instead, they represent the Latin Bible as it was read by many from the eighth through the sixteenth century. Furthermore, in the service of economy, sources for the text are cited according to a hierarchy, and consequently the lists of sources following the lemmas are not necessarily comprehensive. If a reading appears in Weber's text or apparatus, no other sources are cited; if it is not in Weber but is in Quentin, only the sources cited by Quentin are reproduced. The complete list of sources for the Latin text, in their hierarchical order, is Weber, his apparatus, Quentin, his apparatus, the Vetus Latina edition of Pierre Sabatier (1682–1742), the *Glossa Ordinaria* attributed (wrongly) to Walafrid Strabo in the Patrologia Latina, and the database of the Beuroner Vetus Latina-Institut.

When no source can be found for what seems to be the correct Latin, a reconstruction is proposed in the Notes to the Text but the Weber text is generally printed in the edition. Trivial differences between the Weber and Sixto-Clementine editions in word order and orthography, alternative spellings and inflections of proper names, and synco-

pation of verbs have not been noted, nor have many differences that do not affect translation, such as the omission or inclusion of forms of *esse,* variant forms of personal pronouns, conjunctions treated by the Douay-Rheims translators as synonymous, and the omission or inclusion of certain pronouns or possessive adjectives.

Whenever it has been necessary to stray from Weber's text (about one thousand times in the first volume), the departures are recorded in the Notes to the Text. These notes by no means constitute a true *apparatus criticus,* but they enable interested readers to see both the deviations from Weber (whose text is preferable for people wanting to get as close as possible to the earliest versions of the many Latin texts which, combined, form the Vulgate Bible) and significant differences among the Weber, Sixto-Clementine, and Douay-Rheims texts.

When the translation reflects a reading closer to Weber's than to the Sixto-Clementine edition, the Sixto-Clementine variation is printed in the Notes to the Text. Less frequently, there are two readings that would translate the same way but that differ sufficiently to warrant noting, as at Gen 19:6, where Weber reads "umbraculum tegminis" while the Sixto-Clementine version has "umbra culminis."

Often the punctuation of the Douay-Rheims edition reflects an understanding of the Latin different from that of the Weber, Sixto-Clementine, or both editions. The Weber edition has no punctuation marks in most books; rather, the editors inserted line breaks to mark new clauses or sentences, a punctuation style known as *per cola et commata,* which is meant to assist readers without inserting anachronistic markings. These line breaks have been represented in

the notes by slashes (/). In general, differences in punctuation among this edition, the Sixto-Clementine Bible, and Weber's edition have been cited only when they demonstrate considerably different understandings of the Latin. Often Weber's presentation is too equivocal to shed light on his understanding; in these cases, his edition is not cited.

While the Douay-Rheims translation belongs to a tradition of exceptionally literal renderings of the Latin Bible, Challoner's revision contains some divergences from the Latin. Any English that does not square with the text *en face* is italicized, and where possible, Challoner's source has been indicated in the Notes to the Text. When Challoner's source is given, it is not necessarily quoted word for word in the lemma; indeed, the Septuagint is cited as a source, yet almost no Greek is quoted in the notes. Whenever there can be doubt of a source based on a slight difference between its reading and Challoner's, the difference has been recorded following the lemma, either in parentheses or in brackets when containing explanatory material that is not a quotation from the source. Sources for the English text are cited in a hierarchical fashion similar to that of the Latin, in the following order: Douay-Rheims, Sixto-Clementine, King James, Septuagint, Hebrew text; this means that if an English reading is found in the King James Version that may also be in the Septuagint, only the King James Version is cited. Also, if Challoner's translation seems to approximate a source that is cited, the distance between source and translation is indicated by a question mark following the siglum.

Words cited from biblical sources are in italics in the notes, and the sigla and any comments are in roman type. Lemmas precede colons; other readings follow them. Occa-

sionally Challoner indicated that he was adding words to his revision that did not appear in the Latin text; he did this by italicizing the relevant words, much as the authors of the King James Version printed occasional words in roman as opposed to black-letter type to indicate an addition. Bracketed explanations or underlinings draw attention to these typographical variations in the Notes to the Text where necessary.

Notes to the Text

*D-R = Latin text that seems to give rise to the D-R translation but that is not represented in S-C, Weber, the manuscripts cited in those editions, or the Old Latin Bible.

D-R = The Holie Bible: Faithfully Translated into English out of the Authentical Latin (The English Colleges of Douay and Rheims, OT 1609–10, NT 1582)

D-R/C = The Holy Bible: Translated from the Latin Vulgat (Challoner's 1752 revision, Dublin?)

Heb = Hebrew sources for the text

KJV = The Holy Bible, Conteyning the Old Testament, and the New: Newly Translated out of the Originall tongues: & with the former Translations diligently compared and reuised: by his Maiesties speciall Comandement Appointed to be read in Churches (London, 1611, rpr. 1990)

KJVn = marginalia in KJV

PL = J.-P. Migue, ed., Patrologia Latina (Paris, 1844–1865)

Quentin = Biblia sacra: iuxta Latinam Vulgatam versionem (Typis Polyglottis Vaticanis, 1926–[1995])

S = A. Rahlfs, ed., Septuaginta, 2nd ed. (Stuttgart: Deutsche Bibelgesellschaft, 1979)

S-C = Biblia Sacra: Vulgatae Editionis Sixti V Pont. Max. iussu recognita et Clementis VIII auctoritate edita (Vatican City: Marietti, 1959)

Weber = R. Weber, ed., *Biblia Sacra Vulgata,* 5th ed. (Stuttgart, 2007)

The use of sigla from Rahlfs's, Weber's, and Quentin's critical apparatus is indicated in brackets following the sigla.

Other abbreviations follow those found in H. J. Frede, *Kirchenschriftsteller: Verzeichnis und Sigel* (Freiburg: Herder, 1995) and R. Gryson, *Altlateinische Handschriften*, 2 vols. (Freiburg: Herder, 1999), and those sigla are introduced by "Frede" or "Gryson" to indicate their source. Sigla without citations following them are to be understood to refer to the verse indicated by the lemma.

GENESIS

1:4	*a tenebris*: *ac tenebras* Weber
1:12	*adferentem*: *facientem* S-C
1:14	*caeli ut*: *caeli et* S-C
<1:21	*winged* KJV: omitted in D-R>
<1:28	*saying* S: *and saith* D-R>
1:31	*fecerat*: *fecit* Weber
<2:3	*and made* KJV: *to make* D-R>
2:4	*creatae*: *creata* S-C
2:12	*Ibi*: *ibique* Weber
<2:16	*thou shalt eat* KJVn: *eate thou* D-R>
<3:2	*saying* italicized in D-R/C: omitted in D-R>
3:2	*vescimur*: *vescemur* Weber
<3:8	*Adam and his wife hid themselves* KJV: *Adam hid himselfe and so did his wife* D-R>
<3:17	*labour and toil* D-R/C: *much toyling* D-R>
3:17	*ex ea*: *eam* Weber
3:23	*Et emisit*: *emisit* Weber
4:1	*Deum*: *Dominum* Weber
4:6	*iratus*: *maestus* Weber
4:14	*tua abscondar, et*: *tua. Abscondar et* S-C, *tua abscondar / et* Weber
5:22	*et vixit postquam*: *postquam* Weber
5:31	*Ham*: *et Ham* Weber
6:2	*hominum*: *eorum* Weber
<6:13	*through* KJV: *from the face of* D-R>

6:16   *summitatem eius: summitatem* Weber

6:17   *diluvii: diluvii magni* *D-R

7:1   *in arcam: arcam* Weber

<7:2   ends after first *female* D-R/C; the rest of the verse is part of 7:3>

7:2–3   *septena et septena . . . duo et duo . . . septena et septena: septena septena . . . duo duo . . . septena septena* Weber

7:9   *Dominus: Deus* Weber

<7:13   *selfsame* KJV: *verie point of that* D-R>

7:18   *vehementer enim: vehementer* Weber

<7:21–22 *both of fowl . . . earth and all men. And* KJV: *of foule . . . earth: al men, and* D-R>

7:24   *terram: terras* Weber

8:7   *non revertebatur: revertebatur* Weber

8:17   *et universis: et in universis* Weber

<8:19   *and* KJV?: omitted in D-R>

8:21   *ait: ait ad eum* Weber; *animam viventem: animantem* Weber

9:16   *omnem: inter omnem* Weber

9:17   *omnem: inter omnem* Weber

10:1   *Ham et Iafeth: Ham Iafeth* Weber

10:2   *Gomer et Magog et Madai et Iavan: Gomer Magog et Madai Iavan* Weber

10:5   *suam et familias suas: et familias* Weber

<10:18   *families* KJV: *people* D-R>

10:27   *Uzal et: Uzal* Weber

<11:4   *make* D-R/C: *make vs* D-R>

<11:7   *they may not understand one another's speech* KJV: *none may heare is* [sic] *neighbours voice* D-R>

11:27   *Abram, Nahor: Abram et Nahor* Weber

11:29   *nomen* [first time]: *nomen autem* Weber

12:1   *tui, et veni: tui* Weber

12:18   *hoc quod: quod* Weber

13:9   *ego* [first time]: *ego ad* Weber

13:12   *Loth vero: Loth* Weber

13:14   *et meridiem: et ad meridiem* Weber; *et occidentem: et ad occidentem* Weber

<13:14   *to* [both times] D-R/C: omitted in D-R>

13:16   *numerare pulverem terrae*: *numerare pulverem* Weber

<14:11   *their victuals* KJV: *al kind of victuales* D-R>

15:6   *Abram Deo*: *Domino* Weber

15:9   *Et respondens*: *respondens* Weber

15:18   *magnum*: *magnum flumen* Weber

15:19   *Cenezeos*: *Cenezeos et Cedmoneos* Weber

16:7   *Sur in deserto*: *Sur* Weber

16:9   *manu*: *manibus* Weber

<16:10   *I will multiply thy seed exceedingly* KJV: *Multiplying . . . wil I multiplie thy seede* D-R>

16:16   *erat Abram*: *erat* Weber

17:6   *ponam te*: *ponam* Weber

17:10   *pactum meum*: *pactum* Weber

<17:11   *it had ceased to be with Sarah after the manner of women* D-R: literally, *things characteristic of women had stopped happening to Sarah*>

17:24   *Abraham nonaginta et*: *nonaginta* Weber

18:2   *propter*: *prope* S-C

18:5   *Ponamque*: *ponam* Weber

<18:15   *Nay* KJV: *It is not so* D-R>

<18:18   *mighty* KJV: *verie strong* D-R>

18:27   *Respondensque*: *respondens* Weber

18:28   *quadraginta quinque* [first time]: *quinque* Weber; *invenero ibi*: *invenero* *D-R

18:29   *quadraginta ibi*: *quadraginta* Weber

18:32   *Et dixit*: *dixit* Weber

18:33   *Abiitque*: *abiit* Weber

<18:33   *left speaking* KJV (*left communing*): *ceased to speake* D-R>

19:1   *et sedente*: *sedente* Weber; *vidisset eos*: *vidisset* Weber

19:2   *proficiscemini*: *proficiscimini* Weber

19:3   *et coxit*: *coxit* Weber

<19:4   *both . . . and* KJV: *from . . . to* D-R>

19:8   *umbraculum tegminis*: *umbra culminis* S-C

19:9   *iamque*: *iam* Weber

19:15   *Tolle*: *et tolle* Weber

19:17   *ibique locuti sunt ad eum, dicentes*: *ibi locutus est ad eum* Weber

<19:19   *shewn to me in saving my life* KJV: *wrought with me, in that thou wouldest saue my life* D-R>

<19:20 *it is* KJV: omitted in D-R>

19:29 *Abrahae liberavit*: *est Abrahae et liberavit* Weber

19:30 *eius cum eo* [second time]: *eius* Weber

19:35 *patri bibere*: *patri* Weber

20:3 *nocte*: *noctis* Weber

<20:6 *suffered thee not to* KJV: *permitted not that thou shouldest* D-R>

<20:10 *expostulated with him* D-R/C: *expostulating* D-R>

20:18 *Dominus*: *Deus* Weber

21:9 *ludentem cum Isaac, filio suo*: *ludentem* Weber

21:17 *Dei*: *Domini* Weber

21:23 *Deum*: *Dominum* Weber

21:26 *Responditque*: *respondit* Weber

<22:1 *After these things* KJV: *VVhich things being done* D-R>

22:1 *Abraham, Abraham*: *Abraham* Weber; *At ille*: *ille* Weber

22:2 *offeres*: *offer* Weber

22:8 *Dixit autem*: *dixit* Weber

22:12 *timeas*: *times* S-C; *Deum*: *Dominum* Weber; *peperceris*: *pepercisti* S-C

22:16 *unigenito propter me*: *unigenito* Weber

<22:20 *After these things* KJV: *These things so being done* D-R>

22:20 *ita*: *itaque* Weber

22:21 *et Camuhel*: *Camuhel* Weber

23:5 *Responderunt*: *responderuntque* Weber; *Heth, dicentes*: *Heth* Weber

<23:6 *sepulchre* KJV: *monument* D-R>

23:8 *intercedite pro me*: *intercedite* Weber

23:10 *Responditque Ephron*: *responditque* Weber

23:11 *sed tu*: *sed* Weber

23:14 *Responditque*: *respondit* Weber

23:15 *audi me*: *audi* Weber

23:16 *probatae*: *et probati* Weber

23:17 *terminis eius*: *terminis* Weber

<24:1 *advanced* [S] *in age* KJV: *of manie days* D-R>

24:4 *cognationem*: *ad cognationem* Weber

24:6 *Dixitque*: *dixit* Weber

24:7 *iuravit mihi*: *iuravit* Weber

<24:8 *back thither again* D-R/C: *thither againe* D-R>

24:13 *propter*: *prope* S-C

<24:14 *let it be the same* KJV: *she it is* D-R>

24:17   *sorbendum*: *bibendum* S-C

<24:20   *having drawn, she gave* D-R/C: *being drawen gaue it* D-R>

<24:21   *musing* D-R: literally would be omitted>

24:22   *autem*: *ergo* Weber

24:24   *peperit*: *peperit ipsi* S-C

<24:25   *said moreover to him* KJV: *added, saying* D-R>

<24:29   *to the well* KJV: *where the fountaine was* D-R>

<24:30   *that she related* D-R/C: *her words* D-R; *Thus and thus* D-R/C [*Thus* KJV]: *These words* D-R>

24:30   *propter*: *prope* S-C

24:32   *in hospitium*: *hospitium* Weber; *eius*: *camelorum* Weber

<24:37   *Canaanites* D-R: *daughters of the Canaanites* all other sources>

<24:41   *if* KJV: *and* D-R; *one* KJV: *her* D-R>

24:42   *fontem aquae*: *fontem* Weber

<24:43   *who shall hear me say* D-R/C: *when she shal heare me say* D-R, literally, *will have heard from me*>

<24:44   *let the same be* KJV: *that is the* D-R>

24:45   *Dumque*: *dum* Weber

24:48   *perduxit*: *perduxisset* Weber

24:49   *dicite mihi*: *dicite* Weber

24:50   *Responderuntque*: *responderunt* Weber

24:52   *procidens adoravit*: *adoravit* Weber

24:54   *Inito*: *initoque* Weber

<24:54   *And* KJV: omitted in D-R>

24:55   *Responderuntque*: *responderunt* Weber; *frater* Ω^J [Quentin's siglum]: *fratres* S-C, Weber

<24:56   *prospered* KJV: *directed* D-R>

24:57   *Et dixerunt*: *dixerunt* Weber

24:62   *Eo tempore*: *Eo autem tempore* S-C; *Eodem tempore* *D-R

24:65   *Dixitque*: *dixit* Weber

25:7   *Abraham*: *Abrahae* S-C, *eius* Weber

25:15   *et Itur*: *Itur* Weber

25:17   *Et facti sunt anni*: *anni* Weber; *deficiensque*: *deficiens* Weber

25:21   *est Isaac*: *est* Weber

<25:25   *hairy* D-R/C: *al hearie* D-R; *he was called* KJV: *he called him* D-R>

25:26   *sunt ei*: *sunt* Weber

<25:27   *skillful hunter* KJV (*cunning* for *skillful*): *a man cunning in hunting*
D-R>

25:33   *Iuravit ei: iuravit* Weber

<26:3   *to fulfill* D-R/C: *accomplishing* D-R>

26:8   *ibi demoraretur: ibidem moraretur* S-C

<26:11   *surely* KJV: omitted in D-R>

26:14   *possessiones: possessionem* Weber

26:17   *ut veniret: veniret* Weber

<26:17–18   *So he departed and came to the torrent of Gerar to dwell there. And*
D-R/C: *And departing, to come to the Torrent of Gerara, and to dwel there*
D-R>

26:19   *Foderuntque: foderunt* Weber

26:21   *Foderunt autem: foderunt* Weber

26:24   *metuere: timere* S-C

26:28   *nos: nunc* Weber

26:33   *urbis* ΞΩ^S a [Quentin's sigla]: *urbi* S-C, Weber

<26:33   *called* D-R/C: *geuen* D-R>

27:7   *de venatione tua: venationem tuam* Weber

27:12   *inducam: inducat* Weber

27:13   *perge; adfer* CΣT [Weber's sigla, my punctuation]: *pergens affer* S-
C, *perge adferque* Weber

27:17   *Deditque: dedit* Weber

27:18   *At: et* Weber

27:20   *Rursumque: rursum* Weber; *Voluntas: voluntatis* Weber

27:27   *frangrantiam, benedicens illi: flagrantiam benedicens* Weber; *agri pleni:
agri* Weber

<27:31   *what he had taken in hunting* D-R/C: *his hunting* D-R>

<27:34   *in a great consternation* D-R/C: *dismaied* D-R>

<27:37   *made . . . his servants* S: *made subiect to his seruice* D-R>

27:37   *et tibi: tibi* Weber

27:41   *Venient dies luctus patris mei et: veniant dies luctus patris mei ut* Weber

27:43   *fili mi: fili* Weber

<27:46   *choose* D-R/C: *list* D-R>

28:1   *benedixit eum: benedixit* Weber

<28:8   *was not well pleased with* D-R/C [*pleased* is in KJV, but syntax is
different]: *did not willingly see* D-R>

28:14   *semen: germen* Weber; *orientem et: orientem* Weber

28:18   *ergo Iacob: ergo* Weber

29:16   *minor vero: minor* Weber

29:26   *nostro: hoc* *D-R

29:34   *Concepitque: concepit* Weber; *alium filium: alium* Weber

<30:1   *herself without children* D-R/C: *she was vnfruitful* D-R>

30:16   *Dormivitque: dormivit* Weber

30:20   *Dotavit: ditavit* Weber

30:27   *quod: quia* S-C

30:30   *venirem ad te: venirem* Weber

<30:32   *speckled* KJV: *of speckled flyse* [= *fleece*] D-R>

30:34   *Dixitque: dixit* Weber

30:35   *oves et: oves* Weber

<30:37   *so* D-R/C: *and* D-R>

<30:39   *speckled* D-R: literally, *speckled with vaired color*>

30:40   *virgas in canalibus: virgas* Weber

31:7   *Sed et: sed* Weber

<31:8   *speckled* KJV: *young of diuers colours* D-R>

31:14   *Responderuntque: responderunt* Weber

31:16   *praecipit tibi Deus: praecipit* Weber

31:23   *conprehendit eum: conprehendit* Weber

31:24   *Deum: Dominum* Weber

31:25   *cumque: cum* Weber; *consecutus fuisset: consecutus* Weber

<31:27   *privately* D-R/C, not unlike KJV (*secretly*): *without my knowledge* D-R>

31:27   *citharis: cithara* Weber

31:29   *contra: cum* Weber

<31:32   *and if thou find any of thy things with me, take them away." Now when he said* D-R/C: *what soeuer of thy things thou shalt finde with me, and take away. Saying* D-R>

<31:35   *his careful search was in vain* D-R/C: *his carefulnes in seeking was deluded* D-R>

31:36   *peccatum meum: peccatum* Weber

<31:39   *torn* KJV: *caught* D-R>

31:40   *fugiebatque: fugiebat* Weber

31:41   *Sicque: sic* Weber

31:43   *filiae meae*: *filiae* Weber

31:44   *ergo* Σ^M [Quentin's siglum]: *ergo et* S-C, Weber

31:44   *in testimonium*: *testimonium* Weber

31:55   *reversusque*: *reversus* Weber

32:3   *in regionem*: *regionis* Weber

32:5   *et oves*: *oves* Weber

32:6   *Reversique*: *reversi* Weber

<32:7   *Then* KJV: omitted in D-R>

<32:10   *I am not worthy of the least of* KJV: *I am inferiour to al* D-R>

32:10   *tuis et veritate tua*: *et veritate* Weber

32:11   *Esau*: *de manu Esau* Weber

32:14   *et arietes*: *arietes* Weber

32:17   *aut* [both times]: *et* Weber

<32:17   *before thee* KJV: *that thou doest folowe* D-R>

32:20   *interum nostrum*: *post nos* *D-R

<32:20   *after us* D-R: literally, *our path*>

<32:22   *two* KJV: *as manie* D-R>

<32:25–26   bracketed words added in this edition>

33:8   *Dixitque Esau, "Quaenam sunt istae*: *quaenam sunt inquit istae* Weber

33:9   *At*: *et* Weber

33:10   *Dixitque*: *dixit* Weber

<33:11   *He took it at his brother's earnest pressing him* D-R/C: *Scarse at his brothers great instance, taking it* D-R>

33:13   *Dixitque*: *dixit* Weber

<33:13   *to be overdriven* D-R/C [KJV has *over-drive* but syntax is different]: *to ouerlaboure themselues in going* D-R>

<33:14   *softly* D-R: *softly* here means "slowly.">

<33:15   *nothing else but* D-R/C: *this only* D-R>

33:15   *uno*: *unum tantum* S-C; *tuo, domine mi*: *domini mei* Weber

33:19   *tabernacula*: *tabernaculum* Weber

<34:3   *whereas she was sad, he comforted* D-R: literally, *he comforted the sad [girl]*>

34:12   *et munera postulate, et libenter*: *munera postulate libens* Weber

34:22   *quo*: *quod* Weber

<34:22   *we must circumcise* D-R/C: *If we circumcise* D-R; *every male among us* KJV: *our men sexe* D-R>

34:24 *Adsensique*: *adsensi* Weber

<34:28 *they took* KJV: omitted in D-R, which has all the accusatives in the sentence as objects of *vastantes*, except *uxores*.>

34:30 *fecistis me*: *fecistis* Weber

<35:1 *make there* KJV: *make* D-R>

35:7 *loci illius*: *loci* Weber

35:8 *loci illius*: *loci* Weber

35:14 *effundens super eum* X [Quentin's siglum]: *effundens* S-C, Weber

35:15 *loci illius*: *loci* Weber

35:16 *Egressus autem*: *egressus* Weber

36:9 *Hae autem*: *hae* Weber

36:17 *Hii autem*: *hii* Weber

36:21 *et Dison*: *Dison* Weber

36:23 *Hebal et*: *Hebal* Weber

36:40 *nomina ducum*: *nomina* Weber

37:4 *pacifice*: *pacificum* Weber

<37:4 *peaceably* KJV: *any thing . . . peaceably* D-R>

37:21 *Audiens autem*: *audiens* Weber

37:22 *interficiatis*: *interficiamus* Weber

37:24 *cisternam veterem*: *cisternam* Weber

<37:35 *father in his sorrow* D-R/C: *fathers sorowe* D-R>

37:35 *sed*: *et* Weber

38:1 *Eodem*: *eo* Weber

<38:1 *At that* KJV: *The same* D-R; *certain* KJV: *man an* D-R>

38:4 *Rursumque*: *rursum* Weber

<38:9 *be his* KJV: *be borne to himselfe* D-R>

38:17 *Rursumque*: *rursum* Weber

38:22 *mihi numquam*: *mihi: Numquam* S-C [implying direct speech]

<38:24 *she appeareth to have a big belly* D-R/C: *her bellie semeth to swel* D-R>

38:24 *Dixitque*: *dixit* Weber

38:25 *duceretur*: *educeretur* Weber

38:28 *egredietur*: *egreditur* Weber

39:11 *quadam die ut*: *ut quadam die* Weber

<39:11 *any man with him* D-R: literally, *onlookers*>

39:14 *vocavit ad se*: *vocavit* Weber

39:18   *audisset*: *vidisset* Weber; *pallium quod tenebam*: *pallium* Weber

40:4   *Aliquantulum*: *aliquantum* Weber

40:13   *ministerii*: *magisterii* Weber

40:14   *facias*: *facies* Weber; *ut* [second time]: *et* Weber

40:21   *ei*: *regi* Weber

<41:3   *leanfleshed* KJV: *caryan leane* D-R>

<41:4   *whose bodies were very beautiful and well conditioned* D-R/C: *that had the merucylous beautie and good state of bodies* D-R; *so Pharao awoke.* ¶ *He slept again* KJV: *Pharao after he waked, slept againe* D-R>

<41:6   *seven* KJV: *as many* D-R; *blasted* S: *blasted with adustion* D-R>

41:7   *Evigilans Pharao*: *evigilans* Weber

41:8   *ad omnes*: *ad* Weber

<41:15 *art very wise at interpreting them* D-R/C: *doest most wisely interprete* D-R>

41:15   *prudentissime*: *sapientissime* S-C

41:17   *Pharao*: *ille* Weber

<41:21 *were as lean and ill favoured as before* D-R/C: *with the like leanenes and deformitie, looked heauelie* D-R>

<41:23 *blasted* S: *blasted, with adustion* D-R>

41:34   *singulas*: *cunctas* S-C

41:41   *Dixitque*: *dicens quoque* Weber

41:42   *Tulitque*: *tulit* Weber

41:46   *et circuivit*: *circuivit* Weber

41:49   *abundantia*: *multitudo* Weber

<41:57 *seek some relief of their* D-R/C: *moderate the miserie of the* D-R>

42:6   *princeps in terra*: *princeps* Weber

42:9   *ait ad eos*: *ait* Weber

42:13   *At*: *et* Weber

<42:15 *try what you are* D-R/C: *take a trial of you* D-R>

42:16   *ut* $\Lambda\Sigma^M$ [Quentin's sigla]: *et* S-C, Weber

42:25   *Tollensque*: *tollens* Weber; *iussit*: *iussitque* Weber

42:32   *patre est*: *patre versatur* Weber

42:36   *et Beniamin*: *Beniamin* Weber

42:37   *eum tibi*: *eum* Weber

42:38   *et ipse*: *ipse* Weber

<43:1   *was heavy* D-R/C: *did oppresse . . . very sore* D-R>

43:2   *emite nobis: emite* Weber

43:3   *attestatione: testificatione* Weber; *iurandi: iurisiurandi* S-C

<43:11   *Israel* D-R/C: *Israel their father* D-R>

43:11   *stactes* sigla L, C and Vi in Frede CAr ant 2.118 185.1 (*stacten*): *stactes et* S-C, *et stactes et* Weber

43:19   *dispensatorem domus: dispensatorem* Weber

43:20   *audias nos: audias* Weber

43:21   *reportamus: reportavimus* S-C

43:22   *quae nobis: quae* Weber

<43:22   *We cannot tell* KJV: *our conscience is not priuie* D-R>

<43:25   *against* KJV: *until* D-R>

<43:34   *merry* KJV: *inebriated* D-R>

44:4   *et persequere: persequere* Weber

<44:6   *the same words* KJV: *in the same order* D-R>

<44:8   *should it be* D-R/C: *foloweth it* D-R>

<44:9   *my* KJV: *our* D-R>

44:10   *dixit eis: dixit* Weber; *quemcumque: quem* Weber

44:16   *iuste: iusti* Weber

44:18   *Accedens autem: accedens* Weber

<44:20   *he alone is left of his mother* KJV: *his mother hath him only* D-R>

44:27   *Ad quae: atque* Weber

44:32   *tuus sim: tuus* Weber

<44:34   *be* D-R/C: *stand by* D-R>

45:3   *Non: nec* Weber

45:6   *est enim: est* Weber

45:9   *me; ne moreris: me ne moreris* S-C, Weber

45:10   *habitabis: habita* Weber

<45:13   *You shall tell* KJV: *Report* D-R>

45:20   *nec: ne* Weber

45:21   *Feceruntque: fecerunt* Weber

45:23   *addens et: addens eis* Weber

45:26   *Ioseph, flilus tuus: Ioseph* Weber; *audito Iacob: audito* Weber

46:3   *timere: timere et* Weber

46:4   *manus suas: manum suam* Weber

46:5   *Surrexit autem: surrexit* Weber

46:11   *Gerson et: Gerson*

46:16   *Haggi et: Haggi* Weber; *Esebon et: Esebon* Weber

46:21   *Asbel et: Asbel* Weber; *Ros et: Ros* Weber

46:27   *Omnes animae: omnis anima* Weber

<46:32   *have* KJV: *could haue* D-R>

47:2   *constituit: statuit* Weber

<47:9   *pilgrimage* [first time] KJV: *pilgrimage of my life* D-R; *pilgrimage of my fathers* KJV (*of my fathers, in the dayes of their pilgrimage*): *of my fathers, in which they were pilgrimes* D-R>

47:11   *terrae: terrae solo* Weber

<47:13   *more especially* D-R/C: *especially* D-R>

<47:14   *corn which they bought* KJV: *selling of corne* D-R>

47:15   *emptoribus: emptoris* Weber

47:18   *celabimus: celamus* Weber

47:19   *moriemur: morimur* Weber

<47:24   *you shall have* S: *I am content you shal haue* D-R>

48:1   *perrexit* O [Quentin's siglum]: *ire perrexit* S-C, Weber

<48:1   *set out to go to him* D-R/C: *went forward* D-R>

<48:4   *of thee a multitude* KJV: *thee into multitudes* D-R>

48:9   *dedit: donavit* S-C

<48:9   *And* KJV: omitted in D-R>

48:14   *iunioris: minoris* S-C

48:15   *Iacob filiis Ioseph: Ioseph filio suo* Weber

48:16   *pueris istis: pueris* Weber

<48:17   *was much displeased* KJV (*it displeased him*): *tooke it heauily* D-R>

<48:18   *should not be so, my father* D-R/C: *is not conuenient father so to be* D-R>

48:19   *iunior: minor* S-C

49:9   *Ad praedam: a praeda* Weber

49:10   *femore: femoribus* Weber

<50:2   *embalme* KJV: *embawme . . . with spices* D-R>

<50:9   *it was a great company* KJV: *it became no smal multitude* D-R>

50:11   *vocatum est: appelaverunt* Weber

<50:17   *from him* D-R/C: *in his wordes* D-R>

50:18   *proni adorantes: proni* Weber

50:19   *resistere voluntati: rennuere voluntatem* Weber

50:20   *sed: et* Weber

50:21   *metuere: timere* S-C

<50:24 *And he made them swear to him, saying* KJV (*And Ioseph tooke an othe of the children of Israel, saying*): *And when he had adiured them and said* D-R>

<50:25   *embalmed* KJV: *embawmed with spices* D-R>

EXODUS

1:5   *animae* Gryson 100 E, Frede AM 118 Ps 71.12, CAr cpl 1093D , CAr Ps 77.50 725.686, HI ep 22.11.3 158.16: *animae eorum* S-C, Weber

<1:7   *sprung up into multitudes* D-R/C: *as it were springing vp did multiplie* D-R>

1:21   *timuerunt: timuerant* Weber

1:22   *ergo: autem* Weber

<1:22   *ye shall cast . . . ye shall save alive* KJV: *cast . . . reserue it* D-R>

2:1   *et accepit uxorem: accepta uxore* Weber

<2:4   *what would be done* KJV: *the event of the thing* D-R>

<2:5   *for it* KJV (*to fetch it*): omitted in D-R>

2:6   *est hic: est* Weber

<2:7   *Shall* KJV: *Wilt thou that* D-R; *to nurse* D-R/C: *that may nurse* D-R>

2:10   *nomen eius: eum* *D-R

2:11   *egressus est ad fratres suos viditque: egressus ad fratres suos vidit* Weber

2:14   *vis sicut heri: dicis sicut* Weber

<2:14   *to be known* D-R/C [*knowen* is in KJV, but syntax is different]: *abroad* D-R>

2:16   *Erant autem: erant* Weber; *hauriendam aquam: hauriendas aquas* Weber

2:21   *eius, uxorem: eius* Weber

2:22   *peperit ei: peperit* Weber; *Alterum–Pharaonis* omitted in Weber

2:23   *multum vero: multum* Weber

2:24   *pepigit: pepigerat* Weber; *Isaac: et Isaac* Weber

2:25   *Et respexit Dominus: respexit* Weber

3:1   *soceri: cognati* Weber

3:6   *Isaac et: Isaac* Weber

3:8   *liberem: liberarem* Weber; *educam: educerem* Weber; *Amorrei et: Amorrei* Weber

<3:9   *for* D-R/C: *Therfore* D-R>

3:10   *et mittam: mittam* Weber

3:11	*Dixitque*: *dixit* Weber
3:12	*populum meum*: *populum* Weber
<3:15	unto all generations KJV: *into generation and to generation* D-R>
3:15	*generatione*: *generationem* S-C
3:16	*Vade et*: *Vade* Weber; *Abraham*: *Abraham et* Weber; *et vidi*: *et* Weber
3:17	*Amorrei et*: *Amorrei* Weber
3:18	*in*: *per* Weber
<3:19	let you go KJV: *dismisse you to goe* D-R>
3:22	*hospita sua*: *hospita* Weber
4:2	*quod*: *hoc quod* Weber
4:3	*Dixitque Dominus*: *ait* Weber
<4:4	by the tail KJV: *the tayle therof* D-R>
4:5	*Isaac et*: *Isaac* Weber
4:15	*et ego*: *ego* Weber
4:18	*socerum*: *cognatum* Weber; *vivant*: *vivunt* Weber
4:19	*et revertere*: *revertere* Weber; *sunt enim*: *sunt* Weber
4:20	*Tulit ergo*: *tulit* Weber
<4:22	my son, my firstborn KJV: *My first begotten sonne* D-R>
4:22	*primogenitus*: *primogenitus meus* Weber
<4:23	thy son, thy firstborn KJV: *thy first-begotten-sonne* D-R>
4:26	*Sponsus sanguinium tu mihi es* Λ^HΞΣ^{OM}BΘ^{HAM*G}P² Ψ^{BDF}Ω^{SM} arels [Quentin's sigla]: *Sponsus sanguinium* S-C, Weber [without capitalization]
4:27	*desertum*: *deserto* Weber
<4:31	falling down S: *prostrate* D-R>
5:3	*Dixeruntque*: *dixerunt* Weber
5:7	*stipulam*: *stipulas* S-C
5:8	*quam*: *quos* Weber
5:11	*poteritis*: *potueritis* Weber
5:20	*egredientes*: *egredientibus* S-C
5:22	*Reversusque est*: *reversusque* Weber; *et ait*: *ait* Weber
5:23	*in nomine*: *nomine* Weber
6:1	*Dixitque*: *dixit* Weber; *sum*: *sim* S-C
<6:3	by the name of KJV: *as* D-R>
<6:7	I D-R/C: *and I* D-R>
6:7	*sim*: *sum* S-C
6:12	*audiet*: *audiet me* Weber

<6:12   *hear me* KJV: *heare* D-R>

6:13   *Locutusque*: *locutus* Weber

6:15   *Aod et*: *Aod* Weber

7:1   *et Aaron*: *Aaron* Weber

7:2   *loqueris ei*: *loqueris* Weber; *et ille*: *ille* Weber

7:5   *sim*: *sum* S-C

7:9   *vertetur*: *vertatur* Weber

7:20   *Feceruntque*: *feceruntque ita* Weber

<8:3   *bring forth an abundance of* KJV (*bring foorth . . . abundantly*): *bubble with* D-R>

8:6   *Et extendit*: *extendit* Weber

8:8   *dixit eis*: *dixit* Weber

<8:9   *Set me a time* D-R/C: *Appoint me when* D-R>

8:9   *et a servis tuis et a populo tuo* omitted in Weber

8:10   *faciam ut*: *ut* Weber

8:11   *et tantum*: *tantum* Weber

8:17   *manum*: *manu* Weber

8:19   *est hic*: *est* Weber

8:20   *egredietur*: *egreditur* Weber

8:21   *universa*: *in universa* Weber

8:25   *Vocavitque*: *vocavit* Weber; *et sacrificate*: *sacrificate* Weber; *terra hac*: *terra* Weber

8:27   *Via*: *Viam* S-C; *solitudinem*: *solitudine* Weber; *praeceperit*: *praecepit* S-C

8:29   *servis suis*: *servis* Weber

<8:29   *in not letting the people go* KJV: *that thou wilt not dismisse the people* D-R>

8:31   *servis suis*: *servis* Weber

<9:4   *wonderful difference* D-R/C: *merueile* D-R>

9:4   *intereat*: *pereat* S-C

9:8   *illud*: *illum* S-C

<9:9   *both* D-R/C: omitted in D-R>

9:9   *iumentis ulcera*: *in iumentis vulnera* Weber

9:10   *coram*: *contra* Weber; *illud*: *illum* S-C; *ulcera*: *vulnera* Weber; *iumentis*: *in iumentis* Weber

<9:10   *with* KJV: *of* D-R>

9:11   *ulcera*: *vulnera* Weber

9:14   *tuum et*: *tuum* Weber

<9:15   *I will stretch out my hand to* KJV: *stretching forth my hand I wil*
D-R>

<9:19   *which the hail shall fall upon* D-R/C: *and the haile fal vpon them*
D-R>

9:24   *inmixta*: *mista* S-C

<9:24   *was seen* D-R/C: *appeared* D-R>

<9:25   *both . . . and* KJV: *from . . . euen vnto* D-R>

9:25   *cunctamque*: *cunctam* Weber

9:28   *ut desinant*: *et desinant* Weber

<9:32   *other winter corn* D-R: literally, *corn*>

9:33   *ex*: *et ex* Weber

10:5   *ne*: *nec* Weber; *fuit*: *fuerit* S-C

10:9   *senibus*: *senioribus* S-C; *Dei nostri*: *nostri* Weber

10:10   *respondit Pharao*: *respondit* Weber

<10:10   *some great evil* D-R/C: *very wickedly* D-R>

10:12   *fuit*: *fuerit* S-C

10:13   *Et extendit*: *extendit* Weber

10:18   *Egressusque*: *egressusque est* Weber: *oravit ad* Ψ^{B2} [Quentin's sigla,
orauit for *oravit*]: *oravit* S-C, *et oravit* Weber

10:22   *Extenditque*: *extendit* Weber

10:28   *Mosen*: *eum* Weber; *et cave*: *cave* Weber

10:29   *fiet*: *fiat* Weber

11:2   *unusquisque* Frede AU Ex 39 84.526, AU loc 2.60 411.261: *vir* S-C,
Weber

11:3   *populo suo*: *populo* Weber

12:7   *sanguine eius*: *sanguine* Weber

12:10   *residuum*: *residui* Weber

12:11   *et calciamenta*: *calciamenta* Weber; *festinanter*: *festinantes* Weber

<12:12   *both . . . and* KJV: *from . . . euen vnto* D-R>

<12:14   *And this day shall be for a memorial to you* KJV: *And you shal haue this
day for a moniment* D-R>

<12:16   *shall be kept with the like solemnity* D-R/C: *with the like festiuitie shal
be venerable* D-R>

<12:17   *feast of the unleavened bread* KJV [*feast of* is italicized in D-R/C and
in roman type in KJV]: *azymes* D-R>

12:21   *et immolate*: *immolate* Weber

12:22   *in sanguine: sanguine* Weber

12:23   *ostium domus: ostium* Weber

<12:24   *Thou shalt keep* KJV (*ye shall obserue*): *Keepe* D-R>

12:31   *Pharao Mosen: Mosen* Weber; *et egredimini: egredimini* Weber; *Vos: et vos* Weber

12:37   *ferme: fere* S-C

12:39   *occurrerat: ocurrerant* Weber

12:40   *manserunt: manserant* Weber

12:48   *transire: habitare* *D-R

12:50   *Feceruntque: fecerunt* Weber

12:51   *eadem: in eadem* Weber

<13:9   *the land of* D-R/C: omitted in D-R>

13:11   *te Dominus: te* Weber

<13:13   *men* D-R/C: *men among thy children* D-R>

13:14   *terra Aegypti: Aegypto* Weber

13:16   *eduxerit: eduxit* S-C

13:17   *Dominus: Deus* S-C

14:7   *et quicquid: quicquid* Weber

14:12   *erat: est* Weber

14:17   *eius et: eius* Weber

14:19–20 *tergum stetit: tergum. Stetit* S-C

14:20   *ita ut: ut* Weber

14:23   *et omnis: omnis* Weber

14:28   *nec: ne* Weber

<14:29   *sea upon dry land* KJV: *drie sea* D-R>

15:6   *magnificata est: magnifice* Weber

15:7   *tuos: meos* Weber; *ut: sicut* S-C

15:11   *faciens: et faciens* Weber

15:14   *Ascenderunt: adtenderunt* Weber

15:17   *sanctuarium tuum: sanctuarium* Weber

15:19   *eques: equus* Weber

15:20   *prophetissa: prophetis* Weber

15:23   *illud: illum* S-C

15:27   *Helim filii Israhel: Helim* Weber

16:2   *Aaron: contra Aaron* Weber

16:3   *panem: panes* Weber

16:7   *mussitatis: mussitastis* S-C

16:12   *sim*: *sum* S-C

16:13   *operuit*: *cooperuit* S-C

16:16   *sufficiat*: *sufficit* S-C

<16:16   *of it* D-R/C: *vp* D-R>

16:22   *vero*: *autem* S-C

16:23   *est* [third time]: *erit* Weber

16:25   *Domini*: *Domino* Weber

16:26   *Domini*: *Domino* Weber

16:27   *Venitque*: *venit* Weber

16:29   *et nullus* ae [Quentin's sigla]: *nullus* S-C, Weber

17:1   *castrametata est*: *castrametati sunt* S-C

17:3   *pro*: *prae* S-C; *nos et*: *et nos et* Weber

17:4   *pauxillum et lapidabunt*: *paululum et lapidabit* S-C

17:5   *Et ait*: *ait* Weber; *senibus*: *senioribus* S-C

17:6   *super*: *supra* S-C; *senibus*: *senioribus* S-C

17:10   *locutus*: *locutus ei* Weber

17:16   *bellum Domini*: *bellum Dei* Weber

18:1   *et*: *eo* Weber

18:5   *uxor eius*: *uxor* Weber

18:8   *Dominus* [first time]: *Deus* Weber; *universumque*: *universum* Weber; *et quod*: *quo* Weber

18:12   *senes*: *seniores* S-C; *Deo* [second time]: *Domino* Weber

18:13   *de*: *a* S-C

<18:14   *all things* KJV (*all*): *to witte, al thinges* D-R>

18:20   *facere debeant*: *facere* Weber

<18:22   *that* D-R/C: *and* D-R>

19:6   *regnum*: *in regnum* S-C

19:8   *universus*: *omnis* S-C

<19:9   *Lo! Now* KJV (*Loe*): *Now presently* D-R>

19:11   *in die*: *die* Weber

19:12   *dices ad eos*: *dices* Weber

19:15   *et ne*: *ne* Weber

19:16   *iamque*: *iam* Weber; *et timuit*: *timuit* Weber

19:19   *Deus*: *Dominus* Weber

<19:24   *lest* KJV: *lest perhappes* D-R>

19:25   *Descenditque*: *descendit* Weber

<20:4   *the likeness of any thing* KJV: *any similitude* D-R>

20:5   *filiis: filios* S-C

20:10   *sabbatum Domini, Dei tui, est. Non facies omne opus in eo: sabbati*
Domini Dei tui non facies omne opus Weber

<20:10   *nor* [both times] KJV: omitted in D-R>

<20:16   *bear false witness* KJV: *speake . . . false testimonie* D-R>

<20:22   *and* KJV: *moreouer* D-R>

20:22   *sum: sim* S-C

20:23   *facietis* [first time]: *facietis mecum* Weber

20:25   *cultrum tuum: cultrum* S-C

<20:25   *a* D-R/C: *thy* D-R; *tool* KJV: *knife* D-R>

21:4   *pepererit: peperit* Weber

21:8   *fuerit: fuerat* S-C; *habebit: habet* Weber

21:10   *puellae: illi* *D-R

21:13   *quo: in quem* S-C

21:14   *de industria: per industriam* S-C

21:15   *aut: et* Weber

21:17   *vel: et* Weber

<21:18   *keepeth* KJV: *lye in* D-R>

21:19   *percussit: percusserit* S-C

21:28   *percusserit: petierit* Weber

<21:28   *gore* KJV: *with his horne strike* D-R>

21:29   *reclusit: recluserit* S-C

<21:29   *his owner also shall be put to death* KJV: *they shal put to death his*
owner also D-R>

<21:31   *have gored* KJV: *with his horne he strike* D-R>

<22:7   *any* D-R/C: omitted in D-R>

22:8   *latet fur: latet* Weber

22:13   *deferat: deferet* Weber

22:16   *habebit eam: habebit* Weber

22:20   *praeter: praeterquam* S-C

22:25   *urguebis: urgues* Weber

22:26   *reddes: redde* Weber

22:29   *reddere: offere* Weber

<23:1   *bear false witness* D-R/C: *say false testimonie* D-R>

23:3   *iudicio: negotio* Weber

23:6   *iudicio: iudicium* S-C

23:8   *accipies*: *accipias* Weber

23:11   *reliquum*: *reliqui* Weber

23:15   *novarum frugum* Ω^M [Quentin's siglum]: *novorum* S-C, Weber

23:16   *messis*: *mensis* S-C; *seminaveris*: *serueris* Weber

23:17   *Deo tuo*: *Deo* Weber

23:19   *Non*: *nec* Weber

23:20   *in locum*: *ad locum* Weber

23:21   *peccaveris*: *peccaveritis* Weber

23:23   *contribo*: *conteram* S-C

23:31   *in manibus*: *manibus* Weber

23:33   *certo*: *certe* S-C

24:3   *cunctus*: *omnis* S-C

<24:7   *we* D-R/C: *and we* D-R>

24:10   *et sub*: *sub* Weber

<24:36   *shall be of the same beaten work* KJV (*shall be of the same: all it shall bee one beaten worke*): *shal be out of it, al the whole beaten* D-R>

25:2   *offert*: *offeret* S-C

25:5   *pellesque*: *pelles* Weber

25:6   *thymiama*: *thymiamata* S-C

25:10   *duos et*: *duos* Weber

25:17   *eius et*: *eius* Weber

25:22   *propitiatorio*: *propitiatorium* S-C; *ac de*: *scilicet ac* Weber

<25:31   *bowls* KJV: *boules* [i.e., "balls"] D-R>

25:33   *spherulaque simul* [second time]: *spherulaque* Weber

<25:33   *bowl* [both times] D-R/C: *boule* [i.e., "ball"] D-R>

<25:34   *bowls* D-R/C: *boules* [i.e., "balls"] D-R>

25:35   *spherulae*: *spherula* Weber

<25:35   *bowls* D-R/C: *boules* [i.e., "balls"] D-R>

25:36   *spherulae*: *spherae* Weber

<25:36   *bowls* D-R/C: *boules* [i.e., "balls"] D-R>

25:38   *fiant*: *fient* Weber

<25:38   *shall be* KJV: *let them be* D-R>

25:39   *purissimi*: *mundissimi* Weber

26:1   *facies* [first time]: *fiet* Weber

26:5   *cortina*: *unaquaeque cortina* *D-R

26:11   *Facies et quinquaginta*: *quinquaginta* Weber; *ut*: *et* Weber

26:29   *eis: in eis* S-C

26:30   *exemplum: exemplar* S-C

<26:37   *their* KJV: *whose* D-R>

<27:9   *of a hundred cubits long for one side* KJV: *one side shal hold in length an hundred cubites* D-R>

<27:10   *the heads of which with their engraving shall be* D-R/C: *which shal haue heades with their engrauinges of siluer* D-R>

27:11   *Similiter et: similiter* Weber

27:15   *columnae: columnas* Weber

27:17   *argenti: argenteis* S-C

<27:20   *olives* S: *oliuetrees* D-R>

<28:1   *minister . . . in the priest's office* KJV: *doe the function of priesthoode* D-R>

28:2   *Aaron, fratri: fratri* Weber

28:14   *auri purissimi: ex auro purissimo* S-C

28:26   *in oris: et in oris* Weber

28:29   *ingredietur: ingreditur* Weber

28:30   *ingredietur: ingreditur* Weber

28:34   *malum punicum* [first time]: *malum* Weber

28:38   *obtulerint et sanctificaverint: obtulerunt et sanctificaverunt* S-C

28:42   *femora: femina* Weber

29:2   *crustulam: crustula* Weber; *sit: sint* Weber

29:4   *filiis suis: filiis* Weber

29:9   *mihi: mei in* Weber

29:15   *arietem: arietum* Weber

29:18   *Domino: Domini* Weber; *Domini: Dei* Weber

29:21   *ipsis: et ipsis* Weber

29:22   *consecrationis: consecrationum* Weber

29:23   *tortamque: tortam* Weber; *crustulum conspersum: crustulam conspersam* S-C

29:26   *elevatum: elatum* Weber

29:27   *Sanctificabisque: sanctificabis* Weber

29:29   *utetur: utitur* Weber

29:31   *consecrationis: consecrationum* Weber

<29:38   *sacrifice* KJV (*offer*): *doe* D-R>

30:1   *in: ad* S-C

30:7   *fragrans: fraglans* Weber

30:8   *conlocabit*: *conlocat* Weber

30:9   *libamina*: *liba* Weber

30:10   *quod*: *eius quod* *D-R

30:18   *labrum*: *labium* Weber

30:19   *eo*: *ea* S-C

30:23   *aromata*: *primae zmyrnae et electae*: *aromata prima / et zmyrnae electae*
Weber; *zmyrnae*: *myrrhae* S-C; *quinquaginta siclos*: *quinquaginta* Weber

30:36   *Testimonii Tabernaculo*: *testimonio tabernaculi* Weber

31:3   *et intellegentia*: *intellegentia* Weber

31:9   *labrum*: *labium* Weber

31:14   *sabbatum meum*: *sabbatum* Weber

31:18   *Deditque Dominus*: *dedit quoque* Weber

32:3   *Fecitque*: *fecit* Weber

32:6   *comedere*: *manducare* S-C

32:7   *Mosen, dicens*: *Mosen* Weber

32:15   *in manu sua*: *manu* Weber

32:19   *radicem*: *radices* Weber

32:28   *Feceruntque*: *fecerunt* Weber; *tria*: *viginti tria* S-C

<32:28   *three and twenty* S-C: *three* D-R>

32:29   *et in*: *et* Weber

32:31   *magnum*: *maximum* S-C

32:35   *fecerat*: *fecit* Weber

33:1   *Mosen, dicens*: *Mosen* Weber

<33:3   *that* D-R/C: *and* D-R>

33:3   *es*: *est* Weber

33:4   *Audiensque*: *audiens* Weber

<33:10   *tents* KJV: *tabernacles* D-R>

33:13   *faciem*: *viam* Weber

33:15   *praecedas*: *praecedes* Weber

33:21   *et stabis*: *stabis* Weber

34:6   *verus*: *verax* S-C

34:7   *filiis*: *in filiis* Weber

34:10   *populus iste*: *populus* Weber

<34:14   *any* D-R/C: *a* D-R; *he is a jealous God* KJV: *God is an emulatour*
D-R>

<34:16   *son* D-R/C: *sonnes* D-R>

<34:17   *any* D-R/C: omitted in D-R>

<34:22 *keep* KJV (*obserue*): *make to thee* D-R>

<34:27 *Write* KJV (*Write thou*): *Write thee* D-R>

34:28 *Fuit*: *fecit* Weber

34:29 *Domini*: *Dei* Weber

34:31 *est ad eos*: *est* Weber

<34:32 *and* KJV: omitted in D-R>

<34:34 *But* KJV: *Which* D-R>

35:5 *proni animi*: *prono animo* S-C

35:6 *hyacinthum et*: *hyacinthum* Weber

35:15 *vectes et*: *vectes* Weber

35:21 *obtulit*: *obtulerunt* S-C; *ad cultum*: *in cultum* Weber

35:23 *habuit*: *habebat* S-C; *hyacinthum et*: *hyacinthum* Weber

<35:28 *for the lights* KJV: *to maintaine the lights* D-R>

<35:29 *All, both* D-R/C [after S?]: *Al* D-R>

35:31 *sapientia et intellegentia et scientia et omni*: *sapientiae et intellegentiae et scientiae omni* Weber

<35:35 *carpenters' work and tapestry and embroidery* S: *the workes of a carpenter, a tapester, an embroderer* D-R; *blue* KJV: *hyacinth* D-R>

35:35 *plumarii* Ψ^{B*} [Quentin's siglum]: *ac plumarii* S-C, Weber

36:2 *Dominus*: *Deus* Weber

36:18 *ut*: *et* Weber

36:29 *conpagem*: *conpaginem* S-C

36:34 *deauravit*: *deauravit, fusis basibus earum argenteis* S-C; *possint*: *possent* S-C

36:35 *hyacintho et*: *hyacintho* Weber

37:1 *unius cubiti fuit et dimidii*: *uno cubito fuit et dimidio* Weber

37:6 *duo cubiti* O *et dimidium* O (*demedium*) $\Xi\Psi^M$ [Quentin's sigla]: *duorum cubitorum et dimidio* S-C (*dimidii*), Weber; *cubito ac semisse*: *cubiti ac semis* S-C

37:8 *unius*: *huius* Weber

37:9 *respectantes*: *respicientes* S-C

37:12 *auream interrasilem*: *interrasilem* Weber

37:16 *fialas et*: *fialas* Weber; *libamina*: *liba* Weber

37:17 *spherulaeque*: *spherulae* Weber

<37:17 *bowls* KJV: *boules* [i.e., "balls"] D-R>

<37:19 *bowls* [both times] KJV: *boules* [i.e., "balls"] D-R>

<37:20 *bowls* KJV: *boules* [i.e., "balls"] D-R>

37:20 *simul et*: *et* Weber

37:21 *spherulae*: *spherae* Weber

<37:21 *bowls* D-R/C: *boule* [i.e., "ball"] D-R>

37:22 *spherulae*: *spherae* Weber; *de*: *ex* S-C

<37:22 *bowls* D-R/C: *boules* [i.e., "balls"] D-R>

37:23 *ubi*: *ubi ea* S-C; *extinguantur*: *extinguuntur* Weber

<38:6 *And . . . the bars* KJV [*staues* for *bars*]: *the which themselues also* D-R>

38:9 *Fecit et*: *et* Weber

38:11 *septentrionalem*: *septentrionalis* Weber; *eiusdem*: *eiusdem et* Weber

38:12 *quae ad*: *quae* Weber; *et tota operis celatura*: *celata* Weber

38:15 *inter utraque*: *utraque* Weber; *fecit*: *facit* Weber; *columnaeque*: *columnae* Weber

38:16 *torta*: *retorta* S-C

38:17 *cum cunctis*: *cum* Weber

38:19 *in ingressu*: *ingressus* Weber

38:21 *numerata*: *enumerata* S-C; *caerimonias*: *ceremoniis* S-C

38:22 *quas*: *quae* S-C

38:25 *transierunt*: *transierant* Weber

39:3 *possint*: *possent* S-C

39:11 *et iaspis*: *iaspis* Weber

39:12 *et amethistus*: *amethistus* Weber

39:13 *et berillus*: *berillus* Weber

39:19 *laxe*: *laxa* S-C

39:23 *purissimo*: *mundissimo* Weber; *mala granata*: *malogranata* S-C

39:24 *autem aureum*: *aureum* Weber, *scilicet aureum* *D-R; *praeceperat*: *praecepit* Weber

39:28 *bis tincto*: *distinctum* Weber; *praeceperat*: *praecepit* Weber

39:30 *praeceperat*: *praecepit* Weber

39:35 *vasis suis*: *vasis* Weber

39:36 *eorum*: *earum* S-C

39:37 *et thymiama*: *thymiama* Weber

39:43 *completa*: *expleta* Weber

40:15 *prima*: *in prima* Weber

40:25 *Dominus Mosi*: *Dominus* Weber

40:26 *Tabernaculi Testimonii*: *tabernaculi* Weber

<40:30 *Tabernacle* D-R/C: *roofe* D-R>

40:30 *Dominus Mosi*: *Dominus* Weber

40:31 *cuncta*: *omnia* S-C

<40:33 *Tabernacle* S: *roofe* D-R>

40:36 *cunctis populis*: *populis* Weber, *cunctis filiis* *D-R

LEVITICUS

<1:3 *testimony* D-R/C: *tabernacle of the testimonie* D-R>

1:4 *manus*: *manum* S-C

<1:4 *hand* KJV: *handes* D-R>

1:5 *per*: *super* Weber

1:10 *agnum anniculum* Θ^H aels [Quentin's sigla]: *masculum* S-C, *anniculum et* Weber

<1:10 *male* S-C: *lambe of a yeare old* D-R>

1:12 *ponent*: *inponent* Weber

1:14 *Sin*: *Si* S-C; *et*: *aut* S-C

<1:14 *or* KJV: *and* D-R>

1:16 *propter*: *prope* S-C

<2:1 *any one* KJV (*any*): *a soule* D-R>

2:6 *supra eam*: *supra* Weber, *super eam* S-C

2:7 *sacrificium*: *fuerit sacrificium* S-C

2:8 *offerens Domino trades*: *offeres Domino tradens* Weber

2:12 *ponentur*: *imponentur* S-C

2:13 *oblatione*: *oblatione tua* S-C

<2:13 *all thy oblations* KJV (*all thine offerings*): *euerie oblation* D-R>

2:14 *Sin*: *Si* S-C; *torrebis*: *torres eas* Weber

3:2 *Tabernaculi Testimonii*: *tabernaculi* Weber

3:3 *Domino*: *Domini* Weber

3:4 *renunculis*: *duobus renunculis* *D-R

3:17 *adipem omnino*: *adipes* Weber

4:2 *Anima quae*: *anima cum* Weber

4:4 *Tabernaculi Testimonii*: *testimonii* *D-R

<4:8 *offering* KJV: omitted in D-R>

<4:12 *they* D-R/C [after S?]: *which* D-R>

4:14   *peccato suo: peccato* Weber

4:20   *erit eis: erit* Weber

4:26   *eo sacerdos: eo* Weber

<4:27   any one KJV: *a soule* D-R>

4:27   *ut faciat: faciens* *D-R, *de his: ex his* Weber, *derelinquat: derelinquens*
*D-R

4:35   *et cremabit: cremabit* S-C

5:6   *eo: ea* S-C

5:10   *in holocaustum: holocaustum* Weber

5:11   *columbae: columbarum* S-C; *suo similae: similam* Weber

5:12   *ea: toto* Weber; *obtulit: obtulerit* S-C

5:14   *Locutusque: locutus* Weber

5:18   *quod: quia* S-C

6:7   *peccaverit: peccavit* S-C

6:8   *Locutusque: locutus* Weber

<6:10   of that D-R/C: omitted in D-R>

<6:18   ordinance everlasting S: *ordinance and euerlasting* D-R>

6:18   *erit: est* Weber

6:20   *eius vespere: vespere* Weber

<6:21   It shall be D-R/C: *which being* D-R>

6:24   *est autem: est* Weber

6:29   *de carnibus: carnibus* Weber

7:1   *est lex: lex* S-C

7:2   *immolatur: immolabitur* S-C

7:10   *fuerint: fuerit* Weber

<7:12   fine flour fried KJV: *fryed floure* D-R; and mingled with KJV
[without *and*]: *with the mingling of* D-R>

7:16   *quisquam: quispiam* S-C

<7:17   shall be found D-R/C on the third day shall be consumed with fire KJV
[*burnt* for *consumed*]: *the third day shal find, fire shal consume it* D-R>

7:19   *ex ea: ea* Weber

7:28   *Locutusque: locutus* Weber

7:29   *Israhel, dicens: Israhel* Weber

<7:32   to the priest for firstfruits D-R/C [after S?]: *for first fuites of the priest*
D-R>

7:34   *elevationis: elationis* Weber

<7:34   *that is elevated* D-R/C: *of eleuation* D-R>

7:38   *quam: quas* Weber

8:4   *Fecitque* els [Quentin's sigla, my capitalization]: *fecit* S-C, Weber; *fores tabernaculi: fores* Weber

8:7   *induens eum: induens* Weber

8:10   *levit: linivit* S-C

8:13   *balteis: balteo* Weber

8:14   *posuissent: posuisset* S-C

8:16   *autem: vero* S-C

8:17   *pelle et: pelle* Weber

<8:19   *round about upon* KJV: *in the circuite of* D-R>

8:23   *sanguine eius: sanguine* Weber

8:28–29   *Domino. Tulitque: Domini / tulit et* Weber

8:31   *mihi Dominus: mihi* Weber

9:2   *inmaculatos: immaculatum* S-C

9:5   *staret: astaret* S-C

9:7   *Et dixit: dixit et* Weber

9:19   *Adipes: Adipem* S-C; *renunculosque: et duos renunculos* *D-R

9:20   *super altare: in altari* Weber

9:22   *extendens: tendens* Weber; *manum: manus* S-C; *ad: contra* Weber; *eis: ei* S-C

<9:22   *hands* S-C: *hand* D-R>

9:23   *tabernaculum: in tabernaculum* S-C

10:4   *tollite: colligite* Weber

10:6   *Locutusque: locutus* Weber

10:7   *egrediemini: egredimini* Weber

10:9   *intratis in: intratis* Weber

10:15   *elevaverint: elevaverunt* S-C

<10:16   *While these things were a-doing* D-R/C: *Among these thinges* D-R>

11:1   *Locutusque: locutus* Weber

11:14   *et milvum: milvum* Weber

11:18   *et cycnum: cycnum* Weber

11:26   *quicquid: qui* S-C

<11:26   *he that* D-R/C: *whatsoeuer* D-R>

11:29   *Haec: hoc* Weber; *reputabuntur: reputabitur* Weber

11:33   *quod*: *quo* Weber

11:34   *comedetis*: *comeditis* Weber

<11:34   *eat* D-R/C: *shal eat* D-R>

11:35   *huiuscemodi*: *istiusmodi* Weber

<11:35   *oven* KJV: *ouens* D-R>

11:37   *ceciderit*: *ceciderint* Weber; *polluet*: *polluent* Weber

11:38   *Sin*: *si* S-C

11:44   *quoniam*: *quoniam et* Weber, *quia* S-C

11:45   *Ego enim*: *ego* Weber; *quia*: *quia et* Weber

<11:46   verse begins at *You* D-R/C: verse begins twice, once spuriously, in D-R. D-R/C follows first possibility, this edition the second, after also S-C, Weber

12:1   *Locutusque*: *locutus* Weber

12:4   *ingredietur in*: *ingredietur* Weber

12:5   *sex*: *ac sex* Weber

12:7   *orabit*: *rogabit* Weber; *aut*: *ac* Weber

<12:8   *sufficiency* KJVn: omitted in D-R>

12:8   *columbae*: *columbarum* S-C

13:1   *Locutusque*: *locutus* Weber

13:4   *recludet eum*: *recludet* S-C

<13:5   *spread itself in* KJV (without *itself*): *passed the former limites of* D-R>

13:5   *recludet*: *includet* Weber

<13:6   *declare him clean* KJV (*pronounce* for *declare*): *cleanse him* D-R; *but* KJV [italicized in D-R/C and in roman type in KJV]: omitted in D-R>

<13:11   *declare him unclean* KJV (*pronounce* for *declare*): *contaminate him* D-R>

13:11   *perspicue inmunditia*: *perspicuae immunditiae* S-C, *perspicue inmundus* *D-R, not unlike Gryson 100 E and Frede AU Lv 47 209.1229.

13:12   *carnem*: *cutem* S-C

<13:12   *skin* [second time] KJV: *flesh* D-R>

<13:13   *the leprosy which he has is very clean* D-R/C: *he is taken with a most cleane leprosie* D-R>

13:15   *aspergatur*: *aspergitur* S-C

13:18   *Caro autem*: *caro* Weber

<13:24   *hath been burnt* D-R/C: *fire hath burnt* D-R>

<13:25   *if he see it turned white* D-R/C: *loe it is turned into whitenesse* D-R; *declare him unclean* KJV (*pronounce* for *declare*): *contaminate him* D-R>

<13:27   *declare him unclean* KJV (*pronounce* for *declare*): *contaminate him* D-R>

<13:30   *declare them unclean* KJV (*pronounce him* for *declare them*): *contaminate them* D-R>

13:31   *locum: et locum* Weber; *eum: eos* Weber

<13:34   *evil* D-R/C: *plague* D-R>

13:34   *vestibus suis: vestibus* Weber

13:36   *commutatus: immutatus* S-C

13:37   *et capilli: at capilli* S-C

13:38   *sive: et* Weber

13:43   *dubie: dubiae* Weber

13:44   *separatus est: separatus* Weber

<13:55   *colour* KJV: *shape* D-R; *has taken hold of* D-R/C: *is spred in* D-R>

13:58   *aqua ea: ea* Weber

<13:59   *pronounced unclean* KJV: *contaminated* D-R>

14:3   *e: de* S-C

14:4   *quos: quibus* S-C

14:9   *radet: radat* Weber

14:16   *coram Domino: contra Dominum* Weber

14:17   *fusus: effusus* S-C

14:27   *coram Domino: contra Dominum* Weber

14:33   *Locutusque: locutus* Weber

14:35   *et referet sacerdoti, dicens* Gryson 100 E [repunctuated]: *nuntians sacerdoti et dicet* S-C, Weber

14:36   *leprosa: lepra* Weber

14:37   *si* Frede HES 4 963B, TE pud 20 267.26: *cum* S-C, Weber

<14:37   *all the rest* D-R: literally, *the rest of the surface*>

14:40   *locum inmundum: loco inmundo* Weber

14:41   *locum inmundum: loco inmundo* Weber

14:43   *erasus: elatus* Weber

14:44   *aspersos:* for translation as "full," see the gloss, *aspersa, id est diffusa* Frede HES 4 964D

14:45   *locum inmundum: loco inmundo* Weber

14:48   *est: fuerit* S-C

14:51   *intinguet: tinget* S-C

<15:3   *gathereth there* D-R/C: *is congealed* D-R>

15:8   *vestimenta sua: vestem suam* Weber

15:10   *vestimenta sua: vestem suam* Weber

15:14   *conspectum: conspectu* Weber

<15:14   *before* KJV: *into the sight of* D-R>

15:23   *ipse lotus: lotus* Weber

<15:24   *flowers* KJV: *menstrual bloud* D-R>

<15:25   *ordinary* D-R/C: *menstrual* D-R>

15:27   *ea: eam* Weber

15:29   *columbae: columbarum* S-C

16:4   *verecunda: verenda* S-C

16:8   *mittensque: mittens* Weber

<16:9   *to be offered* D-R/C: omitted in D-R>

16:13   *super: supra* S-C

16:24   *vestimentis: vestibus* S-C

16:27   *in sanctuarium ut: ut in sanctuario* Weber

17:2   *dicens* [first time]: *et dices* Weber

17:4   *Quasi: quasi si* S-C

17:5   *occidunt: occident* S-C

<17:10   *cut him off* KJV: *destroy it* D-R>

17:12   *apud: inter* Weber

<17:14   *be cut off* KJV: *die* D-R>

17:15   *vestes suas: vestimenta sua* S-C

17:16   *et: nec* Weber

18:1   *Locutusque: Locutus* S-C

18:4   *praecepta mea: praecepta* Weber

<18:5   *my* KJV: omitted in D-R; *if a man do* KJV: *a man doing* D-R>

<18:18   bracketed words added in this edition>

18:22   *commiscearis: commisceberis* Weber

<18:22   *Thou shalt not lie* KJV: *Companie not* D-R>

18:26   *faciatis: faciat* Weber; *peregrinatur: peregrinantur* S-C

<18:28   *if* D-R/C: *when* D-R>

19:3   *patrem suum et matrem suam: matrem et patrem suum* Weber

19:8   *portabitque: portabit* Weber

19:12   *peierabis: peiurabis* S-C

19:13   *mercennarii tui: mercennarii* Weber

19:14   *Dominum, Deum: Deum* Weber

19:15   *Non consideres: nec consideres* Weber

<19:15   *but* KJV [italicized in D-R/C and in roman type in KJV]: omitted in D-R>

19:16   *nec: et* Weber; *populo: populis* Weber

19:17   *Non: ne* Weber

19:18   *quaeras: quaeres* Weber; *temet ipsum: teipsum* S-C

19:19   *Iumenta tua: Iumentum tuum* S-C; *Agrum tuum: agrum* Weber

19:22   *peccato: delicto* Weber

<19:23   *firstfruits* D-R/C: *prepuces* D-R>

19:24   *Quarto autem: quarto* Weber

<19:25   *thereof* [first time] KJV: omitted in D-R; *increase thereof* KJV: *offspring, that they bring forth* D-R>

19:27   *radatis: radetis* Weber

19:28   *aut: et* Weber

19:29   *ne contaminetur: et contaminetur* Weber

19:32   *Dominum, Deum: Deum* Weber

19:33   *ne: non* S-C

19:35   *pondere, in mensura: pondere aut mensura* *D-R

20:4   *dederit: dedit* S-C

20:5   *cognationem: super cognationem* S-C; *fornicarentur: fornicaretur* S-C

20:9   *aut: et* Weber

<20:10   *defile* D-R/C: *commit aduontrie* [sic, probably for *aduoutrie*] with D-R>

20:10   *moriantur: moriatur* S-C

<20:11   *If a man lie* S: *He that lieth* D-R>

20:12   *moriantur: moriatur* S-C

<20:13   *If any one lie* D-R/C: *He that lieth* D-R>

20:13   *operati sunt: operatus est* S-C

<20:14   *If any man after marrying the daughter* D-R/C: *He that besides his wife the daughter* D-R>

<20:17   *If any man take* D-R/C: *He that taketh* D-R>

<20:18 *If any man lie* D-R/C: *He that compaineth* D-R; *flowers* D-R/C: *menstrual fluxe* D-R>

20:19 *materterae tuae*: *materterae* S-C

<20:20 *If any man lie* D-R/C: *He that compaineth* D-R>

20:21 *liberis*: *filiis* Weber

<20:22 *to dwell therein* KJV: *and inhabite* D-R>

<20:23 *therefore* KJV: omitted in D-R>

20:23 *eos*: *eas* S-C

20:25 *avibus*: *in avibus* Weber

21:7 *ducet*: *ducent* S-C; *consecrati sunt*: *consecratus est* Weber

<21:7 *They* KJV: *he* D-R; *put away from* D-R: literally, *divorced by*>

21:8 *offerunt. Sint ergo sancti*: *offert / sit ergo sanctus* Weber; *eos*: *vos* Weber

21:14 *autem et*: *et* Weber

<21:17 *Whosoever* KJV: *The man* D-R>

21:18 *parvo vel grandi vel*: *vel parvo vel grandi et* Weber

21:24 *ad filios*: *filios* Weber

22:9 *Custodiant*: *custodient* Weber

<22:10 *a sojourner of the priests* KJV: *the priestes* [probably singular] *guest* D-R>

22:17 *Locutusque*: *locutus* Weber

22:18 *ad filios* CΣ [Weber's sigla]: *filios* S-C, Weber

22:19 *ovibus*: *ex ovibus* Weber

<22:19 *of* KJV: omitted in D-R>

22:25 *voluerit*: *voluerint* Weber

23:1 *Locutusque*: *locutus* Weber

23:3 *Domini*: *domini* S-C

23:8 *facietis*: *fiet* Weber

23:14 *offeratis*: *offeretis* S-C

<23:14 *shall* S-C: omitted in D-R>

23:24 *memoriale*: *memorabile* Weber

<23:27 *it shall be* KJV: omitted in D-R>

23:28 *opus servile*: *opus* Weber

23:32 *et adfligetis*: *adfligetis* Weber

<23:34 *same* and *kept* D-R/C: omitted in D-R>

23:35   *facietis in eo: facietis* Weber; *Et septem:* v. 36 begins here S-C, Weber

23:38   *offeretis: offertis* Weber; *tribuetis: tribuitis* Weber

<23:39   *day of* D-R/C: omitted in D-R>

<23:40   *thick trees* KJV: *tree with thicke leaues* D-R>

24:3   *in mane: ad mane* S-C

24:10   *Israhelitis: israelitidis* S-C; *Israhelite: israelita* S-C

<24:18   *killeth* KJV: *striketh* D-R; *make it good* KJV: *render one for it* D-R; *shall give* D-R/C [after S?]: omitted in D-R; *beast for beast* KJV: *soule for soule* D-R>

24:18   *reddet: reddat* Weber

24:19   *sic fiet: fiet* Weber

25:2   *sabbatizes sabbatum Domino: sabbatizet sabbatum Domini* Weber

25:5   *gignet: gignit* Weber

<25:5   *the* D-R/C [typographical error?]: *thy* D-R>

25:6   *peregrinatur* CΣTMΦ [Weber's sigla]: *peregrinantur* S-C, Weber

<25:6   *strangers that soujourn* D-R/C [after S-C?]: *stranger that seiourneth* D-R>

25:12   *oblata: ablata* Weber

25:16   *plus: plures* S-C

<25:16   *is counted* D-R/C: *that thou shal account* D-R>

25:18   *mea, et iudicia custodite, et implete ea ut: mea et iudicia, custodite et implete ea, ut* S-C

25:20   *severimus: seruerimus* Weber

<25:23   *strangers and sojourners with me* KJV: *my strangers and seiourners* D-R>

25:23   *veniet: vendetur* S-C

<25:24   *be* D-R/C: *be sould* D-R>

25:28   *redibit: redit* Weber

25:33   *Levitarum: leviticarum* Weber

25:42   *veneant: venient* Weber

<25:44   *your bondmen and your bondwomen* KJV [*thy* for *your, bondmaids* for *bondwomen*]: *your man seruant, and woman seruant* D-R>

25:49   *redimet: redimat* S-C

26:8   *de vobis: ex vobis* Weber

26:16   *animas vestras: animas* Weber

<26:18   *yet for all this* KJV: *so neither* D-R>

26:21   *usque in*: *in* S-C

26:22   *inmittamque*: *emittamque* Weber; *vos et*: *et vos et* Weber

<26:22   *make you few in number* KJV: *bring al thinges to a smal number* D-R>

<26:23   *amend* D-R/C: *receiue discipline* D-R>

26:25   *in manibus hostium*: *hostium manibus* Weber

<26:27   *not for all this* KJV: *neither by these meanes* D-R>

26:29   *filiorum vestrorum*: *filiorum* Weber

<26:31   *your sweet odours* KJV: *the most sweete odour* D-R>

26:33   *civitates vestrae*: *civitates* Weber

<26:36   *as to them* KJV [*vpon* for *as to*]: *they* D-R>

26:36   *persequente*: *sequente* Weber

<26:44   *And yet for all that* KJV: *Howbeit euen* D-R>

26:45   *Dominus*: *Dominus Deus* Weber

27:3   *vicesimo anno*: *vicesimo* Weber

27:12   *diiudicans*: *iudicans* S-C

27:13   *aestimationem*: *aestimationis* Weber

27:16   *venundetur*: *veniet* Weber

<27:18   *the price shall be abated* D-R/C [*abated* is in KJV]: *there shal be diminished of the price* D-R>

<27:21   *as* KJV: omitted in D-R>

27:22   *emptus est*: *emptus* Weber

<27:22   *that was* D-R/C: *be* D-R>

27:28   *veniet*: *vendetur* S-C

27:32   *bovis et ovis et caprae*: *boves et oves et caprae* Weber, *bo(v)um et ovium et caprarum* *D-R, not unlike Gryson 100 E (*bouum et ouium*) and Frede PS-AM man 11B (*boum et ovium*)

Numbers

<1:20   *eldest son* KJV: *first begotten* D-R; *that were able to* KJV: *of them that* D-R>

<1:22   *that were able to* KJV: *of them that* D-R>

<1:24   *were able to go* KJV: *went* D-R>

<1:44   *who were numbered by Moses and Aaron* D-R/C: *whom Moyses and Aaron numbered* D-R>

1:45   *omnis numerus*: *omnes* Weber

1:49   *pones: ponas* Weber

<1:50   *minister* KJV: *be in the ministerie* D-R>

1:50   *et cuncta: cuncta* Weber

1:51   *castra metanda: castrametandum* S-C

<1:53   *and guard* D-R/C: *in the custodies of* D-R>

2:2   *filiorum: filii* S-C

<2:2   *All the children* S-C: *Euerie one of the children* D-R>

2:4   *sescentorum: sexcenti* S-C

2:16   *suas. In* G [Quentin's siglum, third apparatus]: *suas in* S-C, Weber

2:21   *Cunctusque: cunctus* Weber

2:24   *suas. Tertii* *D-R: *suas tertii* S-C, Weber

2:33   *praeceperat: praecepit* Weber

3:1   *Haec: Hae* S-C

3:4   *sunt enim: sunt* Weber

3:5   *Locutusque: locutus* Weber

3:14   *Locutusque: locutus* Weber

3:22   *quingentorum: quingenti* S-C

<3:26   *Tabernacle* KJV: *roofe* D-R>

<3:27   *Of the kindred of Kohath come* D-R/C: *The kinred of Caath shal haue* D-R>

<3:33   *are* D-R/C: *shal be* D-R>

3:41   *pecorum: pecoris* Weber

3:44   *Mosen, dicens: Mosen* Weber

4:4–5   *Caath. Tabernaculum Foederis et Sanctum Sanctorum ingredientur: Caath: tabernaculum foederis et sanctum sanctorum. Ingredientur* S-C, *Caath / tabernaculum foederis et sanctum sanctorum ingredientur* Weber

<4:13   *They* D-R/C: *But . . . they* D-R>

4:15   *tangent: tangant* Weber

<4:16   *sweet incense* KJV: *incense of composition* D-R>

<4:19   *appoint every man his work* KJV (*appoint them euerie one to his seruice*): *dispose the charges of euerie one* D-R; *the burdens that* D-R/C [*burdens* in KJV with different syntax]: *what* D-R>

4:21   *Locutusque: locutus* Weber

4:37   *intrant: intrat* Weber; *iuxta: uxta* [sic] S-C

4:46   *fecit: recenseri fecit* S-C

5:5   *Locutusque: locutus* Weber

5:11   *Locutusque: locutus* Weber

5:20   *altero viro: altero* Weber

<5:21   *these curses shall light upon thee* D-R/C: *thou shalt be subiect to these maledictions* D-R; *may thy belly swell and* D-R/C [*thy* is in KJV]: *bellie swelling* D-R>

5:21   *uterus tuus: uterus* Weber

5:25   *inponetque illud: imponetque* Weber

6:1   *Locutusque: locutus* Weber

6:2   *fecerint: fecerit* Weber

<6:2   *When a man or woman shall* KJV: *Man, or woman, when they shal* D-R>

6:3   *vino: a vino* S-C

<6:7   *for his father or for his mother or for his brother or for his sister when they die* KJV: *on his fathers and mothers and brothers and sisters corps* D-R>

6:8   *Omnes dies: Omnibus diebus* S-C

6:9   *ilico: ilico et* Weber

<6:14   *one* [all three times] KJV: *a, an, a* D-R>

6:15   *sunt: sint* S-C

<6:18   *shall the hair of the consecration of the Nazirite be shaved off* D-R/C: *shal the Nazareite be shauen . . . from the bush of the haire of his consecration* D-R>

6:19   *manus: manibus* Weber

6:20   *femur: armum* *D-R, not unlike Gryson 100 E (*brachium*)

6:22   *Locutusque: locutus* Weber

6:27   *Invocabuntque: invocabunt* Weber

7:1   *omnia vasa: vasa* Weber

7:2   *praefectique: praefecti* Weber

<7:2   *who were* KJV: *and* D-R>

7:5   *trades: tradas* Weber

<7:13   *his offering was* KJV: *there were in it* D-R>

7:15   *bovem de armento: bovem* Weber

<7:18   *made his offering:* KJV (*did offer.*): *offered* D-R>

7:62   *mortariolum: et mortariolum* S-C

7:85   *haberet una: una* Weber

<7:85   *seventy* KJV: *had seuentie* D-R>

7:88   *in hostias: hostiae* Weber

<7:88 *and* KJV: omitted in D-R>

7:89 *Arcam Testimonii: Arcam* *D-R

8:1 *Locutusque: locutus* Weber

8:2 *candelabrum in australi parte erigatur contra boream ad mensam panum propositionis* omitted in Weber; after *erigatur* S-C adds *Hoc igitur praecipe, ut lucernae* and after *boream* S-C adds *e regione respiciant*

<8:2 *Give orders therefore that the lamps look* S-C: omitted in D-R>

8:4 *cuncta quae: cuncta* Weber

8:8 *tollent: tollant* Weber

<8:12 *sacrifice* KJV (*offer*): *make* D-R>

8:15 *ingredientur: ingrediantur* Weber

8:17 *sunt enim: sunt* Weber; *omnem: omne* S-C

<8:20 *all* KJV: *the thinges* D-R>

8:23 *Locutusque: locutus* Weber

8:26 *Levitis: Levitas* Weber

<8:26 *order* D-R/C: *dispose to* D-R>

9:6 *Phase: pascha* Weber

<9:8 *the Lord what he* D-R/C: *what our Lord* D-R>

9:8 *praecipiet* Φ^R [Quentin's siglum]: *praecipiat* S-C, Weber

<9:10 *by occasion of one that is dead* D-R/C: *vpon a soule* D-R>

9:11 *mense: in mense* S-C

<9:13 *due season* D-R/C [*season* is in KJV]: *his dew time* D-R>

9:14 *fuerint apud vos, facient Phase Domino: fuerit apud vos / faciet phase Domini* Weber

9:20 *quotquot: quot* S-C

9:22 *Si vero: si* Weber

<9:22 *remained* KJV (*were . . . remayning*): *had bene* D-R>

10:1 *Locutusque: locutus* Weber

10:5 *Sin: si* S-C

<10:5 *sound of the trumpets be* D-R/C: *trumpeting sound* D-R>

10:6 *profectione: profectionem* S-C

10:8 *Filii autem: filii* Weber

10:24 *erat dux: dux* Weber, *princeps fuit* *D-R [*dux fuit* Weber's siglum l]

10:27 *princeps fuit: princeps* Weber

10:33 *via: viam* Weber

<11:1   *their fatigue* D-R/C: *labour* D-R>

11:1   *audisset Dominus*: *audisset* Weber

11:2   *ad Dominum*: *Dominum* Weber

11:3   *succensus*: *incensus* S-C

<11:23   *or no* KJV (*or not*): omitted in D-R>

11:25   *Mosen*: *Moyse* S-C

11:29   *Quis tribuat ut*: *Utinam* *D-R

<11:31   *for the space of one day's journey* D-R (without *for*): literally, *as far as can be travelled in a journey of one day*>

12:8   *et non*: *non* Weber

12:12   *lepra*: *a lepra* S-C

12:14   *dierum*: *diebus* S-C

13:1   *Profectusque est populus*: *profectus est* Weber

13:2   *Ibique*: *ibi* Weber

13:19   *pauci*: *si pauci* S-C

13:33   *Terram*: *Terra* S-C; *populum*: *populus* S-C

14:3   *et in*: *et non in* Weber

14:7   *Terram*: *Terra* S-C

<14:10   *Tabernacle* KJV: *roofe* D-R>

14:14   *diem et*: *diem e* [sic] S-C

14:19   *populi tui*: *populi* S-C

<14:19   *this* KJV: *this thy* D-R>

14:24–25 eam, quoniam . . . vallibus. Cras: *eam. Quoniam . . . vallibus, cras* S-C

<14:29   *the* D-R/C: *this* D-R>

14:45   *habitabat*: *habitabant* Weber; *est eos*: *est* Weber

15:1   *Locutusque* ΠΣ^{O2M}Ψ^BΩ^{JM} [Quentin's sigla]: *Locutus* S-C, Weber [without capitalization]

15:6   *arietes*: *arietis* Weber

15:11   *facies*: *facietis* Weber

15:26   *eos*: *vos* Weber

<16:6   *of you your* D-R/C: *their* D-R>

<16:12   *will not come* KJV: *come not* D-R>

<16:14   *will not come* KJV: *come not* D-R>

<16:17   *of you* D-R/C: *your* D-R>

16:18   *Mose*: *Mosen* Weber

<16:28   *head* D-R/C: *mind* D-R>

<16:29 *they be visited with a plague* KJV [without *with a plague*]: *the plague . . . do visite them* D-R>

16:32 *substantia eorum*: *substantia* Weber

16:37 *sacerdotis*: *sacerdoti* S-C

17:3 *eorum*: *seorsum* S-C

<17:8 *it had bloomed blossoms* KJV (without *it had*): *the blossomes were shotte forth* D-R>

17:10 *filiorum Israhel*: *filiorum* Weber

18:2 *sceptro*: *sceptrum* S-C

<18:3 *to do* D-R/C: *vpon* D-R; *nor* D-R/C: *and to* D-R>

18:3 *ad altare*: *altare* Weber

<18:6 *the* KJV: *his* D-R>

<18:7 *the* D-R/C: *your* D-R>

18:8 *Locutusque*: *locutus* Weber

<18:8 *by* KJV: *as* D-R>

18:9 *cedit*: *cedet* Weber

18:11 *filiis tuis*: *filiis* Weber

18:15 *erumpit*: *erumpet* Weber

<18:15 *is firstborn* D-R/C: *first breaketh forth from the matrice* D-R; *shalt* KJV: omitted in D-R>

18:26 *denuntia ad eos* Gryson 100 E, Frede RUF Rm 2.13 904A (*dices* for *denuntia*): *denuntia* S-C, Weber

18:28 *quorum*: *quorum decimas* *D-R

18:29 *offeretis*: *offertis* Weber; *separabitis*: *separatis* Weber

<19:6 *take, and* KJV: omitted in D-R>

<19:14 *tent* KJV: *tabernacle* D-R>

19:17 *Tollentque*: *tollent* Weber

19:18 *eo*: *ex eo* S-C

19:19 *inmundus erit usque*: *mundus erit* Weber

20:2 *coierunt*: *convenerunt* S-C

20:4 *moriantur*: *moriamur* S-C

<20:5 *is there* KJV: *hath* D-R>

20:6 *clamaveruntque ad Dominum atque dixerunt, "Domine Deus, audi clamorem huius populi, et aperi eis thesaurum tuum, fontem aquae vivae, ut satiati cesset murmuratio eorum."* omitted in Weber

<20:6 *they may cease to murmur* D-R/C: *their murmuring may cease* D-R>

20:8   *aquam de petra, bibet*: *aquam, de petra bibet* S-C

20:11   *ut*: *ut et* Weber

<20:13   *strove* KJV *with words* D-R/C: *quarelled* D-R>

20:16   *Nunc in* Gryson 100 E, Frede PS-AM man 33 34D: *in* S-C, Weber

<20:25   *bring* KJV: *thou shalt bring* D-R>

20:26   *Aaron*: *et Aaron* Weber

<20:26   *to his people* KJV [italicized in D-R/C and in roman type in KJV]: omitted in D-R>

<21:1   *overcoming them* D-R/C: *being victour* D-R>

<21:3   *and they cut them off* D-R/C: *whom they slew* D-R>

<21:5   *nor have we any waters* D-R/C: *waters there are none* D-R; *loatheth* KJV: *loatheth at* D-R>

<21:6–7   *which bit them and killed many of them, upon which* D-R/C: *at whose plagues and the deathes of verie manie* D-R>

<21:7   *these* D-R/C: *the* D-R>

21:7   *Oravitque*: *oravit* Weber

21:8   *serpentem aeneum*: *serpentem* Weber

21:9   *posuit eum*: *posuit* Weber

<21:16   *When they went* KJV [without *when*; *When they went* is in italics in D-R/C, and *they went* is in roman type in KJV]: omitted in D-R>

21:18   *Profectique* C [Weber's siglum]: omitted in S-C, Weber; *in Matthana* Gryson 100 E (*Manthapae* for *Matthana*), Frede HI ep 78.40 81.11 and 82.4, RUF Nm 12.3 101.10 and 16 (*Mathanaim* for *Matthana*): *Matthana* S-C, Weber

21:19   *Matthana in*: *Matthana* Weber

21:20   *quod*: *et quod* Weber

<21:24   *the confines of* D-R/C: omitted in D-R>

21:26   *Seon, regis*: *regis Seon* Weber

<21:26   *Amorites* KJV: *Amorheite* D-R>

<21:35   *not letting any one escape* D-R/C: *vnto vtter destruction* D-R>

22:7   *Perrexeruntque*: *perrexerunt* Weber

<22:6   *he whom thou shalt curse is cursed* KJV [*cursest* for *shalt curse*]: *cursed vpon whom thou shalt heape curses* D-R>

22:8   *hic hac* $\Sigma^{\text{T20}}\Omega^{\text{S}}$ cum Lugd. [Quentin's sigla]: *hic* S-C, Weber

22:11   *abigere*: *abicere* Weber

<22:12   *Thou shalt not go, shalt thou curse* KJV: *Goe not, doe thou curse* D-R>

22:13   *Dominus*: *Deus* Weber

22:17   *paratus sum*: *paratum* Weber; *dabo tibi*: *dare* Weber

<22:17   *for* D-R: a literal translation would omit *for*>

<22:19   *that* KJV: *and* D-R>

22:21   *asina sua*: *asina* Weber

22:22   *sedebat*: *insidebat* S-C

22:25   *verberabat eam*: *verberabat* Weber

22:26   *deviare*: *deviari* Weber

22:27   *latera eius*: *latera* Weber

<22:29   *served me ill* D-R/C: *abused me* D-R>

<22:32   *these three times* KJV: *the third time* D-R>

22:37   *vocarent*: *vocarem* S-C

<23:2   *every* KJV [in italics in D-R/C and in roman type in KJV]: *an* D-R>

23:5   *sic* Gryson 100 E: *haec* S-C, Weber

<23:10   *end be* KJV: *endes be made* D-R>

23:11   *inimicis meis*: *inimicis* Weber

<23:11   *sent for* D-R/C: *called* D-R>

<23:22   *whose* = *and his*>

23:24   *accubabit*: *accusabit* S-C

<23:30   *a calf and a ram* KJV (*bullocke* for *calf*): *the calues and the rammes* D-R>

24:6   *propter*: *prope* S-C

24:9   *et ipse*: *ipse* Weber

<24:10   *three times* KJV: *the third time* D-R>

<24:13   *head* D-R/C: *minde* D-R>

24:14   *faciet* MΩ[S] a cum Lugd. [Quentin's sigla]: *faciat* S-C, Weber

<24:18   *he shall possess Edom* D-R/C [KJV has *Edom*]: *Idumea shal be his possession* D-R>

<24:21   *though* D-R/C: *if* D-R>

25:9   *homines*: *hominum* S-C

25:12   *eum*: *eos* Weber

<26:5   *sons were* S: *son* D-R>

26:37   *numerus fuit*: *numerus* Weber

26:41   *numerus fuit*: *numerus* Weber

26:42   *Hae sunt*: *hae* Weber

<26:55   *by lot the land be divided* KJV (*the land shall bee diuided by lot*): *lotte doe diuide the Land* D-R>

26:56   *accipiant*: *accipient* Weber

<26:56   *shall be taken by the more or the fewer* D-R/C: *let either the more take, or the fewer* D-R>

26:62   *possessio est*: *possessio* Weber

<27:3   *and* KJV [italicized in D-R/C]: omitted in D-R>

<28:2   *my bread* KJV: *breades* D-R>

<28:3   *shall* KJV: *must* D-R>

<28:5   *of the measure of* D-R/C: *and shall have* D-R>

<28:10   *regularly* D-R/C: *ritely* D-R>

28:11   *autem*: *autem id est in mensuum exordiis* Weber

28:13   *consparsae* l [Weber's siglum]: *ex* S-C, Weber

<28:14   *and* D-R/C [italicized in D-R/C; after S?]: omitted in D-R>

<28:15   *over and above the* D-R/C: *an euerlasting* D-R>

28:23   *offeretis*: *offertis* Weber

28:26   *offeretis*: *offertis* Weber

29:2   *et agnos*: *agnos* Weber

<29:11   *sin* KJV: *offence* D-R>

29:11   *cum*: *in* Weber

29:17   *offeretis*: *offeres* Weber

<29:18   *for* [third and fourth times] KJV: omitted in D-R>

29:18   *celebrabitis*: *celebrabis* Weber

29:19   *et libamine eius*: *eius et libamine* Weber

29:20   *offeretis*: *offeres* Weber

<29:20   *and* D-R/C: omitted in D-R>

29:21   *celebrabitis*: *celebrabis* Weber

<29:21   *offer* D-R/C: *celebrate* D-R>

29:23   *offeretis*: *offeres* Weber

29:24   *sacrificiaque*: *sacrificiaque eorum* Weber; *celebrabitis*: *celebrabis* Weber

29:26   *offeretis*: *offeres* Weber

29:27   *celebrabitis*: *celebrabis* Weber

29:29   *offeretis*: *offeres* Weber

<29:29   *and* KJV: omitted in D-R>

29:30   *celebrabitis*: *celebrabis* Weber

29:32   *offeretis: offeres* Weber; *septem et: septem* Weber

<29:32   *and* KJV: omitted in D-R>

29:33   *celebrabitis: celebrabis* Weber

<29:36   *and* D-R/C: omitted in D-R>

<29:37   *for* [second and third times] KJV: omitted in D-R>

29:37   *celebrabitis: celebrabis* Weber

30:8   *reddetque: reddet* Weber

<30:10   *fulfil* D-R/C: *render* D-R>

<30:12   *accomplish* D-R/C: *render* D-R>

<30:13   *bound* D-R/C: *holden bound* D-R>

<30:15   *fulfil* D-R/C: *render* D-R>

31:4   *Israhel: ex Israel* S-C

31:5   *singulis: cunctis* Weber

<31:9   *and all their possessions* D-R/C: *whatsoeuer they had bene able to make* D-R>

31:12   *autem: etiam* Weber

31:22   *plumbum et stagnum: stagnum et plumbum* Weber

31:30   *cunctarumque: cunctorum* S-C

31:38   *et duo: duo* Weber

31:43   *ovium: ovibus* S-C

31:47   *excubabant: excubant* Weber

32:1   *animalibus terras: animalibus* Weber

32:4   *terram: terra* S-C; *regionis uberrimae: regio uberrima* S-C

<32:4   *is* S-C: *is of* D-R>

32:5   *nec: ne* Weber

<32:7   *hath given* KJV: *wil geue* D-R>

<32:11   *because* KJV: *and* D-R>

32:15   *Quod: qui* Weber

<32:17   *have* D-R/C: *can haue* D-R>

32:18   *usquequo: usque dum* S-C

32:22   *inculpabiles: inculpabiles et* Weber

32:23   *dubium: dubium est* S-C; *Deum: Dominum* Weber

<32:28   *of all* D-R/C: *by* D-R>

32:30   *transire armati: transire* Weber

32:35   *et Etroth et Sophan et Iazer et: Etrothsophan et Iazer* Weber

32:41 *Avoth Iair: Avothiair* Weber

<33:1 *under* KJV *the conduct* D-R/C: *in the hand* D-R>

33:3 *die fecerunt* ΛΠ^{D²}SBΣ²Ψ [Quentin's sigla]: *die* S-C, Weber

<33:3 *after* KJV: *after they made* D-R>

33:14 *Egressique: egressi* Weber; *in Raphidim: Raphidim* Weber

33:21 *De: et de* Weber

33:22 *Egressique: egressi* Weber

<33:27 *Removing* S: omitted in D-R>

<33:29 *removing* S: omitted in D-R>

<33:31 *removing* S [italicized in D-R/C]: omitted in D-R>

33:32 *Egressique: profectique* S-C

<33:36 *which* KJV: *this* D-R>

33:38 *in Montem: montem* Weber

33:40 *terram: terra* Weber

33:47 *Egressique: egressi* Weber

33:48 *super: supra* S-C

<33:48 *by* KJV: *von* D-R [typographical error for *vpon*]>

33:52 *terrae: regionis* Weber

33:54 *paucioribus* Λ^{L}Ω^{S} arels [Quentin's sigla]: *paucis* S-C, Weber

<33:54 *lesser* KJV (*lesse*): *straiter* D-R>

34:1 *Locutusque: locutus* Weber; *Mosen, dicens: Mosen* Weber

34:4 *in Senna: Senna* Weber; *in meridiem: a meridie* S-C; *usque ad: usque* Weber

<34:5 *limits* S: *border* D-R>

34:8 *venient: venies* Weber

34:9 *usque ad: usque* Weber

34:11 *fontem Daphnim: fontem* Weber

35:1 *super: supra* S-C

<35:1 *by* KJV: *vpon* D-R>

35:3 *pecoribus eorum* S² [Quentin's siglum]: *pecoribus* S-C, Weber

35:5 *similiter erunt: similiter* Weber; *ad occidentem: occidentem* Weber

<35:5 *cubits* KJV: omitted in D-R>

35:6 *et exceptis: exceptis* Weber

<35:8 *of* D-R/C: omitted in D-R; *from them* KJV [italicized in D-R/C]: omitted in D-R>

35:16   *mortuus fuerit qui percussus est, reus erit: mortuus fuerit, qui percussus est reus erit* S-C

35:19   *interficiet* [second time]: *percutiet* Weber

36:13   *praecepit: mandavit* S-C; *super: supra* S-C

DEUTERONOMY

1:2   *usque: usque ad* S-C

1:4   *habitavit: habitabat* S-C

<1:6   *You have stayed long enough* KJV [*dwelt* for *stayed*]: *It is sufficient for you that you haue stayed* D-R>

1:8   *Abraham: Abraham et* Weber

1:10   *plurimi: plurimae* Weber

1:12   *pondus ac iurgia: pondus vestrum ac iurgia vestra* *D-R

<1:13   *Let me have* D-R/C: *Geue* D-R>

1:21   *Deus noster: Deus* Weber; *metuere: timere* S-C

<1:21   *be any way discouraged* KJV [without *any way*]: *dread you any thing* D-R>

1:27   *murmurati estis: murmurastis* S-C; *traderet nos: traderet* Weber; *nos* [fourth time] Gryson 100 E, Frede LUC Ath 1.5 72.16: omitted in S-C, Weber

<1:27   *tents* KJV: *tabernacles* D-R>

1:28   *in statura: statura* S-C

<1:31   *as* D-R/C: omitted in D-R>

1:31   *ambulastis: ambulasti* Weber

<1:32   *yet for all this* D-R/C: *neither so* D-R>

1:38   *dividet: dividat* Weber

<1:44   *do* KJV: *are wont to pursew* D-R>

<2:3   *You have compassed this mountain long enough* KJV: *It is sufficient for you to haue compassed this mountaine* D-R>

<2:6   *water for money* KJV: *bought water* D-R>

2:12   *Horim: Horrhaei* S-C

<2:14   *we passed over* KJV [*were come* for *passed*]: *the passage of* D-R>

2:14   *triginta et: triginta* Weber [D-R reads *thirtie and eight*]

<2:15   *for his* D-R/C [*for* is in KJV, italicized in D-R/C]: *whose* D-R>

<2:23   *were expelled by the Cappadocians* D-R/C: *the Capadocians expelled* D-R>

<2:28   *We only ask that thou wilt let us pass through* D-R/C: *Onlie this that thou wilt graunt vs passage* D-R>

2:29   *ad terram*: *in terram* Weber

2:33   *filiis suis*: *filiis* Weber

3:10   *usque ad*: *usque* Weber

3:12   *tempore*: *in tempore* Weber

3:13   *Manasse, omnem regionem Argob. Cunctaque*: *Manasse. Omnem regionem Argob cunctaque* S-C, *Manasse / omnem regionem Argob / cuncta* Weber

3:14   *Avoth Iair*: *Avothiair* Weber

3:16   *de terra*: *terram* Weber; *confinium*: *finium* Weber

<3:17   *Sea* KJV: omitted in D-R>

3:27   *ad aquilonem*: *aquilonem* Weber

<3:27   *to* [third and fourth times] D-R/C: omitted in D-R>

<4:6   *nations* KJV: *peoples* D-R>

4:7   *Deus*: *Dominus Deus* Weber

4:8   *vestros?*: *vestros.* S-C

4:9   *excidant*: *excedant* Weber

<4:9   *go* D-R/C: *fal* D-R>

4:10   *die* l [Weber's siglum]: *a die* S-C, *diem* Weber; *audiant . . . discant . . . vivunt*: *audiat . . . discat . . . vivit* Weber

<4:10   *from* S-C: omitted in D-R>

4:11   *et nubes*: *nubes* Weber

<4:14   *shall* D-R/C: *should* D-R>

<4:20   *make* D-R/C: *haue* D-R>

4:28   *nec* [all three]: *non* Weber

<4:32   *thy time* D-R: literally, *thee*>

4:32   *caeli*: *caelo* S-C

4:35   *eum*: *unum* Weber

4:42   *nec sibi*: *nec* Weber

<4:48   *called* D-R/C: omitted in D-R>

<5:3   *now present and living* D-R/C: *at this present, and doe liue* D-R>

<5:14   *thy* [all five times] KJV: omitted in D-R>

5:14   *servus tuus*: *servus* Weber

5:25   *moriemur*: *morimur* Weber

5:31   *mandata mea*: *mandata* Weber

6:3   *facias quae praecepit tibi Dominus*: *facias* Weber

<6:3   *that* KJV: *and* D-R>

6:7   *meditaberis*: *meditaberis in eis* S-C

<6:7   *upon them* S-C: omitted in D-R>

<6:11   *riches* D-R/C: *al riches* D-R>

6:13   *ipsi soli*: *ipsi* Weber

6:20   *Cumque*: *cum* Weber

6:24   *ut bene*: *et bene* Weber

7:1   *ingrederis*: *ingredieris* Weber; *et* [before *Chananeum*]: Frede AU Jos 21.2 325.506, Gryson 100 E, PL 21.814C: omitted in S-C, Weber

7:5   *et confringite*: *confringite* Weber

<7:7   *the fewest of any people* KJV [*all* for *any*]: *fewer then* [sic] *al peoples* D-R>

<7:13   *thy* [fourth, fifth and sixth times] KJV: omitted in D-R>

<7:19   *with which the Lord, thy God, brought thee out* KJV [*whereby* for *with which*]: *that the Lord thy God might bring thee forth* D-R>

7:24   *tradetque*: *tradet* Weber

<8:1   *All the commandments* KJV: *Everie commandment* D-R>

8:3   *quem*: *quod* S-C; *de ore Dei*: *ex ore Domini* Weber

<8:7   *land* D-R/C [after S?]: *land, a land* D-R>

8:8   *hordei ac*: *hordei* Weber

<8:8   *and* KJV: omitted in D-R>

<8:9   *where the* D-R/C: *whose* D-R>

8:12   *satiatus fueris*: *satiatus* Weber

8:13   *armenta boum*: *armenta* Weber; *auri et argenti* Ψ^B [Quentin's siglum]: *argenti et auri* S-C, Weber

9:5   *eorum*: *earum* S-C

9:12   *quos*: *quem* S-C

9:14   *de sub*: *sub* Weber

<9:21   *until it was as small as* KJV: *bringing it wholy into* D-R>

<9:22   *place of* D-R/C: omitted in D-R>

10:13   *praecipio tibi*: *praecipio* Weber

<10:17 *taketh* KJV: omitted in D-R>

10:20 *ei soli*: *ei* Weber

<11:2 *chastisements* D-R/C [KJV has *chastisement* but only D-R/C makes it plural]: *discipline* D-R>

<11:9 *a land which floweth* KJV [*a land* italicized in D-R/C]: *flowing* D-R>

11:10 *ingrederis*: *ingredieris* Weber

11:14 *dabit*: *dabo* Weber; *temporivam*: *temporaneam* S-C

11:15 *faenumque*: *faenum* Weber

<11:17 *that* KJV: *and* D-R; *come* D-R/C: *came* D-R>

11:24 *a Libano*: *Libano* Weber

11:27 *ego hodie*: *ego* Weber

11:28 *oboedieritis mandatis*: *audieritis mandata* Weber

11:29 *Cum vero*: *cum* Weber

11:31 *ut habeatis*: *et habeatis* Weber

12:1 *possideas*: *possideatis* S-C

12:3 *earum*: *eorum* S-C

<12:6 *herds* KJV: *oxen* D-R>

12:9 *Deus vester*: *Deus* Weber

12:11 *vovebitis*: *vovistis* Weber

12:12 *vos et*: *vos* Weber

<12:12 *your* [third and fourth times] KJV: omitted in D-R>

12:16 *quod*: *quem* S-C

<12:17 *thy* [third, fourth and sixth times] KJV: omitted in D-R; fifth time would also be omitted in a literal translation>

12:18 *filia tua et*: *filia* Weber

<12:18 *thy* KJV: omitted in D-R>

12:19 *omni*: *in omni* S-C

<12:32 *the* KJV: *their* D-R>

13:4 *et mandata*: *mandata* Weber

13:5 *redemit vos*: *redemit* Weber

13:6 *tuam, clam, dicens*: *tuam, clam dicens* S-C

<13:7 *one end of the earth to the other* KJV [*euen vnto* for *to*]: *the beginning vnto the end of the earth* D-R>

13:9 *post te*: *postea* S-C

<13:9   *afterwards* KJV: *after thee* D-R>

<13:10   *With stones shall he be stoned to death* D-R: literally, *Having been stoned, he will be put to death*>

13:13   *suae: tuae* Weber

<13:14   *diligently the truth of the thing by looking well into it, and* D-R/C [*and* is in KJV]: *diligently, the truth of the thing being looked into, if* D-R>

<13:16   *And all the household goods that are there* D-R/C: *What stuffe also soeuer there is* D-R>

<14:4   *shall* KJV: *ought to* D-R>

14:5   *cervum et: cervum* Weber

14:7   *haec comedere: comedere* S-C; *ut camelum: camelum* Weber; *quia: haec quia* S-C

<14:7   *you* S-C: *these you* D-R>

<14:9   *all that* KJV: *Such as* D-R>

<14:11   *you shall eat* KJV: *eate* D-R>

14:15   *et strutionem: strutionem* Weber

<14:20   *you shall eat* D-R/C: *eate* D-R>

14:21   *quicquid autem: quicquid* Weber

14:22   *quae: qui* S-C

<14:22   *the earth bringeth forth* KJV [*field* for *earth*]: *spring in the earth* D-R>

<14:23   *thy* [second, third and fifth times] KJV: omitted in D-R>

<14:25   *turn them into money* KJV: *bring . . . into a price* D-R; *Lord* D-R/C: *Lord thy God* D-R>

14:27   *Levita: levites* S-C

<14:29   *shall come* [plural] KJV: *shal come* [singular; immediately following the Leuite] D-R>

15:3   *habebis: habes* Weber

15:4   *Dominus, Deus tuus: Dominus* Weber

15:7   *manum tuam* OL [Weber's sigla]: *manum* S-C, Weber

<15:8   *thou* S: *and* D-R>

15:8   *quod: quo* S-C

15:9   *subrepat: subripiat* Weber; *oculos tuos: oculos* Weber

15:14   *gregibus, area: gregibus tuis, area tua* *D-R

15:15   *praecipio: praecipiam* S-C

15:18   *avertas: avertes* Weber

15:19   *ovibus*: *in ovibus* S-C

15:21   *et vel*: *vel* S-C

<15:21   or be S-C: *and either be* D-R>

15:23   *effundas*: *effundes* S-C

<16:1   which is D-R/C: *and* D-R>

16:4   *manebit*: *remanebit* S-C; *usque mane*: *mane* Weber

16:11   *tu et*: *tu* S-C; *et servus*: *servus* S-C; *ancilla tua*: *ancilla* Weber; *tuas et*: *tuas* S-C

16:14   *tu*: *tu et* Weber; *filia tua* $\Lambda^H\Sigma^M$B [Quentin's sigla]: *filia* S-C, *filia et* Weber; *advena et*: *advena* S-C

<16:14   thy [fourth time] KJV: omitted in D-R>

16:16   *azymorum*: *azymorum / et* Weber

<16:16   males KJV: *male* D-R; with his hands D-R/C: omitted in D-R>

16:22   *neque*: *atque* Weber

17:1   *ovem et bovem*: *bovem et ovem* Weber; *Domino, Deo tuo* [second time]: *Domini Dei tui* Weber

<17:7   upon him to kill him, and afterwards, the hands of the rest of the people KJV [put him to death for kill him, all for the rest of]: to kil him, and the hand of the rest of the people shal be layd on last D-R>

17:8   *et non lepram*: *et lepram* S-C

<17:8   leprosy S-C: *not leprosy* D-R>

17:11   *sequerisque*: *sequeris* Weber; *neque*: *vel* Weber

17:17   *inliciant*: *alliciant* S-C

<17:18   is raised D-R/C [after S?]: *shal sitte* D-R>

17:19   *in lege*: *lege* Weber

<18:3   priest's due KJV [Priests may be singular or plural in KJV]: *right of the priestes* D-R>

<18:4   also KJV [italicized in D-R/C, in roman type in KJV]: omitted in D-R>

18:6   *de*: *ex* S-C

<18:6   have a longing mind to D-R/C: *would* D-R>

18:7   *Domini, Dei*: *Dei* Weber

18:10–11   *nec sit . . . nec . . . nec qui . . . nec*: *ne sit . . . ne . . . ne . . . ne* Weber; *et*: *aut* S-C

18:11   *pythones*: *pythone* *D-R

<18:11   or KJV: *and* D-R; pythonic spirits D-R/C: *with pithone* D-R>

<18:13 *before* S: *with* D-R>

<18:16 *neither let me see any more* KJV: *I wil see no more* D-R>

<18:20 *shall* KJV: *wil* [with the sense of wishing] D-R>

18:22 *ille*: *idem* *D-R

19:1 *disperderit*: *disperdiderit* S-C

<19:2 *Lord* D-R/C: *Lord thy God* D-R>

<19:5 *tree* KJV: *wood* D-R>

19:10 *ne*: *nec* Weber

19:13 *Non*: *nec* Weber

<19:14 *landmarks* KJV: *boundes* D-R>

20:1 *equitatum*: *equitatus* S-C; *habes*: *habeas* S-C

<20:1 *numbers, thine* D-R/C: *multitude, thou hast* D-R>

20:6 *de*: *et de* Weber

<20:11 *paying* D-R/C [after S?]: *vnder* D-R>

20:12 *noluerint*: *noluerit* S-C; *coeperint* Φ [Weber's siglum]: *coeperit* S-C, *receperint* Weber

<20:14 *and* D-R/C [after S?]: omitted in D-R>

20:20 *extrue*: *instrue* S-C

21:1 *ignoratur*: *ignorabitur* S-C

<21:2 *where the body lieth* D-R/C: *of the corps* D-R>

<21:4 *head* D-R/C: *necke* D-R>

21:5 *negotium pendet* Λ^H ΣBΨ^{B*DFM}Ω^{SJ*M} arel [Quentin's sigla]: *negotium* S-C, Weber

<21:5 *should be decided* D-R/C [in italics after S-C]: *dependeth* D-R>

21:6 *et venient*: *et* Weber

21:8 *non*: *ne* S-C

21:12 *introduces eam*: *introduces* Weber

21:14 *Sin*: *Si* S-C

<21:14 *thee* D-R/C: *thy mynde* D-R>

<21:22 *committed a crime* D-R/C: *offended* D-R; *for which he is to be punished* D-R/C: *so that he is to be punished* D-R, literally, *which is to be punished*>

<22:1 *Thou shalt not pass by if thou seest* D-R/C [after S?]: *Thov shalt not see . . . and passe by* D-R>

<22:9 *fruit* KJV: *thinges that grow* D-R>

22:17 *imponit*: *imponet* Weber; *senibus*: *senioribus* S-C

<22:18   *that* KJV: *the* D-R>

22:19   *eam omnibus diebus*: *omni tempore* Weber

22:22   *morientur*: *morietur* S-C

<22:27   *help* S: *deliuer* D-R>

22:29   *dimittere eam*: *dimittere* Weber

<23:6   *shalt* KJV: *doe* D-R>

23:6   *quaeras*: *quaeres* Weber

23:14   *et sint*: *ut sint* Weber; *ne*: *nec* Weber

23:16   *Ne*: *nec* Weber

23:18   *voveris*: *voverint* Weber

23:20   *quod*: *quo* S-C

<23:20   *works* S: *worke* D-R>

23:21   *reputabitur*: *reputabit* Weber

<23:24   *thou mayst eat* KJV: *eate* D-R>

24:5   *domui*: *domi* S-C

<24:5   *be free at home* KJV: *attend to his owne house* D-R>

24:6   *adposuit*: *opposuit* S-C

24:7   *acceperit*: *accipiens* Weber

24:8   *plagam*: *in plagam* Weber

24:20   *collegeris*: *colliges* Weber

<24:21   *be for* KJV: *goe to the vses of* D-R>

24:22   *praecipio*: *praecipiam* Weber

<25:1   *men* KJV: *some* D-R>

25:2   *Si* O [Weber's siglum, without capitalization]: *Sin* S-C [probably a typo for *Si*], Weber, without capitalization

25:7   *coniugium*: *coniugem* S-C

25:9   *fiet*: *fit* Weber

25:11   *viri duo*: *viri* Weber; *miserit*: *miseritque* S-C

25:16   *Dominus tuus*: *Dominus* Weber

<25:16   *the Lord, thy God* KJV: *thy Lord* D-R>

26:2   *frugibus tuis*: *frugibus* Weber

26:3   *sim*: *sum* S-C; *in terram*: *terram* Weber

26:4   *eius*: *tua* S-C

<26:4   *thy* KJV: *his* D-R>

<26:5   *thus* D-R/C: omitted in D-R>

26:7   *angustiam*: *angustias* Weber

26:9 *terram hanc* Θ^{G2} [Quentin's sigla]: *terram* S-C, Weber

26:10 *adorato: et adorato* S-C

<26:13 *thus* D-R/C [italicized]: omitted in D-R>

26:13 *et pupillo: pupillo* Weber; *imperii tui: imperii* Weber

26:15 *et de: de* Weber

<27:2 *plaster* KJV: *polish* D-R>

27:4 *erigite: erige* Weber; *eos calce: calce* Weber

<27:4 *plaster* KJV: *polish* D-R>

27:12 *populo: Domino* Weber

<27:13 *shal* D-R/C: *these shal* D-R>

27:13 *Aser et: Aser* Weber

<27:25 *an innocent person* KJV: *soule of innocent bloud* D-R>

28:1 *Sin: Si* S-C

28:4 *armentorum tuorum: armentorum* Weber

<28:12 *rain* D-R/C: *rayne to thy land* D-R>

28:12 *benedicetque: benedicet* Weber

28:13 *si tamen: si* Weber

<28:22 *misearble want* D-R/C: *pouertie* D-R>

28:27 *partem: parte* Weber; *egeruntur: digeruntur* Weber

28:48 *omni: omnium* Weber

<28:48 *want of all things* KJV: *al penurie* D-R>

28:50 *parvulo: parvuli* S-C

<28:51 *nor* [both times] D-R/C: omitted in D-R>

28:52 *tua quam: quam* Weber

28:53 *filiorum tuorum: filiorum* Weber; *dederit: dedit* Weber

<28:63 *bringing . . . to nought* KJV: *subuerting* D-R>

28:68 *dixit: dixi* Weber

29:4 *possint: possunt* S-C

29:5 *Adduxit: adduxi* Weber; *vestrorum: tuorum* Weber

29:7 *occurrens: occurrentes* S-C

29:16 *quomodo: ut* Weber

29:18 *nostro: vestro* Weber

29:19 *adsumat: absumat* S-C

29:20 *deleat Dominus: deleat* Weber

<29:24 *great* D-R/C [after S?]: omitted in D-R; *heat* KJV: *wrath* D-R>

29:28 *furore et in* AL [Weber's sigla]: *in furore et in* S-C, *furore et* Weber

<29:28 *in* KJV: omitted in D-R>

29:29 *aeternum*: *sempiternum* S-C; *verba legis*: *legis* Weber

<30:1 *things* KJV: *wordes* D-R>

30:2 *et reversus*: *reversus* Weber

<30:2 *thou and* KJV: *with* D-R>

30:5 *adsumet*: *adsumet sibi* *D-R

30:6 *ut possis*: *et possis* Weber

30:10 *conscriptae*: *conscripta* S-C

<30:11 *from thee* S: omitted in D-R>

<30:12 *is it* KJV: *situated* D-R; *shouldst* KJV: *maiest* D-R>

30:12 *ascendere*: *conscendere* Weber

30:17 *Sin*: *Si* S-C

30:19 *mortem*: *mortem bonum et malum* Weber

31:6 *ad conspectum*: *a conspectu* Weber

31:13 *ut audire*: *audire* Weber; *transito*: *transmisso* S-C

31:16 *ingreditur ut habitet*: *ingredietur et habitabit* Weber

<31:21 *And* KJV: omitted in D-R; *and* D-R/C: omitted in D-R>

31:21 *sui*: *tui* Weber

31:23 *Dominus Iosue*: *Iosue* Weber

<31:27 *been rebellious* KJV: *done . . . contenciously* D-R>

<31:28 *call . . . to witness* S: *inuocate* D-R>

32:2 *ut pluvia*: *in pluvia* Weber

32:5 *ei et*: *ei* Weber

<32:5 *are none of* D-R/C: *not* D-R>

<32:6 *Is this the return thou makest* D-R/C: *These thinges doest thou render* D-R; *thee* KJV: omitted in D-R>

32:6 *te et fecit*: *et fecit* Weber

<32:9 *lot* KJV: *corde* D-R>

<32:15 *he grew* S: *made* D-R>

32:17 *daemonibus*: *daemoniis* S-C

<32:22 *lowest hell* KJV: *lowest partes of hel* D-R>

32:25 *lactentem*: *lactantem* Weber

32:31 *dii*: *deus* Weber

<32:33 *which is* D-R/C: omitted in D-R>

32:36 *defecerint*: *defecerunt* S-C; *sint*: *sunt* S-C

<32:44 *and* D-R/C: *he and* D-R>

<32:46   *which you shall* KJV: *that you* D-R>

33:9   *Ignoro vos*: *ignoro illos* Weber

33:9–10   *servaverunt, iudicia . . . Israhel. Ponent*: *servaverunt. Iudicia . . . Israel, ponent* S-C

<33:14   *fruits* KJV (*precious fruits*): *pomes of fruites* D-R>

33:16   *de plenitudine*: *plenitudine* Weber

33:23   *benedictionibus*: *benedictione* Weber

33:24   *et tinguat*: *tinguat* Weber

33:26   *Deus alius* S-C: *alius* Weber

<33:26   *He that is mounted upon* D-R/C: *the mounter of* D-R>

<33:27   *before thee* KJV: *thy face* D-R>

34:2   *terram Iuda*: *terram* Weber

<34:8   *in which they* D-R/C: *that* D-R>

Alternate Spellings

In general, the translators of the Douay-Rheims edition of the Bible preserved the transliterations of Hebrew names (and words based on those names) found throughout the textual tradition of the Sixto-Clementine edition of the Vulgate Bible. While these transliterations do reflect the Latin sources for the English presented in this edition, they do not represent what is currently thought to be the likely pronunciation of the Hebrew words or, in some books, words from other ancient languages: for example, the name we see in the New Revised Standard Version (NRSV) as "Ahuzzath" (Gen 26:26) was transliterated by the authors and revisers of the Latin text as "Ochozath." This sort of transliteration renders a few well-known characters harder to recognize, such as Noah, or "Noe" in the Latin tradition. Furthermore, there are frequent inconsistencies in the Douay-Rheims translation as to the spellings of names.

Another quirk of the Douay-Rheims and Vulgate Bibles is that they often identify locations by the names they were understood to have had at the time of the Vulgate's composition rather than the names found in Hebrew scripture. For example, "Mesopotamia of Syria" (Gen 28:2) represents a place referred to in the NRSV as "Paddan-aram."

In presenting the Latin text and the Douay-Rheims transla-

tion, the transliterations in the English have been updated for the sake of accuracy and ease of reference. The Latin has been preserved to reflect its own textual tradition in accordance with the principles stated in the Introduction. However, when names given are not simply a matter of representing vowel and consonant sounds, the Douay-Rheims translation has been left intact so that it remains a genuine translation of the facing text.

There are moments in the Bible where the anachronistic place-names are of significance: at the end of Balaam's last prophetic blessing of Israel, he declares, "They shall come in galleys from Italy; they shall overcome the Assyrians and shall waste the Hebrews, and at the last they themselves also shall perish" (Nm 24:24). The Hebrew word rendered as "Italy" is transliterated in the NRSV as "Kittim," and though the meaning is obscure, it is almost certainly not Italy, for reasons outlined by Milgrom (1990), ad loc. Nevertheless, it is fascinating and important to realize that in the Western European tradition from the fourth century CE until the twentieth century, many read, wrote, and learned that Italians would "waste the Hebrews." Because of this and other instances in which the place-names, however unrepresentative of the Hebrew tradition they may be, are important in terms of what readers of these versions of the Bible may have believed, the Vulgate words have been retained.

Below is list of the names in the English translation of this volume. The names are followed by an alternate spelling (or, in some cases, an alternate word) if there is one. An entry presented in italic text signifies a word retained from the Douay-Rheims translation; all other words are the spellings given by the NRSV. An entry in roman text with no alternative spelling

means that the spellings are identical in the two editions; one in italic text with no alternative spelling means that the name is in the Douay-Rheims translation but no parallel was found in the NRSV. In a few cases, words have been based on the spellings of the NRSV and the form in the Douay-Rheims text. For example, the Douay-Rheims text reads "the Sichemites" (Gen 33:18), where the NRSV has "Shechem." To illustrate the translation of the Douay-Rheims while providing an up-to-date transliteration of the Hebrew word, "the Shechemites" has been printed; similarly, in cases where Jerome translated parts of a Hebrew place-name into Latin where the NRSV left the whole name in Hebrew (such as the "temple of Phogor," as opposed to "Beth-peor" at Dt 3:29), the transliterated part of the name has been updated in this edition, but the Latin and English translations have not been changed, yielding "temple of Peor."

Aaron	Abronah [Hebrona]
Abarim	Accad [Achad]
Abel	Achbor [Achobor]
Abel-shittim [Ablesatim]	Adah [Ada]
Abiasaph	Adam
Abida	*Adar [Hazar-addar]*
Abidan	Adbeel
Abihail [Abihaiel]	Admah [Adama]
Abihu [Abiu]	*Adonai*
Abimael	Adullamite [Odollamite]
Abimelech	Agag
Abiram [Abiron]	Ahiezer
Abraham	Ahihud [Ahiud]
Abram	Ahiman [Achiman]

Ahira

Ahiram

Ahiramites

Ahisamach [Achisamech]

Ahuzzath [Ochozath]

Ai [Hai]

Aiah [Aia]

Akan [Acan]

Almodad [Elmodad]

Almon-diblathaim [Helmon-
    deblathaim]

Alush [Alus]

Alvah [Alva]

Alvan

Amalek [Amalech]

Amalekite [Amalecite]

Amalekites [Amalecites]

Ammiel

Ammihud [Ammiud]

Amminadab [Aminadab]

Ammishaddai [Ammisaddai]

Ammon

Ammon [Ben-ammi]

Ammonite

Ammonites

Amorean [Amorrhean]

Amorite [Amorrhite]

Amorites [Amorrhites]

Amram

Amramites

Amraphel

Anah [Ana]

Anak [Enac]

Anakim [Enacims]

Anamim

Aner

Ar

Arad

Aradian [Arvadites]

Aram

Aran [Aram]

Arbee [Kiriath-arba]

Ard [Ared]

Ard [Hered]

Ardites [Heredites]

Areli

Areli [Ariel]

Arelites [Arielites]

Argob

Arioch

Arkite [Aracite]

Armenia [Ararat]

Arnon

Arod

Arodi

Arodites

Aroer

Arpachshad [Arphaxad]

Asenath [Aseneth]

Ashbel [Asbel]

Ashbelites [Asbelites]

Asher [Aser]

Ashkenaz [Ascenez]
Ashtaroth [Astaroth]
Ashteroth-karnaim
  [Astarothcarnaim]
Asriel
Asrielites
Asshur [Assur]
Asshurim [Assurim]
Assir [Aser]
Assyrians
Assyrians [Asshur]
Atad
Ataroth
Atroth [Etroth]
Avith
Avvim [Hevites]
Azmon [Asemona]
Azzan [Ozan]

Baal
Baal of Peor [Beelphegor]
Baal-hanan [Balanan]
Baal-meon [Ballmeon]
Baal-zephon [Beelsephon]
Babel
Babylon [Babel]
Balaam
Balak [Balac]
Bamoth
Basemath
Bashan [Basan]

Becher
Becher [Bechor]
Becherites
Bedad [Badad]
Beer-sheba [Bersabee]
Beeri
Beeroth [Beroth]
Bela
Bela [Bala]
Belaites
Belial, children of [scoundrels]
Ben-oni [Benoni]
Bene-jaakan [Benejaacan]
Benjamin
Beon
Beor
Bera [Bara]
Bered [Barad]
Beriah [Beria]
Beriah [Brie]
Beriites [Brieites]
Beth-haran [Betharan]
Beth-jeshimoth [Bethsi-
  moth]
Beth-nimrah [Bethnemra]
Bethel
Bethlehem
Bethuel [Bathuel]
Bezalel [Beseleel]
Bezer [Bosor]
Bilhah [Bala]

Bilhan [Balaan]
Birsha [Bersa]
Bozrah [Bosra]
Bukki [Bocci]
Burning, the [Taberah]
Buz

Cain
Calah [Chale]
Caleb
Canaan [Chanaan]
Canaanite [Chanaanite]
Canaanites [Chanaanites]
Canaanitess [Chanaanitess]
Caphtorim [Capthorim]
Cappadocia [Caphtor]
Cappadocians [Caphtorim]
Carmi [Charmi]
Carmites [Charmites]
Casluhim [Chasluim]
Chalanne
Chaldeans [Chaldees]
Chedorlaomer [Chodorlaho-
    mor]
Chemosh [Chamos]
Cheran [Charan]
Chesed [Cased]
Chinnereth [Cenereth]
Chislon [Chaselon]
Contradiction, Waters of [waters
    of Meribath]

Cozbi
Cush [Chus]

Damascus
Dan
Daphnis, fountain of [east side of
    Ain]
Dathan
Deborah [Debora]
Dedan [Dadan]
Deuel [Duel]
Deuteronomy, the [a copy]
Dibon
Dibon-gab [Dibongab]
Dibri [Dabri]
Diklah [Decla]
Dinah [Dina]
Dinhabah [Denaba]
Dishan [Disan]
Dishon [Dison]
Dophkah [Daphca]
Dothan [Dothain]
Dumah [Duma]

Ebal
Ebal [Hebal]
Eber [Heber]
Eden
Edom
Edom [Idumea]
Edomite

Edomites

Edrei [Edrai]

Egypt

Egyptian

Egyptians

Ehi [Echi]

El-paran [Pharan]

Elah [Ela]

Elam

Elamites

Elath

Eldaah [Eldaa]

Eldad

Elealeh [Eleale]

Eleazar

Eli-zaphan [Elisaphan]

Eliab

Eliasaph

Elidad

Eliezer

Elim

Eliphaz

Elishaba [Elizabeth]

Elishah [Elisa]

Elishama [Elisama]

Elizaphan [Elisaphan]

Elizur [Elisur]

Elizur [Helisur]

Elkanah [Elcana]

Elon

Elonites

Elzaphan [Elisaphan]

Elzaphan [Elizaphan]

Emim

Emim [Emims]

En-mishpat [Misphat]

Enan

Enan [Hazar-enan]

Enoch [Henoch]

Enosh [Enos]

Ephah [Epha]

Epher [Opher]

Ephod

Ephraim

Ephrath [Ephrata]

Ephron

Er [Her]

Eran [Heran]

Eran [Heranites]

Erech [Arach]

Eri [Her]

Eri [Heri]

Erites [Herites]

Esau

Eshban [Eseban]

Eshcol [Escol]

Etham

Ethiopia [Cush]

Ethiopian [Cushite]

Euphrates

Eve

Evi

Ezbon [Esebon]
Ezer [Eser]
Ezion-geber [Asiongaber]

Gad
Gaddi
Gaddiel
Gadgad, Mount [Hor-haggidgad]
Gaham
Galeed [Galaad]
Gamaliel
Gatam [Gatham]
Gaza
Gemalli
Gentiles
Gera
Gerar [Gerara]
Gerizim [Garizim]
Gershom [Gersam]
Gershon [Gerson]
Gershonites [Gersonites]
Geshur [Gessuri]
Gether
Geuel [Guel]
Giants, the Land of [a land of Rephaim]
Gideoni [Gedeon]
Gihon [Gehon]
Gilead [Galaad]
Gileadites [Galaadites]

Gilgal [Galgala]
Girgashite [Gergesite]
Girgashites [Gergesites]
Golan
Gomer
Gomorrah [Gomorrha]
Gomorrites [Gomorrhites]
Goshen [Gessen]
Graves of Lust, the [Kibroth-hattaavah]
Great Sea
Gudgodah [Gadgad]
Guni
Gunites

Hadad [Adad]
Hadad [Hadar]
Hadar [Adar]
Hadoram [Aduram]
Hagar [Agar]
Haggi
Haggi [Aggi]
Haggites [Aggites]
Ham [Cham]
Hamath [Emath]
Hamathite
Hamor [Hemor]
Hamul
Hamulites
Hanniel
Hanoch [Henoch]

Hanochites [Henochites]
Haradah [Arada]
Haran
Haran [Aran]
Haserim
Hashmonah [Hesmona]
Havilah [Hevila]
Havilah [Hevilath]
Havvoth Jair [Havoth Jair]
Hazarmaveth [Asarmoth]
Hazazon-tamar [Asason-
   thamar]
Hazeroth [Haseroth]
Hazo [Azau]
Heber
Heberites
Hebrew
Hebrews
Hebrews [Eber]
Hebron
Hebroni
Hebronites
Helek [Helec]
Helekites [Helecites]
Heliopolis [On]
Helon
Heman
Hemdan [Hamdan]
Hepher
Hepherites
Hermon

Heshbon [Hesebon]
Heth
Hezron [Hesron]
Hezronites [Hesronites]
Hirah [Hiras]
Hittite [Hethite]
Hittites [Hethites]
Hivite [Hevite]
Hobab
Hobah [Hoba]
Hoglah [Hegla]
Hor
Horeb
Hori
Hori [Huri]
Horim [Horrhites]
Horite [Horrite]
Horites [Chorreans]
Horites [Horrites]
Hormah [Horma]
Hoshea [Osee]
Hul [Hull]
Hupham
Huphamites
Huppim [Ophim]
Hur
Husham [Husam]
Husham [Husim]

Iezer [Jezer]
Iezerites [Jezerites]

Igal

Imnah [Jamne]

Imnah [Jemna]

Imnites [Jemnaites]

Irad

Iram [Hiram]

Isaac

Iscah [Jescha]

Ishbak [Jesbok]

Ishmael [Ismael]

Ishmaelites [Ismaelites]

Ishvah [Jesua]

Ishvi [Jessui]

Ishvi [Jessuri]

Ishvites [Jessuites]

Israel

Israelite

Issachar

Italy [Kittim]

Ithamar

Ithran [Jethram]

Iye-abarim [Ijeabarim]

Iye-abarim [Jeabarim]

Izhar [Isaar]

Izhar [Jesaar]

Izharites [Jesaarites]

Jaakan [Jacan]

Jabal [Jabel]

Jabbok [Jaboc]

Jabbok [Jeboc]

Jachin

Jachinites

Jacob

Jahaz [Jasa]

Jahleel [Jahelel]

Jahleel [Jalel]

Jahleelites [Jalelites]

Jahzeel [Jaziel]

Jahzeel [Jesiel]

Jahzeelites [Jesielites]

Jair

Jalam [Ihelon]

Jamin

Jaminites

Japheth

Jared

Jashub [Jasub]

Jashub [Job]

Jashubites [Jasubites]

Javan

Jazer

Jebusite

Jebusites

Jemuel [Jamuel]

Jephunneh [Jephone]

Jerah [Jare]

Jericho

Jetheth

Jethro

Jetur [Jethur]
Jeush [Jehus]
Jezer [Jeser]
Jezerites [Jeserites]
Jidlaph [Jedlaph]
Jobab
Jochebed [Jochabed]
Jogbehah [Jegbaa]
Jogli
Jokshan [Jecsan]
Joktan [Jectan]
Jordan
Joseph
Joshua [Josue]
Jotbathah [Jetebatha]
Jubal
Judah [Juda]
Judith

Kadesh [Cades]
Kadesh-barnea [Cadesbarne]
Kadmonites [Cedmonites]
Kain [Cin]
Kedar [Cedar]
Kedemah [Cedma]
Kedemoth [Cademoth]
Kehelathah [Ceelatha]
Kemuel [Camuel]
Kenan [Cainan]
Kenath [Canath]

Kenaz [Cenez]
Kenite [Cinite]
Kenites [Cineans]
Kenizzite [Cenezite]
Kenizzites [Cenezites]
Keturah [Cetura]
Kiriathaim [Cariathaim]
Kittim [Cetthim]
Kohath [Caath]
Kohathites [Caathites]
Korah [Core]
Korahites [Corites]

Laban
Lael
Lamech
Lasha [Lesa]
Leah [Lia]
Lehabim [Laabim]
Letushim [Latusim]
Leummim [Loomin]
Levi
Levite
Levites
Levitical
Libanus [the Lebanon]
Libnah [Lebna]
Libni [Lebni]
Libni [Lobni]
Libnites [Lebnites]

Lot

Lotan

Lud

Ludim

Luz [Luza]

Maacah [Maacha]

Maacah [Machati]

Machi

Machir

Machirites

Madai

Magdiel

Magog

Mahalalel [Malaleel]

Mahalath [Maheleth]

Mahanaim

Mahlah [Maala]

Mahli [Moholi]

Mahlites [Moholites]

Makheloth [Maceloth]

Malchiel [Melchiel]

Malchielites [Melchielites]

Mamre [Mambre]

Mamre [Manahat]

Manasseh [Manasses]

Marah [Mara]

Mash [Mess]

Masrekah [Masreca]

Massa

Matred

Mattanah [Mathana]

Me-zahab [Mezaab]

Medad

Medan [Madan]

Medeba [Medaba]

Mehetabel [Meetabel]

Mehujael [Maviael]

Melchizedek [Melchisedech]

Merari

Merarites

Mesha [Messa]

Meshech [Mosoch]

Mesopotamia [Aram-naharaim]

Mesopotamia [Paddan-aram]

Mesopotamia [Paddan]

Mesopotamia in Syria [Pethor of
Mesopotamia]

Mesopotamia of Syria [Paddan-
aram]

Mesraim

Mesram [Egypt]

Methuselah [Mathusala]

Methushael [Mathusael]

Mibsam [Mabsam]

Mibzar [Mabsar]

Michael

Midian [Madain]

Midianite [Madianite]

Midianites [Madianites]

Migdol [Magdal]

Migdol [Magdalum]

Milcah [Melcha]
Miriam [Mary]
Mishael [Misael]
Mishael [Mizael]
Mishma [Masma]
Mithkah [Methca]
Mizzah [Meza]
Moab
Moabite
Moabites
Molech [Moloch]
Moserah [Mosera]
Moseroth
Moses
Most Salt Sea [Dead Sea]
Muppim [Mophim]
Mushi [Musi]
Mushites [Musites]

Naamah [Noema]
Naaman
Naaman [Noeman]
Naamites [Noemanites]
Nadab
Nahaliel
Nahath
Nahbi [Nahabi]
Nahor [Nachor]
Nahshon [Nahason]
Nahshon [Nahasson]
Naphish [Naphis]

Naphtali [Nephtali]
Naphtuhim [Nepthuim]
Nazirite [Nazarite; not
    treated as a proper noun in
    NRSV and at times trans-
    lated as "set apart"]
Nebaioth [Nabajoth]
Nebo
Nebo [Nabo]
Nehelescol [Wadi Eshcol]
Nemuel [Namuel]
Nemuelites [Namuelites]
Nepheg
Nethanel [Nathanael]
Nimrah [Nemra]
Nimrod [Nemrod]
Nineveh [Ninive]
Noah [Noa]
Noah [Noe]
Nobah [Nobe]
Nophe
Nun

Obal [Ebal]
Oboth
Ochran
Og
Ohad [Ahod]
Oholiab [Ooliab]
Oholibamah [Oolibama]
Omar

On [Hon]
Onam [Oman]
Onan
Ophir
Ozni
Oznites

Pagiel [Phegiel]
Pallu [Phallu]
Palluites [Phalluites]
Palti [Phalti]
Paltiel [Phaltiel]
Paran [Pharan]
Parnach [Pharnach]
Pathrusim [Phetrusim]
Pau [Phau]
Pedahel [Phedael]
Pedahzur [Phadassur]
Peleg [Phaleg]
Peleth [Pheleth]
Peniel [Phanuel]
Penuel [Phanuel]
Peor [Phogor]
Perez [Phares]
Perezites [Pharesites]
Perizzite [Pherezite]
Perizzites [Pherezites]
Pharaoh [Pharao]
Phicol
Philistia [Philisthiim]
Philistines

Philistines [Palestines]
Phinehas [Phinees]
Pi-hahiroth [Phihahiroth]
Pildash [Pheldas]
Pinon [Phinon]
Pisgah [Phasga]
Pishon [Phison]
Pithom [Phithom]
Pontus [Ellasar]
Potiphar [Putiphar]
Potiphera [Putiphare]
Puah [Phua]
Punites [Phuaites]
Punon [Phunon]
Put [Phuth]
Putiel [Phutiel]
Puvah [Phua]

Raamah [Regma]
Rabbah [Rabbath]
Rachel
Rameses [Ramesse]
Rameses [Ramesses]
Ramoth
Raphu
Reba [Rebe]
Rebekah [Rebecca]
Red Sea
Rehob [Rohob]
Rehoboth [Rohoboth]
Rekem [Recem]

Rephaim [Raphaim]
Rephidim [Raphidim]
Resen
Reu
Reuben [Ruben]
Reuel [Raguel]
Reuel [Rahuel]
Reumah [Roma]
Riblah [Rebla]
Rimmon-perez [Rem-
    momphares]
Riphath
Rissah [Ressa]
Rithmah [Rethma]
Rodanim [Dodanim]
Rosh [Ros]

Sabtah [Sabatha]
Sabteca [Sabatacha]
Salecah [Selcha]
Salem
Salu
Samlah [Semla]
Sarah [Sara]
Sarai
Scorpion [Akrabbim]
Seba [Saba]
Sebam [Saban]
Seir
Senir [Sanir]
Sephar

Serah [Sara]
Sered [Sared]
Seredites [Saredites]
Serug [Sarug]
Seth
Sethur [Sthur]
Shammah [Samma]
Shammua [Sammua]
Shaphat [Saphat]
Shaul [Saul]
Shaulites [Saulites]
Shaveh [Save]
Shaveh-kiriathaim [Save of
    Cariathaim]
Sheba [Saba]
Shechem [Sechem]
Shechem [Sichem]
Shechemites [Sechemites]
Shechemites [Sichemites]
Shedeur [Sedeur]
Shelah [Sale]
Shelah [Sela]
Shelanites [Selaites]
Sheleph [Saleph]
Shelomi [Salomi]
Shelomith [Salumith]
Shelumiel [Salamiel]
Shem [Sem]
Shemeber [Semeber]
Shemida [Semida]
Shemidaites [Semidaites]

Shemuel [Samuel]

Shepham [Sephama]

Shepher [Sepher]

Shepho [Sepho]

Shephupham [Supham]

Sheshai [Sisai]

Sheth [Seth]

Shillem [Sallem]

Shillem [Sellem]

Shillemites [Sellemites]

Shimei [Semei]

Shimeites [Semeites]

Shimron [Semran]

Shimron [Semron]

Shimronites [Semranites]

Shinab [Sennaab]

Shinar [Sennaar]

Shiphrah [Sephora]

Shiphtan [Sephtan]

Shittim [Settim]

Shobal [Sobal]

Shophan [Sophan]

Shua [Sue]

Shuah [Sue]

Shuham [Suham]

Shuhamites [Suhamites]

Shuni [Suni]

Shunites [Sunites]

Shuphamites [Suphamites]

Shur [Sur]

Shuthelah [Suthela]

Shuthelahites [Suthelaites]

Sibmah [Sabama]

Sidon

Sidonians

Sihon [Sehon]

Simeon

Sin

Sinai

Sinite

Sion [Sirion]

Sirion [Sarion]

Sithri [Sethri]

Sodi

Sodom

Sodomites

Succoth [Soccoth]

Succoth [Socoth]

Susi

Syria. See *Mesopotamia in Syria*
    and *Mesopotamia of Syria*

Syrian [Aramean]

Tahan [Thehen]

Tahanites [Thehenites]

Tahash [Tahas]

Tahath [Thahath]

Talmai [Tholmai]

Tamar [Thamar]

Tanis [Zoan]

Tarshish [Tharsis]

Tebah [Tabee]

Tema [Thema]
Teman [Theman]
Temanites [Themanites]
Temptation, the Place of [Massah]
Temptation [Massah and Meribah]
Terah [Thare]
Tidal [Thadal]
Tigris
Timna [Thamna]
Timnah [Thamnas]
Tiras [Thiras]
Tirzah [Thersa]
Togarmah [Thogorma]
Tola [Thola]
Tolaites [Tholaites]
Tophel [Thophel]
Tubal [Thubal]
Tubalcain

Ur
Uri
Uz [Hus]
Uz [Us]
Uzal
Uzziel [Oziel]
Uzzielites [Ozielites]

Valley of the Cluster [Wadi Eshcol]

Vophsi [Vapsi]

Zaavan [Zavan]
Zaccur [Zechur]
Zamzummim [Zomzommims]
Zeboiim [Seboim]
Zebulun [Zabulon]
Zedad [Sedada]
Zelmonah [Salmona]
Zelophehad [Salphaad]
Zemarite [Samarite]
Zepho [Sepho]
Zephon [Sephon]
Zephonites [Sephonites]
Zerah [Zara]
Zerah [Zare]
Zerahites [Zarites]
Zered [Zared]
Zibeon [Sebeon]
Zichri [Zechri]
Zillah [Sella]
Zilpah [Zelpha]
Zimran [Zamran]
Zimri [Zambri]
Zin [Senna]
Zin [Sin]
Ziphion [Sephian]
Zippor [Sephor]
Zipporah [Sephora]
Zoar [Segor]

Zohar [Seor]

Zohar [Soar]

Zuar [Suar]

Zur [Sur]

Zuriel [Suriel]

Zurishaddai [Surisaddai]

Zuzim

Bibliography

Carleton, J. G. *The Part of Rheims in the Making of the English Bible.* Oxford: Clarendon, 1902.

Cartmell, J. "English Spiritual Writers: x. Richard Challoner." *Clergy Review* n.s. 44, no. 10 (October 1959): 577–587.

A Catholic. "A new Version of the Four Gospels, with Notes, Critical and Explanatory." *Dublin Review* 2, no. 2 (April 1837): 475–492.

Biblia Sacra: Vulgatae Editionis Sixti V Pont. Max. iussu recognita et Clementis VIII auctoritate edita. Vatican City: Marietti, 1959.

Challoner, R. "The Touchstone of the New Religion: or, Sixty Assertions of Protestants, try'd by their own Rule of Scripture alone, and condemned by clear and express Texts of their own Bible." London, n.p.: 1735.

———. ed. *The Holy Bible translated from the Latin Vulgat: Diligently compared With the Hebrew, Greek, and other Editions in divers Languages. And first published by The English College at Doway, Anno 1609. Newly revised, and corrected, according to the Clementine Edition of the Scriptures with Annotations for clearing up the principal Difficulties of Holy Writ.* 4 vols. Dublin(?): 1752.

———., ed. *The Holy Bible, translated from the Latin Vulgate, Diligently compared with the Hebrew, Greek, and other editions in divers languages. The Old Testament, First published by the English College at Douay, A.D. 1609 and The New Testament, First published by the English College at Rheims, A.D. 1582. With annotations, references, and an historical and chronological index. The whole revised and diligently compared with the Latin Vulgate Published with the approbation of His Eminence James Cardinal Gibbons Archbishop of Baltimore.* Baltimore: John Murphy, 1899.

———., ed. *The New Testament of Our LORD and SAVIOUR JESUS*

CHRIST. Translated out of the Latin Vulgat; diligently compared with the original Greek: and first published by the English *College at* Rhemes, *Anno 1582. Newly revised and corrected according to the* Clementin *Edition of the Scriptures. With Annotations, for Clearing up modern Controversies in Religion; and other Difficulties of Holy Writ.* 2 vols. Dublin(?): 1752.

Cotton, H. *Rhemes and Doway: An Attempt to shew what has been done by Roman Catholics for the Diffusion of the Holy Scriptures in English.* Oxford: University Press, 1855.

de Hamel, C. *The Book: A History of the Bible.* London: Phaidon, 2001.

Dodd, C. [H. Tootell]. *The Church History of England, From The Year 1500, to The Year 1688. Chiefly with regard to Catholicks.* 8 vols. Brussels [London], 1737–1742.

Duffy, E., ed. *Challoner and His Church: A Catholic Bishop in Georgian England.* London: Darton, Longman & Todd, 1981.

English College of Doway. *The Holie Bible Faithfully Translated into English, out of the Authentical Latin. Diligently conferred with the Hebrew, Greeke, and other Editions in diuers languages. With Arguments of the Bookes, and Chapters: Annotations. Tables: and other helpes, for better understanding of the text: for discoueirie of corruptions in some late translations: and for clearing Controversies in Religion.* 2 vols. Doway: Lavrence Kellam, at the signe of the holie Lambe, 1609–1610.

English College of Rhemes. *The Nevv Testament of Iesvs Christ, Translated Faithfully into English, out of the authentical Latin, according to the best corrected copies of the same, diligently conferred vvithe the Greeke and other editions in diuers languages: Vvith Argvments of bookes and chapters, Annotations, and other necessarie helpes, for the better vnderstanding of the text, and specially for the discouerie of the Corrvptions of diuers late translations, and for cleering the Controversies in religion, of these daies.* Rhemes: Iohn Fogny, 1582.

Frede, H. J. *Kirchenschriftsteller: Verzeichnis und Sigel.* Freiburg: Herder, 1995.

Gilley, S. "Challoner as Controvertionalist." In E. Duffy, ed., *Challoner and His Church: A Catholic Bishop in Georgian England.* London: Darton, Longman & Todd, 1981, pp. 90–111.

Greenslade, S. L., ed. *The Cambridge History of the Bible: The West, from the Reformation to the Present Day.* Rev. ed. Cambridge: Cambridge University Press, 1975.

Gryson, R. *Altlateinische Handschriften: Manuscrits Vieux Latins.* Freiburg: Herder, 1999.

The Holy Bible, Conteyning the Old Testament, and the New: Newly Translated out of the Originall tongues: & with the former Translations diligently compared and reuised: by his Maiesties speciall Comandement Appointed to be read in Churches. London: Robert Barker, Printer to the Kings most Excellent Maiestie, 1611; rpr. Thomas Nelson, 1990.

Kaske, R. E. *Medieval Chirstian Literary Imagery: A Guide to Interpretation.* Toronto: University of Toronto Press, ca. 1988.

Knox, T. F. Introduction. In *The First and Second Diaries of the English College, Douay, and an Appendix of Unpublished Documents, Edited by Fathers of the Congregation of the London Oratory, with an Historical Introduction.* Records of the English Catholics under the Penal Laws. Chiefly from the Archives of the See of Westinster 1. London: David Nutt, 1878.

Metzger, B. M., and R. E. Murphy. *The New Oxford Annotated Bible: New Revised Standard Version.* New York: Oxford University Press, 1991.

Milgrom, J., comm. *The JPS Torah Commentary: Numbers.* Philadelphia: The Jewish Publication Society.

Pope, H., and S. Bullough. *English Versions of the Bible.* St. Louis: Herder, 1952.

Quentin, H. *Biblia sacra: iuxta Latinam Vulgatam versionem.* Typis Polyglottis Vaticanis, 1926–[1995].

———. *Mémoire sur l'établissement du texte de la Vulgate.* Collectanea Biblica Latina 6, 1922.

Rahlfs, A., ed., and R. Hanhart, rev. *Septuaginta: Id est Vetus Testamentum graece iuxta LXX interpretes, Editio altera.* Stuttgart: Deutsche Bibelgesellschaft, 2006.

Sabatier, P. *Bibliorum Sacrorum Latinae versiones antiquae, seu Vetus Italica, et Ceterae quaecunque in Codicibus Mss. & antiquorum libris reperiri poterunt: Quae cum Vulgata Latina, & cum Textu Graeco comparantur. Accedunt Praefationes, Observationes, ac Notae, Indexque novus ad Vulgatam è regione editam, idemque locupletissimus.* 3 vols. Rheims: Apud Reginaldum Florentain, Regis Typographicum & Bibliopolam, sub signo Bibliorum aureorum, 1743–1749.

Weber, R., ed. *Biblia Sacra Vulgata.* 5th ed. Stuttgart: Deutsche Bibelgesellschaft, 2007.